PEACE, REFORM AND LIBERATION

A HISTORY OF LIBERAL POLITICS IN BRITAIN 1679–2011

PEACE, REFORM AND LIBERATION

A HISTORY OF LIBERAL POLITICS IN BRITAIN 1679–2011

Edited by
ROBERT INGHAM
and
DUNCAN BRACK

Liberal Democrat History Group

Biteback Publishing

First published in Great Britain in 2011 by
Biteback Publishing Ltd
Westminster Tower
3 Albert Embankment
London SE1 7SP

ISBN 978-1-84954-043-8

10 9 8 7 6 5 4 3 2 1

A CIP catalogue record for this book is available from the British Library.

Designed and typeset in Bembo by Duncan Brack.
Cover design by Namkwan Cho.

Printed and bound in Great Britain by TJ International Ltd, Padstow, Cornwall

Contents

Background text sections

Foreword

Rt Hon. Nick Clegg MP,
Leader of the Liberal Democrats and Deputy Prime Minister

'Peace, reform and liberation',
Be our triune aspiration,
Till we win them for the nation,
And our land be free.

These words, the refrain from 'The Liberal March', written for the 1892 general election, form a fitting title for this book.[1] 'Peace, reform and liberation' is an apt summary of what Liberals have sought through the centuries – and still strive for today.

The British Liberal Party, and, by extension, its successor, the Liberal Democrats, has a good claim to be regarded as the oldest political party in the world. The much-missed Conrad Russell asserted for us an organisational continuity from the Whigs of 1679 to the formation of the Liberal Party in 1859, and then to 1988, and the merger with the Social Democratic Party to form today's Liberal Democrats.[2]

Politicians of all these different labels displayed a continual adherence to a set of core liberal principles: the belief in individual liberty, the quest for an equitable society, both at home and abroad, and the ceaseless pursuit of reform, in the economic and social spheres as much as the political, with the aim of enlarging freedom for all.

One can see these principles in action throughout the centuries. The Whigs fought to curb the power of the monarchy, for equality before the law, and for the rights of conscience, religion and thought. In the eighteenth century Fox made the case for reform instead of repression, in the face of the threat from revolutionary France. The liberal belief in the right of dissent and the protection of civil liberties echoes down the centuries to our own day.

In the nineteenth century, John Stuart Mill led the intellectual charge for a society allowing the 'greatest amount of human liberty and spontaneity'. Russell and Grey began the long series of political reforms, extending the franchise, tearing down the barriers to participation in the civil service, the universities and the military. Gladstone continued this assault on privilege, establishing free trade and freedom of commerce. Abroad he supported peoples struggling to be free from imperial oppression, and tried to create an international system that respected the rights of all states, however small, and where trade bound nations together, rendering conflict less likely.

The realisation that true freedom could not be achieved without releasing the shackles of poverty, unemployment and ill-health underlay the New Liberalism of the twentieth century. Asquith and Lloyd George fought to build a fairer society, where government acted to create the conditions in which individuals could realise their full potential.

Even after the party fell from power in the 1920s, Liberals continued to influence the governance of Britain. Keynes and Beveridge provided the intellectual underpinnings for an economic policy aiming at full employment, and a welfare state providing for those in need. Liberals were the first of the major parties to call for British entry into Europe, the first to argue for the codification of human rights and the first to campaign for the protection of the natural environment.

These beliefs, and the policies that sprang from them, were sufficient to keep the party alive in the dark days of the 1940s and 1950s. They underpinned successive waves of Liberal revivals, the formation of the SDP and the Alliance and the merger and dramatic growth of the Liberal Democrats. At the start of a new decade, they still inspire us as we take part in government once again, and write a new chapter in Liberal history.

This book is the most comprehensive and most up-to-date guide to the story of those who called themselves Liberals, what inspired them and what they achieved over the last 300 years and more. I congratulate the Liberal Democrat History Group for its work to produce *Peace, Reform and Liberation*, and I commend the book wholeheartedly to all those wishing to learn the history of Liberal politics in Britain.

Nick Clegg MP
August 2011

Notes

1   To be sung to the tune of 'Men of Harlech'; for the full song, see www.liberator.org.uk/ article.asp?id=7703871.
2   Conrad Russell, *An Intelligent Person's Guide to Liberalism* (Duckworth, 1999).

Editors' Notes and Acknowledgements

Duncan Brack and Robert Ingham

The first four books produced by the Liberal Democrat History Group have all been reference sources: *Dictionary of Liberal Biography* (1998), *Dictionary of Liberal Quotations* (1999), *Great Liberal Speeches* (2001) and *Dictionary of Liberal Thought* (2007). For some time, however, we have wanted to produce a narrative history of British liberalism and the parties that adhered to it, particularly since, in our view, all the other single-volume histories available either cover only a limited period or concentrate on one aspect of party history to the exclusion of others. We aimed to present a comprehensive but accessible treatment of events in the party's history, its election record, its leaders and key personalities, its evolving ideology and policy platform, its impacts on government and politics, and its membership and structure. Readers can judge for themselves whether we have succeeded!

Throughout the book, the main text is supplemented by a series of background sections, containing more detail on personalities, policies or other issues of interest; these are picked out in a different typeface.

Each chapter is followed by a list of further reading, for those interested in pursuing the topics covered in more detail; the Introduction lists a number of books which are of particular use in studying the history of Liberal politics in Britain.

Note on election results

General election results are included in full in the chapters, and Appendix 2 summarises the Liberal performance throughout the entire period. The details are taken from Colin Rallings and Michael Thrasher (eds.), *British Electoral Facts* (Total Politics, 2009), and are based on the work originally undertaken by F. W. S. Craig. For more recent elections, House of Commons Library figures have been used. Party labels were principally derived from *Dod's Parliamentary Companion*. Percentages may not also sum to 100 because of rounding.

The exact numbers of Liberal (and other) MPs in all elections before 1945 need to be treated with care. Describing the situation in the nineteenth century, Craig wrote that 'during a period when party ties were often tenuous and changes of party allegiance after election were frequent and rarely reported in the national press, there is no doubt that some errors will have occurred, but these are unavoidable. There were always a number of candidates who could equally well have been classed as Liberal or Conservative.'[1]

Even in the twentieth century, and particularly in the 1920s and 1930s, a confused period of coalitions and divisions in the Liberal Party, it was not always clear which faction particular MPs belonged to, and different sources give different totals. We have stuck to Craig's analysis throughout.

It should also be remembered that in the nineteenth and early twentieth centuries, many seats went uncontested. The vote totals given in the tables may not, therefore, completely reflect party support in the country. Appendix 2 includes the total of Liberal MPs elected without a contest.

The party or parties that formed the government after each election are indicated in the tables in **bold**.

Note on terminology

For the name of parties and their ideologies, we have used the following conventions: 'Liberal' and 'Liberalism' is used only where the reference is clearly to the political party and its programme, and 'liberal' and 'liberalism' in all other cases. Similarly for Social Democrat(ic), and social democrat(ic).

Acknowledgements

The support and encouragement of the History Group's executive has been vital to the successful completion of this book, and we place on record our thanks to them. Iain Dale, Sam Carter and Hollie Teague, at Biteback Publishing, have been consistently encouraging and tolerant of our changing production schedule. Hannah McBain and Charlotte Littleboy have been both consistently supportive and remarkably good-natured at seeing their partners disappear for hours at a time to write and edit the book. Michael Steed was of considerable assistance in its early planning. Above all, the chapter authors have not only written their own chapters but commented on each others', to maintain consistency of treatment and a continuous narrative. Our warmest thanks go to them all.

Notes

1   F. W. S. Craig, *British Electoral Facts 1832–1987* (Ashgate, 1989), p. xv.

Authors

Eugenio Biagini is Reader in Modern History at Cambridge and a Fellow of Sidney Sussex College. He has published extensively on the history of Liberalism in Britain, Ireland and Italy. His publications include *Liberty, Retrenchment and Reform: Popular Liberalism in the Age of Gladstone, 1860–1880* (CUP, 1992), *Gladstone* (Palgrave Macmillan, 2000) and *British Democracy and Irish Nationalism, 1876–1906* (CUP, 2010), a study of the way in which the home rule crisis affected the debate on democracy and human rights among popular liberals and democrats in the two countries.

Duncan Brack is the Editor of the *Journal of Liberal History*, and has co-edited and contributed to all four of the Liberal Democrat History Group's previous books (all published by Politico's): *Dictionary of Liberal Biography* (1998), *Dictionary of Liberal Quotations* (1999), *Great Liberal Speeches* (2001) and *Dictionary of Liberal Thought* (2007). A former Director of Policy for the Liberal Democrats, he is currently special adviser to Chris Huhne MP, Secretary of State for Energy and Climate Change.

David Brown is Senior Lecturer in History at the University of Strathclyde. He has written widely on nineteenth-century British politics and his most recent book is *Palmerston: A Biography* (Yale University Press, 2010). His previous works include *Palmerston and the Politics of Foreign Policy 1846–55* (Manchester University Press, 2002) and the two volume co-edited *Palmerston Studies* (University of Southampton, 2007).

Matt Cole is a Visiting Fellow of the Hansard Society and Head of Modern History and Politics at King Edward VI College in Stourbridge. He has written widely on party and electoral politics, and is the author of *Democracy in Britain* (Edinburgh University Press, 2006) and *Richard Wainwright, the Liberals and Liberal Democrats: Unfinished Business* (Manchester University Press, 2011). In 1987 he worked in the Social Democratic Party's General Election Unit.

Philip Cowley is Professor of Parliamentary Government at the University of Nottingham. He is author (with Dennis Kavanagh) of *The British General Election of 2010* (Palgrave Macmillan, 2010). His other publications include *The Rebels* (Politico's, 2005) and *Developments in British Politics 9* (Palgrave Macmillan, 2011, co-edited with Richard Heffernan and Colin Hay).

David Dutton retired recently as Ramsay Muir Professor of Modern History at the University of Liverpool. He has written widely on the history of the Conservative and Liberal parties. His more recent books include *A History of the Liberal Party in the Twentieth Century* (Palgrave Macmillan, 2004) and *Liberals in Schism: a History of the National Liberal Party* (I. B. Tauris, 2008).

Stephen Farrell is a former senior research fellow at the History of Parliament, where he contributed extensively to *The House of Commons, 1820–1832* (D. R. Fisher (ed.), CUP, 2009). With Melanie Unwin and James Walvin, he edited *The British Slave Trade: Abolition, Parliament and People* (Edinburgh University Press, 2007). He now works as a committee reporter for House of Commons Hansard.

Michael Freeden is Professor of Politics and initiator and first director of the Centre for Political Ideologies at the University of Oxford, and Professorial Fellow at Mansfield College, Oxford. He has founded, and edits, the *Journal of Political Ideologies*. Among his books are *The New Liberalism: An Ideology of Social Reform* (Clarendon, 1978); *Liberalism Divided: A Study in British Political Thought 1914–1939* (Clarendon, 1986); *Reappraising J. A. Hobson: Humanism and Welfare* (ed.) (Unwin Hyman, 1990); *Rights* (Open University Press, 1991); *Ideology: A Very Short Introduction* (OUP, 2003); and *Liberal Languages: Ideological Imaginations and Twentieth Century Progressive Thought* (Princeton University Press, 2005). He is currently completing a book on 'the political theory of political thinking', and is also engaged in developing an international project on comparative political thought, and in co-organising a research programme on European conceptual history.

Ian Hunter lives in west London and has contributed to a number of publications relating to Liberal history. He is currently working as editor on the collected correspondence between Churchill and Lloyd George, and a collection of Lloyd George's speeches, to be published in 2012 and 2013 respectively. He studied history at Bristol and Oxford universities and is now director of a business consultancy.

Robert Ingham has written extensively for the *Journal of Liberal History* in recent years and is the *Journal*'s Biographies Editor. He has also contributed a number of entries on twentieth-century Liberals (and others) to the *Oxford Dictionary of National Biography*.

Tony Little is Chairman of the Liberal Democrat History Group. He jointly edited *Great Liberal Speeches* with Duncan Brack and contributed entries on the Victorian era to the *Dictionary of Liberal Thought* and *Dictionary of Liberal Biography*. Between 1982 and 1990 he led the Liberal/SDP Alliance group on Hillingdon Council. He twice stood unsuccessfully as a parliamentary candidate in Hayes and Harlington. Professionally he has worked as a fund manager and corporate governance specialist for fund management companies in the City.

Mark Pack has contributed to several books as an author or editor, mainly on British history and politics. He originally studied nineteenth-century English elections for his PhD and subsequently broadened out into electoral law, co-authoring the standard reference works for Liberal Democrat agents and organisers. He was Head of Innovations at the Liberal Democrats and is now Head of Digital at MHP Communications. He is Co-Editor of Liberal Democrat Voice, the most well-read Liberal Democrat blog in the UK.

Martin Pugh was Professor of Modern British History at Newcastle University until 1999, when he made his escape and has worked as a freelance historian ever since. He is the author of thirteen books on nineteenth and twentieth-century political and social history. His most recent works are *'We Danced All Night': A Social History of Britain Between the Wars* (Bodley Head, 2008) and *Speak for Britain! A New History of the Labour Party* (Bodley Head, 2010).

Jaime Reynolds has written extensively on Liberal history and also Eastern European politics. He studied at the London School of Economics and Warsaw University. He works for the European Commission on international environmental policy.

Martin Ryder is a freelance writer and editor, and occasional contributor to the *Journal of Liberal History*.

Sarah Whitehead studied the history of the Liberal Party as both an undergraduate and a postgraduate and focused on the Liberal Party's split over free trade in the 1930s as part of her MA in modern history from the University of East Anglia. She started her career as a parliamentary researcher and is now a senior communications officer in the NHS.

Introduction

Michael Freeden

The British Liberal Party was, in its prime, the most successful of its kind, both in Europe and beyond. Associated with political and social reform and with the spread of an immensely influential set of political ideas, its impact permeated the politics and culture of the Western world – its ideology becoming one of Britain's most durable and significant exports. Institutionally, its dominance was determined not only by the internal drive and policies it generated, but by its shifting relative position among rival parties on the right and the left – tracing an arc whose rise and partial decline can be charted. In terms of ideas, the liberalism for which it served as a major, though not sole, conduit established standards of civilised behaviour and reflection that were saluted with worldwide acclaim, and many of its major legislative achievements were enshrined as fundamental features of a good society, irrespective of the minutiae of Liberal politics.

Yet the Liberal Party's flexibility, foresight and remarkable innovative capacity were not attained without difficulties, controversy and the mundanities of political struggle and intrigue. As a political organisation, the party suffered crises of leadership and schisms of support, rivalries and betrayals of principles and, ultimately, a catastrophic downturn in electoral appeal. What may nevertheless be surprising is the degree to which it resisted the pressures and strains that, far more emphatically, undermined and choked continental liberalisms. While the latter tended to be crowded out by a range of social democratic, socialist and centrist groups, in Britain the Liberal Party initially succeeded in occupying the large space available for a moderate radicalism without fear of competition – abetted not only by the first-past-the-post electoral system but by a culture of political minimalism and the simplicity of crisp antagonisms. By the twentieth century, as a result, it was alternating with Labour as a site of social democracy. It did so only through the continuous realignment of its internal coalitions, dispatching its right wing in the direction of the Conservative (and Unionist) Party when its powers were in the ascendant. When the slow decline of the Liberal Party began, it was exacerbated by losing most of its left wing through gradual attrition to a Labour Party many of whose members and policies were consequently infused with left-liberal visions.

The humanism and culturedness of the Liberals were an asset that ensured the continued attractiveness of British political values at home and abroad. But that very commitment to civility and to responsible citizenship also took the edge off a radicalism that could never compete with the more energetic and iconoclastic versions of the European left, however watered down were their British manifestations. The tameness

I

and decency of liberalism ceased to be clarion calls to political action, once Lloyd Georgite rhetoric had waned and the emotionalism of both Conservatives and Labour took over as mobilisers of patriotism or of class solidarity. Liberalism failed to transcend class as a political movement – even as its rhetoric dismissed class and sectionalism – while continuing to inject its political and ideological rivals with creative programmes and suffering a haemorrhaging of its membership. As Keynes wryly observed in 1926: 'Possibly the Liberal Party cannot serve the State in any better way than by supplying Conservative Governments with Cabinets, and Labour Governments with ideas'. Even that gem of Liberal theory and legislative achievement, the welfare state project, was hijacked by Labour, despite its pre-1914 Liberal origins and despite its crystallisation through two major political documents with a definite Liberal pedigree: *Britain's Industrial Future* ('The Yellow Book', 1928), written among others by Keynes, and the Beveridge Report (1942).

The antecedents of the Liberal Party are visible in a proto-liberalism that typified ideological and political developments from the seventeenth century onwards. At its forefront stood the issues of rising middle class self-assertion, the toleration of religious diversity and liberty, and the redistribution of political power. Its inspiration was grounded in the claims of the dispossessed to inalienable rights and to political recognition. The dualism of British political life – reformers and conservers, periodically, though by no means consistently, mirrored in the confrontation of Whigs and Tories – created a constructed polarity which appeared to don a natural garb. That benefited future liberalism, utilising its structural ability to attract dissenters and carriers of social change. However, the breakdown of that dualism, with the strengthening Labour Party offering radicalism an alternative home, played a significant role in weakening the Liberal cause, though not the cause of broader liberal thinking. A liberalism stressing first and foremost individual enterprise, property and constitutional liberties eventually allowed itself to be taken over by the forces of conservatism, while a liberalism whose crowning glory was the welfare state and the attempt to impart a public conscience to politics overlapped with moderate redistributionary tendencies within the Labour camp.

The roots of institutional British liberalism may be found, as with British politics in general, in a paternalist and exclusivist political culture that relied heavily on leading lights and on cliques that pursued a limited agenda. The early political, as distinct from philosophical, successes of the liberal tradition revolved around the rise of Parliament as a challenge to kingly authority. From the mid-nineteenth century onwards, however, the now officially named Liberal Party had begun to distinguish itself on four fronts. First, it deepened its effort at political reform, seeking a fairer distribution of representation on a national level as well as within the party itself, and attempting to further the cause of home rule and retreat from constitutional centralism. In the latter case, the emergence of broader decision-making bodies was accompanied by the development of political programmes that offered voters choices and the semblance of an obligatory contract between the party and those who supported extensive political progress. Second, it introduced practices of financial probity and good budgeting into public life. Third, it launched the notion of an ethical foreign policy as well as insisting on the maintenance of such foreign policies in other lands, admittedly some time before equivalent ethical demands were directed fulsomely towards British domestic politics. Fourth, it established free trade as a non-negotiable doctrine, effectively extending the hallowed principle of personal, legal and religious liberty into economic conduct. John Stuart Mill's eccentric individuals had become the Victorian entrepreneurs – men (though rarely acknowledging women) of initiative, daring, foresight, efficiency and invention. That confident and assertive liberalism rode on the crest of Empire and the white man's civilising mission, enacted for the main part in good faith, and secularising a profound Nonconformist religious impulse. When the Liberal Party was in office, moreover, it recalibrated the role of government as a focus of political activity, as initiator and reformer not only on constitutional but eventually on social and economic issues as well, thereby creating the administrative attitudes and structures that were to launch the welfare state a century ago.

The Liberal Party also benefited immeasurably from the availability of a body of high-quality home-grown philosophical and ideological liberal theory, from which it could draw – with appropriate simplifications – and to whose reputation it could harness itself. No other political movement in the UK has been blessed with such intellectual power at its disposal, even if the liberalism of the party often lagged behind that of the thinkers. Sporadically from John Locke onwards, and consistently during the nineteenth and early twentieth centuries, British philosophers and theorists crafted and explored a creed of compelling political import. The proto-liberal doctrine of natural rights, and the even older but rejuvenated right to resist tyranny, identified impermeable spheres of individual liberty and offered justification for accountable government. The utilitarianism of philosophic radicalism epitomised by Jeremy Bentham advocated the maximisation of individual pleasure and happiness, soon to be translated into the pursuit of human and social well-being, but it also instilled a critical and constructivist attitude towards public affairs as a permanent norm of enlightened civic conduct. Mill's commanding investigations into the possibilities and limits of liberty, combined with the extolling of progress and individual development, became beacons for exploring the political relationship between the private and the public. Finally, the New Liberals – L. T. Hobhouse and J. A. Hobson in particular – helped to motivate the Liberal Party towards redefining the art of government as that of providing socially desirable goods, combined with a strong sense of collective responsibility in which welfare and liberty became mutually sustaining values.

The gradual democratisation of British politics had two immediate effects on the Liberal Party. Its centre of gravity shifted to an emerging professional middle class, in which the press and the free professions played a salient role, replacing the landed and urban aristocracies that had spearheaded Whiggism. And it was suddenly and sharply confronted with incontrovertible evidence of the squalid living conditions of the newly politicised working class, conditions that constituted a grave threat not only to constitutional stability but to national prosperity and to human decency. The end result was an unprecedented internal agitation within the Liberal camp that culminated in the reforms of 1906–14 – the most important and enduring of the party's concrete achievements in the twentieth century, and arguably the nineteenth as well.

The thinking behind the welfare state was an eminent example of liberalism at its best. It was premised on the recognition of individualism, group voluntarism, and state regulation as three cornerstones of a national partnership. It extended the idea of human flourishing by redefining the removable barriers to its attainment – not merely those of will and character but economic, social and cultural impediments as well – and in doing so acknowledged the ubiquity of human vulnerability alongside human ingenuity. Above all, it envisaged a communal spirit in which the recognition of mutual interdependence, guided by a benevolent state, would release individuals of all walks of life to pursue their own development, to their benefit and to that of their fellow citizens. Alongside the sanctification of individual freedom and rights, that must count as British liberalism's proudest intellectual accomplishment.

As the twentieth century progressed, the liberal emphasis on universal and abstract argument also came at a price: the cerebral nature of liberal argument found itself at a disadvantage in an age of mass politics and increasing appeals to the emotional rather than the rational side of citizens. No working people's clubs, or Primrose League tea parties, came to the rescue of an apparently desiccated and elitist language of politics. The Liberal Party did itself no favours either. After the First World War, especially from the 1930s, it suffered what can only be termed an intellectual decline and an obscuring of political vision, thus undermining itself in the very sphere that had been its source of strength. The Ramsay Muirs of liberalism were no match for its Mills and Hobhouses.

Politics is also about leadership, and for a while the Liberal Party produced leaders of national standing second to none, the most illustrious of which was Gladstone, followed closely by Lloyd George. If Gladstone was a case of a conscientious, even visionary, intellectual in politics with a hard head for finance, but one who could not transcend mid-nineteenth century Liberal premises and prejudices, Lloyd George was a moderniser, an acute practitioner of political tactics and populist rhetoric who understood the rise of democracy but often sailed close to the winds of intrigue and corruption. Both stood head and shoulders above their political contemporaries, inside as well as outside the party, though Joseph Chamberlain might have been – had fortune smiled and his ambition kept in check – the only other Liberal to rival their reputations.

The Liberal Party was, however, plagued with two leadership rifts. The first, between Gladstone and Chamberlain in 1886, resulted in a sea change as the hitherto radical Chamberlain took the Unionist wing of the party into a partnership with the Conservatives. Nevertheless, Gladstone and the party survived easily, freed from the cumbersome weight of an ever more reactionary and nationalistic Whiggism. However, the second rift – between Lloyd George and Asquith in the aftermath of the First World War – hastened the political collapse of the Liberal Party, as personal enmities fatally

eroded its internal coalitions. That was compounded by the discomfort of a traditionally supportive middle class, now voicing growing alarm at the redistribution of private
property and the spectre of socialism, rather than enthusiastically locked into their
former radical struggle with a decaying aristocracy. It was further accelerated by the
impatience of the active radical wing, disillusioned with the lack of reforming pace and
imagination into which the party had lapsed. Consequently the social (and financial) base
of the party narrowed, and it was unable to find alternative resources. In addition, the
Liberals failed to conjure up charismatic national politicians with sufficient electoral pull
from their midst, a weakness that has now characterised them, with a handful of exceptions, for the past eighty years.

Thus, in addition to being an internal coalition that altered over time, the Liberal Party
had increasingly to consider the possibility of external coalitions in a political system fundamentally hostile to political coalitions. Lloyd George formed one and attempted more,
and the 1930s and the post-Second World War period saw that issue as a staple item in party
debates. The problem was that mounting electoral frailty trapped the Liberals between the
Scylla of identity loss as a junior coalition member and the Charybdis of independent invis-
ibility – a dilemma that has now, after the 2010 election, reappeared.

A small-scale revival took place from the late 1950s, with a number of by-election
results proclaimed as the turning of the tide, but proving rather to be a false dawn. But
the Liberal Party appeared then to be little more than an assortment of protesting individuals – and individualists – who became disgruntled when the promise of radical
welfarism turned into an increasingly stagnant complacency, burdened with not always
endearing eccentricities. Be that as it may, Liberal aims and policies were dwarfed by the
power and duopoly of Conservatives and Labour. If Jo Grimond knocked some Liberal
policies into shape, particularly on Europe and on the increasingly attractive promise of
nuclear disarmament, the party nonetheless failed to shed its by now chaotic image or to
regulate its patchy and erratic performance. It was still burrowing away in the margins
of both public interest and the public interest.

By contrast, the 1980s rebranding of the Liberal Party – as the Liberal Democrats –
may have been a tactical decision following a part-merger with the Social Democratic
Party, but it rang true to the British liberal tradition and to the residue of social democracy contained within its policies. Recent years have shown it to be a left-of-centre party,
and a worthy upholder of its nineteenth and early twentieth-century principles, but with
increasing calls to resurrect entrepreneurial initiatives and to appeal to the private sector.
Concerns with civil liberties have reoccupied centre stage, but they have not sidetracked
the Liberal commitment to public services and to the idea of communal responsibility
promoted by twentieth-century British liberalism. Nonetheless, that credibility boost
has been, as always, partly a function of the weaknesses exhibited by the other major parties and the consequent space cleared by them, enabling the Liberal Party to recolonise
an important segment of public political discourse. In so doing, it has rediscovered an
audience for its voice of radical moderation.

The liberal revival was thus sparked off by two paradoxical phenomena. In the 1980s, the radicalisation of British politics, both rightwards and leftwards, opened up a gaping central area that Liberals attempted to fill, with some success. Following the rise of New Labour, however, a converse movement occurred in which the two big parties appeared to converge on major issues, thus leaving room for manoeuvre for a left-of-centre Liberal Party, often encountering a Labour Party to its right on key issues. The advent of the 2010 coalition suggests that the party's focus may change again, but at the same time affords the party the chance it has been denied, for most of a century, to express what political liberalism means in practice.

All this demonstrates yet again that a two-party system is ill-fitted to reflect the broader and increasingly more subtle spread of political opinion in the UK, and that British party alignment has for the past century not matched the available range of ideological variety. Indeed, the two-party system often encourages an institutional dumbing-down of the complexities of political understandings that obtain in modern, educated polities. Undoubtedly, though, liberal ideology still constitutes a fundamental feature of British political culture in general, whether disseminated through the organisational form of a party – no negligible shaping force, of course – or outside it, and the underlying liberality of British political life has so far survived attacks at its margins. In a political world of partial successes and more frequent failures that must surely count as a resounding achievement.

Guide to further reading

The list below provides a brief guide to some of the best concise histories of the Liberal Party, SDP and Liberal Democrats. Guides to further reading relating to each of the periods covered in this book can be found at the end of each chapter.

For a general survey, two of the reference sources produced by the Liberal Democrat History Group are useful companions: Duncan Brack et al. (eds.), *Dictionary of Liberal Biography* (Politico's Publishing, 1998) and Duncan Brack and Tony Little (eds.), *Great Liberal Speeches* (Politico's Publishing, 2001). Alan Sykes, *The Rise and Fall of British Liberalism 1776–1988* (Longman, 1997), covers the period from the American Revolution to merger.

On ideology, Duncan Brack and Ed Randall (eds.), *Dictionary of Liberal Thought* (Politico's Publishing, 2007) offers a comprehensive guide to the key people, ideas and organisations associated with liberalism. Conrad Russell, *An Intelligent Person's Guide to Liberalism* (Duckworth, 1999), traces the evolution of Liberal philosophy from the seventeenth century to the present day, and is elegantly and accessibly written. Kevin Hickson (ed.), *The Political Thought of the Liberals and Liberal Democrats since 1945* (Manchester University Press, 2009) is comprehensive and well argued, with contributions from a wide range of Liberal Democrats, including current politicians as well as academics. Tudor Jones, *The Revival of British Liberalism: From Grimond to Clegg* (Palgrave Macmillan, 2011) examines Liberal ideas as they have been embodied in the writings of Liberal politicians and thinkers and in party policy and strategy.

For for the period to the end of the nineteenth century, Leslie Mitchell, *The Whig World* (Hambledon Continuum, 2005) offers a political and cultural portrait of the Whigs in the eighteenth and nineteenth centuries. Jonathan Parry, *The Rise and Fall of Liberal Government in Victorian Britain* (Yale University Press, 1993) analyses the successes and crises of moderate, or Whig, Liberalism from 1830 to 1886. John Vincent, *The Formation of the Liberal Party, 1857–68* (Constable, 1966) is a seminal text looking at the origins of the party from a grassroots perspective, while Ian Bradley, *The Optimists*, (Faber and Faber, 1980) presents the ideological perspective of Victorian Liberalism throughout the nineteenth century. Key biographies include Richard Reeves, *John Stuart Mill: Victorian Firebrand* (Atlantic Books, 2007) and Colin Matthew, *Gladstone 1809–1898* (OUP, 1996).

Moving on to the twentieth century, Geoffrey Searle, *The Liberal Party: Triumph and Disintegration, 1886–1929* (2nd edn, Palgrave, 2001) is an excellent summary of the period from the Third Reform Act to *We Can Conquer Unemployment*. George Dangerfield, *The Strange Death of Liberal England* (Serif, 1997; reprint, first published 1935) is debatable history but a great polemic. Biographies of the key Liberal leaders include Roy Jenkins, *Asquith* (Collins, 1988) and Martin Pugh, *Lloyd George* (Longmans, 1988). Mark Egan, *Coming into Focus: The Transformation of the Liberal Party, 1945–64* (VDM Verlag, 2009) is a comprehensive treatment of a neglected period, examining how the party survived and laid the foundations for revival.

Peter Barberis, *Liberal Lion: Jo Grimond – A Political Life* (I. B. Tauris, 2005) contains a thorough and comprehensive political biography of the most important of the post-war Liberal leaders. Vernon Bogdanor, *Liberal Party Politics* (OUP, 1983) gives a portrait of the revived Liberal Party just before it embraced the SDP in the 1980s, while the SDP is comprehensively covered in Ivor Crewe and Anthony King, *SDP: The Birth, Life and Death of the Social Democratic Party* (OUP, 1995).

On the Liberal Democrats, Don MacIver (ed.), *The Liberal Democrats* (Prentice Hall Harvester Wheatsheaf, 1996) is the only thorough study so far of the merged party. Andrew Russell and Edward Fieldhouse, *Neither Left nor Right? The Liberal Democrats and the Electorate* (Manchester University Press, 2004) presents a detailed examination of where the Liberal Democrats derived their support in the 1997 and 2001 elections. Paddy Ashdown, *The Ashdown Diaries* (Penguin, 2000 (Vol. 1, 1988–97) and 2001 (Vol. 2, 1997–99)) concentrate heavily on 'The Project', Ashdown's ultimately futile attempt to bring the Liberal Democrats and Labour closer together. Ashdown's autobiography, *A Fortunate Life* (Aurum Press, 2009) is also worth a look.

Chapter 1

The Glorious Revolution to the Great Reform Act (1679–1832)

Mark Pack and Stephen Farrell

When the Liberal Party was formed in the nineteenth century, people did not view either the party or its policies as a wholly new entity without historic roots. Rather, it was seen as emerging from a long historical tradition which featured figures and events that were often quoted as being part of the party's inheritance. Many saw it as having deep roots, stretching back to the seventeenth century.

The extent to which political parties existed in the preceding two and a half centuries, the appropriate names to be used for them and how important they were have long been sources of debate among historians. Without delving too far into these debates, this chapter looks at the philosophical, policy and organisational roots which came together to help form the Liberal Party in the nineteenth century and which those at the time saw as key parts of its heritage.

The emergence of parties

Political parties emerged as part of the English political model in the seventeenth century, although precisely when a party system first came into being remains subject to academic debate. For centuries politicians have naturally formed into groups, for protection, support, patronage and power. Usually centred on an individual, or sometimes around a family, such groupings merge into the concept of party as they acquire a life of their own – beyond that of the individual or family – with an organisation and set of political beliefs that help define its existence.

There are numerous grey areas on the spectrum that runs from a loose collection of colleagues to a fully formed political party, and a resulting multitude of interpretations as to whether particular groupings at particular times should qualify for the name 'party'. A range of other terms, including 'factions', have been deployed by historians seeking to describe something more than a collection of political acquaintances but less than a party.

In English parliamentary history, one of the main catalysts for the formation of such factions was the question of 'supply'. The monarch had to secure parliamentary approval to approve funding ('supply') for his or her government's policies where they involved expenditure. Such decisions to grant or withhold supply in the end came down to a yes or no vote, and this binary choice encouraged the formation of groups either in support of the monarch's proposals – often assisted by the exercise of the crown's power of patronage – or in opposition to them.

Under Charles I these disputes ended in a bloody fashion: the ousting and execution of the monarch. Following the Restoration, similar pro- and anti-monarch factions, often fluid in their form, were again present. 'Court' and 'country' become popular terms for describing them. The court faction comprised those supporting the monarchy and its government, whilst the country faction saw themselves as standing up for other interests, such as those of the landed gentry, against the monarchy. By definition, these two groupings could not alternate in power – the court was always the government – though individuals could move between the two.

The court and country factions of the seventeenth century were of a very different nature from political parties in a modern democracy. Not only was party organisation outside Parliament largely absent, but even within Parliament many MPs and peers belonged to no party. At election times there was no national party machine, many seats went uncontested, sometimes for decades, and the political affiliation of many MPs can only be assessed by examining their behaviour in Parliament rather than how they presented themselves to their electors. Political labels were in part a matter of social self-identity as well as of ideology.

The exclusion crisis of 1678–81 was the midwife for the emergence of organisations in a form that makes them recognisable predecessors to the parties of the mid- to late nineteenth century. The crisis occurred over the question of who would inherit the throne after Charles II. Faced with the prospect of his brother James, a Roman Catholic, a group of powerful figures wished Parliament to legislate in order to exclude him from the succession. The conflict had a clear objective, and a clear means of achieving it – the passage of the exclusion bill through Parliament. The struggle to get the bill passed brought together a range of politicians and thinkers, unified by their hostility to unbridled monarchical power, particularly if the monarch was a Catholic.

The exclusion crisis also saw 'Whig' and 'Tory' labels spread into the political vocabulary, both originally as terms of abuse.[1] 'Whig' was used to describe those fighting to exclude James from the succession and 'Tory', previously applied to opponents of Cromwell in Ireland, was now used to describe those who opposed the exclusion legislation.

For those called Whigs the political drama gave a sense of identity and belief, essential for any developing grouping of politicians. Fear of what would happen under a strong Catholic monarch brought opponents together, not yet into what would now be called a party but into something more than the fluid groups of the past. Though monarchs and politicians would change, the Whigs over the next century and a half would retain a sense of self-identity born in the exclusion crisis; they would remain critical of the monarchy's power, even if at times they were the then monarch's preferred politicians.

From 1679, when the Earl of Shaftesbury first introduced the exclusion bill, a trial of political strength was waged with Charles, who repeatedly dissolved Parliament in an effort to secure a legislature that would not pursue the issue. Though the dissolutions did not in themselves succeed in this respect, Charles retained solid support in the House of Lords which, in 1680, rejected the exclusion bill on the one occasion that it progressed that far. After 1681 he changed tactics and simply did not summon Parliament, thereby removing from the Whigs their main political platform. Accompanied by the use of the crown's power to harass its opponents, this was sufficient to see the issue recede, and James II's succession protected.

Although the Whigs failed to prevent James from ascending the throne, his coronation did not place him firmly in control. As King, he continued to face scepticism from the Whigs, but he also antagonised many Tories with the extent of his pro-Catholic policies and his preference for aggregating more power to the monarchy. James did not help himself with his maladroit policies; although popular when he took the throne, he failed to appreciate the extent to which his support was conditional on the belief that, despite being a Catholic, he would support the Church of England's role and status. As a result of his failure to do so, his support ebbed away, particularly among Tory Anglicans. Despite their differences, Tories and Whigs increasingly came to share a common cause – opposition to James. Ultimately this resulted in the 'Glorious Revolution' of 1688 in which James was deposed, mostly (and unusually for the time) peacefully,[2] and replaced with a newly invited king and queen, the Dutch Prince William of Orange and his wife Mary, James II's daughter. Though it had Tory support, the revolution was very much a Whig event – driven by the Whigs and subsequently embraced by them as part of their heritage.

The Glorious Revolution

During James II's reign (1685–88) the issues of religion and the powers of the crown deeply split the country. Many Protestants were opposed to James, an open Catholic, and this fuelled an additional conflict over the relative powers and roles of Parliament and the monarch. In 1688, James fathered a son, who took precedence in the line of succession over his Protestant daughter Mary. This triggered a conspiracy by Protestants – both Whig and Tory – to depose James and replace him with Mary, whose husband, William of Orange, was also a Protestant. Seven Tory and Whig notables invited Mary and William to assume the throne. William's home country, the Netherlands, was at war with France, so the prospect of coming to power and thereby acquiring a new ally in this conflict appealed to him.

William and Mary, backed by a Dutch army, landed in Devon in November 1688. From the start the invasion gathered widespread support. James massed his forces near Salisbury but a combination of defections, doubts about the loyalty of his remaining troops and an evil omen (nosebleeds) led him to withdraw after only a minor skirmish. Power slipped further from James's grasp with the defection of the Duke of Marlborough, one of his military commanders, followed by his other daughter, Princess Anne. With William advancing on London, James decided to flee, but was caught by fishermen. He was imprisoned at Rochester, but escaped to France on 23 December 1688.

There followed some debate over how to proceed – should James be recalled under strict conditions, should a regency be installed or should his flight be deemed to have been an abdication? The last was settled on and in 1689 William and Mary became joint sovereigns. The Bill of Rights of that year asserted the power of Parliament and laid down the terms on which they could exercise power. The continuation of the monarchy, accompanied by some subsequent legal restrictions on its power, along with the coup's relatively peaceful nature, led its supporters to call the event the 'Glorious Revolution'. They saw it as the defining moment in the establishment of a constitutional monarchy and religious toleration.

The period from the late seventeenth to the early eighteenth century has often been called 'the first age of party',[3] with periods of government largely drawn from either Whig or Tory politicians. Although from a later perspective, it looks rather like a two-party system it was, however, different in a number of important respects to the Victorian and subsequent party systems. There continued to be a strong court versus country dimension, with attitudes on topics such as the power of the crown and levels of national expenditure still playing an important part in politics, tending to reflect who was in or out of power. Views on issues such as religion and commerce, however, were more clearly differentiated between Whig and Tory, regardless of who was in or out, and hence who was court or country, at any particular time.

Although Parliament was elected, the combination of significant monarchical power, infrequent constituency contests, a limited electorate and the lavish use of patronage to influence electors meant that politics was much more about the intrigues of a small group of individuals than influencing public opinion to achieve electoral success. What was significantly different about the Whig/Tory split, compared to the court and country division, was the possibility of power being transferred from one group to the other.[4]

There was much that was not clear about the distinction between Whigs and Tories. Some Tories had supported the Glorious Revolution, while others had opposed it (and there were enough of the latter to keep William III suspicious of all Tories). There were, however, many distinguishing Whig characteristics. For the Whigs, the Glorious Revolution was increasingly seen as 'their' event; a justifiable case of Parliament acting against an over-mighty monarchy to restrain and restrict its powers. This was to be a continuing theme of Whig beliefs and the Glorious Revolution was their collective lodestone, idolised as being an example of the wise use of political power in support of liberty against absolute monarchy. 1688 was seen – by them – as bringing about the most perfect form of government, a careful balancing act between crown and Parliament with sufficient checks and balances to preserve both liberty and property. Belief in this balancing act was one reason why many Whigs proved subsequently to be lukewarm over any significant extension to the vote; the franchise needed to be wide enough to ensure that the crown could not control the outcomes of elections, but not so wide as to upset the balance they desired. The stability of Britain's governing system after 1688, along with trial by jury, a relatively free press, the inability of government arbitrarily to jail its citizens, and hundreds of years of parliamentary government, compared favourably with the experience of other European countries, so reinforcing the Whigs' pride in what they saw as their own achievement in creating such a system.

William initially created a balanced ministry in terms of party composition. The Whigs manoeuvred themselves into a greater share of power as the 1690s progressed, with William turning to them increasingly as his need for financial support to pay for his wars grew; the Whigs had strong links with the financiers who controlled the money the King needed. These political manoeuvrings were in many ways unexceptional and were not obviously the harbinger of a major development in the country's party and political structure. Yet the connection between the Whigs and finance was to have a strong long-term influence on the development of the party system. This nexus meant that, despite their social conservatism in some areas, the Whigs became more closely aligned with industrial progress and development than did the Tories. This was never a neat and tidy division, and counter-examples abound, but as the industrial revolution gathered pace it helped explain how the Whigs became increasingly associated with progress and change, and the Tories with conservatism, tradition and rural life.

At the same time as these political developments, the Whigs were acquiring a set of distinctive philosophical ideas which were more enduring than the factors which led to transient coalitions for or against a particular monarch or political leader. John Locke, for the last third of the seventeenth century a follower of the leading Whig Lord Shaftesbury, both in office and in exile overseas, was their first major ideological thinker. Moving on from a defence of religious toleration, he developed a theory of natural rights and natural laws which led to a distinction between legitimate and illegitimate government and use of state power. It justified revolt against tyrannical authorities, such as an over-bearing monarch, and on a more modest scale justified opposing monarchs, on occasion, and restricting their powers – as in the Glorious Revolution. His *Two Treatises of Government* argued for two basic sets of rights, those of property and of thought. In practice, for Whigs, this meant opposing high-taxing, interfering kings (and so protecting property) whilst also supporting some religious toleration (distinguishing them from the Tories) for different forms of Protestantism.

John Locke (1632–1704)

Born in 1632, Locke spent many years in his youth in and around Oxford; he studied at Christ Church and was awarded degrees in 1656 and 1658. He became associated with Lord Shaftesbury in 1666 after treating him for a liver infection. Shaftesbury was to become Lord Chancellor in 1672, and Locke benefited from a series of influential government posts.

In contrast with Thomas Hobbes's *Leviathan* (1651) – which based a theory of government on the pooling of natural rights, and justified monarchies on the basis of a need for order and restraint so as to produce a peaceful society ('the people manifests itself as a unit through the single royal will') – Locke argued for the rights of individuals, accompanied by a responsibility to respect the rights of others. His theories of natural law and natural rights could justify the overthrow of governments that infringed them. Government was a necessary evil, to be tolerated only when needed.

His major work in this regard – *Two Treatises of Government* – is now dated to the 1680s, preceding the Glorious Revolution and making it a radical expression of views for the time. It provided Whigs with an intellectual legacy and a justification for the Glorious Revolution. Promoting the powers of Parliament and limiting the powers of the monarch were not merely a matter of personal political manoeuvring; they could also be viewed as protecting the natural order and reflecting a belief that government should be based on the consent of the governed.

Locke's writings also expressed support for religious toleration – which became a defining feature of Whig politicians – and hostility to organised factions in Parliament. He would not have been a supporter of the emergence of political parties.

At the turn of the century, the Tories returned to office, helped by William III's dislike of the Whigs' fondness for power, and also his immediate need to ensure that, in the absence of a direct male heir, a bill was passed to keep the monarchy in Protestant hands. It was unclear if the weakened Whig ministry could secure the passage of such a bill, but the Tories were willing to promise their support in return for power. The bill, which was to become the Act of Settlement of 1701, provided for the crown to pass to the Electress Sophia of Hanover – a niece of Charles I – and her Protestant descendants, rather than to revert to James II and his son, in the event of William and Mary, and Mary's sister Anne, dying without issue.

The Whig ascendancy

The two parties continued to crystallise during Anne's reign (1702–14). The question of who should succeed her as monarch continued to play a major role in politics, as did European wars. Anne's own political preferences were Tory, with the result that the Tories continued in power early in her reign. The strength of the Whigs in Parliament, however, especially after the 1707 Act of Union with Scotland, meant that they could not be ignored when, indeed, the Whigs briefly returned to office in 1708.

Religion was an important source of division between the parties, albeit not in a completely straightforward way. The Whigs were advocates of religious toleration, at least as far as Protestants were concerned. They tarred all Tories as closet Jacobites, supporters of James II and his descendants. Painting the Tories as Catholic sympathisers, unworthy of political office, was an effective political tactic, but not an entirely fair characterisation. Although there were Tory Jacobites, their political influence was waning and there were also some Scottish Whigs who supported the 'King over the Water'. Despite the Catholic sympathiser tag, the Tories were staunch defenders of the Church of England, largely hostile to Nonconformists and the principle of religious toleration, and consequently were able to portray the Whigs as a threat to the established church.[5]

The Jacobites

Replacing James II with a direct relative reduced the scope for questioning the legitimacy of the new monarchy, but the Glorious Revolution was still clearly a departure from the traditional line of inheritance. James II fled to France, where he died in 1701. He retained followers who intermittently plotted to return him to the throne, including through an invasion of Ireland (1689–90) which ended in failure at the Battle of the Boyne.

After James's death his son, whom supporters knew as James III, continued to live abroad, plotting to regain the throne, often in alliance with other countries. There were major uprisings in his support in 1715–16 and 1745–46. It was only with the failure of the latter revolt, led by James III's son Charles ('Bonny Prince Charlie'), that the Jacobite threat finally faded away.

Most support for the Jacobite cause came from Catholic Highlanders, though a handful of Whigs, such as the Earl of Mar, saw Jacobitism as a way of reducing the English dominance of Scotland. Even in the Highlands, however, such Whigs were very much the exception; Protestant lowlanders, whether Whig or Tory, largely supported the Glorious Revolution and its consequences.

Finance continued to be the other main source of division. The Whigs tended to attract support from those able to lend money, which was borrowed in large quantities by the government to pay for its wars. The Tories, in contrast, were increasingly the party of the small landowner, likely to be hit hard by taxation but, unlike the Whig financiers, unable to make money from lending to government.

Anne's death in 1714 brought George I to the throne under the terms of the Act of Settlement, and initiated a long period of Whig supremacy. Important though the era was in many ways, its role in the formation of the Liberal Party was less than that either of subsequent periods, nearer to the party's birth, or to the earlier period of the Glorious Revolution, with its legacy for Whig thought and traditions.

George's immediate preference was for the Whigs, largely because of his suspicion, reinforced by the failed Jacobite rebellion of 1715, that many Tories were hostile to his accession. Early in his reign, party divisions seemed to be clear and increasingly entrenched as the Whigs enjoyed power and tried to marginalise the Tories. However, the dominance of Robert Walpole – Britain's first 'Prime Minister' – ended up confusing the former party system, as politics increasingly revolved around support for or opposition to him. Some Whigs were consistent opponents of Walpole; these were the so-called country Whigs, who sought to resist the encroachments of royal and executive power by campaigning against the continuation of placemen in the Commons, trying to reduce corruption at elections, making efforts to scrutinise government expenditure, and expressing a profound unease at the maintenance of a peacetime army and a general distrust of British involvement in European wars.

Walpole took office in 1721 and held it until 1742. His long political career was a testament to his influence over people (particularly the kings he served), his oratorical skills and his adept handling of political crises, at least until the last few years of his premiership. Early successes included managing the political fall-out from the South Sea Bubble and retaining his position when George II took the throne in 1727. His main policy was to avoid foreign wars, which helped keep taxes low and also secured the position of the Hanoverian dynasty, thereby containing the Jacobite threat. Ironically, Walpole's fall from power came about after he reluctantly entered into war with Spain in 1739. The conflict did not go well and a mediocre election result in 1741 – caused in part by the personal hostility of the King's eldest son, Frederick, Prince of Wales, who exercised his patronage against Walpole – combined with Walpole's increasing age, encouraged many court Whigs to seek a new and more vigorous leader.

The court Whigs remained in power, with Henry Pelham and his brother, the Duke of Newcastle, becoming the dominant figures of the 1740s and 1750s. The Tories were a significant minority in Parliament, but remained on the fringes of power while George II lived. The Whigs continued to be divided, with William Pitt the Elder, for example, being a consistent critic of Newcastle. Ideological differences between the parties became blurred during this period, although the policy of avoiding continental entanglements continued. Maintaining the balance of power in Europe was an identifiable Whig concern, and the alliance with Austria and a commitment to diplomacy to secure peace became known as the Newcastle System.

Parties in the mid-eighteenth century

The mid-eighteenth century is a contentious period for tracing the origin of the Liberal Party. As the study of the history of British political parties took off in the late nineteenth century, the overwhelming view was that parties had originated in the late seventeenth century and had existed continuously ever since. It was only with the work of Lewis Namier and his followers in the early twentieth century that more attention was paid to the mid-eighteenth-century gaps in this supposed story of progress,[6] as a result of which the field is open for historians to pick a wide range of dates from the seventeenth, eighteenth or nineteenth centuries for the formation of modern political parties.

In recent years, more attention has again been paid to the existence of the party structure during the long period of one-party rule in the eighteenth century. Crucially, the social divisions between court Whigs and their Tory opponents helped keep the parties in existence. The Whigs were 'an interrelated leadership' centred around the 'Bedfords, Russells, Devonshires, Granvilles, Spencers and Westminsters ... whose connections with the commercial interests of the City of London, part of the provincial manufacturing elite and Old Dissent allowed them to serve as intermediaries between the parliamentary and public political worlds'.[7]

The political landscape changed when George III ascended to the throne in 1760. He did not share his grandfather's preference for the court Whigs and his accession accordingly led to a period of instability, as he attempted to end their monopoly on power and to lift the proscription of the Tories. However, the court Whigs remained strong in Parliament, and the hundred-odd Tories elected to the 1761 Parliament soon merged into the indistinguishable mass of country gentlemen in the House of Commons. The Earl of Bute, George III's former tutor and a leading advocate of the non-party ideas associated with the new King's father Frederick, Prince of Wales, became Prime Minister in 1762, but his government soon foundered and was replaced by a succession of ministries drawn from the different factions of the old court Whigs.

The governments of the 1760s

Bute's government of 1762–63 lasted less than a year; it foundered through lack of support in Parliament and Bute's own political ineptitude. He was replaced as Prime Minister in April 1763 by George Grenville, closely associated with William Pitt the Elder, who had served as Leader of the Commons under Bute. Grenville's government passed the Stamp Act, which was to bring tensions with the American colonies to a head, prosecuted John Wilkes (see below) and pursued an aggressive foreign policy. George III disliked Grenville and replaced him with the Marquess of Rockingham in July 1765. His ministry lasted for only a year and he was succeeded in turn by Pitt (who became Earl of Chatham).

William Pitt was a colossus of eighteenth-century politics, and was particularly popular with the general public as a 'patriot' – a lover of his country and a defender of liberty. An opponent of Walpole in the 1730s and 1740s, he served as a Cabinet minister after Walpole's fall, despite earning the enmity of George II for opposing a British subsidy to Hanover. During the 1750s he was the 'Great Commoner', the senior minister in the Commons, noted for his oratory and firm leadership, particularly in international affairs. He was seriously ill, however, by the time he formed his own administration, in 1766, and his popularity waned when he accepted a peerage. His government comprised talented individuals, almost regardless of party, but Pitt was unable by this stage to meld them into an effective team. He retired, through ill-health, in 1768, and was succeeded by the Duke of Grafton, a Whig acolyte of Pitt's. His ministry was short-lived and undistinguished, and gave way, in 1770, to Lord North's government.

Stability was achieved in 1770 when Lord North was appointed Prime Minister. Although in many ways he was an orthodox court Whig, he would later be characterised as a Tory because of his close identification with the royal influence within his government, a bolstering of the power of the executive that strengthened his hold over

Parliament. In the face of a monarch antagonistic to the power they had accumulated, the court Whigs who were now excluded from office ended up rediscovering their enthusiasm for an independent Parliament and for limiting the powers of the monarch.

John Wilkes and the American Revolution

By the 1770s, the political mood of the country was changing, with the opposition Whigs increasingly coming to believe that liberty itself was under threat. This was not just hostility to the powers of a king who now favoured their political rivals, but a reaction to the treatment of the colonists in America which culminated in the American Revolution.

In addition, it was the legacy of John Wilkes, the journalist who had provoked two *causes célèbres* during the previous decade. Although he was a man of authentic radical principles, his prominence in these two episodes owed more to his genius for controversy and his innovatory techniques of popular demagoguery than to any belief in the advancement of individual rights as such. With his scurrilous journalism, his unashamed libertinism and his insolent self-assertiveness, he easily alienated more moderate thinkers, polite 'middling rank' supporters and self-restrained Whig parliamentarians.

The North Briton, established in 1762, was Wilkes's vehicle for weekly articles attacking the government of John Stuart, the Earl of Bute, for its adoption of the arbitrary tendencies of the Stuart dynasty. In issue no. 45, dated 23 April 1763, he condemned the King's Speech, and was subsequently prosecuted for seditious libel. However, the law officers chose to proceed using a 'general warrant', a power enabling a search to be made not only of the printers' and publishers' property, but also of any other property. That proved to be a tactical error, for it gave the mob a ready cry ('no general warrants'), and the warrants were ruled to be illegal. As Wilkes broke his bail terms by absconding to the continent, the Commons expelled him as MP for Aylesbury on 20 January 1764. His – temporary – removal from the scene allowed the opposition Whigs to argue Wilkes's case for freedom of publication and freedom from arbitrary arrest without the dishonour of associating with such an unsavoury character.

Forced by his lack of money to return to England, Wilkes audaciously stood for Parliament at the 1768 general election. As an outlaw, his return for Middlesex was rejected by the House. He stood in the consequent by-election and, having run an extraordinarily popular campaign, was easily re-elected. The Commons expelled him again and, after he had once more won back his seat, simply seated his ministerialist opponent in his place. Wilkes's astute identification with the cause of the common man, or at least of the middling sort of freeholder, turned his personal situation into a call for protecting the rights of electors. The gravity of the affair allowed it to become a campaigning issue for metropolitan radicals, such as the Society of the Supporters of the Bill of Rights, and for hundreds of county electors who signed petitions to the Commons and who won the endorsement of the parliamentary opposition.

As an alderman of the City of London, Wilkes delighted in his corporation's defiance of Parliament over the printing of parliamentary debates, which at the time was unlawful. With the Lord Mayor, Brass Crosby, and another City magistrate, Richard Oliver, he obstructed attempts by the Commons to arrest the newspaper publishers whose papers persistently reproduced accounts of debates. Crosby and Oliver were imprisoned by the Commons, but their actions meant that from then onwards parliamentary debates could effectively be printed with impunity. Wilkes re-entered the Commons in 1774 and became Lord Mayor of London in the same year. Although he was later a steady supporter of Pitt the Younger's ministry, he sided with the opposition over the war with America.

The War of American Independence (1775–83) further helped to re-establish clear divisions between the ministry, the 'party of the crown', and the opposition, which now emerged as a party in its own right. The war provided a high-profile political issue on which the opposition could take a clear stance – support for the colonists' views – that was at variance from that of the government. As was the case with the Wilkes affairs, the war also provided a major stimulus to the radicalisation of political discourse in Britain and the development of extra-parliamentary activism.

At the heart of the disputes that led to the rebellion of the American colonies lay the issues of taxation and representation. Given the growing cost of paying for imperial defence, successive British governments sought ways of raising revenue in America, either in the form of customs duties on staple commodities such as sugar and tea, or through more intrusive excise taxes, such as the famous stamp duty, which provoked major colonial riots in 1765. The Stamp Act was repealed in 1766 by the short-lived Rockingham administration. The same government also passed legislation declaring the supremacy of Parliament over the colonies, demonstrating that almost all parliamentarians and most of the political establishment were united in their abhorrence of American claims for self-determination. Even Pitt the Elder, who argued that British taxes should only be laid on the colonies' external trade, and not raised internally, was adamant that they had to submit to the overall authority of the mother country.

Most Americans were prepared to accept the right of the British Parliament to regulate trade by varying excise duties, but they rejected its claim to be able to impose taxes for the purpose of raising revenue for the state. Most of the colonies possessed their own assemblies, which to varying degrees shared the exercise of power over local affairs with royal governors. However, the Americans had no direct representation at Westminster, which would have been impractical, and they were increasingly reluctant to accept the doctrine of 'virtual representation' which was broadly accepted in Britain. It may have been possible to believe that unenfranchised Britons had their concerns looked after in Parliament by MPs who knew them and had their interests at heart; it was much harder to convince Americans that their immediate needs and desires were capable of being understood and safeguarded by politicians in London. The great cry of 'no taxation without representation' was so effective partly because settlers and their descendants seemed to be deprived of the rights in America that had long been enjoyed by their contemporaries in Britain.

The war that the American colonies eventually won was ultimately fought over the extent of Parliament's authority. Even George III, whose obstinacy prolonged the war for several years, declared that he was 'fighting the battle of the legislature' in resisting for so long the likely outcome of American independence. It was ironic, therefore, that Americans interpreted their struggle for liberty in terms of the Lockean right of resistance: taking up arms to exercise their right to remove (or, in this case, to seek separation from) a constitutional monarch who they considered to have turned into a tyrant. The American Declaration of Independence of 1776 was in many ways a personal attack on the recent policies of George III, but it was also a classic restatement of the principle of government by consent – of the authority of government being based on the support of the people.

The American Revolution had a huge impact, not least in Ireland, where the Volunteers, a defence force armed against external invasion, posed an implicit threat to the colonial authority of Britain. Ireland might have gone the same way as America had not commercial and constitutional concessions been made, particularly the granting in 1782 of legislative independence, with what was later called 'Grattan's Parliament' lasting until the Union of 1801.

By 1779, mounting dissatisfaction at the expense and controversy of the war – for instance, over the employment of German mercenaries – helped fuel calls in Britain for changes to the way in which Parliament operated. The Rev. Christopher Wyvill's association movement, which began in Yorkshire that year, built on the Wilkesite agitation of the previous decade. It was a campaign led by respectable property owners that nonetheless made radical demands for economies in public expenditure, an additional 100 county MPs and annual parliaments. Although reformers such as these concentrated on Parliament, their purpose was to strengthen its independence to counterbalance the perceived increase in the power of the crown. The opposition Whigs in Parliament had slightly different views, especially on parliamentary reform, from the Wyvillites, but they adopted the same diagnosis of the ills facing the body politic in these years.

The Rockingham Whig Party

At the heart of the Whig opposition sat the group around the Marquess of Rockingham, the Rockingham Whigs, who, crucially, developed a set of political beliefs in which party organisation was no longer something to be deprecated or disguised, but instead became a positive virtue.

The Rockingham Whigs grew out of the Pelhamite court Whigs who were forced from office in the early 1760s. Their early identity derived from a sense of grievance at their mistreatment by George III, with the King's petulant dismissal of the Duke of Devonshire in 1762 being particularly hard to stomach.[8] But the Rockingham Whigs also took in those, such as the old Tory William Dowdeswell, who brought a particular country tinge to the party. This manifested itself in a growing sense of unease at the power exercised by the government on behalf of the crown. However, it was in developing the myth of so-called 'secret influence', of the King being misled by a 'minister behind the curtain', that the party was able to elevate an explanation for its own exclusion from office into a set of principles and policies for future application in government.

The Marquess of Rockingham (1730–82)

Charles Watson-Wentworth, second Marquess of Rockingham, was a leading Whig from the time he entered the House of Lords in 1751 until he died, during his second brief term as Prime Minister, in 1782. Not a great orator or political thinker, he was nevertheless effective in organising local Whig supporters, particularly through the Whig Club in York, which was named after him from 1753. A staunch supporter of Newcastle's court Whigs, he resigned as a Lord of the Bedchamber in 1762 in protest at the political actions of George III.

During the political turmoil of the early part of the new reign, Rockingham was briefly Prime Minister in 1765–66 before spending sixteen years as leader of the Whigs in opposition. Although he displayed limited abilities as a party leader in the Lords, proving to be weak in some of the organisational areas associated with the position, he became much more adept at managing his party more widely and in projecting its image beyond Westminster.

He was Prime Minister again for fourteen weeks before his death, during which time his government acknowledged the independence of the United States for the first time. Edmund Burke was a close associate of Rockingham for many years, first as his private secretary, and later as his Commons mouthpiece and the party's political philosopher.

Principal among the Whig thinkers at this time was Edmund Burke, an MP who was an outspoken supporter of the American colonists. His 1770 work, *Thoughts on the Cause of the Present Discontents*, was an attack on corruption and poor government that identified interference by the monarch as the root cause of the problems. From this perspective, an organised group of politicians – usually denounced as a 'faction' at that time – became a virtuous necessity, as an organisation that was required to keep the monarch in check. Burke famously defined, and at the same time justified, 'party' as 'a body of men united, for promoting by their joint endeavours the national interest, upon some particular principle in which they are all agreed'. The opposition Whigs therefore possessed a distinctively different set of beliefs from the ministerialist supporters of government, which justified them in forming an organised opposition. On the other hand, an important restraint on the development of party was the belief, most eloquently put by Burke, that MPs should be able to exercise their own judgment, free from outside interference – as representatives rather than delegates of their constituents. This was a view which did not encourage the creation of party organisation.

Not only did the Rockingham Whigs possess a party mentality, but they behaved as one, for example in their refusing to enter office in 1780 without guarantees over policies and personnel. When Rockingham did regain power, two years later, he implemented the first real legislative programme to have been conceived in opposition. His brief second administration set in train the negotiations for American independence that culminated in the following year's peace treaty, and it oversaw the passage of several items of economic reform, or anti-corruption legislation, including in particular Burke's measure to abolish redundant government offices and sinecures. In addition, in a move which had not been foreseen and which was rushed through Parliament under the pressure of events, Ireland's Parliament in Dublin was granted a greater degree of autonomy.

Fox versus Pitt

In the early 1780s there also emerged a potent personal debating duel to help clarify the party divisions: Charles James Fox, the first acknowledged 'leader of the opposition', versus William Pitt the Younger.[9] Fox himself was a member of a distinct social set. He and his fellow Whigs formed a community of their own with their own habits, forms of speech and thought patterns.[10] They were also predominantly a group in opposition. This was not just a reflection of their parliamentary record, but also of their mindset, for their liberalism was 'a doctrine of opposition, whether to the pretensions of a monarch, a corrupted Parliament, a self-serving aristocratic elite, an established church, or, indeed any authority or regulation that restricted the legitimate liberty of the individual'.[11]

Yet the liberalism espoused by the opposition Whigs was not simply a means of defining their own identity on the margins of politics. In Fox, they found a champion of the kind of religious and political liberty that had so exercised their seventeenth-century predecessors. In the 1770s, he supported the attempts to remove the civil disabilities imposed on religious Dissenters, at last achieved in 1779, and the highly controversial, though relatively minor, Catholic Relief Act of 1778, which provoked the Gordon riots in 1780. Fox also expressed much sympathy with the moderate proposals for parliamentary reform that Pitt tried to introduce in the early 1780s but abandoned in 1785 after his failure to carry them.

Behind these endeavours for improvements in society and government lay a shared sense of optimism. For Whigs, progress was both inevitable and generally welcome. They were more instinctively accepting of change, religious toleration and industrial developments than their opponents – though broad agreement on principles such as these did not prevent numerous disagreements between Whigs over specific policies.

Charles James Fox (1749–1806)

Fox, who entered the House of Commons in 1768, before he was of age, was the son of the ambitious office-hunter and man on the make, Henry Fox, Baron Holland. A spoilt child, he developed into a reckless gambler and, for all his personal charm, his vanity and arrogance made him an object of suspicion and an easy target for the satirists. Yet his vigorous intellect, his brilliant oratory and his persistent support for the cause of liberty turned him into a heroic parliamentarian and earned him a reputation as 'a man of the people'.

Having briefly held office in 1782, when he became the first man to hold the (renamed) office of Foreign Secretary, Fox's career was essentially one of failure. He was Foreign Secretary twice more, but only for brief periods, and never became Prime Minister. This failure was heavily shaped by his support for, and friendship with, George III's heir, the Prince of Wales (later Prince Regent and George IV), which earned the King's hostility. This was not just a matter of politics; with some justice, George blamed Fox for leading his son into a life of dissolution. As with many other leading Whigs, life was generally good for Fox, and pleasure-seeking may well have taken the edge off his, and his colleagues', political campaigning.

Fox maintained his opposition to the war against France in the 1790s and to the repression of the radical movement in Britain during that period. He did not live long enough to fulfil his ambition of making a lasting peace with Napoleon Bonaparte, but his return to office in Lord Grenville's 'Ministry of All the Talents' achieved another long-term aspiration. Largely at his bidding, the Commons approved his policy of abolishing the slave trade, which was implemented by legislation in 1807. In this and other respects, Fox was a bridge between the late-eighteenth century Whig opposition and the emergence of a Liberal Party in the early nineteenth century. He personified the way in which the aristocratic Whigs acted as a moderating force between radicals and reactionaries at the turn of the century.

Lord North's government lasted until 1782, but fell because of dissatisfaction with the conduct of the American war. The Whigs returned to power under Rockingham, who soon died, and then the Earl of Shelburne, until Fox and his supporters threw in their lot with North in a new government led by the Duke of Portland.

George III demonstrated that he was an active participant in British politics by intervening in the debate about Fox's India Bill and then by dissolving Parliament in 1784 for an early general election. The Fox–North coalition had brought in a bill to give control of the management of Indian affairs to a board based in London that would be filled with Fox's cronies. Granting the lucrative patronage of the sub-continent to his friends was seen as despicably grasping and self-serving on the part of Fox, which was ironic given that ten years earlier the opposition Whigs had objected to the 1773 India Bill as interference with the chartered rights of the East India Company.

Taking advantage of the bill's controversial nature, the King influenced the natural supporters of the court in the Lords to vote the measure down. He gave his full backing to the new Prime Minister, Pitt, and granted him an early dissolution to benefit from the disarray of the opposition. At just twenty-four years of age, Pitt was a risky choice, but he had one clear attribute: he was dependent on royal backing, and his appointment removed many of the shackles on the King. Pitt faced a Parliament that was overwhelmingly opposed to his government, but early signs of competence in the job, combined with royal backing, ensured that he could both form a ministry and keep it together. The result of the general election was a rout of the opposition and a majority for the now well-established Prime Minister. This display of royal power also further defined the party system. It was the King, Pitt, royal power and government privileges against the Whigs, fighting for restrictions on regal power and curbs on corruption.

The 1784 Parliament lasted six years, and in that period there was a consistent body of around 130 votes for the Whig opposition in the Commons. The Whig Club was formed in May 1784 as an embryonic party headquarters, and Brooks's Club provided a useful social centre for the leading Whigs – and continued to do so well into the nineteenth century. In Parliament a whipping system emerged, while outside Parliament William Adam assumed the role that would later be titled national party agent. Adam had an office and full-time staff, and sought to establish political clubs in the constituencies to support the Whig cause. His organisation's tasks included the corralling of MPs to attend Parliament, the matching up of candidates with seats and the encouragement of (limited) campaigning to win the support of voters. Organisation and fundraising were supplemented by a media operation of sorts – funding newspapers to ensure favourable coverage.

The Whigs came close to power in 1788, when George III suffered his first serious mental health difficulties. The Prince of Wales who, it was expected, would act as regent in place of his father, was a friend of Fox and a supporter of the Whigs. It was only George III's recovery in early 1789 that forestalled the Whigs' return to power. This episode damaged the Whigs, however, because Fox's enthusiasm for transferring unrestricted regency powers to the Prince undermined his apparent commitment to the supremacy of Parliament. Nevertheless, the general election of 1790 confirmed the developments in the party system over the preceding fifteen years. Before then, the normal pattern had been for the ruling group to gain in power over time as the lure and perks of office attracted support, until royal intervention or some other external event overturned the existing political order. With a clear ideological background to their position, however, the Whigs were able to maintain their strength at this election despite remaining in opposition.

The French Revolution

The outbreak of the French Revolution in 1789 did not at first shake up the political system in Britain. Appalling though it seemed to many of the other monarchies in Europe, the revolution initially appeared, at least in Britain, to be similar to England's Glorious Revolution – an exercise of unconventional power to restrain an overweening monarch. As such, it attracted some support from the British political establishment. This perception changed, however, as the revolution became more radical and more bloody. In January 1793 Louis XVI was executed and in the following month war with France broke out. As the revolution became more violent, the British reaction polarised.

For some, the descent into violence was a reason to disavow events in France. Burke, for example, moved away from the Whigs to become a leading conservative thinker because of the revolution. For others, the violence was caused by a brutal monarchy that had refused to give way gracefully to demands for reform. That was seen as an illustration of what could happen in Britain if pressure for moderate reform was resisted.

Events in France gave hope to some of those outside traditional political circles that more radical change was possible in Britain, and in 1791–92 this led to the spread of corresponding societies across the country, many including people from the working classes. The corresponding societies argued for radical political reform, including universal manhood suffrage; they took their name from one of their principal activities – corresponding, by means of letters, with each other and with like-minded radicals in France. *The Rights of Man* by Thomas Paine was their main ideological inspiration. The development of such a network caused many in the ruling classes to fear the outbreak of violence and rebellion, particularly once Britain was at war with France.

Thomas Paine (1737–1809)

Born in Norfolk in 1737, Thomas Paine became one of the most influential political thinkers of the late eighteenth century, with a legacy lasting long beyond his lifetime.

With its clear and emphatic writing style, his anonymously published *Common Sense* (1776) encouraged the American Revolution. In turn *The Rights of Man* (1791) defended the French Revolution and many of its ideals against critics and was a reply to Burke's *Reflections on the Revolution in France*, an argument for pragmatic and incremental policies which Burke described as at odds with the abstract ideas of the revolution. Paine defended abstract rights and radical change, though he stopped short of supporting such violent acts as executing the king.

In contrast with earlier writers such as Locke, who emphasised the protection of property as part of a natural free society, Paine stressed the rights of individuals. He argued that men were born free and equal, and from this he developed a withering critique of European monarchies and their social and political structures. He linked together absence of democracy with dictatorial ruling cliques, wars and financial hardship.

Until well into the nineteenth century, Paine's ideas were largely ignored by the Whigs. But as the party became broader, encompassing those who called themselves radicals, reformers and liberals, its tenets could increasingly be traced back to Paine. In particular, his beliefs easily led on to the view that democracy, peace and low taxation were a harmonious and self-reinforcing trio. In the guise of 'peace, retrenchment and reform', these views would become a central part of Gladstonian Liberalism.

Unlike the previous generation of radicals and advanced Whigs, whose ambition had been to restore the best parts of Britain's former political and social structures, Paine's generation of radicals worked from first principles of morality and government towards a new constitutional model. Thereafter, politics increasingly became a conflict between those arguing for universal, inalienable rights and those trying to protect established authority and order against what they saw as the danger of anarchy. This crude distinction underlay political discussion and the structure of the party system throughout much of the nineteenth century.

There has been much historical debate about the extent of the threat of revolution in Britain at that time – how many plotted revolution, what were their aims and what was their real level of support? Even though revolution was in reality never likely, the opposition Whigs were torn apart by revolution abroad and the tensions this caused domestically. Some switched to support the government, some remained in opposition but became more conservative, some continued to advocate modest reforms and some toyed with supporting much more radical reform, linking up with radical campaigners outside Parliament.

The most famous proponent of the conservative anti-French case was, ironically, the former Whig standard-bearer, Edmund Burke. In his 1790 work, *Reflections on the Revolution in France*, he warned of increasing violence and extremism in France, arguing that order and stability could only come from respect for, and the preservation of, the social order. Rooted in the past, in deference and in customs and habits, the established order provided the basis for stable and peaceful government. In contrast, he believed that reformers wished, to varying degrees, to do away with the current order to allow for the better demonstration of basic rights that everyone (although often this meant every man rather than every person) had by virtue of their birth.

Burke's own views were too sophisticated and subtle to be pigeonholed as reactionary. He was, after all, a firm believer in equal rights for Catholics, a view that did not find favour with stoutly Protestant supporters of the government. Yet he did mark out a road that many other Whigs followed, scared off reform by the events in France and by fear of revolution at home. Burke and Fox split after a dramatic scene in Parliament in 1791, and although few Whigs followed Burke at the time, the party lost support with every report from Paris of the worsening violence and chaos.

Part of the pressure on the Whigs in opposition derived from the role of property in debates over reform. Many Whigs were significant landowners and were inevitably attracted to arguments over the protection of the rights of property-owners and of their importance in protecting society from extremism. In the past, such debate had focused on resistance to the monarchy, and its demands for tariffs and taxation; property-owners were seen as the key defenders of liberty, for they possessed sufficient independence (and means) to be able to stand up to the monarch. The French Revolution changed the way in which their role was perceived, with many revolutionaries coming to condemn them as the enemy, underpinning an oppressive state. At the same time conservatives praised them and sought to defend their position, seeing those with a stake in the country as best placed to defend it against wild and dangerous – and foreign – ideas. No longer were property-owners the bulwark of independent Englishmen against the monarch; now they were the defenders of the social order against revolutionaries and foreigners.

In 1792 several leading Whigs, generally those who were younger and more radical, set up the Association of the Friends of the People to push for parliamentary reform; this was supported in the Commons by, among others, Charles Grey. The Association was a self-consciously elitist body; its annual subscription was set at two and a half guineas, far higher than most people could afford. It argued for moderate reform led by moderate people, who would help control and temper the more extreme campaigners for political change. For its members, the lesson from France was that opposing change would lead to far worse consequences than would a process of managed reform.

Other Whig thinkers were more inclined to protect the existing order than risk undermining it by arguing for change. In 1793 there came a formal split, when William Windham, the MP for Norwich, who had spoken in favour of Fox's position during the regency crisis of 1788–89, led around thirty Whigs into an independent parliamentary faction opposed to reform. In the same year, Lord Loughborough, the Whig leader in the Lords, switched to the government, enticed in part by the post of Lord Chancellor. The political realignment was completed in 1794, when not only Windham but the Duke of Portland and many other Whigs crossed the floor to support the government. Over the previous two years, Portland had increasingly differed from Fox over questions such as the summoning of the militia, war with France and reform of the electoral system, which was the subject of a vote in Parliament in 1793. In Pitt's new government, Portland became Home Secretary, while Windham and three other Whigs also joined the Cabinet; indeed, the new Cabinet split nearly equally between past supporters and opponents of Pitt.

The Duke of Portland (1738–1809)

William Cavendish-Bentinck, third Duke of Portland, was a conservative Whig, whose alliance with Pitt from 1794 was instrumental in cementing Pitt's hold on power and in continuing the development of what became the Tory party of the nineteenth century.

Born of an established Whig family, wealthy and showered with titles, Portland was associated with Rockingham and held positions in both his short-lived administrations. He emerged in 1783 as an acceptable candidate to serve as Prime Minister in the Fox–North coalition government, but he later broke with Fox over the French Revolution, joining Pitt's government as an unfairly under-rated Home Secretary in 1794. He held ministerial office until 1806 and was again chosen to head a coalition government from 1807 until shortly before his death in 1809.

Whig wilderness

Many historians have seen the events of 1794 as signalling the formation of a new Tory party, the antecedent of the Conservative Party. What was left of Fox's party was small, but ideologically more coherent. As the Tories became more clearly the party of patriotism, stability and the defence of property, the Church of England and the constitution,

Fox's Whigs became more clearly the party of reform, religious equality and greater political rights for a larger part of the population.

In the mid-1790s there were only around forty to fifty followers of Fox, though they managed to muster 91 votes (against 256) on Grey's parliamentary reform motion in 1797. Although only a parliamentary rump, and despite Fox's secession from the Commons in the late 1790s, the Foxites kept the flame of liberty alive by offering opposition to the suspension of habeas corpus and other repressive policies pursued by Pitt's government during that decade.

The party structure was shaken up again in 1801. Unrest in Ireland, a Catholic country colonised by Protestant settlers whose elite held tight to political power, persuaded Pitt of the need to grant Catholics more civil and political rights. He promised to legislate for Catholic emancipation during the negotiations over the union between Great Britain and Ireland. The King, though, did not agree and as a result Pitt resigned. Not until Lord Liverpool became Prime Minister in 1812 was there another long-serving government. Instead, the intervening period witnessed a myriad of administrations – six in total, many short-lived, as Pitt's coalition splintered. Pitt's difficulties raised the hopes of Fox and his followers, but the Whigs remained divided during this period of ministerial manoeuvrings. Though in some votes the Foxites could attract much higher support than during the lean years of the mid-1790s, Fox was too closely associated with reform to attract the support of those Whigs who had drifted under the wing of Pitt.

Pitt returned to power in 1804 after Henry Addington, as Prime Minister, first negotiated a highly controversial peace with France and then saw it fail. This provided only a brief respite from the manoeuvrings, as Pitt died in January 1806. The opposition to Pitt's final ministry in Parliament was still small but, briefly after Pitt's death, the Whigs did recombine to gain power. George III had little choice but to accept the return of Fox, who served briefly as Foreign Secretary in the short-lived 'Ministry of All the Talents' (1806–07) until his death in September 1806. Neither on parliamentary reform nor religious equality did this government do anything to distinguish itself from a Pittite government; it was simply a ministry of those who had not supported Pitt. It was headed by Pitt's cousin Lord Grenville, whose small band of supporters remained allied to the Whigs for over a decade.

The Grenville government fell apart in 1807, leading to a twenty-three-year period of Pittite dominance.[12] The ministry formed under Portland received a clear endorsement in the 1807 general election, with many of the supporters of the previous government going down to defeat. Ill-health saw Portland stand down in 1809 and when his successor, Spencer Perceval, was murdered in 1812, Lord Liverpool became Prime Minister. He inherited a government supported by all shades of ministerialist opinion that were strongly anti-reform and committed to continuing the war with France.

In the first few years of Liverpool's administration, the opposition remained split over the war, with some Whigs wanting immediate peace and others being in favour of fighting until military victory was secured. Victory in 1815 brought an end to this division and made it easier for advanced political thinkers to argue for domestic reform. This helped bring the Whigs together, and the opposition to Liverpool evolved into a relatively unified group which favoured moderate parliamentary reform and religious freedoms – though they were less willing than before to associate with extra-parliamentary reform campaigns.

Radicals

Outside Parliament, but with some supporters within it, the Society for Constitutional Information was one of the leading organisations of radicals in the late eighteenth century. John Cartwright is generally recognised as its founder, and it included such notable writers and polemicists as John Horne Tooke, Richard Price, Capel Lofft and Richard Brinsley Sheridan, a close friend of Fox. Its purpose was not so much to promote radical activism directly as to provide for the dissemination of political knowledge through printed publications in order to encourage such activism more widely. However, the society was central to the advancement of the more radical agenda of political change inspired by the French Revolution, including the attempts to establish a national convention (or anti-Parliament), and it was suppressed by Pitt's wartime coalition in 1794, when Horne Tooke was tried (and acquitted) of treason.

Women thinkers played an important role in the world of radical ideas. Several of the leading 'bluestockings' had marked radical leanings, including the republican historian Catherine Macaulay, and the feminist writer Mary Wollstonecraft, who published her *Vindication of the Rights of Woman* in 1792. Women such as Anna Letitia Barbauld, who in 1791 addressed to William Wilberforce a verse satire on the defeat in Parliament of the slave trade abolition bill, were prominent in the campaign to end the trafficking of enslaved Africans in British ships. Anti-slavery was an issue that cut across party divisions, uniting as it did both evangelical Pittites, like Wilberforce, and more advanced Whig figures such as Thomas Clarkson. It was also the arena in which black Britons, such as Olaudah Equiano, contributed significantly to the development of liberal ideas on race and equality.

Economic liberalism and foreign affairs

Industrialisation provided an important impetus to the reform movement. The growth of large cities with no, or minimal, parliamentary representation, such as Manchester and Sheffield, made it increasingly difficult to argue that parliamentary reform should remain out of the question. Social and economic change meant that defending the status quo was no longer as safe an option as it had been in the 1790s, and it proved much more difficult to argue against reform when society was undergoing a period of rapid change. For the Whigs, opposition to arbitrary monarchical power was translating into opposition to the arbitrary exclusion of the rising commercial interests from political power. There was increasing scope for a broad coalition bringing together both ardent reformers and those who wished to see only limited reform to deal with the extremes brought on by industrialisation and population change. Liverpool's political skills, however, ensured that this was only a theoretical threat to the Tories' dominance, and he kept the Whigs firmly out of power.

The end of the war with France had an immediate economic impact: government spending was massively cut, deflating the economy, wheat prices rose sharply after a period of bad weather, and around 300,000 members of the armed forces lost their jobs as the army and navy were scaled back. Economic hardship triggered unrest around the country. There were many meetings, petitions and demands, but no coherent movement or central organisation to apply pressure to the government. The Whigs, centred on Parliament and nervous of inciting mass violence, were neither able nor willing to provide a lead.

Their failure to present a coherent alternative to Liverpool's economic policy perhaps reflected their intellectual roots in the new economic thinking in Scotland. Many Whigs were educated at Edinburgh and Glasgow, and The *Edinburgh Review* (founded in 1802) was essentially a Whig journal. As a result, there was considerable crossover between the Scottish intellectual establishment, including the followers of the economist Adam Smith, and leading Whigs. The Whigs' tendency to believe in the inevitability of beneficial progress was consistent with the theories of Adam Smith and the 'invisible hand' he saw at work in the marketplace.[13] This easily translated into a belief that the government could not and should not seek to intervene in economic matters.

Laissez-faire economics

Although the Corn Laws of 1815 (duties on imports of grain) remained in place until 1846, the early nineteenth century witnessed a gradual opening or liberalisation of commerce between the United Kingdom and other trading nations. This was largely the fruit of the developing discipline of political economy, which saw the lifting of restrictions on trade, including import duties and export bounties, as the most likely way to produce the greatest expansion of activity and profits. One of the most economically literate MPs of the time was William Huskisson, and it was during his spell as President of the Board of Trade in the mid-1820s that the most extensive moves towards free trade were implemented, notably in the relaxation of the old Navigation Laws and the opening of colonial markets to foreign competition.

In economic and social contexts, liberalism came to mean less the defence of the liberty of the people in terms of politics or religion, but rather the freedom (almost in the libertarian sense) for some to gain in wealth or status at the expense of others; indeed, economic liberalism aimed to exclude the least successful in society, whereas political liberalism was meant to be inclusive of the weakest minorities. This distinction between liberalism as a political creed (the moral duty to advance the cause of constitutional and religious freedom) and as an economic system (the right to promote individual financial and social autonomy) has long confused the historical debate over the nature of liberalism in Britain, and still marks a profound fissure within the broader liberal movement.

The Whigs adopted a principled stand during this period against government measures which, in the name of preserving law and order, infringed on people's rights. The repressive Six Acts of 1819,[14] for example, were opposed by the then Whig leader in the Commons, George Tierney, whose theme of protecting individual liberties even at times of disorder and threats to national security would resonate throughout subsequent liberal history.[15]

In general, however, the leadership of the Whigs at this time was unimpressive, and the party remained weak. That was largely because the nominal leader, Lord Grey (as Charles Grey had become), was unwilling either to leave control of the party to others while he remained at his home in the country, or to take a sufficiently active interest in politics to compensate for the lack of a strong party spokesman in the Commons. The resulting vacuum in Parliament was filled by figures such as the erratic Henry Brougham, who was capable of launching forensic oratorical criticism of ministers, as well as of alienating the opposition's backbench supporters.

The Peterloo Massacre

The repressive Six Acts were a direct response to the Peterloo Massacre of 16 August 1819. A crowd of around 60,000 – 80,000 gathered at St Peter's Field, Manchester, to demonstrate in favour of parliamentary reform. The crowd was made up of contingents from numerous towns and villages near Manchester and represented up to half of the population of the area. They intended to elect a 'Member of Parliament' and listen to the radical orator, Henry Hunt.

The government attempted to ban the meeting; shortly after it began, magistrates ordered the arrest of Hunt and the meeting's organisers. In the ensuing charge by the yeomanry cavalry, fifteen people were killed and hundreds were injured. The carnage caused outrage across the country, and its long-term effect was to bolster support for radical political change and for a more tolerant approach to policing and protest.

In the early nineteenth century, the party labels of Tory and Whig came back into general usage, albeit with rather different connotations than their original meanings. Throughout much of the previous century, almost all politicians would have described themselves as 'Whig', a word encompassing such a panorama of views that its use is almost meaningless without the addition of a qualifying term such as court, country or opposition. The political philosophy of the late seventeenth-century Tories and Whigs was hard to discern in their nominal successors over a century later, but in common historical parlance, a continuity of sorts – if not necessarily of personnel – can be discerned. After the accession of George III, the description 'Tory', although it surfaced occasionally, was generally reserved for a term of abuse until Robert Peel and George Canning began cautiously to adopt it to describe themselves and the Liverpool government of 1812–27.

Following the reshuffles between 1821 and 1823 that brought Peel to the Home Office, Canning to the Foreign Office and Huskisson to the Board of Trade, the administration entered what was later described as a 'liberal Tory' phase. This usage emphasised the more liberal attitude behind some of the reforms of those years, for instance Peel's beneficial changes to the criminal laws. However, 'liberal' itself emerged as a distinct term in the 1820s. One significant example comes from Francis Jeffrey, the editor of the *Edinburgh Review*, who described Canning's ministry of 1827, a coalition of pro-Catholic Tories and moderate Whigs, as a 'new and bold experiment of a liberal or rational government'. 'Liberal' as a descriptive term for a politician was probably used for the first time in May 1828, when the ex-Canningites, now led by Huskisson, were forced out of the Duke of Wellington's administration; Lord Palmerston referred to himself and his fellow former ministers as 'the ejected liberals'.[16]

Liberal foreign policy

One of the key areas of 'liberal Toryism' in the 1820s was the foreign policy associated with the name of George Canning. Some of his decisions – for instance, to support the Greeks in their war of independence against Turkey, or to use British forces to defend the liberal constitution of Portugal in 1826 – showed a surprising willingness to go out on a limb in favour of populist aims and more democratic forms of government. However, his policy was still governed by the need to defend British interests, and some of his apparently 'liberal' policies were thinly disguised attempts to do down the influence of other European powers. Of his backing for the independence of several of Spain's colonies in South America, he boasted in the Commons that he had 'called the new world into existence to redress the balance of the old'.

Canning's attitude to foreign affairs was similar to Grey's, and his period as Foreign Secretary prefigured the long occupancy of that post by Palmerston, who transmitted some of Canning's principles of government to what became Gladstonian Liberalism. Palmerston, too, was adept at making the most of appearing to be liberal in his foreign policy, while at the same time proving the ultimate patriot in upholding Britain's unchanging national interests.

Catholic emancipation and parliamentary reform

The political situation was turned on its head when Daniel O'Connell's Catholic Association in Ireland forced the issue of Catholic emancipation back into the mainstream of debate in the 1820s. The government was so deeply split on the issue that Liverpool was unable to hold his ministers to a collective line. He was strong enough to remain in office, but when a stroke forced his resignation in April 1827, the splits became more significant.

Liverpool's successor as Prime Minister, Canning, a man noted for insults and personal antagonisms, was far from the ideal candidate to deal with a delicate political situation. With several key hard-core anti-emancipation Tories unwilling on personal grounds to serve under him, he tried to build a 'liberal' coalition with the Whigs, based on the common ground of religious toleration. The Whigs in turn split, some backing Canning and some not. To make matters worse, Canning died in August 1827, leaving two divided parties and a vacancy in the premiership. His successor, his Chancellor of the Exchequer Frederick Robinson (now Viscount Goderich) was unable to hold the ministry together and the King asked him to step down in early 1828.

Catholic emancipation

Catholics in Ireland had been able to vote in parliamentary elections since 1793, but they were unable to stand for election to Parliament or to hold government office. Once Wellington accepted that there were unanswerable practical reasons for conceding emancipation, the parliamentary arithmetic became highly favourable. Although he lost his right wing (the Ultra Tories), he could of course count on the votes of the Whig opposition to help carry the Roman Catholic Relief Act of 1829.

Many opponents of the measure had hoped to obtain concessions, for example a royal veto over the appointment of Catholic bishops, but in the end the only accompanying compromise was the Irish Franchise Act, whereby the voting qualification for freeholders in Irish counties was raised from 40s. to £10. That reduced the size of the Irish county electorate by about four-fifths, but aroused little controversy. By 1832 there were sixteen Irish Catholic MPs, including Daniel O'Connell, who contributed a distinctively radical element to the Irish contingent in the Commons. Some, though not all of them, followed O'Connell in advocating repeal of the Union.

George IV now turned back to the conventional Tories, trying to rebuild the grouping which Canning had split asunder. With Wellington, the hero of Waterloo, as Prime Minister, Robert (later Sir Robert) Peel as Home Secretary and the liberal Tories under Huskisson back on board, it was a combination that might have prospered. But Wellington did not like the Huskisson faction and, anyway, the ministry was deeply divided over the religious question. A disagreement over parliamentary reform – what to do about corruption at East Retford – provided the trigger for Huskisson's followers to resign from the government in May 1828. This left a narrow, hard-line government that was unsure of a majority in Parliament and lacked public support. Economic distress added to the pressure and then O'Connell intervened again, contesting and winning the by-election caused by William Vesey Fitzgerald's promotion to replace Huskisson's colleague and fellow resigner Charles Grant.

Despite his victory, O'Connell was not legally permitted to take his seat in Parliament since he was a Catholic. Peel, despite his hard-line reputation, advised Wellington that changing the law was the only way to avoid revolution, as otherwise

O'Connell would trigger mass civil unrest in Ireland. When Wellington and Peel subsequently pushed Catholic emancipation through Parliament, it left the Tory party thoroughly shattered. The liberal Huskissonites had already decamped. Now the hardline Ultra Tories felt betrayed, and even willing to contemplate parliamentary reform in the (probably correct) belief that a Parliament more representative of public opinion would also have been more hostile to Catholics.

The drama in this saga centred on the Tories and O'Connell; the Whigs continued to be supporters of religious toleration throughout. In 1828 Lord John Russell (later to be Prime Minister) finally secured the repeal of the Test and Corporation Acts, so removing restrictions on non-Anglicans holding public office. As with other areas of reform, although the Whigs were often too conservative for radical reformers, they usually wished to move in roughly the same direction. At the time of the Glorious Revolution the Whigs' conception of religious toleration had not extended fully to Catholics, as shown by their exclusion from the 1689 Act of Toleration. But as the political threat from Catholics to the governing order declined, the Whigs became increasingly supportive of allowing rights for their religion too. As with reform, although there were periods when Tories supported greater religious toleration, it was an issue that was distinctively Whig rather than Tory.

The small band of Wellington and Peel loyalists had now lost the support of both the Huskissonites and the hardliners in the government. The period 1829–30 also saw an upsurge in demands for parliamentary reform, pushed on by the harvest failure of 1829 and a series of skilful campaigners, such as the founder of the Birmingham Political Union, Thomas Attwood, who harnessed middle-class and lower-class discontent into combined pressure for change. The year 1830 also saw the overthrow of another French monarch, Charles X, a reminder of the threat to stability if reform was persistently refused. Added pressure came from the agricultural (or 'Swing') riots of 1830–31 in southern England, fuelled by food and job shortages.

The unreformed electoral system and MPs' political allegiances

The Reform Act of 1832 created a (more) uniform borough franchise (the £10 resident householder qualification) to match the standard 40s. franchise in the counties. Before that date there was a bewildering variety of different rights of voting in the six basic types of English borough constituencies, while further differences applied in Wales, Scotland and Ireland. Not only did this mean that there was a whole spectrum of constituencies in terms of size and validity – from the almost non-existent electorates in the rotten boroughs or the entirely closed pocket boroughs at one end of the scale, to the large freemen boroughs and the comparatively open counties at the other – but also that it was nearly impossible for contemporary observers to discern the party or political background of the members elected, especially since candidates might make no reference to national politics in their campaigns and could be either inactive or independent in Parliament.

Reformers made exhaustive efforts to identify who controlled each constituency, with a view to highlighting the abuses in the unreformed system; a much quoted example was T. H. B. Oldfield's *Representative History of Great Britain and Ireland*, which was published in six volumes in 1816. Radicals were also keen to point out the connections and voting patterns of MPs, in an attempt to shed light on the workings of the Commons. One of the most famous such volumes was *The Black Book* (1823), which had a 'Key to the Lower House'. From 1833 there was a new reference work – one which exists to this day – in the form of *Dod's Parliamentary Companion*. This work confidently attributed party labels to all the MPs elected at the 1832 general election. It made some, in fact fairly temporary, supporters of the reform bills into Liberals and restricted the term 'Radical' to only the most advanced parliamentary reformers, but it marked a key advance in contemporary understanding of Parliament and of party strengths.

George IV's death in 1830 triggered a general election. In those seats that were contested, the tide ran clearly against the government. Parliamentary reform featured in some, though not many, contests; most spectacularly, Henry Brougham, an outsider, won one of the symbolically potent county seats of Yorkshire on a reform ticket, pushing aside the more conservative Whig establishment.

However, more importantly, Wellington then badly misjudged the political mood and over-played the anti-reform line by making a hard-line declaration against any parliamentary reform. Even cautious Whigs and many Ultra Tories, scared by thoughts of revolution and worried about losing power to candidates like Brougham, saw justification for implementing some degree of reform. Although even a more skilled politician than Wellington would have faced difficulties in this situation, his own political inexperience made them worse. He was not well suited to managing a Cabinet or a party, rather than an army; as he said of his first Cabinet meeting: 'An extraordinary affair. I gave them their orders and they wanted to stay and discuss them.'

Lacking the political skills to navigate the situation, Wellington stumbled out of office. The Tories were now so deeply split that William IV had no choice but to ask the Whigs, under Grey, to form a new government, although with support from some Ultra Tories. The exit of Wellington having been triggered by the issue of parliamentary reform, there was widespread expectation that the new ministry would introduce some measure of reform, though it was to turn out to be far more radical than many expected.

Earl Grey (1764–1845)

Charles Grey entered Parliament as MP for Northumberland in 1786 and held that seat until he succeeded his father, becoming the second Earl Grey in 1807. Politically his origins were Foxite; he served as First Lord of the Admiralty (1806) and Foreign Secretary (1806–07). Despite occupying a prominent position in Whig ranks in the 1810s and 1820s, he did not hold further office until he became Prime Minister in 1830, a post he occupied until 1834. He is remembered chiefly as the premier who oversaw the introduction and passing of the Great Reform Act of 1832, although his government enacted many other liberal measures, notably the abolition of slavery in the British colonies in 1833 (finally completed in 1838).

In addition to domestic reform, he also supported self-determination abroad. Sitting in a tradition that stretched from sympathy for the American colonists in the previous century through to liberal support for self-determination in a range of countries in the years after him, his views on the topic were most eloquently expressed in his 1814 speech on the independence of Norway.[17] For him and his colleagues, authoritarian and illiberal government in any country was wrong – and he wished them all to have the same benefits as he believed derived from the Glorious Revolution in Britain.

The Whigs offered a credible alternative in 1830 because of their long-standing support for parliamentary reform and religious toleration. The limitations of the party, however, were demonstrated by the fact that it was Wellington's fall that brought them in government; they did not take power but had it handed to them. Since the French Revolution, the Whigs had frequently been deeply divided on reform questions and those of religious tolerance had not been central to forming or defeating governments (save for Pitt's demise in 1801). This left the Whigs as a party of almost permanent opposition, enjoying only brief glimpses of power as a result of the failings of others and without a credible alternative programme to attract positive support.

When both parliamentary reform and religious tolerance returned to the fore in the late 1820s, the Whigs were well placed to exploit the situation as a moderate and reasonably coherent reform party. But it was not yet as the Liberal Party that they did so. There were many radicals and reformers who did not see themselves as Whigs – allies, frequently, maybe, but not of the same ilk. Though generally willing to support Grey's premiership from 1830, it was only later events – and the impetus to organise brought on by the changes to the electoral system in the 1830s, especially the introduction of electoral registration – that brought all of them together into one party.[18]

Conclusion

The politics of the long eighteenth century can often seem like a confusing mélange of the power struggles of ambitious aristocrats, putting the search for monarchical approval ahead of anything resembling political principle. Walpole, Pitt and North were among the great political survivors, making and remaking coalitions to stay in power. Fox was the great loser, backing the wrong horse – the Prince of Wales – and dying well before George III finally left the stage. But underpinning the manoeuvrings of this elite were political principles, forged in the decades after the English Civil War, which were to form the bedrock of the nineteenth-century party system.

Trends in Whig thought are evident at numerous key moments throughout the period: opposition to the power of the monarch and other vested interests; religious toleration; a close association with the financial sector, which created connections with the men who drove the industrial revolution; sympathy for the rights and liberties of people overseas; a pacific foreign policy; suspicion of government expenditure, which was often in this period linked to abuse of power and privilege; and a willingness to countenance political reform, again in order to curb the power of the crown.

From the later part of the eighteenth century there are very early signs of the organisational roots which would help subsequently to form the Liberal Party. For both Foxite Whigs and nineteenth-century radicals such as Joseph Hume, extra-parliamentary organisation was a part of their political approach, whether to win elections in the more open constituencies or to marshal popular support to their causes.

At the time, however, no one was predicting the strengthening of those organisational roots into a form that would make a recognisable modern political party. Nor were people predicting that a collection made up of radicals, reformers and Whigs would permanently coalesce into a new and long-lasting political force. That would take several more decades of political development, but when it did occur it was an evolution of these earlier stages, and the Liberal Party adopted as its history that of these predecessors.

Further reading

The history of the Whigs is closely intertwined with the more general history of the period. A comprehensive general survey is Frank O'Gorman's *The Long Eighteenth Century: British Political and Social History, 1688–1832* (Bloomsbury, 1997), while a good starting general history of political parties is B. W. Hill, *The Growth of Parliamentary Parties 1689–1742* (HarperCollins, 1976). For the Glorious Revolution, Robert Beddard (ed.) *The Revolutions of 1688* (OUP, 1991) covers not just the events themselves but also its place in Whig history. Edward Vallance's *The Glorious Revolution: 1688 – Britain's Fight for Liberty* (Abacus, 2006) is a modern work of synthesis whilst some of the latest research is to be found in Tim Harris's *Revolution: The Great Crisis of the British Monarchy 1685–1720* (Allen Lane, 2006). Steven Pincus, *1688: The First Modern Revolution* (Yale University Press, 2009) also seeks to overturn earlier perceptions of the Glorious Revolution as a peaceful coup, and covers Whig politics up to 1696.

Conrad Russell's *An Intelligent Person's Guide to Liberalism* (Duckworth, 1999) traces a continuous strand of liberal thought and a Liberal Party 'in its various forms' from 1679, and is a very good starting point for further discussion of liberal thought. Alan Sykes's *The Rise and Fall of British Liberalism 1776–1988* (Longman, 1997) presents a rather more sceptical view of liberalism, and emphasises the elitist roots of much liberal thought. A useful supplement to both is H. T. Dickinson's *Liberty and Property: Political Ideology in Eighteenth-Century Britain* (Weidenfeld and Dickinson, 1977).

For a description of the mid-eighteenth-century electoral system, Lewis Namier, *The Structure of Politics at the Accession of George III* (Macmillan, 1929) was the standard, path-breaking work – challenging the previous view of a continuous two-party system through the period. His iconoclasm was hugely influential, though subsequently some historians have returned (more cautiously than their pre-Namier predecessors) to seeing some continuity of parties through the century. For a more modern treatment of politics in this period, see Linda Colley, *In Defiance of Oligarchy: The Tory Party 1714–60* (CUP, 1982).

For activity outside Parliament during the second half of the eighteenth century, see John Brewer, *Party Ideology and Popular Politics at the Accession of George III* (CUP, 1976), and E. C. Black, *The Association: British Extraparliamentary Political Organisation, 1769–1793* (Harvard University Press, 1963). For the Rockingham Whigs, see W. M. Elofson, *The Rockingham Connection and the Second Founding of the Whig Party, 1768–1773* (McGill–Queen's University Press, 1996), and Stephen Farrell, 'The Practices and Purposes of Party Leadership: Rockingham and the Lords, 1765–82', in R. W. Davis (ed.), *Leaders in the Lords: Government Management and Party Organisation in the Upper Chamber, 1765–1902* (Edinburgh University Press, 2003).

Donald Ginter's *Whig Organisation in the General Election of 1790* (Berkeley, 1967) is one of the first detailed accounts of Whig 'party' organisation before the nineteenth century. Moving into the nineteenth century, W. A. Hay, *The Whig Revival, 1808–1830* (Palgrave, 2005) is a good survey of the political manoeuvrings (and failings) of Whigs in this period, but again with an emphasis on organisational details. Clyve Jones (ed.), *Party and Management in Parliament, 1660–1784* (Leicester University Press, 1984) supplements these two with its earlier period.

For radicals, see the entries in the *Oxford Dictionary of National Biography* on the Society for Constitutional Information (act. 1780–1795), the Bluestocking Circle (act. c.1755–c.1795), the Society for the Purpose of Effecting the Abolition of the Slave Trade (act. 1787–1807) and Equiano, Olaudah (c.1745–1797).

There are many biographies of the major Whig political figures in this period, including for Chatham, Jeremy Black, *Pitt the Elder* (CUP, 1992); for Wilkes, P. D. G. Thomas, *John Wilkes: A Friend to Liberty* (Clarendon Press, 1996) and Audrey Williamson, *Wilkes, A Friend of Liberty* (Allen and Unwin, 1974); for Burke, F. P. Lock, *Edmund Burke* (Clarendon Press, 2 vols, 1998 and 2006); for Fox, David Powell, *Charles James Fox, Man of the People* (Hutchinson, 1989) and Stanley Ayling, *Fox* (John Murray, 1991); for Portland, David Wilkinson, *The Duke of Portland: Politics and Party in the Age of George III* (Palgrave Macmillan, 2003); and for Grey, E. A. Smith, *Lord Grey, 1764–1845* (Clarendon Press, 1990).

Finally, L. G. Mitchell has made a career out of writing on the Whigs, including a biography of *Charles James Fox* (OUP, 1992). Most important of his books is *The Whig World* (Hambledon Continuum, 2005) which gives a description of the social and cultural meanings to being a Whig that are often lacking from other works. For sophisticated analyses of the development of Whiggism into liberalism and of the varieties of meanings attached to liberalism, see Jonathan Parry, *The Rise and Fall of Liberal Government in Victorian Britain* (Yale University Press, 1993) and Boyd Hilton, *A Mad, Bad, and Dangerous People? England, 1783–1846* (Clarendon Press, 2006).

Notes

1 A Whig was a Scottish horse thief; the term was first used during the English Civil War. A Tory was an Irish papist outlaw.

2 There is some debate about how peaceful the Glorious Revolution was; for example see Steven Pincus, *1688 – The First Modern Revolution* (Yale University Press, 2009) and Edward Vallance, *The Glorious Revolution: 1688 – Britain's Fight for Liberty* (Abacus, 2006).

3 For example, *Britain in the First Age of Party 1680–1750: Essays presented to Geoffrey Holmes* (Hambledon Continuum, 2003).

4 A good survey of the development of parties in this period is B. W. Hill, *The Growth of Parliamentary Parties 1689–1742* (HarperCollins, 1976).

5 Although at times it was difficult to discern this political dividing line was consistently present, as W. A. Speck, *Tory and Whig: The Struggle in the Constituencies, 1701–1715* (Macmillan, 1970), demonstrates.

6 Particularly Lewis Namier, *The Structure of Politics at the Accession of George III* (Macmillan, 1929).

7 John Belchem and Richard Price (eds.), *A Dictionary of Nineteenth Century History* (Penguin, 2001) p. 657.

8 For more on the origins and significance of the Rockingham Whigs, see W. M. Elofson, *The Rockingham Connection and the Second Foundation of the Whig Party* (McGill–Queen's University Press, 1996).

9 Indeed, Robert Blake points out in the introduction to his *The Conservative Party from Peel to Thatcher* (Fontana, 1985) that at this time the most common labels in use in the Commons were 'Pittite' and 'Foxite' rather than 'Tory' and 'Whig'.

10 See Leslie Mitchell, *The Whig World* (Hambledon Continuum, 2005) for more on this: 'By instinct a man either had the caution of the conservative or the confidence of the reformer' (p. 6).

11 Alan Sykes, *The Rise and Fall of British Liberalism 1776–1988* (Longman, 1997), p. 1.

12 During this period Byron quipped that, 'Nought's permanent among the human race / Except the Whigs not getting into place [i.e. office]'. See W. A. Hay, *The Whig Revival, 1808–1830* (Palgrave, 2005), which is also a good survey of this period.

13 Adam Smith wrote that, 'commerce and manufactures gradually introduced order and good government, and with them, the liberty and security of individuals' (quoted in J. M. Beattie, *Crime and the Courts in England, 1660–1800* (OUP, 1986), p. 137).

14 These were the Training Prevention (or Unlawful Drilling) Act, the Seizure of Arms Act, the Misdemeanors Act, the Seditious Meetings Prevention Act, the Blasphemous and Seditious Libels Act and the Newspaper and Stamp Duties Act.

15 The speech is included in Duncan Brack and Tony Little (eds.), *Great Liberal Speeches* (Politico's, 2001).

16 D. R. Fisher (ed.) *The History of Parliament: The House of Commons, 1820–1832* (CUP, 7 vols, 2009), vol. 1, pp. 333–37 and vol. 4, p. 566.

17 The speech is included in *Great Liberal Speeches* (2001).

18 However, Hay, *The Whig Revival*, makes a persuasive case for the importance of Henry Brougham's organisational skills in 1827–30 when he reached out to provincial merchants and manufacturers, tapping into their frustration at their political exclusion, and so transforming the Whigs into an organisation with a national reach.

Chapter 2

Reform, Free Trade and the Birth of the Liberal Party (1830–1859)

David Brown

Introduction: chronology of a birth

In his review of the Liberal Party's record over half a century, offered in 1885 to voters newly enfranchised under the terms of the Third Reform Act, John Bright laid particular emphasis on the extent to which that party had brought 'political freedom … and a real representation of the People, rich and poor', yet crucially he saw the roots of this liberation primarily in the 1830s, 1840s and 1850s.[1] Significantly, it was during this period, he argued, that the Liberals had engineered the repeal of the Corn Laws (even if that was largely because, by backing Robert Peel, they had given Peel 'the power to repeal this wicked and cruel law'), and, rather more convincingly, inaugurated a new era of free trade and consequently improved standards of living.

Bright's letter was an unremarkable piece of electioneering propaganda, and yet his ebullient assessment of the party's achievements might be seen to have bordered on sophistry; at least his identification of a Liberal Party throughout this period displays a certain confidence in the stability and even existence of a Liberal Party not always borne out in subsequent analyses of the period.

Whigs, radicals and Nonconformists

The terms 'Whig' and 'radical' were used throughout the Liberal heyday to describe factions within the party, but these factions were not formally organised and shifted from time to time and issue to issue. As we have seen, 'Whig' described the descendants of the aristocratic families who backed the Glorious Revolution of 1688 and their adherents. These aristocratic families provided the backbone of administrative and leadership skills to the Liberal governments of this period. But to those in the more 'advanced' or 'independent' sections of Liberalism, the term Whig could be used to describe Liberals to their political right who were cautious about the immediate introduction of democracy or reforms of property laws.

Also under the 'liberal' umbrella were assorted radicals who, just as the Whigs saw themselves as the defenders of liberties in the face of royal power, viewed themselves in turn as the opponents of Whiggish aristocratic government. Consolidating their strength after 1832, Benthamite 'philosophic' radicals espoused political reform, especially the introduction of the secret ballot (as a way of undermining aristocratic influence at elections), as well as educational reforms to prepare the country for a more mature, even perhaps democratic, political system. However in composition and outlook they remained elitist and metropolitan, distanced from the majority of the population in tastes and manners. Regarding political parties as the organs of corruption, radicals never coalesced into a coherent parliamentary force, and despite arguing for political reform, were never friends of 'the people', sharing Whig concerns about the maturity and reliability of the lower classes.

Nonconformist elements within radicalism could on some levels establish a rapport with Whig desires to champion religious liberty, building on measures such as the 1828 repeal of the Test and Corporation Acts allowing Nonconformists into public life. But within Nonconformity – Wesleyan Methodist, Baptist, Congregationalist, Quaker, Unitarian – the range of liberal views, from the more conservative wings of liberal thought to the more radical, were evident and tended against any homogeneous 'Nonconformist' outlook.

These varied elements underlined the broad-based nature of liberalism in early Victorian Britain. Whigs and radicals shared overlapping views of what represented progress, such as free trade, sufficient to form an alliance; but differences over tactics, priorities and the details of legislation were often crucial. Attempts to take the party too far in a radical direction were always vulnerable to a Whig revolt. Too much timidity left the leadership vulnerable to radical rebellions and mass demonstrations. Riding the Whig and radical horses in tandem was no easy task for Palmerston, Russell and Gladstone.

Indeed, so laboured was the so-called birth of the party in the early nineteenth century that some historians have even been prompted to ask whether in fact that birth took place at all. Rather than the emergence of an identifiable party, implying unity of purpose and outlook, in this view the Liberal Party in the early Victorian period only really existed in a negative sense, as a collection of loosely connected political interests joined by a shared aversion to Toryism, but lacking in its own right any genuine sense of party cohesion and structure. It is certainly striking that Conservative disunity plays almost as much of a role in this history as Liberal concord.[2] Yet while it has been suggested that the liberal hegemony of the mid-Victorian period was little more than a 'political mentality',[3] and that it was one of the great paradoxes of the years 1832–59 that Liberal governments failed to capitalise sufficiently on this strong ideological hold, it is true that by the end of the 1850s more people were talking confidently and unproblematically of a Liberal Party and of the progress of liberal politics.

Traditionally the Liberal Party is taken to have been born in 1859, when at a meeting in Willis's Rooms in London on 6 June, the Whigs, radicals and Peelites, that is, those with broadly liberal leanings, gathered to agree how best to confront the protectionist government of Lord Derby, and for that purpose determined to unite under the 'Liberal' banner. However, there are grounds for arguing that the party existed already by this point, and that it had emerged, depending on one's perspective, in the early 1830s, during the 1840s, or perhaps in the early 1850s. The Reform Act of 1832 has been seen by some, including some of the party's great luminaries such as William Gladstone, as marking the point at which liberal politics and, by extension, a Liberal Party first emerged as the dominant feature of the political landscape, although later commentators have been a little sceptical of such a teleology. Subsequently, historians have dated the birth of the party at various points from the mid-1830s to the later 1850s. In 1835 Whigs, radicals and Irish Members of Parliament met at Lichfield House to hammer out the grounds on which they would combine to defeat Peel's minority Conservative government of 1834–35 and many have been tempted to see in this alliance the origins of a Parliamentary Liberal Party. At the same time, Whig agreement, following damaging differences of opinion in 1834, over the principle of the redistribution of the surplus revenue of the established Church of Ireland for the benefit of the entire population, seemed further to underline the importance of the mid-1830s as the point at which liberal values were starting to coalesce in a more formalised Liberal Party. Certainly the language of the period was adapting to such perceived new alignments and the term 'Liberal' gained currency as liberals sought not only to define themselves as 'not Conservatives', but also, more carefully, as parliamentary and social reformers of some sort.

By 1846, when Peel tore the Conservatives asunder in his determination to repeal the punitive Corn Laws, the process of Liberal consolidation seemed only to be further advanced.

Free trade, the Corn Laws and the politicians

Since 1815, in an attempt to maintain agricultural incomes, the Corn Laws, a system of protection which restricted the import of corn while the domestic price remained below eighty shillings per quarter, had been in force. Though the Corn Laws could not moderate fluctuations in agricultural yields, which inevitably impacted on prices, they were seen by the landed classes as an important sign of government commitment to upholding the agricultural interest. The measure by definition privileged the interests of the landed classes over those of the labouring population, for whom basic foodstuffs were often prohibitively expensive as a result.

Despite a sliding scale introduced in 1828 by Wellington's government, the perceived inequities of the system remained, and attitudes to the Corn Laws themselves became an increasingly important indicator of political alignment, determining a politician's general position on the principle of free trade and unfettered commerce. Popular middle-class pressure in the form of the Anti-Corn Law League from the mid- to the late 1830s added to growing parliamentary interest in repeal of the Corn Laws, although by the early 1840s the Whigs, generally more pro-free trade than the Conservatives, were out of office.

The Anti-Corn Law League, founded in 1838–39, proved to be a highly effective lobbying organisation. Backed by Manchester cotton manufacturers, led by Richard Cobden, assisted by John Bright and Charles Villiers, the League exploited the economic recession of the late 1830s, using public meetings, newsletters and regular parliamentary debates to blame bread prices for the poverty of working families; significantly, its campaigns often incorporated women.

It fell to Robert Peel (Prime Minister 1841–46) to deal with the issue and, in an act of political bravery – or suicide, according to taste – he finally steered repeal through Parliament in 1846. Such was the importance of the question that he destroyed his party in the process. 'Protectionists', who saw themselves as adherents of true Tory politics and guardians of the landed interest, broke away, only to find themselves in an increasingly marginal parliamentary position. Meanwhile, free-trade 'Peelites' clung to the politics and ideas of Peel, many eventually finding a political home under the 'liberal' umbrella.

Free-trade Peelites now moved towards the Whig-Liberal ranks and as the protectionist rump of the old Conservative Party slumped to near electoral and parliamentary oblivion (forming only two governments between that point and the mid-1860s, both of very short duration, in 1852 and 1858–59) it seemed, if only by virtue of overwhelming numerical superiority and the consequent sense of liberal supremacy, that some sort of dominant liberal parliamentary presence had been achieved. Yet still there were divisions and tensions, and a weak Conservative opposition served only to focus attention on the divisions among the non-Conservatives.

The years 1834–35 might have seen tactical alliances to defeat a government, and even the laying down of some sort of ideological foundations of a Liberal Party, but still there was a prevailing ambiguity about the nature of liberal government. Some saw themselves as Liberals, yet many whom psephologists might place within that camp preferred instead still to see themselves distinctly as Whigs, or radicals, or Nonconformists. Liberal disunity in the face of liberal hegemony has led some historians to argue that the conscious attempts made to address the issue in 1852, leading to the coalition of Peelites and Whigs under Lord Aberdeen between 1852 and 1855, in fact represent the true birth of the party. Far from a coalition, then, that government might be seen as a 'fusion' of the two groups. The case is persuasive, and yet, still, following the débâcle of the Crimean War and the collapse of Aberdeen's government in early 1855, the Liberal Party train seemed to have been derailed once more. Such was the degree of this disunity that in the 1850s the leader of the protectionists, Lord Derby, judged it to be so potentially damaging to his opponents' interests that he adopted as his preferred parliamentary strategy an approach of 'masterly inactivity' by which the Whigs, radicals, Peelites and others might be given enough rope with which to hang themselves. Thus might we look, in turn, to 1859, when once again liberal politicians met to settle their differences and agree to work in harmony to overcome a common political opposition.

Parliamentary reform and the emergence of Liberal government in Victorian Britain

By the late 1820s pressure for reform of Parliament was gathering pace, and by the early 1830s was arguably the primary political issue of the day. The question of reform brought together a number of single-issue pressure groups which saw in parliamentary reform a potential panacea for a multitude of ills and grievances. The demand for reform was varied. Within Parliament radicals combined, unusually, with the ultra-Tories, the latter believing that Parliament's increasingly unrepresentative character made change necessary, especially in relation to Catholic emancipation. Furthermore, direct popular pressure seemed to strengthen the case for reform, as radical critics of the existing system became more vociferous, and in cities such as Birmingham political unions which sought to orchestrate public opinion in favour of reform through meetings and petitions gathered momentum. Added to this, the economy, and especially the agricultural sector, was depressed during these years, leading, especially in southern England, to rural disturbances in 1830 and 1831 known as the 'Swing Riots' in which agricultural labourers reacted to low wages and poverty by attempting to destroy the 'labour-displacing' threshing machines.

The existing franchise was indeed out of keeping with an increasingly industrialised country. Important industrial towns such as Manchester, Birmingham and Leeds, though they had a combined population approaching half a million by the early 1830s, lacked direct representation. Smaller boroughs, returning members on the smallest of franchises (or even on none at all, as in the infamous case of Old Sarum, where two members were returned by a 'field and ancient earthwork') or under the patronage of local political magnates, also emphasised the rottenness of the system.

Yet it was the Whigs who undertook a programme of reform following the Tory Duke of Wellington's refusal to brook the idea of change in 1830. Rather than jeopardise strong government and social order, a measure of moderate reform was conceived that would remove existing abuses within the political system without recklessly handing power to the masses. The 1832 Reform Act was designed to be a timely though moderate concession. Lord John Russell, who was later to claim that the measure had finally settled the question, declared in 1832 that: 'If great changes accomplished by the people are dangerous, although sometimes salutary, great changes accomplished by the aristocracy, at the desire of the people, are at once salutary and safe'.[4]

The terms of the reform, however, were profound. Parliament was still effectively structured on the principle of representing property, rather than people, but the Act took account of the shifting demographic and economic patterns within the country. The extension of the franchise to the £10 householder (all adult males who occupied, as either tenant or owner, property with an annual value of £10), and extensions to the electorate in the counties to include certain copyholders and long-leaseholders as well as those tenants who paid an annual rent of £50 to their landlord, nearly doubled the size of the electorate; but significantly the Act also redistributed the seats for which they elected representatives. Fifty-six old rotten boroughs were disenfranchised out-right while a further thirty boroughs were reduced from two members to one. In all, 143 seats were lost to the small boroughs in this process; sixty-five new seats were created in industrial and commercial towns, particularly in the industrial midlands and north, while a further sixty-five extra seats were granted to the counties and thirteen more were given to Scotland and Ireland.[5]

William Gladstone, elected as a Tory in 1832, regarded the passing of the 1832 Reform Act by the Whigs as having, in effect, marked the birth of a Liberal Party when he observed in 1874 that it had been 'forty, or more exactly forty-three, years since the Liberal Party acquired the main direction of public affairs'.[6] While that landmark Act may well have been seen to have set in motion an era of progressive change, it may be to exaggerate slightly to insist that such legislation actually marked the establishment of a political party. For while the impact of the Act was profound, not least in terms of setting a precedent for change and showing that the political system could be adapted; nonetheless in real terms it was a modest piece of legislation. Its terms were essentially Whiggish, privileging property over citizenship, and as an avowedly 'final' measure scarcely laid out an ongoing agenda for a Liberal Party. Some sense of party interest was certainly fostered by the terms of the Act, not least in its requirements that voters be registered, which in turn generated considerable activity on the part of quasi-party activists to secure the fullest representation of 'their' voters. Party identity was clearly evident in the actions of those who sought not only to make sure voters were registered, but to remove, where possible, the names of those thought hostile.

1832 general election (8 December 1832 – 8 January 1833)			
	Votes	%	MPs
Liberal	554,719	67.0	441
Conservative	241,284	29.2	175
Irish Repeal	31,773	3.8	42
Total	827,776		658

However, it is clear that the election of 1832 turned in many constituencies on local issues, and if there was a liberal agenda emerging at Westminster it had not yet found its full expression on the ground in terms of conscious electioneering for a Liberal Party. But if voters were not choosing a Liberal Party candidate, there was a growing sense of support for liberal values. A key concern, and indeed achievement, of Earl Grey's government of 1830–34 was the abolition of slavery in 1833, and there was in addition a growing commitment to financial reform. A Liberal Party might not yet have existed, but the language of liberalism was gaining ground and liberal politics were winning support. It was perhaps this sense of a project begun that added urgency to calls for some sort of concerted action among 'liberals' when, contrary to expectations, Robert Peel's Conservatives stole a march on the reformers and won power in 1834.

Peel, the Irish Church and the path to Lichfield House

Having reformed the House of Commons in 1832, it was becoming increasingly difficult for those charged with driving what had been termed the 'reform coach' to see clearly the road ahead and what course to steer. Having rallied to an essentially negative agenda – a recognition of the need to reform Parliament in order to contain radical demands and a desire to seize the advantages inherent in pressing for that change – the non-Tory elements at Westminster all too often afterwards betrayed their differences and divisions. Far from challenging or even undermining the principle of aristocratic government, the reformed House sustained ministries just as socially 'top-heavy' as had been the case previously, and aristocratic Whig paternalism continued to hold considerable sway in the face of the very limited calls for a more democratic (or accountable) franchise. Meanwhile, the label 'reformers', let alone 'liberals', had still to transcend the distinctions of 'Whigs', 'radicals', 'Nonconformists', and 'Irish repealers'[7] to create a genuine sense of a broadly conceived common purpose; parliamentary reform brought them together, it was not sufficient to keep them so. These tensions within Grey's ministry came to a head over the government's policies in Ireland. Calls for social and economic reforms in Ireland highlighted just how divergent were views on questions of state intervention and the role of an established church as well as the extent to which high-profile ministers were prepared to put personal ambition ahead of government.

Lord John Russell had visited Ireland in the autumn of 1833 and, disturbed by what he had witnessed, returned to London determined to press for changes to ameliorate Irish social conditions. Russell's solution was for the government to appropriate any surplus revenue of the established Church of Ireland and use such funds for lay purposes, such as education. He spoke with moderation to his colleagues in Cabinet, telling them in a memorandum that 'future inquiry may lead to some diminution of the revenues of the Established Church after all its proper uses have been provided for. But this subject requires long and patient investigation before any decision is made.'[8] However, Russell had already decided that such an investigation would have to conclude in favour of lay appropriation.

Lord John Russell (1792–1878)

The son of the sixth Duke of Bedford, Russell was born into one of the great Whig families of the period and as such enjoyed a prominent position within political circles often defined as much by blood as political ties; talk of the 'great grandmotherhood' of Whigs was not uncommon in this period.

Educated at Edinburgh University, the nursery of many future prominent Whigs, Russell entered Parliament in 1813 and remained an MP until his elevation to the Lords in 1861 as the first Earl Russell. A proponent of religious liberty (he was the leading advocate of repeal of the Test and Corporation Acts in 1828) and parliamentary reform, Russell introduced the bills for franchise reform in the early 1830s (there were three bills proposed between 1830 and 1832). Despite acquiring the nickname 'Finality Jack' for his supposed indifference to further reform, his commitment to parliamentary reform remained a central feature of his political outlook.

Russell held office in all the 'liberal' governments of the period, as Home Secretary 1835–39, Colonial Secretary 1839–41, Prime Minister 1846–51 and again, briefly, 1865–66, and Foreign Secretary on two occasions in 1852–53 and 1859–65, latterly serving under his erstwhile colleague and rival, Palmerston.

Initially this seemed a good 'liberal' cause – indeed, post-1832, perhaps the best ground on which to base claims for continued liberal progress. Few MPs not personally connected with Ireland troubled themselves to discover much about the situation there as Russell had done but, as Jonathan Parry has observed, 'what mattered was the upbeat combination of activity, integration, liberality and anti-clericalism which appropriation seemed to offer'.[9] Such were the hopes, at least. In the short term, however, the question of Irish appropriation seemed only to divide the reformers. Anglican feeling within government in particular remained hostile to the scheme, while Russell's own Protestantism did not endear his proposals to the Catholic clergy in Ireland. The after-effects of this issue were dramatic: it would effectively end any lingering hopes that Grey's government could continue to work together, provoke William IV to exercise his prerogative powers to dismiss a ministry, revitalise the Conservatives and ultimately, as some historians have argued, force such a re-evaluation of the reformist agenda as to allow one to see the actual birth of a Liberal Party in Britain.

When Russell first introduced his plans to the Cabinet his arguments fell on stony ground and, indeed, when the government addressed the tithe issue in Parliament in 1834, no mention was made of appropriation. Russell was appalled and was willing to resign over the issue, prompting Lord Stanley, the Colonial Secretary, to observe, somewhat melancholically, that 'John Russell has upset the Coach. We cannot go on after his declaration that "if ever a nation had a right to complain of any grievance it is the people of the Church of Ireland".'[10] It was not Russell who went, however, but Stanley, accompanied by Sir James Graham (First Lord of the Admiralty) and the Duke of Richmond, who quit the government over the appropriation question in May. In July they were followed by the Prime Minister, Grey, himself, to be replaced by Lord Melbourne.

Melbourne's approach was to consolidate the government's position, but the question of Irish Church revenues continued to divide the political nation. It led, indeed, to one of the last decisive examples of monarchical intervention in British politics. In November 1834, William IV dismissed the government because he objected to the appointment of Russell as leader of the House of Commons on the grounds that Russell stood as one of the ministry's most prominent advocates of lay appropriation. Melbourne's position was untenable and he had no alternative but to offer his resignation.

Lord Melbourne (1779–1848)

William Lamb, the second Viscount Melbourne, was descended from one of the great Whig families. A Whig MP before his elevation to the peerage, Melbourne made his name as Canning's Secretary for Ireland, 1827–28, and as Home Secretary in Grey's government of 1830–34. When Grey fell from power in 1834 Melbourne assumed the premiership and, although soon defeated by Peel in 1834, he returned as Prime Minister in 1835, remaining in that post until 1841.

He was thus Prime Minister at the moment of Victoria's accession to the throne and he became personally very close to the young Queen, tutoring her in the ways of politics. As a result Melbourne and the Whigs were exposed to allegations of becoming too close to monarchy while the Queen's political independence was likewise brought into question.

Meanwhile, the Conservatives had not been altogether idle. Wellington sensibly refused to form a government when the King called on him in November 1834, but the Duke did suggest Robert Peel be invited to try his hand. Although faced with forming a government from among a parliamentary minority, Peel recognised that he was offered a good opportunity to consolidate a distinctive Conservative identity, particularly as the King was willing to grant a dissolution of Parliament. Thus in December 1834 Peel launched his 'manifesto' at Tamworth. In fact he faced no real opposition in Staffordshire and as such had no particular need to produce what he described as 'a declaration of my views of public policy'; rather, his speech to electors was intended to be, and was taken to be, a statement of a 'party' view.

Although he had come forward claiming to speak to 'that great and intelligent class of society ... which is much less interested in the contentions of party, than in the maintenance of order and the cause of good government', at the same time, in setting out a 'frank exposition of general principles and views which appears to be anxiously expected', he was in effect articulating an agenda of 'conservation', committing only to 'a careful review of institutions, civil and ecclesiastical, undertaken in a friendly temper combining, with the firm maintenance of established rights, the correction of proved abuses and the redress of real grievances'. When Peel and the Conservatives subsequently gained approximately 100 seats at the general election in January 1835 it seemed that there was indeed a definable and successful Conservative agenda emerging.

1835 general election (6 January – 6 February)			
	Votes	%	MPs
Liberal	349,868	55.2	385
Conservative	261,269	40.8	273
Total	611,137		658

1837 general election (24 July – 18 August)			
	Votes	%	MPs
Liberal	418,331	51.7	344
Conservative	379,694	40.8	314
Total	798,025		658

Once again, the non-Conservatives had a common antagonist, a renewed sense of something to act in concert to oppose or change. And beyond the shared antipathy towards a Peelite government, there was in addition the renewed threat of unchecked monarchical authority to draw the reformers together. William IV's arbitrary dismissal of the government in 1834 might have been constitutionally justifiable from a technical point of view, but it seemed only to underline just how far the existing system of government had to go if traditional Whig concerns about royal power were to be allayed.

The role of the crown

When she came to the throne in 1837, aged only eighteen, Victoria was in need of instruction in the arts of government. The task of educating the new Queen fell largely to Lord Melbourne, the incumbent Prime Minister at the time of her accession. The relationship soon became a close personal as well as political one; Melbourne, by this time a widower and with no surviving children of his own, gladly took the young fatherless Queen under his wing.

He schooled the Queen in what he conceived to be Whig political theory and was able therefore to exercise considerable influence over the political role of the court. While the Queen became during these early years of her reign both politically and personally reliant on Melbourne, the closeness of this relationship combined with political scandals in the later 1830s brought the integrity of the court into question, and made the Queen herself deeply unpopular. When Prince Albert married the Queen in 1840 the image of the monarchy was already tarnished and, while the Queen's marriage represented a rupture in her relations with Melbourne, it simultaneously introduced an important new element into British political life, and more specifically, to the political outlook of the Queen, which was to have important ramifications for the future of the British monarchy.

As Melbourne's ministry foundered in 1841, the Prince was able to establish himself as more than just the Queen's private secretary, and became effectively her chief political adviser, guiding her through the troubled months surrounding the end of the government. Albert had no desire to fashion the British monarch into an apolitical functionary of the state; in fact quite the reverse, as his explicit demonstrations of support for Peel's attempts to repeal the Corn Laws bear testimony. Though he considered that the monarch had an 'immense moral responsibility' to 'watch and control' the government, he recognised that this did not signify a right to influence the selection of ministers themselves.

In many respects the limitations on royal power and authority had been becoming evident for some time. In 1834, before Victoria ascended the throne, William IV had exercised his 'right' to dismiss a government by ejecting Melbourne in favour of Peel, but the short-lived nature of Peel's government of 1835 only underlined the fact that the monarch could not impose ministers on Parliament arbitrarily. With royal influence being arguably therefore more important than formal royal prerogative rights, the role of

Melbourne in the later 1830s and of Albert in the 1840s and 1850s in terms of fashioning a sense of monarchical authority were therefore critical in shaping the role of the crown during Victoria's reign. To offset the apparent decline in royal power, it was necessary to assert its ability to guide and offer wise counsel.

In 1867 Walter Bagehot published *The English Constitution*, in which he identified a distinction between the 'dignified' and the 'efficient' parts of the constitution, the dignified parts being those which 'excite and preserve the reverence of the population' while the efficient parts were 'those by which … [the constitution], in fact, works and rules'. Thus, he reasoned, the 'crown is, according to the saying, the "fountain of honour"; but the Treasury is the spring of business'. While seeking to draw attention to what he perceived as the ultimate subjugation of the monarch's governing power, Bagehot was nonetheless keen to illustrate the valuable, indeed indispensable, role the crown still had to play in the government of the country. The monarchy offered distractions from the hurly-burly of politics, represented religious strength, continuity, and national morality and provided a façade of stability in a period of change and upheaval. The Bagehotian monarchy therefore had no legislative power, nor did it form the executive; it had ultimately only three rights: 'the right to be consulted, the right to encourage, the right to warn'.

Sobered from their Reform Bill hangover by Peel's success in 1835, the erstwhile reform colleagues began seriously to consider tactics anew. In February and March 1835 Whig, radical and Irish Repeal MPs met at Lichfield House in order to look for ways to defeat Peel's new administration. It was a tactical alliance more than an ideological one; there was concurrence that they would oppose Peel's nominee for the post of Speaker of the House for the coming session and there was a broad consensus over Irish appropriation (although no formal pledges on behalf of a future Whig government were made), but beyond agreeing that a Whig government was more desirable than Peel's little else of substance was established during these meetings. Nonetheless, this was recognisably party behaviour. Differences were to a large extent set aside, there were some general hints at a liberal tone (if not a specific policy platform) and there was careful discussion of how to turn out the government.

On these grounds, 1835 has been seen by some as the date at which a recognisable Liberal Party emerged. Norman Gash first insisted on this view a generation ago,[11] and, as Jonathan Parry has more recently argued, this 'was not a professionally managed party, nor were its principles embodied in regular policy packages', but nonetheless, the 'Liberal Party was a liberal party' and 'it was effective enough'.[12] Certainly contemporaries, both within Parliament and in the newspaper press, were starting to define or describe these groups as 'liberal' instead of 'reformer' or 'radical' or 'Whig', and in linguistic terms at least there appears to have been a developing sense of party. More than this, the diarist Charles Greville discerned something else separating the opposing groups at Westminster. The pen portraits may have been less than flattering, but nonetheless they are suggestive of collective, party, behaviour. Peel's party, Greville wrote:

Is in great part composed of the rich and fashionable, who are constantly drawn away by one attraction or another, and whose habitual haunts are the clubs and houses at the west end of the town; and it is next to impossible to collect his scattered forces at a moment's notice. The Opposition contains a dense body of fellows who have no vocation out of the walls of the House of Commons; who put up in the vicinity; either do not dine at all, or get their meals at some adjoining chop-house, throng the benches early, and never think of moving until everything is over ...[13]

Yet however much the events of late 1834 and early 1835 can be seen to have reinvigorated reformist and liberal spirits, still the 'party' was a thinly conceived one. Despite appearances at Lichfield House, divisions continued to plague the 'liberals'. Although Peel's government was quickly overturned, it soon became clear that the Whigs' readiness to accommodate their radical and Irish associates was a limited one. Lord John Russell, by now a leading voice in Whig politics, was quick to declare that Melbourne's second government, which replaced Peel's in 1835, would comprise the 'Whiggest part of the Whigs' and would be able to 'hold our own Whig course'.[14] Such a determination may have been a natural reaction to Russell's own fear, as he would later put it to Melbourne in 1837, that it was the 'very old difficulty of Whig administrations, that their friends expect them to do more than is possible; so that if they attempt little, their friends grow slacker, and if they attempt much, their enemies grow strong'.[15] Yet this commitment to Whiggery sat ill with supposed attempts to broaden the base of liberal politics.

Back in government in 1835 as Home Secretary, Russell soon returned to the theme of lay appropriation of Irish Church revenues. The question continued to divide Protestant and Catholic opinion and in this sense remained controversial, but it has also been suggested that Russell pursued the matter as much to force or emphasise the breach with Stanley and other rivals for influence in Whig circles. Whatever the case, the question did nothing for Whig unity. This was important at a time when, by the later 1830s, the Whigs seemed squeezed on all sides. Peel and the Conservatives continued to oppose the government, of course, but so too, increasingly, did many erstwhile supporters. Chartist calls by the later 1830s for a more thoroughgoing reform of the system of political representation tended only to encourage the Whigs to treat 1832 as a final solution, but in turn, as a result, radicals grew dissatisfied with the lack of further reform while moderate opinion became concerned that such questions were still being raised at all and dismayed at the apparent inability of the government to keep a lid on calls for more change. When Russell insisted in 1839 that the Whigs were not 'the party of movement',[16] it seemed only to confirm to many how seriously the Whigs had lost their way. Radicals were becoming concerned. Historian George Grote, for example, complained that:

The Whig Government has been, ever since the accession of our present Queen [in 1837], becoming more and more confirmed in its Conservative tendencies; in fact, it is now scarcely at all distinguished, either in its leanings or in its acts, from Peel and his friends … Lord Melbourne's majority is a very inconsiderable one, and he maintains himself in the House of Commons chiefly by making use of the Radicals against the Tories, and of the Tories against the Radicals.[17]

If an important part of the liberal ambition had been to forge a closer compact between government and the people through more effective representation of those people, the fact that popular discontent with the Whig governments of Lords Grey and Melbourne was growing further undermined the sense of liberal harmony at the political centre. For while the development of liberalism and a Liberal Party at Westminster is a crucial part of this history, it was operating against, or in relation to, an equally dynamic (and multi-faceted) extra-parliamentary 'liberal' history.

Reform of the political system in 1832 had, in many respects, altered little. While an important precedent had been set, and while the Act had ushered in significant shifts in the balance of representation, removing many of the anachronisms of the old political system, on other levels nothing had changed. Members of Parliament were still drawn largely from the same social groups as before; for example, more than one third of all MPs in Parliament between the two reform acts of 1832 and 1867 had blood ties to the aristocracy, while in the Parliament of 1841–47 something like 71 per cent of parliamentarians were direct descendants of peers, baronets or gentry families. Meanwhile, the electorate both before and after the 1832 Act was dominated by artisans, skilled craftsmen and shopkeepers. The landed elites maintained a tight grip on power, supported by the middle or skilled professional classes: how and where MPs were elected might have changed; who they were had not to any great extent.[18]

For all the post-1832 rhetoric of the reformers that they now more obviously and fairly represented the population, therefore, this held true only within the narrow confines of the political class. Liberal elements, according to historians of popular radicalism, were distanced from those they supposedly represented. Middle-class radicalism now enjoyed a more secure parliamentary voice, but used that primarily to argue for further reform along the lines of the introduction of the secret ballot, while popular calls outside Parliament were still for the need to address the fundamental question of the franchise itself. Whigs, meanwhile, still impressed by the notion of the 'finality' of 1832, and led by the unequivocally and unapologetically aristocratic Grey and Melbourne, did little to convince 'the masses' of their commitment to liberal progress. The Reform Act had in some respects further alienated the working classes – highlighting the fact that Parliament would only ever extend a welcome to 'respectable' middle-class opinion – and as a result, radicalism became increasingly divided along class lines. A developing working-class political consciousness, therefore, came to define itself in a meaningful way as being the 'victim of the Whigs' and in the plethora of working-class pressure groups of the 1830s – political unions, trade unions, assorted groups for the education of the working classes and protection of working-class interests – progressive politics seemed ever more fragmented.

Although there had been much talk of liberal harmony (at Westminster) post-1832, after the Lichfield House meeting, this seemed, from a working-class and extra-parliamentary point of view, only to illustrate the establishment of a Whig hegemony or ascendancy in parliamentary terms. Despite the limitations of Whig leadership and Whig conceptions of popular liberalism, this was more than a match for the 'philosophic' or middle-class radicals in Parliament. In addition, middle-class radicalism's failure to tackle the perceived need for further reform of the franchise meant that radicalism, far from being a broad-church alliance of advanced, progressive reformers, remained a divided and discontented collection of sometimes competing interests. Middle-class radical attempts to reduce taxes on newspapers, for example, which were an integral part of a mission to educate and elevate the working classes, seemed patriarchal and patronising, a betrayal of popular interests which demanded reform of political structures rather than accommodation within the established system. As Bronterre O'Brien, a leading Chartist, would put it: 'The only knowledge which is of any service to the working people is that which makes them more dissatisfied, and makes them worse slaves. This is the knowledge we shall give them.'[19]

Utilitarianism and philosophic radicalism

Middle-class radicalism in the early nineteenth century drew inspiration from experience and observance of a developing, more industrial, mobile, urban society, which generated a range of humanitarian impulses for reform. A far stronger, and for some consistent, impulse, especially once changes in the political system gave them a clearer voice, were the intellectual underpinnings of a radical critique of government and society provided by Jeremy Bentham (1748–1832). The work of Bentham was crucial, and gave rise to the 'philosophic radicals' in Parliament, among whose number many had been closely connected with Bentham personally during the 1820s.

At the heart of Bentham's utilitarian philosophy was a belief that the role of government should be to realise 'the greatest happiness of the greatest number'. Drawing on a wide range of European and American influences Bentham provided the philosophical foundations for a wide-ranging system of rational improvement, producing both pamphlets and examples, such as schemes for reform, constitutions, and model prisons, to inspire such reforms. This was, significantly, a world view in man-made terms to which, by definition, man-made remedies were possible. Through his own work and that of others, such as, in particular, James Mill, and periodicals such as the *Westminster Review*, the utilitarian critique of privilege and corruption gathered significant middle-class support, coalescing around a broadly defined project of political reform, including widening the suffrage, the introduction of the secret ballot and improvements in education.

Benthamite utilitarianism was also a major inspiration to reformers such as Edwin Chadwick in their work on poor laws and public health. While the early to mid-Victorian period has sometimes been labelled the 'age of improvement', to some, this is simply evidence of the extent to which it might equally be described as the 'age of Bentham'.

There was one area, however, in which all liberal interests might find common cause. If the Conservatives stood for the vested interests of land, the 'liberals' could at least position themselves as opponents of protectionism. It suited the liberal tone of earlier discussions and by the later 1830s was seen by some as the one hope for liberal unity. As the historian T. B. Macaulay, at that point a member of Melbourne's government, put it, 'all the chances of our party depend on [free trade] … We shall play double or quits.'[20]

Although the stakes were high it made sound political sense to adopt a free trade stance. The turning point, then, in the history of liberalism was centred on trade and commercial policy; this was an area of public life that had an impact on all levels of society, from landlords to merchants and consumers, and in an era of rising prices for basic commodities such as food, and notably corn, the subject became very much a central if not the defining issue of the time. The year 1839 saw the establishment of the Anti-Corn Law League (ACLL), an extension of the National Corn Law Association formed in London in 1836 and the Manchester Anti-Corn Law Association of 1838, which became a rallying point for radical politics. In origin, the ACLL grew out of middle-class parliamentary radicalism and its leading lights were Richard Cobden and John Bright, but in moving away from a focus on the ballot this middle-class radicalism now seemed more relevant to the working classes and a more useful means of attacking aristocratic government. As Cobden enthused: 'I think the scattered elements may yet be rallied round the question of the Corn Laws. It appears to me that a moral and even a religious spirit may be infused into that topic, and if agitated in the same manner that the question of slavery has been, it will be irresistible.'[21]

Richard Cobden (1804–65)

Born in Sussex, Richard Cobden was more commonly associated with Manchester politics, having become during the 1830s and 1840s a leading advocate of commercial and industrial interests in Lancashire, initially as a partner in a calico-printing works and subsequently as a local politician. By the late 1830s he had emerged as a key figure in the Manchester campaign against protectionism as embodied in the Corn Laws, which seemed to demonstrate the continuing over-representation in Britain of landed interests at the expense of entrepreneurial ones. His campaigning at the head of the Anti-Corn Law League was said to have been particularly important in influencing Robert Peel to adopt repeal, particularly once Cobden had taken the message into Parliament as MP for Stockport from 1841.

Following the repeal of the Corn Laws in 1846, Cobden continued to be a vocal advocate of free trade, both domestically, in Parliament, and increasingly on the continental European stage, where he toured in 1846–47. His commitment to free trade and peace brought Cobden into ever more frequent conflict with what he took to be Palmerston's interventionist and meddlesome foreign policy and he became one of Palmerston's most persistent critics, in Parliament and through the press, particularly with the establishment of the Cobdenite *Morning Star* in 1856. The breach with

Palmerston's vision of liberalism was profound, and Cobden declined an invitation to serve in Palmerston's second government in 1859. He did, however, undertake a mission to France where, along with Michel Chevalier, he drafted the Commercial Treaty of 1860 that was designed to create something approximating to a common market and, by extension, lasting peace and prosperity.

A hero of some middle-class liberals at home and a celebrated European figure, Cobden offered an alternative to the dominance, in parliamentary terms, of the liberalism associated with Palmerston and Russell.

Based in Manchester, site also of the Peterloo massacre of 1819, the ACLL had strong symbolic ties with radical history. By using the press, petitions and strikes as well as parliamentary platforms to argue for cheaper bread through the abolition of the punitive duties on corn, the ACLL not only advanced a radical liberal agenda, but also provided something of a model for future radical activity, as seen, for example, in Chartism and in the Nonconformist pressure group the Liberation Society. As John Belchem has argued, changes in the culture of middle-class radicalism, as evidenced by the shift from the ballot to corn and the work of the ACLL, meant that 'middle-class radicalism was transforming itself into Victorian liberalism, a vehicle of political moralism in which the extension of the franchise was not a matter of constitutional balance or citizenship rights but a question of "character", of moral entitlement'.[22] For some, then, the ACLL was the authentic voice of Victorian liberalism. But it also paved the way for further radical action. Chartist demands for far-reaching reform of the political system drew from the ACLL at least in terms of campaigning methods, and even if Chartism displayed many of the old working-class/middle-class tensions (characterised as physical force versus moral force), at least the extra-parliamentary radical (or perhaps liberal) agenda was finding a more effective and coherent voice.

The Anti-Corn Law League had been both effective and popular in its campaigns against the high price of corn and the 'liberals' sought to exploit this. The price of corn had increased from 39s. 4d. per quarter in 1835 to 70s. 8d. in 1839, with inevitable consequences for the price of bread. The question of economic policy was squarely on the table, and with the depression of 1838–39 giving further impetus to Chartist radical critiques of government, so too were the Whigs' and liberals' claims to be able to manage the economy under scrutiny. The issue was not straightforward, however. Orthodox Whig commitment to political economy made it relatively easy to challenge the system of protective tariffs embodied in the Corn Laws, as an unnatural monopoly serving a narrow range of vested interests. On the other hand, many Whigs subscribed to the view that abandoning the Corn Laws would only see Britain flooded with cheap imports and leave the country vulnerable to blockades in the event of war, while from a purely political standpoint it made little electoral sense deliberately to alienate the agricultural sector. Circumstances forced the Whigs' hands, however, as disquiet in the country over the high and rising price of bread did little to support Whig claims to serve as efficient managers of the economy in the national interest. By the later 1830s, then, despite their reservations, Whigs were reviewing their approach to economic policy and in 1841 they proposed a more moderate tariff on corn; it was a compromise that 'nodded to free trade theory but did not undermine protection in practice', but one that, nonetheless, would 'guide agitation and demonstrate government responsiveness'.[23]

1841 general election (29 June – 22 July)			
	Votes	%	MPs
Liberal	273,902	46.9	271
Conservative	**306,314**	**50.9**	**367**
Irish Repeal	12,537	2.1	20
Others	692	0.1	0
Total	593,445		658

It was a critical shift for the Whigs that would facilitate an important accommodation with the more liberal branch of Toryism in the coming years and which would in turn have a key impact on the development of a more prominent and even coherent liberal identity. For all of the sense of a developing party unity, however, it is well to remember Greville's description of the state of parties in the aftermath of the 1841 general election, in which he observed that:

> When the 300 men who compose the opposition consist of three distinct sections of politicians, the great Whig and moderate Radical body, owning John [Russell] for their leader, the ultra radicals following Roebuck, and the Irish under O'Connell, and that the Whig leader abhors the Roebuck doctrines, can hardly be restrained from attacking O'Connell, and is resolved to be meek and gentle with his Tory antagonists, it does seem as if Peel's difficulties, whatever may be their nature or magnitude, would not be principally derived from the compact union of his opponents.[24]

Clearly not all observers felt a Liberal Party's existence could be taken for granted.

Sir Robert Peel (1788–1850)

Although a Tory at the beginning of the period, Peel's destruction of the Conservative Party over free trade in repealing the Corn Laws in 1846 in fact made him an important figure in the development of liberal politics.

Having served, briefly, as Prime Minister in 1834–35 Peel's commitment to administrative and financial efficiency as the watchwords of government, as outlined in his 'manifesto' delivered to constituents in Tamworth in 1834, saw him emerge as the leading figure within Conservative ranks and took him back to the premiership in 1841–46. By the end of this period, however, his determination to repeal the Corn Laws effectively ended Conservative hopes of achieving a parliamentary majority for a generation as the party divided acrimoniously and the more liberal, free-trade, 'Peelite' elements moved, slowly, towards an accommodation with the Whigs and radicals.

Indeed, in leaving office Peel made it possible for his followers to explore the possibilities for collaboration with Liberal elements in Parliament among whom leading
lights such as Palmerston held Peel in high regard. Peel died in 1850 following a riding
accident, which was a dramatic further blow to Peelite ambitions to act as an independent political force, but his name lived on among his erstwhile supporters.

Russell, Palmerston and mid-Victorian liberalism

Peel's government of 1841–46 was, of course, in many ways an exercise in the destruction of the old Conservative Party and the hammering out of Tory differences over trade
policies. Peel had come to the conclusion that the protectionist duties on corn had to be
removed and was willing to jeopardise his government's future in order to achieve this.
By 1845, it had become painfully clear that the free-trade Peelites could not continue to
work alongside die-hard protectionists and would have to acknowledge that to some
extent their long-term future lay in conjunction with the liberal elements in Parliament.
Whig inabilities to form a ministry in 1845, however, forced Peel to continue on his
collision course with his own party and only in the midst of the wreckage of the old
Conservative Party, now split irreparably between Peelite free-traders and protectionists
in the aftermath of the repeal of the Corn Laws in 1846, was the Whig Lord John Russell
able to put together an alternative ministry.

Russell finally accepted the Queen's commission on 6 July 1846 and the new ministers
assumed their seals of office at Osborne. Yet Russell's government was not a particularly
strong and united one, and it seemed that factionalism still plagued the liberal interest.
Even to Prince Albert the splintered nature of the new ministry was obvious:

> There is the Grey Party, consisting of Lord Grey, Lord Clarendon, Sir George Grey,
> and Mr Wood; they are against Lord Lansdowne, Lord Minto, Lord Auckland,
> and Sir John Hobhouse, stigmatising them as old women. Lord John leans entirely
> to the last-named gentlemen. There is no cordiality between Lord John and Lord
> Palmerston, who, if he had to make a choice, would even forget what passed in
> December last [when Grey refused to serve alongside Palmerston and prevented
> Russell from forming a government], and join the Grey Party in preference to Lord
> John personally. The curious part of all this is that they cannot keep a secret, and
> speak of all their differences.[25]

Modern analyses of Whig-liberal politics have agreed with the Prince in viewing this as
a period of factions. Clearly the ministry was susceptible to internal division but more
than this, within Parliament, too, support for the new government was weak. While
acknowledging the difficulties in assessing party strength at Westminster between the
time of Peel's fall and the dissolution of 1847, it has been observed that, taking the division lists for the third reading of the Corn Bill and the second reading of the Coercion
Bill in Hansard, the 'nominal supporters of the Government were in a minority and

probably numbered altogether something like 270 to 280 members. The protectionist party represented about 270 and the Peelites about 110.'[26] It was an inauspicious beginning, something which the Queen recognised. 'The present Government is weak, and I think Lord J. does not possess the talent of keeping his people together', she observed a few days after its formation.[27]

1847 general election (29 July – 26 August)			
	Votes	*%*	*MPs*
Liberal	**259,311**	**53.8**	**292**
Conservative (including Peelites)	205,481	42.6	325
Irish Repeal	14,128	2.9	36
Others	3,509	0.7	3
Total	*482,429*		*656*

Yet, by many estimates, the Liberal Party was not only born by this point but had already celebrated its tenth birthday some months before. But while radicals and Whigs generally saw common interest in opposing the protectionists, the mix was now a slightly more complicated one, as Whigs flirted with the disaffected liberal Tories associated with Peel and his supporters in the aftermath of the repeal of the Corn Laws. It would be a few more years before the Peelites and Whigs would share power, but already the liberal agenda was evolving. Sir George Cornewall Lewis, a future Liberal Chancellor of the Exchequer, observed at this time that: 'There is a genuine repugnance and difference of *Grund-ausichten* [basic views] between the Peelites and Protectionists. If they shook hands over the corn-law quarrel, they would part company upon some new question within a month. A junction between the Peelites (or some of them) and the Whigs is possible; a junction between the Peelites and Protectionists, I look upon as impossible.'[28]

This impossible junction was crucial to Whig or liberal success or even, perhaps, survival as the party of government in the later 1840s. Lacking serious heavyweight political leadership, the protectionists became increasingly ineffective, leaving the Whigs a clear run. In such circumstances a certain pragmatism prevailed, as Geoffrey Searle noted: 'For the Whigs were determined to hold on to their political hegemony, and a sufficiently large number of them viewed the problems of the day with the sort of detachment which allowed them to give ground to the urban radicals when it seemed patriotic or expedient to do so.'[29]

Yet it would be wrong to dismiss Whig advances in these years as simply the other side of the coin of Tory failures. Although frequently divided among themselves, Russell's government did much to consolidate the liberal agenda of mid-Victorian Britain, at least in terms of an ongoing (if not particularly active) commitment to some sort of review of the nature of parliamentary representation and a clear adherence to free-trade policies. In the end, however, there seemed an essential lack of vitality; the government could have fallen, it seemed, at almost any time in 1850 or 1851 before it finally collapsed in early 1852. As the Duke of Argyll, a Peelite, observed: 'During 1851 the Government of Lord John Russell was evidently tottering to its fall. The Peelites did all they could to support it, for the sake of keeping Lord Stanley out; but it was difficult. Parties were demoralised, and adverse divisions on particular questions placed the Government in occasional minorities.'[30] But if the sense of stagnation or lack of inspiration described the later 1840s, the situation was not to last. It might have been that the problem was one of continued division and disagreement, but the ten months between February and December 1852 during which Lord Derby held the reins of government failed to impress a protectionist stamp on politics and hopes of liberal revival were not extinguished. However, it was clear that such a revival would call for some reassessment of priorities.

1852 general election (7–31 July)			
	Votes	%	MPs
Liberal	430,882	57.9	324
Conservative (including Peelites)	311,481	41.9	330
Others	1,541	0.2	0
Total	743,904		654

The Aberdeen coalition (1852–55)

Although active in the search for an alternative to the Derby government, the various factions sitting opposite the Treasury benches were not particularly well placed to challenge the government. There was a need for some sort of realignment of parties. The Peelites and the protectionists were no longer united under the Conservative banner, and the Whigs, who were led in opposition by Russell, were equally incapable of supplanting Derby themselves. Russell could not command the loyalty and respect of sufficient colleagues and could no longer claim to be able to carry the Whigs forward as a united body.

Lord Palmerston (1784–1865)

Never quite a Whig, never quite a Tory, Henry John Temple, the third Viscount Palmerston, has troubled biographers seeking to pin down his politics. Opponents such as Lord Derby would complain, in exasperation, that Palmerston was 'a political chameleon, which offers a different hue and colour to the spectator according to the side from which he gazes', but he would also come to be regarded as the first truly Liberal Prime Minister.

Though educated in the classic Whig tradition at Edinburgh University, Palmerston's early career was dominated by Tory patronage before he broke away from Wellington's Tories as part of the more liberal wing led by adherents of George Canning's politics in the late 1820s. He became Foreign Secretary in Lord Grey's government (1830–34) and from that point dominated British foreign policy, either as minister or critic, serving as Foreign Secretary 1830–34, 1835–41 and 1846–51. In 1852 he became Home Secretary in Aberdeen's ill-fated government. It was not long before the Crimean War (1853–56) brought him back into the limelight and, popularly at least, he was heralded as the country's saviour as the dismal conduct of the war was revealed. He became Prime Minister in 1855 and held that post until his death in 1865 (apart from a brief spell out of office in 1858–59).

Now was the time when a new arrangement was called for, be that a union of the opposition members, or some sort of coalition. The Duke of Newcastle imagined this was a watershed in British politics and sought, 'with a view to real fusion of all Liberals', to abandon the names 'Whig' and 'Peelite'. A new party, he believed, must be established 'not by one party joining another. With this view all old names as well as old jealousies must be abandoned.'[31] He was only expressing what the Earl of Aberdeen had already said when he had written to Newcastle expressing his dissatisfaction with the Derby administration: 'I cannot look to the continuance of the present Government in power with any degree of satisfaction', he said, concluding that, since Russell alone could not regain his old position:

> I think therefore the time is come when we ought to act in cordial concert with Lord John and the Whigs. I am not aware of any real difference between us. Free Trade, with all its legitimate consequences, is quite safe; and I do not anticipate anything but agreement on the subject of our financial policy. Different views may be entertained respecting education, and the Church; but perhaps these are more theoretical than practical, and in which the necessity of mutual forbearance will be strongly felt. It is to be hoped, after the lesson of last year, that we shall have nothing to apprehend from any hostile interference on the part of the Whigs with religious freedom.[32]

Newcastle pressed on Aberdeen in August that in the present 'peculiar' circumstances, 'the state of parties [is] unprecedented, and I believe that, if *all* will lay aside selfish and personal views and wishes, you can better serve the Queen and the Country than any other person'.[33] At the same time, Russell declared that he was 'quite ready to support Lord Aberdeen as Prime Minister, if the Liberals prefer him to me'.[34] Aberdeen, however, displayed less confidence in his ability and prospects. There had been talk of him replacing Russell in 1848 which, he had declared, 'would be a dreadful affair, and I trust will never be realised', maintaining that if the Russell government did fail 'it is my determination to preserve my own freedom'.[35]

Lord Aberdeen (1784–1860)

George Hamilton Gordon, the fourth Earl of Aberdeen, never really recovered his reputation after his failure to provide clear leadership as Prime Minister during the Crimean War.

One of the sixteen Scottish representative peers from 1806, Aberdeen's career was characterised by his involvement in foreign affairs, as ambassador extraordinary at Vienna in 1813 and as the Tory Foreign Secretary 1828–30. He shifted towards Peel and served as Peel's Secretary for War and Colonies in 1834–35, returning to the Foreign Office in 1841–46. Traditionally seen as Palmerston's great rival in diplomatic terms,

Aberdeen had emerged as the leading light among the Peelites by the early 1850s. In the search for a more 'liberal' government in 1852 he was prevailed upon to form a government, at which point he sought to downplay his differences with Palmerston and head a genuine coalition (or even fusion) of Whigs and Peelites.

The war with Russia, however, finished an otherwise promising premiership and following his resignation in 1855, when pressed for a committee of inquiry into the mismanagement of the war, Aberdeen held no further important office of state.

By 1852, however, the ground had shifted. Aberdeen was quite clearly the leading light among Peel's old colleagues and there was also considerable support within the Peelite ranks for an Aberdeen government. Still, Aberdeen was a reluctant candidate, preferring a Russell-led administration which he could support though without being 'in office myself',[36] and even in the autumn he distanced himself from the attempts to supplant Derby. He would not attempt to construct a government which would stand little or no chance of survival purely for the sake of replacing Derby, and he seems not to have felt confident of his ability to do otherwise.

In December 1852, however, Aberdeen was prevailed upon to form a government. This administration is frequently described as a coalition of Whigs and Peelites and it was never really any more than that; both Whigs and Peelites adhered to their separate identities for the time being. Leading Peelites seemed generally amenable to collaboration with the Whigs, but as Gladstone pointed out, while he was not 'unconditionally committed against any alliance or fusion', he did not feel that 1852 was the right time to press ahead with such a scheme.[37] Certainly Russell and other prominent Whigs were reluctant to surrender their name. Despite numerical imbalances within Parliament between the groups, in the new Cabinet of thirteen, six seats each went to the Whigs and Peelites (and one to a radical) but this was not indicative of fusion; it was a prudent attempt to satisfy the demands of each competing group.

Aberdeen recognised that this Whig–Peelite 'coalition' was a 'great experiment, hitherto unattempted, and of which the success must be considered doubtful. In the meantime, the Public have regarded the new administration with singular favour.' Nevertheless, he could not deny that while the coming parliamentary session would be difficult, 'I am sanguine in my belief, that our good measures will procure for us sufficient majorities in Parliament, as well as the support of the country'.[38] Even the Whigs could find grounds for a small measure of optimism. They recognised that this was a government of talented individuals who had more in common with each other than there were grounds of difference.

On many issues, as diverse as reform of the currency, railways, universities, and the civil service, not to mention parliamentary reform, the government worked well and old party divisions did indeed seem to have been forgotten. Walter Bagehot went further, describing the Aberdeen Cabinet as 'the ablest we have had, perhaps, since the Reform Act', but as he also noted, it was 'a Cabinet not only adapted, but eminently adapted, for every sort of difficulty save the one that it had to meet'.[39] That difficulty, significantly, was one of foreign affairs; this was the government that faced a renewed crisis in the Ottoman Empire that would escalate into war in the Crimea.

The history of Aberdeen's government of 1852–55 ultimately reveals the failure to fuse its disparate parts. The roots of the coalition were exposed as Whigs and Peelites adopted differing stands over foreign policy, or at least over the Eastern Question. Greville recorded the observation made to him by the Foreign Secretary, Clarendon, that far from the continuity in foreign affairs of which Aberdeen had initially spoken, the Foreign Secretary found himself, by the summer of 1853, 'mediating between Aberdeen and Palmerston, whose ancient and habitual ideas of foreign policy are brought by this business into antagonism'.[40] The rivalry between Aberdeen and Palmerston was reflected more widely in the general division between Peelites and Whigs into doves and hawks respectively. During the spring and summer of 1853 the Aberdonian outlook gained ground within the Cabinet and frequently Palmerston was obliged to back down, but Aberdeen was being premature when he expressed his hopes that now 'all *polémiques*' should cease between them.[41] Palmerston had not given up in his attempts to influence foreign policy, and nor for that matter had Russell.

Though Aberdeen's policy was deemed inadequate, however, neither Russell nor Palmerston had the ability or the desire to push the point too far, offering only a sporadic and piecemeal alternative. In the middle of everything was Clarendon, striving to strike a balance between the competing factions in the government. In early October, he complained to Aberdeen that the 'difficulty is very great of reconciling the opposite views held in the Cab[ine]t & of satisfying my own notions of moderation & firmness'.[42]

By late 1853 Palmerston's more bellicose approach was gaining ground and by early 1854 even Aberdeen was prepared to accept that a rather more forceful approach to Russia was required, but it was too late to hide the divisions within the government. These were not simply between Peelite and Whig, but also personal, not least between Palmerston and Russell, who both saw themselves as the legitimate leader of Whig (or even liberal) opinion and who both sought to make political capital out of the war by identifying themselves with a popular and clear-sighted foreign policy.

Yet although Peelites, Whigs and radicals had not yet agreed to become 'liberals', they had recognised some common interests, not least in matters of financial policy, and above all in their shared aversion to protectionism and faith in free trade, and they seemed not too far apart on matters of, for example, education, or parliamentary reform. If 1852 did not quite represent the unequivocal establishment of a Liberal Party in Parliament, it did at least bring the non-Conservatives closer together. For although Aberdeen's government collapsed disastrously over the Crimean War and Aberdeen's own reputation never recovered from the debacle, when Palmerston was commissioned to form a new government to replace Aberdeen in 1855, he did so using largely the same personnel as Aberdeen had employed, even though resignations would quickly turn Palmerston's first government into a largely Whig one.

The first Palmerston government (1855–58)

Palmerston emerged in February 1855, as he put it himself in a letter to his brother, as *l'inévitable* choice for the premiership. However much it might have distressed the Queen to turn to Palmerston – she was determined to exhaust every possible arrangement before she turned to the man she regarded as a most dangerous and cavalier minister – in the end she seemed to have no alternative. Aberdeen and Russell were both damaged by the disastrous war; Aberdeen as Prime Minister was unequivocally guilty by association, and Russell, having chosen to resign rather than face Roebuck's motion of censure of the government in January 1855, had lost standing in the eyes of his political colleagues. Thus did the Queen ask Palmerston to form a government:

> I know this would be very objectionable in many respects, and personally not agree-
> able to me, [she wrote] but *I* think of *nothing* but the country, and the preservation
> of its institutions, and *my own* personal feelings would be sunk if only the efficiency
> of the government could be obtained. *If* the *Peelites* and *Whigs* would serve *under*
> Lord Palmerston, *I should not* apprehend the consequences – for they would restrain
> him from mischief, and Palmerston *himself* in *that position* would feel the weight and
> responsibility of *such a position* in a manner that would make him feel very differently
> to what he has hitherto done, as a subordinate.[43]

Clearly the supposed 'fusion' of liberal interests had still some way to go. Yet, whether Whigs and Peelites reined Palmerston in, or whether Palmerston remained his own man, the subsequent four years would be crucial to the development of liberal politics in Britain. If the 'birth' of the party had been disputed up until this point, by 1859 the issue was much more clearly defined, and by most estimates the end of the decade did finally see the establishment of a Parliamentary Liberal Party that was widely recognised as such.

Central to this process was the role of Palmerston. Palmerston had made his name in the world of foreign policy. Uniquely this could be presented as an area of business of pre-eminently national significance in which even the most oppressed British subjects could share in the reflected 'glory' of the *Pax Britannica*. Indeed, Palmerstonian foreign policy can be seen, to a degree, to have exploited a sense of Protestant, and liberal, providentialism, at least rhetorically. Palmerston frequently played upon notions of Britain as a model of constitutional freedom and commercial prosperity able, and in certain cases perhaps obliged, to elevate the condition of less favoured parts of the world. Thus Palmerston's foreign policy could appeal to a sense of a higher purpose, transcending domestic difficulties and offering a rallying point for national cohesion.

However superficial it might have been, Palmerstonian foreign policy suggested a concern with promoting liberalism all over the world, and although subsequent commentators have been quick to question Palmerston's sincerity and point to the inconsistencies in his policies, these flaws were not always apparent to a population easily swayed by emotive Palmerstonian grandiloquence. Rather, Palmerston was remembered for promises such as that Britain would be 'the champion of justice and right: pursuing that course with moderation and prudence, not becoming the Quixote of the world, but giving her moral sanction and support wherever she thinks justice is, and whenever she thinks that wrong has been done'.[44] He garnished his diplomacy, then, with frequent appeals to the need to champion the rights of smaller European states to self-determination and of the people of Europe to enjoy liberal constitutional government, and he made great play of his commitment to humanitarian concerns, notably the abolition of the slave trade. This all tended to generate a sense of liberal values embodied in a certain kind of British patriotism and associated in particular with one of the period's leading Whig, or liberal, figures. And although he has sometimes been presented as a conservative politician by instinct, Palmerston was cognisant by the early 1850s of the need to commit to the cause of 'the great Liberal Party, (not in the H[ouse]. of C[om]m[on]s, nor at Brooks's nor at the Reform Club) but in the United Kingdom'.[45] This professed commitment to 'the great Liberal Party' is important.

In Jonathan Parry's narrative of the 'rise and fall' of Liberal government in the Victorian period, with liberal forces in the mid-1850s in need of a clear focus, there were three competing strategies: Russellite schemes for a Liberal–radical coalition based on constitutional and religious reform; a Peelite-inspired 'programme of economy and good administration'; and, the 'most successful' in the event, a Palmerstonian third way.[46] The race was essentially between Russell and Palmerston, but as Parry argues, Russell fell at three separate fences: he was not 'sufficiently prime ministerial', he continued to embody Whiggish social exclusiveness; and he managed to alienate radical support through his perceived 'impulsiveness'.[47]

Palmerston's strategy, such as it was, was for the impression of activity to stand in lieu of real accomplishments. Palmerston continued to place foreign policy at the head of his agenda during the first couple of years of his premiership and for the most part left domestic politics alone. In later years he would joke that 'we cannot go on adding to the statute book *ad infinitum*' and this has all too often been taken to signify a reactionary spirit hostile to change. In fact it was a symbol of Palmerston's moderation; his desire to hold things in check and establish a reputation for responsible, safe management of the nation's affairs. Walter Bagehot would call Palmerston's approach 'dull', but he meant it as a compliment; it served well the needs of the booming, successful workshop of the world.[48]

Palmerston could survive, prosper even, on this basis because his government faced little real opposition. The protectionists led by Derby and Disraeli, though starting to get their act together at Westminster, remained a lukewarm challenge to the government. There was a sense that Whig–Peelite government continued by default as much as anything else. As Sir James Graham, formerly a First Lord of the Admiralty, put it in April 1856, 'the government goes on because there is no organised opposition prepared and able to take its place, and the government receives a sufficiency of independent support, because all feel that the business of the country must be carried on'.[49]

In fact Palmerston did much to consolidate non-Conservative strength and position at Westminster during these years. He demonstrated commitment to administrative efficiency, including civil service reform (he gave the Northcote-Trevelyan proposals for competitive entry into the service a favourable hearing) and educational reforms and, in contrast to the perception of stasis, made energetic use of Royal Commissions to investigate various aspects of government efficiency.

Palmerston's popular touch did not desert him in these years either. In advance of the much more familiar stumping around the country undertaken by Gladstone in the 1860s and 1870s, Palmerston was an energetic speaker, taking advantage of the parliamentary recess in 1856 to speak in northern towns such as Liverpool, Salford and Manchester. Of course this did much to cement his own personal rapport with the population; it also served a broader purpose of confirming the non-Conservatives as those most closely interested in the country at large. Palmerston's view of society remained essentially a patrician one, and he never did abandon his suspicion of democracy, but he made quite clear his commitment to 'progressive improvement' in Britain, asking his audiences in Lancashire in November 1856:

> Why should we not endeavour to be perpetually ameliorating ... laws and institutions, which, being human, cannot be perfect, but which, according to the progress of society and the change of circumstances must be continually in need of emendation and extension?[50]

Whether or not Palmerstonian liberalism demonstrated a sincere commitment to developing a more accountable political structure – and in recent revisionist accounts his governments have been presented as a 'conscious introduction to the new era' of democratic politics[51] – in terms of political style and technique there was emerging a clearer sense of bringing politics to the people, and even if representation remained limited in a formal sense, in an informal one it was nonetheless real.

Democracy and the role of government

In 1854 Palmerston warned the Prime Minister, Lord Aberdeen, that extension of the franchise would be a dangerous thing for British government. 'Can it be expected', he asked, 'that men who murder their Children to get nine Pounds to be spent in Drink will not sell their vote for whatever they can get for it?' Although he expressed himself more vehemently than many others did, Palmerston was not alone in his wariness of 'democracy'.

Many Whigs who had been educated in Enlightenment Scotland and who now formed a crucial backbone to Victorian liberalism, had been schooled, as Palmerston had, in the merits of a more representative system. As Dugald Stewart, a former student of Adam Smith and himself tutor to many future prominent Whigs, had counselled, the 'happiness of mankind depends, not on the share which the people possess, directly or indirectly, in the enactment of laws, but on the equity and expedience of the laws that are enacted'. It was a plea for the sort of virtual rather than direct representation of which Edmund Burke would have approved. Mid-Victorian liberals therefore frequently drew a distinction between representation and democracy; even when franchise reform was proposed, it rested still on the primacy of property, and thus kept political power in the hands of a narrow section of society.

Meanwhile, government continued to grow dramatically throughout this period as laissez-faire ideals gave way to something more interventionist. If Utilitarian hopes for achieving 'the greatest happiness of the greatest number' were to be realised, then it would become, it seemed, increasingly necessary for the state to act in such a way as to level the playing field. Evangelical and humanitarian impulses also drove governments to address not just the inequalities but also the iniquities of Victorian society. Allied to this were greater knowledge and understanding of social problems, for example as a result of investigations of the urban condition such as Chadwick's Sanitary Report of 1842, and technological advances which made reform of such conditions possible as well as desirable.

Although there was still considerable resistance to centralised state intervention, this position seemed increasingly untenable, and liberal consciences were drawn to improve society through greater involvement in, or regulation of, working conditions (particularly in factories and mines), education, public health, and the relief of poverty. The developing machinery of the state, including the origins of a more professional, meritocratic, civil service, has led some to talk of a 'revolution in government' in this period. Revolutionary or not, the state was coming much closer to the people and was having a much greater impact on their everyday lives. In some ways this was an extension of Whig/liberal notions of *noblesse oblige*, but at the same time, in bringing government to the people, it raised important questions about the extent to which the people might thus in turn expect to be brought closer to government.

Palmerston's administrative efficiency drive took much of the wind out of Peelite sails and they found it increasingly difficult to decide on a clear line of opposition to his government; indeed, as has been argued, this led pretty quickly to 'the destruction of Peelism as a separate political identity'.[52] Only Gladstone, among the Peelites, continued to present any kind of threat to Palmerston's ascendancy.

Historical fashion today, then, is to portray Palmerston as the quintessential mid-Victorian liberal. As Parry concludes:

> In administrative, financial and foreign policy, Palmerston squared the circle. He presided over far-reaching change in the image of the state. To a much greater extent than before, its ministers seemed disinterested, its taxes justifiable, its fiscal stance neutral as between interests, its success in promoting liberal commercial, constitutional and religious values cheap at the price. The sting was drawn from radicalism; it sought increasingly to participate with dutiful aristocrats in sober administration.

Liberalism came to look responsible. Again, much more than in the 1830s, the 'permanent interests' of the country could place trust in it. Where national and propertied interests were concerned, Palmerston seemed to have as safe a pair of hands as one could expect in a liberal age.[53]

In terms of the management of Parliament and consolidating some sense of administrative stability, Palmerston's mix of bombastic nationalist rhetoric and his populist instincts, combined with an innate cautiousness and desire to ensure responsible, careful, government, did much to secure Whig and liberal claims to be the natural power-brokers in mid-Victorian Britain. Yet the 'liberal ascendancy' of this period, such as it was, was not just about technique; beyond a certain commitment to 'progressive improvement', Palmerston's contribution to the evolution of liberal politics remained ambiguous, more valuable in a symbolic sense than in terms of his contribution to the ideological drive to policy. That role fell, perhaps inevitably, to Russell and, to a degree, Gladstone.

Although Russell's personal interests had not been well served by his appointment as Britain's representative at the negotiations to settle the Eastern crisis, and his consequent association with the rather hollow Treaty of Paris of 1856 which brought the war in the Crimea to an anti-climactic conclusion, his continued presence in government provided him with a platform from which to focus attention on the course of liberalism. He had long since abandoned the notion that 1832 represented a final solution of the franchise question and as recently as 1853 had brought forward plans for another, more extensive, measure of parliamentary reform. His decisive victory at the general election of 1857 in the City of London, in which he came forward on a platform of parliamentary reform, underlined the extent to which there remained a vital debate about the cause of progress still to be conducted within the party. His advocacy of reform garnered considerable support within Whig, radical and liberal circles. However, though setting down something of a marker, Russell's impressive showing in London in 1857 did not stimulate the sort of re-evaluation of liberal politics that he might have hoped for.

1857 general election (27 March – 24 April)			
	Votes	%	MPs
Liberal	464,127	64.8	377
Conservative (including Peelites)	239,712	33.4	264
Others	12,713	1.8	13
Total	716,552		654

The election had come about as a direct result of attacks on Palmerston's government from two other important sources within non-Conservative ranks: Cobden and Gladstone. At the beginning of the year, Gladstone had attempted to discredit the government's fiscal policy by means of a thorough critique of the Chancellor, Cornewall Lewis's, handling of the income tax. Cornewall Lewis, an extremely able politician, side-stepped Gladstone's attack with a budget that harked back to Peelite remedies with a reduced fixed rate, but although Gladstone failed to land a blow on the government, his actions marked the start of a turbulent year in politics. Russell had already raised the reform standard again when Cobden brought forward a third line of attack on the government, the altogether more successful challenge to Palmerston's cavalier treatment of China, whereby a minor perceived insult to British honour had brought forth a typically forthright Palmerstonian gunboat response in the bombardment of Canton. Conservatives, radicals and disaffected Whigs rallied to Cobden's call and successfully brought Palmerston's responsibility and liberal credentials into question. Palmerston was mocked by the radical Thomas Milner Gibson, for example, for having abandoned the cause of 'Peace, Retrenchment and Reform', in favour of 'Bombardment of Canton and No Reform', while Disraeli from the opposition benches taunted the ministry for its policies of 'No Reform! New Taxes! Canton blazing! Persia invaded!'[54]

However, in making the attacks on the government highly personal ones on Palmerston, the attempts to mark out a distinct liberal agenda were somewhat lost from view. While not strictly a plebiscite on Palmerston himself, the election that followed the government's defeat over Cobden's motion was frequently taken to have been just that and while many of the 'liberal' gains at the election were made on the back of promises about parliamentary reform, the resounding liberal victory at the polls seemed only to reaffirm Palmerston's claims to stand as the best interpreter of the national mood.

Nonetheless, the mood had clearly changed, and when Palmerston's government reconvened in May 1857 it was no longer possible to maintain a complacent faith in the virtues of administrative efficiency and vague commitments to 'progress' to serve as the bedrocks of government. It seemed to many observers that the reform issue was quite clearly back on the table: 'the immediate victory is Palmerston's,' observed one Whig, but he added, 'the second is the Liberal Party's, and the third will be Lord John's'.[55] For the rest of the year it seemed that the Russellite reform agenda would force a significant reassessment of liberal politics. Had it not been for an extraordinary diplomatic incident, Russell might well have got his way.

In January 1858 Felice Orsini, an Italian nationalist, tried to assassinate Emperor Napoleon III in Paris. However, it soon emerged that he had done so using bombs which had been made in Britain and according to a plan apparently hatched by refugees in London. This did not play well in France, and Palmerston came under intense pressure from the French government to introduce a Conspiracy to Murder Bill in February 1858 that stiffened the penalties against such conspirators. For once, Palmerston's popular touch abandoned him and he stood exposed to the public, not as the champion of national self-determination, but as the Prime Minister who did the bidding of France. Palmerston started to look vulnerable and, facing at the same time another defeat over his conduct of the government's handling of mutiny in India, he chose to fall on his sword and resign.

Politics were left in a state of flux. Derby, who replaced Palmerston, enjoyed a fifteen-month period of government but his Conservative ministry never really looked likely to last long. But what might replace it? Palmerston looked badly damaged and yet there seemed few other obvious leaders on the liberal side ready to take his place.

1859: the birth of the Liberal Party

The omens were not good in 1858 for liberal politics; Palmerston and Russell were more determined to make sure that the other did not return to the head of government than to turn out Derby, while a number of independent radicals, perhaps as many as 120, worked to make sure that Palmerston, as an opponent of parliamentary reform, was not returned to power, thereby giving the lie in the process to any suggestion that the 1857 election had underscored Palmerston's personal inviolability.

Yet just as in the past a sense of being anti-Conservative had trumped any doubts about the identity of liberalism, so would the events of 1858 and 1859 reinforce this process of liberal development. But this time the determination to work together seemed more urgent, and the results were more clearly formalised: if the party's origins in the 1830s, 1840s and early 1850s are debateable, few would deny that the later 1850s saw a more explicit and systematic attempt to give the Liberal Party a distinct form.

Two issues gave the liberals their opportunity. An extremely modest proposal for parliamentary reform was made by Derby's government in 1859 in response to the evident popular demand for further change, not least as such demands were being whipped up by people like John Bright who spoke around the country in late 1858 and early 1859 in favour of reform. The government's projected legislation, however, was so weak as to allow almost all liberal opinion to oppose it without having to map out a more radical alternative. The government's defeat over its Reform Bill provoked another general election, but this time it took place in the midst of an international crisis that was ripe for Palmerstonian bluster. France and Austria had gone to war over the future of Italy, and Palmerston could exploit his track record of dealing with international crises to the liberals' advantage while buttressing it with grand liberal rhetoric about the defence of Italian nationalism in the face of Derby's apparent sympathy for Austrian ambitions to retain influence in northern Italy.

1859 general election (28 April – 18 May)			
	Votes	%	MPs
Liberal	372,117	65.8	356
Conservative	193,232	34.2	298
Others	151	0.0	0
Total	565,500		654

At a meeting in June 1859 at Willis's Rooms in London, then, liberals gathered once again to decide how to turn out a Conservative government.

The Willis's Rooms Meeting, June 1859

An extract from *The Times*' report (7 June 1859) of the meeting in Willis's Rooms in St James Street, London, held on 6 June 1859.

A meeting of the Liberal members of the House of Commons was held yesterday afternoon, at Willis's Rooms, and was attended by 274 gentlemen, representing the various sections of that party. The proceedings were opened by Lord Palmerston, who observed that the issue upon which the Government had dissolved Parliament was not the question of Reform, or any other matter of legislation, but simply and solely whether or not they possessed the confidence of the country. He thought that the late election had given a conclusive answer to that question, and that it was the business of the Liberal Party to determine whether or not they should accept the challenge which had been given them. He believed it would be the more manly and straightforward course to do so, and he briefly sketched out the terms of the proposed amendment, expressive of a want of confidence in the present Government, which he stated that Lord Hartington and Mr Hanbury were respectively willing to propose and second, should the meeting deem it advisable for them to do so. In adverting to the war in Italy, his Lordship dwelt on the signal failure which the Government had met with in their endeavours to maintain peace between the contending parties and contended that a Cabinet, which had manifestly lost all weight in the Councils of Europe upon so momentous a question as that of peace and war, was not fit to be any longer intrusted with the conduct of our foreign relations. He also insisted very strongly on the duty of maintaining a strict neutrality, which he said that the speech of Lord Derby, previous to the outbreak of the war, had tended to impair; and declared that he could not foresee any circumstance which would render the hostile intervention of England necessary.

Lord John Russell next addressed the meeting and, after strongly deprecating the continuance of the Government in the hands of a minority, which he characterised as most unconstitutional and dangerous, expressed his hearty desire either to co-operate with Lord Palmerston, in the event of that noble Lord being called upon to form an Administration; or to avail himself of his assistance, in the event of his being required to conduct the affairs of the country himself. His Lordship adverted in the course of his speech to the state of the Liberal Party, and expressed his opinion that in the event of a Liberal Government being formed it was essential that the three great sections of that party – the old Whigs, the Peelites, and the advanced Liberals – should each be represented in it.

Mr Bright, who followed Lord John, spoke of the dissensions which had hitherto existed in the Liberal Party, for which he considered himself in some measure responsible, but which he both accounted for and vindicated, on the ground that the old members of that party, who had carried the Reform Bill of 1832, had not acted up to the principles which inevitably flowed from that measure, but had made a point of excluding from any share of power all those independent members who usually sat below the gangway, and who considered that they had duties to perform to their constituents as well as to the nominal leaders of the party to which they belonged. If, however, they were willing to act henceforth on a more comprehensive system, he should have no hesitation in sinking minor differences, and in giving such a Government his most cordial support. He was not quite satisfied, however, with what had fallen from Lord Palmerston on the subject of our foreign relations; and if he thought that peace was more likely to be secured by keeping the present Government in office, nothing should induce him to assist in turning them out.

Lord Palmerston explained that, in his opinion, nothing was so conducive to the interests of Europe and the preservation of peace as the maintenance of a strict alliance between England and France.

Mr Sidney Herbert strongly advocated a decided movement on the part of the Liberal members, and said that even if unsuccessful it would do them no harm, and would at least have the effect of determining the question as to whom the country was to be governed by.

As Palmerston argued, in addressing the meeting, it was the only 'manly and straight-forward course' available to the liberal Members of Parliament to accept the challenge to form a new government, while other speakers, such as John Bright, expressed a willing-ness to set aside past disagreements and finally to put into practice liberal values first put forward in the early 1830s.[56] Crucially, however, whereas earlier meetings, like that at Lichfield House, had masked disagreements through ambiguity, in 1859 the mood was altogether more constructive. Palmerston and Russell had already met in private and agreed that in the interests of liberal harmony they would work together and serve in the other's Cabinet, as fate dictated (although they would not agree to work under anyone else – which, significantly, kept liberal politics in the hands of those who were either by background or instinct, or both, Whiggish in their outlook for the foreseeable future).

Although the move was driven by a negative impulse, once again, when the new Parliament met in the summer of 1859, there existed a Liberal Party in both name and spirit. It was led by the irascible Palmerston and driven by the petulant Russell but none-theless finally, after a protracted birth of almost three decades, the foundations for a 'Liberal heyday' had been laid.

Further reading

The mid-Victorian period is well-served with general surveys of the political landscape. For the Liberals in particular, good starting points are Alan Sykes, *The Rise and Fall of British Liberalism, 1776–1988* (Longman, 1997), T. A. Jenkins, *The Liberal Ascendancy, 1830–1886*

(Palgrave Macmillan, 1994) and especially Jonathan Parry, *The Rise and Fall of Liberal Government in Victorian Britain* (Yale University Press, 1993). An older study that examines specifically the fortunes of the Whigs is Donald Southgate, *The Passing of the Whigs, 1832–1886* (Macmillan, 1965). Compare this with the more recent, and sophisticated, Peter Mandler, *Aristocratic Government in the Age of Reform: Whigs and Liberals, 1830–1852* (Clarendon Press, 1990). To place these studies in a broader parliamentary context see Robert Stewart, *Party and Politics, 1830–1852* (Macmillan, 1989) and Angus Hawkins, *British Party Politics, 1852–1886* (Macmillan, 1998).

As indicated in this chapter, there remains some debate about the date on which the party was 'born'. Norman Gash located the birth in the mid-1830s in his *Reaction and Reconstruction in English Politics, 1832–52* (OUP, 1965) and a more recent study, Jonathan Parry's *Rise and Fall of Liberal Government*, echoes this view to some extent. Meanwhile, the view that the party was established in the early 1850s can be read in Muriel Chamberlain's *Who Founded the Liberal Party?* (University of Wales Press, 1991). These studies might profitably be contrasted with John Vincent's splendid examination of *The Formation of the British Liberal Party, 1857–68* (Constable, 1966).

The 1832 Reform Act has been the subject of much scholarly interest, but for a study of the Act in detail, still worthwhile is Michael Brock, *The Great Reform Act* (Hutchinson, 1973). The functioning of parliamentary politics is examined in T. A. Jenkins, *Parliament, Party and Politics in Victorian Britain* (Manchester University Press, 1996) and this might be compared with Walter Bagehot's celebrated contemporary analysis of *The English Constitution* (1867), although Bagehot should be read in the light of a current preface provided in one of the recent modern editions (for example by Miles Taylor in the Oxford World's Classics 2009 edition or Paul Smith in the CUP 2001 edition).

Excellent studies of the governments of Aberdeen and Palmerston are provided in J. B. Conacher, *The Aberdeen Coalition, 1852–1855* (CUP, 1968), E. D. Steele, *Palmerston and Liberalism, 1855–1865* (CUP, 1991) and D. F. Krein, *The Last Palmerston Government* (Iowa State University Press, 1978), all of which offer valuable guides to the development of liberal politics in this period. Also worth consulting are G. R. Searle's *Entrepreneurial Politics in Mid-Victorian Britain* (OUP, 1993) and Anthony Howe's *Free Trade and Liberal England, 1846–1946* (Clarendon Press, 1997).

Examining the period from a biographical perspective, the following all have much to say about liberal politics: L. G. Mitchell, *Lord Melbourne, 1779–1848* (OUP, 1997); T. A. Jenkins, *Sir Robert Peel* (Palgrave Macmillan, 1998); Norman Gash, *Sir Robert Peel* (Routledge and Kegan Paul, 1972); Richard Gaunt, *Sir Robert Peel: The Life and Legacy* (I. B. Tauris, 2010); John Prest, *Lord John Russell* (Macmillan, 1972); M. E. Chamberlain, *Lord Aberdeen* (Addison Wesley, 1983); Jasper Ridley, *Lord Palmerston* (Constable, 1970); David Brown, *Palmerston: A Biography* (Yale University Press, 2010); and Donald Southgate, *'The Most English Minister': The Policies and Politics of Palmerston* (Macmillan, 1966).

Notes

1   *The Work of the Liberal Party During the last Fifty Years. A letter from the Right Honourable John Bright, M.P.* (1885), pp. 4–5.

2   The Tory Party became known as the Conservative Party under the leadership of Sir Robert Peel in the 1830s.

3   Alan Sykes, *The Rise and Fall of British Liberalism, 1776–1988* (Longman, 1997), p. 20.

4   Robert Stewart, *Party and Politics, 1830–1852* (Macmillan, 1989) p. 20.

5   Ibid., pp. 22–23; David Thompson, *England in the Nineteenth Century* (Penguin, 1978), pp. 74–75.

6   Quoted in Sykes, *British Liberalism*, p. 19.

7   Supporters of Daniel O'Connell who advocated repeal of the Act of Union.

8   Quoted in John Prest, *Lord John Russell* (Macmillan, 1972), p. 61.

9   Jonathan Parry, *The Rise and Fall of Liberal Government in Victorian Britain* (Yale University Press, 1993), pp. 108–09.

10   Quoted in Michael Bentley, *Politics without Democracy 1815–1914* (Blackwell, 1984) p. 85.

11   Norman Gash, *Reaction and Reconstruction in English Politics, 1832–52* (Clarendon Press, 1965) and *Aristocracy and People, 1815–1865* (Edward Arnold, 1979).

12   Parry, *Liberal Government*, p. 128.

13   Greville's diary, 24 March 1835, quoted in Bentley, *Politics without Democracy*, p. 99.

14   Russell to Lord Howick, 1 February 1835 and to Grey, 1835, quoted in T. A. Jenkins, *The Liberal Ascendancy, 1830–1886* (Palgrave Macmillan, 1994), p. 25.

15   Russell to Melbourne, 10 August 1837, quoted in ibid., p. 29.

16   Russell made the case in an open letter to his constituents at Stroud in May 1839, quoted in ibid,, p. 30.

17   Grote to John Austin, February 1838, quoted in ibid., p. 32.

18   John Belchem, *Popular Radicalism in Nineteenth-Century Britain* (Macmillan, 1996), p. 67.

19   O'Brien, quoted in ibid., p. 67.

20   Quoted in Bentley, *Politics without Democracy*, p. 111.

21   Cobden quoted in Belchem, *Popular Radicalism*, p. 71.

22   Ibid., p. 82.

23   Parry, *Liberal Government*, pp. 143–47.

24   *Greville Memoirs,* 12 August 1841, quoted in Jenkins, *Liberal Ascendancy*, pp. 36–37.

25   Memorandum by Prince Albert, 6 July 1846, A. C. Benson and Viscount Esher (eds.), *The Letters of Queen Victoria: a selection from Her Majesty's correspondence between the years 1837 and 1861,* 3 vols. (John Murray, 1911) [hereafter *LQV*], vol. 2, pp. 101–03.

26   F. A. Dreyer 'The Russell Administration, 1846–52', (unpublished D.Phil thesis, University of St. Andrews, 1962), p. 80; for more detail on voting patterns and party allegiance see pp. 80–82.

27   Queen Victoria to the King of the Belgians, 14 July 1846, *LQV*, vol. 2, pp. 103–05.

28   G. F. Lewis (ed.), *The Letters of the Right Hon. Sir George Cornewall Lewis, Bart.* (1870), pp. 191–92.

29 G. R. Searle, *Entrepreneurial Politics in Mid-Victorian Britain* (OUP, 1993), p. 45.

30 George Douglas Campbell, Eighth Duke of Argyll, *Autobiography and Memoirs*, edited by the Dowager Duchess of Argyll, 2 vols. (John Murray, 1906), vol. 1, p. 341.

31 Newcastle to Aberdeen, 3 August 1852, Aberdeen Papers, British Library, Add. Mss. 43197.

32 Aberdeen to Newcastle, 25 July 1852, Aberdeen Papers, BL, Add. Mss. 43197.

33 Newcastle to Aberdeen, 2 August 1852, Aberdeen Papers, BL, Add. Mss. 43197.

34 Russell to Graham, 18 August 1852, quoted in C. S. Parker, *Life and Letters of Sir James Graham, Second Baronet of Netherby, 1792–1861*, 2 vols. (John Murray, 1907), vol. 2, p. 174.

35 Aberdeen to Lady Haddo, 30 June, 8 July 1848, quoted in M. E. Chamberlain, *Lord Aberdeen* (Addison Wesley, 1983), p. 418.

36 Aberdeen to Newcastle, 25 July 1852, Aberdeen Papers, BL, Add. Mss. 43197.

37 Gladstone to Aberdeen, 5 August 1852, quoted in M.E. Chamberlain, *Who Founded the Liberal Party?* (University of Wales Press, 1991), p. 19.

38 Aberdeen to Edward Everett (US Cabinet minister and friend of Aberdeen), 13 January 1853, quoted in J. B. Conacher, *The Aberdeen Coalition, 1852–1855* (CUP, 1968), p. 49.

39 Walter Bagehot, *The English Constitution* (1867; 1993 edn., Cornell University Press) p. 81.

40 C. C. F. Greville, *The Greville Memoirs: third part*, 2 vols. (Longmans, Green, 1887), vol. 1, p. 71 (22 June 1853).

41 Aberdeen to Palmerston, 15 July 1853, quoted in Conacher, *The Aberdeen Coalition*, p. 160.

42 Clarendon to Aberdeen, 8 October 1853, Aberdeen Papers, BL, Add. Mss. 43188.

43 Memorandum by the Queen, 1 February 1855, quoted in G. B. Henderson, *Crimean War Diplomacy, and other historical essays* (Jackson, 1947; 1975 edn.). p. 81.

44 Palmerston speaking in the House of Commons, 1 March 1848.

45 Palmerston to Sullivan, 31 December 1852, quoted in David Brown, *Palmerston and the Politics of Foreign Policy, 1846–55* (Manchester University Press, 2002), p. 146.

46 Parry, *Liberal Government*, p. 170.

47 Ibid., pp. 173–75.

48 Ibid., p. 178.

49 Quoted in Angus Hawkins, *British Party Politics, 1852–1886* (Macmillan, 1998), p. 60.

50 Quoted in E. D. Steele, *Palmerston and Liberalism, 1855–1865* (CUP, 1991), p. 26; see also pp. 24–42 for further development of this theme.

51 Ibid., p. 367.

52 Parry, *Liberal Government*, p. 177.

53 Ibid., p. 191.

54 See Hawkins, *British Party Politics*, p. 62.

55 Quoted in ibid., p. 64.

56 *The Times*, 7 June 1859.

Chapter 3

The Liberal Heyday (1859–1886)

Tony Little

On 7 June 1859, as instructed by the meeting at Willis's Rooms, Lord Hartington moved the Liberal motion of no confidence in Derby's Conservative minority government. In the course of his speech he confessed: 'we have learned a lesson from adversity, and the leaders of all sections of our party are prepared to co-operate for the advancement of what they consider the good of their country'.[1] The Tories were defeated by 323 to 310 and Derby resigned. The smooth Liberal takeover was temporarily obstructed by Queen Victoria, however, who 'felt it an invidious task to select' either Lord Palmerston or Lord John Russell and that 'it might be more easy for the party to act together under a third person', so chose Lord Granville, Whig leader in the Lords, instead.[2] Granville failed to form a government but the obstructive way in which Russell reacted to this quirk of the Queen's determined that the premiership fell to Palmerston.

The government formed by Palmerston in June 1859 had an initial majority of only thirteen. The factions forming this majority – Whigs, radicals, Liberals, Peelites and Irish – contained the same clashing agendas and ambitions that had led to the instability of the previous decade. In the quarter of a century that followed, none of these groups was wholly to lose its identity under the Liberal umbrella. Yet Palmerston's government survived until 1865 and won the general election in that year. His principal legatee, William Ewart Gladstone, led the party through the century's greatest reforming government between 1868 and 1874 and headed three further administrations. But the factionalism was not entirely dead. Palmerston's inheritance was partially squandered less than a year after his death by a Liberal revolt, and Gladstone's governments were all destroyed by Liberal insurrections.

Why was Palmerston so successful between 1859 and his death in 1865, and why did the Liberal Party dominate the political battlefield despite its factionalism and squabbling? Three principal reasons are suggested: first, the leadership of the party; second, the adaptation of the Liberal Party to changing circumstances; and third, and linked to this, the inadequacies of the opposition.

One of the peculiarities of mid-Victorian politics is that the principal party leaders had their origins in the opposite party. Lord Derby was a Whig before joining Peel's Tories, and Benjamin Disraeli was a somewhat romantic radical before coming to embody a certain style of Conservatism. Both Gladstone and Palmerston served in Tory

Cabinets before leading the Liberals and both remained profoundly conservative in their political intentions, seeking to preserve the roles and responsibilities of aristocracy while undertaking reforms to incorporate new wealth and classes into full citizenship on a gradual, non-revolutionary basis. As in more recent politics, the battleground was in the centre, and the Liberal Party's two most dominant leaders were able to mobilise support that went beyond the natural heartlands of their party, though in very different ways.

The political system within which Palmerston had to operate was shaped by the 1832 Reform Act but remained dominated by older elements of the constitution. The primary skill that he required was to construct and manage a majority within the House of Commons, but Palmerston went beyond this in seeking to shape public opinion through his management of newspaper commentary on his government and through direct appeals to the public, addressing large public meetings outside the immediate demands of an election. In this, he anticipated and pioneered the techniques that would be more widely required after the passing of the Second Reform Act in 1867. Gladstone proved an apt pupil, perfecting the creation of public opinion through the reporting of his meetings which he then used to shape the political agenda and if necessary to coerce the parliamentary party and reinforce his leadership.

Palmerston in government

In the summer of 1859, Palmerston's immediate tasks were to create a government, incorporating all the appropriate factions in the right proportions, and to ensure its survival. The long years of infighting had served to ensure that the will to co-operate was stronger than the desire to plot, and most alternative combinations of individuals had already been tested to destruction. The adherence of Lord John Russell as Foreign Secretary came at the expense of Lord Clarendon, Palmerston's preferred candidate, but kept a major source of potential difficulty under the constraints of Cabinet responsibility. Despite Cobden's refusal of office, places were found for two radicals and three Peelites, including Gladstone, who had not attended the meeting in Willis's Rooms, who indeed had been a hot-tempered critic of Palmerston over the previous four years and who had sided with the Conservatives in the motion of no confidence. Italy, the issue that brought the Liberal factions together, served to cover Gladstone's blushes in accepting office as Chancellor of the Exchequer. But his underlying motivation was expressed in a letter to his fellow Oxford MP Sir William Heathcote: 'for thirteen years, the middle space of life, I have been cast out of party connection ... How could I, under these circumstances, say, I will have nothing to do with you, and be the one remaining Ishmael in the House of Commons?'[3] His feeling that this might represent a last chance was probably common to a number of the government's supporters and a significant factor in its success.

Constructing a government was not the same as keeping it together. Palmerston's jaunty personality was a great strength, and his age also worked in his favour; as Lord Acton suggested in 1862, 'he is tolerated because he is cheerful and wounds no pride, and because he is old and excites no envy'.[4] Palmerston, 'with his long experience and consequent knowledge of mankind, knew the value of a great man's smile, and was quite aware that a hearty shake of the hand, or a familiar pat on the back, or a little delicate flattery, or even an anxious inquiry after health, would often do as much to win a half-hearted friend as the presentation of a place'.[5] These man-management skills were put to good effect in the key political tests faced by the government.

The efficient part of the English constitution

Walter Bagehot's pioneering work on the constitution describes government at the time of Palmerston:

> The efficient secret of the English Constitution may be described as the close union, the nearly complete fusion of the executive and legislative powers. No doubt by the traditional theory, as it exists in all the books, the goodness of our constitution consists in the entire separation of the legislative and executive authorities, but in truth its merit consists in their singular approximation. The connecting link is the cabinet. By that new word we mean a committee of the legislative body selected to be the executive body ... It chooses for this, its main committee, the men in whom it has most confidence. It does not, it is true, choose them directly; but it is nearly omnipotent in choosing them indirectly ... At the death of Lord Palmerston it is very likely that the Queen may have the opportunity of fairly choosing between two, if not three statesmen. But, as a rule, the nominal prime minister is chosen by the legislature, and the real prime minister for most purposes – the leader of the House of Commons – almost without exception is so ... We have in England an elective first magistrate as truly as the Americans have an elective first magistrate. The Queen is only at the head of the dignified part of the constitution. The prime minister is at the head of the efficient part.
>
> The leading minister so selected has to choose his associates, but he only chooses among a charmed circle. The position of most men in Parliament forbids their being invited to the cabinet; the position of a few men ensures their being invited ... A prime minister's independent choice in the formation of a cabinet is not very large; it extends rather to the division of the cabinet offices than to the choice of cabinet ministers.
>
> The most curious point about the cabinet is that so very little is known about it. The meetings are not only secret in theory, but secret in reality. By present practice, no official minute in all ordinary cases is kept of them. Even a private note is discouraged and disliked ... No description of it, at once graphic and authentic, has ever been given. It is said to be sometimes like a rather disorderly board of directors, where many speak and few listen – though no one knows ...
>
> But a cabinet, though it is a committee of the legislative assembly, is a committee with a power which no assembly would – unless for historical accidents,

and after happy experience – have been persuaded to entrust to any committee. It is a committee which can dissolve the assembly which appointed it ... Though appointed by one Parliament, it can appeal if it chooses to the next.[6]

Palmerston's vision of government was primarily that of administration rather than legislation, and he had no great domestic programme he sought to achieve. He is reported to have said to Goschen that 'we cannot go on adding to the statute book *ad infinitum*', but it would be a mistake to see him as wishing nothing to change. In his second government, the Companies Act of 1862 laid the foundation on which modern companies rely, the criminal law was codified through the 1861 Offences Against the Person Act and changes were made to alleviate the worst of the workhouse system of poor relief.

Nor did Palmerston neglect his wider political obligations. A central Liberal Registration Association was formed in 1861, the first glimmerings of formal party organisation. Based in London, the Association was under the control of the party whips; it sought to stimulate activity to ensure the registration of Liberal voters on the electoral roll and prevent the registration of Conservative voters. From its offices, the whips were able to effect the introduction of suitable potential candidates to constituencies and, often more importantly, to mediate between local Liberal factions to prevent them nominating too many candidates and splitting the vote.

Palmerston's addresses to large public meetings in major cities helped to reconcile both the middle classes and the disenfranchised to the continued rule of a mostly aristocratic elite. In religious matters, still an important element in politics, he had little of the personal commitment of a Gladstone, but he was able to deprive Conservatives of their traditional 'church in danger' rallying cry by using the prime minister's ecclesiastical patronage to appoint 'Low Churchmen' to moderate the supposed papist influence of 'High Churchmen', while at the same time expressing sympathy for the complaints of the Nonconformists, thereby helping to bind them to the Liberal Party.[7]

The foremost challenges faced by the new government were in foreign policy. Russell's price for participation in Palmerston's government had been the Foreign Office and the opportunity to bring forward a reform bill but surprisingly, given their long-standing rivalry, Russell and Palmerston worked well together in Cabinet. Palmerstonian foreign policy – assertiveness in favour of British overseas trading interests, and frequent threats uttered against the European powers – was managed with sufficient discretion to avoid a war with another major power, for which the army was not equipped, and to retain the allegiance of the more pacific radicals such as Bright, a Quaker, and Cobden, for whom war was illogical and wasteful.

The struggle for Italian unity, which had brought the Liberals together, was resolved to their satisfaction with little need for British participation. But, as a result of Louis Napoleon's acquisition of Nice and Savoy (his reward for supporting the Italians), the public was alarmed by fears of French expansion. Alleviating these concerns about Napoleon's ambitions was a continuing source of tension within the Liberal government, particularly between Palmerston and Gladstone; Palmerston insisted on strengthening Britain's coastal defences, while Gladstone resisted the increased expenditure. As an alternative, the Chancellor promoted a trade agreement with France, using Cobden as an intermediary. He argued that growing commercial links would reduce tensions and avert military spending – a common theme of the Liberal belief in free trade. Palmerston's position was popular, but complicated by the expensive Anglo-French naval competition in the development of ironclad steam battleships. The combination of the trade treaty, military preparedness and more regular diplomacy reduced Anglo-French rivalry but residual suspicion handicapped active co-operation.

Gladstone's approach built links with the radicals which would prove useful for his future, but he compounded his difficulties by using his budgets for the simplification of indirect taxes, including, in 1860, a proposal for the abolition of the paper tax, denigrated as a tax on knowledge. Increased military expenditure and the elimination of indirect taxes inevitably placed a greater burden on income tax. Gladstone and Palmerston pushed their relationship to the brink of Gladstone's resignation but, despite Palmerston's collusion in the defeat of the paper tax proposals by the House of Lords, Gladstone held back from a move that would end his career. In the following year, Gladstone contrived to incorporate all the budget measures, including the paper tax changes, into a single measure which the Lords were unwilling to challenge, establishing a precedent sustained until Lloyd George's budget of 1909. Gladstone's policy of minimising indirect taxes, in particular those on imported products, made Britain the leading free trade nation, another orthodoxy that was not seriously challenged until the twentieth century.[8] The redistributive effects of the switch from regressive indirect taxes to a more progressive income tax represented the major domestic policy accomplishment of the Palmerston government.

Free trade

Free trade was a fundamental Victorian Liberal belief whose political and emotional importance transcended its significance as economic policy because it incorporated the rejection of protection for special interests, the endorsement of self-help and the promotion of world peace, and identified the party with the growing urban population rather than a declining rural Britain.

Early nineteenth-century economic policy, in so far as government consciously had one, assumed that world trade and monetary resources were largely fixed. Government protected the share of its domestic merchants through tariffs (duties and taxes) on imports and restrictions on shipping (through the Navigation Acts). This attitude was challenged by Enlightenment economists, such as Adam Smith and David Ricardo, who developed the theory of comparative advantage, the idea that nations can maximise their output and wealth by specialising in the production of goods at which they are relatively most efficient, trading with other countries to realise the gains from such specialisation.

The struggle for the repeal of the Corn Laws is described in Chapter 2; Peel finally abolished them in 1846, splitting his party in the process. In 1849, Lord John Russell's Whig government discarded the Navigation Acts. Peel's political heir, Gladstone, Chancellor of the Exchequer in the 1850s and 1860s, used income tax revenue to simplify the tax system and eliminate the duties on a wide range of imported goods, particularly those used by the poorer classes. After Gladstone's budget of 1860, only sixteen dutiable articles remained in the British tariff, compared to more than a thousand in 1852. The subsequent growth in British exports, particularly of manufactured products, formed the basis of the long mid-Victorian economic boom. Disraeli abandoned any attempt to reintroduce protection, and free trade became a Victorian orthodoxy.

As lower tariffs meant cheaper food, together with higher employment and bigger profits in manufacturing, the doctrine of free trade appealed to the growing manufacturing and business interests, precisely those groups most attracted to the nascent Liberal Party – and was opposed by the predominantly Tory land-owners whose estates produced the grain. Liberals, however, always saw much more than economic justification for open markets. Abolishing protection for agriculture was part of the process of tearing down the remnants of the feudal order and putting an end to the special treatment enjoyed by the land-owners. Cobden and the Anti-Corn Law League argued, by extension, for an end to special treatment for *any* industry; commercial success should be the outcome of hard work and natural talent alone, not the protection of vested interests. The campaign for free trade formed an important part of the liberal assault on economic, and therefore political, privilege.

The removal of tariff barriers also had benefits on the international scene. Liberals looked to free trade as the agency which would promote internationalism and end war. 'For the disbanding of great armies and the promotion of peace', wrote John Bright, 'I rely on the abolition of tariffs, on the brotherhood of the nations resulting from free trade in the products of industry.' Trade promoted interdependence and a sense of international community, building links between peoples and nations and rendering conflict less likely.

Free trade remained an article of Liberal faith for decades, even after British pre-eminence in world markets began to wane in the 1870s. In 1959, the Liberal election manifesto ended with the slogan: 'exchange goods, not bombs'. The Cobdenite vision of trade building links between peoples was an important factor underlying Liberal support for British participation in the European Economic Community.

Britain maintained an uneasy neutrality during the American Civil War of 1861–65. Radicals sided with the North's stance against slavery, but the North adopted a hostile policy towards British interests in Canada, and its blockade of Confederate cotton exports badly hurt the Lancashire textile industry. Gladstone's unfortunate, and later regretted, declaration, at a public banquet in Newcastle, that the Confederates 'have made a Nation' seemed to presage a recognition of the South. The North's seizure of Southern officials from a British ship, the *Trent*, could have provided the government with an excuse for war had Palmerston wished to 'send a gunboat'. The acquisition by the South of a British-built commerce raider, the *Alabama*, caused considerable damage to Union shipping and provided a grievance that the United States pursued long after the war had ended. Palmerston's caution, together with disagreement within the party, prevented a hasty decision and enabled Britain to avoid a damaging entanglement in a conflict which, as time soon showed, the North would inevitably win.

John Stuart Mill, *On Liberty*, 1859

The son of the philosopher James Mill, John Stuart Mill was born in 1806 and was writing for publication as a teenager. After an illness in his early twenties, his philosophical thought developed new directions, softening and broadening the austerities of his father's utilitarianism.

On Liberty was published in 1859, the year of the Willis's Rooms meeting. It provided the classic argument for freedom of speech, the rights of the individual against the tyranny of the majority, and the criteria to be used in justifying interference by the state:

> There is, in fact, no recognised principle by which the propriety or impropriety of government interference is customarily tested. People decide according to their personal preferences. Some, whenever they see any good to be done, or evil to be remedied, would willingly instigate the government to undertake the business; while others prefer to bear almost any amount of social evil, rather than add one to the departments of human interests amenable to governmental control. And men range themselves on one or the other side in any particular case ... but very rarely on account of any opinion to which they consistently adhere, as to what things are fit to be done by a government.
>
> The object of this Essay is to assert one very simple principle, as entitled to govern absolutely the dealings of society with the individual in the way of compulsion and control, whether the means used be physical force in the form of legal penalties, or the moral coercion of public opinion. That principle is, that the sole end for which mankind are warranted, individually or collectively, in interfering with the liberty of action of any of their number is self-protection. That the only purpose for which power can be rightly exercised over any member of a civilised community, against his will, is to prevent harm to others.[9]

In 1865, Mill was elected as the radical Liberal MP for Westminster. In the debates on the Second Reform Act, he advocated votes for women, but lost his seat in 1868 and died in 1873.

Palmerston was less fortunate, though equally cautious, in European foreign policy. While the Italian question was satisfactorily resolved and the French threat minimised, British support for a Polish rebellion against the Russians was vocal but ineffective. Similarly, when Palmerston threatened to intervene in support of Denmark over Bismarck's plans to incorporate the duchies of Schleswig and Holstein into Prussia, Bismarck called his bluff. Bismarck recognised that without joint intervention by Russia or France, Britain lacked the land-based military resources to prevent the Prussians defeating the Danes. Palmerston and Russell backed away from confrontation. The government's embarrassment led to a strong Conservative attack which caused a defeat for the Liberals in the Lords in July 1864, though they survived the Conservative attack in the Commons.

For most of the period between 1859 and 1865, Palmerston and his colleagues received an easy ride from the Conservatives. Tory MPs were quite comfortable with Palmerstonian foreign policy and his steady, even cynical, approach to domestic admin- istration. After more than a decade spent largely in opposition, they had yet to develop a compelling narrative to replace protectionism. Some, no doubt, would have preferred Palmerston to their own leader in the Commons, the flamboyant and volatile Disraeli. But Conservative intentions were not benign. Disraeli and Derby were well aware of the fragility of the Liberal coalition and by supporting Palmerston against radical or Gladstonian initiatives hoped to precipitate a split. Where opportunity offered, for example over Schleswig-Holstein, they did not hesitate to attack.

Although Bismarck exposed the limits of British power in continental Europe the diplomatic defeat he inflicted did little to dent Palmerston's popularity 'out of doors', which was built more on his belligerent rhetoric than its practical results. In the general election of 1865, Palmerston was rewarded with an increased majority – more for the efficiency of his administration, the tax and civil service reforms of his Chancellor and the efforts he had made to conciliate the Nonconformists rather than the modest but progressive legislative achievements of the government.

1865 general election (11–24 July)			
	Votes	*%*	*MPs*
Liberal	**508,821**	**59.5**	**369**
Conservative	346,035	40.5	289
Total	*854,856*		*658*

Dishing the Whigs

Palmerston did not live to meet the new Parliament, dying, aged eighty, at Brocket Hall from the after-effects of a chill. He was succeeded by the 73-year-old Earl Russell. Russell's second government was short-lived and ineffective, doomed by his single- minded pursuit of electoral reform and Gladstone's inexperience as Leader of the House.

Russell had managed the passage of the 1832 Reform Act in the Commons. Although it had been intended as a lasting solution, he had gradually come to realise that those left out would continue to agitate for admittance to the franchise. In the 1850s, support for a further reform bill formed part of Russell's efforts to reclaim the leadership from Palmerston, enabling him to reach out to the radicals from the narrow Whiggery in which he had been born.

Reform formed part of the battleground of the 1859 election campaign, but although many Liberals were pledged to widen the franchise, their support reflected grass-roots pressure and was not aligned behind any specific measure.[10] As Cobden wryly commented:

> I rather think there is quite as much agitation about parliamentary reform in the House of Commons as in the country. It has got into the House of Commons, and they don't know what to do with it. It is bandied from side to side, and all parties are professing to be reformers; everybody is in favour of an extension of the suffrage; and, upon my honour, I think in my heart no one likes it much, and they don't care much about it.[11]

In accordance with their compact in 1859, Palmerston allowed Russell to introduce a reform bill but when it became obvious to both men that support was at best tepid, the bill was allowed to drop; for the next six years Palmerston avoided bringing the issue to the test.

Reform was helped back to life by Gladstone's 1864 speech, in which he exceeded his brief by venturing 'to say that every man who is not presumably incapacitated by some consideration of personal unfitness or of political danger, is morally entitled to come within the pale of the constitution'.[12] Frustrated by the lack of progress, John Bright, Cobden's closest parliamentary ally, organised a campaign to demonstrate the popular demand for the vote, 'the question that will not sleep'. Speaking at Birmingham at the beginning of 1865, he claimed that 'England is the mother of parliaments', before pointing out that, 'An Englishman, if he goes to the Cape can vote; if he goes further, to Australia, to the nascent empires of the New World, he can vote ... It is only in his own country, on his own soil, where he was born, the very soil which he has enriched with his labour and with the sweat of his brow, that he is denied this right.'[13] His agitation kept the issue in play for the 1865 election, but provoked a reaction among some hesitant Whigs.

William Ewart Gladstone (1809–98)

Gladstone dominated the Victorian Liberal Party, both as a long-serving Chancellor of the Exchequer and as a four-term Prime Minister.

Gladstone was born in Liverpool, the son of a wealthy trader. He was educated at Eton and Oxford, where he opposed the 1831 Reform Bill in the Union debates, leading his friend Lord Lincoln to arrange with his father, the Duke of Newcastle, for Gladstone to stand as a Tory for Newark. Gladstone was given junior office in Peel's 1834 ministry and in Peel's second government of 1841 he was appointed to the Board of Trade, entering the Cabinet in 1843. Here he became converted to free trade and, with his fellow Peelites, broke with the Conservatives over the Corn Laws in 1846. In Aberdeen's 1852 coalition he served as Chancellor of the Exchequer and resumed that office when he joined the Liberals under Palmerston in 1859.

He served as Prime Minister between 1868 and 1874, but retired from the leadership after losing the 1874 general election. His campaign against the Bulgarian atrocities after

1876 made inevitable his return to office in 1880–85, for a short time in 1886, and finally between 1892 and 1894. The period between 1886 and 1892, which Gladstone spent campaigning for home rule, was his only prolonged period as leader of the opposition.

Like his mentor Peel, Gladstone laid great stress on administrative competence and sought to preserve by timely reform. In the process, he created the ethos of the Liberal Party and was largely responsible for its main achievements, including free trade, disestablishment of the Church of Ireland, electoral reform and state primary education.

His Christianity gave him a strong sense of moral purpose, and in turn this gave him a powerful public appeal, particularly to Nonconformists. His drive and urgency to communicate made him a pioneer in electoral campaigning, particularly when he relied on the comprehensive reporting of his speeches in the press to convert his 1879–80 battle to win the Edinburgh seat of Midlothian into a national debate on the iniquities of Disraeli's government.

Gladstone was blessed with considerable physical energy, and with the surplus left over from politics he was able to participate in most of the religious controversies of his time, publish extensively on Homer, rescue prostitutes and chop down trees at Hawarden, collect china and take lengthy walks. The rescue work remains controversial; Gladstone, who clearly admired female beauty, admitted temptations to his diaries. He never hid his involvement, his wife worked with him, and the efforts of advisers to deter him were only intermittently successful; but, on balance, historians have tended to give him the benefit of the doubt.

Russell's government met Parliament in February 1866 and, although aware of the need for caution, brought forward a modest reform bill in March. 'Intended as a rallying-call to the boroughs and a precursor of educational, social and Irish measures',[14] Russell proposed lowering the property qualification to vote from £10 p.a. to £7 p.a. It was estimated that the electorate of England and Wales would increase from around 1 million to 1.5 million.

A Whig clique, dubbed the 'Cave of Adullam'[15] by Bright, which was led by Lords Lansdowne, Grey and Grosvenor and whose spokesmen in the Commons were Edward Horsman and Robert Lowe, engaged in a sustained attack on the bill. The Adullamite Whigs feared that Parliament would be swamped by an uneducated working class unable to distinguish their own interests from the interests of the nation. Lowe wound up a speech against Russell's bill by declaiming, 'we are about to barter maxims and traditions that have never failed, for theories and doctrines that have never succeeded. Democracy you may have at any time. Night and day the gate is open that leads to that bare and level plain, where every ant's nest is a mountain and every thistle a forest tree.'[16]

The Tory strategy of exploiting divisions in the Liberal ranks, which had failed in Palmerston's time, now paid dividends. In June 1866, the discontented Whigs brought down the government. But they reaped a poor reward from their rebellion. Instead of the centrist Whig–Conservative coalition sought by the Adullamites, Derby formed a minority Tory government. Riots in London and further agitation throughout the country forced the Tories to introduce their own reform bill. Although this provoked ministerial resignations, Disraeli, as Leader of the House, persisted with the proposals, accepting whatever amendments were necessary to keep the bill afloat and the Liberals disunited. The unintended outcome, defended by Derby as dishing the Whigs,[17] was the Second Reform Act. Much more radical than originally envisaged, the act extended the franchise to most householders and some lodgers, nearly doubling the electorate in England and Wales and more than doubling the number of Scottish electors. Most significantly, the case against democracy had been lost.

The failure of the reform bill of 1866 led to Lord Russell's withdrawal from political leadership. Gladstone, then Leader of the House as well as Chancellor, had piloted the bill through the debates, and his failings had contributed to its defeat but, to the annoyance of the dissident Whigs, his energy, administrative and oratorical skills still marked him as the Liberal Party's future leader. After some reflection on his relations with the party, he reunited the Liberal forces with calls for the disestablishment of the Church of Ireland. Despite Tory hopes, the 1868 election brought them little reward and Gladstone won the contest with a majority in excess of 100.

1868 general election (17 November – 7 December)			
	Votes	*%*	*MPs*
Liberal	**1,428,776**	**61.2**	**387**
Conservative	903,318	38.7	271
Others	1,157	0.1	0
Total	*2,333,251*		*658*

Local government

At the beginning of the nineteenth century, local government reflected a series of historical developments from Tudor times which bore little relationship to the needs of an industrialising and urbanising population. In the counties, much reliance was placed on the bench of magistrates. In urban areas there was little logic behind which towns or cities had corporations and which relied on the activities of parish vestries. As the century developed the new waves of social reform created ad hoc local bodies for their implementation, such as the Poor Law Unions (1837), Local Boards of Health (1848) and School Boards (1870), while central government increasingly recognised a need for a more rational form of local administration accountable to the area in which it was situated.

The 1835 Municipal Reform Act, the counterpart of the 1832 Reform Act, rationalised the corporations to ensure election by ratepayers and the publication of accounts by town councils. Both of these reform acts were of benefit to the Whigs, or Liberals, by reducing the influence of the old, corrupt and predominantly Tory corporations on national elections and opening up not only an incubator for budding politicians but a new source of patronage.

In 1869, Liberal MP Jacob Bright secured an amendment allowing women ratepayers the vote in borough elections, though the courts narrowed this to unmarried women ratepayers in 1872. Women were not only allowed to vote for the election of the school boards established by Forster's 1870 Education Act but themselves stand for election and by 1879 some seventy had been elected. The first woman was elected to a London Poor Law Board in 1875.

The best known exploiter of the opportunities opened up in local government was Joseph Chamberlain. In 1873, Chamberlain became mayor of Birmingham, a post he held for three years, acting more as chief executive than local dignitary. Through the purchase and profitable operation of gas and water companies for the municipality, he was able to generate the resources for local improvements, including the paving and lighting of streets, new parks and the demolition of the town centre slums. The example set by Chamberlain was imitated by cities as diverse as Bath and Leeds.

Although Gladstone's 1880–85 administration had intended to reform local government, it was the Conservatives who passed the Local Government Act of 1888, incorporating a wide range of local functions into elected county councils, including road maintenance, lunatic asylums and poor relief. The London County Council was established the following year, with a Progressive administration led by Lord Rosebery, later Liberal Prime Minister. Gladstone's last government created urban and rural district councils in 1894. Gladstone made his last speech in the Commons, as Prime Minister, accepting the Lords amendments to this legislation under protest.

Gladstonian Liberalism 1868–94

William Gladstone led the Liberal Party in four governments over a quarter of a century (1868–74, 1880–85, 1886, 1892–94). He brought to fruition a wide range of reforms and in his own personality came almost to personify Liberalism. In a party which combined radical reformers with a Whig land-owning elite which entertained a worldly scepticism of enthusiasts but provided the bulk of ministerial talent, Gladstone's role was pivotal: his moral purpose and oratorical passion inspired the wider electorate while the conservative intent of the reforms generally reconciled the Whigs to his innovations.

During this period, the Second Reform Act of 1867 and the Third Reform Act, passed by Gladstone's government in 1884, enfranchised the bulk of both urban and agricultural male householders and transformed the nature of party politics. In the 1865 general election, campaigning was essentially local; the government proposed no programme and voting took place in public, facilitated by bullying and bribery. By 1868, Liberal leaders had agreed a key issue for the campaign and by 1874, the first general election under a secret ballot, the leader felt the need to write a defence of his past record and hint at tax cuts to retrieve his popularity. The National Liberal Federation (NLF) was founded in 1877 to coerce the leadership into embracing more radical policies, but was co-opted by Gladstone and gradually became the foundation of a popularly based central party organisation. For the 1885 election, an extensive manifesto covering the main areas of controversy was published for the new and more working-class electorate, and by 1892, Gladstone found it advisable to endorse the policies agreed by the annual conferences of the NLF as the programme for the election.

Party organisation

Each of the nineteenth-century electoral reform acts spurred political polarisation and party organisation. However, local influence and patronage remained significant even while the new politics developed, though its decline was accelerated by the secret ballot in 1872 and the effective outlawing of bribery and intimidation in the 1883 Corrupt and Illegal Practices Act.

The 1832 Reform Act regularised the electoral register but retained open voting in public, which aided accurate canvassing. Consequently, the key battles were fought over who qualified to be included on the register, with legal agents employed by local parties to encourage registration of supporters and prevent the registration of opponents. London political clubs such as the Reform acted as clearing houses to match constituencies in search of candidates with candidates in search of seats. They also supplied modest and occasional funding for local campaigns.

Among the features of the 1867 Act was the allocation of three seats to Birmingham, but each elector had only two votes. The intention was to facilitate the representation of both political parties, but the Liberals were determined to win all three seats and organised their supporters to vote for different candidate combinations in different wards. Their discipline paid off. The ward organisations were also used to win the school board elections, which followed the 1870 Education Act, and other municipal contests. Chamberlain and his associates in Birmingham built a constituency organisation on to the wards with ward committees sending delegates to the central constituency management committee.

Chamberlain's ambitions were not just to win elections but to influence policy in a more radical direction. Drawing on the experience of fighting the Forster Education Act through the National Education League, the National Liberal Federation (NLF) was formed in 1877, headquartered in Birmingham, supplied with officers and with a staff also from Birmingham. Opponents of the new disciplined approach, or of the radical direction to which it tended, decried the innovation as a 'caucus', an insult drawn from allegedly corrupt and democratic US practices. Despite Chamberlain's powers as a propagandist, and Whig fears, the NLF never became the alternative power base he hoped. Always individualists, other radicals resented Chamberlain's presumption to lead them, depriving the NLF of the breadth of support it needed.

At first there were only forty-six federated associations, and even in 1884 a majority of associations were not members, although the largest metropolitan areas were.[18] Meanwhile, the official leadership of the party gradually co-opted the Federation to its own ends. The first annual meeting of the NLF was given respectability when it was addressed by Gladstone, and it became the base from which the modern political party organisation and conference derived.

When the party split over home rule in 1886, the National Liberal Federation remained with the Gladstonians, and its secretary moved to London. In time the NLF became the foundation for an ideologically more broadly based campaigning body and the forerunner of the party's central organisation and annual assembly. (See further in Appendix 1.)

Judging the achievements and failures of Victorian administrations in the light of the scale and role of government after the two world wars of the twentieth century would be misguided. Neither the intellectual environment nor the capabilities of the bureaucratic machinery would have facilitated modern levels of direction from Whitehall, while the demand for heavy government intervention was confined to a small 'socialistic' fringe. Ministers still saw government as the pragmatic administration of the Queen's business tempered by the need to accommodate parliamentary or public pressure. Nevertheless, it was in this period, and led by Liberals, that government began to assume the responsibilities of a modern executive and began to give shape to coherent programmes of reform.

In one of the best known speeches of his first Midlothian campaign, Gladstone drew attention to a banner in the hall bearing the slogan 'peace, retrenchment and reform', words which he 'connected with the promotion of human happiness'.[19] If used with care, peace, retrenchment and reform also offer a framework in which to consider the achievements of the Gladstonian period.

No Liberal government of the period was pacifist, and Gladstone's governments were involved in Victoria's 'little wars' of unintended (at least by the metropolitan government) colonial expansion. This is particularly true of Gladstone's second government between 1880 and 1885, which took office on a policy of repudiating Disraeli's aggression in Southern Africa and Afghanistan, but inherited wars in those territories. In 1882 the government reluctantly intervened in Egypt to protect the Suez Canal and became embroiled in the Mahdi's revolt in Sudan which resulted in the death of General Gordon at the beginning of 1885, severely damaging the government's popularity.

Peace was seen as the dividend that flowed from free trade – which, although it came under attack by some Conservatives in reaction to the growth of the protected US and German economies, remained the cornerstone of Gladstonian finance. In his famous Midlothian campaign in 1879, Gladstone argued for a concert of nations inspiring Liberal internationalism – which later led to the League of Nations – but, in practice, Liberal governments largely avoided continental entanglements; in particular, they stayed out of the Franco-Prussian war of 1870. To maintain peace, Gladstone was prepared to make sacrifices. He accepted arbitration to settle the dispute with the United States over the depredations of the British-built Confederate commerce raider, the *Alabama*, not only in preference to a military solution but to demonstrate the practicality of international civil justice, despite the cost to the exchequer and the government's popular standing.

Considered even in its narrowest form as the gradual improvement of the constitution, reform remained a continuing aspiration for Liberals, particularly those more radically inclined. In 1872, Lord Hartington piloted the secret ballot through Parliament and in 1883 the second Gladstone government introduced the Corrupt and Illegal Practices Act which proved much more effective at reducing bribery and intimidation than previous efforts. The Third Reform Act of 1884 was tied to a Redistribution Act which converted traditional multi-member constituencies to the single-member seats which have continued into the twenty-first century. Despite its passing mention in the 1868 'manifesto', local government was neglected and Lord Salisbury's Tory government was allowed to claim the credit for the creation of county councils, though Gladstone's final government consoled its supporters with the establishment of smaller scale urban and rural district councils in 1894.

At heart, Gladstone was always the careful, cheeseparing Chancellor, and retrenchment remained central to his approach to government and Liberalism; wealth should be left 'to fructify in the pockets of the people'. Gladstone's keenness to cut military spending was the cause of his final resignation in 1894. It would be a mistake, however, to assume that his preference for promoting individual responsibility meant a pathological aversion to government intervention. Gladstone was too restless a politician and too effective an administrator to shut his eyes to change. But this attitude did predispose ministers towards reforms which improved the efficiency of government and towards interventions which would enable individuals to undertake their own economic or moral self-improvement.

Who were the Liberals?

Harcourt defined the Liberal Party as like the Biblical kingdom of heaven – 'a house of many mansions' – and, like heaven, the mid-Victorian party is more easily depicted anecdotally than in statistical detail.

MPs were not paid and therefore needed to be independently wealthy. The electorate was expanding throughout the period but it too remained constrained by property qualifications and its voting affected by bribery and intimidation. Consequently MPs were not representative of the electorate and the electorate was not representative of the population.

Gladstone's first, 1868, government had fifteen Cabinet positions, of whom six were peers, and it is estimated that seven were Whigs. Only one was a Nonconformist. His second, 1880, government also consisted of fifteen Cabinet members, including six peers and five Whigs, but this underestimates the Whig influence. Of the twenty ministers who served in Cabinet between 1880 and 1885, nine were Whigs. Two Cabinet ministers were Nonconformists. H. C. G. Matthew claims only one Roman Catholic ever sat in a Gladstonian Liberal Cabinet.[20]

As the Liberal Party came together in 1859, around two-thirds of its MPs were connected to the aristocracy or the land, with only 16 per cent having a predominantly commercial or financial background and just over one in ten coming from the legal profession. By 1886, the aristocratic and gentry component of the parliamentary party had fallen to just over a third, and the businessmen constituted a further third. The proportion of lawyers remained largely unchanged, but the balancing miscellaneous group now included around a dozen men from working-class backgrounds.[21]

Liberals were a party of the regions rather than the home counties. Scotland, Wales (except in 1859), the West Country and the north (except Lancashire), were areas of Liberal strength. In Ireland a Liberal majority was replaced by a home rule majority after 1874. Liberals were a party of the English boroughs rather than of the English counties, which then, as now, represented the heartland of Conservative strength, and the Liberals were especially strong in the larger boroughs, i.e. the cities. This geographical distribution of strength reflects the underlying identification of the parties with particular issues. The Tories were the defenders of the agricultural interest, while free trade was seen as of benefit to urban areas. The identification of the Liberals with issues of significance to Nonconformists can be overestimated, both because of differences between denominations and the tendency of high-profile lobby groups to overestimate their strength.[22]

Gladstone's first government

In retrospect, Gladstone's first administration has been seen as one of the most dynamic and accomplished of the Victorian period. However, its achievements should not be considered as the outcome of any pre-planned programme for government and, although its first task was to implement the campaign pledge to disestablish the Irish Church, it was not intent on liberalising religion in the way that Gladstone had liberalised trade in the 1850s and 1860s. The Church of Ireland, privileged as the national church, represented no more than 10 per cent of the population, and its disestablishment righted an undoubted injustice to Irish Catholics, who made up more than 80 per cent of the Irish people, in a manner which united all sections of the Liberal Party. The Nonconformists welcomed the weakening of Anglicanism, and the Whigs escaped the alternative of endowing Catholicism with state funding. Gladstone saw disestablishment as renewing the Church of Ireland's sense of mission. The accompanying disendowment of church funds provided substantial sums for the relief of Irish poverty.

Granville George Leveson-Gower, second Earl Granville (1815–91)

Granville led the Liberals in the Lords for most of the period from 1855 until his death and was twice a potential premier. Granville's family connections placed him at the heart of the Whig cousinhood which, together with his good-humoured quiet diplomacy, was crucial to keeping the party together under Gladstone's sometimes acerbic leadership.

After Eton and Oxford, Granville served for a short period at the Paris embassy under his father before becoming MP for Morpeth in 1836, and later for Lichfield. In 1840 he married Lady Acton, the mother of the historian Lord Acton, and in 1846 he succeeded to the earldom. An ardent free trader, he held junior office in Russell's 1846 government, where he helped promote the Great Exhibition of 1851. After Russell sacked Palmerston as Foreign Secretary, Granville was appointed to the post. He acted as Leader of the Lords under Palmerston in 1855 and when Queen Victoria sought to avoid appointing either Palmerston or Russell in 1859 it was Granville she approached, unsuccessfully, to form a government.

In Gladstone's first government, Granville was the Colonial Secretary who persuaded New Zealand and Canada to assume responsibility for their own defence. His tact and diplomacy was key to securing the disestablishment of the Church of Ireland. On Clarendon's death in 1870, he again became Foreign Secretary, unsuccessfully offering to mediate in the Franco-Prussian war but securing Belgian neutrality.

After Gladstone resigned in 1875, Hartington and Granville jointly led the Liberal opposition, with Granville's satirical criticism of Disraeli's foreign policy proving quietly effective. In 1880 Granville was unwilling to stand in Gladstone's way, and returned to the Foreign Office, but he struggled with the increased volume of work. In 1886, Gladstone persuaded Granville to take the less onerous Colonial Office, allowing Rosebery the Foreign Office.

Granville was one of the few Whig peers who stood by Gladstone in the home rule debacle. In his final years, he struggled with financial problems and ill health, dying in 1891 as the result of gout and an abscess in his face.[23]

The 1868–74 administration was also responsible for significant reforms of government. In the aftermath of the American Civil War and the Franco-Prussian War, both the army and the civil service were opened up to promotion by merit rather than by wealth and influence. The purchase of military commissions was abolished, the Commander-in-Chief was subordinated to the Minister of War, and the War Office was reorganised by Cardwell. Outside the Foreign Office, civil service posts were opened to entrance by examination. Similarly, the workings of the law courts were rationalised and the local government legislation of 1871–72 brought tentative steps towards a stronger Whitehall organisation to tackle public health and establish local sanitary authorities, the forerunners of the urban and rural district councils.

During the debates on the 1867 Second Reform Act, Robert Lowe had sardonically argued that 'it will be absolutely necessary that you should prevail on our future masters to learn their lessons'. It may be thought that Gladstone's government had taken the advice literally when it embarked on a series of education reforms, but of more weight with ministers were concerns over US and German economic competitiveness, reinforced by the easy Prussian victories over the French in 1870. The best remembered of the government's achievements was the Forster Education Act of 1870 but this was in reality the culmination of a series of reforms. At the end of 1868 the governing bodies of Britain's best-known public schools were reformed and in 1869 it was the turn of the grammar schools. In 1871 Nonconformists were enabled to receive scholarships and hold teaching posts at the ancient universities.

The bulk of primary schools in Britain were built and operated by the churches, though they did not have the resources to provide places for all children of the appropriate age range, and their teaching on matters of faith did not meet the requirements of the increasingly vocal and organised Nonconformist communities. The Forster Act provided for the establishment of elected school boards to manage schools paid for out of local taxation and prohibited from teaching the particular tenets of the various religious denominations. These 'board' schools charged fees, except in the poorest districts, and co-existed with the church schools, a mixed system that still survives. The Act provided the impetus which in time delivered state-funded education for all children.

What may be seen as the Liberal government's greatest achievement, however, also exemplifies the reason the government eventually failed. Gladstone's moral crusading campaign on Irish Church disestablishment focused on the single issue around which all the sections of the party could reunite after their Reform Act splits in 1866–67. Many of the other reforms proposed by the government either went too far for the more Whiggish section of the party or not far enough for the radicals. The compromises necessary to carry the 1870 Education Act disappointed the radicals, who sought the elimination of church-based primary education, and the most disenchanted were prepared to see Liberal seats fall to the Conservatives rather than support Liberal candidates who tolerated church schools. Irish land reform disturbed some aristocrats in the party who feared its extension to England, while the trade union reforms, giving union funds protection but outlawing picketing, did not go far enough to satisfy working-class activists looking for legal protection for strike action. Changes in the alcohol licensing arrangements multiplied the party's enemies in the brewery trade – often a vital element in sometimes rowdy and disreputable Victorian elections – while disappointing the temperance campaigners, a well-organised pressure group within the liberal movement.

The culmination of the government's problems came when it proposed to reform university education in Ireland to assist Catholic integration. Irish university legislation had been in Gladstone's mind since the beginning of his premiership, but he made insufficient effort to prepare the way for his proposals to create a central authority under which Catholic, Presbyterian and Church of Ireland university colleges would shelter. To escape religious controversy, there would be no professorships in modern history, philosophy or theology within this federated university. The idea pleased none of the English Liberal factions, nor the Irish MPs, who reflected the views of a Catholic hierarchy which had expected endowment of a Catholic Irish university.

When the bill was defeated in March 1873, Gladstone resigned, but Disraeli refused to accept office while in a minority at the tail end of a Parliament's life merely to give the Liberals a target to fire at and so rebuild their unity. Reluctantly, Gladstone resumed office and a tired and bedraggled ministry soldiered on until early in 1874, when the premier surprised colleagues with a snap election and a manifesto hinting at the abolition of income tax; Gladstone hoped that a 'cry' for sound finance would be the banner under which squabbling Liberals could all campaign. The disagreements within the party were too great to be overcome in the short term and the party organisation was less prepared for the election than its Conservative rival. When it was over, the Conservatives had gained seventy-six seats from the Liberals, who had lost an additional fifty-eight seats to a new Irish Home Rule party. Disraeli formed the first majority Conservative government since 1842.

1874 general election (31 January – 17 February)			
	Votes	*%*	*MPs*
Liberal	1,281,159	52.0	242
Conservative	**1,091,708**	**44.3**	**350**
Home Rule	90,234	3.7	60
Others	2,936	0.1	0
Total	*2,466,037*		*652*

Gladstone's analysis of the defeat of his first government

At the end of the 1874 election Gladstone wrote to his brother Robertson:

> For many years in the House of Commons I have had more fighting than any other man. For the last five years I have had it almost all, and of it a considerable part has been against those 'independent' liberals whose characters and talents seem to be much more appreciated by the press and general public, than the characters and talents of quieter members of the party. I do not speak of such men as ___, who leave office or otherwise find occasion to vindicate their independence, and vote against us on the questions immediately concerned. These men make very little noise and get very little applause. But there is another and more popular class of independent liberals who have been represented by the *Daily News,* and who have been one main cause of the weakness of the government, though they (generally) and their organ have rallied to us too late during the election. We have never recovered from the blow which they helped to strike on the Irish Education bill.
>
> But more immediately operative causes have determined the elections. I have no doubt what is the principal. We have been borne down in a torrent of gin and beer. Next to this has been the action of the Education Act of 1870, and the subsequent controversies. Many of the Roman Catholics have voted against us because we are not denominational; and many of the dissenters have at least abstained from voting because we are. Doubtless there have been other minor agencies; but these are the chief ones. The effect must be our early removal from office. For me that will be a very great change, for I do not intend to assume the general functions of leader of the opposition, and my great ambition or design will be to spend the remainder of my days, if it please God, in tranquillity, and at any rate in freedom from political strife.

6th Feb 1874[24]

The Liberals in opposition

At the end of 1874, Gladstone resigned the leadership of the party, convincing himself that at the age of sixty-five he 'deeply desired an interval between Parliament and the grave'.[25] But he did not resign his seat. Lord Granville, a close friend of Gladstone's and known for his diplomatic skills within the party, assumed command of the opposition in the Lords, and Lord Hartington, the heir to the Duke of Devonshire, led in the Commons. Hartington, an enthusiast for horse racing and a member of the 'fast' Marlborough House set, maintained an air of gruff indifference to conceal his devotion to politics. Both were Whigs and moderates – indeed, Hartington was described by Goschen as a 'violently moderate man'. Hartington's modesty and self-deprecation have led many to underestimate his skills as leader, though modern scholarship tends to view the position of the Whigs within Liberalism up to 1886 favourably.[26] It was Hartington's misfortune to succeed and to compete with the most charismatic orator of his age.

Spencer Compton Cavendish, eighth Duke of Devonshire (1833–1908)

Lord Hartington, as he was known for most of his career, epitomised the Whigs – progressive, rich, aristocratic but driven by duty to take public office. When he broke with Gladstone in 1886 it symbolised the drift of the landed classes towards Conservatism. Hartington thrice rejected the premiership. His position in the party was built not on brilliance but on his obvious integrity and common sense.

Hartington gained an MA from Cambridge in 1854 and for a few years hunted a good deal and served in the militia. In 1857, he was elected for North Lancashire, and in 1866 entered the Cabinet as Secretary of State for War. He later served as Postmaster-General, where he nationalised the telegraph system. When Gladstone resigned the leadership in 1875, Hartington reluctantly filled the vacancy offered him at a party meeting in the Reform Club. He felt no great objection to Disraeli's chief accomplishments and his under-rated and moderate opposition was eclipsed by Gladstone's energetic Midlothian campaign.

Following Disraeli's defeat in April 1880, the Queen sent for Hartington but he stepped aside for Gladstone, who had refused to serve under him. He served instead as Secretary of State for India and then for War. He clashed repeatedly with Dilke and Chamberlain and disagreed with the conciliatory policy for Ireland. In 1882 Irish rebels assassinated his brother, Lord Frederick Cavendish, newly appointed Chief Secretary for Ireland, a tragedy that reinforced his resistance to Irish demands. He stood aloof from Gladstone's 1886 government and moved the rejection of the Home Rule Bill. Despite their antipathy Hartington and Chamberlain then combined to form the Liberal Unionist party, agreeing an electoral pact with the Conservatives and winning seventy-seven seats in the 1886 election.

Hartington twice refused the premiership of a Conservative/Liberal Unionist coalition but lent support to Salisbury's government. In December 1891, he became eighth Duke of Devonshire and, shortly afterwards, he married the widowed Duchess of Manchester, his long-term mistress.

In 1893, the Duke moved the rejection of Gladstone's second Home Rule Bill in the Lords, where it was defeated by 419 to 41. He became President of the Council in Salisbury's 1895 administration, responsible for state education and for the Cabinet's defence committee. He retained office under Balfour, succeeding Salisbury as leader in the Lords. When Chamberlain adopted protectionism, the Duke fought for free trade and resigned from the Cabinet in October 1903, and from the Liberal Unionist leadership in May 1904. The Liberals won the ensuing election, ending the Duke's public career.

During the early part of Disraeli's government, Gladstone gratified himself with his Homeric studies and indulged in religious controversy, while Hartington allowed the party a period for quiet recuperation. The time was productively used in Birmingham's grassroots organisational innovations and municipal enterprise, spearheaded by Joseph Chamberlain.

Joseph Chamberlain (1836–1914)

Innovative and radical, Joseph Chamberlain created municipal socialism and transformed electoral campaigning, but his dynamism put policy before party, splitting the Liberals in 1886 and the Conservatives in 1903.

Chamberlain was born in July 1836, the son of a London shoemaker. In 1854 he joined his uncle, John Nettlefold's, screw-manufacturing business in Birmingham, where the success of his entrepreneurial talents allowed him to devote himself full-time to politics after 1874. In 1873, he became mayor of Birmingham. Through the purchase and profitable operation of gas and water companies for the municipality, he was able to finance the paving and lighting of streets, new parks and the demolition of the slums.

As a Unitarian, Chamberlain opposed the 1870 Education Act's support for Anglican schools and organised the National Education League (NEL), a step towards national politics completed when 'Radical Joe' was returned as MP for Birmingham in 1876. He established the local Liberals as an effective campaigning organisation, capturing most of the seats in the West Midlands for the party. Building on the NEL, he established the National Liberal Federation, intending to capture the whole party for radicalism.

Gladstone selected Chamberlain to represent the new generation of radicals in the 1880 Cabinet, as President of the Board of Trade. His prickly personality and disregard for political conventions amplified the Cabinet's political differences. He fought coercion in Ireland, sided with Hartington against Gladstone over Egypt/Sudan and annoyed most colleagues by the way he promoted government intervention in social reform. In 1883, he organised the series of articles later published as *The Radical Programme* and the basis of Chamberlain's 'unauthorised' election campaign in 1885, a forerunner of today's programmatic election manifestos.

Chamberlain believed that an Irish Parliament would damage imperial unity and joined Hartington to defeat Gladstone's Home Rule Bill in 1886. Despite round-table talks in 1887, the split in Liberalism proved permanent and in 1895, Radical Joe joined

Salisbury's Cabinet as Secretary of State for the Colonies. In 1903, he launched a proposal for preferential tariffs for the colonies, in order to consolidate the Empire and to fund old-age pensions. His scheme split the Conservatives, caused his resignation from Balfour's government and galvanised the Liberals to win the 1906 election.

A serious stroke in 1906 removed him from active politics, although he did not die until 1914. Both of his sons led the Conservative Party, with the younger, Neville, becoming Prime Minister in the 1930s.

As the Conservative government became bogged down in foreign affairs, and the ageing Disraeli's health began to fail, a gap opened up in domestic policy. Hartington seized the opportunity to create a moderate programme, including representative local government for the counties, land reform and an extension to the county franchise, which all sections of the party, including radicals, could support. The onset of an economic slowdown, particularly acute in agriculture, confirmed the unpopularity of the government and Liberals began to hope for a return to administration when the government's term expired.

But the election did not turn primarily on these domestic concerns. In 1876, a rebellion broke out in the Turkish province of Bulgaria. The suppression of this insurrection with massacres and ill-treatment of Balkan Christians filled the British press with lurid tales of brutality. For the government, these events were unfortunate. Traditionally, Britain was a defender of the Ottoman Empire as a bulwark against expansion by Russia, which liked to portray itself as a defender both of Orthodox Christians and Slavs, the communities represented in the rebellion. Unwisely, Disraeli tried to play down the accounts of the slaughter.

A country-wide agitation developed, especially among Nonconformists, an explosion of moral indignation which the Liberal leadership was slow to recognise and unwilling to exploit. A good Palmerstonian, Hartington was no more willing than Disraeli to weaken Turkey or further Russian ambitions. Gladstone, however, had no such qualms. He did not lead the agitation but he recognised its importance and sympathised with its aims. In September 1876 he dashed off a pamphlet, *Bulgarian Atrocities and the Question of the East*, which became an instant best seller. Gladstone had found a cause which compelled his return to politics.

Despite the popular support for the campaign, Gladstone found little backing from the Whig leadership when, in 1877, he set out to move a series of resolutions condemning the government. The divisions within the Liberal Party were offset when Disraeli's aggressive stance appeared to risk war with Russia, causing the resignation of his Foreign Secretary, Lord Derby (who later joined the Liberals and served in Gladstone's second government). The Eastern Question was resolved at the Congress of Berlin in 1878, which gave Disraeli (now Lord Beaconsfield) the opportunity to manoeuvre upon a world stage, acquiring Cyprus as an addition to the British Empire, further annoying Gladstone. However, worse was to follow. At the end of 1878, imperialist enthusiasm among the British pro-consuls in India and South Africa provoked unnecessary wars with the Afghans and Zulus respectively. Both the human and financial costs appalled Gladstone.

In 1879, Gladstone accepted an invitation to contest the Scottish county seat of Midlothian, traditionally held by the Tories but winnable if vigorously fought, and in November set out to introduce himself to his prospective constituents. By this stage, it was not unusual for senior politicians to address large public meetings, but Gladstone's first Midlothian election was innovative; he created a well-publicised and coherent campaign through a series of pre-planned orations that assaulted all aspects of what Gladstone termed 'Beaconsfieldism' – the foreign and colonial policies of Lord Beaconsfield. Whether asking his audience to 'remember the rights of the savage' or setting out the six 'right principles of foreign policy', Gladstone's moral indignation burnt through not just to the people on the spot but to the newspaper readers who were a more important audience in this appeal direct to the people over the heads of the party. Gladstone's trip to Scotland became a triumphal procession with a number of short addresses given to crowds at railway stations along the way. Once in Edinburgh, he gave a planned series of speeches to audiences totalling nearly 87,000, with accompanying parades and processions.

'Inspired by the love of freedom' – Gladstone's six 'right principles' of foreign policy

'The first thing is to foster the strength of the Empire by just legislation and economy at home, thereby producing two of the great elements of national power – namely, wealth, which is a physical element, and union and contentment, which are moral elements ...

My second principle of foreign policy is this – that its aim ought to be to preserve to the nations of the world ... the blessings of peace.

In my opinion the third sound principle is this – to strive to cultivate and maintain, ay, to the very uttermost, what is called the concert of Europe; to keep the Powers of Europe in union together.

My fourth principle is – that you should avoid needless and entangling engagements.

My fifth principle is this, gentlemen, to acknowledge the equal rights of all nations. You may sympathise with one nation more than another. Nay, you must sympathise in certain circumstances with one nation more than another ... But in point of right all are equal ...

In my opinion, subject to all the limitations that I have described, the foreign policy of England should always be inspired by the love of freedom. There should be a sympathy with freedom, a desire to give it scope, founded not upon visionary ideas, but upon the long experience of many generations within the shores of this happy isle, that in freedom you lay the firmest foundations both of loyalty and order; the firmest foundations for the development of individual character, and the best provision for the happiness of the nation at large.'[27]

The process was repeated during the general election campaign itself, in the spring of 1880. The Liberals won by a much greater margin than anticipated, gaining 112 seats and, despite the continuing strength of the Irish nationalist party, a majority of over fifty against all other parties. The scale of the success was attributed to Gladstone's intervention. In spite of Queen Victoria's effort to appoint Hartington as premier, it had become inevitable that Gladstone would resume the office a second time.

1880 general election (31 March – 27 April)			
	Votes	%	MPs
Liberal	1,836,423	54.7	352
Conservative	1,426,351	42.5	237
Home Rule	95,535	2.8	63
Others	1,107	0.0	0
Total	3,359,416		652

The second Gladstone government

The Liberal government of 1880–85 had its successes, and the third Reform Act of 1884, with its accompanying redistribution of seats, was a major achievement; but overall this administration has not been celebrated in the same way as its Liberal predecessor. Most commentary, coloured by hindsight of the events of 1886, has focused on its difficulties.

Despite its substantial majority, the government operated in a difficult environment and had its own inherent weaknesses. Gladstone returned to office to cleanse the country of the evil consequences of Disraeli's unfettered period in power, as he had outlined in his Midlothian Campaign; essentially a negative objective that left him without a positive personal programme for government. This did not mean that ministers were bereft of ideas but rather that their leader did not impose priorities on the government in the way he had in his first ministry; the government was accordingly more than usually vulnerable to the pressure of events.

Secondly, his negative programme, age and frequent expression of his inclination to retire deceived the Cabinet into anticipating Gladstone's early departure, leading to a jostling for the succession; the principal protagonists were Hartington for the more moderate Liberals and Chamberlain for the radicals. When personal competition for the leadership was combined with ideological differences the impression was conveyed of a party about to split apart. But, as later events proved, the differences between the major contenders should not be exaggerated – Hartington's obduracy on some issues masked an underlying flexibility, while Chamberlain's outrageous public speeches inflated his support and exaggerated his unwillingness to compromise if he could secure at least part of his agenda.

External constraints on the government should also be recognised. Charles Stewart Parnell's accession to the leadership of the Irish nationalist (Home Rule) party combined a mastery of parliamentary tactics with exploitation of the violent agrarian campaigns in Ireland to promote Irish issues. On the death of Lord Beaconsfield in 1881, the Tory leadership battle was resolved in favour of Lord Salisbury, but in the Commons, Sir Stafford Northcote proved to be too reasonable to lead an opposition effectively. The consequent indiscipline of some of his followers, centred on Lord Randolph Churchill, proved a trial and distraction both to Northcote and the Liberal government. House of Commons procedures relied on the self-restraint of honourable gentlemen, a weakness that Churchill and Parnell exploited fully, particularly over Charles Bradlaugh, a case almost heaven-sent to cause embarrassment to a Gladstonian government.

Charles Bradlaugh (1833–91)

Charles Bradlaugh proved to be both a trial to the Liberal Party and a triumph for Liberal values in the 1880s. He espoused republicanism and atheism at a time when both were anathema to the party's leadership, and battled prejudice to win his place in the Commons despite the half-hearted support of fellow-Liberal MPs.

The son of a London solicitor's clerk, Bradlaugh received only an elementary education. Doubting Christian doctrines, in 1850 he began a career as a free thought lecturer, interrupted by a short spell in the army. In 1860 he became editor of the *National Reformer,* and later its owner. He formed the National Secular Society in 1866, took a leading part in the Reform League, established the National Republican League in 1873 and assisted Annie Besant to publish a birth control pamphlet in 1877, which led to his prosecution for obscenity.

An effective radical orator, Bradlaugh stood for Northampton against official Liberal candidates, taking sufficient votes in 1874 to allow the Tories to capture one of the two seats. Rather than face defeat again, in 1880, the local party endorsed Bradlaugh. On entering the Commons, he asked to make an affirmation, instead of taking the oath, on the grounds of his unbelief. When a select committee ruled against this, Bradlaugh offered to take the oath, but was refused. There followed a series of expulsions from the Commons, after each of which Northampton re-elected him – in 1881, 1882, 1884 and 1885. In 1883, Gladstone tried to break this cycle with a bill permitting members to affirm. The opposition derived much pleasure from hearing the High Church Gladstone argue the case for permitting unbelievers to be legislators in a Christian nation, but the bill was defeated by three votes.

The Speaker allowed Bradlaugh to take the oath at the beginning of the 1886 Parliament, before any hostile resolutions could be introduced, and he settled down as a diligent backbencher, acting as unofficial spokesman for Indian nationalism. In 1888 an Affirmations Bill was passed. Bradlaugh's Westminster career was short-lived, however, as he died of Bright's disease in January 1891.[28]

The government's first year was its most productive for domestic legislation, including the first Employers' Liability Act, which provided compensation for employees injured at work, and Mundella's Education Act, which made primary education compulsory and established truancy officers to enforce attendance. The Burials Act of the same year, permitting the burial of Nonconformists by their own ministers in Anglican churchyards, satisfied a long-standing Nonconformist grievance. The Ground Game Act and the abolition of the malt tax gave some relief to the suffering caused by the agricultural depression, and the Irish Land Act formed the major legislative achievement of 1881. The 1883 Agricultural Holdings Act helped English tenants, building on earlier permissive Conservative legislation.

The passage of the 1884 Representation of the People Act and the accompanying Redistribution Act is crucial to the understanding of party positions in the 1885 general election. The Third Reform Act was the first to treat all parts of the United Kingdom equally. It lowered the county franchise to the level of the borough franchise, increasing the electorate by two-thirds in England and Wales and three-quarters in Scotland, and tripling the Irish electorate. The main beneficiaries of the Act were agricultural labourers.

Since, outside Ireland, the restricted county electorate had returned a majority of Conservative members, Liberals expected the proposed reform bill to afford them a great opportunity. The same assessment led the Tory majority in the House of Lords to obstruct the bill until Gladstone, Charles Dilke and Salisbury could negotiate the Redistribution Bill. The resulting move from largely two-member to mostly single-member constituencies eliminated the cosy division of the two-member seats equally between the parties, to save the cost of an election, or between Whig and more radical factions within Liberalism. The abolition of the smallest boroughs was used to augment the number of constituencies in the principal cities and the counties. Subsequent analysis suggests that Salisbury got the better of the bargain. The delays over the Reform Act also squeezed the introduction of representative local government for the counties out of the government programme.

Sir Charles Wentworth Dilke (1843–1911)

Dilke was a leading representative of the radicals until his ministerial career was ended by a divorce scandal.

After a Cambridge education, Dilke undertook a tour to Australia, Canada, New Zealand and the US, subsequently publishing *Greater Britain* in 1869 and helping to inspire enthusiasm for empire among younger Liberals. Elected as MP for Chelsea in 1868, he came to believe that Gladstone's first government was insufficiently ambitious and in 1870 organised the Radical Club to press for electoral and education reforms. He espoused republicanism, and his 1872 Commons motion for a parliamentary enquiry into the Civil List was attacked by Gladstone and suffered a 276–2 vote defeat, also earning Dilke the life-long hostility of Queen Victoria.

Dilke rehabilitated himself with the party leadership during the period of opposition in the later 1870s and was appointed Under-Secretary to the Foreign Office in 1880, acting as spokesman in the Commons. In 1882 he entered the Cabinet as President of the Local Government Board, acting in partnership with Chamberlain in many of the quarrels that beset the 1880–85 government. He was the key Liberal spokesman in the successful negotiations over constituency boundaries which facilitated the passage of the 1884 Reform Act.

He failed to clear his name of what were probably false accusations of adultery in the Crawford divorce case, and lost his seat in 1886. Although Dilke returned to the Commons in 1892 and continued to support labour, women's suffrage and other advanced causes, he never again held office. Some biographers see Dilke as a lost Prime Minister, but his radicalism and the enmity of the Queen make this implausible.[29]

The agricultural depression that had hurt the British economy had a greater impact on Ireland, where lower grain prices combined with a drop in potato production reduced tenant incomes and risked a return of famine. When landlords introduced cost savings, tightened rent collection and consolidated their holdings through evicting tenants, violence, a regular feature in nineteenth-century rural Ireland, resurfaced in the worst-hit communities. But in 1879 there were two differences. Firstly, the protesting tenants were better organised, under Michael Davitt, a former Fenian, and second, they forged strong links with the Irish Parliamentary Party. In 1875, Parnell was elected as a Home Rule MP for Meath in a by-election. Together with a small number of colleagues, he developed techniques of obstructing government business in the Commons, and by defending Fenian terrorists in Parliament established communications with those revolutionaries. In 1880, Parnell took over the leadership of the Irish nationalist MPs and became president of the Irish National Land League. He promoted the shunning of Captain Boycott, a land agent, a technique as effective in extra-parliamentary campaigning as obstruction was within Westminster.

Home rule

'Who are the Unionists? Who are the Separatists?' (W. E. Gladstone)[30]

Ireland, essentially a British province since the sixteenth and seventeenth centuries, was incorporated politically into the United Kingdom in 1800, when the British government passed the Acts of Union following the suppression of the 1798 United Irishmen rebellion. The Union abolished the Irish Parliament and gave the Irish representation at Westminster, but at the cost of creating a persistent sense of grievance in Ireland.

The first to mobilise this discontent successfully was Daniel O'Connell, whose 1820s Catholic emancipation movement secured the vote for the predominant religious group in Ireland. In the 1830s, O'Connell worked with the Whigs, but dissatisfied with the pace of progress, founded the Repeal Association in 1840, attacking the union through a series of 'monster' meetings. This campaign failed when O'Connell cancelled a mass meeting at Clontarf in 1843 rather than risk provoking violence.

Thereafter repealers can be considered in two groups. On one side were the advocates of violence such as Young Ireland, the Fenians and later the Irish Republican Army (IRA)/Sinn Fein. There were further attempted uprisings in 1848, 1867 and 1916, together with much lower level agrarian disturbance throughout the Victorian period. On the other side, the failure of the 1867 Fenian uprising inspired Isaac Butt to establish a Home Rule Association, later the Home Rule League, and secure the election of fifty-nine

Home Rule MPs in 1874. Too gentlemanly for his colleagues, Butt was replaced initially by William Shaw and in 1880 by Charles Stewart Parnell.

Parnell combined obstructive tactics in the House of Commons with mass agitation in the Irish countryside over land tenancy issues to keep Ireland at the head of the British political agenda. In the 1885 election, Irish nationalists or Home Rulers won 85 out of the 103 Irish seats, completely displacing the Liberals and securing the balance of power in the Commons.

Part of Parnell's success may be attributed to the ambiguity with which his party defined 'home rule'. Was it a restoration of the eighteenth-century Irish Parliament (Grattan's Parliament), full independence, a form of local government or a devolved parliament subject to the Imperial Parliament in Westminster? The 1885 election tempted the Liberals to solve this puzzle, splitting the party. Gladstone judged that Parnell was at heart a constitutionalist and decided that trusting the Irish with substantial devolved powers, including policing and taxation, but reserving defence and foreign affairs to London, would preserve the union. Chamberlain was prepared to concede local government through a 'national board', while Hartington and other Liberal Unionists concluded that home rule was a step towards Irish independence and the break-up of the British Empire. Gladstone's proposals underestimated the difficulties of Ulster and did not resolve whether Irish MPs should remain at Westminster.

Home rule bills were rejected in 1886 and 1893. A third bill was carried in 1914 when a Liberal government again depended on Irish parliamentary support, but this time was able to override the Tory House of Lords' veto; its implementation was postponed by the First World War. The Easter Uprising of 1916 and subsequent IRA/Sinn Fein campaigns led to Irish independence after 1922, with the exception of Northern Ireland, which remained within the UK.

Gladstone's concession of the principle of home rule led to demands for the same treatment for Scotland and Wales, which the party would have conceded. Devolution has been a part of Liberal policy ever since.

Britain had traditionally dealt with Irish problems by a combination of 'coercion' and compassion. Normal legal procedures were suspended to allow violent protesters to be locked up when local juries refused to convict. After order was restored, ameliorative measures were offered. At the beginning of its term of office, the second Gladstone government allowed these special legal powers to lapse, and in 1880 proposed a Compensation for Disturbance Bill to help small tenants. When this was defeated overwhelmingly in the Lords (it would have failed even if the Tories had abstained), there was a rise both in Irish violence and in obstruction in the Commons. Prosecution of Parnell and his chief lieutenants failed at the beginning of 1881, and W. E. Forster, Chief Secretary for Ireland, introduced new coercive legislation which was met by greater obstruction and more interminable filibustering. Ultimately the Speaker of the House peremptorily curtailed the debate, and not long afterwards a number of the Irish members arranged to have themselves temporarily expelled. Commons procedures were reformed and standing committees were introduced to deal with the detailed consideration of some legislation. Parnell was imprisoned in Kilmainham jail.

Coercion needed to be balanced by further conciliation. Gladstone initiated a further round of land reform designed to meet Irish demands for fixity of tenure, freedom of sale and fair rent. The Act, which was passed in 1881, created the opportunity to undermine the Land League by offering a legitimate method of securing rent reductions as an alternative to the League's intimidation. For both political and personal reasons, Parnell was anxious to secure his release. Third parties approached the Cabinet on his behalf, most notably Captain O'Shea, the husband of his mistress. The resulting understanding, the so called 'Kilmainham Treaty', secured Parnell's co-operation with the implementation of the Land Act and gave him further legislation to protect tenants with arrears of rent from eviction. Parnell recognised the need to reduce the direct action rural campaign and converted the Land League into the National League to campaign for home rule.

The Land Act cost Gladstone the resignation of the Duke of Argyll, who was concerned about interference in the rights of land-owners, and the Kilmainham Treaty brought about the resignations of Lord Cowper and Forster – the Lord Lieutenant and Chief Secretary for Ireland – who had fought for a further dose of coercion. Forster's replacement, Lord Frederick Cavendish, the husband of Mrs Gladstone's niece and the brother of Lord Hartington, was assassinated almost immediately on his arrival in Dublin. The shock almost caused Parnell to withdraw from politics but did not deter the government from implementing the Arrears Act, though inevitably strengthened with a further dose of coercion. But lasting damage had been done to English attitudes to Ireland, and a link between Gladstone and Hartington had been broken.

Joseph Arch (1826–1919)

As the first agricultural worker to become an MP, Joseph Arch was clearly exceptional; but he was also representative of the working men who were inspired by the Liberal creed that, as Gladstone put it, 'the best thing that government can do for the people is to help them to help themselves'.[31]

Arch was the son of a poor agricultural worker whose wife had been in domestic service and had inherited a small cottage. From his mother, he took his faith as a Primitive Methodist, and from her he also learnt to read and write, saving pennies to buy newspapers to read the speeches of Cobden and Bright. From the 1860s he was playing a part in Warwickshire Liberal politics, canvassing in the 1868 general election. He earned his living as a hedger and ditcher, and was also a lay preacher.

In the early 1870s he combined his oratorical skills with his Nonconformist and political contacts as the organiser of the National Agricultural Labourers' Union. Previous attempts to unionise had been defeated by the inability to mobilise the scattered workforces of a widely distributed industry on the scale necessary for effective wage bargaining. Arch's greater ambitions, combined with a labour shortage and resentment at the 1870 Education Act's threat to child earnings, bought temporary success and a membership approaching 100,000.[32] The depression later in the decade undermined this achievement, however, leading to a decline in membership and squabbling among the leaders. Attention was switched to providing friendly society activities and political campaigning.

Arch benefited from the 1884 Reform Act, winning a Norfolk seat in the short-lived 1885–86 Parliament and again in 1892–1900. From 1889 to 1892, Arch was a councillor in his native Warwickshire. He remained a conventional Liberal, writing in his autobiography, 'I do not believe in State Aid and land nationalisation … Self-help and liberty, order and progress – these are what I advocate.'[33]

Although elected on a searing critique of Disraeli's foreign policy, the record of the 1880–85 government on foreign and colonial affairs was at best mixed. The Afghan war soon faded but tension with Russia on India's northwest frontier remained until after the Panjdeh incident in 1885 when it was resolved by arbitration without obliging Britain to undertake further territorial expansion. Despite initial defeats, the war with the Zulus was quickly won, only to precipitate a struggle with the Boers for predominance in Southern Africa. Fudged at this point, the contest was finally decided by the Boer War at the end of the century. In spite of himself, Gladstone had added to Britain's territorial responsibilities.

Worse was to come at the other end of Africa. Egypt, an outpost of the Ottoman Empire, was badly run and European efforts to enforce the repayment of loan financing provoked a nationalist revolt led by Arabi Pasha. Gladstone had some initial sympathy for Arabi, but he turned down an offer from the Sultan to run Egypt under Turkish suzerainty, as he hoped to concert action with the French. Disorder at Alexandria, and Arabi's fortification of the city, provoked a bombardment by a British fleet stationed in the harbour, followed by the occupation of Egypt by a British army. The bombardment of Alexandria in 1882 was the occasion of the radical John Bright's resignation from the Cabinet, and also damaged British relations with the French and Italian governments.

Responsibility in Egypt brought further difficulties. Sudan was an Egyptian possession that from 1881 had itself been in revolt. In November 1883, the rebel leader, the Mahdi, destroyed an Anglo-Egyptian army under Hicks Pasha. General Gordon was sent to evacuate British forces but, in disobedience to his orders, chose to stay and was besieged in Khartoum. Naturally reluctant to intervene, the government prevaricated and it was not until Hartington threatened to resign that a relief force was authorised. It arrived at Khartoum on 28 January 1885, two days after the garrison had fallen. To many of his opponents, Gladstone was known thereafter as the MOG (Murderer of Gordon) rather than the GOM (Grand Old Man). As the government became more deeply embroiled in Egypt, the Cabinet became increasingly fractious.

As the next general election loomed, two elements in the new electoral environment were obvious: the rural bias of the expanded electorate would favour the home rulers in

Ireland but also offered an opportunity for new radical thinking in the rest of the United Kingdom. Chamberlain was ready for both eventualities. Between 1883 and 1885 he had organised a series of articles in the *Fortnightly Review*, which were published as a book in 1885 under the title of *The Radical Programme*. In Cabinet he introduced a proposal for local government for Ireland in the form of an elected central board based in Dublin, which he mistakenly believed would satisfy Parnell's demand for home rule. Hartington welcomed neither Chamberlain's British nor his Irish ideas, while the Prime Minister rebuked both his provocative language in his public speeches expounding *The Radical Programme* and his departure from the etiquette of joint Cabinet responsibility.

The Radical Programme

Joseph Chamberlain built a national reputation as mayor of Birmingham, but, as a Cabinet minister, he was frustrated by what he saw as Gladstone's lack of domestic policy ambition and Whig obstructionism. The growing working-class electorate necessitated new, radical, ideas, a view reinforced by the first stirrings of socialism among working men and their enthusiasm for Henry George's land tax. Chamberlain persuaded the editor of the *Fortnightly Review*, T. H. S. Escott, to commission a series of anonymous articles between July 1883 and July 1885. In 1885 the collected articles were published as *The Radical Programme*.

Chamberlain supervised the whole project, bringing in his close allies John Morley to write on 'Religious Equality', Jesse Collings on 'The Agricultural Labourer', Frank Harris on 'The Housing of the Poor in Towns' and Francis Adams on education and taxation. A scheme for local government completed the series.

'The community as a whole, co-operating for the benefit of all, may do something … to make the life of all its citizens, and above all, the poorest of them, somewhat better, somewhat nobler, somewhat happier', Chamberlain proclaimed at Ipswich, in 1885. He proposed:

- The disestablishment of the Church of England to create religious equality.
- Free schools, to be funded from the endowments of the Anglican Church.
- Reformed local government, including elected councils for the counties and London. (For Ireland, Chamberlain proposed to the Cabinet an elected central board to sit in Dublin.)
- Slum clearance through powers to direct landlords to make improvements and compulsory purchase.
- Powers for rural authorities to buy land for the creation of smallholdings for peasant proprietors (known as 'three acres and a cow').
- Graduated income tax – 'taxation, on equitable principles, for objects which the nation approves, cannot be on too liberal a scale'.
- Reformed local rates to take account of the rental value of properties.
- Manhood suffrage in equal-sized constituencies, with MPs paid by their constituents.

Radicals, as Escott wrote, advocated the 'intervention of the state on behalf of the weak against the strong, in the interests of labour against capital, of want and suffering against luxury and ease'. The controversy generated by the programme derived from this sponsorship of constructive government intercession, as Chamberlain's bitter comment at Birmingham on 5 January 1885 reveals: 'What ransom will property pay for the security which it enjoys? What substitute will it find for the natural rights it has ceased to recognise?'

His later use of the term 'insurance' instead of 'ransom' came too late to prevent damage to his relations with the Queen and Cabinet colleagues. Speaking for the Whigs, George Goschen disowned Chamberlain's speeches as an 'Unauthorised Programme', while Lord Hartington wrote to the Queen that Chamberlain's language 'almost amounted to socialism'. In tribute to *The Radical Programme*, however, the official Liberal manifesto, when it appeared, was longer and more detailed than its predecessors had been, but its contents owed little to the ideas of Radical Joe.[34]

Shortly after the government had seen the reform and redistribution measures safely on to the statute book, it suffered a defeat on the budget and resigned. Lord Salisbury was allowed the doubtful privilege of leading a minority Conservative government while Liberal forces were given the opportunity to regroup.

The defeat in June 1885 was certainly convenient. It absolved Liberals from renewing the Irish coercion legislation, gave a breathing space for the resolution of the conflicts that had developed in Cabinet, and allowed Chamberlain to campaign free of ministerial responsibility. Gladstone was provided with an opportunity to think about whether he wanted to continue leading the party and if so, his justification for doing so at the age of seventy-five. His manifesto for the 1885 election was three times the size of Hartington's in 1880; Chamberlain's *Radical Programme* had had its effect. Even so, the extensive defence of the late government's foreign and colonial policies outweighed the number of concrete promises for the future, while other issues such as disestablishment of the English Church were gently punted into the long grass.

The home rule crisis

Neither the Conservative government nor the November 1885 general election accorded with Liberal expectations. To woo Irish support, Salisbury allowed the Coercion Act to lapse. Without informing the Cabinet, he also allowed one of his colleagues, Lord Carnarvon, to meet Parnell in secret, giving the Irish leader rather more grounds for calling on Irish voters to support the Tories in British constituencies than Salisbury had intended. The Liberals gained seats in the counties, suggesting that the new rural electorate welcomed *The Radical Programme*'s 'three acres and a cow', though unexpected losses in the boroughs and new single-member city seats resulted in a House of Commons of

86 Irish Nationalists, around 250 Conservatives and around 320 Liberals, not all of whom could be relied on to support the party whip.

1885 general election (24 November – 18 December)			
	Votes	*%*	*MPs*
Liberal	**2,199,998**	**47.4**	**319**
Conservative	2,020,927	43.6	249
Irish Parliamentary	310,608	6.7	86
Others	106,702	2.3	16
Total	*4,638,235*		*670*

The fine balance in the Commons meant that once again Irish issues occupied centre stage. Initially Gladstone hoped that the problem could be resolved by Salisbury's government with Liberal support, and put out feelers through Arthur Balfour, Salisbury's nephew. Gladstone recognised that more than half a century of alternating repression and conciliation had failed to dampen the Irish appetite for repeal of the union with Britain, but he also recognised that the party led by Parnell was essentially constitutional. Home rule in the form of a devolved subordinate parliament in Dublin, dealing with local but not imperial matters, would satisfy Irish demands and remove the principal source of obstruction to legislative progress in the British Parliament. He hoped that his offer to the Conservatives would take the issue out of party contention. However, Gladstone's son Herbert undermined what little chance this strategy had of success. Fearing a coup for the leadership by Chamberlain, he briefed a friendly journalist on his father's conversion to home rule, a conversation which became known as the 'Hawarden kite' after the family residence at Hawarden Castle.

When Salisbury realised, despite Gladstone's half-hearted denials, that he had been outbid for Irish support he forced the pace by declaring that a coercion bill would be introduced. The Liberals carried an amendment to the Queen's Speech based not on Irish policy but on a demand for 'three acres and a cow', an attempt to ensure continued radical support. However, despite achieving a majority of 71, 18 Liberals voted against the motion and a further 51 abstained or were absent without a pair. Unfortunately the kite also undermined Gladstone's fall-back position, which was to take his party towards home rule one step at a time, converting key colleagues one by one if necessary. Gladstone's third government was therefore formed on the basis of examining 'whether it is or is not practicable to comply with the desire, widely prevalent in Ireland … for the establishment by Statute of a Legislative Body, to sit in Dublin'.[35] While this was sufficient to attach Chamberlain and Trevelyan to the government, Lords Hartington, Selborne, Derby and Northbrook could not be enticed to join – a serious weakness.

Between February and June 1886, Gladstone sought to devise a home rule bill and an Irish land bill which would keep the Liberal Party together. His speech winding up the debate on the second reading of the Home Rule Bill on the night of 7–8 June recognised the historic opportunity: 'This, if I understand it, is one of the golden moments of our history – one of those opportunities which may come and may go, but which rarely return, or, if they return, return at long intervals, and under circumstances which no man can forecast.' But he also recognised the imminence of defeat: 'Think, I beseech you, think well, think wisely, think, not for the moment, but for the years that are to come before you reject this Bill.'[36] The bill was defeated by 341 to 311, with 94 Liberal MPs voting against the government. The dissidents included both Hartington and Chamberlain, though in terms of numbers Whig dissenters predominated.

In party terms, what was unusual was not that a Liberal government had been defeated with the assistance of dissident Liberal MPs – after all, this was how Russell's government in 1866 and both of Gladstone's previous governments had ended – but what followed. Rather than make way for another minority Conservative government, the Cabinet quickly decided to call another general election. Rather than wait on the sidelines for an opportunity to reunite with the bulk of the party or for Gladstone's retirement, both Hartington's lieutenants and Chamberlain set up separate Liberal Unionist parties and despite their acute differences on domestic policy sought to co-operate with each other and with the Conservatives. Chamberlain was defeated in his efforts to retain control of the National Liberal Federation, but retained his dominance over the politics of Birmingham. The House of Lords did not have the opportunity to vote on the 1886 bill, but the revolt in the Commons was accompanied by a quieter defection of Whig lords which was of even greater long-term significance: a loss not just in numbers but in administrative experience and the wealth which provided party funding.

The outcome of the election was inevitable. Caught by surprise and without the opportunity to replenish funds or choose fresh candidates, the parties left 219 seats uncontested. The Conservatives gained 66 seats, the Irish Nationalists consolidated their position and 77 Liberal Unionists were returned. Geographically, the Liberal Unionists were strong in Devon, Cornwall, parts of Scotland (especially around Glasgow) and East Lancashire – areas where a more militantly Protestant tradition continued to have an influence. Chamberlain's organisational skills ensured a solid block of loyal unionist voters in the West Midlands.[37] The Gladstonian Liberal Party was reduced to just 192 members.

1886 general election (1–27 July)			
	Votes	*%*	*MPs*
Liberal	1,353,581	45.5	192
Conservative and Liberal Unionist	**1,520,886**	**51.1**	**393**
Conservative			*316*
Liberal Unionist			*77*
Irish Parliamentary	97,905	3.3	85
Others	1,791	0.1	0
Total	*2,974,163*		*670*

Further reading

The mid-Victorian period has been well studied, though the focus has been on high politics involving the chief actors in government rather the operation of parties. Angus Hawkins, *British Party Politics, 1852–1886* (Macmillan, 1998) gives an understanding of both sides of the political hill. A good brief guide to the Liberal achievement is found in T. A. Jenkins, *The Liberal Ascendancy 1830–1886* (Palgrave Macmillan, 1994), while Jonathan Parry, *The Rise and Fall of Liberal Government in Victorian Britain* (Yale University Press, 1993), is a somewhat more substantial canter across the same period.

For the interactions of the factions within Liberalism, Ian Bradley, *The Optimists: Themes and Personalities in Victorian Politics* (Faber and Faber, 1980), provides a good introduction. For the early part of the period depth, density and insight into Palmerston's methods are provided in E. D. Steele, *Palmerston and Liberalism, 1855–1865* (CUP, 1991), while Jonathan Parry demonstrates the interaction between British Liberalism, Englishness and foreign policy in *The Politics of Patriotism* (CUP, 2006). The intrigues of the 1866–67 Reform Act are investigated in Maurice Cowling, *1867: Disraeli, Gladstone and Revolution* (CUP, 1967), and F. B. Smith, *The Making of the Second Reform Bill* (CUP, 1966), while the complexities of the Gladstonian period are conveyed in Jonathan Parry, *Democracy and Religion, Gladstone and the Liberal Party, 1867–1875* (CUP, 1986), and T. A. Jenkins, *Gladstone, Whiggery and The Liberal Party, 1874–1886* (Clarendon Press, 1988). Jenkins and Parry help redress the balance of earlier accounts by focusing on the continuing vitality of the moderates and Whigs.

The Irish home rule crisis of 1886 remains the most controversial event of the period. It can be approached via the texts already suggested and the biographies of the key participants, but it also useful to consider the more technical W. C. Lubenow, *Parliamentary Politics and the Home Rule Crisis, The British House of Commons in 1886* (Clarendon Press, 1988), and Thomas William Heyck, *The Dimensions of British Radicalism: The Case of Ireland, 1874–1895* (University of Illinois Press, 1974). The 'high politics', conspiratorial approach is explored in A. B. Cooke and John Vincent, *The Governing Passion: Cabinet Government and Party Politics in Britain, 1885–86* (Barnes and Noble, 1974).

For an understanding of politics at the grassroots level, John Vincent, *The Formation of the British Liberal Party 1857–68* (Constable, 1966), and H. J. Hanham, *Elections and Party Management: Politics in the Time of Disraeli and Gladstone* (Longman, 1959) are essential, while K. T. Hoppen, *Elections, Politics and Society in Ireland, 1832–1885* (Clarendon Press, 1984), supplements Hanham's work from an Irish perspective. The significant pressure groups which influenced Liberal policy are dissected in D. A. Hamer, *The Politics of Electoral Pressure: A Study in the History of Victorian Reform Agitations* (Harvester Press, 1977). Insight into a subaltern politics inherited from earlier 'independent' and 'puritan' traditions rather than class can be gained from Eugenio Biagini, *Liberty, Retrenchment and Reform: Popular Politics in the Age of Gladstone, 1860–1880* (CUP, 1992) and Eugenio Biagini and Alistair Reid, (eds.), *Currents of Radicalism: Popular Radicalism, Organised Labour and Party Politics in Britain, 1850–1914* (CUP, 1991).

Gladstone dominated British politics in this period; Colin Matthew, *Gladstone 1809–1898* (OUP, 1996), written in conjunction with his work on the Gladstone diaries, is the best introduction, while Richard Shannon's two volumes, *Gladstone: Peel's Inheritor* and *Gladstone: Heroic Minister* (Penguin, 1999) are more critical of his later career. More specialist are David Bebbington, *The Mind of Gladstone: Religion, Homer and Politics* (OUP, 2004), and David Bebbington and Roger Swift (eds.), *Gladstone Centenary Essays* (Liverpool University Press, 2000).

Chamberlain is well served by Peter T. Marsh, *Joseph Chamberlain: Entrepreneur in Politics* (Yale University Press, 1994). By comparison Hartington has been less well covered; Patrick Jackson, *The Last of the Whigs* (Farleigh Dickinson University Press, 1994) focuses almost entirely on his politics rather than his personality. For Cobden there is the choice of Nicholas C. Edsall, *Richard Cobden: Independent Radical* (Harvard University Press, 1986), or Wendy Hinde, *Richard Cobden: A Victorian Outsider* (Yale University Press, 1987), while the most recent biography of Bright is Keith Robbins, *John Bright* (Routledge, 1979). Palmerston deserves a modern biography of the same calibre as recent works on Gladstone, but there is a tendency for foreign affairs to overwhelm domestic politics. The most recent assault on the mountainous resource left by Palmerston is David Brown, *Palmerston: a Biography* (Yale University Press, 2010). The relationship with Gladstone may be explored through their correspondence in Philip Guedalla (ed.), *Gladstone and Palmerston* (Victor Gollancz, 1928).

For those who prefer their politics in small doses and informal, the three volumes derived from the diaries of the Earl of Derby are rewarding and add a dose of immediacy and reality sometimes missing in more academic analyses: John Vincent (ed.), *Disraeli, Derby, and the Conservative Party: Journals and Memoirs of Edward Henry, Lord Stanley 1849–1869* (Harvester Press, 1978); John Vincent (ed.), *A Selection from The Diaries of Edward Henry Stanley, 15th Earl of Derby (1826–93) between September 1869 and March 1878* (Camden Fifth Series, Vol. 4, 1994); and John Vincent (ed.), *The Diaries of Edward Henry Stanley, 15th Earl of Derby (1826–93) between 1878 and 1893: A Selection* (Leopard's Head Press, 2003).

Notes

1 Bernard Holland, *The Life of Spencer Compton, Eighth Duke of Devonshire* (Longmans Green, 1911), vol. 1, p. 33.

2 A. C. Benson and Viscount Esher (eds.), *The Letters of Queen Victoria 1837–1861*, vol. III (John Murray, 1911), p. 345.

3 16 June 1859; quoted in John Morley, *Life of Gladstone* (Macmillan, 1903), vol. 1, p. 627. Ishmael was an exiled son of Abraham.

4 Quoted in Angus Hawkins, *Parliament, Party and the Art of Politics in Britain, 1855–59* (Palgrave Macmillan, 1987), p. 278.

5 William White, *The Inner Life of the House of Commons* (1897, reprinted Richmond Publishing Co., 1973), vol. ii, p. 116.

6   Walter Bagehot, *The English Constitution* (1872), pp. 81–86.

7   The statement to Goschen is taken from Jasper Ridley, *Lord Palmerston* (Constable, 1970), p. 506. The argument that Palmerston aimed to build national social cohesion as premier is elaborated in E. D. Steele, *Palmerston and Liberalism, 1855–1865* (CUP, 1991).

8   For the correspondence between the premier and his Chancellor of the Exchequer, see Philip Guedalla, *Gladstone and Palmerston* (Victor Gollancz, 1928).

9   J. S. Mill, *On Liberty*, in J. S. Mill, *Utilitarianism, Liberty, Representative Government* (Dent, 1972), p. 72.

10   See Kristin Zimmerman, 'Liberal Speech, Palmerstonian Delay, and the Passage of the Second Reform Act', *English Historical Review*, November 2003.

11   Speech at Rochdale, 18 August 1859, from John Bright and J. E. Thorold Rogers (eds.), *Speeches on Questions of Public Policy by Richard Cobden* (1870).

12   House of Commons 11 May 1864; cited in Morley, *Life of Gladstone*, vol. II, p. 126.

13   J. E. Thorold Rogers (ed.), *Speeches on Questions of Public Policy by John Bright MP* (Macmillan, 1869), vol. 2, pp. 112–14.

14   Jonthan Parry, 'The later career of Lord John Russell', in T. C. W. Blanning and David Cannadine (eds.), *History and Biography: Essays in Honour of Derek Beales* (CUP, 1996), p. 169. Russell has not been as well served as Palmerston or Gladstone for biographies; Parry's essay serves as a useful background to Russell's political views.

15   The biblical King David took refuge from Saul in caves near the city of Adullam – 'and every one that was in distress, and every one that was in debt, and everyone that was discontented, gathered themselves unto him'. 1 Samuel 22 verse 2.

16   James Winter, *Robert Lowe* (University of Toronto Press, 1976), p. 225.

17   W. F. Monypenny and G. E. Buckle, *The Life of Benjamin Disraeli* (John Murray, 1929), vol. 2, p. 285.

18   H. J. Hanham, *Elections and Party Management: Politics in the Time of Disraeli and Gladstone* (Longman, 1959), pp. 138–39.

19   W. E. Gladstone, *Midlothian Speeches 1879* (reprinted Leicester University Press, 1971), p. 90.

20   H. C. G. Matthew, *Gladstone 1809–1874* (Clarendon Press, 1986), p. 174; H. C. G. Matthew, *Gladstone 1875–1898* (OUP, 1995), p. 112.

21   T. A. Jenkins, *The Liberal Ascendancy 1830–1886* (Palgrave Macmillan, 1994).

22   Derived from Henry Pelling, *Social Geography of British Elections 1885–1910* (Palgrave Macmillan, 1967), Michael Kinnear, *The British Voter, An Atlas and Survey since 1885* (Batsford, 1968) and Michael Winstanley, *Gladstone and the Liberal Party* (Routledge, 1990).

23   The standard but dated biography of Granville is Lord Edmond Fitzmaurice, *The Life of Lord Granville 1815–1891* (Longmans Green, 1905). A sense of his easy relationship with Gladstone is given in Agatha Ramm (ed.), *The Political Correspondence of Mr Gladstone and Lord Granville 1868–1876* (Royal Historical Society, 1952) and Agatha Ramm (ed.), *The Political Correspondence of Mr Gladstone and Lord Granville 1876–1886* (Clarendon Press, 1962).

24   Morley, *Life of Gladstone*, vol. 2, pp. 495–96.

25   Ibid., p. 498.

26 See particularly, Jonathan Parry, *The Rise and Fall of Liberal Government in Victorian Britain* (Yale University Press, 1993), and T. A. Jenkins, *Gladstone, Whiggery and The Liberal Party, 1874–1886* (Clarendon Press, 1988).

27 From Gladstone's speech on 27 November 1879, at West Calder; Gladstone, *Midlothian Speeches 1879*, pp. 115–17.

28 Walter L. Arnstein, *The Bradlaugh Case* (OUP, 1965).

29 Roy Jenkins, *Sir Charles Dilke: A Victorian Tragedy* (Collins, 1958); David Nicholls, *The Lost Prime Minister: A Life of Sir Charles Dilke* (Hambledon Continuum, 1995).

30 Speech in House of Commons, 7 June 1886, in Duncan Brack and Tony Little (eds.), *Great Liberal Speeches* (Politico's, 2001), p. 185.

31 *The Times*, 5 February 1877.

32 E. H. Hunt, *British Labour History, 1815–1914* (Weidenfeld and Nicolson, 1981).

33 Joseph Arch, *From Ploughtail to Parliament* (reprinted Ebury Press, 1986), p. 404.

34 Joseph Chamberlain (ed.), *The Radical Programme* (1885, reprinted Harvester Press, 1971, D. A. Hamer (ed.)). See also J. L. Garvin, *The Life of Joseph Chamberlain* (Macmillan, 1935), vol. 1, p. 545 onwards.

35 Matthew, *Gladstone 1875–1898*, p. 239.

36 Brack and Little, *Great Liberal Speeches*, pp. 194–95.

37 Kinnear, *The British Voter*, p. 98 and associated maps.

Chapter 4

Gladstonianism, Imperialism and the Origins of New Liberalism (1886–1899)

Eugenio Biagini and Robert Ingham

The period surveyed in this chapter is one which is often studied in terms of the 'decline and fall' of the 'great' Victorian Liberal Party. In purely electoral terms this is of course a legitimate interpretation: the party split in 1886, lost the election of that year, and went on to lose the general elections of 1895 and 1900. Its victory in 1892 was narrow and the Liberals' return to power achieved little.

The period from 1886 to 1892 was the only one in which Gladstone served as leader of the opposition, and it was dominated by Ireland, relations with the Liberal Unionists, the Liberals' response to the social reforms initiated by Salisbury's government and organisational changes within the Liberal Party.

Despite supporting the Conservatives in government the Liberal Unionists commenced the 1886 Parliament sitting with the Liberals on the opposition benches. Liberal reunion seemed possible and there were negotiations to that end in 1887, but home rule remained the inevitable stumbling block. The parties' views on how to govern Ireland polarised during the late 1880s. The Conservative government combined a more forceful policy on coercion and suppression of the Irish National Land League with various new land reform schemes which failed to dampen Irish enthusiasm for home rule and often annoyed Tory landowners. The Liberals, on the other hand, were now firmly committed to home rule in some form and the loose alliance between the Liberals and Parnell's Irish nationalists, which was to help bolster the Liberal governments of the Edwardian era, was fashioned during this period. Liberal reunion in these circumstances, particularly with Gladstone still leading the party, was impossible and Chamberlain ruled it out completely when he replaced Hartington as Liberal Unionist leader in 1891.

The Liberal Unionists

Those Liberals who opposed Gladstone's policy of home rule for Ireland were known as Liberal Unionists, but it took some time for them to separate unambiguously from the Gladstonian Liberals, and the Liberal Unionist party lasted only until 1912.

When Gladstone declared for home rule he immediately opened up a breach with a large proportion of the leading Whigs, including Lords Hartington and Lansdowne.

They were joined by a radical element, led by Joseph Chamberlain, who had resigned from Gladstone's brief 1886 government in protest at his home rule scheme. However, the Whigs and radicals maintained separate political organisations, with Chamberlain founding the National Radical Union and the Whigs creating the Liberal Unionist Council.

Hartington declined Salisbury's invitation to join (or even lead) the Conservative government formed after the 1886 election, although George Goschen was later appointed Chancellor of the Exchequer. The two Liberal Unionist groupings remained on the opposition benches with the Gladstonian Liberals throughout the 1886 Parliament. Discussions about Liberal reunion foundered on the rock of home rule and the Liberal Unionists developed closer ties with the Conservatives. The Liberal Unionists joined Salisbury's government in 1895, which was usually described as Unionist.

Joseph Chamberlain emerged as the leading Liberal Unionist, particularly with his campaign for tariff reform from 1903, which drove some of his free trade colleagues back to the Liberals and further eroded differences between the unionist parties. The Liberal Unionists were strongest in Birmingham, Chamberlain's base, and Scotland, but their numbers in Parliament fell from seventy-seven in 1886 to around twenty-five in 1906. The Liberal Unionists lacked a grassroots organisation from which to expand, and their separate existence came into an end in 1912 when the party's funds were merged with the Conservatives to form the Conservative and Unionist Party.

Acting to some extent under the influence of Chamberlain, the 1886–92 Conservative government passed a number of political and social reform measures, for example to establish county councils, introduce free elementary education, and reduce working hours in factories. The Liberals responded by agreeing a broad statement of their political priorities at the National Liberal Federation's annual assembly in Newcastle in 1891. The Newcastle Programme, which is discussed in detail below, included political and economic reform measures and was an important step in the development of more ambitious social reforms by 'New Liberal' thinkers and politicians in the 1890s and 1900s.

The Newcastle Programme may have helped the Liberals return to power in 1892 but their election victory was narrow. The Liberals were damaged in particular by the Parnell divorce scandal in 1890, followed by the split of the Irish Parliamentary Party the following year, which discredited the home rule alliance and demoralised home rule supporters. Even so, the party recovered most of the losses of 1886. The net result was that in the House of Commons there were some forty fewer Liberal MPs than the combined total of Conservatives and Liberal Unionists. Gladstone depended for his majority on the external support of the Irish nationalists, a fact which was held, by the overwhelmingly Unionist House of Lords, to deprive his government of legitimacy, thereby justifying it in obstructing and frustrating much of the legislation passed by the Commons.

1892 general election (4–26 July)			
	Votes	%	MPs
Liberal	**2,088,019**	**45.4**	**272**
Conservative and Liberal Unionist	2,159,150	47.0	313
Conservative			268
Liberal Unionist			45
Irish Parliamentary	311,509	6.8	81
Independent Labour	22,198	0.5	3
Others	17,443	0.4	1
Total	4,598,319		670

Return to government

Gladstone was eighty-two when he took up office for the fourth and final time in 1892. Sir William Harcourt was appointed Chancellor of the Exchequer; Lord Rosebery was Foreign Secretary; and H. H. Asquith was made Home Secretary, his first ministerial post. Gladstone retained close control over Irish policy, appointing his friend and later biographer John Morley to the post of Chief Secretary for Ireland. As in 1886, Gladstone took personal charge of drafting the Home Rule Bill, which proposed a bicameral Irish Parliament to control domestic affairs and allowed Irish MPs to remain at Westminster to vote only on bills affecting Ireland. The bill was approved at second reading in the Commons in April 1893 by a majority of forty-three, but its passage was stormy and its credibility was undermined when a miscalculation about the Irish contribution to the British exchequer was revealed during the committee stage. The only surprising factor in the bill's rejection by the Lords on 8 September 1893 was in the scale of the government's defeat, by 419 votes to 41.

Gladstone remained as Prime Minister for a further six months, resigning in 1894 after differences emerged with his Cabinet colleagues over public expenditure on naval expansion – 'the most wanton contribution … to accursed militarism that has yet been made in any quarter', as he described it in a secret autobiographical memorandum.[1] He was also uneasy about Harcourt's budget, which included the introduction of a graduated death duty to help raise the money required for a larger navy. The Queen did not seek Gladstone's advice before asking Lord Rosebery to form a government, effectively handing him the party leadership. Had Gladstone been consulted, he would have suggested Lord Spencer, who was more senior than Rosebery and more enthusiastic about Irish home rule. However, it is likely that the party would have approved of the Queen's choice had members been consulted.

Rosebery was certainly the natural leader of the younger generation of MPs who were to dominate early twentieth-century politics, including H. H. Asquith, R. B. S. Haldane, and Edward Grey. Wealthy and well-connected, the Scottish peer was a formidable speaker, championing radical (the Queen thought 'communistic') social reform in order to increase 'national efficiency' in both industrial and military terms.

Gladstone was not particularly upset about the new leader's 'communism', but found his foreign and colonial policy very alarming. This had become evident from September 1892 when the Cabinet was discussing whether Britain should formally annex or evacuate Uganda, which was then run by a chartered company, the Imperial British East Africa Company, locally represented by the energetic Captain Frederick (later Lord) Lugard. Rosebery insisted on annexation. His motivations were both humanitarian (he wanted to put down the slave trade and defend Christian missionaries and their many converts from Muslim persecution) and strategic (to consolidate British control over north-east Africa). Many other Cabinet ministers took a different line. They were sceptical about the benefits of the proposed British occupation, including the 'humanitarian' dimension; as Sir William Harcourt put it, 'Captain Lugard has probably with his Maxim gun slain more Catholic Christians than are likely to be killed in his absence'.[2] However, outmanoeuvring Gladstone, Harcourt and Morley, Rosebery managed to get his way and Uganda was secured for the British Empire. His skills as a negotiator were further displayed in 1894, when he successfully mediated a major industrial dispute and persuaded the coal owners and the Miners' Federation to reach agreement.

Rosebery was not, however, a success as Prime Minister, and after failing to make much impact he seemed to lose interest in politics. He mismanaged the 1895 election in an unsuccessful attempt to mobilise public opinion against the House of Lords.[3] Dominated by the Conservatives, the latter had become a purely partisan branch of the legislature, rejecting most of the legislation passed by the Commons in 1892–95. Its powers were obviously inconsistent with the democratic expectations of the age and even Gladstone had recommended a parliamentary dissolution on the reform of the Lords in 1894. The Unionist victories at the elections of 1895 and 1900 postponed, but did not solve, the problem, which was eventually addressed by Asquith and Lloyd George in 1911.

1895 general election (13 July – 17 August)			
	Votes	%	MPs
Liberal	1,765,266	45.7	177
Conservative and Liberal Unionist	**1,894,772**	**49.0**	**411**
Conservative			340
Liberal Unionist			71
Irish Parliamentary	152,959	4.0	82
Independent Labour	44,325	1.1	0
Others	8,960	0.2	0
Total	3,866,282		670

The Earl of Rosebery (1847–1929)

The Earl of Rosebery is one of the least known British Prime Ministers. Born Archibald Primrose in 1847, and educated at Eton and Oxford, he succeeded his grandfather to become the Fifth Earl of Rosebery in 1868. Despite not completing his degree, Rosebery was well read, well travelled and a prolific writer. He also owned champion racehorses.

At university Rosebery was asked to stand for the Liberals but declined, due to his uncertainty as to which party he preferred. Nevertheless, he served as a Home Office minister in 1881 and was appointed to the Cabinet as First Commissioner for Works and Lord Privy Seal in 1885. He became the first chairman of the new London County Council in 1889.

Rosebery soon became the leader of the Liberals' Imperialist faction and in Gladstone's third and fourth administrations he served as Foreign Secretary. On Gladstone's resignation in 1894, Rosebery became Prime Minister, though this was largely a consequence of the Queen disliking most of the other leading Liberals of the day.

Rosebery's period as Prime Minister was brief and unsuccessful. Although he had developed an image as an energetic and visionary politician, he proved to be a poor leader. Pessimistic, introspective and self-absorbed, he never learned how to deal with either criticism or opposition. He failed either to unify the party or to provide any new direction for it. His legislative record was thin, thanks to the Conservative-dominated House of Lords, and he caused controversy within his party by advocating the expansion of the fleet and calling an unnecessary election, which was convincingly lost in 1895.

Rosebery stood down as Liberal leader in 1896. He remained active in the Lords, although he became increasingly distant from, and critical of, his party's leadership. In 1901 the Liberal Imperial Council was formed by his supporters, and in 1902 the Liberal League was founded with him as president; although his adherents were keen to see his return to the leadership, he failed to give them any consistent lead and in reality had no clear alternative to Campbell-Bannerman's agenda.

A stroke in 1918 ended his active political career and he died in 1929.

Three leaders in five years

Rosebery remained party leader for another year, eventually resigning on 6 October 1896, in protest against Gladstone's partial and temporary return to politics. The veteran Liberal leader, now eighty-six, had been persuaded to speak at Liverpool, where he addressed a public meeting called to protest against the 'ethnic cleansing' of the Armenian subjects of the Ottoman Empire, over 100,000 of whom were killed by the Sultan's troops in 1894–96 in a successful attempt to crush Christian separatism. The massacres – the beginning of a genocide – had been debated by the Cabinet from the end of 1894. Many ministers insisted that Britain should intervene to stop the atrocities and Rosebery took action through the usual diplomatic channels, without achieving much. In any case, as a Liberal Imperialist, he was more concerned about the demands of *realpolitik* and the need to preserve peace in Europe than about humanitarian crises in the East. Electoral defeat in 1895 relieved Rosebery from the responsibility of dealing with the 1895–96 Armenian massacre, but not from the embarrassment of leading a party which remained essentially Gladstonian in its attitudes to foreign affairs.[4] When he realised the extent to which he was out of touch with both rank-and-file Liberals and a significant number of the party's MPs he resigned.

Liberal Imperialism

A moderate, centrist faction within the Liberal Party during the late Victorian and early Edwardian period, Liberal Imperialism was less an intellectual movement than an expression of a strategy for reviving the party's electoral fortunes and ensuring the success of future Liberal governments. Liberal Imperialists argued for a more positive attitude towards empire and imperialism, ending the overriding commitment to Irish home rule and distancing themselves from 'faddist' minority causes. They supported the idea of 'national efficiency' as an organising principle for domestic policy.

The divisions between the Liberal Imperialists and others within the party came to a head over the Boer War, where Asquith, Grey, Haldane and, more distantly, Rosebery, attempted to prevent the party leader, Campbell-Bannerman, from tilting towards the 'pro-Boers' in the party, such as Lloyd George. The ending of the Boer War, the increasing detachment of Rosebery and the disintegration of Balfour's government all helped to heal the divisions, but the Liberal Imperialists had some success in ensuring that Irish home rule was not pursued until after the Liberals lost their majority in 1910, and in abandoning commitments to fringe issues, such as temperance or Welsh and Scottish disestablishment. Grey's appointment as Foreign Secretary also ensured a substantial measure of continuity in foreign policy.

In many ways the Liberal Imperialists can be seen as the political descendant of the Whigs, seeking to act both as a brake on radicalism and as a progressive alternative to Toryism.

Rosebery's successor was Sir William Harcourt, who disagreed with his predecessor over imperialism and most other policy issues. Although Harcourt was a good leader of the opposition in the Commons, his front-bench colleagues never wholeheartedly supported him, partly because they feared to antagonise Rosebery. His leadership was further undermined by his failure to capitalise on the Jameson Raid – Joseph Chamberlain's first attempt to seize the territories of the Boer Republics in South Africa. The attempt was completely illegal and an official inquiry was called to establish government responsibilities. As a leading member of the relevant committee Harcourt could have exposed Chamberlain's role in this episode of international piracy. Instead he handled the Colonial Secretary with incredible restraint. As a consequence, the inquiry's report was inconclusive. When its results were published, many in the party were very disappointed. H. W. Massingham expressed his frustration in the columns of the influential *Daily Chronicle* and it was rumoured that the National Liberal Federation would censure the party leader at the next meeting of the General Council, due in December 1898. Harcourt, who had been struggling to assert his authority against the Liberal Imperialists, was now also losing the support of the radicals. Not surprisingly, he decided to resign.

Sir William Harcourt (1827–1904)

Harcourt was at the forefront of British politics for almost twenty years and held some of the top political offices during this time, yet never succeeded in developing the personal following needed, with either his party or in the country as a whole, to enable him to become Prime Minister.

The second son of a landowning clergyman whose ancestry stretched back to many of the great English houses, Harcourt gained a first from Cambridge and was called to the bar in 1854. He entered Parliament in 1868 for Oxford City, briefly served as Solicitor-General in 1873–74 and was Home Secretary in 1880–85. Briefly Chancellor of the Exchequer in 1886, he again took up the post from 1892 to 1895. His 1894 budget included the reform for which he was chiefly remembered, the introduction of graduated death duties on both real and personal property.

He was an impressive public speaker and debater, and steadily became more radical in his politics despite his aristocratic background, supporting the wide range of radical measures contained in the Newcastle Programme. He proved a tough and effective Liberal partisan, and effectively acted as Gladstone's deputy in the Grand Old Man's later years.

Harcourt's political nemesis was the Earl of Rosebery who, despite being twenty years younger than him, succeeded Gladstone as Prime Minister in 1894. Harcourt became Leader of the Commons as well as Chancellor, but the combination was unstable. Rosebery's premiership was brief and, when he resigned as Liberal leader in 1896 following disagreement with Gladstone and Harcourt over the Turkish massacres of Armenians, Harcourt succeeded him. Increasing difficulties in dealing with the Roseberyite Liberal Imperialists, however, caused Harcourt to abandon the leadership in 1899. He died in 1904.

The party had now had three leaders in five years and continued to be divided over its future direction and approach. Gladstone had recently died, but his policies and ideas still found enthusiastic supporters within the rank and file. On the other hand, the brightest and most promising parliamentary leaders were all Liberal Imperialists. Asquith was perhaps the strongest candidate for the leadership, but he was as yet unwilling to quit his lucrative law practice and was perhaps too closely identified with Rosebery to be acceptable to the other side. Instead the party chose Sir Henry Campbell-Bannerman. Unlike his predecessors, he was neither a charismatic leader nor a great social or financial reformer. However, he was patient, resilient and imperturbable. He proved the right man to lead the party out of factionalism and anarchy.[5] A man of solid common sense, strong Liberal principles and nerves of steel, he gradually asserted his authority.

Sir Henry Campbell-Bannerman (1836–1908)

Henry Campbell was born in Glasgow and after university worked for his father's retail drapery firm, of which he became a director. 'Bannerman' was added to his name in 1871 as a condition of benefiting from his uncle's will; after this he was often known as 'CB'. Although his family were Conservatives he was elected as Liberal MP for Stirling

Burghs in 1868 and held the seat until his death. He was a minister in Liberal governments from 1871, entering the Cabinet as Chief Secretary for Ireland in 1884 and serving as Secretary of State for War in 1886 and 1892–95.

Popular with politicians in both parties, he was spoken of as a possible Speaker of the House when a vacancy arose in 1895, but the party would not let him; he was one of the few Liberal leaders who was not hopelessly committed to one faction or another. In 1899 he reluctantly took on the Liberal leadership after the resignation of Harcourt. Although he faced constant carping from Rosebery and some hostility from the Liberal Imperialists, he proved to be a highly effective party manager, gradually bringing the party's warring factions together. He was an effective leader of the opposition to the government's tactics in the Boer War, criticising the use of 'methods of barbarism' in the British camps for Boer civilians in South Africa.

In 1905, the Liberal Imperialists Asquith, Grey and Haldane plotted to send Campbell-Bannerman to the Lords so that Asquith could become Prime Minister following Balfour's resignation. Campbell-Bannerman saw off this attempted coup and was appointed Prime Minister, leading the Liberals to victory in the 1906 landslide. He was an effective chairman of a highly talented group of ministers but his health failed and he died in 10 Downing Street shortly after handing over the reins to Asquith in April 1908.

Taking stock

Despite these difficulties, the final decade and a half of the nineteenth century was also a time of enormous importance in the making of modern democratic liberalism. Consequently, at this point we take stock of three of the most salient themes of the period: the continuing impact of home rule; the development of the party's internal organisation; and new approaches to the creed of liberalism.

The most divisive issue of this period, Irish home rule, involved important principles – that the views of a people, expressed in free elections, should be respected; that self-government was better than empire; and that the old parliamentary centralism on which the United Kingdom was based should be replaced by something like a federation of self-governing nations. Related to this debate about the future of the UK there was the broader debate about the Empire and free trade, which elicited a variety of different Liberal responses and culminated with J. A. Hobson producing one of the most perceptive and penetrating analyses of imperialism ever conceived by a radical (one which was largely plagiarised by Lenin a few years later).[6] Hobson himself drew his inspiration from Richard Cobden's classically Liberal anti-imperialism, and sought to link foreign policy to new answers to the 'social questions' of poverty, unemployment and sickness.

The years 1886–99 also saw a lively debate about internal party democracy. The National Liberal Federation (NLF) and the Liberal Central Association (LCA), the Chief Whip's office for placing and supporting parliamentary candidates, were brought together under the secretaryship of Francis Schnadhorst in 1886. Although the LCA was to continue into being until after the Second World War, this move clarified the party's institutional structure and went some way towards placing the NLF at the heart of the party's national organisation. However, as we shall see below, tensions continued between the NLF and the parliamentary party, especially over the former's claim to shape the Liberal programme. With the NLF becoming a model of what a party machine, based on the principle of representation and democratic control over the parliamentary party, could achieve, the party was forced to update its political agenda by adopting a broad range of democratic causes (most significantly with the 1891 Newcastle Programme) and revise its understanding of citizenship to include women (a cause autonomously championed by the Women's Liberal Federation, established in 1887, again as a response to the home rule crisis).

In parallel to these political changes, there were important developments in the social philosophy behind liberalism, with German idealism replacing utilitarianism – a change which was accompanied by a greater emphasis on state intervention in social reform and on 'positive' liberty, that is, on enabling citizens to enjoy rights, rather than merely encouraging competition within a free market context. In short the party became much more radical, perhaps inevitably as an opposition force, a development which paved the way to the successful experiment of the New Liberalism in the twentieth century.

Women's Liberal Federation

The doctrine of 'separate spheres', whereby men took responsibility for public life and restricted women to responsibility for domestic, family and charitable life, was probably only ever a male fantasy. Women have always been involved in politics, whether as powers behind the throne, managers of aristocratic family salons or participants in Chartist demonstrations. Women managed constituency interests while their husbands or fathers were at Westminster, carried out politically motivated 'good works' and canvassed at elections. Women often provided leadership in pressing social reforms such as nursing (Florence Nightingale), housing (Octavia Hill) or prostitution (Josephine Butler).

The secret ballot and the enlarged electorate which resulted from the 1867 and 1884 Reform Acts, however, required an enhanced organisational response from the political parties. The first organised attempt to enlist the services of women in the Liberal cause was made in 1880. By 1886, there were fifteen women's Liberal Associations, with 6,000 members, and the Women's Liberal Federation (WLF) was formed in June, at the height of the home rule crisis. Its aims were 'to organise women's Liberal associations throughout the country, and to secure the admission of women as members of existing Liberal associations; to promote the adoption of Liberal principles in the government of the country; to advance political education; and to promote just legislation for women, and protect the interests of children'.[7] The ordering of the objectives suggests that organising within the party and public campaigning were the top priorities.

By 1889 there were seventy branches and by 1912 membership totalled 133,000. Even in 1920 membership exceeded 95,000, spread over 732 branches. The first president, rather 'against her better judgement', was Catherine Gladstone, wife of the Grand Old Man.[8] Other prominent parts on the central committee were played by the wives and other relatives of major Liberal politicians.

The WLF was soon embroiled in controversy over women's suffrage, with Lady Carlisle pushing support for the vote to the point of splitting the organisation in the early 1890s, leading to the resignation of Mrs Gladstone, who reflected her husband's unenthusiastic attitude, and the establishment of a breakaway group. By 1897, the National Liberal Federation had adopted women's suffrage as part of its platform.

Although women did not gain the vote at parliamentary elections until 1918, women were entitled to vote for School Boards in 1870 and for county councils in 1889. Two Liberal women were elected to London's first county council, but their right to sit was successfully challenged by the Tories and it was not until 1907 that a Liberal government corrected this injustice.

The fortunes of the WLF reflected those of the party more broadly, with membership probably peaking just before the Great War and declining in the 1920s. It maintained a separate organisation until it merged with Women for Socal Democracy to form the Women Liberal Democrats.

Home rule and the Newcastle Programme

Historians have tended to regard Gladstone's adoption of home rule as one of his worst political mistakes, attributable to his personal 'obsession' with Ireland and wish to retain the party leadership. Allegedly, by imposing home rule on his followers, Gladstone first split the party, then lost his working-class supporters – thus creating a margin of manoeuvre for the nascent Labour Party – and eventually led British Liberalism towards its terminal 'decline and fall'. This interpretation is consistent with some of the evidence about the 'high politics' of the proposal – most systematically presented by Cooke and Vincent.[9] They see the whole home rule crisis as either a pawn in the ruthless game for the party leadership in 1885–86, or as a figment of Gladstone's excited imagination. They focus on the secretive way in which the proposal was prepared, the extraordinary circumstances under which it was leaked to the press, and the extent to which Gladstone marginalised Hartington and Chamberlain, his two rivals for the party leadership. He certainly managed to 'dish the Whigs' and retain the leadership for eight more years. But was this really his aim?

There are good reasons to reject this view. The main problem with it is that it takes little note of the fact that until 1921 the United Kingdom included the whole of Ireland, and that the total number of Irish MPs accounted for about one sixth of the membership of the House of Commons. In the 1880s the Irish question could not be ignored; indeed, more than social reform or anything else debated in Parliament, Ireland was the pressing question of the day. In this respect, let us bear in mind that while there was not a single socialist or independent Labour MP in Parliament in 1885, there were as many as eighty-six Irish nationalists. Even within the *British* electorate, mass immigration from Ireland from the 1840s meant that the Irish comprised a sizeable proportion of working-class voters in many constituencies – a well-organised minority which could affect election results in marginal seats. It is also important to observe that, in radical circles, sympathy for home rule went back to 1874, when several prominent radical leaders – including the two Lib-Lab MPs – first expressed their support for the idea. In fact, Gladstone himself, far from being 'converted' to home rule at the end of 1885, had been thinking about it for years – from as early as 1877 or 1882.[10]

Thus, if it is true that the announcement of Gladstone's adoption of home rule came as a surprise to many party members and supporters, it was one which delighted those who had already come to regard it as the only alternative to coercion. The use of more severe and widespread measures of coercion by the Liberal government of 1880 in the vain attempt to preserve law and order in Ireland was both politically embarrassing and seemed to indicate that the Irish problem was not simply political, but constitutional and systemic, suggesting that the centralised parliamentary system on which the United Kingdom was based was fundamentally inconsistent with liberalism. By 1885 Gladstone and many others became convinced that there was no alternative to home rule.

Were there alternatives? In terms of imperial government, despite land reform, the situation in Ireland was not getting any better, with mounting rural outrage and the violently anti-English 'Gaelic' revival. It was safer to grant limited self-government than to resist the demands of Parnell's National Party, which was the moderate alternative to revolutionary Fenianism. In party political terms, it may also be wondered whether, had home rule not been adopted by the Liberal Party, it would have become the rallying point of the radical left under Joseph Cowen and Keir Hardie, including the Social Democratic Federation and from 1893 the Independent Labour Party. Although this is a counterfactual on which it would not be profitable for the historian to dwell, we know that between 1881 and 1885 coercion had generated considerable resistance among Gladstone's followers in the country, and after 1887 Unionist coercion was the single most important factor in building up support for home rule.

Whatever the case, Gladstone had gradually reached the view that Ireland could only be effectively ruled through her own people. Only the timing was in question. This was eventually decided by the election of 1885, at which the overwhelming majority of the Irish electors voted for Parnell. However, while for Gladstone this was a vote for home rule, for the Whig leader Lord Hartington and even for some of the radicals, in particular Joseph Chamberlain and John Bright, it was little less than a rebellion on the scale of the one which had disrupted the United States in 1861–65, which should be resisted in the way President Lincoln had resisted the claims of the Confederacy. Hartington, Chamberlain and Bright felt that only the British Parliament could ultimately guarantee civil and religious liberty in a country like Ireland, which was deeply divided along sectarian and ethnic lines. In particular, they distrusted Parnell and his party, which had been prepared to encourage violence and unrest for years and was unlikely to behave better in future. Chamberlain, although in favour of local government, was concerned about the overall unity of the Kingdom and indeed the Empire. Furthermore, he and his allies were genuinely concerned about the fate of the Irish Protestant minority.

The latter was the single weakest point in Gladstone's scheme. He believed that in choosing the way in which Ireland should be governed, politicians ought to bear in mind the views of the local population. His main mistake was in dismissing the importance of Protestants in Ulster and the extent of their opposition to home rule. Over the next forty years this would become a major stumbling block for both Liberals and Irish Nationalists, reaching a climax in the agitation led by Sir Edward Carson in 1912–14.

There is no doubt that Gladstone did not want independence for Ireland any more than he did for India (despite the fact that Dadabhai Naoroji, the first Asian MP in 1892–95, was then trying to adapt Gladstonianism to Indian nationalist purposes). His aim was to make the Empire more flexible and less vulnerable to nationalist movements and easier to run by the traditional landed elite (which, in Ireland, was well represented by Parnell himself). Always hostile to 'metropolitan centralism', Gladstone believed that the United Kingdom should experiment with the strategy already implemented with the so-called 'white' colonies: representative devolution. Its success in Canada – a society which, like Ireland, was divided not only between Protestant and Catholics, but also between distinct language groups and opposed national histories – encouraged a similar experiment in Ireland.

Dadabhai Naoroji (1825–1917)

Dadabhai Naoroji was the UK's first Asian MP, sitting as a Liberal for Finsbury Central from 1892 to 1895. An Indian academic and Zoroastrian priest, he was a partner in the first Indian company to be established in the UK, in 1855, and founded his own cotton trading firm in 1859. He was also appointed Professor of Gujarati at University College, London. Naoroji founded the East India Association, which was a forerunner of the Indian National Congress and helped counter academic arguments in the 1860s that Asians were intrinsically inferior to Europeans.

Although he was based in the UK until 1907, Naoroji's political career spanned two continents. He was a prominent Indian politician in the 1870s and 1880s, serving as President of the Indian National Congress in 1886, 1893 and 1906. In 1885 he stood for election in Holborn but was defeated. Referring to this result three years later, Prime Minister Lord Salisbury said that: 'I doubt if we have yet got to the point where a British constituency will elect a black man', but he was proved wrong when Naoroji succeeded at Finsbury in 1892. He campaigned for a range of radical causes, including women's suffrage and temperance reform, but lost the seat in 1895.

Home rule became the single most important catalyst in the remaking of popular radicalism after the extension of the franchise to the county householders in 1884. The 1886

Home Rule Bill, together with the subsequent agitation and electoral campaigns, polarised British and Irish politics and the crisis created a new political awareness even among subjects – including women – who hitherto had been marginalised. Animosity and partisanship under the recently enlarged franchise stimulated the rise of the party machine and caucus politics. The latter had contrasting effects on popular radicalism – simultaneously increasing and limiting effective participation in national politics – but became an essential device of mass mobilisation in both Britain and Ireland.

At the beginning of the home rule crisis Chamberlain expressed the view that: 'in this great controversy there are three powerful influences all working in favour of the [sic] Gladstone's Bills'. These were: 'first ... the Liberal feeling in favour of self-government; the second is the impatience generally felt at the Irish question & the hope to be rid of it once for all; and the third is the tremendous personality of Mr Gladstone himself'. He concluded that the 'last of these three has had the greatest effect in causing Liberals to accept the proposals without careful personal investigation of them'.[11] Historians have tended to agree with him. By contrast, the present writer argues that, although Gladstone's charisma was significant in swaying many electors, the old radical preference for self-government was more important.

The radical understanding of liberty was rooted in participatory citizenship and democracy – which is what popular liberalism was primarily about – and involved government 'by the people' as well as 'for the people'. Thus for many radicals 'self-government' implied more than a set of elective local authorities deriving their legitimacy from a decision taken by a majority in the imperial parliament. It meant that government legitimacy depended on popular support, and that the latter's permanent withdrawal would result in the former's loss of legitimacy. It was on grounds of popular demand that the franchise and the electoral system of the United Kingdom had been reformed several times since 1832 – most recently in 1884–85. Now, if a large majority of the Irish electorate demanded further constitutional change, on what grounds could their demand be rejected? While the clash between Liberal Unionists and Liberal home rulers was a conflict between parliamentary and popular sovereignty, reports about the suspension of civil liberties in Ireland reawakened memories of past persecution and discrimination among British Nonconformists, who had long been at the receiving end of parliamentary sovereignty in a non-democratic society.

This went together with a deeper transformation in the meaning of liberalism, which, from a creed of free market economics and moderate constitutional reforms became increasingly dominated by a concern for human rights. It was a transformation that was to pave the way both for the New Liberalism and for twentieth-century understanding of international law. Gladstone played a key role in propelling the first stages of such change, in particular during the 1876 Bulgarian agitation and his 1879 Midlothian campaign. His redefinition of Liberal foreign policy as the politics of humanitarianism (in the third Midlothian speech) was not welcomed by the parliamentary party – and especially not by Whig front-benchers such as Lord Hartington. However, activists in the country revelled in the sense that the party stood for 'righteousness' and 'truth'. The notion that 'justice' was the only principle which would ensure both civil freedom and political stability had wide-ranging implications and was obviously relevant in Ireland. In 1886 Gladstone believed that he could mobilise the electorate by linking the Irish cause to the broader politics of humanitarianism; home rule, he claimed, was the only alternative to coercion and the permanent suspension of civil liberties.

Indeed, between 1886 and 1893 the connection between liberty and home rule developed into an article of faith among the Liberal rank and file, a moral crusade which empowered new and emerging groups of activists – such as women – although it lost a sizeable number of less politically aware voters to the Liberal Party. The NLF played an important role in this, by organising a number of political demonstrations in 1886 and 1887 in which a close link was established between home rule and the reforms desired in the various regions of the United Kingdom, and especially in the traditional Liberal strongholds. In other words, the NLF adapted radical policies to build enthusiasm for home rule. In this way a synergy was created whereby home rule came to stand for further steps towards democracy, not only in Ireland but within the United Kingdom as a whole. These involved the abolition of the legislative power of the House of Lords, the reform of the registration laws, one man one vote, full religious equality (or at least the disestablishment of the Church in Wales and of the Church of Scotland), land reform, taxation of ground rents and mining royalties, and better housing for the working classes. In the process the Liberal Party developed an increasingly democratic outlook and programme, culminating with the adoption of the Newcastle Programme by the NLF in 1891.

The Newcastle Programme

The Newcastle Programme was a set of policy proposals agreed at the annual meeting of the National Liberal Federation at Newcastle-upon-Tyne in 1891. It included compulsory powers for local authorities to acquire land, rating reform, proposals to enable agricultural workers to become small-scale tenants, disestablishment of both the Welsh and Scottish Churches, and a localised prohibition on the sale of alcohol.

The most well-developed ideas in the Newcastle Programme concerned electoral reform. Popularly elected district and parish councils were advocated, along with faster electoral registration for those that moved home and the payment of MPs in order to encourage more from working-class backgrounds. Finally, proposals to change death duties, limit working hours and make employers liable for accidents to employees were also included.

The development and publication of the programme reflected concern that the Liberal Party needed to broaden its appeal following several years in which debate within the party had focused principally on home rule. It also marked a further stage in the evolution of mass party politics, although the extent to which the programme was binding on a Liberal government was debatable. Some of the programme's proposals were put into effect by the 1892 Liberal government, including those relating to employ-er's liability, district councils and death duties, but others were not, either because of the weaknesses of the 1892–95 government or the party leadership's lack of enthusiasm for particular measures.

Thus, as the years went by, the prolonged home rule crisis consolidated new identi-ties, political cultures and party allegiances. Politics became concerned less with local issues than with a national debate. Traditionally, historians have stressed the 'negative', anti-British dimension of Parnellism, and have dismissed Irish liberalism as a dwindling Unionist pressure group. Yet, when the language and demands of Parnell's Irish National League are studied in their own terms and context, what is most striking is the ideologi-cal and cultural ground shared by rank-and-file Irish nationalism with British popular liberalism, especially in the Scottish Highlands and in North Wales. They all insisted on civil rights under the 'constitution', praised responsible local government in contrast to central control, and were against militarised police forces and coercion laws. Moreover, they all included a strong Christian dimension and an affinity with Gladstone's 'ethical' foreign policy.

By the late 1880s home rule for Scotland and Ireland was part of a broader pro-gramme for a federal reconstruction of the United Kingdom. Such a programme was vocally supported by the Scottish Home Rule Association with increasingly separatist undertones. In 1892 James Reith, its secretary, proposed to the Irish Nationalist leader Edward Blake the formation of a 'Joint Parliamentary Party of the Representation of Scotland, Ireland and Wales' to demand 'Home Rule All Round' as the only just solution to the home rule question.[12]

The National Liberal Federation and internal party democracy

When Joseph Chamberlain formed the Liberal Unionist party, not a single constituency organisation, save in Birmingham, rejected a Gladstonian candidate.[13] The decision to endorse Gladstone's home rule policy was a turning point in the history of the NLF, for it was only then that the NLF became a focal point for Gladstonian loyalism.

The number of federated Liberal associations increased after 1886 and not just because of the increase in the number of constituencies after the adoption of the single-member system in 1885. The sheer enthusiasm that the party continued to inspire and the determined effort on the side of the leadership to strengthen the organisation was also important; by 1890 there were 850 federated associations. Furthermore, the secession of most of the Whigs cleared the way for the NLF to blossom as a power within the party as a whole. On the one hand, it forced the party further to develop its electoral machine in order to compensate for the loss of the Whigs' wealth, patronage and influence. On the other, it purged the party of most of its non-radical components, thus increas-ing the scope for the adoption of those policies with which the NLF was identified.

These developments reached their climax during the years 1888–95. For the first time the rank and file of a major party was able to challenge not only the system of aristocratic patronage at constituency level, but also the authority of its leaders in Parliament, and claimed the right to define party policy and priorities.

Yet the relationship with the party leaders remained ambiguous, with the NLF asserting both its loyalty and its independence, and indeed sovereignty, as a policy-making body. Such ambiguity was a reflection of the way in which the party machine had developed during its early years. By contrast with the intellectual debate generated by the NLF from the 1880s, there was little theoretical preparation for its establishment in 1877. No blueprint had been drawn up by 'the lights of liberalism'. Even John Stuart Mill had been comparatively silent on the question of mass party politics. This omission is somewhat surprising when we consider that during his lifetime there flourished well-organised pressure groups, including the National Education League, with which he was well acquainted, and the Land Tenure Reform Association, of which he was a member. The NLF, launched only four years after Mill's death, drew heavily on the experience of such leagues and associations, some of which it tried to co-ordinate.

The NLF's constitution was based on a form of direct democracy, which sat uneasily with the relationship between the Liberal leadership, Liberal MPs and their electors in the constituencies. It was frequently amended, often with important consequences for the party's identity. Indeed, the constitution was significantly redrafted at least sixteen times between 1877 and 1935. There were major changes in 1880, 1885, 1886, 1887, 1890, annually between 1895 and 1897, and more drastically at various stages between 1903 and 1907. Though the ultimate aim was to reorganise the party as a whole on a federal, representative basis, the means of achieving this result were not specified by the constitution. Nor was it clear how it would affect the internal authority structure as between the parliamentary party and the leader on the one hand, and the mass party on the other. By contrast, the political aims of mass agitation were discussed in detail – thus creating a situation in which the party Assembly generated policies which the parliamentary party was not prepared to implement.

From the beginning, the NLF had given rise to misgivings among both rank and file and national leaders, though for different reasons. The then party leader, Lord Hartington, far from welcoming the new development, rightly saw it as a challenge from the periphery to the power at the centre. Moreover, many MPs and candidates feared that their 'independence' was now being threatened in the constituencies, having already been curtailed at Westminster. Critics of the NLF included several working-class leaders and their supporters, who complained that the 'caucus' was an exclusive, elitist device which destroyed the 'open' system of the traditional 'constitution' and the 'independence' of the electors.

'Independence' seemed to be what Liberals were most concerned about. Not only were MPs jealous of their right to vote according to conviction, sometimes against the wishes of their leaders and constituents, but also local Liberal associations were keen to safeguard their own freedom from interference by the Whips. Furthermore, Liberal activists and voters in general were jealous of their own independence from local associations or anybody else.

On the other hand, both critics and supporters of the 'caucus' tended to exaggerate its effectiveness. Far from being a leviathan, the new organisation was often chaotic, possessed an insufficient professional bureaucratic structure which would have been essential to allow prolonged political effort, and relied instead on voluntary workers and the support offered by social and religious groups on the basis of local allegiances.

The weakness of the 'machine' was compounded by the fact that the NLF as a whole was financially independent of the Liberal Central Association. This arrangement had two consequences: on the one hand, it meant that the Whips had little institutional influence over the mass party, a restriction which was indeed a matter of pride for the NLF. It also implied that the financial resources of the NLF were severely limited, however, and this affected its performance as an electoral organisation. In the long run, real problems were to arise not from the efficiency of the mass party and its allegedly coercive powers, but from its endemic anarchy and ineffectiveness. Liberal localism was a questionable asset to the party's electoral performance and prospects. It meant, for instance, that the NLF was unable to control candidatures, a fact that frustrated attempts to accommodate trade union demands for political recognition, and arguably contributed to hastening the rise of independent Labour politics.

Yet, from the beginning the NLF did have a working-class component, both in terms of individual membership and corporate representation on the executives of federated caucuses. In 1886 the NLF vice-presidents included Lib-Lab worthies such as Henry Broadhurst, Thomas Burt, William Crawford, Charles Fenwick, Benjamin Pickard, Joseph Arch, and even George Howell, who, only a few years earlier, had been one of the bitterest labour critics of the 'caucus'. In 1891 it was Thomas Burt, the Lib-Lab MP for Morpeth, who was chosen to deliver the welcome address to Gladstone at the commencement of the famous Newcastle meeting of the NLF. Moreover, in the areas where the trade union movement was strongest – such as in the coalfields of County Durham and the Rhondda – labour managed to 'colonise' the local Liberal (sometimes called 'Liberal and Labour') associations. This resulted in the formation of trade union caucuses, which dominated local Liberal Party councils with their block vote, and which can be seen as early experiments in what would become the constitutional framework and 'machine' of post-1918 Labour politics. These were important developments, but they took place not because of but *despite* the efforts of the Liberal associations directly involved, and independently of the NLF. The latter was ready to bestow honours on those representatives who were already successful anyway – a strategy amounting to little more than laissez-faire in the politics of party organisation. It was inadequate for what the labour movement needed, which was a political machine which would actively foster working-class interests and a wider 'direct' parliamentary representation of the trade unions.

Lib-Labs

Lib-Labs were a distinct group in the Parliamentary Liberal Party from a working-class and trade union background. Whilst accepting the Liberal whip they exercised the right to utilise their experience to speak freely about labour issues.

The first Lib-Lab MPs were Thomas Burt and Alexander Macdonald, elected in 1874. By 1898 there were eleven Lib-Lab MPs though thereafter the growth in their numbers was stilted by the establishment of the Labour Party. By 1910 the majority of Lib-Lab MPs had aligned themselves with Labour, although the latter had not yet developed a distinct identity or ideology, and was little more than 'a cork on the Liberal tide', as George Bernard Shaw described it in 1906.

Besides antagonising frustrated labour Liberals, and thus reducing the electoral effectiveness of the organisation, the NLF's passion for decentralisation also hampered the formulation of coherent policies based on broad strategies. It did not help the party to deal with 'faddism', one of the problems which the Federation had set out to solve in the first place. While all interests were freely voiced, Liberal energies could only be focused on a single long-term effort when either a charismatic leader took charge (as happened, in 1886–94, with Irish home rule, under Gladstone) or when a spontaneous rising of the rank and file occurred to defend some threatened Liberal dogma (as in 1903–06 with free trade). It seems that members realised that they *needed* a charismatic leader for the Federation to be effective, for they endeavoured to become a sounding board for Gladstone even when they effectively tried to push him beyond Gladstonian Liberalism.[14]

The novelty of the NLF lay in the adoption of the principle of rank-and-file sovereignty by a party whose primary expression remained the parliamentary group. But one of the problems with internal democracy was that – being based on unrealistically high expectations of popular participation – it represented only party activists. With a few exceptions such as Birmingham, the claim that the caucus was the forum for popular Liberalism was rather inaccurate, in view of both the comparatively small size of the NLF and the fact that local Liberal associations were often resented, or even resisted, by working-class radicals.[15]

The years 1886–91 represented a very exciting period in the history of the NLF. Yet, as we have seen, in electoral terms the outcome of internal party democracy was disappointing. Despite victory at the 1892 election, the Newcastle Programme as such was unrealistically ambitious: it could not be implemented by any one government, and certainly not by Gladstone's fourth administration (1892–94), with its slim majority in the Commons and hopeless minority in the Lords. Later, the crushing electoral defeat of 1895 was regarded by some as an indication of the shortcomings of internal party democracy, and led to a new constitutional debate in 1895–97.

In 1895, in his addresses to the NLF Council, the new leader, Lord Rosebery, argued that the NLF should limit itself to thrashing out 'the various issues that lie before the

Liberal Party',[16] and thus leave policy-making to the parliamentary front bench and the Cabinet. This was the model of the mass party organisation as 'a great educational assembly' rather than a 'sovereign' body.[17] The revised constitution approved that year was a compromise between rank-and-file democracy and parliamentary centralism. It emphasised the principle of regional representation, but turned the NLF into the 'sounding board' for the leaders' rhetoric and for decisions taken elsewhere. In this way it institutionalised a tendency which, as we have seen, had emerged during Gladstone's last years. Under the new constitution, members were to be mere delegates, rather than representatives, and the Liberal MPs were now ex officio members of both the Council and the General Committee of the NLF. Since only a minority of the elected delegates either cared, or were able, to attend meetings,[18] MPs would constitute a sizeable proportion, especially of the General Committee. In conclusion, the proposed reforms implied a dramatic shift of the party's internal balance of power towards both the parliamentary party and the local notables and a major departure from the original NLF rhetoric of participatory citizenship and a 'Parliament outside the Imperial Parliament'.

It seemed as if the old dream of a free assembly ruling the Liberal Party had been abandoned. However, delegates thought otherwise, and continued to give a tough time to the party leaders throughout the period up to 1906. Despite their efforts to strengthen the hand of the parliamentary party, the post-Gladstone leadership was unable to prevent a three-way division of power between the party assembly (the NLF), the parliamentary party and the leader. This created a margin of uncertainty as to where ultimate legitimate authority rested. The party leader was not responsible to the representative assembly, though the latter could censure policies and MPs, thus embarrassing the leader and even jeopardising electoral prospects. Since the leader could exercise only limited control over the deliberations of the Council, this system encouraged radicalism without responsibility within the NLF. Before 1894 a constitutional impasse was avoided thanks to Gladstone's charisma, to which the NLF, like all other branches of popular Liberalism, was very responsive. In this sense Gladstone's rhetoric was neither a development from, nor a counterbalance to, the 'caucus' system; rather, the NLF was an instrument of Gladstone's style of political communication, and party unity was based on charismatic rhetoric.

While these were real problems from an electoral point of view, throughout the 1890s the NLF rank and file continued to raise concerns of a different character. They were worried about the accountability of the parliamentary party to the Council and a reduction of bureaucratic centralisation. Such demands showed the extent to which many members of the NLF wanted it to remain 'a Parliament outside Parliament', rather than to become a modern party machine. When Gladstone retired, R. B. Haldane and other younger leaders insisted that 'the future programme could not be fashioned by the officials of the National Liberal Federation, but only by a statesman with an outlook which was fresh and appreciative of this country as the centre of an Empire' – alluding to Rosebery.[19] Herbert Samuel told the 1897 Council that there were three ways forward for the NLF if they wanted 'to make that assembly the real parliament of the Liberal Party':

One was that there should be subordinate federations, which would discuss in provincial assemblies the various resolutions, and, after sifting them, send them up to the General Council. A second proposal was that they should do as the Trade Union Congress did, and sit a week for the discussion of the various questions in which they were interested; and the third proposal was that the assembly should, by some means, be split up into committees for the discussion of the various groups of questions that went to the formation of the programme of the party.[20]

The second alternative would have been consistent with the tradition of charismatic democracy; the third would have been the most innovative and democratic, as well as the closest to a more modern model of a political party. However, it is significant that it was the first one – the effective dismemberment of the Council in regional federations – which eventually triumphed, with the Herbert Gladstone reforms at the turn of the century. Such a solution favoured concerns of 'representation' and direct participation over those of national debate and rank-and-file control over the party. Members would be better able to 'voice' their views; however, the NLF became less able to influence the parliamentary party and the programme. Effectively, it was deprived of a national voice, and made more similar to the mass organisations of the Irish National Party, but without the electoral advantage they enjoyed – i.e. centralisation under decisive parliamentary leadership.

Liberal Imperialism and Liberal Unionism

When home rule split the Liberal Party, the radicals' main casualty was Joseph Chamberlain, but this was far from a fatal blow to the Liberals' commitment to social reform.[21] Although Chamberlain had long been the champion of social reform, for as long as the issue remained a matter of municipal competence there was little to divide him from Gladstone. The growth of local government was promoted by Gladstone through the 1870 Education Act, one of the most expensive domestic reforms adopted in nineteenth-century Britain. In addition, both supported 'retrenchment' in national expenditure; Chamberlain demanded strict economy in the areas for which the Treasury was directly responsible – mainly the army, navy and national debt – in order to free up resources for new social reforms.

Far more divisive were issues pertaining to Ireland and foreign and imperial policy, on which the Liberals *nearly* split in 1876–79 (over the UK's relationship with the Ottoman Empire) and1894–98 (over various colonial questions in Uganda and Sudan), and *actually* did so in 1886, 1899–1902 (Boer War) and finally in 1916–23. The clash was often presented as one between the majority of the Nonconformists (allegedly cosmopolitan and pacifists) and the more 'patriotically' minded Anglicans. In fact, the situation was far more complex. For example, the missionary zeal and hatred for the slave trade shared by all churches could easily foster imperial expansionism. Chamberlain was a further example of this complexity. Despite the fact that he was a dissenter by birth, his Unitarian politics did not emphasise peace, and indeed his family had made a fortune out of Britain's past wars. The Unitarians embraced utilitarianism and philosophical radicalism, traditions which prized individual liberty of judgement, and tended to scrutinise religious as well as social practices in the cold light of reason. In this respect, as Peter Marsh has pointed out, Chamberlain was the political heir to Joseph Priestley, the polymath founder of Unitarianism. For a Liberal, this heritage came with obvious benefits, but also a few *dis*advantages. Like the education of the young J. S. Mill (who also moved in Unitarian circles), Chamberlain's upbringing did not include a cultivation of the poetic imagination. The resulting emotional impoverishment cut him off from the other Dissenters, who were by then fired by evangelicalism, a powerfully emotional form of Christianity.

This is well exemplified by the events of 1876, when Chamberlain supported the Bulgarian agitation without sharing the emotions which played such an important role in mobilising Nonconformist support for Gladstone. To Chamberlain the agitation was not a 'moral crusade', but a matter of party politics in a situation in which – despite the claims of the Tory government – national interest was not really at stake. After the opening of the Suez Canal in 1869 and Disraeli's purchase of the Khedive's shares in the Canal Company in 1875, the Mediterranean kernel of British imperial defence had shifted from the Dardanelles to Suez. In apparent breach of Gladstone's 'Midlothian Principles', the Liberal government decided to invade Egypt in 1882. Chamberlain fully endorsed this policy and – unlike Gladstone – never changed his mind afterwards. British intervention, he claimed, would 'liberate' the Egyptian people, enable them to choose constitutional and representative forms of government, and, meanwhile, stop 'anarchy' and restore 'law and order'. These slogans were repeated from every Liberal platform and by most Liberal newspapers; Egypt's alleged lawlessness and the claim that it was swayed by a military dictatorship without popular support were offered as the supreme justification for liberal imperialism. Chamberlain claimed that Britain had a mission in the East but, as Gladstone knew well (and as was to become clear again in the twenty-first century) 'exporting western and beneficent [sic] institutions' to Muslim countries was not easy.[22]

The political priorities and idealism characterising the Liberal Party could justify imperialism, but did not help to preserve imperial control. British liberalism was concerned with civilisation, progress and individual liberty, which were supposed to be the essential prerequisites of self-government. For many radicals, the British government was justified in enforcing law and order, retrenchment and financial accountability on reluctant or corrupt subjects. It is remarkable that even J. S. Mill – who was an ardent supporter of national self-government – believed that countries such as India were not yet ready for representative institutions, let alone independence. He accepted the notion of a hierarchy of cultures within which 'inferior' ones should be trained for 'order and progress' by those which were 'superior'. Interestingly, he was prepared to apply this reasoning to the Europeans as well – for example, he suggested that in response to foreign despotic rule the Italians had recently emerged from anarchy and foreign domination as a united and independent country. For Mill's successors in the 1880s, including Chamberlain, Ireland and Egypt were cases in point. In both instances, irrespective of ethnic or religious differences, people needed to be *coerced* to be free.

Moreover, liberalism insisted on the normative concept of the 'public interest', which ought to be pursued relentlessly as the pinnacle of good government. Chamberlain agreed and often appealed to the 'public' interest to defend his views on municipal socialism, educational change and land reform. Certainly during the Egyptian crisis of 1882 he was eager to be perceived as standing up for the 'public' interest, in contrast to the 'sectional' concerns of the bondholders. He argued that there could be 'no doubt' that European control was in Egypt's public interest. The only question was whether this rational consideration should be allowed to overrule the Egyptian people's misguided and emotional inclination to prefer native administration with its 'corruption' and oppression, to the 'order', 'honesty' and individual rights which British rule would offer.

In the case of the Irish crisis from 1886, when Chamberlain stood for the union and abandoned the Gladstonians, his views were more complex, but relied on a similar logic: the priority of preserving law and order as a prerequisite of the 'common good', a concern for the liberty of all those who had been at the receiving end of agrarian terrorism and the rights of the Protestant minority in Ulster. He identified the 'Ulster Scots' as a distinct group within Ireland, a group with its own views and rights to self-determination. He was convinced that it was his duty as a Liberal to defend these rights against the home rule proposal, fearing that the latter, if implemented, would 'hand over' the Protestant Unionist minority, 'bound hand and foot', to a Dublin government staffed by former terrorists, law-breakers and quasi-anarchists. He played the anti-terrorist card very eloquently, and stressed the extent to which the party of the bomb, the enemy within, was not really Irish, but foreign and supported by a foreign conspiracy.

His fears for civil and religious liberty were compounded by his alarm at the fiscal and commercial implications of home rule: Ulster, 'industrious and prosperous' under the union, would be heavily taxed by the Dublin Parliament, which would introduce protectionism to benefit the backward agriculture of the south. His views were echoed by many contemporary observers whose life-long liberalism was now shaken by what the famous Cambridge historian Sir John Seeley regarded as Gladstone's betrayal of the basic values of the Liberal Party – namely, the preservation of personal liberty through the rule of law. Concern for minority rights and the defence of property was both publicly and privately voiced even by a few Gladstonian Liberals both in 1886 and 1892–93. Liberal Unionists reckoned that there was no future for Irish Protestant liberties without Britain, no future for the Irish economy outside the union, and no future for the United Kingdom if it allowed a noisy but insignificant minority of short-sighted farmers and self-interested politicians to break away at the periphery. National interest, individual liberty, the cause of economic progress in Ireland and the greatness of Britain in the world, all depended on the preservation of the union. While the Liberal Unionists agreed that there was still much to do in terms of removing grievances and reforming unjust laws, this could be done more speedily and more fairly by 'one united democracy as a first motive power, with a simple sense of justice springing from the bosom of the people'.[23] From this point of view, the Liberal Unionists were faithful to the tradition of the Liberal Party, while the Gladstonians were the real 'seceders'.[24]

If radical politics was now about improving the lot of the people through land reform and popular education, and if poverty was to be reduced – as Chamberlain had demanded in his 1885 'Unauthorised Programme' – then what was required, the Liberal Unionists argued, was not devolution, but the rational reconstruction and empowerment of the imperial executive at the centre. By contrast, home rule would degrade Ireland to the level of a 'colony', while simultaneously spreading the virus of disintegration throughout the Empire. This argument was perfectly consistent in its own terms and also consistent with the Anglo-American and European liberal traditions, which sought improvement by means of the consolidation of regions and provinces into larger and more economically feasible nations. Separatism, especially when it came with the request of special privileges for the Catholic church, was regarded as the very opposite of both nation-building and progress, especially in the Irish case, because, as the radical W. J. Linton (and Giuseppe Mazzini) had argued, Ireland was not a nation. The solution was not to be sought by placing Ireland and England on a footing of complete equality.

Viewed in this context, coercion was nothing more than the administration of deserved retribution to dangerous criminals, and the preservation of the rights of the honest portion of the people. Indeed, as an anonymous Irish Liberal claimed in a letter to *The Scotsman*, there was considerable hypocrisy in the Gladstonian outrage at government coercion: 'How is it that the coercion or punishment of criminals raises such pious horror in England and there is not a word of sympathy for the honest labourer, tradesman or farmer coerced grievously by the National League? (For, recollect, it is hardly the wealthy aristocrat that is boycotted.)'[25] While Gladstone's advocacy of home rule was denounced as necessarily conducive to parliamentary impotence and imperial disintegration, Lord Salisbury's readiness to accommodate Liberal demands between 1886 and 1892 – with the 1887 Land Act, the county councils in 1888 and free education in 1891 – was welcomed as the vindication of the principle behind the Liberal Unionist strategy: 'Liberal principles in legislation, by whomsoever they are carried out'.[26]

The impact of philosophical idealism

Whatever the case, in the 1890s social concerns such as 'the plight of the unemployed' and the need for further and more radical state intervention in social reform came to dominate both the Liberal Unionist and the Gladstonian camps. Simultaneously the old demand for the 'remission of taxation' now became a demand for a more equitable distribution of taxation, which, on the whole, was expected to increase. In 1892–95 Gladstone and Harcourt played an important role in this process, first by unsuccessfully trying to contain the increase in central government's expenditure, and then by stressing that, if expenditure was going to increase, taxation should be distributed in a socially equitable way.

This new phase in the development of Liberalism was exemplified by Sir William Harcourt in a speech in the House of Commons in 1893:[27]

> I believe the Prime Minister [Gladstone] and myself are the last representatives of the vanished creed [economy]. The saying has been attributed to me that everyone is a socialist now. I do not know whether I ever said that, but this I will say – there are no economists now … anyone who comes forward with a proposal for increased expenditure is welcome as if he had discovered a new pleasure. … Private members with large hearts and small responsibilities … desire that the State should undertake new duties, fresh responsibilities, larger expenditure. We are eager to create new empires here and annex fresh territories there … I belong myself, as I have said, to the old school, and I would gladly see less money spent, for I think a good deal of it is wasted. But, if I may reverse the old saying, I would say that those who call the tune must pay the piper.

It is not clear what 'socialism' or collectivism meant at the time, nor how these concepts were used by both Liberals and Liberal Unionists. For example, Chamberlain regarded himself as a 'socialist', but dismissed Marxism as 'collectivism' and hated class struggle. Chamberlain's 'collectivism' (or 'socialism') was an aspect of what was in reality his *anti*-socialist strategy, which insisted on nation-building and was partly inspired by the example of Bismarck's Imperial Germany. This strategy, which was shared by many Gladstonian Liberals of the younger generation, was certainly imperialist and saw both Britain and her overseas dominions as forming a natural unit or community. There was a close link between imperialism, social reform and increased taxation. For, although the increase in central government spending was partly due to 'grants in aid' to local authorities – to support free education, public works and other 'socialist' initiatives – it was largely caused by the increased demands of the military establishment necessary to sustain Britain's imperial role. Significantly it was not on social expenditure but on the ever-growing naval estimates that Gladstone chose to resign in 1894, while Harcourt stayed on and adopted a budget which, by introducing the principle of graduated taxation, became a milestone in the history of the British tax system.

These debates on imperialism and fiscal reform were accompanied by important transformations in the intellectual and philosophical landscape of British liberalism, which moved away from the old utilitarian individualism towards what we would nowadays describe as 'communitarianism'. In particular, the revival of Platonism, a growing interest in German idealism, the impact of social Darwinism and the continuing influence of Christianity all supported a tendency to regard society as an organism. The latter metaphor had obvious political implications. As the parts of an organism are mutually dependent and the value and definition of each part is derived from the whole, so the whole is in some ways different from the sum of its parts. Thus society was something more than the sum of the men and women who composed it. It was made up of individuals fashioned by their place within the whole, and, since society shaped the moral self, citizens should be devoted to the common good, in whose pursuit they could develop their uniquely human capacity for self-improvement. This was the essence of a moral organicism which brought into particular prominence the old Aristotelian notion that the key to ethical life was membership of a community, and that virtue was best cultivated within a social context.

From the 1850s Herbert Spencer had played an important and often neglected role in preparing the ground for liberal organicism. Many liberal idealists came to agree with him that, through an evolutionary process, society tended to encourage co-operation, altruism, responsibility and whatever else enhanced the common good. However, the idealists rejected Spencer's rational calculation of utility and argued that political obligation was rooted in the notion of the common good, which D. G. Ritchie, in *Natural Rights* (1890), defined as 'the highest development of individual capacities compatible with coherence and continuance of society as a whole'.

Herbert Spencer (1820–1903)

Herbert Spencer was born in Derby in 1820, the son of a Quaker with a passionate interest in science. Largely self-educated, he worked as a railway engineer before becoming a journalist with *The Economist*. His first book, *Social Statics*, was published in 1851 and by the 1860s he was recognised as one of the leading philosophers of the age. He was a polymath but he is best known for applying the evolutionary concepts being developed in scientific study by Charles Darwin and others to the study of society. He coined the phrase 'survival of the fittest' having read Darwin's *On the Origin of Species*.

Spencer regarded society as a living organism, with its own internal laws of development. He suggested that societies progressed from a primitive stage, where co-operation between individuals was limited, through military and industrial stages to a liberal utopia where the state withered away and individuals recognised that altruism and the recognition of mutual rights were in everyone's best interests. Initially regarded as a radical, he became disillusioned with Gladstone's Liberals, who he regarded as embracing socialistic principles which would entrench the state in society. He is regarded by some as a founder of modern libertarianism.

While this could be interpreted as implying that 'rights are the creation of society', the leading liberal idealist of the period, Thomas Hill Green, defended the individual's right to stand up against the state for the common good. Like the utilitarians, he dismissed the notion of 'natural' rights, if this meant rights which existed independent of social attachment. Instead, he saw rights as historical phenomena embodied in an increasingly wider range of social institutions, which defined the conditions under which moral action was possible.

Thomas Hill Green (1836–82)

Green was born in Yorkshire, where his father was a clergyman. He studied at Oxford and remained there as an academic until his early death. An English empiricist, his work provided a response to Spencer's utilitarianism. Green's key breakthrough was to show the positive role the state could play in enhancing liberties and, as such, he was the founding father of New Liberalism.

A product of the Oxford University system, Green exercised his influence on generations of Oxford students, including the likes of Asquith and Herbert Samuel. He was also an influence on Labour and social democrat politicians in the twentieth century. Green was active in Liberal politics in Oxford, speaking out on temperance reform and reform of the franchise.

While for Spencer liberty was simply the absence of external impediments or restraints, to Green it was a 'positive power or capacity of enjoying, and that, too, something which we enjoy in common with others'. Indeed, the removal of external restraints to individual action did not constitute an adequate liberal strategy because there was no guarantee that the opportunities thus created would be used for worthwhile purposes. Thus social and legal control of individual momentary decisions might be necessary. This was best exemplified by temperance legislation, which Green – like many other liberals at the time – supported on the principle that:

> until the English people were a sober people they could not be a free people. He should like to consider the word 'freedom'. If it was doing exactly what a person pleased ... then all he could say was, if that was the sort of freedom they desired they must go back to the naked savage in order to find it. By freedom he meant every man to make the most of himself, to turn to the best account all the talents and capabilities God had given him. Only in that sense was freedom worth having.[28]

While, Green argued, excessive supervision of a paternalistic kind should be avoided because it might hamper individual self-development and stultify initiative and responsibility, society should create an environment in which it was more feasible for all citizens to pursue a moral course of action. The province of law concerns whatever 'is really necessary to the maintenance of the material conditions essential to the existence and perfection of humanity'.

Thus, Green's notion of liberty had strong 'positive' connotations. Far from focusing on the removal of external constraints it was about 'the liberation of the powers of all men equally for contributions to a common good'[29] – or the power to realise those capabilities, which were part of humanity. He wanted to foster conditions under which the formation of intelligent patriots would be possible – by this meaning citizens aware of their duties and social obligations as well as their rights. His strategy centred on democracy and participatory citizenship, which would strengthen the connection between obedience to the law and freedom in a politically significant way. This applied not only to all men, but to women too, and, consistently, Green and his wife co-operated to increase the sphere of women's participation in the 'public sphere' chiefly through local government and the opening up of Oxford education to women students.

The other great pioneer of new liberal thinking in these years was the Cambridge economist Alfred Marshall, whose reputation and prestige in the period 1880–1914 was comparable to that J. S. Mill had enjoyed earlier in the century. Mill and Marshall shared considerable common ground, including a deep conviction that a liberal state – and indeed, a liberal social and economic system – required active participatory citizenship. Even more openly than Mill, Marshall conceived of social improvement as a process to be kept under the close supervision of the intellectual elite. He was concerned to educate his students to go forth and improve the world outside the university. As he said in his inaugural lecture as Professor of Political Economy at Cambridge, in 1885, 'it will be my cherished ambition ... to increase the number of those, whom Cambridge ... sends out into the world with cool heads and warm hearts willing to give some at least of their best powers to grappling with the social suffering around them'.[30] Like Mill and Green, Marshall – at least in his early career – conceived of this elite as one comprising both men and women. Thus, from 1873 Marshall was involved in the movement for university reform, with the aim of opening up Cambridge to women.

Alfred Marshall (1842–1924)

Alfred Marshall was perhaps the founder of modern economics; his theoretical work underpinned political economy for decades. Marshall hailed from a London middle-class family of strong Anglican evangelical traditions. Like T. H. Green, Marshall lost his faith but attained both an evangelical-style concern for the poor and a puritanical drive to change things.

Marshall's *Principles of Economics* was published in 1890 and popularised the concepts of supply and demand as influencing individuals' economic decisions and, thus, wider macroeconomic questions. Capable of expressing complex ideas in an accessible form, and a respected teacher at Cambridge, Marshall's well-disguised unorthodoxy was highly influential. Although believing that private gain was necessary for industrial progress, Marshall argued that the enormous fortunes accrued by successful men and passed to their children were likely to hold back economic growth in the long run. He thus supported taxes levied on the rich, especially graduated death duties, to provide a good and varied education and open air recreation for working-class children – who might do more in open competition to increase the national wealth than less motivated inheritors.

Marshall also argued against the idea that unemployment reflected the existence of a class of 'idle poor', instead suggesting that it was a symptom of structural problems with the economy which the state could seek to overcome. A social reformer, he was no socialist; he believed that continuous economic growth was possible and would solve social problems. Like Green, Marshall postulated that ignorance was the main cause of both crime and pauperism. In contrast, cultivated people would be morally, intellectually and socially 'superior', as well as civically aware, socially useful, and economically efficient. Most importantly, Marshall's emphasis was ultimately on a new kind of fuller citizenship, which included *social* rights and duties, as well as political ones.

In Marshall's view, civic virtue and participatory citizenship should be fostered by state intervention as well as the operation of various voluntary institutions sustaining what nowadays we would call 'civil society'. In particular, Marshall praised both the Charity Organisation Society, which mobilised middle-class human and financial resources, and the trade unions, which trained the workers 'to sacrifice individual interests for a common object ... to bind [themselves] to treaties and adhere to them'. The latter generated a discipline which in itself was a first step towards the transformation of manual work and all forms of labour into meaningful expressions of the human personality. Such 'professionalisation' of labour would make it consistent with the mindset of an industrious gentleman: 'The question is not whether all men will ultimately be equal – that they certainly will not – but whether progress may not go on steadily if slowly, till the official distinction between working man and gentleman has passed away'. *Working*-men could become *gentle*-men; to Marshall this was not a utopia, but a forecast.[31]

In this sense Mill and Marshall really belonged to two different eras. Marshall emphasised moralised capitalism based on evolution as a central explanatory mechanism. He was thus able to escape the problem that had so baffled Mill – that is, how would men be persuaded to strive for the 'higher' rather than the 'lower' pleasures? For Marshall history itself solved the problem; like Herbert Spencer, he saw in history a transition from self-interest to self-sacrifice and altruism. Marshall's study of ethics led him to economics, which he saw first of all as the study of poverty and its remedies. Marshall's writings mapped the delicate period of transition from the mid-Victorian Liberals' laissez-faire optimism to various experiments in state intervention and public control, and eventually the welfare state.

Although Marshall and Green justified a growing role for the state in social reform, there is no evidence to suggest that either of them abandoned liberalism for socialism. Their collectivist tendencies are rather to be explained in terms of their defence of participatory citizenship. Though Herbert Spencer and many others were deeply upset by this development of collectivist rhetoric, they were wrong in fearing that liberal philosophy was losing its individualism. For these forerunners of the 'New Liberalism' rejected Spencer's own brand of democratic individualism, and retained a firm commitment to older 'aristocratic' values.[32] Indeed, one might conclude, there was an elitist and deeply individualist component in their concern for social justice. It can, of course, be argued that the Liberals helped to shore up the capitalist system, but they also contributed to its radical reform, and ensured that in its operation it would be more humane and more compatible with classical notions of citizenship and human development. As this was what Mill, Marshall and Green hoped to achieve, one has to conclude that their efforts were – in the end – largely successful.

Further reading

There is a wealth of further reading on this period in the history of the Liberal Party and on the themes covered in this chapter. The best survey of the political history of this period is Martin Pugh, *The Making of Modern British Politics, 1867–1945* (Wiley-Blackwell, 2002), and the best introduction is G. R. Searle, *The Liberal Party; Triumph and Disintegration, 1886–1929* (Palgrave, 2nd edn, 2001), but see also Michael Bentley, *The Climax of Liberal Politics, 1868–1918* (Edward Arnold, 1987).

D. A. Hamer is the author of two important works which analyse 'high' and 'low' Liberal politics in the 1880s and 1890s: *Liberal Politics in the Age of Gladstone and Rosebery: a Study in Leadership and Policy* (Clarendon Press, 1972) and *The Politics of Electoral Pressure: a Study in the History of Victorian Reform Agitations* (Harvester Press, 1977). The latter is still the most important work on Liberal pressure groups, such as the United Kingdom Alliance (temperance) and the Liberation Society (separation between church and state).

The politics of the Nonconformists – so important for liberalism throughout the nineteenth and early twentieth centuries – are best discussed in D. W. Bebbington's indispensable *The Nonconformist Conscience: Chapel and Politics 1870–1914* (HarperCollins, 1982) and James Munson, *The Nonconformists: in Search of a Lost Culture* (SPCK, 1991). On popular liberalism, the Lib-Labs and Gladstone's magnetic appeal to working-class and Nonconformist culture see Eugenio Biagini and Alistair Reid (eds.), *Currents of Radicalism* (CUP, 1991) and Eugenio Biagini's systematic work *Liberty, Retrenchment and Reform: Popular Liberalism in the Age of Gladstone 1860–80* (CUP 1992 and 2004). The reforms of 1884–85 extended the franchise to the county householders: some of the new challenges and opportunities which this created are examined in Patricia Lynch, *The Liberal Party in Rural England* (OUP, 2003), as well as in Chapter 6 of Biagini's *Liberty, Retrenchment and Reform*.

The question of Irish home rule and its impact on both British and Irish liberalism has been the subject of a considerable number of studies: the context is presented in Alvin Jackson's masterly *Home Rule: An Irish History 1800–2000* (OUP, 2003). W. C. Lubenow, *Parliamentary Politics and the Home Rule Crisis: the British House of Commons in 1886* (Clarendon Press, 1988) is the best work on how the question affected the parties at Westminster; among other things. For the impact of the home rule debate on Liberal politics and culture see Patricia Jalland, *The Liberals and Ireland: the Ulster Problem in British Politics to 1914* (Gregg Revivals, 1993) and James Loughlin, *Gladstone, Home Rule and the Irish Question 1882–93* (Macmillan, 1986). On the impact of the crisis on Liberalism and the NLF see Michael Barker, *Gladstone and Radicalism, 1886–1894* (Harvester Press, 1975) and Eugenio Biagini, *Ireland and the British Nation: Home Rule and the remaking of popular radicalism in the British Isles, 1876–1900* (CUP, 2007) – the latter focusing on popular politics, the significance of women and the politics of humanitarianism as a central dimension of modern liberalism.

The best work on Gladstone is H. C. G. Matthew's two-volume study *Gladstone, 1809–74* (Clarendon Press, 1986) and *Gladstone, 1875–98* (OUP, 1995). The statesman's intellectual development is analysed in D. W. Bebbington's fundamental *The Mind of Gladstone* (OUP, 2004). Roy Jenkins, *Gladstone* (Macmillan, 1995) is a 'popular' biography, but a very good one. On Chamberlain, the best work is Peter Marsh, *Joseph Chamberlain: Entrepreneur in Politics* (Yale University Press, 1994). On Lord Hartington, there are important insights in Jonathan Parry, *The Rise and Fall of Liberal Government in Victorian Britain* (Yale University Press, 1993).

For the development of Liberals after Gladstone and the evolution of a new social reform agenda, see H. C. G. Matthew, *The Liberal Imperialists* (Clarendon Press, 1973). The origins of the New Liberalism has inspired a substantial number of publications, including I. M. Greengarten, *Thomas Hill Green and the Development of Liberal Democratic Thought* (University of Toronto Press, 1981), Sandra Den Otter, *British Idealism and Social Explanation* (Clarendon Press, 1996), Stefan Collini, *Liberalism and Sociology: L. T. Hobhouse and Political Argument in England, 1880–1914* (CUP, 1979), and David Boucher (ed.), *The British idealists* (CUP, 1997). On the later development of the New Liberalism see Michael Freeden, *The New Liberalism* (Clarendon Press, 1978), and especially the fundamental works by Peter Clarke, *Lancashire and the New Liberalism* (CUP, 1971) and *Liberals and Social Democrats* (CUP, 1978).

Notes

1 19 March 1894, in H. C. G. Matthew (ed.), *The Gladstone Diaries*, vol.13 (OUP, 1994), p. 402.

2 Peter Stansky, *Ambitions and Strategies: The struggle for the leadership of the Liberal Party in the 1890s* (Clarendon Press, 1964), p. 7 n.

3 Leo McKinstry, *Rosebery: Statesman in Turmoil* (John Murray, 2005) pp. 328–31, 381–82.

4 Eugenio Biagini, *Ireland and the British Nation: Populism and democracy in the Home Rule crisis, 1874–1906* (CUP, 2007).

5 John Wilson, *C.B. – A life of Sir Henry Campbell-Bannerman* (Constable, 1973).

6 See Peter Cain, *Hobson and Imperialism: Radicalism, New Liberalism and Finance 1887–1938* (OUP, 2002).

7 *Liberal Year Book 1889*, p. 96.

8 Georgina Battiscombe, *Mrs Gladstone* (Constable, 1956), p. 210.

9 A. B. Cooke and John Vincent, *The Governing Passion* (Harvester Press, 1974) and R. T. Shannon, *Gladstone, Vol. 2, Heroic Minister* (Penguin, 1999).

10 Eugenio Biagini, *Gladstone* (St Martin's Press, 2000), pp. 98–99.

11 Joseph Chamberlain to Thomas Gee, 26 April 1886, National Library of Wales, T.Gee MSS, 8305D, 15a.

12 James Reith to Edward Blake, 9 August 1892, in National Archives, Dublin, Blake Letters, [221] 4684. Enclosed with the letter Reith sent an 'Outline of a Federal Union League for the British Empire'.

13 W. C. Lubenow, *Parliamentary Politics and the Home Rule Crisis. The British House of Commons in 1886* (Clarendon Press, 1988), p. 246.

14 For Gladstone's charismatic power see Eugenio Biagini, *Liberty, Retrenchment and Reform: Popular liberalism in the age of Gladstone, 1860–1880* (CUP, 1992 and 2004 (paperback)), Chapter 7.

15 Joseph Chamberlain, 'A New Political Organisation', *Fortnightly Review*, n.s., XXII (July 1877) p. 126.

16 Proceedings of the Annual Meeting, Portsmouth, 13–14 February 1895, p. 111 in NLF Annual Reports. Cf. also Rosebery's speech in Proceedings of the Annual Meeting, Huddersfield, 26 March 1896, pp. 109–10 in NLF Annual Reports.

17 William Harcourt, in Proceedings of the Annual Meeting of the Council, Manchester, 3 December 1889, p. 120 in NLF Annual Reports.

18 For concerns about attendance see ibid., pp. 35–36.

19 R. B. Haldane, *An Autobiography* (Hodder and Stoughton, 1929), p. 100.

20 NLF Annual Report 1897, pp. 78–79.

21 In general, as Parry and others have argued, in Victorian Britain social reform was not politically controversial; see Jonathan Parry, *Democracy and Religion* (CUP, 1986).

22 Gladstone to Lord Rosebery, 15 November 1883, in *Gladstone Diaries*, vol. 11, p. 59.

23 Letter by a 'A Scottish Workman' to *The Scotsman*, 28 June 1886, p. 10.

24 For example, see the address by Lord Hartington to a meeting of Liberal Unionists in Glasgow, *The Northern Whig*, 26 June 1886, p. 5.

25 Letter by 'An Irish Radical', *The Scotsman*, 29 April 1886, p. 7.

26 Leading article, 'The session and the Union', *Lloyd's Weekly*, 24 July 1887, p. 1.

27 Chancellor of the Exchequer Sir William Harcourt in the House of Commons, 24 April 1893, cit. in A. G. Gardiner, *The Life of Sir William Harcourt*, Vol. 2 (Constable, 1923), p. 231.

28 T. H. Green, *The Oxford Chronicle*, 13 March 1875, p. 6.

29 T. H. Green, 'Liberal legislation', *Collected Works of Thomas Hill Green*, vol. 3 (Continuum, 1997), p. 372.

30 Cit. in Peter Groenewegen, *A Soaring Eagle: Alfred Marshall 1832–1924* (Edward Elgar, 1998), p. 311.

31 Alfred Marshall, 'The future of the working classes' (1873) in Tiziano Raffaeli, Eugenio Biagini and Rita McWilliams Tullberg (eds.), *Alfred Marshall's Lectures to Women* (Edward Elgar, 1995), pp. 156–75.

32 See Peregrine Worsthorne, *In Defence of Aristocracy* (HarperCollins, 2004).

Chapter 5

The Triumph of the New Liberalism (1899–1914)

Martin Pugh

The origins of the New Liberalism

At the disastrous general election of 1895 the Liberals won a mere 177 seats, and despite a subsequent by-election revival the 1900 election saw only a slight improvement to 183. These dismal results underlined the point that since the Liberal split over home rule in 1886 the mood of politics had turned against the party. In particular, the brief and frustrating ministries led by Gladstone and Lord Rosebery between 1892 and 1895 had undermined the Liberals' credibility among voters who looked to them to deliver domestic reforms. Since the 1880s many of the party's financial backers had left and the organisation in the country had dwindled, with the result that many Tory seats were left uncontested; even in 1900 only 406 Liberal candidates stood for 670 seats. Some Liberals blamed Gladstone for alienating moderate, middle-class voters to appease the 'faddists' and home rulers: 'Mr G. thoroughly demoralised the Liberal Party by the policy of sop-throwing in the years before 1892', wrote Richard Haldane.[1]

1900 general election (25 September – 24 October)			
	Votes	*%*	*MPs*
Liberal	1,572,323	44.6	183
Conservative and Liberal Unionist	**1,767,958**	**50.2**	**402**
Labour	62,698	1.8	2
Irish Parliamentary	91,055	2.6	77
Others	29,448	0.8	6
Total	*3,523,482*		*670*

Although with Gladstone in retirement home rule, which was increasingly regarded as an electoral handicap, lost its centrality in Liberal politics, his successors, Rosebery (1894–96), Sir William Harcourt (1896–99) and Sir Henry Campbell-Bannerman (1899–1908) proved largely unable to give the party a fresh sense of purpose. Younger Liberals, including Charles Trevelyan, Herbert Samuel and Walter Runciman, regarded the leading parliamentarians with despair. 'Neither Harcourtian iconoclastic crusades nor Roseberian grand panjandrum secretiveness will do any good', complained Trevelyan.[2]

Nor did he see much prospect of a social reform programme from the National Liberal Federation which was 'merely reiterating its approval of the Newcastle Programme'.

However, the Liberals used their lengthy periods in opposition to re-evaluate the ideas and programme of the party. This process was more obvious at local than at parliamentary level. The Progressive (in effect, Liberal) majority on the London County Council adopted innovatory policies including the direct employment of labour on conditions agreed with the trade unions. Several councils experimented with free school meals for schoolchildren. In the north many poor law boards offered outdoor relief to deserving elderly people – tantamount to paying an old age pension. The abolition of property qualifications for poor law guardians in 1894 also helped to widen the recruitment of guardians to include many more women and working men, who often adopted a wider view of their responsibilities. This pattern of experimentation with collectivist social policies locally was strengthened by the revelations about the extent of urban poverty in Britain in studies by Charles Booth and B. S. Rowntree. Combined with setbacks in the Boer War (1899–1902) and threats to Britain's position abroad, their findings generated an obsession with 'national decadence' by the end of the decade; increasingly it was recognised that Britain's position as a great industrial and imperial power could not be sustained on the basis of an unhealthy, ill-educated population. But tackling the extensive weaknesses highlighted by Booth and Rowntree was beyond the scope of local authorities, whose resources were limited by an archaic system of rates which fell heavily on householders with modest incomes. This situation clearly pointed to greater intervention by national government in social policy.

In rethinking the role of the state, the basis of national taxation and the relationship between the individual and society, late-Victorian Liberals felt torn in several directions, as did contemporary Conservatives and socialists. Some, following Herbert Spencer's liberalism, believed that maximising individual liberty implied reducing the role of the state. Increasingly, however, this view became associated with Lord Salisbury's Conservative Party. As set out in the preceding chapter, at Oxford the Liberal philosopher T. H. Green argued that collective action could serve to promote individual liberty, not restrict it. Liberals were already familiar with the idea of municipal control of utilities such as gas and water as more likely to serve the public interest than private ownership; it was a question of deciding where to draw the line. 'Laissez-faire is not done with as a principle of rational limitation of state interference', wrote J. M. Robertson, later MP for Wallsend, 'but it is quite done with as a pretext for leaving uncured deadly social evils which admit of curative treatment by state action'.[3]

The obvious objection to state intervention in social policy was that it meant higher taxes, which were assumed to be damaging to the economy and thus counter-productive; the uneven distribution of wealth and income was widely held to be desirable because it created a class of people capable of investing in industry and commerce. However, this was challenged by J. A. Hobson, who argued that the maldistribution had two unhelpful consequences: it led to excessive concentrations of surplus capital which stimulated imperialist expansion, and, by reducing consumption it weakened demand for the goods generated by industry. This put a fresh complexion on the traditional radical argument that certain forms of wealth, notably in land, could and should be taxed for the benefit of the community. The sharp rise in the value of land as a result of urban development and the spread of population strengthened the demand to tax what radicals called the 'unearned increment'. This was defended on the grounds that it did not involve the expropriation of wealth, but merely the collection of a fair share; the larger the income or size of an estate, the higher the tax levied upon it. In his famous budget of 1894 Harcourt had gone some way to putting this into effect by his scheme of graduated death duties.

J. A. Hobson (1858–1940)

Hobson was an author, journalist and lecturer who became a leading Liberal theorist and economist. In *Imperialism: A Study* (1902) he wrote that:

> The fallacy of the supposed inevitability of imperial expansion as a necessary outlet for progressive industry is now manifest. It is not industrial progress that demands the opening up of new markets and areas of investment, but mal-distribution of consuming power … If we may take the careful statistics of Mr Rowntree for our guide, we shall be aware that more than one-fourth of the population of our towns is living at a standard which is below bare physical effi-ciency. If, by some economic readjustment, the products which flow from the surplus saving of the rich to swell the overflow streams could be diverted so as to raise the incomes and the standard of consumption of this inefficient fourth, there would be no need for pushful Imperialism, and the cause of social reform would have won its greatest victory.[4]

In this way, although the New Liberalism did not amount to a precise programme, it began to reflect assumptions very different from those of the Conservatives: the state should undertake an obligation to maintain a minimum standard of life for its citizens; financial retrenchment and the repayment of the national debt were no longer the priorities of a Liberal government; and taxation should be shifted from taxes on expenditure to taxes on income and wealth. More generally, the advocates of New Liberalism were redefin-ing the scope of politics by moving beyond the moral, constitutional and religious issues that had been central to Victorian Liberalism to embrace social and economic questions. This represented a break with Gladstonian traditions though, as Liberals such as Herbert Samuel were keen to emphasise, there was continuity, too, in that New Liberalism sought to promote individual freedom by accepting that freedom had a material dimension.

Sir Herbert Samuel (1870–1963)

Samuel was a leading figure in the Liberal Party for over fifty years from its zenith before the First World War to the beginnings of its revival in the 1950s. A respected statesman, mediator and administrator, and notable intellectual, his term as Liberal leader from 1931 to 1935 was nevertheless calamitous.

He was born into a wealthy Jewish banking family from Liverpool and was able to live comfortably on his private income, dedicating himself to public service. He became active in progressive Liberal politics while still at Oxford in the 1890s and was involved in the Fabian–social-liberal 'Rainbow Circle'. His *Liberalism*, published in 1902, was one of the prominent works of the New Liberal wing of the party. In it he explained how New Liberalism had arisen:

> In the first place, the State itself has become more competent ... Now democracy has been substituted for aristocracy as the root principle of the constitution. Court influence and the grosser kinds of corruption have disappeared, efficient local authorities and an expert Civil Service have been created ... In the second place ... the social conscience was becoming more fully awake to the urgent need of improvement, and the inability of the laissez faire policy to bring it about was gradually becoming more plain ... the condition of the poorer classes seemed in many respects to be hardly at all the better ... Another influence was also at work. So far as questions of labour regulation were concerned, there was arising a new doctrine of the true meaning and the best guarantee of liberty. It was urged that legal restrictions might after all be made to extend rather than to limit freedom ... Because the law does not interfere with his actions a man is not necessarily free. There is economic restriction as well as legal restriction ... The State must intervene in the interest of liberty itself.[5]

Elected to Parliament in 1902, he was a leading progressive minister in the Asquith government and rose to the post of Home Secretary in 1916. He declined to serve under Lloyd George and lost his seat in the 1918 election.

A pro-Zionist, Samuel served as High Commissioner for Palestine in 1920–25. In 1926 he played a key role in mediating the deal that ended the General Strike, and as Lloyd George's head of organisation helped to reunite and revitalise the Liberals in the run-up to the 1929 general election. However, as leader from 1931 he was powerless to prevent the fragmentation and marginalisation of the Liberals, and lost his own seat in the 1935 election.

As Viscount Samuel he served as Liberal deputy leader (1937–44) and leader (1944–55) in the Lords, and into his eighties was still one of its most prominent public faces. Samuel's intellectual, rationalist approach to life and politics, his diligence and rather dry, uncharismatic personality did not inspire the voters. He was happiest writing philosophical studies, and for many years served as President of the Royal Institute of Philosophy.

Of course, the Liberal Party was by no means completely or suddenly captured either by the ideas or by the personnel of the New Liberalism; it was a gradual process right up to 1914. New Liberalism's agenda was promoted partly through pressure groups of intellectuals such as the Rainbow Circle,[6] which included Samuel, Hobson, Trevelyan and Robertson as well as several socialists, partly by the writings of journalist-politicians such as Charles Masterman, author of *The Heart of Empire* (1901), *From the Abyss* (1902) and

The Condition of England (1909), and partly through the support of Liberal editors, including A. G. Gardiner of the *Daily News*, W. H. Massingham of the *Daily Chronicle*, C. P. Scott of the *Manchester Guardian*, and J. A. Spender of the *Westminster Gazette*. Although many of the New Liberals entered Parliament and the Cabinet after 1906, the party still contained many businessmen who had reservations about the new agenda; indeed, some leading figures left the party, including Alfred Pease, whose interests included railways, collieries and banking, and James Joicey, the north-eastern coal-owner. Conversely, many of the most successful employers were enthusiastic advocates of a progressive programme of state welfare, notably William Lever (soap), Sir John Brunner (chemicals) and the Cadbury and Rowntree families; they backed the Edwardian Liberal programme both financially and as parliamentary candidates.

L. T. Hobhouse (1864–1929)

An academic and journalist, Hobhouse was one of the leading social theorists of his generation, noted for his prominence in the field of sociology. He was a major exponent of the New Liberalism, developing ideas on the enabling purposes of state power to further liberty. In *Liberalism* (1911), he sought to explain the social programmes and taxation policies of the Liberal government as an extension, not a reversal, of the economic principles of earlier Liberals such as Mill. He wrote:

> The struggle for liberty is also, when pushed through, a struggle for equality. Freedom to choose and follow an occupation, if it is to become fully effective, means equality with others in the opportunities for following such occupation. This is, in fact, one among the various considerations which leads Liberalism to support a national system of free education, and will lead it further on the same lines.[7]

Perhaps his most famous quotation, from the same book, is: 'liberty without equality is a name of noble sound and squalid result'.

The Liberal revival in the early 1900s

The Edwardian Liberal revival benefited greatly from the divisions and confusion among its rivals. Largely in office since 1886, the Conservative and Unionist Party under Lord Salisbury offered a mixture of domestic populism, a vigorous patriotic-imperialism and some judicious social reforms. It combined traditional landed support with the votes of middle-class suburbanites and working-class Tories; the alliance with Liberal Unionism had attracted most of the Whigs and extra middle-class support and strengthened the party in areas of weakness like Scotland and the West Midlands. But by 1900 this alliance was disintegrating, although Salisbury managed to obscure the trend by holding a 'Khaki' election in 1900 to capitalise on the patriotic mood.[8]

The Conservatives found it increasingly impractical to combine low taxation and minimal state intervention with the needs of the British state at home and abroad.

The South African war had underlined the neglect of the army and navy, and Britain had become terribly vulnerable in a world dominated by two alliance systems from which she had excluded herself. Some Tories had responded to the evidence of poverty and tried to boost their own popularity by promising old age pensions, but Salisbury had failed to deliver. Their reputation was further damaged by the notorious Taff Vale judgment in 1902, which made trade unions liable for the costs of strike action and helped to alienate the party from organised labour. By 1903 the crisis caused by the Boer War had prompted Joseph Chamberlain to recognise the inadequacy of the Victorian tax system and to seize the opportunity to launch a fresh programme involving the abandonment of free trade in favour of tariff reform. This, Chamberlain argued, would protect British manufacturers (and thus jobs) from imports, raise additional revenue to help pay for social reforms, and unite the Empire in a common trading bloc.

It was a bold vision but it played into the hands of the Liberals. Although a majority of Conservatives adopted protectionism, the issue divided the party and destabilised Balfour's leadership. By contrast the Liberals rediscovered their unity by rallying to the free trade cause. During the late-Victorian period they had championed the 'free breakfast table', which meant levying no duties on the staple food items of working families, but while free trade was not under threat there was little mileage in this message. Suddenly Liberals had the opportunity to defend cheap food for millions of ordinary people.

Industry was more divided. Manufacturers who suffered from German competition welcomed tariffs, but most employers appreciated that dearer food would expose them to higher costs in the form of increased wages; and major industries such as cotton textiles relied heavily on free trade to allow them to buy their raw material cheaply and to export a high proportion of their output.

Free trade gave the warring factions within Liberalism the opportunity to unite and thereby restored party morale. H. H. Asquith, who had become involved with party infighting as a supporter of Rosebery and Liberal Imperialism, worked his passage back into Liberal affections by chasing Chamberlain all over the country to refute his protectionist propaganda. The revival was also boosted by the controversy engendered by Balfour's Education Act of 1902 which antagonised Nonconformists by abolishing the school boards and obliging some of them to contribute towards the maintenance of Anglican schools. There followed a campaign of civil disobedience in which some Nonconformists refused to pay rates. Although few participated directly, the issue helped to galvanise a community whose wealthier members had been drifting towards Conservatism during the 1890s.

The effects of free trade and Nonconformist revivalism were evident in some dramatic Liberal by-election gains in places such as North Leeds and Brighton, which had been strong Tory seats. The backlash against the South African war also discredited the imperial cause, usually exploited by the Conservatives. Despite her costly military victory, it was far from obvious that Britain had really gained anything. When the High Commissioner, Sir Alfred Milner, began to import indentured labourers from China to work in the mines of the Rand, he discredited the claim that British control of South Africa would create jobs for British miners. At the ensuing election the Liberals drama- tised the issue by parading pig-tailed 'coolies' through the streets to remind voters that 'Chinese slavery' was another example of Tory deception.

Herbert Henry Asquith (1852–1928)

Asquith was born in Morley, Yorkshire, in 1852, into a solid middle-class Nonconformist background; he was educated at Oxford University and became a barrister. Elected as Liberal MP for East Fife in 1886, he held the seat for thirty-two years. Although he had a footing in Gladstonian Liberalism, Asquith was attracted to Liberal Imperialism and, as a student of T. H. Green at Oxford, was familiar with the ideas of New Liberalism.

With his barrister's command of his brief, Asquith became a formidable parliamen- tary performer and was appointed Home Secretary in 1892. He could have become Liberal leader after Rosebery, but as he needed the income from his legal practice, he declined the opportunity. In opposition after 1895, Asquith was nicknamed the 'sledge- hammer' because of his debating prowess, which was deployed with particular effect against Joseph Chamberlain. He was touted as a potential Prime Minister in 1905 as part of the Relugas compact to send the ageing Campbell-Bannerman to the Lords, but when that failed he served under CB as Chancellor of the Exchequer. As Chancellor his intel- lectual grasp and capacity for systematic work enabled him to prepare the ground for the Liberal revolution in taxation.

Asquith succeeded Campbell-Bannerman as Prime Minister in 1908. He was notable for recognising talent and allowing his ministers to get on with their jobs; in particular, his co-operation with Lloyd George proved to be the key to his government's success. On the other hand, contemporaries thought he was damaged by his marriage to Margot Tennant, who accelerated his abandonment of his modest West Riding, Nonconformist origins for the fast life of London; Asquith delivered brilliant speeches on temperance with all the insight of a rather heavy drinker (one of his nicknames was 'Squiffy'). He also suffered from several blind spots: he refused to give the press, even the Liberal press, the attention it deserved, and he failed to understand the desire to enfranchise women.

One of Asquith's greatest achievements was to have prepared Britain for the military crisis posed by the First World War, and to have taken the country and his party into the war in 1914 without experiencing serious divisions. Though very skilful in leading the Liberals into accepting policies, such as conscription, that many of them disliked, he was unlucky in that neither his naval nor military commanders managed to score any clear victories in the first half of the war. By forming a coalition with the Conservatives and Labour in 1915 he undermined his support among Liberals, and by his subsequent refusal to cooperate with Lloyd George he became responsible for dividing the party. He was overthrown as Prime Minister in 1916 and took half his party into opposition.

His reluctance to resign as party leader after 1918, when he lost East Fife, and even after 1924, when he was defeated at Paisley (where he had been re-elected in 1920), perpetuated the party split into the mid-1920s; this proved disastrous because it greatly delayed the Liberal recovery.

Asquith was raised to the peerage as the Earl of Oxford and Asquith in 1925, finally relinquished the Liberal leadership to Lloyd George the following year and died in 1928.

While Liberal campaigns in the country gathered momentum, the party in Parliament was less impressive. Campbell-Bannerman was not a skilful leader of the opposition, and the government's large majority made it difficult to inflict serious damage. The leading Liberal Imperialists, Grey, Haldane and Asquith, plotted to push Campbell-Bannerman out of the leadership, but they lacked support among the rank and file who respected CB for his loyalty to traditional causes, including home rule, disestablishment and educational reform. However, as party fortunes revived Campbell-Bannerman's position grew more secure. Moreover, though not a great parliamentarian, the Liberal leader was a skilful tactician and under his leadership the party effected two crucial alliances which prepared the ground for victory in 1906.

For several years the Tory free traders fought the protectionist majority inside their own party before eventually accepting the new programme. But some, including twelve MPs, were ready to leave the party altogether. Though not on the same scale as the Liberal Unionist revolt in 1886, this had important consequences, not least because it brought the young Winston Churchill into the Liberal ranks in 1904. 'I am an English Liberal', he told Lord Robert Cecil in October 1903, 'I hate the Tory party, their men, their works, their methods'.[9] As an indefatigable platform speaker and as an innovative minister, Churchill proved to be a huge asset to his new party – at least until 1914.

Winston Churchill (1874–1965)

Churchill was the son of Lord Randolph Churchill who had resigned as Salisbury's Chancellor of the Exchequer in 1886. As Conservative member for Oldham (1900–04) he believed that his father had been badly treated and took up the issue of economies in military spending which had occasioned his downfall. To contemporaries his decision to quit the Conservative Party over free trade in 1904 appeared typically impulsive and opportunist. In fairness, Churchill remained loyal to free trade for decades to come. But 1904 was a good time to leave the Conservatives.

He was adopted by the Liberals in North West Manchester, a marginal Tory seat dominated by commercial interests to whom free trade appealed. He won it in 1906, and, after being defeated at a ministerial by-election in 1908, was returned for Dundee, which he retained until 1922. The Liberal leaders were quick to recognise Churchill's talent, making him Under-Secretary for the Colonies in 1905, President of the Board of Trade in 1908, Home Secretary in 1910 and First Lord of the Admiralty in 1911. This swift rise provoked jealously among colleagues who questioned his Liberal credentials. His enthusiasm for building Dreadnoughts made him seem a warmonger, and his bizarre behaviour as Home Secretary, when he personally directed operations at the siege of

Sidney Street, where the police had cornered a gang of anarchists, suggested an excessive thirst for publicity.

Churchill certainly had to learn his Liberalism in 1904. 'What I want to know', Charles Trevelyan told him, 'is how much common ground can you find with reforming Liberals on economic and social questions?'[10] In fact, at the Board of Trade Churchill proved to be an ardent reformer, introducing labour exchanges and the unemployment insurance scheme, though even this looked like opportunism to some. 'He is full of the poor whom he has just discovered', commented Charles Masterman.[11]

Admittedly, Churchill's rationale for state welfare betrayed his Tory background; he justified reform in Bismarckian rather than humanitarian terms, arguing that it would strengthen the loyalty of the citizens towards the state. The truth is that Churchill was a man of enthusiasms, always eager to pick up a new idea; hence the lengthy memoranda he inflicted on Asquith on everything from national insurance to the development of tanks. But on some issues he showed a genuine liberalism. In 1904, when Conservatives were demanding legislation against alien immigration he publicly argued for retaining 'the old tolerant and generous practice of free entry and asylum to which this country has so long adhered and from which it has so greatly gained'; he also condemned the police for harassing immigrants and political refugees.[12]

His career damaged by the Dardanelles disaster, Churchill resigned in 1915 and fought in the trenches for two years. In 1917 he returned to government under Lloyd George, but lost his seat on the fall of the coalition. After 1922 he returned to the Conservatives, although it was thought that he remained sympathetic to the Liberals and he was close in particular to Violet Bonham Carter. He offered Liberal leader Clement Davies a Cabinet post in 1951, although this was primarily motivated by a desire to win Liberal support for the Tories at a time when the two main parties were evenly matched in the country.

These recruits from the right attracted less interest than the pact with the newly formed Labour Representation Committee, which called itself the Labour Party from 1906 onwards. Negotiated in 1903 by the Liberal Chief Whip, Herbert Gladstone, and Ramsay MacDonald, Secretary of the Labour Representation Committee, it was not a comprehensive pact but a limited agreement designed to avoid splitting the anti-Conservative vote in certain constituencies. In some single-member seats either Labour or the Liberals gave the other a free run, and in several two-member seats, including Newcastle, Blackburn, Bolton, Preston, Derby and Leicester, each party ran one candidate against two Tories.

In retrospect it became clear that the Liberals would have won in 1906 without the pact, and as twenty-four of Labour's twenty-nine members were elected in the absence of a Liberal, it was easy to argue that the party had made an unforced error in helping its rival to its first real foothold in Parliament. However, the pact proved very effective for the Liberals not just in 1906 but also in 1910, when the revival of the Conservative vote to over 46 per cent made it essential to combine Liberal and Labour support. Also, lack of funds meant that the Liberals had failed to contest many Tory seats in the 1890s;

Labour candidatures now saved the Liberals the cost of doing so. In any case, Gladstone regarded most Labour MPs as essentially working-class Liberals, similar to the existing trade union members who took the Liberal whip as 'Lib-Labs'; they were loyal free traders and backed the Liberal reform programme. In 1906 few people saw the new Labour MPs as a potential governing party.

Meanwhile, Balfour's Cabinet became so fractious that eventually he attempted to wrong-foot his opponents by resigning in December 1905 in the hope that Campbell-Bannerman would not manage to form a united government. In fact, the Liberal leader incorporated the Liberal Imperialists into his Cabinet without difficulty and held a general election in January 1906 which led to a Liberal landslide, the party's most resounding election victory in its history. The Liberals won almost 400 seats, and their Labour allies a further twenty-nine. The Conservatives lost more than half of the constituencies they had won in 1900; even their leader, Balfour, was defeated (though he was re-elected for another seat later in the month-long poll).

1906 general election (12 January – 8 February)			
	Votes	%	MPs
Liberal	2,751,057	48.9	399
Conservative and Liberal Unionist	2,422071	43.0	156
Labour	321,663	5.7	29
Irish Parliamentary	35,031	0.6	82
Others	96,269	1.7	4
Total	5,626,091		670

As the campaign focused on free trade, financial retrenchment, education and licensing it had the appearance of a traditional Victorian election, the last triumph of Gladstonianism. In fact, however, although these issues undoubtedly helped the Liberals, the election reflected long-term shifts in the agenda and in personnel. As Trevelyan had reminded Churchill in 1903, 'the Liberal Party is not a free trade party. It is only satisfied with Free Trade as an economic base to work from … The whole raison d'etre of present-day Liberalism is constructive reform.'[13] In 1906 some 69 per cent of Liberal candidates included old age pensions and poor law reform in their election addresses, 68 per cent land reform and 59 per cent reform of trade union law.[14] As Chief Whip Gladstone had used his resources to place rising younger men, including Charles Masterman, Herbert Samuel, Christopher Addison, and W. M. Robertson, in winnable constituencies. Among the 397 Liberals elected in 1906 no fewer than 205 had never sat in Parliament before. A new generation of Liberals had arrived, and with them the agenda of the New Liberalism.

The emergence of the Liberal state 1906–14

As Campbell-Bannerman took office without a legislative plan, the reforms that emerged reflected initiatives taken by individual ministers and the pressure exerted through the party itself. Two of the early measures were the result of joint demands by Liberal and Labour backbenchers. In 1906 the Trades Disputes Act relieved the unions of the legal disabilities placed on them by the Taff Vale judgment. In the same year a bill to allow local authorities to provide free school meals for needy children was also enacted. In retrospect this seems a modest measure – not until 1914 was the meals service made compulsory – but at the time it represented an important break with Victorian thinking because it seemed to undermine parents' responsibility for the welfare of their children, and it did not disqualify them from voting, as was the case with poor relief. It thus symbolised a retreat from the traditional assumption that poverty was necessarily a sign of moral failings.

'There is a tremendous policy in Social Organisation'

Churchill's approach to social reform is exemplified in this letter to Asquith, dated 29 December 1908:

> There is a tremendous policy in Social Organisation. The need is urgent and the moment ripe. Germany with a harder climate and far less accumulated wealth has managed to establish tolerable basic conditions for her people. She is organised not only for war, but for peace. We are organised for nothing except party politics. The Minister who will apply to this country the successful experience of Germany in social organisation may or may not be supported at the polls, but he will at least leave a memorial which time will not deface of his administration ... 1. Labour Exchanges and Unemployment Insurance 2. National Infirmity Insurance 3. Special Expansive State Industries – Afforestation – Roads 4. Modernised Poor Law 5. Railway amalgamation with state control and guarantee 6. Education compulsory till 17 ... I say – thrust a big slice of Bismarckianism over the whole underside of our industrial system, and await the consequences whatever they may be with a good conscience.[15]

Further progress towards social reform could not be made without major innovations in taxation. The way was opened by H. H. Asquith, as Chancellor of the Exchequer from 1905, until he replaced Campbell-Bannerman as Prime Minister in 1908. Asquith introduced the requirement for an annual declaration of all income by every individual. He forced the Treasury to accept the need for a super tax on incomes over £5,000, and he set a lower rate of income tax on earned incomes under £2,000 compared to income above that level. He also prepared a scheme for non-contributory old age pensions paid at the maximum rate of five shillings weekly to people over seventy whose income was not above £21 a year. 'It is of course Socialism pure and simple', complained Lord Rosebery. Although Asquith's civil servants had calculated that 572,000 people would be eligible, by 1914 no fewer than 967,000 were drawing the pension. Pensions proved immensely popular, not least because they were administered through post offices and kept separate from the poor law. New Year's Day 1909 was dubbed 'Pensions Day' by the press, and Liberals raised flags and organised celebrations to mark the event; Liberal agents also advertised their willingness to assist any claimants who had difficulty in completing their application forms. As the new pensioners retained their vote (though two-thirds were women and thus unenfranchised) they and their relatives became an asset in the general elections of 1910.

However, as pensions cost the government £8 million any further reforms required extra revenue; moreover, other aspects of poverty such as health and unemployment were far more complicated because they unsettled so many vested interests. Following Lloyd George's visit to Germany in 1908 to study the insurance system operating there, he and Churchill co-ordinated their plans. They decided that the first step was the introduction of labour exchanges – a recognition that the free market in labour failed to work efficiently. The government overcame trade union objections by allowing men to apply voluntarily, permitting them to refuse jobs paying below union rates, and even employing union officials in the new bureaux. In 1909 the Trade Boards Act introduced minimum wages for very poorly paid occupations, many dominated by women workers, where unions were weak. Ministers also legislated on behalf of the coal miners, who won an eight-hour day in 1908 and a minimum wage in 1912. As these measures interfered with the management of privately owned businesses they aroused controversy; but they reflected growing support in the Liberal ranks for the idea of a national minimum standard guaranteed by the state.

In the 'People's Budget' of 1909 Lloyd George imposed some extra duties on consumption of drink and tobacco; but the main thrust was to redistribute income by taxing the wealthy by means of motor car licences and petrol duties, higher taxation on unearned income over £700 and on earned income above £2,000, a 'super tax' on income above £5,000, a higher rate of death duties and a levy on undeveloped land. It is worth remembering that as liability for income tax started at £150 annual income, most people did not pay it at all. Most employees paid no additional tax as a result of the budget, and Lloyd George introduced a tax allowance of £10 for children under sixteen for anyone whose income was below £500.

The innovations of 1909 had a lasting effect in shifting the burden of taxation from indirect taxes on consumption, which were largely paid by the poor, to direct taxes on income, paid by the wealthy; they also enshrined the principle that the rate of tax one paid should reflect one's ability to pay. In addition, Lloyd George established a Development Commission with a remit to use its funds to invest in forestry, experimental farming and land reclamation – sectors in which private investment had failed to materialise. In the event Britain enjoyed fairly full employment during the last few years before the war and so these funds were not much used. However, the policy was the precursor of new bodies such as the Forestry Commission after the war and it heralded the pump-priming strategy for stimulating the economy in periods of depression.

The controversy over the 1909 budget delayed the National Insurance scheme which was eventually introduced in 1911. This was based on the principle of contributions, paid by employees, employers and the state, an idea familiar to a generation of people who subscribed to Friendly Society policies. The health scheme, which was compulsory for those earning under £160, brought a weekly benefit of ten shillings and access to a panel doctor. Unemployment insurance was an experiment applying initially to only 2.5 million higher paid workers, but it was extended to twelve million, representing a majority of the labour force, in 1920. For a time the National Insurance scheme made the government unpopular, so much so that Charles Masterman, the acknowledged expert on the legislation, lost two ministerial by-elections, at Bethnal Green and Ipswich. Such setbacks encouraged the view that the Liberals had gone as far as they dared in promoting the new agenda by 1911. This, however, is debateable. By 1912 the government was winning by-elections again, and several ministers were pioneering new reforms. In 1914 Herbert Samuel initiated local maternity and child-care clinics, supported by government grants, a policy that was to be rapidly developed after 1918. Lloyd George's 1914 budget extended most of the taxation innovations of 1909 even further, and in the autumn of 1913 he seized the initiative by launching his land campaign. His proposals involved creating boards to set minimum wages for agricultural labourers, and building houses with an acre of land to free workers from tied cottages and compulsory purchase powers. Even the Conservatives acknowledged privately that Lloyd George's campaign was popular and threatened to undermine their hold on rural constituencies.[16]

David Lloyd George (1863–1945)

Lloyd George was born in the heartland of Victorian, Welsh, Nonconformist Liberalism. From an early age, however, he was a somewhat wayward Liberal; attracted by Chamberlain's Radical Programme, he was tempted to join the Liberal Unionists in 1886. After narrowly winning Caernarvon Boroughs at a by-election in 1890, he served his apprenticeship as a rebellious backbencher, but won national prominence as an opponent of the Boer War.

In 1905 Campbell-Bannerman brought Lloyd George into the Cabinet as a representative of Gladstonian radicalism. In his two years at the Board of Trade he revealed key aspects of his approach to politics. He approached free trade pragmatically, rather than as a moral good, as many Liberals did. When preparing legislation he consulted the vested interests, both employers and labour, with the object of offering an agreed measure to Parliament.[17]

Lloyd George also played a key role in settling some of the major strikes of the Edwardian period, usually by persuading recalcitrant employers to negotiate with the workers and to accept a permanent conciliation scheme. His attacks on landed wealth were powerful, sometimes even vitriolic, but they in no way inhibited his respect for successful industrialists and entrepreneurs; and his penchant for using experts and businessmen was to culminate in his wartime government when he appointed them, instead of party politicians, to the new ministries.

Lloyd George's role in the controversy over the 1909 'People's Budget' and the House of Lords obscured his bi-partisanship and the extent to which he was driven by a desire to find solutions to each problem. This became obvious during the summer of 1910, when he took a remarkable initiative to break the constitutional log-jam by offering the Conservatives a coalition which would settle tariff reform, naval expansion and compulsory military service in return for acceptance of devolution for Ireland, Scotland and Wales, among other things.[18] This initiative prepared the ground for his coalition with them from 1916 to 1922.

Lloyd George was appointed Minister for Munitions in 1915 and then Secretary of State for War, moves which were intended to intensify the British war effort following criticism of Asquith's government for not organising the country's military and industrial resources to win an all-out war. Lloyd George used his reputation as a man of vision and action to replace Asquith at the head of the government at the end of 1916, but this ultimately split the Liberal Party and left Lloyd George dependent on Conservative support.

The Liberal split was confirmed at the 1918 election, when Lloyd George and the Conservative leader, Bonar Law, jointly endorsed coalition candidates. Tentative moves to create a new political grouping came to nothing and Lloyd George became even more dependent on Conservative backing until the Tory backbenchers overthrew the coalition in 1922. Although his coalition government enacted various measures of social reform it struggled to cope with post-war unemployment as well as moves towards Irish independence and the international ramifications of the First World War.

The Liberals reunited uneasily under Asquith to fight the 1923 election in defence of free trade, and Lloyd George became party leader after Asquith's retirement in 1926. He regained the intellectual initiative by launching a series of new policy initiatives, including *Britain's Industrial Future* (the 'Yellow Book'), written by, among others, John Maynard Keynes, which proposed to use public spending to reduce unemployment. Although this helped underpin a revival in the 1929 election, the party was by then too firmly established in third place.

Lloyd George also remained personally unpopular with, and was distrusted by, many leading Liberals; one source of contention was his personal control over a sizeable political fund derived from the sale of honours. He opposed the formation of the National Government in 1931 and formed an independent Liberal grouping. He remained a brooding presence on the back benches into the 1940s, though his speech in the Norway debate contributed to the fall of Chamberlain's government in 1940. He was elevated to the peerage shortly before his death on 26 March 1945.

The constitutional crisis

Their landslide victory in 1906 convinced many Liberals that the House of Lords would not dare to frustrate their legislative programme. However, the peers judged shrewdly that they could risk rejecting bills dealing with education and licensing, which were narrowly partisan measures, as long as they were careful to avoid interfering with trade union or school meals legislation. As a result, by 1908 considerable frustration had built up among Liberal MPs. The answer to their dilemma was eventually found in Lloyd George's budget of 1909, which at last gave Liberals a sufficiently big issue on which to challenge the peers in the country.

However, it would be a mistake to think that Lloyd George devised it with rejection in mind; rather, he intended it as a Trojan Horse, enabling him to smuggle through measures dealing with licensing and land valuation previously mangled in the upper house. Lloyd George boasted that he had 'some exquisite plans for outwitting the Lords', assuming that by convention they did not reject financial legislation.[19] As the government faced a revenue deficit of around £16–17 million, somewhat exaggerated by the Chancellor to suit his purposes, no one could dispute that major measures were required. Lloyd George believed that his budget would restore the initiative to the Liberals and thus 'stop the electoral rot'.

However, many landed aristocrats interpreted the budget as a fundamental threat to their order. The proposal to raise half a million pounds from new land taxes was purely nominal, but its purpose was to justify a scheme to conduct a complete valuation of land ownership which would subsequently form the basis for an effective taxation of landed wealth. But the more immediate threat was reflected in the effect the budget had in galvanising the Conservative tariff reformers, who saw that Lloyd George threatened to render their whole strategy irrelevant. Once the Liberals had opened up fresh sources of revenue they would be able to finance social welfare measures *and* offer voters the benefits of free trade at the same time – which the protectionists had calculated to be an impossibility. Consequently, within days of the introduction of the budget, Viscount Ridley, chairman of the Tariff Reform League, was claiming that the peers did enjoy the right to reject budgets and condemning the Liberal proposals as socialism and revolution.

Asquith and Lloyd George, however, noted the enthusiasm generated by the budget among Liberals and in the Labour Party, and, to judge from their success in defending four seats at by-elections in July 1909, among the voters too. In a famous speech at Limehouse on 30 July, Lloyd George stoked up the controversy by employing language not used since 1885, when Joseph Chamberlain had attacked the idle rich, by condemning wealthy landowners for refusing to contribute a fair share to the costs of pensions and national defence; he warned that their selfishness would encourage society to 'reconsider the conditions' under which land was privately held. By this time the Chancellor had begun to realise that more was at stake than the budget. By manoeuvring the Tory peers into becoming apologists for the wealthy, Liberals would gain a weapon with which to attack the powers enjoyed by the House of Lords. Lloyd George therefore maintained the pressure in even more extreme speeches, such as one at Newcastle where he appeared to set class against class. By now the Tories found it embarrassing to withdraw from the trap.

'They are forcing a revolution, and they will get it'

One of Lloyd George's most controversial speeches on the House of Lords was made at Newcastle-upon-Tyne on 9 October 1909:

There has been a great slump in dukes … They have been making speeches lately. One especially expensive duke made a speech, and all the Tory press said, 'Well, now, really, is that the sort of thing we are spending £250,000 a year on?' Because a fully equipped duke costs as much to keep as two Dreadnoughts – and they are just as great a terror – and they last longer … Let them realise what they are doing. They are forcing a revolution, and they will get it … The question will be asked whether five hundred men, ordinary men chosen accidentally from among the unemployed, should override the judgement of millions of people who are engaged in the industry which makes the wealth of the country.

That is one question. Another will be: who ordained that a few should have the land of Britain as a perquisite? Who made ten thousand people the owners of the soil and the rest of us trespassers in the land of our birth? Who is it who is responsible for the scheme of things whereby one man who is engaged through life in grinding labour to win a bare and precarious subsistence for himself, and when, at the end of his days, he claims at the hands of the community he served a poor pension of eight pence a day, he can only get it through a revolution, and another man who does not toil receives every hour of the day, every hour of the night, whilst he slumbers, more than his poor neighbour receives in a whole year of toil? … The answers are charged with peril for the order of things the Peers represent.

Though Balfour was aware of the danger of rejecting the budget, he also knew that retreat would mean splitting his own party and undermining his leadership. Accordingly, at the end of November the peers voted down the budget by 350 to 75. 'With all their cunning, their greed has overborne their craft', exulted Lloyd George, 'We have got them at last.'[20] The House of Commons denounced the peers' action as unconstitutional and Asquith proceeded to seek a dissolution, in effect inviting voters to overrule the upper house.

'The absolute veto which it at present possesses must go'

Speaking at the Albert Hall on 10 December 1909, H. H. Asquith set out the Liberals' view about what the election was about:

I tell you quite plainly and I tell my fellow countrymen that neither I nor any other Liberal ministers supported by a majority in the House of Commons is going to submit to the rebuffs and humiliations of the last four years. We shall not assume office and we shall not hold office unless we can secure the safeguards which experience shows us to be necessary for the legislative utility and honour of the party of progress … We are not proposing the abolition of the House of Lords, but … the absolute veto which it at present possesses must go. The power which it claims from time to time of, in effect, compelling us to choose between a dissolution and – so far as legislative projects are concerned – legislative sterility must go also. The people in future when they elect a new House of

Commons, must be able to feel, what they cannot feel now, that they are sending to Westminster men who will have the power not merely of proposing and
debating, but of making laws.

In the pre-Christmas campaign Asquith, Lloyd George and Churchill stormed the country, forcing the Conservatives on to the defensive; among other things they argued that
the Tories' opposition to the new taxes would make it impossible for them to finance
the pensions that were so popular. However, in an eight-week campaign interrupted by
Christmas, the Liberals peaked too soon. Some colleagues also felt that Lloyd George
and Churchill went over the top in attacking the wealthy, allowing their opponents
to frighten some middle-class voters into feeling threatened even though the budget
placed no extra tax on them. The Liberals were bound to lose many of the seats won
in 1906, but they were a little disappointed to emerge with almost the same number as
the Conservatives. However, backed by the Labour and Irish members the government
remained firmly entrenched in office.

January 1910 general election (15 January – 20 February)			
	Votes	*%*	*MPs*
Liberal	**2,866,157**	**43.0**	**274**
Conservative and Liberal Unionist	3,104,407	46.6	272
Labour	505,657	7.6	40
Irish Parliamentary	126,647	1.9	82
Others	64,532	1.0	2
Total	*6,667,400*		*670*

The flaw lay in the fact that while the election had settled the budget issue, it had not
resolved the role of the House of Lords, despite the expectations aroused during the campaign. Notwithstanding Asquith's insistence on safeguards before taking office, he could
not reform the upper chamber against the peers' wishes unless around five hundred new
Liberal peers were created to overcome the Tory majority; the King made it clear that
he would agree to the new creations only after a second election had been won. After a
summer of fruitless negotiations in search of a compromise, another election was held in
December. This almost took the form of a referendum on the upper chamber and virtually reproduced the January result.

December 1910 general election (3–19 December)			
	Votes	*%*	*MPs*
Liberal	**2,293,869**	**43.8**	**272**
Conservative and Liberal Unionist	2,420,169	46.2	271
Labour	371,802	7.1	42
Irish Parliamentary	131,720	2.5	84
Others	17,678	0.3	1
Total	*5,235,238*		*670*

The Cabinet decided to formalise the convention that the Lords had no powers over financial legislation; ordinary legislation could be delayed for two years but would be enacted if passed in three sessions by the Commons; finally, the length of a parliament's life was reduced from seven to five years. The revelation that the King had agreed to create new peers sobered some Tories and angered others; but Balfour accepted that the game was up and on 10 August 1911 the peers reluctantly passed the Parliament Act by 131 votes to 113.

This was a brilliant triumph for the Liberals, resolving a problem that had obstructed reforming governments since Gladstone's time. And by giving the Liberals the radical high ground the controversy had effectively forced Labour to maintain its status as a client of the Liberal Party. It had also divided the Conservatives and forced them into a negative and extremist position which alienated them from urban working-class support up to 1914. However, there was a downside. The Liberals had thrown away their huge 1906 majority three years early. By shortening the life of Parliament they had curtailed the amount that any reforming government could achieve. This became obvious because now that the Irish members held the balance of power the home rule issue was revived. Finally, the reforms of 1911 meant that Asquith's government would be due to face the electorate again in 1915, which, as things turned out, was not a good time for Liberals.

Irish home rule

During the 1890s the Liberal commitment to home rule had weakened, so much so that Rosebery had urged abandoning it altogether. However, in many urban constituencies the small but well-organised Irish vote was crucial in sustaining the party's majority – and after the 1910 elections the Liberal government became dependent on Irish nationalist support in the Commons.

The third Home Rule Bill, announced in the King's Speech in February 1912, proposed a two-chamber parliament in Dublin comprising an elected House of Commons with 164 members and a 40-strong Senate nominated by the government. It was to handle domestic matters, not including social welfare and policing, and enjoy the power to raise income tax, death duties and customs by 10 per cent. The Irish members at Westminster were to be reduced to 42 in number.

As the Bill had to be passed three times between 1912 and 1914 to overcome the peers' opposition, some Liberals complained that too much time was being devoted to Ireland; but it was not damaging on the mainland. In northern Ireland the story was different, however; led by Sir Edward Carson the Ulster Unionists used this period to mobilise a violent resistance, proposing to establish a provisional government for Ulster and organising an Ulster Volunteer Force armed with 20,000 rifles in 1914. Yet despite gaining influential support in Britain, their position was not strong; even in Ulster they had only seventeen seats compared to sixteen for the Nationalists, and one of those was lost at a by-election in Londonderry in 1913.

At a notorious speech at Blenheim Palace in July 1912 the new Conservative leader, Andrew Bonar Law, condemned the government as 'a revolutionary committee which has seized by fraud upon despotic power', and offered Tory support for any opposition to home rule, however violent. In March 1914 Asquith offered to allow the Ulster counties to opt out of home rule for six years, after which they would join Dublin unless Parliament decided otherwise; but he refused demands to hold yet another general election before the enactment of the bill. Beyond this he declined further compromise, and moved troops and naval reinforcements to check any rebellion. Although by the summer of 1914 there was a real prospect of the two sides engaging in a civil war, the government was probably correct in thinking that the Tories were damaging themselves by their extremism and irresponsibility and that their leadership was being undermined by the 'radical right'.

The weaknesses in Edwardian Liberalism

Edwardian Liberalism achieved great success in the social and economic sphere; its failures lay more in political, constitutional and legal matters where the government departed from liberal traditions. Of these the most demoralising was its handling of the campaign to give women the vote. Since 1867, when John Stuart Mill launched the cause in Parliament, female suffrage appeared to be a natural extension of the work of Victorian radicals in extending participation to every section of society; by 1906 a majority of Liberal MPs and ministers supported it. However, suffragists had become impatient with prevarication by the politicians: 'we have been hewers of wood and drawers of water for the Liberal Party for too long', as one woman put it in 1909.[21] In 1902 even the Women's Liberal Federation (WLF) decided to impose tests on all Liberal by-election candidates, refusing support for those who failed to advocate women's suffrage. In 1902 T. A. Brassey (Devonport) and Colonel Seeley (Isle of Wight) became the first victims of this policy; and between 1904 and 1914 five others were proscribed and only thirteen actively supported among the twenty considered by the WLF.[22]

In 1906, when Emmeline Pankhurst's suffragettes embarked on a campaign of heckling Liberal Cabinet ministers and intervening against Liberal candidates, they played into the hands of Asquith, a die-hard anti-suffragist. Relations deteriorated after 1909 when the suffragette hunger strikes began; the authorities responded with forcible feeding in prison and eventually with the 'Cat and Mouse Act' which permitted the release of hunger strikers for a week or so, if their lives were in danger, and their re-imprisonment to continue serving their sentences. From 1912 onwards the Home Secretary, Reginald McKenna, effectively suppressed the Women's Social and Political Union by raiding its headquarters, seizing its papers, diverting its mail, cutting off its telephones, censoring its journal and prosecuting its publishers. Such an illiberal policy proved very damaging to the party and demoralising for women Liberals. The WLF lost about 18,000 members between 1912 and 1914, 105 branches lapsed and 47 withdrew from the organisation.[23]

Similar, though less damaging, controversies were aroused by the government's handling of the wave of strikes that engulfed Edwardian Britain. Though largely motivated by material grievances, some strikers advocated syndicalism – the overthrow of parliamentary government by direct action. The situation became dangerous when troops were called out to keep order, leading to the death of two miners at Ton-y-pandy in South Wales in 1910 and two men in the Liverpool dock strike in 1911. The imprisonment of Tom Mann for urging soldiers not to fire on strikers, and Jim Larkin of the Dublin transport workers, angered Charles Trevelyan, the left-wing education minister, who felt that Asquith and Churchill were too aloof from the labour movement. However, syndicalism was more embarrassing to the Labour Party leaders than to the Liberals, and in any case, the party continued to win industrial seats at by-elections while Labour usually ran third.

The Edwardian governments also dismayed some of their supporters over external affairs. They inherited an army and navy in dire need of reform, fears about the German naval building programme, and a widespread belief that thousands of German spies had been infiltrated into Britain as clerks, waiters and hairdressers. One response to this was the notorious Official Secrets Act which was enacted by an empty House of Commons on a Friday afternoon in 1911. It empowered the authorities to arrest anyone on mere suspicion of harbouring an intention 'prejudicial to the safety or interests of the state'; it was not necessary to prove that the accused was a spy or had committed an act of subversion. At the time it was not realised how this illiberal measure would enable governments to stifle legitimate criticism on the plea of protecting national security.

More controversy was aroused by preparations for a continental war. Richard Haldane reorganised the army so as to create a British Expeditionary Force; however, as he saved money in the process this was not entirely unwelcome to Liberal MPs. They were more alarmed by the huge costs of the programme to rebuild the Royal Navy with Dreadnought-type battleships, though as Lloyd George found the money without jeopardising social reform, their criticism was contained. However, many critics correctly feared that the government was making policy behind their backs. The Committee of Imperial Defence, which had been deliberately designed by Balfour in 1902 to bypass Parliament, developed a new strategy to dispatch a British force to support France in any war with Germany.

This was complemented by a reappraisal of diplomatic relations under the Foreign Secretary, Sir Edward Grey, who believed it was in Britain's interests to prevent Germany inflicting a further defeat on the French. Although the *Entente* of 1904 was not an alliance, Grey turned it into one by sanctioning discussions between the French and British navies. Many Liberals also disliked Britain's support for Belgium because she seemed to turn a blind eye to the exploitation of the Congo by King Leopold, which had been exposed by the Liberal backbencher E. D. Morel. Above all, they detested the *Entente* with Russia in 1907, partly because it looked like an attempt to encircle Germany and partly because they loathed the Tsarist regime for its violent suppression of democratic opinion and institutions. Over 100 Liberal MPs joined the Liberal Foreign Affairs

Group led by Arthur Ponsonby, who argued that Britain had not done enough to retain the friendship of Germany and that by prosecuting an arms race the UK was actively bringing war about. However, Lloyd George's commitment to Grey's policy deprived the backbench rebels of a major anti-war leader, and when war came they felt reluctant to split the party to the advantage of the Tories. But they were dismayed by the political implications of the drift towards war which allowed Labour to enjoy 'the whole honour of voicing the best traditions of Liberal foreign policy';[24] their misgivings were proved justified during the First World War.

Sir Edward Grey (1862–1933)

Grey was MP for Berwick from 1885 to 1916, when he was raised to the peerage as Viscount Grey of Fallodon. A descendant of Earl Grey, he was a Liberal Imperialist who served in the Foreign Office in the Liberal government of 1892–95 and was Foreign Secretary in 1905–16. Problems with his eyesight affected his later career but he served as the British ambassador to the United States in 1919–20 and led the Liberals in the Lords in 1923–24. Grey played a crucial role in European diplomacy in the run-up to the outbreak of war in 1914. Speaking in the House of Commons on 3 August 1914 he said:

> I come first to the question of British obligations … In this present crisis, up till yesterday, we have given no promise … of more than diplomatic support. Now I must make this question of obligation clear to the House … For many years we had a long-standing friendship with France [An Hon. Member: 'And with Germany!'] … The French Fleet is now in the Mediterranean, and the Northern and Western coasts of France are absolutely undefended … in these compelling circumstances, yesterday afternoon I gave to the French ambassador the following statement: 'I am authorised to give an assurance that if the German Fleet comes into the Channel or through the North Sea to undertake hostile operations against French coasts or shipping, the British Fleet will give all the protection in its power. This assurance is, of course, subject to the policy of His Majesty's Government receiving the support of Parliament.' … I ask the House, from the point of view of British interests, to consider what may be at stake. If France is beaten in a struggle of life and death, beaten to her knees, loses her position as a Great Power, becomes subordinate to the will and power of one greater than herself … then would not Mr Gladstone's words come true, that just opposite to us there would be a common interest against the unmeasured aggrandisement of any Power?

Survival, adaptation or decline?

With the benefit of hindsight many earlier historians assumed that the origins of the decline of the Liberal Party during and after the First World War lay in the Edwardian period. All over Europe liberal parties were squeezed between parties of the right and left, and this made Liberal decline in Britain appear inevitable. A classic example was the vivid, impressionistic account by George Dangerfield, *The Strange Death of Liberal England*, published in 1935, which said more about inter-war Europe, in which liberal democracy was giving way to fascist and communist regimes, than it did about the Edwardian period. During the 1950s, when the Liberal Party came close to extinction, the two main parties won over 90 per cent of the vote, and academic orthodoxy held that in an industrial society like Britain politics was largely determined by social class; hence the polarisation between Labour and Conservatives.

Today all this looks very dubious. Class voting is very obviously an inadequate explanation for party loyalties. In addition, research on the early Labour Party from the 1960s onwards suggested that it was little more than a client of the Liberals; its failure to attract a majority of the working-class vote even in the 1920s and 1930s makes the inevitability of its rise seem implausible. Conversely, pre-1914 Liberalism has emerged not as a party stuck in a Victorian cul-de-sac but as one capable of adapting its programme and personnel to a new agenda and successful in combining working-class and middle-class support. Indeed, we now recognise that it was the Edwardian *Conservatives* who struggled to adapt; they felt reluctant to compete with the Liberals on social reform, were thwarted by public hostility towards tariffs, and became frustrated because their attacks on government policies only consolidated the alliance between the Liberals, Labour and the Irish that kept them out of power.

Nonetheless, despite the achievements of the Edwardian governments, there are legitimate doubts about how far the Liberal Party's organisation was able to respond to the challenge of a mass electorate, and in particular how far it could encompass an increasingly organised working class. Liberals still followed tradition in making the Chief Whip responsible for the party both in Parliament and in the constituencies, a role too onerous for one man to fill; the post was held by Herbert Gladstone (1899–1905), George Whiteley (1905–08), Jack Pease (1908–10), Alexander Murray (1910–12)[25] and Percy Illingworth (1912–15). One of their main functions was to raise funds from a small number of wealthy Liberals; Sir William Lever, Joseph Rowntree, Baron Henry de Worms, George Cadbury and Sir John Brunner were among those willing to donate as much as £5,000 and £10,000 at a time. The shortage of money at constituency level had made local Liberal associations reluctant to adopt working men as candidates during the 1890s, though Herbert Gladstone tried to overcome this by directing central funds to assist needy constituencies.

The party organisation was also still cumbersome, being divided between the Liberal Central Association, which was effectively the Chief Whip's office, and the National Liberal Federation, which included the Chief Agent who published the *Liberal Agents' Journal*, a handbook of tips on electoral law and registration of voters for the paid constituency agents. The NLF was by now past its prime and was neglected by Asquith. Party membership is not known, though the Women's Liberal Federation frequently published its own figures which reflected some decline towards the end of the Edwardian period.

Women's Liberal Federation membership 1894–1915					
1894	1895	1903	1906	1908	1910
76,000	82,000	51,000	81,000	94,000	104,000
1911	1912	1913	1914	1915	
120,000	133,000	121,000	115,000	107,000	

Scotland retained a separate organisation and its own Women's Liberal Federation, and in some respects asserted its independence from Liberal views south of the border. For example, the Secretary of State, Lord Pentland, declined to adopt forcible feeding of suffragettes in Scottish prisons, probably in deference to the pro-suffrage opinions of Scottish Liberals.[26] Also, the electoral pact with Labour did not apply north of the border, largely because Liberals like Alexander Murray, the Member for Midlothian, regarded Labour candidates as extreme socialists; Churchill, who represented Dundee after 1908, characteristically described them as 'an obscure gang of malignant wirepullers'.[27]

Perhaps the biggest question mark over the Edwardian Liberal Party centres around the fact that although it won three successive elections, it did so under an electoral system in which only six out of every ten men were eligible to vote. In fact, the party wanted to create a simplified system to register all adult males and to abolish the plural voters, who numbered half a million of the eight million total, and were thought to favour the Conservatives. When consulted by the Chief Agent the local organisations replied that the enfranchisement of all men would help the party, though in two northern regions the agents thought that some younger voters would support Labour.[28]

The government certainly assisted the Labour Party by introducing salaries for MPs in 1911 and by creating a system that in 1912 required trade union members to con-tract out if they did not want to pay a political levy to the Labour Party; this eventually boosted Labour funds considerably. These advantages might have been expected to encourage Labour to abandon its pact with the Liberals and contest more than the fifty-nine seats fought in December 1910; by splitting the non-Conservative vote this could easily have led to the defeat of the Liberal government. Significantly, however, Ramsay MacDonald insisted on retaining electoral co-operation, despite pressure from some of his supporters, because without it Labour stood to lose most of its seats through Liberal intervention. When Labour intervened in working-class Liberal seats in the north of England at by-elections between 1912 and 1914 its candidates always came bottom of the poll; there was, thus, no compelling evidence that by 1914 Labour was in a position to oust the Liberal Party.

The Marconi scandal

The Marconi scandal arose from a contract for the construction of a chain of wireless stations awarded in March 1912 to the English Marconi Company by the government, represented by the Postmaster-General, Herbert Samuel, who was a wholly inno-cent party. One of the company's directors, Godfrey Isaacs, was also a director of the American Marconi Company, which had no holdings in the English company but stood to benefit from its success. In April Isaacs offered shares in the American company to his brother, Rufus Isaacs, the Attorney General, Lloyd George, and Alexander Murray, the Liberal Chief Whip. Lloyd George unhesitatingly bought 1,000 shares at £2 each before they went on sale to the public for £3.50.

By July rumours were circulating about ministerial speculation, notably in *Eye Witness*, a journal edited by Cecil Chesterton, a fanatical anti-Semite who portrayed what he dubbed 'the Marconi Scandal' as part of a Jewish-Radical conspiracy. In June 1913 Godfrey Isaacs successfully sued Chesterton for libel, but in March another libel suit brought by Isaacs and Samuel revealed information about the *two* companies which ministers had hitherto concealed. A parliamentary select committee exonerated them but as this reflected the party majority it exacerbated the bitterness of Liberal–Conservative relations during the closing years of peacetime, not least because Murray had invested Liberal Party funds in Marconi before disappearing to Bogota in South America.

In fact, despite the problems it faced, the Asquith government appeared well prepared to face another general election in 1915. It intended to abolish plural voting, which alone was expected to deliver twenty or more Tory seats to the Liberals. More importantly, Lloyd George's land campaign had enabled it to seize the initiative again with a programme that seemed certain to enable Liberals to gain some marginal Conservative constituencies in rural areas without doing anything to assist Labour. Consequently, when war broke out in July 1914, a remarkable fourth victory for the Liberal Party seemed a realistic prospect.

Further reading

The revisionism in Liberal thinking is ably analysed in H. V. Emy, *Liberals, Radicals and Social Politics 1892–1914* (CUP, 1973) and Michael Freeden, *The New Liberalism* (Clarendon Press, 1978). Peter Clarke's *Lancashire and the New Liberalism* (CUP, 1971) argues the case that the party had successfully adapted to a working-class electorate, and Neil Blewett's *The Peers, the Parties and the People* (University of Toronto Press, 1972) discusses the 1910 elections in detail. For a study of local Liberal strength and organisation in three constituencies see Patricia Lynch, *The Liberal Party in Rural England 1885–1910* (OUP, 2003). Electoral fortunes, changing ideas and tactical issues are covered in G. R. Searle, *The Liberal Party: Triumph and Disintegration 1886–1929*, 2nd edn. (Palgrave, 2001) and Martin Pugh, *The Making of Modern British Politics 1867–1945*, 3rd edn. (Wiley-Blackwell, 2002).

For correctives to the revisionist view of Edwardian Liberalism that cast doubt on the extent to which the Liberals had adapted, see G. R. Searle, 'The Edwardian Liberal Party and Business', *English Historical Review*, 98, 1983, and George Bernstein, *Liberalism and Liberal Politics in Edwardian England* (Allen and Unwin, 1986).

On Liberal social reforms, see Bruce K. Murray, *The People's Budget 1909–10* (Clarendon Press, 1980), J. R. Hay, *The Origins of the Liberal Welfare Reforms 1906–1914* (Macmillan, 1975), Pat Thane, 'The working class and state welfare in Britain 1880–1914', *Historical Journal*, 27, 1984, and Martin Pugh, 'Working-class experience and state social welfare 1906–1914: old age pensions reconsidered', *Historical Journal*, 45, 2002.

Several collections of essays discuss Liberal thinking, the backbench critics and the land campaign including: Paul Readman, *Land and Nation in England* (Boydell Press, 2008), A. J. A. Morris (ed.), *Edwardian Radicalism* (Routledge and Kegan Paul, 1974), and *Radicalism Against War 1906–1914* (Longman, 1972), and A. J. P. Taylor (ed.), *Lloyd George: Twelve Essays* (Hamish Hamilton, 1971). On the Liberals' difficulties over women's suffrage and the Marconi scandal see, respectively, Martin Pugh, *The March of the Women* (OUP, 2000), and G. R. Searle, *Corruption in British Politics 1895–1930* (Clarendon Press, 1987).

Useful biographies include: Roy Jenkins, *Asquith* (Collins, 1964); S. E. Koss, *Asquith* (Allen Lane, 1976); John Grigg, *Lloyd George: the People's Champion 1902–11* (Eyre Methuen, 1978), and *Lloyd George: From Peace to War 1912–1916* (Methuen, 1985); Paul Addison, *Churchill on the Home Front* (Cape, 1992); Bernard Wasserstein, *Herbert Samuel: A Political Life* (Clarendon Press, 1992); A. J. A. Morris, *Charles Trevelyan: Portrait of a Radical* (Blackstaff Press, 1977); and Keith Robbins, *Sir Edward Grey* (Cassell, 1971).

Notes

1   R. B. Haldane to Lord Rosebery, 23 April 1895, National Library of Scotland: Rosebery Papers 24.

2   C. P. Trevelyan to Herbert Samuel, 2 October 1898, Newcastle University Library: Trevelyan Papers 4.

3   J. M. Robertson, *The Meaning of Liberalism* (Methuen, 1912), p. 64.

4   J. A. Hobson, *Imperialism: A Study* (James Nisbet and Co., 1902), p. 85.

5   Herbert Samuel, *Liberalism* (Richards, 1902), pp. 27–29.

6   Its deliberations may be followed in Michael Freeden (ed.), *Minutes of the Rainbow Circle 1894–1924* (Royal Historical Society, 1989).

7   L. T. Hobhouse, *Liberalism* (first published 1911; reprint, Galaxy Press, 1964), p. 21.

8   For a comprehensive account of their dilemmas see E. H. H. Green, *The Crisis of Conservatism: the politics, economics and ideology of the British Conservative Party 1880–1914* (Routledge, 1995).

9   Letter from W. S. Churchill to Lord Hugh Cecil, 24 October 1903, cited in R. S. Churchill (ed.), *Winston S. Churchill*, vol. II 1900–1914 (Heinemann, 1967).

10   C. P. Trevelyan to Winston Churchill (draft) undated 1903, Newcastle University Library: Trevelyan Papers 13.

11   Lucy Masterman, *C. F. G. Masterman* (Nicholson and Watson, 1939), p. 97.

12   See Paul Addison, *Churchill On The Home Front 1900–1955* (Cape, 1992), pp. 42–44.

13 C. P. Trevelyan to Winston Churchill (draft) undated 1903, Newcastle University Library: Trevelyan Papers 13.

14 A. K. Russell, *Liberal Landslide* (David and Charles, 1973), p. 65.

15 Churchill to Asquith; R. S. Churchill (ed.), *Winston S. Churchill*, companion vol. II, part 2 (Heinemann, 1969), p. 863.

16 Leslie Scott to David Lloyd George, 29 September 1913, House of Lords Record Office (HLRO): Lloyd George Papers, C/8/2/1.

17 See John Grigg, *Lloyd George: The People's Champion 1902–1911* (Eyre Methuen, 1978), pp. 100–22.

18 'Memorandum on the Formation of a Coalition', 17 August 1910: Sir Charles Petrie, *Life and Letters of Austen Chamberlain*, vol. II (Cassell, 1940) pp. 381–88.

19 David Lloyd George to W. G. George, 6 May 1908, cited in William George, *My Brother And I* (Eyre and Spottiswoode, 1958), p. 220.

20 David Lloyd George, speech at the National Liberal Club, 30 November 1909.

21 *The Common Cause*, 7 October 1909, p. 329.

22 Women's Liberal Federation *News*, November 1902, April 1904; Women's Liberal Federation executive minutes, 30 June 1911, 31 October 1911: Bristol University Library.

23 Women's Liberal Federation *Annual Reports*, 1912, 1913, 1914.

24 George Young to C. P. Trevelyan, 28 June 1906, in the Trevelyan Papers (Newcastle University Special Collections), Vol. 16.

25 Murray was usually known as the Master of Elibank.

26 D. Crombie, Note, 22 October 1909, National Archives of Scotland: Scottish Prison Commission HH/16/619.

27 Alexander Murray to Lord Knollys (copy), 7 November 1906, and 'Memorandum on the Socialist and Labour Movements' by D. A. Wood and W. Webster, National Library of Scotland: Elibank Papers 8801.

28 National Archives, CAB 37/108/148, 16 November 1911.

Chapter 6

Personality Politics and the Break-up of the Party (1914–1929)

David Dutton

B y any criteria the fifteen years between the outbreak of the First World War and the general election of 1929 were a traumatic period in the history of the Liberal Party. What happened is clear enough. During this decade and a half the Liberals moved from the status of governing party to that of third party in a political system whose electoral structure and operation favour the interests of no more than two contenders. By contrast, *why* this happened is a matter of considerable historiographical debate in which no consensus has yet been reached.

It is tempting to attribute major, if not exclusive, responsibility to the impact of the First World War, portrayed in Trevor Wilson's graphic phrase as a 'rampant omnibus' which, mounting the pavement of British politics, knocked down and killed the pedestrian which was Liberalism, a victim who, whatever his minor ailments dating from the pre-war era, was otherwise in no obvious danger of demise. The supporting evidence is seductively strong. The scale and nature of the war – the first total conflict in British military history – inevitably disrupted all existing patterns of political development. Liberal ministers such as Herbert Samuel had quickly to abandon plans for a further tranche of social reforming legislation. 'These are not days', he declared to a conference of county councillors early in 1915, 'in which any minister can sketch out an ambitious legislative programme'.[1] The general election anticipated for 1915 never took place. At this contest Liberal strategists had hoped that their land campaign would recapture urban working-class votes from Labour while prising a number of marginal rural seats from the Conservatives. Had it resulted in a fourth successive defeat for the Conservatives, a 1915 election might have led to that party's total disintegration. As it was, within weeks of the armistice of November 1918, the party of Herbert Asquith, the Prime Minister of 1914, had been reduced to a mere rump of fewer than thirty MPs.

There is also a strong case for suggesting that historical morticians have been premature in their assumption of the death of the Liberal Party. The general election of 1918 was held in such unique circumstances that it was unlikely to provide an accurate barometer of the underlying strength of the three main political parties. Moreover, if the 'coupon' election was a triumph for the Conservative Party, it was also an overwhelming victory for a Prime Minister who continued to stress his Liberal credentials and who undoubtedly attracted a sizeable proportion of the Liberal vote. Many coalition candidates seem to have based their appeal upon Lloyd George himself, displaying posters which urged voters to support the Prime Minister, with their own names printed beneath his in much smaller letters. Furthermore, the Liberal Party remained a major player in the political encounters of the 1920s. As late as 1929 it still succeeded, at a time when the electorate was encouraged to believe that it had the choice of three potential governments, in attracting almost a quarter of the popular vote. Whatever the war did to the Liberal Party, it is difficult to suggest that it killed it outright.

The impact of war

In fact, while some contemporaries were quick to predict that the coming of war would prove a fatal blow – 'Liberalism is dead', muttered the Chief Whip as news came through of the outbreak of hostilities – the objective historian has to be struck by the comparative equanimity with which both the government and the parliamentary party overcame the crisis of July and August 1914. Indeed, it is striking that the coming of war seemed to have a far more damaging effect upon the unity of the Labour Party – the body which is ultimately judged to have derived most advantage from the conflict – than it did upon the Liberals. Convinced that the ostensible *casus belli*, the German violation of Belgian neutrality, was compelling and in full knowledge that an alternative Conservative government was waiting, eager and willing, in the wings, the vast majority of Liberal ministers and backbench MPs swallowed whatever misgivings they had and agreed to give the government their full support in waging the war. Such signs of dissent as there were, including the ministerial resignations of Lord Morley, John Burns and C.P. Trevelyan, caused hardly a ripple of disturbance, certainly nothing to suggest that the party had been mortally wounded.

John Burns (1858–1943)

Burns was born in Lambeth in 1858, joining the Amalgamated Society of Engineers in 1879. After being horrified by the racist treatment of Africans, Burns turned to socialism and formed a Battersea branch of the Social Democratic Federation in 1881.

He was involved in a demonstration against unemployment in 1886 and was arrested; a year later he was involved in a demonstration against coercion in Ireland which led to his imprisonment for six weeks. By 1889 Burns had left the SDF and helped win the London dock workers dispute. He was elected to represent Battersea in the London County Council elections.

In 1892 Burns was elected MP for Battersea North as an Independent Labour member, though aligned to the Liberal Party. Campbell-Bannerman appointed him President of the Local Government Board in 1906; he thus achieved the distinction of being the first working-class person to serve as a government minister. He was responsible for the important Housing and Town Planning Act 1909 and the Census Act 1910 which sought to obtain for the government information about family structure and urban conditions which had not previously been collected, to help tackle infant mortality.

In 1914 Burns was appointed President of the Board of Trade but the soon-to-be-declared war on Germany meant his tenure was brief; he opposed Britain's involvement in a European conflict and resigned from the government. This in effect put an end to his political career. He no longer had the support of the Labour or Liberal parties and the British public were largely hostile to politicians that did not support the First World War. He spent the rest of his life pursuing other interests, and died in 1943.

Over the next few months the ever-escalating demands of war compelled the government to enact a series of measures which, according to abstract principle, flew in the face of traditional liberalism. The Defence of the Realm Act swept away many of the liberties of the individual; the freedom of the press was inevitably curtailed; enemy aliens were interned; the National Registration Bill of July 1915 was widely interpreted as preparing the way for full-scale conscription; and the budget of Reginald McKenna in October 1915 tore into the very ark of the Liberal covenant, the doctrine of free trade. But what is surely most striking is the readiness – enthusiasm would be too strong a word – with which these measures were embraced by Liberals at Westminster and even more by the party in the country. In short, the wartime party proved altogether more pragmatic and adaptable than has sometimes been allowed. There were, as at all times, internal divisions within Asquith's government, but these were of varying contours depending upon the issue at stake at any given moment and in no way suggestive of a party approaching ideological catastrophe. Indeed, when Britain's last Liberal government came to an end with the formation of the first coalition in May 1915, it did not do so as the inevitable culmination of a process of decay. Rather the new government emerged out of the blue, a matter of bewilderment to most contemporary observers.

Eight Conservatives and one Labour MP, Arthur Henderson (the first member of his party to serve as a minister) joined the new coalition. Both Churchill and Haldane were sacrificed, while Lloyd George moved to the newly created Ministry of Munitions. Precisely why Asquith agreed to admit members of the opposition parties into his administration is unlikely ever to be established with any certainty. At all events, the government remained dominated, as far as the distribution of high offices was concerned, by Liberals. Yet the formation of the coalition did more damage to the party's cohesion and self-assurance than had any previous demand of wartime necessity. A meeting of Liberal MPs led to a unanimous resolution condemning the proposed coalition. Asquith found it necessary to put in a personal appearance and to appeal for support. 'Certain things', he declared oracularly, 'had happened; certain things had been divulged; and certain things had emerged as probable'.[2] On this somewhat flimsy explanatory basis the Prime Minister saved the day and the hostile resolution was withdrawn.

Liberal critics of the government now felt emboldened in their attacks upon a Cabinet which had become contaminated by partnership with the Conservatives. Dissident groups began to coalesce. 'The Government and the House are settling down', noted Richard Holt, MP for Hexham, 'the latter to watch the former rather in an anxious and puzzled frame of mind'. But 'the unpleasant suspicions remain and it is obvious that the public has not been told the whole truth'.[3] Much of that suspicion surrounded the issue of conscription, which was finally introduced for single men at the beginning of 1916. This prompted greater opposition within the Parliamentary Liberal Party than had any previous issue. Thirty-five Liberal MPs voted against the government in January 1916, while forty-one dissented when conscription was extended to married men the following summer. Many voiced the opinion that the government had now gone too far, infringing the basic right of a man to decide for himself whether he was prepared to fight, and quite possibly die, for his country. But many more, including some of the dissenters, still viewed the issue in purely pragmatic terms. At the end of 1915 McKenna, the Chancellor of the Exchequer, submitted a memorandum opposing conscription to his Cabinet colleagues:

> In my judgement the policy approved by the Cabinet entails the maintenance of an Army of a size which will gravely embarrass the country in giving the support to our Allies in directions which are of greater importance in the common prosecution of the war to a successful conclusion. Demands have been made and are being met which I admit can only be met by compulsion, but they are demands which, however met, are in my opinion inconsistent with other and not inferior obligations into which we have already entered.[4]

Herbert Samuel, who might have been expected to voice traditional Liberal sentiments, found himself 'driven to support this Bill against all my predilections, against my strong bias in favour of voluntary service, by the hard, cold logic of facts'. Arguments against compulsion were 'valid in normal times' but could not 'be pressed today ... We must give up this much liberty in order to save the rest.'[5]

The parting of the ways

At much the same time as the crisis over conscription, and probably not unconnected with it, relations between Lloyd George and Asquith, the two most important figures in the government and in many ways the essential axis of the party's pre-war ascendancy, began to decline. In the face of mounting disquiet about the conduct of the war, in Parliament and in public, Lloyd George (by now Minister for War after Lord Kitchener's death at sea) increasingly pressed for more effective direction of the war effort by a small committee. When, in December 1916, Bonar Law informed Asquith that he could not continue in the government unless the War Committee proposal was adopted, the Prime Minister realised that his position had become untenable. On 7 December, Asquith resigned, and was replaced by Lloyd George.

Ever since R. C. K. Ensor penned his influential Oxford history, some writers have sought to uncover in the quarrel and eventual split between the two men a fundamental clash between the Whig and radical traditions of the historic party.[6] Yet the quest is essentially futile. The issue which ultimately drove the two men and their respective followers apart was the efficient management of the British war effort and a mounting conviction among Asquith's critics that the Prime Minister's ways were ill-suited to the pressing demands facing the country in 1916. The diary of Frances Stevenson, Lloyd George's secretary and mistress, details the latter's increasing frustration with Asquith's 'business-as-usual' approach. On the other side was a growing belief that Lloyd George was not a man with whom to go tiger shooting. He had, admitted Asquith, 'many qualities that would fit him for the first place, but he lacks the one thing needful – he does not inspire trust'. When the parting of the ways came in December 1916 – variously described as the product of a 'palace revolution' or the result of the 'disillusion' of Asquith's friends – the impact on the fortunes of the Liberal Party was immense. This was less because of the revelation of a fundamental ideological rift, but simply because the party would remain divided to the end of the war and beyond. It would fight the next two general elections as two separate groups and, even when reunion was belatedly effected in 1923, it was at best partial and incomplete: in Asquith's telling words, 'a fiction if not a farce'.

Little of this was immediately apparent. Most of the apparatus of the Liberal Party organisation remained firmly in Asquith's hands. The majority of the party's leading figures, including the Chief Whip, also stayed loyal. Those Liberals who agreed to join the Lloyd George coalition were largely figures of the second rank. In some ways a precarious unity was maintained. Liberal whips continued to canvass the whole of the parliamentary party and from time to time tentative approaches were made to see whether Asquith might be prepared to rejoin the government. For his part Lloyd George insisted that he would not follow the example of Joseph Chamberlain by wrecking the party. As C. P. Scott of the *Manchester Guardian* noted, 'he held to all the essential principles of Liberalism and was most anxious to avoid a split'.[7]

Circumstances ensured that the Asquithians never moved into full opposition. Asquith himself was prepared to be seen as ineffectual rather than risk the charge of disloyalty during the emergency of the war. But while it perhaps held out the prospect of ultimate reconciliation, his attitude had a disillusioning effect on those Liberals who felt alienated from Lloyd George's Conservative-dominated administration and now looked vainly to the former Prime Minister for a reassertion of Liberal principles. The Liberal Party at this time lost much of its credibility as the standard-bearer of the radical left in British politics. Many, such as C. P. Scott, came to place their hopes for the future in an association between the radical wing of the Liberal Party and moderate Labour. A process of transfer from the Liberal to the Labour Party, which had begun among anti-war Liberals at the outbreak of hostilities via such bodies as the Union of Democratic Control, now gathered momentum, particularly after November 1917 when Labour formally adopted a UDC-style approach to the conduct of the war.

The celebrated Maurice debate of 9 May 1918 hardened the lines of division between the two Liberal groups. Sir Frederick Maurice, until recently Director of Military Operations at the War Office, claimed that Lloyd George had misled Parliament about the true strength of the British army on the Western Front. For the first time Asquith openly opposed the Prime Minister in the House of Commons and his whips marshalled their forces against the government. Though Lloyd George won the division reasonably comfortably, more Liberal MPs supported Asquith than the Prime Minister. The event emphasised Lloyd George's dependence upon Conservative backing and engendered a greater degree of bitterness in relations between the two Liberal factions than had been present hitherto. *The Times* described the 'debut of an organised Opposition' and suggested that a first step might have been taken 'towards what may become a permanent cleavage'.

The coupon election

During the second half of 1918 the Prime Minister's mind turned increasingly towards a general election, a contest which, if it took place with the Liberals still divided and the Conservatives dominating the government, was bound, in a mood of fervent nationalism, to harm the Liberal Party. While Lloyd George would not cut himself adrift from the Conservatives, whose support and loyalty since December 1916 he much respected, he continued to make overtures to Asquith to return to the fold. The latter, however, nurtured a sense of grievance about the way he had been treated in 1916 and rejected all advances. Nonetheless, Lloyd George told a meeting of almost 200 Liberal MPs on 12 November that he was as strong a Liberal as he had ever been, committed still to free trade and Irish home rule. 'I'm too old to change', he assured them. 'I cannot leave Liberalism. I would quit this place tomorrow if I could not obtain the support of Liberals.' Furthermore, when the election was fixed for December, the two Liberal factions seemed set to campaign on programmes that were virtually interchangeable.

The situation was transformed following a speech made by Lloyd George at Wolverhampton. Here he seemed to suggest that no one who had voted against him over Maurice could be regarded as a reliable supporter of the government. Matters were compounded when Lloyd George accepted the bargain struck with the Conservatives by his whip, Freddie Guest, that only 150 Liberal candidates would receive the letter of endorsement, the notorious 'coupon', signed by the Tory leader, Bonar Law, and himself. Inevitably, this meant that many Liberals, who regarded themselves as every bit as committed to the Liberal creed as the Prime Minister, were bound to be opposed and in all probability defeated by couponed Conservatives. Thus were lines of demarcation created altogether more significant and damaging than any drawn up in 1916. Nor, as the campaign progressed, could Asquithians compete, even had they wished to, with the increasingly shrill demands of coalition candidates for a punitive peace with Germany.

In what was effectively a khaki election, and one, furthermore, among an expanded electorate (the 1918 Representation of the People Act had enlarged the electorate to all men over twenty-one and all women over thirty), many of whom had of course never voted Liberal before, the outcome was entirely predictable. From a Liberal point of view it could scarcely have been worse. 133 Coalition Liberals were returned to the new Parliament, but they were easily swamped by 335 Conservatives. Only twenty-eight independent Liberals took their seats when the Commons reassembled, overtaken now by sixty-three Labour MPs. Over the years that followed, many Liberals, including Asquith himself, came to see this as the seminal moment in their party's decline. Writing in 1926, at the time of his retirement from the leadership, Asquith declared that 'the disintegration of the Liberal Party began with the Coupon Election ... It then received a blow from which it has never since recovered.'[8]

1918 general election (14 December)[9]			
	Votes	%	MPs
Liberal	1,298,808	12.6	28
Coalition Liberal	**1,455,640**	**14.2**	**133**
Coalition Conservative	**3,504,198**	**34.1**	**335**
Coalition Labour	**161,521**	**1.6**	**10**
Conservative	370,375	3.6	23
Irish Unionist	292,722	2.9	25
Labour	2,385,472	23.2	63
Irish Parliamentary	238,477	2.3	7
Sinn Fein	486,867	4.7	73
Others	72,503	0.7	10
Total	10,266,583		707

The party's subsequent record makes it difficult to dispute this judgement, but a number of qualifying comments need to be made. In the euphoria of military victory, the outcome of the 1918 election represented above all else the nationalistic enthusiasm of the electorate for a government which had just brought the war to a successful conclusion and even more for 'the man who had won the war'. Only secondarily was it a verdict expressed in traditional party political terms. It seems therefore reasonable to speculate that any political grouping headed by Lloyd George, including a reunited Liberal Party, would have performed well at this time. Then, despite the symbolic importance of Labour's advance, that party's performance under a newly widened franchise was worse than anyone had predicted. Its results in England were particularly disappointing, where only in the Midlands did it made any real advance in new areas compared with the pre-war era. To some extent Liberals would use their electoral collapse in 1918 as an excuse for the lethargy into which they now relapsed, thereby depriving themselves of the possibility of recovery which arguably still existed.

Discord and disunity

In the remaining four years of coalition government neither part of the divided Liberal Party prospered. The shattered Asquithian remnant – without Asquith himself, who had been defeated after more than thirty years as MP for East Fife – seemed devoid of ideas for the future, intellectually bankrupt and bound together by little more than personal loyalties and historic memories.

It had, of course, been difficult for the party to move forward on questions of policy during the war. Nonetheless, in the spring of 1918 Asquith had asked Herbert Samuel to chair a committee of ex-ministers and MPs to draw up a social and economic programme for the post-war era. But little of that sort of thinking was now apparent. The selection, in Asquith's absence, of Donald Maclean as sessional chairman of the parliamentary party was scarcely designed to inspire. At a time when radical voices wanted to build a land fit for heroes to live in, Maclean insisted that a Liberal government would impose rigid and detailed economy. 'They would go right back to the Gladstonian policy of saving the pence and even the ha'pence.'[10] Not surprisingly, Charles Masterman, one of the ministerial architects of the pre-1914 New Liberalism, concluded that 'the poor old Liberal Party is dead or dying'.[11]

Donald Maclean (1864–1932)

Maclean was born in Farnworth, Lancashire in January 1864. A solicitor by profession, he, like many of his generation, was first elected to Parliament in the Liberal landslide of 1906. After a relatively undistinguished parliamentary career he shot to prominence as a result of the destruction of the independent Liberal Party in the coupon election of December 1918. Unusually for an uncouponed Liberal he found himself without a couponed opponent and returned to Westminster as one of a group of around thirty Liberal MPs who supported Asquith rather than Lloyd George. As such, he was elected chairman of the Parliamentary Liberal Party, a position he retained when Asquith returned to the Commons after victory in the Paisley by-election of February 1920. With his pronouncement in March 1920 that independent Liberals were in no sense obliged to vote for Coalition Liberal candidates at by-elections, he played a not unimportant role in confirming the divisions in the party's ranks.

Maclean lost his seat at Peebles and South Midlothian in 1922 and did not return to Parliament until he was victorious in North Cornwall in the general election of 1929. Despite his earlier career as an Asquithian, he now worked well under Lloyd George's leadership of the party. With the formation of the National Government in August 1931 Maclean became President of the Board of Education, outside the Cabinet. It was a position for which his long-term interest in child welfare had well prepared him, but he found himself having to defend the government's stringent policies of reduced expenditure. At the general election in October, which Maclean opposed, he faced and defeated a Conservative opponent and then joined the Cabinet. Along with his Liberal colleagues he stayed in office, when the government introduced tariffs early in 1932, through the so-called 'agreement to differ'.

Maclean died suddenly from a heart attack in June 1932. He is probably best remembered because of his notorious son of the same name who became a diplomat, Russian spy and defector.

Asquith himself, diminished by the trials of war and particularly by the loss on the Western Front of his eldest son, Raymond, clung obstinately to the party leadership at a time when he had little that was constructive to offer. Even his official biographers concede that, during the last decade of his life, Asquith's 'mind was rarely "extended"; there was a visible slackening, not so much of its fibre, as of the will to use it'. Lloyd George was more blunt. 'There was no life in him. He was like a great boulder blocking the way.' Asquith could not even reconcile himself to the limited enfranchisement of women in 1918. They were, he wrote of the female voters in the Paisley by-election of 1920 which secured his return to Parliament, 'a dim, impenetrable, for the most part ungettable, element – of whom all that one knows is that they are for the most part hopelessly ignorant of politics, credulous to the last degree, and flickering with gusts of sentiment like a candle in the wind'.[12]

Many independent Liberals – or 'Wee Frees' as they came to be called – began the quest for a new leader who could breathe life into a dispirited party. But it was not at all clear from which direction salvation would come. Sir John Simon was in some respects Asquith's natural successor. He had the talent and intellect that were required, but failed to attract universal trust, let alone affection. Other potential candidates such as Samuel and Lord Reading were tending to drift away from the domestic political arena. Most attention focused on the former Foreign Secretary, Edward Grey, still under sixty at the end of the war and a politician of undoubted stature. But Grey's failing eyesight gave him an understandable reason to reject all approaches. For want of a better alternative, and with a personal determination to block any chance of a prodigal Lloyd George returning to inherit the succession, Asquith soldiered on.

Reunion was in practice the necessary precondition of Liberal revival. To begin with, there appeared to be few ideological barriers in the way of reconciliation. Liberal influence was fully apparent in the government's policies of reconstruction and social reform, and a joint committee to promote unity met on several occasions early in 1919. Gradually, however, the dominant Conservative voice within the coalition became clear. Masterman bemoaned that the government had 'dug a grave wide and deep' for the Liberals' pre-war land policy and complained of Lloyd George's apostasy in going along with it. The government decided to remove the land taxes, which Lloyd George himself had first introduced a decade before, on the grounds that the revenue raised was of negligible importance.

It was the coalition's repressive policy in Ireland which, more than anything else, stuck in the gullets of any true Liberal, especially as it was 'maintained under a Prime Minister with a following still claiming to be Liberal, and living in the tradition of Gladstone'.[13] In the period before the ceasefire with the Irish Republican Army in July 1921, and the establishment of the Irish Free State in December, the coalition tried to stamp out terrorism using the tactics of the terrorists themselves. The activities of the 'Black and Tans', auxiliaries brought in to support the Royal Irish Constabulary, alienated moderate Liberal opinion. Yet many Asquithians needed no excuse to keep Lloyd

George at arm's length. They nurtured a visceral hatred, believing that by his actions in 1916 and ever since he had deliberately set out to wreck the Liberal Party. As a result, the divisions within the Liberal fold tended only to deepen during the remainder of Lloyd George's premiership. Matters came to a head at a meeting of the National Liberal Federation General Committee in Leamington in May 1920, at which the Coalition Liberal delegation walked out in protest at the hostile attitude taken up by the Wee Frees. The result was something like civil war in the party's local constituency associations, with the Asquithians for the most part holding the upper hand. Coalition and Wee Free Liberals opposed one another at by-elections to the confusion of potential Liberal voters and the inevitable advantage of their political opponents.

Lloyd George himself, increasingly aware that he was at the mercy of his Conservative colleagues and likely to be ditched if they ever judged him to be no longer an electoral asset, seemed unsure which course to follow. 'D[avid] at present is very silent', noted Frances Stevenson in January 1920, 'which means that he does not quite see his way'. Though he lived and would die calling himself a Liberal, Lloyd George's primary purpose in politics was always to secure concrete objectives and his adherence to any particular party label took a poor second place to this goal. As Robert Boothby once put it, he had a 'penchant for ad hoc solutions provided they would work'. Lloyd George's preferred option was the fusion of moderate politicians from all parties into a new centre grouping designed to hold back the tide of doctrinaire socialism. Speaking in Manchester in December 1919, he suggested that there were no longer any differences of substance between Liberals and Conservatives and that they should join together to fight the new menace on the political left. But when his own Coalition Liberal ministers made it clear that they had no interest in permanent fusion with Conservatives, the plan was still-born. By the spring of 1920 Lloyd George had little alternative but to try to convert the Coalition Liberals into a permanent organisation. Guest was now given the task of setting up a local Coalition Liberal party in every parliamentary constituency.

The Coalition's social policy

It was once common to denigrate the social policy of the coalition government and to see it as part of a broader failure to build a 'fit country for heroes to live in'. Christopher Addison, whose embittered departure from the government in July 1921 seemed to symbolise the coalition's abandonment of its promises of reform, contributed significantly to this picture, using his long political career, much of it spent inside later Labour governments, to present the coalition's record as an illustration of what to avoid. Yet Kenneth Morgan, in particular, has argued that the Lloyd George government's record is one of considerable achievement, largely but not exclusively secured by its Liberal members.

The Unemployment Insurance Act of 1920 extended benefits to those trades already covered by the health insurance scheme, thereby bringing twelve million workers into its coverage for the first time. Old age pensions were significantly increased, while the creation of the Ministry of Health was a brave attempt to impose a measure of centralised control over a range of uncoordinated services. At the Board of Education H. A. L. Fisher introduced a valuable school-building programme, supported day continuation schools and improved teachers' pay. Addison's own housing schemes saw the completion of over 170,000 houses and introduced the principle, important for the future, that housing was a social service, and one where the government would support local authorities in footing the bill.

For some time the social programme withstood the pressures of economic restraint, but it inevitably slowed down during the winter of 1920–21, the victim of rampant inflation and a subsequent economic slump. In the circumstances it is doubtful whether any government could have done better. Indeed, Morgan judges that 'until forced off course by overwhelming economic and political pressures, the government made a genuine effort to build on the wartime consensus with vigorous social policies'.[14]

The Liberal Party's internal split might not have been fatal had it not been combined with the rise of another party enjoying mounting electoral support. No analysis of Liberal decline can ignore the fact that Labour's great advance came in those years *after* the coupon election when the Liberals remained divided. In the context of Britain's two-party system, this was the critical era of transition during which Labour emerged as the main alternative to the Conservatives within the national polity. Margot Asquith was among those who failed to appreciate the importance of what was happening. Writing from Paisley in 1920, where her husband was fighting a successful by-election, she warned against the 'snob movement towards Labour ... like the snob movement towards Ugliness in Art, Discord in Music and Sexlessness in Women'. There was, she insisted, 'nothing eternal in chic'.[15] But the growing strength of the Labour Party was no passing fad. By the fall of the coalition in October 1922 the Liberal Party had lost its claim to be the main party of change and progress. With Lloyd George's position undermined by too close association with Conservatives and the Asquithian leadership languishing in a state of intellectual stagnation, Labour took its chance. Before 1914 its threat to Liberalism had been largely theoretical, a potential challenge if the Liberals should lose their predominant claim to the working-class vote. Now that potential was transformed into reality.

Labour's path was eased by its very 'liberalism'. Rather than representing the challenge of dogmatic socialism, as Lloyd George and many other contemporaries claimed, Labour found it easy to draw away Liberal support because of its inherent moderation. Beatrice Webb's assessment of Arthur Henderson would serve for most of the Labour hierarchy of this time: 'right down in his consciousness is the old Liberal who does not himself want any considerable change in social structure and is contented with a very moderate measure of social reform within that present system'.[16]

Long before the collapse of the coalition in October 1922, the Conservative Party's rank and file had become increasingly hostile to its continuation, and particularly to the prospect of fighting another election under its banner. Although most of the leading Conservatives in the government remained loyal to Lloyd George, the majority of

Conservative MPs did not. At a meeting in the Carlton Club on 19 October 1922, Tory back-benchers revolted against the coalition, overthrowing their own leadership in the process.

With the fall of the coalition, the new Conservative Prime Minister, Andrew Bonar Law, called an immediate general election to secure legitimacy for his purely Conservative administration. In a handful of constituencies Liberals made common cause, but for the most part ongoing divisions prevailed and, as Lloyd George later recalled, 'Liberals spent a great part of their strength in fighting each other'. Yet, with just 328 candidates for a House of Commons of over 600 seats, Asquith's Liberals could only present themselves as serious aspirants for power in conjunction with Lloyd George and his followers. In the event the Wee Frees secured 62 seats, a considerable improvement on their 1918 performance. The Lloyd Georgeites won just 53, as against 133 in 1918, and performed particularly badly in industrial areas. But even taken together the forces of Liberalism were now outnumbered by Labour, with 142 seats.

1922 general election (15 November)			
	Votes	*%*	*MPs*
Liberal	2,668,143	18.5	62
National Liberal	1,471,317	10.2	53
Conservative	**5,502,298**	**38.2**	**344**
Labour	4,237,349	29.4	142
Others	513,223	3.6	14
Total	*14,392,330*		*615*

It seems reasonable to conclude that a genuinely unified Liberal Party could have performed sufficiently strongly to deprive Labour of the title of official opposition to which it now justifiably laid claim. For the future the electorate's choice seemed to lie between a Conservative or a Labour government, and contemporaries increasingly spoke of the Liberals being crushed between the upper and nether millstones of the two other parties. They had in fact already fallen into the third-party trap with all the disadvantages that this status carries with it. The combined Liberal Party had secured almost 30 per cent of the popular vote but less than 20 per cent of the seats in the new House of Commons. Moreover, the British electoral system makes it difficult for a party to escape from this predicament. A third party is no longer the alternative government in waiting and the electorate becomes disinclined to support it because it wishes to cast its vote for a realistic contender for power.

High-profile defections

In the kaleidoscopic political maelstrom of the 1920s, as Liberalism sought – largely unsuccessfully – to establish a clear and viable identity within the political spectrum, it was scarcely surprising that the mass haemorrhaging of Liberal votes to the right and to the left was accompanied by a series of high-profile defections at the top of the party.

Indeed, this process was one of the most obvious manifestations of Liberal decline. It began while the First World War was still in progress as disillusioned radicals such as C. P. Trevelyan (a junior minister in 1914) and Josiah Wedgwood severed their formal links with Liberalism. Others went down to defeat as Liberals in the coupon election before transferring their political allegiance. Noel Buxton, defeated as a Liberal in North Norfolk in 1918, re-emerged as Labour MP for the same constituency in 1922. The Unionists' *Constitutional Year Book* (1923) suggested that eleven former Liberal MPs stood as Labour candidates in the general election of 1922.

Christopher Addison, who fell out with Lloyd George in 1921, was the only leading Coalition Liberal to join Labour. He was elected for Swindon in 1929 and held office in the Labour governments of 1929–31 and 1945–51. More logically, Winston Churchill found his way back to the Conservative ranks. Defeated as a Liberal in Leicester West in 1923, he opposed the decision to install a Labour government and stood unsuccessfully as an independent anti-socialist in a by-election in the Abbey division of Westminster in March 1924. Later that year he was elected as a 'constitutionalist' in Epping and soon took office in Baldwin's Conservative government.

Another prominent defector was William Wedgwood Benn, whose mounting hostility towards Lloyd George led to his resignation as Liberal member for Leith in 1927. In 1928 he was elected Labour MP for Aberdeen North. Commander Kenworthy switched to Labour after Asquith's retirement in 1926, while Sir Alfred Mond joined the Conservatives in the same year in opposition to Lloyd George's land policy. Perhaps most strikingly, William Jowitt, elected as Liberal MP for Preston in the general election of 1929, immediately accepted the office of Attorney-General in the new Labour government formed by Ramsay MacDonald.

Uneasy reunion

At least the disappointing outcome at the polls had the effect of concentrating more Liberal minds on the question of reunion. In the new Parliament several MPs asked to receive both whips, while petitions for reunion went the rounds of the House of Commons. Meanwhile Liberal peers of all hues seemed happy to accept Lord Grey as their common leader. The two principals, however, were more wary. Asquith recognised that reunion might well be coming, but was 'all against forcing the pace and surrendering any of our ground'.[17] For his part, Lloyd George still seemed to be hankering after political realignment. In a statement to the *Daily Chronicle* he called for 'men of progressive outlook in all parties' to act together. By the spring of 1923, however, he had become convinced of the need for Liberal reunion, though privately insisting that he would 'not crawl on my belly' to achieve this result. Speaking in Edinburgh on 14 March he claimed that the coalition had stood by Liberalism during the previous six years, but stressed that he was neither seeking nor claiming the party leadership for himself. Nevertheless, it was, he said, necessary for Liberals to form a common front against the Labour threat.

The annual meeting of the National Liberal Federation at Buxton turned a blind eye to insistent demands for reunion from the constituencies, but by September more than fifty local Liberal and Lloyd Georgeite Liberal associations had merged.

It needed an outside agency to complete the process. When in October 1923 the new Conservative Prime Minister, Stanley Baldwin, called another general election to secure a mandate for the introduction of tariffs, in line with a pledge given by his predecessor, the divided forces of Liberalism were brought together almost overnight. So easily was reunion secured that some Labour observers suggested that Baldwin's initiative had been designed to revive the Liberal Party as the best way of defeating Labour. The defence of free trade could still rally the party's disparate strands in a way that no other issue could. A combined committee of Liberals quickly hammered out a joint election manifesto and agreed that the party would fight as a single body across the country. The Lloyd Georgeite party was abruptly wound up without its rank and file being consulted, but it was significant that no steps were taken to merge the private political fund which Lloyd George had accumulated during the years of his premiership with the Liberal Party's own accounts. Lloyd George and Asquith even appeared together on the same platform, though the latter at least found the experience somewhat uncomfortable.

Though free trade had, as in 1903, served a definite political purpose, there were those such as Masterman who regretted the party's concentration on this old creed. Free trade had in any case lost the moral purchase on the country as a whole that had been a key factor in the strength of the Edwardian party. Many still saw it as an important economic tool; fewer as an article of quasi-religious faith. Its association with prosperity and the maintenance of democracy and peace had been badly shaken in the course of the First World War. At the outset of the campaign, the *Liberal Magazine* warned that 'Liberals want more than Free Trade can give ... We shall do well to beware of talking all the time on the least positive feature of our programme.' Yet in practice this is what happened. The Liberals waged an almost entirely negative campaign, in opposition to the government's tariff proposals. Of a fifteen-paragraph report on Asquith's speech at Walsall on 14 November, only one was concerned with constructive issues, fourteen with an attack on protection.

Nonetheless, the outcome of the election represented the Liberal Party's best performance in the whole of the inter-war period and left it in the superficially enviable position of holding the balance in the new Parliament. With 30 per cent of the popular vote, 158 MPs were elected. The Conservatives remained the largest single party but, after an election fought specifically on the issue of tariffs, were comfortably outnumbered by the combined free trade strength of Labour (191 seats) and the Liberals. The latter had done well against the Conservatives, especially in rural and middle-class areas and particularly where Labour had not put up a candidate. By contrast, the Liberals were still giving ground in industrial areas, with a net loss of ten seats to Labour. Every new seat was, of course, welcome, but this pattern scarcely suggested that the Liberal Party was still managing to portray itself as the leader of left-of-centre progressivism.

1923 general election (6 December)			
	Votes	%	MPs
Liberal	4,301,481	29.6	158
Conservative	5,514,541	37.9	258
Labour	**4,439,780**	**30.5**	**191**
Others	291,893	2.0	8
Total	14,547,695		615

Working with Labour

Asquith had not expected to win the election. 'I have been going through the general list of candidates', he wrote before the contest, 'and I cannot for the life of me see how we are going to come back more than 200 strong, it may be less'.[18] Yet surprisingly, little advance thought appears to have been given to what the Liberals would do if they held the balance of power, their most realistic aspiration. 'The Liberal Party is divided on the question of supporting Labour', reported Lloyd George. 'Quite a number of the "important and influential" emphatically dislike it, but if Ramsay [MacDonald] were tactful and conciliatory I feel certain that the party as a whole would support him in an advanced Radical programme.'[19] *The Nation* was of the same mind. 'Liberalism will fail to do its work unless it succeeds eventually in re-establishing co-operation and fundamental agreement with the great mass of Labour opinion.' Such thinking may have been well grounded in ideological terms – a cautious Labour administration, possessing no independent majority in the House of Commons, was unlikely to do much of which radical Liberals would disapprove – but it failed to take account of the changes which had occurred in the Liberal–Labour relationship since the pre-war era. Addressing the parliamentary party on 18 December, Asquith adopted a positive tone. Liberals were not going to become a wing or adjunct of any other party, but 'it is we, if we really understand our business, who really control the situation'. He seemed to hold out the prospect of a Liberal government not too far down the line, the result presumably of the early collapse of the new Labour administration.

Thus, with only this limited amount of planning and certainly with no systematic attempt to hammer out an agreed legislative programme, Liberal support enabled Labour to take office, for the first time, in January 1924. In practice, the Liberal position was an extremely difficult one. As there were more Conservative MPs than Labour, the Liberals did not have the option of simply acquiescing in a Labour government; they had positively to support it. Abstention would be impossible if Labour were to survive for any length of time.

If, however, the Liberals had given insufficient thought to their political and parliamentary options, the same could not be said of Labour, and particularly of its new Prime Minister. Among Ramsay MacDonald's clearly defined aims on taking office was to move a stage further towards the destruction and disappearance of the Liberal Party. The Liberals might have been the radical party of the past, but Labour must occupy that place in the future. The new premier soon showed his prejudices. 'He could get on with the Tories ... They were gentlemen, but the Liberals were cads.'[20] His reasoning, however, was rather more subtle. MacDonald understood full well the bias in the political system against third parties. His task now was to govern long enough and responsibly enough to entrench Labour in the mind of the electorate as the main party of the progressive left and to nip in the bud any Liberal aspiration to recover that position. In his vision, the pre-war era of Liberal-Labour co-operation was definitively over. Labour was no longer content to be the junior partner in a progressive alliance. Its role now was as a party of government and there could not be two major British parties of the left at the same time. As MacDonald confided to his diary a few years later, 'our immediate duty is to place every obstacle we can in the way of the survival of the three-party system'.[21]

Labour, then, would not play the game according to Liberal rules. Lloyd George expressed his disappointment at the way in which the Liberal hand of friendship was rebuffed. Speaking in his constituency in April 1924 he asked:

> How has that support been acknowledged? With unmitigated hostility in Parliament, out of Parliament, in the constituencies. Whilst Liberal members are voting for the Labour Government, Labour candidates have been put up against them throughout the constituencies, and Liberalism in the country is being hunted, if possible, to death ... When we support them, our support is received with sullen indifference. If we dare to criticise them, we are visited with a peevish resentment.[22]

In any case, not all Liberals favoured the policy of sustaining a Labour government in office. Continuing divisions of opinion reflected the central dilemma of this period – of whether the party's basic inclination, now that it was positioned in most people's minds somewhere between the left and the right of British politics, was to lean towards the Conservatives or towards Labour. It was a dilemma which had not really existed while the party remained the main alternative to Conservative government. Its effect during the Parliament of 1924 was that Liberals sometimes divided three ways between support, opposition and abstention in relation to individual measures put forward by the Labour government. This ludicrous spectacle reflected no credit on the party as a serious participant in the political arena.

Overall, it seems unlikely that the Liberals derived any benefit from their months of holding the parliamentary balance. The Conservative Party looked increasingly the natural home for those who feared the advent of socialism, while Labour enhanced its credentials as the vehicle for radical progress. When the Labour government came to an end, Lloyd George expressed regret at the way things had worked out. 'With a little more wisdom', Labour could have 'formed a working alliance with Liberalism that would have ensured a progressive administration of this country for twenty years'.[23] Perhaps so, but these remarks displayed a complete misunderstanding of Labour's strategic purpose.

The fall of the Labour government in October 1924 freed the Liberal Party of the burden of sustaining in office a government which offered them nothing in return.

At the same time, it made inevitable a third general election in the space of two years, something for which Liberals were unprepared and which they could ill afford. Indeed, the party's precarious financial situation was a major cause of its difficulties throughout the 1920s and merits some attention.

Back in 1910 the *Manchester Guardian* had rhetorically asked, 'What would be the state of the Liberal Party chest if it depended on the voluntary subscriptions of the rank and file?' In practice, this was the situation that had come to pass by the 1920s. After 1916 the rich men who had kept the Edwardian party afloat tended to fund Lloyd George rather than the party of which he remained nominally a member. As a result, Lloyd George had built up a large personal fund, subscribed to for political purposes but in practice often in exchange for honours. The fund had been swollen by the Prime Minister's shrewd investment in a group of newspapers, including the *Daily Chronicle*. Inevitably, the money became Lloyd George's chief bargaining counter within the party's ongoing power struggles. He tried to keep it within his personal control while using it to exert influence over the party as a whole. By the middle of the decade no single issue caused such dissension within Liberal ranks. The Asquithian journalist A. G. Gardiner was scathing. It was, he said, 'a source of personal influence which can be directed to any occult end, an *imperium in imperio*, as sinister and disruptive in its possibilities as it is ... unprecedented in the whole history of British political life'.[24] There was some truth in this, but the fund was also essential to the Liberal Party's continued viability as a national force in British politics.

In April 1924 Asquith was advised of the pressing need to secure enough financial support to enable Liberals to field a sufficient number of candidates at the next general election. There was no option but to court Lloyd George, and difficult negotiations proceeded throughout the year. But in August Lloyd George informed Asquith that he would not feel able to ask the trustees of his fund to make a contribution until the whole organisation of the party had been overhauled, leaving him confident that the money would be well spent. In the end, Lloyd George agreed to donate just £50,000 to the campaign of October 1924, less than half what the party needed. The result was that only 340 Liberal candidates entered the contest. In effect, the party was disqualifying itself from the start as a serious contender for power.

Even allowing for the reduced number of candidates, the Liberals waged a feeble campaign. Asquith insisted that the party was 'neither manoeuvring for position nor angling for votes by the abandonment of a single one of its characteristic beliefs'. The party, he said, stood for liberalism undiluted – but precisely what that now meant was unclear. Calls for temperance and free trade had a limited appeal. 'I doubt', wrote Charles Hobhouse, a former Cabinet minister, 'if [the Liberal Party] any longer stands for anything distinctive'.[25] Against the background of a 'red scare' occasioned by the Zinoviev Letter (a forged communication, supposedly from the Soviet government, welcoming the normalisation of relations with Russia which MacDonald's government was pursuing as increasing the chance of revolution in Britain), Conservatives won a landslide victory with over 400 MPs. Labour lost forty seats, but its percentage of the overall poll actually increased; it was the main opposition party and likely to remain so. The Liberals on the other hand were reduced to just forty MPs, with Asquith again one of the casualties.

1924 general election (29 October)			
	Votes	%	MPs
Liberal	2,928,737	17.6	40
Conservative	**7,854,523**	**47.2**	**412**
Labour	5,489,087	33.0	151
Others	367,932	2.2	12
Total	16,640,279		615

Almost all the gains of a year earlier, and more, were now lost. Liberals themselves were increasingly aware of the seismic change which had overtaken the political landscape. As Asquith's daughter put it, 'a new generation of young men who had ripened into voters, almost it seemed, since the last Election, were determined to give a solid class-vote to Labour, no matter what we said or did'.[26] The political objective, to which both Labour and the Conservatives had subscribed, of pushing the Liberals out of the front line of British politics had largely been achieved.

Lloyd George takes the reins

'Unless something is done', mused a dispirited Lloyd George, 'the party is doomed to extinction'.[27] That something, he was increasingly convinced, was that he himself should capture control of the party and mould it in his own image. And that image, notwithstanding his flirtation with Conservatism during the days of the coalition, was of a radical party of the left, building upon the New Liberalism of the pre-war era to respond to the social and economic needs of industrial Britain. Over the following four and a half years Lloyd George would indeed achieve a partial revival in Liberalism's fortunes – without, however, managing to overturn the new balance of party political power established by the 1924 general election.

Lloyd George's task was not easy. The mood of the post-election party was one of bitterness and recrimination. At a meeting of defeated candidates Lloyd George was sharply criticised for his financial meanness. Asquith, though beaten at Paisley and now into his eighth decade, soldiered on as an increasingly ineffectual party leader in the House of Lords. Meanwhile leading Asquithians, heedless of Lloyd George's warning that, unless past grievances were forgotten, Liberalism would never again become a dominant force in the life of the country, showed few signs of abating their hostility. Even when, after some opposition, Lloyd George was elected sessional chairman of the parliamentary party, eleven MPs led by Walter Runciman formed the singularly ill-named 'Radical Group', effectively disowning Lloyd George's authority. Gradually, however, more and more Liberals were won over by the remorseless logic of the situation. Even if they did not like Lloyd George, they were doomed without him and especially without his money.

The final trial of strength came over Liberal attitudes to the General Strike of 1926. This event opened up yet another predictable schism within the party hierarchy, with Lloyd George blaming the government for the crisis while right-wing Asquithians insisted that society had an obligation to defeat the strikers. It was rumoured that Lloyd George's sympathetic attitude towards the strikers was part of a secret bargain with Labour which might result in his becoming a minister in the next Labour government. The Liberal economist Hubert Henderson, who argued that on the issue of the strike Lloyd George was 'triumphantly and unmistakably in the right', floated the idea in *The Nation* of a new progressive alliance between the Labour and Liberal parties. More significantly, those around Asquith saw in this latest spat a final opportunity to break with Lloyd George, or at least to destroy his influence within the party once and for all. As Frances Stevenson noted, 'it was obvious that the Old Gang thought D[avid]'s luck and popularity were down as a result of the strike, and that this was a time to get rid of him'.[28] In the wake of John Simon's portentous declaration that the strike was illegal, Lloyd George pointedly stayed away from a meeting of the Liberal Shadow Cabinet on 10 May, informing the Chief Whip that he did not wish to be associated with any party statement which failed to condemn the government's handling of the situation.

The row became public with an acrimonious exchange of letters being published in the press. This culminated in a letter on 31 May from twelve members of the Shadow Cabinet, pledging their support to Asquith while denouncing Lloyd George's conduct since the reunion of 1923. 'We have done our best', they insisted, 'in the highest interests of the cause of Liberalism to work with Mr Lloyd George in the consultations of the party and we regret to say that we cannot any longer continue to work with a colleague who, in our judgement, is not worthy of the trust.' But the Asquithians had misjudged the situation. The wider party had no stomach for a further bout of intra-party strife. On 8 June the parliamentary party effectively disowned Asquith by voting for unity. Just over a week later the annual meeting of the NLF at Weston-super-Mare expressed the same sentiments. As John Simon heard, 'the preponderating desire of the delegates was that the recently published correspondence should not split the Party. While reaffirming its confidence in Lord Oxford [Asquith's new title] as leader, the conference was equally emphatic that Lloyd George must be associated with the Party ... All they were concerned with was that the Party should not be torn asunder.'[29]

In between these two events fate intervened, when Asquith suffered a stroke. With the leader out of action, most Liberals appreciated their need for Lloyd George. Lord Reading summed up the mood within the party: 'The aim should be to achieve, if not a complete and cordial unity, at least a unity which would satisfy the public and lay the lines for closer and more harmonious working between the various sections of the Parliamentary Liberal Party.'[30] For his part, Asquith had no desire to take the fight any further. 'The alternatives', he wrote to his wife, 'are to lead a squalid faction fight against LlG in which he has all the sinews of war; or to accept his money and patch up a hollow and humiliating alliance. I am quite resolved to do neither, so I shall *faire mes paquets* for which I have ample justification on other grounds, age, etc.'[31] In October he finally resigned the leadership of the party.

Momentarily, other names were considered for the succession. In practice, there was no alternative to Lloyd George. The key factor, predictably enough, was money. The party's financial position had never been more precarious. Following the 1924 general election the NLF had launched the so-called Million Fund Appeal, designed to make the party independent of Lloyd George's intermittent and insufficient subventions. But the appeal had been a failure, not least because the existence of the Lloyd George Fund was now a matter of public knowledge. 'A big fund might have been raised on the basis that there was no money, but it could not be raised on the basis that there was a large sum of money which for reasons impossible to explain could not be drawn upon.'[32] By the end of 1926 the Million Fund Administration Committee had accepted Lloyd George's terms for a massive grant from his political fund. 'The position is terribly difficult', noted Richard Holt, 'as the money is badly needed and few have the courage to refuse it and take the consequences'.[33] The terms amounted in practice to a wholesale shake-up of the party organisation, the flushing out of senior Asquithian officials and the installation of Lloyd Georgeite replacements. But as a gesture of reconciliation Lloyd George arranged for the widely respected Herbert Samuel to become chairman of the party organisation, with a clear remit to build bridges between the contending factions. Samuel's recent absence from the domestic political scene had left him virtually the only leading Liberal not publicly committed to any one grouping.

Even now, however, there were those who refused to be reconciled. Edward Grey took the lead in organising remaining dissidents into a Liberal Council, with officers and funds separate from those of the party. Its stated aim was 'to enable Liberals who desire to uphold the independence of the Party to remain within it for the furtherance of the aims of Liberalism', a declaration presumably of Lloyd George's incapacity any longer to espouse Liberal values. Some therefore remained committed to fighting the Liberal civil war, whatever the effects upon the party's prospects, but the majority were content, in Asquith's dismissive phrase, to go 'a-whoring after LlG'.[34]

The return of ideas

Over the next two years, therefore, the Liberal Party became Lloyd George's party. He poured into it not just money but also energy and ideas, qualities which had been largely lacking in the fag-end of Asquith's leadership. The most impressive feature of the Liberal revival of this period was an intellectual renaissance. In an often-quoted statement, Charles Masterman declared that 'when Lloyd George came back to the party, ideas came back to the party'. There is an element of truth here, but it demands qualification. Masterman does insufficient justice to the efforts of Manchester Liberals and Cambridge economists, earlier in the decade and largely independent of the party leadership, to devise and publicise a constructive liberalism relevant to the post-war era rather than to the nineteenth century.

Masterman's own work, *The New Liberalism*, published as early as 1920, was an attempt to reconcile the principles of traditional liberalism with the demands of a modern, industrialised economy. Such endeavours had led to the setting up of the annual Liberal Summer Schools, which brought together some of the best minds in the British intelligentsia. What Lloyd George did was not to create this movement but rather to bring it to the heart of the party's activities, very much as he had helped bring the pre-war New Liberalism to the political and legislative forefront for a few brief years around 1911.

The Liberal Summer Schools

The Liberal Summer Schools provide the best evidence that, whatever was happening to the Liberal Party in the 1920s, liberalism as a political philosophy was far from dead. A group of Manchester businessmen began meeting in the winter of 1918–19 at the home of E. D. Simon, a local manufacturer with a special interest in housing issues. At a meeting at Simon's Herefordshire farm early in 1921, attended by Ramsay Muir, then Professor of History at the University of Manchester, and Edward Scott, son of the editor of the *Manchester Guardian*, the notion of the Summer Schools came to life. Muir's idea was to introduce an annual conference at which current social and economic problems could be discussed and analysed from a Liberal perspective. Importantly, the intention was to operate outside the framework of party organisation, though party policy might subsequently be influenced. 'The thing I care about', Muir later wrote, 'is to set on foot an active process of criticism and discussion – an intellectual activity independent of formal associations.'

The movement got under way when about a hundred younger Liberals were invited to spend a week at Grasmere in the Lake District in September 1921. 'I am really hopeful', recorded Simon, 'that it will be the beginning of a genuine awakening of thought and study in Liberal circles.' In addition to Muir and Simon, the schools attracted such leading Cambridge intellectuals as Maynard Keynes, Walter Layton and Hubert Henderson.

The aim was to build upon the foundations of the New Liberalism of the pre-war era, advocating greater state intervention but avoiding the paths of doctrinaire socialism. As Keynes put it in 1925, 'we have to invent a new wisdom for a new age'. The result was that the party managed to hang on to at least some of those more constructive minds who might otherwise have transferred their allegiance to Labour. In the second half of the decade the Summer Schools were more closely (though still informally) associated with the party leadership. Men such as Muir and Simon came to see in Lloyd George someone who, like themselves, was trying to infuse the Liberal Party with a programme of practical policies for the modern age.

Appropriately, as it was the issue from which his fertile brain had been diverted by the coming of war in 1914, Lloyd George had turned first, before his struggle with Asquith was finally resolved, to the issue of the land. *Land and the Nation*, the report of the Land Inquiry Committee, was published in October 1925. Known as the 'Green Book' because of the colour of its cover, it concluded that the state should take over ownership of all rural land and give tenant farmers security of tenure. The 'Brown Book', *Towns and the Land*, followed in November and focused on policy for urban areas. It proposed that local authorities should be given extensive powers of compulsory acquisition to buy land for housing. The aim was to eliminate slum dwellings and overcrowding. The proposals of the 'Green Book' in particular aroused much enthusiasm among radical Liberals, but also much opposition within the Asquithian old guard. But at this stage Lloyd George was not in a position to dictate policy to the party as a whole.

Ramsay Muir (1872–1941)

One of the unsung heroes of British Liberalism, who helped to keep alive the flame of intellectual vigour during years of political decline, Ramsay Muir was born in Northumberland in September 1872, the son of a Presbyterian minister. After originally intending to train for the church, he read history at University College, Liverpool. According to legend, it was only after the external examiner had lain on his back surrounded by examination scripts, kicked his legs in the air and refused to budge that it was agreed that Muir be awarded a first. Thereafter, he more easily secured firsts in Greats and modern history at Balliol College, Oxford. An academic career took him to chairs in Liverpool and then Manchester, but in 1921 he left university life to follow a career in politics.

Along with a small group of Manchester colleagues, including the businessman, Ernest Simon, Muir was instrumental in constructing a modern industrial policy, paving the way for the Liberal Industrial Inquiry and the subsequent 'Yellow Book'. 'Liberalism stood for nothing', he later recalled, 'but complaints of LG, and therefore it sank to futility … It had to be given a "constructive programme", not as a bait to catch the electorate, but as a means of keeping its soul alive.' He also helped in the establishment of the Liberal Summer Schools in 1921.

Eight attempts to enter Parliament resulted in just one success, and Muir served as MP for Rochdale between 1923 and 1924. He also served as chairman and president of the National Liberal Federation and vice-president of the Liberal Party Organisation. But his greatest contribution was as a thinker and writer. Before the First World War he had criticised multi-party coalition governments on the grounds that they encouraged corrupt deals behind the back of the electorate. In the 1920s, however, as the Liberal Party dropped to third place, he became an articulate advocate of proportional representation. Much of the influential book *The Liberal Way*, published in 1934, was his work.

By 1926–27 the situation was different. The Liberal Industrial Inquiry brought together an impressive array of academics and politicians, including E. D. Simon, Walter Layton, Ramsay Muir, Hubert Henderson, Keynes, Samuel and Lloyd George himself. Its report, *Britain's Industrial Future* (the 'Yellow Book'), was published in February 1928 and put forward radical new proposals to deal with unemployment and economic stagnation.

These included putting vital industries under public boards, the creation of an economic general staff within Whitehall, the use of the Bank of England to encourage investment and large-scale programmes of public works to soak up the country's surplus labour. Further proposals called for national minimum wages to be set for each industry, compulsory profit-sharing schemes for the benefit of employees, and workers' councils to be involved in industrial management. A small committee headed by Lloyd George, Lord Lothian and Seebohm Rowntree then refined these ideas and in March 1929 produced the document *We Can Conquer Unemployment*, designed as the basis for the party's next general election campaign.

John Maynard Keynes (1883–1946)

The most influential economist of the twentieth century and an optimistic believer in the capacity of government to do great things for the benefit of its people, Keynes was born into an academic family in Cambridge in June 1883. After Eton and King's College, he served briefly as a civil servant in the India Office before taking up a teaching post in his old university in 1908.

During the First World War he entered the Treasury and was given extensive responsibility for the external finance of the war. He went to the Paris Peace Conference as an official Treasury representative, but resigned in June 1919 over the scale of reparations to be demanded of Germany. Keynes, however, did not keep his misgivings to himself. His study, *The Economic Consequences of the Peace*, published later that year, argued that Germany had been saddled with a burden of debt which she could only hope to repay by securing that economic domination of Europe which the Allies wished to deny her. The book enjoyed a wide circulation and played an important part in undermining the moral credibility of the peace treaty.

Keynes had been president of the Cambridge Liberal Club and a strong advocate of free trade, but it was only in the 1920s that he became prominent in Liberal Party politics. From 1923 he served as chairman of the weekly *Nation* and played an active role in the Liberal Summer Schools. Together with Hubert Henderson he helped convert Lloyd George to the idea that unemployment could be solved by large-scale schemes of public works, especially road-building, to stimulate economic recovery. It was the beginning of what became 'Keynesianism', the notion that the economy need not be left to the market but could be managed by the state with the overriding aim of maintaining full employment. His ideas were given their fullest expression in *The General Theory of Employment, Interest and Money* (1936).

By the end of the 1920s, however, Keynes had lost faith in the Liberal Party's capacity ever to implement his ideas. He became an official adviser to the second Labour government of 1929–31 and showed support for the proposals of the Chancellor of the Duchy of Lancaster, Sir Oswald Mosley, to deal with unemployment. He came to the conclusion that, in an imperfect world, tariffs were, for the time being at least, a necessity, and his abandonment of the principle of free trade completed his formal separation from Liberalism.

Keynes's views had a limited impact upon the economic policies of the National Government, but he returned to the Treasury in 1940, where he served as an adviser for the rest of his life. His was the dominant influence in the Churchill government's White Paper on Employment of 1944. He took a leading role in the Bretton Woods conference of that year which, by setting up the International Monetary Fund and the World Bank, set in place the economic superstructure of the post-war world. He was also responsible at the end of the war for negotiating a loan from the United States and Canada to cope with the impact of the abrupt termination of lend-lease by the Truman administration in Washington.

Keynes died suddenly in the spring of 1946, but his influence was at its greatest over the following three decades, as governments across the western world implemented his policies (or what they claimed were his policies) of demand management and deficit financing.

The 'Yellow Book' represented a decisive break with existing economic thought. It revealed the Liberals as the first major party to take up the Keynesian belief that the ups and downs of the economic cycle could be controlled, and it seemed to offer the party a viable identity in opposition to the protectionism of the Conservatives and Labour's theoretical commitment to socialism. Many of its ideas would come to underpin the policies of later Conservative and especially Labour governments. As Alan Sykes has written, 'the years 1927–29 saw the last flourishing of progressive liberalism in association with the Liberal Party before its ideas were annexed by Labour as the basis of its reforms after 1945'.[35] Yet it is doubtful whether the Liberals themselves derived any political benefit from this rejuvenation.

In all probability Lloyd George's initiative had come too late. Too much damage had been done during the first half of the decade, and Labour was now too well entrenched in the mind of the electorate as the party of radical progress and more particularly of the working-class vote. Even some of those at the heart of Liberalism's intellectual revival were sceptical of the party's capacity to convert ideas into political action. 'If one regards the existence of the Liberal Party as a route to power', wrote Keynes at the time of the publication of the 'Yellow Book', 'one is probably wasting one's time'.[36] He did not believe that the party would disappear, but doubted whether it would ever again become a major force in Parliament. Its role now might well be to supply 'Conservative governments with cabinets and Labour governments with ideas'. Hubert Henderson put the point rather more graphically. 'We are', he suggested, 'the manufacturing establishment of politics and, if we are compelled for a time to let others do the retailing, we must not try to deprive them of good salesmen and handsome shop-walkers.'[37]

Catastrophe confirmed

For a while, however, Lloyd George's energy and dynamism seemed to have inspired a political as well as an intellectual upsurge. 'After years of defeat and depression', wrote

Herbert Samuel, 'there is now a feeling of buoyant optimism … Although we have only about forty members in the present Parliament, out of 615, there is a growing feeling in the country that we shall dominate the next one'.[38] The party won an encouraging series of by-elections between March 1927 and March 1929, but there were always limits to this Liberal revival. The gains were largely in rural areas at the expense of an increasingly unpopular Conservative government and it was striking that Labour did even better in terms of by-election victories over the Parliament as a whole. It was noticeable too that Lloyd George himself had no real expectation of a Liberal triumph in the general election, and was still thinking in terms of some sort of co-operation with Labour. The very existence of the Liberal Party, he confided to C. P. Scott in December 1928, would force Labour to come to terms since it would deprive Labour of any hope of an independent majority over the other two parties. Labour and the Liberals could 'go together a long way along the road to progress' and it was 'very sad' that they should fight each other 'for the benefit of the reactionaries and the revolutionaries'.[39]

Nor had the Liberal Party's own divisions entirely disappeared. Samuel's efforts to win round the members of the Liberal Council were largely unsuccessful. Nonetheless, by the time that Baldwin called an election for 30 May 1929, the party seemed to have a greater sense of purpose than at any time since before the First World War. Most observers believed that, at the very least, the Liberals would double their parliamentary representation. Speaking to Liberal candidates at the Connaught Rooms on 1 March, Lloyd George issued his famous pledge that a Liberal government would 'reduce the terrible figures of the workless in the course of a single year to normal proportions'. Richard Holt believed that Lloyd George had 'made things very difficult for sober-minded Liberals by [his] reckless promise', but within a fortnight was writing of a strong feeling that 'LlG has touched the popular imagination and that we ought not to throw cold water on his schemes'.[40] In early May Keynes and Henderson published the pamphlet *Can Lloyd George Do It?*, a question to which they responded with an emphatic 'yes'. At least in public, Liberals presented a solid front. A campaign poster showed a united group of Liberal leaders comprising Lloyd George, Grey, Samuel, John Simon, Walter Runciman and Lord Beauchamp. But it was all to little avail.

With more than three-quarters of all constituencies witnessing three-cornered contests, this was the most competitive general election of the decade and thus provides the best guide to the Liberal Party's underlying strength. It fielded 513 candidates, polled more than five million votes (23.6 per cent of the total), but secured just 59 seats. This was, of course, an improvement on 1924, but the party had contrived to lose 19 of the seats won in that year while gaining 35 new ones. This complexity reflected the fact that, despite gains from the Conservatives, the Liberals were still giving ground to Labour, especially in industrial Britain. Indeed, it was striking that, despite its focus on unemployment, the party had done least well in the areas most affected by it. Moreover, the Liberal vote was now too thinly spread to be effective in Britain's first-past-the-post electoral system. While the party's total vote had inevitably gone up from 1924 because of the increase in the number of seats contested, its average share of the vote in those contested seats had actually gone down, from 30.9 to 27.7 per cent.

1929 general election (30 May)			
	Votes	*%*	*MPs*
Liberal	5,308,738	23.4	59
Conservative	8,656,225	38.2	260
Labour	**8,370,417**	**37.0**	**287**
Others	312,995	1.4	9
Total	*22,648,375*		*615*
Average vote per Liberal candidate (%)			27.4
Strong Liberal performances (20 per cent or above in three-cornered contests, 33.3 per cent or above in straight fights)			359

Beyond the statistics, however, 1929 was of enormous symbolic importance for the Liberal Party. For the first time in its history Labour became the largest single party in the House of Commons. It had confirmed its status as the first-choice party of the British working class. Meanwhile the electorate had underlined the Liberals' position as the third party in a polity best suited to the interests of just two competitors. It would not be an easy predicament from which to escape.

Local politics

It is important to note that the fortunes of the national party at Westminster in the decade after the First World War were matched by an equally depressing performance at a local level. A Labour advance at Liberal expense was evident as early as the municipal elections of 1919. Significantly, these were held under a franchise which excluded three-quarters of the newly enfranchised parliamentary electors, evidence which suggests that Labour was gaining ground among existing voters rather than just winning over new ones.

In a long history of decline the Liberals suffered a net loss of seats every year during the 1920s, except for 1922. Thus minor revivals in national elections were not matched in municipal contests. Part of the problem lay in the collapse of local party organisations, particularly after the 1924 general election. As early as April 1923 it was noted that 'Liberalism as an active missionary force is almost dead in numbers of constituencies and needs strengthening in almost all'. A study undertaken in 1927 revealed that the party was effectively dormant in two-thirds of constituencies.

Not surprisingly, Liberals contested an ever-declining proportion of municipal seats. By 1929 less than one in eight of those standing in provincial borough elections was a Liberal. In many towns Liberals formed anti-socialist municipal alliances with the Conservatives, a fusion which almost invariably worked to the Conservative advantage and in which it was the Liberal identity which disappeared. Such a development merely encouraged the transfer of Liberal allegiances to one or other of the two main parties.

Where did it all go wrong?

This narrative has already given many indications of the reasons for the Liberal Party's downfall, but it is now time to look rather more systematically at some of the conflicting theories of decline put forward by historians. Too much of this historiographical debate has been conducted in terms of alternatives, as if one single secret of the Liberal Party's difficulties awaits discovery. But a mono-causal explanation is improbable.

Can the nature and scale of the problem first be defined? At the end of the day, the Liberal Party declined because it lost existing voters to the other two parties, because it failed to do as well among the voters of the post-war generation as it had with their fathers, and because it failed to pick up enough votes from the newly enfranchised following the Representation of the People Act of 1918 and its successor of 1928, which between them created universal adult suffrage in the United Kingdom. Comparisons are somewhat dangerous, because of the differing numbers of uncontested seats and, above all, because of the vastly increased post-war franchise, but it may be noted that the Liberal Party secured 43.2 per cent of the total vote in December 1910, the last occasion on which it emerged victorious from a general election, and just 23.6 per cent in 1929. As we are dealing with the individual voting decisions of literally millions of citizens, it seems unlikely that all were moved by the same set of determinants. A multi-dimensional explanation, in which perhaps half a dozen key factors each accounted for a relatively small percentage of the Liberal decline, would seem the most likely scenario.

It would be perverse to ignore the impact of the war. But defining precisely what that impact was is no easy matter. The idea that an individualist political philosophy reached an impasse in the face of the collectivist demands of modern warfare – that the First World War acted as an intellectual cul-de-sac as far as the British Liberal Party was concerned – is less than convincing. It does scant justice to the manner in which the party had already, before 1914, adapted to the demands of modern society, shaking off its non-interventionist inheritance from the nineteenth century. It also ignores the way in which the majority of (though, it must be admitted, not all) Liberals reacted flexibly to the encroachments of war, with few signs of ideological crisis. The Liberal Party had not 'died strangely' in the last years before 1914; and it did not 'die strangely' between 1914 and 1918. What the war did do was to open up a divide between the party's two leading figures and their followers, a divide which subsequent events deepened, confirmed and entrenched. This schism lasted until at least 1923 and, even after that, left a legacy of bitterness which some Liberals could never forget. Indeed, as one observes the differing political strategies offered in the late 1940s to the by then pathetically weak Liberal Party by Lady Violet Bonham Carter and Lady Megan Lloyd George, daughters of the two principals of the 1916 split, it is difficult not to conclude that the division lasted into a second generation.

Most importantly, the split took place and continued on a political canvas in which there was an alternative force waiting in the wings, ready to take the Liberals' place. Had the Labour Party of this period been of the same mould as that of pre-1914, the damage to Liberalism would have been less marked. As it was, it was the Labour Party which changed, ceasing to be a mere party of protest, the largely willing junior partner within the progressive alliance. By the end of the war Labour was, in its own estimation and increasingly in that of the electorate, a serious aspirant for power. It seems likely that the war initiated, or at least accelerated, processes of social change in which Liberalism, having coped perfectly well before 1914, found itself outflanked by the advancing Labour Party. The war helped to develop a more unified class consciousness, in which earlier distinctions between skilled and unskilled workers were less sharp and which increasingly translated into a conviction that Labour represented the natural vehicle for working-class aspirations. Wartime inflationary pressures and changing conditions in the workplace stimulated recruitment to trade unions and correspondingly enhanced the importance and self-confidence of their political wing, the Labour Party. It was striking that, at Labour's conference of June 1918, Arthur Henderson called upon the movement to seize the political opportunity which beckoned, break out of the progressive alliance and reformulate the party's electoral strategy. In the post-war decade many Liberals looked back wistfully to the years of Liberal–Labour co-operation and dreamed of their re-creation. In this they grievously misunderstood Labour's changed purpose. The fact that there was often little in policy terms to distinguish radical Liberals of the 1920s from their non-doctrinaire Labour counterparts was not so much an indication of scope for renewed collaboration but rather evidence of Labour's imperative need to eliminate Liberalism as an independent political force.

Some writers have presented Labour's rise and Liberalism's decline in terms of near inevitability. The rise of class-based politics is pictured as a remorseless process against which the vain efforts of mortal Liberal politicians could not hope to prevail. As divisions between capital and labour became more pronounced, British politics slid naturally into a Conservative–Labour confrontation in which the Liberal Party, more suited to appeal to the Nonconformist vote in earlier religious divides, now looked increasingly irrelevant. Yet 'inevitability' is a concept of which wiser historians are justifiably suspicious. And in any case, Peter Clarke has argued persuasively that class-based politics were well established before 1914 and that the Liberal Party was adapting successfully to this development. Thus, he suggests, there was nothing inevitable about the loss of the Liberals' claim to the working-class vote.

That said, the international context of Liberalism's demise would suggest that some inexorable forces of change were in play. Britain was by no means unique at this time in having a Liberal party in a state of serious decline. Only in countries which had adopted proportional voting systems did Liberal parties of this era tend to survive as effective operators on the political stage. Some overseas comparisons are striking indeed. In New Zealand, for example, disillusioned trade unionists abandoned their existing Liberal affiliations and organised a new party to give labour separate parliamentary representation. By the mid-1920s this new party had captured much of the old voting strength of the Liberals.

At the opposite extreme from explanations which suggest that there was something approaching inevitability about Liberal decline lie theories of contingency, the idea that it was all a question of accidents and avoidable mistakes. Lloyd George, looking back on what had happened from the vantage point of the mid-1930s, put it in its most extreme form. As Frances Stevenson recorded:

> Last night at dinner, arising out of a discussion on food, and fish in particular, D[avid] said: 'I attribute the downfall of the Liberal Party to an oyster'. He went on to explain that Percy Illingworth [Chief Whip 1912–15] died of typhoid caused by a bad oyster. Had he lived, he would never have allowed the rift between D and Asquith to take place. He would have brought them together, patched the quarrel up, cursed them and saved the Liberal Party … After his death, there was no one who could take his place, and could put the party before persons and personalities.[41]

Few would join Lloyd George in attaching such significance to Illingworth's death, important though the latter was in oiling the wheels of the pre-war party. But it is easy enough to point to a series of events and developments which could have been avoided or mitigated with the result that their damaging effects might have been eliminated, reduced or at least postponed.

If, as Lloyd George originally suggested, Asquith had stayed on as Prime Minister within a reorganised government in December 1916, the original split might never have taken place. Failing that, if Asquith had responded to Lloyd George's advances and returned to the government before the end of the war, the damaging effects of the coupon election might have been averted. If at least the contending Liberal factions, seeing the warning signs, had come together sooner and not left open the door of Labour advance until 1923, the transition in the respective fortunes of the two parties would surely have been delayed. If Asquith had served his party instead of himself and made way for Lloyd George, with the energy and imagination the latter displayed in the second half of the 1920s, to take over the leadership at an earlier date, the moribund post-war party might not have driven so many of its more enthusiastic members into the arms of its political opponents. Then, if Lloyd George had made his political fund more readily available, the Liberal Party could have presented itself as a viable aspirant for power at all of the general elections of the post-war decade. And, finally, if the Liberals had seen more clearly the long-term intentions of their Labour opponents, they might not have supported so readily the formation of Ramsay MacDonald's first government without at least securing safeguards for themselves, possibly in terms of a commitment to electoral reform. None of these forays into counterfactual history defies the limits of possibility; but each would surely have had a beneficial impact upon British Liberalism.

None of these changed events, on its own, could have saved the Liberal Party. But, writing in the 1970s, a trio of historians believed that they had uncovered the single, elusive and, as it seemed, surprisingly simple factor in explaining the replacement of the Liberals by Labour as the main force of the British political left.[42] It is easy to forget that the successive parliamentary reforms of the nineteenth century had in no sense created universal manhood suffrage. Difficult residential qualifications meant that only about 60 per cent of adult males were on the electoral register at any one time. The majority of the disenfranchised were, it was believed, at the bottom of the social pile, members of the manual working class. So, argued Colin Matthew, Ross McKibbin and J. A. Kay, a restricted pre-war franchise, which effectively denied the vote to about half the working class, was bound to limit Labour's ability to tap into its natural constituency of support. Once full male suffrage was achieved, the effect would be dramatic. And this is what happened in time for the coupon election of 1918. The Representation of the People Act passed earlier in the year produced an electorate three times as large as that which had existed at the last contest in December 1910. Allowing for intervening deaths and for people who had only reached voting age in time for the post-war contest, only about a quarter of the electorate of 1918 had voted before. Thus, in the post-war era a predominantly working-class electorate turned to Labour, as it would have done before 1914 had it had the chance to do so. A truly democratic franchise in Edwardian Britain would have enabled Labour to challenge the Liberals far more effectively than had been the case. The conclusion seemed inescapable. Although 'we cannot say how many votes the introduction of universal franchise was worth to Labour ... we can say that it was a critical element in the emergence of the party as a major political force'.

This is an attractive theory, but the argument is flawed. Most obviously, it pays insufficient attention to the fact that the majority of the new electorate of 1918 were female voters, drawn from all classes of society. Then, it seems unlikely that the disenfranchised men of the pre-1918 era were solidly working-class would-be Labour voters. The old franchise discriminated against those who did not own their own homes, irrespective of class or income. Many middle-class men had not been able to vote before the war because the mobility of their employment prevented them from acquiring the necessary residential qualification. Furthermore, those who subscribe to the so-called 'franchise factor' tend to assume that what happened in 1918 would also have happened before the war had the franchise permitted. This overlooks the success of the Edwardian Liberal Party in presenting itself as the natural party of the working class. Why it failed to maintain this image is not necessarily explained by reference to changes in the franchise.

Finally, as has been noted, the Labour performance in the general election of 1918 was far from spectacular. Labour's advance was one of steady growth throughout the 1920s, a fact which sits uneasily with an explanation based on a one-off change to the electorate in 1918. It may be that Liberals suffered less from the sudden arrival of a huge tranche of working-class Labour voters in 1918 than from their own inability to secure in sufficient numbers the allegiance of successive cohorts of new electors as they qualified, by age, to vote over the following decade. The 'franchise factor' may, on balance, have worked in Labour's favour, but it is far from being an all-embracing explanation of Liberalism's demise.

Of probably greater significance was an obvious but often overlooked change in the geographical representation of the Westminster Parliament. Even in its heyday the

Liberal Party had always found it difficult to secure a majority of English seats, relying heavily upon its strength in Scotland, Wales and Ireland. With the creation of the Irish Free State in 1921, the balance of advantage from Irish seats, which had been heavily in the Liberals' favour when the whole of the country was represented, shifted to a small but not insignificant advantage for the Conservatives, now that only the six counties of Northern Ireland sent MPs to Westminster.

The truth behind the decline of the Liberal Party probably lies within a synthesis of some or all of the explanations offered here. What can be said with a degree of certainty is that by 1929 the party had ceased to be a major player on the political stage. A by-election won a few weeks before the general election turned out to be the last by-election gain secured by the party for almost thirty years. Though he could obviously not have known with any certainty of the electoral desert which lay ahead, the veteran Liberal MP, George Lambert, expressed the thoughts of many. 'The future of the old party', he wrote four days after the general election, 'hardly bears thinking about'.[43]

Further reading

Trevor Wilson, *The Downfall of the Liberal Party 1914–1935* (Collins, 1966), though somewhat dated, remains an essential starting point for the impact of the First World War. John Turner's *British Politics and the Great War: Coalition and Conflict 1915–1918* (Yale University Press, 1992) is not easy reading, but opens up interesting lines of enquiry on the second half of the war.

Kenneth Morgan's *Consensus and Disunity: The Lloyd George Coalition Government 1918–1922* (OUP, 1979) is unlikely to be surpassed as a study of the post-war coalition. Michael Bentley, *The Liberal Mind 1914–1929* (CUP, 1977) traces the evolution of Liberal thought through this period, while John Campbell, *Lloyd George: The Goat in the Wilderness 1922–1931* (Cape, 1977) offers a controversial interpretation of the Welshman's role after leaving office.

Frank Trentmann, *Free Trade Nation* (OUP, 2008) exhaustively and compellingly traces the erosion of free trade within the pantheon of Liberal thought. Don Cregier, *Chiefs without Indians* (University Press of America, 1982), contains some useful essays, while Garry Tregidga, *The Liberal Party in South-West Britain since 1918* (University of Exeter Press, 2000) is an important regional study. A. J. P. Taylor (ed.), *Lloyd George: A Diary by Frances Stevenson* (Hutchinson, 1971) offers a perspective on events through the eyes of the Liberal leader's secretary and mistress.

Useful biographies include Peter Rowland, *Lloyd George* (Barrie and Jenkins, 1975) and David Dutton, *Simon: A Political Biography of Sir John Simon* (Aurum Press, 1992).

Notes

1 Bernard Wasserstein, *Herbert Samuel: a political life* (Clarendon Press, 1992), p. 165.

2 Stephen McKenna, *Reginald McKenna, 1863–1943* (Eyre and Spottiswoode, 1948), p. 222.

3   David Dutton (ed), *Odyssey of an Edwardian Liberal: the Political Diary of Richard Durning Holt* (Sutton Publishing, 1989), p. 39.

4   McKenna, *McKenna*, p. 255.

5   Wasserstein, *Samuel*, pp. 176–77

6   For an introduction to the debate see Martin Farr, 'Left, Right: December 1916 – the forward march of Liberals halted', *Journal of Liberal History* 47, summer 2005, pp. 31–35.

7   Trevor Wilson (ed.), *The Political Diaries of C. P. Scott 1911–1928* (Collins, 1970), p. 257.

8   Asquith to Spender 6 October 1926, cited in Stuart Ball, 'Asquith's Decline and the General Election of 1918', *Scottish Historical Review*, LXI, 171 (1982), p. 61.

9   Election results are taken here from David Butler and Gareth Butler, *Twentieth-Century British Political Facts 1900–2000* (Macmillan, 2000). This groups together various smaller factions and independents into supporters or opponents of the coalition in a way which is more easily comprehensible than to present the full breakdown, as Rallings and Thrasher do.

10 Wilson, *Political Diaries of C.P. Scott*, p. 419.

11 Eric Hopkins, *Charles Masterman: Politician and Journalist – the Splendid Failure* (Edwin Mellen Press, 1999), p. 185.

12 Desmond MacCarthy (ed.), *H.H.A.: Letters of the Earl of Oxford and Asquith to a Friend*, vol. 1 (Geoffrey Bles, 1933), pp. 124–25.

13 Charles Masterman, *The New Liberalism* (Leonard Parsons, 1920), p. 173.

14 Kenneth Morgan, *Consensus and Disunity: The Lloyd George Coalition Government 1918–1922* (OUP, 1979), p. 106.

15 Robert Skidelsky, *John Maynard Keynes: The Economist as Saviour 1920–1937* (Macmillan, 1992), p. 21.

16 Norman MacKenzie and Jeanne MacKenzie (eds.), *The Diary of Beatrice Webb*, vol. 3 (Virago, 1984), pp. 432–33.

17 MacCarthy, *H.H.A.: Letters*, vol. 2 (1933), p. 39.

18 Ibid., pp. 90–91.

19 Lloyd George to C. P. Scott, 27 December 1923, Lloyd George MSS G/17/11/8, HLRO.

20 Wilson, *Political Diaries of C. P. Scott*, p. 460.

21 David Marquand, *Ramsay MacDonald* (Cape, 1977), p. 483.

22 Peter Rowland, *Lloyd George* (Barrie and Jenkins, 1975), p. 608.

23 Ibid., p. 612.

24 Don Cregier, *Chiefs without Indians*, p. 135.

25 Wilson, *Political Diaries* of C. P. Scott, p. 468.

26 J. A. Spender and Cyril Asquith, *Life of Herbert Henry Asquith, Lord Oxford and Asquith*, vol. 2 (Hutchinson, 1932), p. 349.

27 Lloyd George to Lord Incheape, 5 November 1924, Lloyd George MSS G/30/3/35, HLRO.

28 A. J. P. Taylor (ed.), *Lloyd George: a Diary by Frances Stevenson* (Hutchinson, 1971), p. 246.

29 Memorandum by J. Rowland Evans, 20 June 1926, Simon MSS, SP 60, Bodleian Library, Oxford.

30 Denis Judd, *Lord Reading* (Weidenfeld and Nicolson, 1982), p. 237.

31   Spender and Asquith, *Asquith*, vol. 2, p. 369.

32   J. A. Spender, *Sir Robert Hudson: a memoir* (Cassell, 1930), pp. 172–73.

33   Dutton, *Odyssey*, p. 93.

34   MacCarthy, *H.H.A.: Letters*, vol. 2, p. 186.

35   Alan Sykes, *The Rise and Fall of British Liberalism 1776–1988* (Longman, 1997), p. 247.

36   Vernon Bogdanor (ed.), *Liberal Party Politics* (OUP, 1983), pp. 1–2.

37   Skidelsky, *Keynes*, p. 137.

38   Wasserstein, *Samuel*, p. 299.

39   Wilson, *Political Diaries of C. P. Scott*, p. 494.

40   Dutton, *Odyssey*, pp. 102–03.

41   Taylor, *Lloyd George: a diary*, p. 320.

42   H. C. G. Matthew, R. L. McKibbin, and J. A. Kay, 'The Franchise Factor in the Rise of the Labour Party', *English Historical Review* 91 (1976), pp. 723–52.

43   Trevor Wilson, *The Downfall of the Liberal Party 1914–35* (Collins, 1966), p. 351.

Chapter 7

Decline and Disintegration (1929–1955)

Jaime Reynolds and Ian Hunter

The 1929 general election was a disappointment for the Liberal Party and confirmed its third-party status at national level.[1] Nevertheless, apart from 1922–23 it was the party's strongest performance in terms of vote share at any election between 1910 and 1983. The Liberals remained a significant force, winning almost a quarter of the votes cast overall and nearly 30 per cent in the seats they contested. In many regions they challenged the new Tory-Labour duopoly. The parliamentary party, though much smaller than its opponents, was impressive, with thirteen former or future Cabinet ministers in its ranks.

A quarter of a century later the party appeared close to extinction, maintaining a tenuous Commons representation thanks largely to Conservative indulgence and polling a significant vote (20 per cent plus) in fewer than a score of constituencies. Moreover, the Liberals no longer seemed relevant to the political concerns of the electorate. In 1929 they had been the champions of distinctive and popular causes such as free trade and the proto-Keynesianism of Lloyd George's 'Yellow Book', and they retained the support of significant social and economic groups. By the early 1950s they were stranded on the margins of British politics, identified with what to many were outdated and even cranky ideas, and representing only a few isolated rural and Nonconformist communities.

The Liberal decline is generally seen as a steady and inexorable slide downwards, and the gradual fall in the number of Liberal MPs seems to bear this out. However, the small number of Liberal candidates in four of the general elections of the period, the party split from the early 1930s, and the confusing party alliances and pacts of the period all obscured the trend in the party's true support. After 1929, the Liberals' strength was only really tested in 1945 and 1950, when they fought on a broader front. The average Liberal share of the poll in comparable three-party contests fell by 12.6 per cent between 1929 and 1945, but by only 2.7 per cent between 1935 and 1945. In other words, the real collapse was between 1929 and 1935, when average Liberal poll shares fell by some 10 per cent, with one in three of its 1929 voters deserting.

Thus the true nadir of the Liberals' fortunes in the period covered by this chapter was 1931–35 when, divided and suffering a calamitous loss of votes, the party seemed close to disintegration. Archibald Sinclair's leadership from 1935 to 1945 marked at least a stabilisation, and also a return to government office in the wartime coalition. A concerted attempt at revival in the late 1940s expired at the 1950 general election. The party again came close to collapse in the early 1950s, but by 1955 the first signs of a recovery that presaged the Liberal renaissance under Jo Grimond could be discerned.

This chapter looks at the reasons for the decline, but also examines the reasons for the Liberals' survival. How, for more than two decades, did the party avoid the complete disintegration and collapse that seemed to be imminent in the early 1930s?

The political landscape from the 1930s to the 1950s

The rise of bipolar class-based party politics peaked in Britain in the early 1950s. In the general election of 1951, 80 per cent of the electorate turned out to vote for the two major parties (the comparable figure in 2010 was 42 per cent). This reflected electoral trends evident since 1918, if not earlier, with Labour's increasing dominance among the unionised working class, and the Tories' strengthening grip on middle-class and rural Britain. Their core votes provided both parties with a solid platform to reach out to other groups of voters in order to build majorities. The Conservatives did this very successfully in the 1930s and again in the 1950s, and Labour broadened its appeal in 1929 and 1945–51. This core vote also provided these parties with a cushion of support in the bad years; even in the Labour meltdown of 1931 the party polled over 30 per cent of the votes, while the Conservatives were still close to 40 per cent in the debacle of 1945. Lacking such a mass voting base, there were fewer and fewer seats in which the Liberals were capable of building a challenge. The groups in which they retained significant support – Nonconformists, small businessmen, small farmers and the commercial middle class – were a winning force in only a handful of constituencies.

Moreover, the Liberals were conspicuously weak in the economically dynamic areas of the country, particularly the new industrial centres and suburbs in the south of England and the Midlands. Their dwindling support was concentrated in declining inner-city and old industrial Britain, and in rural Wales, Scotland and the West Country. The party's old-fashioned image had little appeal in the expanding areas, and it was not until the late 1950s that a modernised party was able to begin to break out of its traditional strongholds.[2]

The fact that politics was becoming more national in character in the period also played against the Liberals. Radio and cinema were having an impact by the 1930s, and the early 1950s saw the beginnings of the age of television politics. Local and regional factors, the provincial press, and the popularity of local candidates were of declining importance. Elections were fought on a national scale by the two major parties. In 1924 Labour and the Conservatives had each left some 80 seats uncontested in England, Wales and Scotland. By 1950 Labour fought all but one, and the Conservatives and their allies all but six. From the retirement of Lloyd George to the advent of Jo Grimond, the Liberals lacked leaders who could project their cause effectively at the national level, while locally the other parties left them less and less political space.

The intense polarisation between the two main parties and the squeeze on third parties under Britain's first-past-the-post electoral system also took their toll after 1929 as the credibility of the Liberals' claims to be a party competing for government collapsed. It was only after 1945 that the Liberals began to carve out a niche for themselves in the system as a party of protest and started to experiment with the tactics needed to exploit this role.

Throughout the period the other parties skilfully, energetically and, to a considerable extent successfully, targeted the Liberal constituency. The Conservatives, in particular, sought to absorb the Liberal Party through the Liberal Nationals in the 1930s and various enticements, including pacts and government posts, in the 1940s and early 1950s. They adopted non-partisan 'National' and 'Liberal and Conservative' labels designed to appeal to Liberal voters, as well as policies such as the social reformism of Neville Chamberlain and R. A. Butler, the coalitions of the 1930s and the war years, and the 'set the people free' rhetoric of the early 1950s. As Roy Jenkins remarked, 'Baldwin was a liberal Tory Prime Minister', while many of Churchill's colleagues in the Conservative leadership remained convinced that he was still a Liberal at heart. There was a steady drain of Liberals to the Conservatives throughout the period, and also significant losses to Labour. Labour flirted with the Liberal left (David and Megan Lloyd George especially) but somewhat ambivalently, conscious that the majority of Liberals would side with the Tories if the party collapsed.

These factors would have damaged the Liberal Party whatever strategy it had followed, but the disasters of the period 1929–35 greatly deepened its crisis.

Lloyd George's last stand and the Liberal split: 1929–31

Despite the party's failure at the 1929 election, Lloyd George contrived to retain at least some of the political initiative until the fall of the second Labour government in 1931. After a brief honeymoon, the course of Ramsay MacDonald's second administration was dominated by the economic crisis unleashed by the Wall Street crash in October 1929 and the government's inability to deal with spiralling unemployment. The slump and the financial crisis that followed in the summer of 1931 broke the government. The Liberals were the big losers from the 1931 political crisis: the party split into three fragments, suffered a crisis of leadership, organisation and finance, and saw its traditional political platform collapse.

Stanley Baldwin's decision to resign immediately following his election defeat in June 1929 and Ramsay MacDonald's formation of a minority government deprived Lloyd George of the opportunity to attempt to strike a deal with Labour. The Liberals, though dejected by the outcome of the election and despite the continuing distaste of some hardcore Asquithians, mostly backed the leadership of Lloyd George and his strategy of conditional support for the government with the aim of securing proportional representation. At this stage the Conservative threat was subdued as Baldwin struggled to contain a rebellion over protectionism and India led by Beaverbrook, Rothermere, Leo Amery and Tory die-hards.

Lloyd George began to increase the pressure on the government at the turn of 1929–30, pushing for a more energetic response to the economic crisis and concessions on electoral reform. The battleground was the Coal Mines Bill, which Lloyd George and Herbert Samuel thought should aim for a far more radical restructuring of the industry. However, a few Asquithian and left-wing Liberal dissidents undermined this strategy by siding with the government in crucial votes on the bill. In March 1930 Lloyd George abandoned his campaign against the government, following its announcement of an electoral reform bill, and shifted towards closer co-operation with Labour aimed at drawing MacDonald into a common Lib-Lab programme based on the ideas of the 1929 'Yellow Book'. The growing paralysis of the Labour Cabinet in the face of the escalating unemployment figures and the recovery of the Conservatives as Baldwin united the Tories around an increasingly protectionist platform posed both an opportunity and a threat for the Liberals and for free trade. Lloyd George responded positively to MacDonald's call for co-operation between the three parties and a series of Lib-Lab talks began. In November 1930 the Liberals refrained from opposing the King's Speech, which included a measure of electoral reform based on the alternative vote, rather than proportional representation.

Lloyd George argued that Labour should be sustained in office until trade revived, thereby invalidating the Conservative calls for protection. Defeating the government would open the way for the Tories to return to office, damaging the Liberals electorally and undermining free trade, which had in the Labour Chancellor of the Exchequer, Philip Snowden, one of its stoutest defenders. Liberals were acutely aware that free trade was under threat. Its potency as a mobilising ideology uniting commerce, civil society and consumerism, so evident in Edwardian times and still significant in the early 1920s, was fading rapidly.[3] As Peter Clarke has put it:

> The march of protectionist ideas in 1930–31 made more headway than in the whole of the previous quarter-century. It was the unlikely sources from which they now gained support that was significant. This was not just the familiar song from the industrialist lobby but a swelling chorus from the City of London, academic economists, trade unionists, even partisan Liberals who had now lost faith in the old cries of Free Trade.[4]

Many of the leading Liberal free traders were looking for a compromise, conceding limited, 'temporary', tariffs to raise revenue from 'luxuries' or to safeguard industries affected by foreign 'dumping'. Such protectionism could be reconciled with free trade principles especially if it was used to negotiate reductions in foreign tariffs. However 'food taxes', a general industrial tariff or a system of imperial tariff preferences remained beyond the pale.

Most of the Asquithian group fell in with Lloyd George's courting of Labour, but opposition arose from another quarter – Sir John Simon, who voted against the King's

Speech, together with Sir Robert Hutchison, who resigned as Chief Whip. Simon had hitherto been heavily occupied with chairing an inquiry into Indian constitutional reform, but had been generally supportive of Lloyd George. His disenchantment seems to have arisen for a mixture of political and personal reasons. In the negotiations on Indian self-government that culminated in a deal between the Viceroy Lord Irwin and Gandhi in March 1931, his report had been largely ignored. Sidelined, Simon found himself aligned with the Tory critics of the deal against the Labour government, Irwin (a liberal Tory) and the Marquess of Reading, a leading Liberal who had helped to broker the final agreement.[5] Simon also regarded the Labour government as incapable of deal- ing with the economic crisis and by late 1930 was ready to compromise his previously unshakeable commitment to free trade in favour of an emergency revenue tariff, which he regarded as preferable to the land tax and other tax increases favoured by Labour and Lloyd George. After more than a decade of unrewarding loyalty to the Liberal cause, he was also coming to the conclusion that it no longer offered a realistic prospect for him to fulfil his undoubted political talents. His hold on his marginal seat of Spen Valley depended on Conservative support. Nevertheless, Simon hesitated to break with the party, partly because his personal following was weak. Only five Liberal MPs joined him in voting against the Trades Disputes Bill in January 1931, and his equivocal and suave personal manner alienated even his political sympathisers.

Sir John Simon (1873–1954)

Sir John Simon had perhaps a strong claim to being the 'Liberal Prime Minister who never was'. Widely seen as Asquith's natural successor, his early career as a radical Liberal, until his resignation in 1916 in protest at the introduction of conscription, was meteoric, taking him into the Cabinet at the age of just forty. He then followed and stuck with the Liberals in the political wilderness for fifteen years until resuming his ministe- rial career as a Liberal National, in alliance with the Conservatives, in 1931. He served as Home Secretary (twice), Chancellor of the Exchequer, Foreign Secretary and Lord Chancellor, a record unique in British politics. He was also one of the most brilliant bar- risters of the period.

Simon came from a humble Manchester background where his father was a Congregationalist minister, and through scholarships reached Oxford University, where he was President of the Union and graduated with a first. Elected to Parliament in 1906, in the inter-war years he sat for the marginal seat of Spen Valley in Yorkshire, where he benefited from the absence of Tory opposition in general elections. A leading figure in the National Governments of the 1930s, he was tainted with the failed policy of appeasement. In 1940 he became Viscount Simon and served as Lord Chancellor in the Churchill coalition.

He was known for his formidable intellect and silky lawyer's skills, but also for his lack of human warmth or a common touch. It was said that his personality chilled after the tragic death of his first wife in 1902. His break with official Liberalism in 1931 marked him with the reputation of being a calculating and careerist politician that is hardly justified by his career up to that point. His complex mind, which enabled him to see all aspects of a problem, did not lead to decisive decision-making. After Simon's defection, Lloyd George said that he had 'sat on the fence so long that the iron has entered his soul'.

Party indiscipline was exacerbated by undercurrents of hostility to Lloyd George's strategy. The rebels comprised the Simon-Hutchison group, a group around Ernest Brown, hitherto a stalwart of the Nonconformist mainstream of the party, and others linked with the Asquithian Liberal Council. A crisis meeting of the parliamentary party in March backed Lloyd George by thirty-four votes to seventeen. The rank and file overwhelmingly supported Lloyd George's line at the party conference in Buxton in May. On 26 June Simon, Hutchison and Brown finally resigned the party whip.

Lloyd George continued to pursue a deal with MacDonald in order to energise the government's economic policy. His biographers, Frank Owen and John Campbell, have argued that by early July 1931 the Liberal and Labour leaders were on the brink of agreeing to form a coalition in which Lloyd George might expect to emerge as a key figure. The direct evidence for this is shaky but it does seem that a Lloyd George-Labour bloc was close to realisation at this stage.[6]

On 27 July Lloyd George, suddenly incapacitated by illness, was removed from the scene at the critical moment when the financial crisis and that of the Labour government came to a head. It was left to Herbert Samuel to lead the Liberals into disaster.

The Liberal crash (1931–35)

The 1931 crisis and the formation of the National Government was one of the periodic sea-changes in British politics – comparable with those in 1886, 1905–06, 1945, 1979, 1997 and 2010 – when new ideas gain ascendancy and parties regroup. In many ways it was the most profound of these shifts. The 1931 election saw a landslide victory for the Conservative-dominated coalition that dwarfed all other election landslides in British political history. It marked the end of the hegemony of free trade that had lasted since the mid-nineteenth century, and the shattering of the Liberal Party that had championed this cause. It opened a period of Tory-led coalitions that lasted until 1945 and consolidated the Conservative hold on a large section of traditional Liberalism that persisted into the 1950s.

The 1931 crisis was curious in the sense that its outcome seemed almost accidental and unintended by the main actors. Modern historians have questioned both the depth of the financial crisis faced by the Labour government and MacDonald's failure to find a solution that would have kept his party intact. Indeed, the purpose for which the National Government was ostensibly formed – to defend the parity of the pound – was almost immediately abandoned when Britain came off the gold standard in September. This forced devaluation, rather than the government's expenditure cuts, revived the economy. Unemployment peaked in late 1932, after which prosperity grew, outside the depressed areas. The 1931 cuts were restored by 1934. Lloyd George was probably right in thinking that if the progressive free-trade camp had been able to ride out the 1931 crisis, economic events might well have turned in its favour in time for an election in 1933–34.

The Conservatives, confident by 1931 of victory in the next election, were lukewarm about sharing power in a coalition government. For Ramsay MacDonald and Philip Snowden, the events turned out to be a tragic negation of political careers that had been dedicated to building the Labour movement, while for the Labour Party 1931 represented a massive political setback and trauma. For the Liberals, the National Government at first seemed a welcome escape route from their political dilemma and was supported by the whole party. But it soon became clear that it was a lethal trap that fragmented the party and almost destroyed its political raison d'etre.

The Liberals had unwittingly planted the seeds of the crisis in February 1931 when they took the sting out of a Conservative vote of censure on the government with an amendment to establish a committee to examine the scope for public spending cuts. This was the May Economy Committee that reported in July, at the same time as the government was struggling to staunch a run on the pound caused by European banking failures. May recommended sharp public expenditure cuts to meet a widening deficit as unemployment benefit costs soared. In mid-August MacDonald and Snowden demanded delivery of much of this package from their Cabinet colleagues while negotiating with Samuel and Chamberlain for the support of the Liberals and Conservatives. A 10 per cent cut in unemployment benefit became the crunch issue resisted by the rebel Labour ministers and demanded by Neville Chamberlain and Samuel. On 23–24 August MacDonald abandoned his efforts to force the cuts through his Cabinet. It appeared that a Conservative–Liberal government would take Labour's place, but at the last moment MacDonald agreed to the urging of the King, Chamberlain and Samuel to lead an emergency National Government.

Samuel as Home Secretary and Lord Reading as Foreign Secretary represented the Liberals in the Cabinet, and Maclean, Sinclair and Crewe were also appointed ministers. The Liberal leadership, including Lloyd George, Simon and Lord Grey, were in complete accord in supporting the government, which was seen as a temporary coalition of the leaders of the three parties with the task of enacting the expenditure cuts and saving the pound. This trade issue and the timing of a general election were put to one side for the time being.

The formation of the government only briefly halted the run on the pound, however, which resumed in mid-September, exacerbated by uncertainty over an election as the Conservatives insisted on an early poll. On 21 September the gold standard was suspended – permanently, as it transpired. The Conservatives now argued that – as the original justification for the coalition was no longer valid – an election should be held to provide the government with a mandate to continue its economic measures. Herbert Samuel resisted these moves, with initial support from MacDonald, who was anxious not to lose the Lloyd George Liberals.[7] However Samuel was unwilling to press the issue to the point of resignation, as urged by Lloyd George. On 5 October the Cabinet agreed to an election, with each party fighting on its own programme under a general statement issued by MacDonald. Samuel extracted an empty promise that an inquiry would be held before any proposal could be made to introduce a general system of tariffs.

Lloyd George was furious with Samuel, protesting that he had 'sold every pass'. With his small 'family group', Lloyd George went into opposition, and for the next four years missed no opportunity to blame 'Samuel and his rabbits' for the party's troubles. Samuel was convinced that he had little choice and that the Tories were manoeuvring to oust him and his followers from the government and replace them with the Simonites, who in mid-September began taking serious steps towards forming their own grouping, which now included Walter Runciman.[8] Runciman, hitherto a pillar of the Asquithian free traders – who had taken an independent anti-Lloyd George position for some time – had gained wide attention with a speech on 10 September which suggested a compromise formula that reconciled demands for protection with key principles of free trade.[9] Samuel feared that if his followers were pushed into opposition, Simon and Runciman would gain the support of middle Liberal opinion and the official party would be pushed to the periphery of politics. The Samuelites continued to hope for the return of a considerable body of free-trade Liberals that would act as a moderating force in the government or the nucleus of a second opposition.

Walter Runciman (1870–1949)

One of the great survivors of Liberal politics, Walter Runciman's political career extended over four decades. He was first elected to Parliament in 1899 and only left the Cabinet for the last time at the outbreak of the Second World War in September 1939.

After reading history at Trinity College, Cambridge, he entered his father's shipping firm. He was a Liberal Imperialist at the time of the Boer War and was appointed to junior office by Campbell-Bannerman when the Liberals formed a government in December 1905, rising to the Cabinet, President of the Board of Education, in 1908. With the outbreak of hostilities he became President of the Board of Trade, where he argued for a limited British commitment to the military effort and opposed the introduction of conscription. He lost office when Lloyd George became Prime Minister and also lost his seat in the coupon election of December 1918. He returned to Parliament in 1924, and two years later formed the 'Radical Group' in opposition to Lloyd George's take-over of the party – though there was precious little that was radical about his views at this time. He was chairman of the Liberal Council under Grey from 1927.

He later became associated with the Liberal National group under John Simon, and his support for the National Government, formed in 1931, led to his return to the Board of Trade that autumn. With successive Prime Ministers, MacDonald and Baldwin, anxious to preserve the national credentials of what became an increasingly Conservative administration, Runciman remained an important figure within the government for the next five and a half years. To the surprise of many, he went along with the introduction of tariffs, though he sought to reduce their impact.

He was dropped from the government when Neville Chamberlain became Prime Minister in May 1937 and took the title of Viscount Runciman of Doxford. Yet the most celebrated episode of his career was still to come. Chamberlain called upon his negotiating skills in the summer of 1938 to act as a so-called 'independent mediator' in the dispute between the Czechoslovakian government and its Sudeten German minority. In practice, his task was to push the Czechs as far as they would go in the quest to secure a peaceful resolution to the crisis. His failure opened the way for Chamberlain himself to negotiate the Munich settlement at the end of September. As a 'reward' for his efforts Runciman returned to government as Lord President of the Council, a post he held for the next eleven months. He died at Doxford Hall, Sunderland, in November 1949.

These hopes soon proved forlorn. The results of the election was a landslide for the National Government, but particularly for the Conservatives: 32 Samuelite Liberals were left uneasily tied to 470 Conservatives and 35 Simonite Liberal Nationals, whose leaders were now brought into the Cabinet.[10] Simon replaced Reading as Foreign Secretary and Runciman became President of the Board of Trade. Samuel remained Home Secretary. His followers, Sinclair (Scottish Secretary) and Maclean (President of the Board of Education) remained in their posts but entered the Cabinet.

1931 general election (27 October)			
	Votes	%	MPs
Liberal	1,372,595	6.3	32
Liberal National	809,302	3.7	35
Independent Liberal	103,528	0.5	4
Conservative	11,905,925	55.0	470
National Labour	341,370	1.6	13
Labour	6,649,630	30.7	52
Others	474,023	2.2	9
Total	21,656,373		615
Average vote per Liberal candidate (%)			36.8
Strong Liberal performances (20% or above in three-cornered contests, 33.3% or above in straight fights)			90

The Tories, with the compliance of Runciman, who continued to seek a middle course between protection and free trade, immediately began to press for emergency tariffs. Neville Chamberlain chaired a Cabinet committee that duly reported in favour of a general tariff of 10 per cent, which was introduced in January 1932. The Samuelites, who with some justice argued that this cursory exercise fell far short of the assurances they had been given in October, came very close to resignation, but were persuaded to accept the so-called 'agreement to differ' whereby they stayed in the government but were free to speak and vote against such measures, thus suspending the principle of collective Cabinet responsibility.

This stance underlined the free traders' impotence and was unpopular with the Liberal rank and file. In September 1932, Samuel, under strong pressure from the party membership, pulled his supporters out of the government in protest at the Ottawa agreements through which the Conservative protectionists attempted – unsuccessfully – to realise their dream of an imperial trading bloc with preferential tariff agreements between Britain and the dominions. Yet, desperate not to lose public support or risk further defections, the Liberals continued to support the National Government from the back benches before finally crossing the floor to join the opposition in November 1933.

Liberal Nationals

For Liberals like Sir John Simon who were frustrated by the party's powerlessness, disdained Labour, and no longer saw free trade as a paramount issue, the realignment of Liberalism within the Conservative camp made compelling strategic sense. The Liberal National group formed in 1931 drew its support from across the party. It embraced older radical Asquithians like Simon and Walter Runciman, ex-Lloyd Georgeites like Hutchison and Geoffrey Shakespeare, veteran pillars of the party like George Lambert (first elected in 1891) and Sir Godfrey Collins, and rising stars like Leslie Hore-Belisha and Clement Davies. Several leading Nonconformist stalwarts such as Ernest Brown, Alec Glassey and Roderick Kedward also sided with the group. Although the Liberal Nationals never produced a significant intellectual case for their position, they undoubtedly represented a large and important current in the Liberal movement.

Except for a few cases in 1931 the Conservatives did not oppose Liberal National candidates and the Liberals did so very rarely until 1945. A Liberal National Council was established in 1932 and some area organisations from 1933, but at local level it was often unclear which side of the fence the Liberal association was on. Although Simon did not encourage the expansion of the Liberal Nationals, and after relinquishing the leadership to Ernest Brown in 1940 became increasingly detached from the party, it would be wrong to see the group as purely a facade to win Liberals over to the Tories. As the only significant non-Tory element in the National Government their influence and share of ministerial posts exceeded their numbers, though this influence waned with the formation of the Churchill coalition in 1940.

There were abortive talks on reunion with the Liberals in 1943–44. The Liberal Nationals maintained their separate identity and organisational independence, in some areas fiercely, until the 1947 Woolton–Teviot agreement, which encouraged the formation of joint Conservative and Liberal National (from 1948 National Liberal) constituency associations. The party was finally wound up in 1968.

The party was in a parlous state. The dire results of the events of 1931–32 left the Liberals diminished in all aspects of activity and were to have profound long-term effects. The party's leadership was gravely weakened by the departure of Lloyd George, its most charismatic figure, and Simon, long the heir-apparent. Moreover, its future leadership potential was damaged as rising stars such as Ernest Brown, Leslie Hore-Belisha and Leslie Burgin joined the Liberal National group, while others such as Isaac Foot, Walter Rea, Ernest Simon, Norman Birkett and Frank Owen lost their seats in the elections of the 1930s. Samuel and Sinclair were not in the same league as Lloyd George and Simon, while other party notables in the 1930s, such as Harcourt Johnstone, Percy Harris and Lords Reading, Lothian and Crewe, made little public impact.

The Foot family

The Foots were one of the most remarkable families in modern British politics. Isaac (1880–1960) was the son of a Plymouth carpenter who set up his own solicitor's practice in 1903. A long-standing member of Plymouth City Council, he stood for Parliament on thirteen occasions, serving as MP for Bodmin in 1922–24 and 1929–35. He was briefly a minister in the 1931 National Government and later served as vice-president of the Methodist Conference and president of the Liberal Party.

Isaac married Eva Mackintosh and four of their sons became parliamentarians. Michael (1913–2010) started off as a Liberal before becoming Labour MP for Plymouth Devonport 1945–55 and Blaenau Gwent 1960–92. A minister under Wilson and Callaghan, Michael led the Labour Party in 1980–83. Dingle (1905–78) was Liberal MP for Dundee in 1931–45 and a minister in the wartime coalition government. Later defecting to Labour, he was MP for Ipswich 1957–70, serving as Solicitor-General 1964–67. Hugh (1907–90) was a diplomat who was Governor of Cyprus in 1957–60. Raised to the peerage as Baron Caradon in 1964, he was a minister in Harold Wilson's first government. Hugh's son, Paul (1937–2004) was a prominent campaigning journalist. John (1909–99) was a solicitor who stood unsuccessfully for Parliament as a Liberal on four occasions before being raised to the peerage in 1967. He was an active Liberal Democrat peer into the 1990s.

Although many in the universities, the City, and the media inclined towards the Liberal tradition, and the Liberal press, particularly the *News Chronicle*, the *Manchester Guardian* and *The Economist*, continued to express Liberal ideas, their support for the Samuelite party as such was often tenuous. Despite the efforts of Ramsay Muir, Elliott Dodds, and others, the party no longer set the intellectual agenda as it had under Lloyd George, and much of its thinking appeared outdated and backward-looking. The Liberal Summer Schools of the 1930s were uninspired and tame affairs.

For many, the collapse of the international free trade system and the gold standard in the early 1930s was regarded as proof that liberal economics had failed. On the right, protectionism was seen as the answer, while many on the left saw economic management and rationalisation as the means to avoid slumps and market 'chaos'.

Regardless of its waning economic and popular force, free trade was championed as the Liberals' defining political platform, the cause for which they had resigned from the National Government and rejected the Simonite alliance with the Conservatives.

Any attempts by the leadership to edge away from the pure milk of free trade and fiscal retrenchment were met with fierce opposition from grassroots free traders, who loomed large in the reduced party.[11] Over 90 per cent of Liberal candidates at the 1935 general election gave prominence to free trade in their election addresses. The party's *Ownership for All* programme of 1938 was described later by one of its authors as raising 'the flag of classical liberalism for the last time in the Liberal Party'. It advocated the radical diffusion of property ownership (rather than social ownership), and called for free trade, rating reform, inheritance tax and voluntary co-ownership. The role of the state was to 'create the conditions for liberty', but the emphasis was on market solutions, not state intervention.[12] Keynes's influence on the Liberal Party had waned after 1929,[13] while Sinclair left economic policy to Harcourt Johnstone, an old-style free-trade radical.

As Lloyd George departed with his fund, and several wealthy donors switched to the Simonites, the Samuelites were left in a very weak financial state. Lloyd George had largely funded the national headquarters up to 1930 and supported some individual candidates who backed his 'Council of Action' in the 1935 election campaign, but otherwise cut off his financial lifeline. Following the 1931 election, Johnstone, who was in charge of fund-raising, estimated that to survive the party needed about £10,000 per annum (equivalent to £400,000 today) for running costs and a further £20,000 for an election fund, whereas annual income stood at only £1,000 and there was no more than £4,500 in the election fund. He often bailed out the party from his own pocket to pay bills and subsidise candidates. A key reason for the small number of Liberal candidates in 1931 and 1935 was lack of money; for example, the income of the Western Counties Federation fell from over £3,000 in 1929 to just £525 in 1934.[14] This was only the start of the perennial financial problems that were to dog the party for decades.

Harcourt Johnstone (1895–1945)

Known by the nickname 'Crinks', Johnstone was a leading Asquithian opponent of Lloyd George within the Liberal Party in the 1920s, Sinclair's closest adviser during his leadership and, as Minister for Overseas Trade in the wartime coalition government, the Liberals' last economics minister until Vince Cable. Related to Sir William Harcourt, Liberal leader in the 1890s, he came from a very affluent aristocratic background, and used much of his wealth to subsidise the cash-strapped Liberal Party in the 1930s when he headed the party organisation. He was an MP in 1922–24, 1930–35 and 1940–45. A large man, fond of food, fine wine, racing and art, he also had considerable, though well-hidden, intellectual ability and was a pivotal figure in the party until 1945.

His appointment as a minister in 1940 owed much to his close friendship with Sinclair and Churchill and caused some resentment among the other Liberal MPs. A free-trade economic liberal, he had opposed Lloyd George's economic interventionism in the 1920s and was sceptical about Beveridge's post-war plans. A poor parliamentary performer, his impact on the government seems to have been limited, partly because of his increasingly poor health. He sat on the key Cabinet reconstruction committee where he commented critically on the massive cost of post-war reconstruction plans. With other Liberals, he was excited by the drive of the US Secretary of State, Cordell Hull, to base the post-war international economic system on free trade and undo the British imperial preference system established from 1932.

Had he lived, Johnstone would have focused the Liberals' 1945 election campaign on international economic issues, but the impact of Beveridge would probably have prevented this in any case.[15]

Party organisation in the constituencies further declined. In many areas such as the mining districts of Yorkshire, Lancashire, Staffordshire, and Durham, working-class Liverpool and Sheffield, and South Wales and Clydeside the Liberal Party ceased to exist and did not revive for decades. Many former strongholds defected to the Liberal Nationals, or were otherwise co-operating closely with the Conservatives. Formal or tacit pacts with the Tories in local government were increasingly common and were frequently extended to parliamentary elections. A striking feature of the elections of the 1930s was the large number of seats which the Liberals abandoned, including in areas where they had previously enjoyed strong support. The ideological confusion sown by the creation of the National Government and lack of funds were part of the explanation for this supine attitude. Fear of splitting the vote and allowing Labour to win was also a factor, although the Liberals stood aside in many seats where Labour offered little competition before 1945, and in a handful of rural constituencies were still given a free run by Labour.

In these circumstances the party singularly failed to develop an effective strategy to recover its electoral position. It might be thought that, in view of the Labour Party's collapse in 1931, its weak leadership and shift to the left, the Liberals could – as Lloyd George advocated – have revived on a radical opposition platform. However, the Keynesian programme of 1929 was largely abandoned as the party focused on traditional free-trade slogans to defend its remaining urban strongholds. These were indeed concentrated in towns and cities dependent on exports and shipping.[16] Overall the Liberals continued to lose ground in working-class areas. A partial exception to this was in the East End of London, where for a time the party with some success targeted the Jewish vote. By the mid-1930s however, MPs Harry Nathan and Barnet Janner had defected to Labour.[17] In local government Labour made big gains in the towns and cities in 1932–34, while the Liberals fell back. The main study of the subject has found that: 'for the Liberals the decade after 1930 saw a continuous and almost uninterrupted decline. By 1938, despite an occasional stronghold in Yorkshire and Lancashire, the party had almost ceased to be represented on many borough councils.'[18] Lloyd George's lavish attempt to rally the opposition behind the progressive 'New Deal' programme of his Council of Action in 1935 made virtually no impact.

Nor was the Liberals' opposition to the National Government a vote-winner. While they had been relatively successful in by-elections up to their break with the National

Government in late 1933, thereafter the results were disastrous. By the time of the 1935 general election the mid-term unpopularity of the National Government was subsiding and it was gaining credit for the economic recovery, pay rises and a house-building boom. The dominance of the centre ground by Baldwin, Prime Minister from 1935 (assisted by Simon), and the constructive social drive of Neville Chamberlain left little space for the Liberals. They were also unable to repeat their 1920s successes as a party of rural protest, even though feeling against tithe payment was running high in some agricultural areas.[19] The election was a major defeat for the Liberals. The number of Liberal MPs was reduced to twenty-one, of whom nineteen had majorities under 2,000; Samuel was one of the defeated MPs. The Liberals lost between a third and a half of their 1929 vote, most of it to the Conservatives.

1935 general election (14 November)			
	Votes	%	MPs
Liberal	1,443,093	6.6	21
Liberal National	866,354	3.9	33
Conservative	10,496,300	47.7	387
National Labour	339,811	1.5	8
Labour	8,325,491	37.8	154
Others	526,005	2.4	12
Total	21,997,054		615
Average vote per Liberal candidate (%)			25.3
Strong Liberal performances (20% or above in three-cornered contests, 33.3% or above in straight fights)			85

Many in the leadership had expected this failure. The party came nowhere near its target of contesting 400 seats, fatally undermining its claims to be an alternative government. Shortly before the election Ramsay Muir, the party president, had written to Lord Lothian that: 'I take a most gloomy, almost a despairing view of our prospects. We are beaten in advance by the public's idea that we are done for, and this affects our own people.' He toyed with the idea of forming a non-party Liberty League to carry on the Liberal tradition. Lothian also wondered whether the Liberal Party had outlived its usefulness and that the progressive Conservative element in the National Government had assumed its role. Harcourt Johnstone argued that: 'we must try to keep up the bluff until the last moment, or decide here and now to disband the Liberal Party as an organised entity'. Sinclair, who had tried to energise the demoralised Samuel before the election, now replaced him as leader and set about rallying the party to continue the fight.

Last outpost: Percy Harris (1876–1952) and Bethnal Green

Sir Percy Harris was a pillar of the Liberal Parliamentary Party until he finally lost his seat in 1945. He was Chief Whip from 1931 to 1945 and while Sinclair was Air Minister during the war acted as leader in the Commons and ran the party organisation in the country.

A businessman of Jewish origin with interests in New Zealand, Harris sat as Progressive member for Bethnal Green on the London County Council from 1907 to 1934. During the First World War he was deputy chairman of the London County Council and was briefly an Asquithian MP.

Bethnal Green was the Liberals' last outpost in London, all that remained by 1945 of a belt of lower middle- and working-class strongholds in south and east London that fell in the 1920s and 1930s. Harris sat as MP for Bethnal Green South West from 1922 until his defeat by Labour in 1945, and the North East division was Liberal into the 1930s. In 1946 Harris regained the same seat on London County Council and held it until his death in 1952. Liberal support in Bethnal Green was built on a socially progressive tradition personified by Harris, his assiduous nursing of the constituency, a strong presence in local government, and a populist appeal – it was said that the Liberals were helped by the fact that they ran the largest drinking club in the area.

Bethnal Green politics were extreme. The Communists ran the local Labour Party in the 1920s and attracted significant support in the 1930s, as did Mosley's fascists. The weakness of the Conservatives in the borough enabled Harris to corner the moderate vote.

Despite massive redevelopment, the remnants of the Liberal tradition were still evident in elections in Bethnal Green after Harris's death and re-surfaced in the 1980s when the Liberals, for a time, controlled Tower Hamlets council.

Stabilisation: the leadership of Sir Archibald Sinclair (1935–45)

The new leader, Sir Archibald Sinclair, inherited an unenviable task. Nevertheless, between 1935 and the outbreak of war in 1939 he can be credited with stabilising the party's position and at least preventing further decline.

A hopeful start was made immediately when Lloyd George's family group rejoined the fold; with Sinclair, whose background was on the Lloyd Georgeite wing of the party, as leader, and Samuel out of the Commons, Lloyd George ended his exile. Sinclair recognised that he needed to reform the archaic internal organisation of the party. A committee under Lord Meston made proposals for significant changes in 1936. A single policy-making body was created with the replacement of the National Liberal Federation with the Liberal Party Organisation (LPO). Sinclair also oversaw a review of the party's finances, which aimed to cut central expenditure so that the party could exist on income from donations, preferably from local associations and ordinary members rather than the declining handful of wealthy supporters and, indeed, Sinclair's extensive personal wealth.

Sinclair's efforts to rebuild the Liberals' credibility centred on opposition to the appeasement and defence policies of the Baldwin and Chamberlain governments. Historians have consistently overlooked the anti-appeasement role played by the Liberal Party between 1936 and 1939, instead focusing on the internal dissent within the Conservative Party and on Winston Churchill's campaign. The Liberal Party, and

Sinclair in particular, played a major part in developing and proposing clear alternatives to the government's foreign policy. Sinclair's international policy can be stated in simple terms as a strategy of collective security through strong defence, resistance to aggression through collective agreements, and solving disputes through international conferences, rather than Munich-style deals between Britain, France and the dictators. All of this was underpinned by the traditional Liberal belief that compliance with international law should form the basis of international relations.

When Sinclair took over the Liberal leadership in 1935, he accepted the position only after he had obtained a promise from his fellow MPs that the party would give priority to defence policy. The Liberals consistently raised the issues of defence and rearmament, especially in relation to the air force. Throughout 1936 and 1937, in the face of a significant surge in German rearmament, Sinclair urged the government further to increase spending on the armed forces.

With the remilitarisation of the Rhineland and the March 1938 Anschluss with Austria, Sinclair, Attlee and Chamberlain met to see if any joint policy could be developed in response to Germany's territorial ambitions, but failed to agree a united position. In the summer of 1938 Germany pressed its claims for the annexation of the Sudetenland, then part of Czechoslovakia, to the Reich. In Parliament Sinclair initially argued that the Czechoslovaks might have to make concessions to avoid conflict but swiftly realised that this would reduce Czechoslovakia's ability to defend herself from further aggression and by September 1938 had reversed his position, vigorously opposing any deal over the Sudetenland. Sinclair argued that a general European settlement was necessary and that Britain had to prove to Germany that aggression would be resisted.

In the Munich debate of 3 October 1938, Sinclair was one of the most damning critics of the deal. Calling Chamberlain's approach a 'policy of successive retreats in the face of aggressive dictatorships', he made clear that Munich had been a humiliating surrender in the face of threatened force. The Munich crisis allowed Sinclair and Churchill to cooperate more openly. Throughout the rest of 1938 and into the spring of 1939, they worked closely together in condemning the Munich agreement, urging the formation of a Ministry of Supply (reflecting their experience of the Ministry of Munitions in 1918) and arguing that Britain's foreign policy must focus on isolating and encircling Germany by forging an understanding with the Russians in the face of a common threat. However, no matter how effective Sinclair's arguments were in the Commons, he failed to convince many outside the House and, indeed, a few in his own party, such as Herbert Samuel and J. A. Spender, supported Chamberlain's policy.

John Alfred Spender (1862–1942)

Spender was the son of a Kent doctor and was educated at Balliol College, Oxford, where he was taken under the wing of Benjamin Jowett. He edited the *Westminster Gazette* from 1896 to 1922, during which time it was one of the most influential political newspapers of the day. Spender's editorials carried enormous weight. A party loyalist, Spender sought to build consensus between the Liberal Party's various factions.

After leaving the *Gazette*, which had suffered a long period of decline following the First World War, Spender wrote numerous books, including biographies of Asquith and Campbell-Bannerman.

During 1936 Sinclair came under pressure from some Liberals to back the concept of a Popular Front to co-ordinate the opposition of the non-Conservative parties to the domestic policy of the National Government. Some suggested that the Popular Front platform should be extended to international policy. Sinclair was hesitant about an initiative which risked compromising the integrity of the party, but he shared a plat- form with Churchill and some Labour leaders at the December 1936 'Arms and the Covenant' rally in London and offered Liberal support to anti-appeasement can- didates at by-elections, including the Duchess of Atholl, a Conservative MP, who resigned her seat to fight an unsuccessful by-election in protest at Chamberlain's handling of international relations. However, the campaign against Munich lacked momentum because the Munich agreement enjoyed enormous support throughout the country.

By 1939 there were signs – such as the retention of the North Cornwall by-election by a Liberal fighting with anti-appeasement Labour and Tory support – that Sinclair's policy stance was turning into a vote-winner, and that the Liberals might have gained ground in the general election due by the end of 1940. Some left-wing Liberal MPs such as Dingle Foot, Richard Acland and Megan Lloyd George felt that Sinclair should have worked more closely with other parties in order to position the Liberal Party as the pivot around which Labour and Conservative dissenters might have gathered. But it would have been a risky initiative, requiring, at the very least, electoral cooperation with the Labour Party, and it was a risk that Sinclair did not feel able to take for fear that the Liberals would fragment.

Sir Archibald Sinclair (1890–1970)

Archie Sinclair was leader of the Parliamentary Liberal Party from 1935 to 1945, and was the last Liberal MP to attend Cabinet until 2010, serving as Churchill's Air Minister from 1940 to 1945.

His career was intertwined with that of Churchill. He had been Churchill's second- in-command in the trenches in the First World War and was his private secretary when he was Colonial Secretary in the Lloyd George Coalition in 1918–22. In 1922 Sinclair was elected as the Lloyd George Liberal MP for Caithness and Sutherland, where he was the local laird. He was a Liberal loyalist, who gamely struggled to hold the fractious par- liamentary party together as Chief Whip in 1930–31 and he served as Secretary of State for Scotland in the National Government in 1931–32. He accepted the post of leader of the party after Samuel's defeat in 1935.

Churchill appointed him as Air Minister in May 1940; although not a member of the War Cabinet he attended 80 per cent of its meetings. His dedication to his government duties in London limited his active leadership of the party during the war, and seems to have been a factor in his narrow defeat in Caithness in 1945 (which was repeated in 1950). In 1951 he was elevated to the peerage as Viscount Thurso, but a series of strokes in the 1950s ended his political career. His grandson, the third Viscount Thurso, was elected for Caithness and Sutherland in 2001 after the reform of the House of Lords allowed hereditary peers to stand for election to the Commons.

As the historian Paul Addison wrote, 'Sinclair had two great loyalties which account for his two main contributions to public life. He believed in Liberalism and revived it when it was down; and he believed in Churchill and revived him when he was down.'[20]

At the outbreak of war in September 1939 Neville Chamberlain invited Sinclair to join his government on behalf of the Liberal Party. Sinclair declined the offer, in part because of his mistrust of Chamberlain but also because it did not include a seat in the War Cabinet. Sinclair and Lloyd George both urged Churchill not to accept office under Chamberlain, but their advice was ignored and Churchill returned to the Admiralty.

The parliamentary arithmetic did not enable the Liberal Party as such to play a significant role in the ending of the Chamberlain government. However, both Lloyd George and Sinclair made key speeches during the critical Commons debate on 7–8 May 1940 concerning the military ineptitude shown in the Norway campaign in April. Sinclair led for the Liberals in the debate with a highly charged and openly critical attack on Chamberlain's conduct of the war. Following shortly afterwards Lloyd George, in his last truly significant intervention in the House of Commons, observed that Chamberlain had appealed for national sacrifice and argued that: 'the nation is prepared for every sacrifice so long as it has leadership ... I say solemnly that the Prime Minister should give an example of sacrifice, because there is nothing which can contribute more to victory in this war than that he should sacrifice the seals of office.' These attacks, together with the speeches of Attlee for Labour and Leo Amery for the dissident Tories, led to the government's majority being dramatically reduced, with over seventy Tory MPs either abstaining or voting with the opposition.

The most significant individual in orchestrating the fall of Chamberlain, however, was probably Clement Davies, at that time the independent MP for Montgomeryshire and a future leader of the Liberal Party. Increasingly frustrated with the conduct of the war by the National Government, in early 1940 Davies had resigned the Liberal National whip. Davies, who had friends in all of the major parties, chaired a parliamentary action committee that pressed for a reorganisation of the government on a truly national basis and a more aggressive handling of war policy. He was active behind the scenes during the Norway debate, encouraging anti-government rebels and organising speakers who could be relied upon to push a strongly anti-Chamberlain line. According to Lord

Boothby, then a Tory MP and first-hand observer of these events, Davies was 'one of the architects – some may judge the principal architect' of the coalition government led by Churchill that emerged.[21]

Churchill appointed Sinclair Secretary of State for Air, but outside the War Cabinet. He attended the vast majority of War Cabinet meetings and was also a key member of the important Defence Committee (Supply), where the majority of strategic decisions were taken.[22] Harcourt Johnstone was appointed as Minister of Overseas Trade and Dingle Foot, MP for Dundee, was appointed Parliamentary Secretary at the Ministry of Economic Warfare.

Sinclair is widely counted as a successful minister in the post he held throughout the war. He fought his corner in Whitehall turf wars and when necessary stood up to Churchill. His first major test came at the height of the Battle of Britain in September 1940, when losses of fighters cut deeply into the remaining reserves. This led to clashes with Lord Beaverbrook, Minister for Aircraft Production in 1940–41, with whom Sinclair had a stormy relationship. Frequently Churchill was called on to intervene in order to resolve inter-departmental disputes. One of Sinclair's most significant contributions as Air Minister was to fight for the allocation of manpower needed to sustain the bomber offensive, which was extremely costly in terms of aircrews' lives. From 1942 he stoutly defended his air marshals in the policy of strategic bombing of Germany, which was controversial both at the time and later.

Some Liberals grew disenchanted with the direction of the wartime coalition, especially as the threat of invasion receded after 1940–41. Some traditionalists criticised the increase in public expenditure, regulation and bureaucracy and supported Sir Ernest Benn's *Manifesto on British Liberty*. Other activists focused on pressing the leadership to take more energetic and radical steps towards shaping a Liberal programme for the post-war world, and a tougher line against the Tories. The Radical Action group was formed in 1941 to work for 'the revival of Radicalism within the Liberal Party and for the mobilisation of men and women of radical opinion inside and outside other political parties'. It declared the Conservative Party 'its natural enemy' and demanded equality of opportunity, adoption of the Beveridge Report on social security and control and regulation of enterprise to prevent social injustice and privilege, while rejecting 'government by bureaucracies'. It claimed the support of six MPs and twenty-four candidates.[23] Radical Action was particularly critical of the wartime electoral truce and lent support to independent Liberals in by-elections – two of which, Chippenham and Darwen, were lost only very narrowly.

A few radicals followed Sir Richard Acland, Liberal MP for Barnstaple since 1935, into a new party, Common Wealth, formed in July 1942. Common Wealth was essentially an ethical anti-capitalist party, reflecting Acland's radical Christian idealism. Acland's party harnessed left-wing and protest votes, winning three seats in wartime by-elections. Common Wealth's propaganda reflected some Liberal themes, but it was largely a proxy Labour Party, and with the return of party politics in the 1945 election its support collapsed. Acland joined Labour, where he continued his maverick political career for another decade.

The wartime disintegration of the Liberal Nationals, due to the identification of their leaders, Sir John Simon and Ernest Brown, with Neville Chamberlain's policy of appeasement, led to MPs such as Clement Davies and Edgar Granville rejoining the Liberals and brief, though ineffectual, negotiations for reunification in August 1943. However, these foundered on the continuing unwillingness of the Liberal Nationals to stand for election other than in alliance with the Tories.[24]

Optimism that the Liberals could revive as an independent force was strengthened when Violet Bonham Carter recruited Sir William Beveridge to the party in July 1944. The Liberals had greeted his 1942 social insurance plan enthusiastically and since then had wooed Beveridge, who had been inclined to throw in his lot with Labour. Apart from what he called 'the bow and arrow brigade', most Liberals were delighted with this coup and Beveridge was put in charge of the party's campaigning in 1944–45, a task that he took up with typical gusto. The prominence of Beveridge and the radical mood in the country at the end of the war pushed the Liberal platform to the left, as reflected in the 1945 manifesto. The pre-war leaders were overshadowed, and traditionalist free traders and land taxers were sidelined.

Without underestimating the influence of Beveridge on post-war Liberal thinking, his immediate impact within the party was short-lived. After the 1945 election, when he lost his seat, he became a Liberal peer, but his party activity wound down.[25] Liberals proudly identified with the contribution of Beveridge – and that of Keynes – but these sometimes co-existed uneasily with an attachment to traditional Liberal economics. Keynesian policies, which then included exchange and import controls, were at odds with the free-trade principles that many Liberals continued to proclaim. One Liberal veteran recalled that 'experience of the Liberal Party ... leads me to guess that in both 1945 and 1950 (and even more so at earlier elections) there were legions of old-style free-traders going to the polls under a Keynes/Lloyd George/Beveridge policy that they neither understood nor really supported'.[26]

William Beveridge (1879–1963)

Generally considered as the father of the modern welfare state, Beveridge joined the Liberals in 1944 after a distinguished career as a civil servant and academic.

Beveridge was born in India, where his father was in the Indian civil service. He took a first at Balliol College, Oxford, and in 1902, after a brief and unsatisfying spell as a barrister, became sub-warden of Toynbee Hall. He worked with Sidney and Beatrice Webb in campaigns for old age pensions and to combat unemployment and from 1908 as a civil servant developed social legislation leading to the establishment of labour exchanges and national insurance. By 1919 – gaining the hostility of the trades unions on the way – he had risen to be Permanent Secretary at the Ministry of Food, but resigned to take up the post of Director of the London School of Economics, where, though often 'despotic and high-handed' in his methods, he remained until 1937 when he became Master of University College, Oxford.

In 1940 he joined the Ministry of Labour, expecting to take charge of managing the wartime manpower programme, but due to trade union objections he was sidelined to chair an inquiry into the social services. He published reports in 1942 and 1944 that proposed a comprehensive national insurance system to slay what he described as the five 'giant evils' of want, disease, ignorance, squalor and idleness. This work provided the blueprint for the welfare system established by the Attlee government as well as the goal of full employment pursued by successive governments until the 1970s.

The Liberals pinned great hopes on Beveridge at the 1945 general election but to no avail, and he lost his own seat, Berwick-upon-Tweed, which he had represented since 1944. In 1946 he accepted a peerage.

Great expectations (1945–51)

Churchill called a general election for July 1945, after the defeat of Germany but before victory over Japan. Under considerable pressure from his party, Sinclair ruled out an electoral pact or continuing in coalition with the Conservatives, even though the war had not yet ended. The Liberals fought the election independently and, although unprepared, managed to put forward 306 candidates, some twice as many as in 1935.

In most respects the election was a further setback. Sinclair's distinguished war service as Air Minister, the high public profile of Sir William Beveridge, and the unpopularity of the Conservatives might have been expected to pay dividends for the Liberals. Indeed, as late as June, some newspapers anticipated that the Liberals would almost double their number of MPs and hold the balance of power in the post-election Parliament. In the event, however, their vote was largely static as Labour surged. In contesting just 306 seats, less than half the total, the Liberals could not be regarded as serious contenders for power. Furthermore, the party gained no significant advantage from Beveridge's support, as his proposals were broadly endorsed by all the main parties. It was Labour, not the Liberals, who benefited from the country's mood for change.

Only twelve Liberals, seven of whom were from Wales, were elected, and Sinclair, Beveridge, Sir Percy Harris and Dingle Foot were among the defeated. Those who survived were an odd and ill-disciplined bunch. Gwilym Lloyd-George was already a Conservative in all but name, while the left-wing Tom Horabin, elected with Labour support in North Cornwall, defected to the Labour Party in 1947. Megan Lloyd George and two of the other MPs were broadly sympathetic to the government and were ultimately to join the Labour Party, while another later defected to the Tories. The eminent Celtic scholar Professor W. J. Gruffydd represented a university seat, which was to be abolished in 1950, and was much preoccupied with his academic duties, while the new Welsh MPs Roderic Bowen (Cardigan), a lawyer, and Emrys Roberts (Merioneth), a businessman, were also distracted by their outside careers. Rhys Hopkin-Morris, who had gained Carmarthen from Labour against the trend, was a much-loved relic of unbending Gladstonian Liberalism.

1945 general election (5 July)			
	Votes	*%*	*MPs*
Liberal	2,252,430	9.0	12
Liberal National	737,732	2.9	11
Conservative	9,101,099	36.2	197
Labour	**11,967,746**	**47.7**	**393**
Others	1,036,188	4.1	27
Total	*25,095,195*		*640*
Average vote per Liberal candidate (%)			18.6
Strong Liberal performances (20% or above in three-cornered contests, 33.3% or above in straight fights)			92

It was with some justification that Lady Violet Bonham-Carter thought the party's 'lack of men of distinction & personality' was its biggest problem, complaining to Megan Lloyd George that the parliamentary party only contained four 'effectives'.[27] From this limited choice, Clement Davies was elected to chair the parliamentary party, initially on a temporary basis, as Sinclair was expected to make a quick return to the Commons. Sinclair's opponent in 1945 went back on an election pledge to stand down after the end of the war in the Far East, however, and Sinclair was again narrowly defeated in the 1950 general election, so Davies ended up as the party's permanent leader. He was supported as Chief Whip by Horabin until his resignation in 1946 and thereafter by Frank Byers, the most promising of the new intake, who had captured North Dorset.

Clement Davies (1884–1962)

Clement Davies came from a modest farming background in Montgomeryshire, through scholarships achieving a place at Trinity College, Cambridge, where he graduated with a first. He had a highly successful career as a barrister. He entered Parliament at the age of forty-five as a radical Lloyd-Georgeite Liberal for his home county, but in 1931 sided with his friend, Sir John Simon. In the 1930s he mainly pursued a business career.

In 1940 he was an architect of the manoeuvres that led to Chamberlain's replacement by Churchill, but was not invited to join the government, and became associated with the group of parliamentarians that acted as an unofficial opposition to the wartime coalition. He rejoined the Liberals in 1942 and was active on its radical wing.[28]

When Sinclair was defeated in 1945, Davies became de facto leader, a post he held until 1956. A radical evangelist rather than a party manager, he struggled to hold the left and right of the party together in the 1945–51 period. In 1951 his refusal of Churchill's offer of a place in the Cabinet as Minister of Education preserved the Liberal Party's independence at its lowest ebb.

From the 1920s he struggled with a severe drinking problem.[29] His personal life was overshadowed by the deaths of three of his four children, all (coincidentally) at the age of twenty-four.

There were some faint silver linings in the 1945 results. First, the party was still in business and had fought fully independently and on a broad front for the first time since 1929. Although the Liberal vote was a shadow of its former glories, the party had nevertheless polled close to 20 per cent on average in the seats that it fought. There are indications that the party was subtly broadening its appeal, holding its own or gaining votes in its weaker constituencies, thus arguably laying the foundations for its role over the next decades as a catch-all party of protest even in seats where it had little chance of winning. The obverse of this was that it was continuing to slip badly in its better seats, where its traditional sources of support crumbled and the credibility of its challenge collapsed. This made it hard to see where it could win back seats in the future. Finally, despite the losses and defections, the Liberals attracted many young ex-service recruits who were to sustain the party over the next decade.[30]

Possibly influenced by Tom Horabin, Clement Davies seems initially to have pursued a strategy of outflanking the new Labour government on the left.[31] The Liberals gave general support to the social reforms of the Attlee government until 1947, though with increasing objections to measures which infringed civil liberties. However, Horabin, who insisted that the Liberals should give whole-hearted backing to what he regarded as a truly radical administration, resigned as Chief Whip in March 1946, and in October left the Liberal Party, joining Labour a year later. He claimed that the Liberal Party organisation was 'all too quickly ridding itself of its radical associations and seems to think that by preaching a merely negative anti-socialist crusade and avoiding any positive expression of policies it can secure more tactical advantage'.[32]

There was little chance of a left-wing course succeeding given the continuing strength of the traditionalists and economic liberals in the party. Some Liberals almost despaired of the party's future and argued for an understanding – though not a merger – with the Conservatives. Asquith's daughter Violet Bonham Carter, encouraged by her friend Churchill, favoured such an understanding in the late 1940s. At the 1950 election Churchill offered her one of the Tories' five election broadcasts to make an anti-socialist call to the voters; she refused.[33]

There were also further abortive talks about reunion with the Liberal Nationals in 1946. They were, however, an ailing force. Of their few remaining 'big hitters', Lord Simon was in his mid-seventies and increasingly detached from the party; Leslie Hore-Belisha had left the party and lost his seat; Ernest Brown had also lost his seat; and Leslie Burgin died in August 1945. The party was ageing: almost a half of its MPs in 1945 were in their sixties or seventies. The Liberal Nationals were only interested in reunion on an anti-socialist platform under the protective umbrella of a pact with the Conservative Party. The Woolton–Teviot pact of 1947, which cemented the alliance between the

Conservatives and Liberal Nationals (who became National Liberals at this point) put an end to any possibility of reunification.

Although both before and after 1945 the Liberals often gave the impression of being little more than a loose gathering of individuals who fought elections together, highly dependent on a few wealthy supporters to keep going, this perhaps ignores the latent potential of the party if only it could get its act together. Michael Steed has estimated that if the Liberals had fought all the seats in general elections, they would have gathered 14.5 per cent of the votes in 1945 and 11 per cent in 1950. This is broadly confirmed by their support in the early Gallup opinion polls, which mostly fluctuated between 10 and 15 per cent in the period 1945–51, not so very different from the level of support the Liberals enjoyed for much of the 1960s and 1970s.[34]

The party had not yet adopted the tactics of third-party campaigning that were to sustain it in the years of revival. It did not use by-elections and local government effectively to win attention and build up its strength, and had yet to develop 'community politics' as a means to win local footholds.[35] Most Liberal organisations of this time give the impression of being very staid. One writer, describing the party in Newcastle-under-Lyme, noted that:

> The Liberals of the 1940s and early 1950s inevitably give the impression of being a hangover from the great days of liberalism of twenty and thirty years earlier. The leadership, though it lacked the mass following of the former period, had the same rather narrow social base – small shopkeepers and businessmen, and the lower ranks of the professional classes. Their political ideals had a flavour of the past about them; a document of 1942 put forward the rallying cries of liberty, the fight against monopoly, and the taxation of land values.[36]

Recalling a Liberal assembly in 1949, David Butler remembered 'a sense of talking to people who had been brilliant young men in 1906, or were the sons of those brilliant young men, and who were looking back fondly to that time'.[37]

Nevertheless, a concerted attempt was made in the later 1940s to energise the party. A key figure in this was Edward Martell, who was attracted to the party after the war and joined up with Frank Byers and Philip Fothergill in a drive to broaden the party's financial resources and revive its constituency organisation. In 1946 he and Sir Percy Harris recaptured the two seats for Bethnal Green South West in the London County Council elections and later the same year Martell stood in a parliamentary by-election in Rotherhithe, a Labour stronghold. Following a well-organised and highly populist campaign Martell won second place, a major achievement compared with other by-elections of these years.

A Reconstruction Committee was set up that produced the *Coats off For the Future!* report to the 1946 Liberal assembly. This advocated a 'grand revivalist campaign', infused with the evangelical passion of a crusade. A military-style organisation plan was launched and a 'Foundation Fund' established in May 1946. The initiative was relatively successful. Headquarters annual income had run at between £7,000 and £15,000 in the

1935–45 period, but Martell's fund-raising flair brought in over £58,000 within the first eight months of its existence. Martell also launched the weekly *Liberal News*, intended primarily as a vehicle for eliciting small but regular financial contributions from the membership, although this fell short of expectations. By 1949 annual party income was up to £50,000.

Great efforts were made to reactivate constituency organisations. By 1947 the party claimed 500 candidates at the next election and held out the prospect of a Liberal government. Sinclair and some others who advocated a more targeted, 'guerrilla', approach did not favour this broad-front strategy, partly because they inclined towards anti-socialist pacts with the Conservatives. Nevertheless, Martell, who masterminded the 1950 general election campaign, found 475 candidates and expectations were very high.

The results of the 1950 election were a devastating disappointment and humiliation for the party, which lost 319 deposits and returned only nine MPs, as Labour's majority was reduced to five. In fact the election was so close that the Liberal vote was critical: a slightly stronger Liberal performance could have given Labour a working majority, possibly avoiding another election and the further heavy Liberal setback in 1951.[38] In fact, the Liberals had overstretched themselves. Many of their candidates were nominated at the last moment and were of low quality. Constituency organisations were mostly no match for the highly effective Conservative and Labour machines. A narrower front might well have been more successful.

1950 general election (23 February)			
	Votes	*%*	*MPs*
Liberal	2,621,487	9.1	9
National Liberal	985,343	3.4	16
Conservative	11,507,061	40.0	282
Labour	**13,266,176**	**46.1**	**315**
Others	391,057	1.4	3
Total	*28,771,124*		*625*
Average vote per Liberal candidate (%)			11.4
Strong Liberal performances (20% or above in three-cornered contests, 33.3% or above in straight fights)			48

Turn of fortune? (1951–56)

Once again the Liberals were in crisis. Their band of nine MPs was caught in the intensive Labour-Tory struggle in the 1950 Parliament that cruelly exposed the party's political divisions and weak leadership. Davies complained that judging by the wayward behaviour of his colleagues anyone 'would come to the conclusion that there is no Party today, but a number of individuals who ... come together only to express completely divergent views'. He admitted that only by following a deliberate policy of 'supine weakness' could he hold the party together.[39] Some prominent Liberals defected to the Tories, while others such as Violet Bonham Carter, Sir Archibald Sinclair and, at times, Lord Samuel, concluded that the party could only survive by entering a broad alliance with Churchill's Conservatives, encouraged by hints of pacts and electoral reform. Davies ruled out any central agreement that would compromise the party's independence.

By 1951 the Liberals were at their lowest ebb since the early 1930s, and the existence of the Liberals as a political party was in grave doubt. When Labour returned to the electorate in October 1951, the Liberals, with little money and less enthusiasm, were able to contest a mere 109 seats. Only six MPs were elected, and only Jo Grimond won in a three-way contest.

1951 general election (25 October)			
	Votes	%	MPs
Liberal	730,546	2.6	6
National Liberal	**1,058,138**	**3.7**	**19**
Conservative	**12,659,712**	**44.3**	**302**
Labour	13,948,883	48.8	295
Others	199,315	0.7	3
Total	28,596,594		625
Average vote per Liberal candidate (%)			14.7
Strong Liberal performances (20% or above in three-cornered contests, 33.3% or above in straight fights)			20

The Conservatives had targeted the Liberal vote in the 1951 election, aware that it had played a pivotal role in the 1950 poll. As then, they deliberately sowed confusion among voters by running candidates with a variety of 'Liberal and Conservative' labels, ignoring protests from Clement Davies. In a few constituencies genuine local co-operation was established between the Liberals and Conservatives. Donald Wade had won Huddersfield West through such an understanding in 1950, and Arthur Holt now won Bolton West through a similar pact. Both MPs, committed Liberals, greatly reinforced the parliamentary party until the pacts broke down and they were defeated in 1964. However, Violet Bonham Carter, who was given a free run in Colne Valley where Churchill came to speak on her behalf, was defeated. There were very few seats where the Tories were willing to contemplate such deals, and inevitably they constrained the independence of any MPs elected. At best they offered a limited lifeline to help preserve the tiny Liberal representation in Parliament, but they were no basis for wider revival.

Last redoubt: Huddersfield and Elliott Dodds (1889–1977)

Huddersfield was the epicentre of the Liberal strength in the Pennine textile belt which survived through the years of the party's collapse from the 1930s to the 1960s. Huddersfield, Halifax and Rochdale were the only sizeable towns where the Liberals remained the leading party in local government during these years. By the 1950s, 90 per cent of the remaining Liberal local councillors were elected in these and nearby Yorkshire, Lancashire and Cheshire mill towns. Many of the key figures in the party's survival and recovery, such as Dodds, Philip Fothergill, Donald Wade, Arthur Holt, Richard Wainwright, Cyril Smith and Michael Meadowcroft, were closely associated with this area.

Pennine Liberalism was traditional and individualist, heavily influenced by Nonconformism and the distinctly anti-Labour economic liberalism of the mill-owning families. In some areas, such as Huddersfield, the local Liberals supported a Liberal National MP in the 1930s and 1940s, but support for an independent Liberal Party was difficult to extinguish. Co-operation with the Tories in local elections often contributed to the party's survival, and pacts were responsible for the election to Parliament of Wade (Huddersfield West, 1950–64) and Holt (Bolton West, 1951–64). The prominence of Pennine Liberalism declined as the party revived in other areas from the 1960s.

George Elliott Dodds was the leading publicist of the Liberalism of the northern counties. The son of a tea merchant, he took a first in history at Oxford. For more than four decades as a journalist and later editor of the *Huddersfield Examiner*, he played a central role in the debates in the party over the boundaries between liberalism and socialism. He chaired the 1938 anti-statist 'Ownership for All' committee but in the 1940s Dodds cautiously welcomed Beveridge's welfare state reforms and backed compulsory co-ownership in industry. He was a prime mover in the foundation in 1953 of the Unservile State Group, which sought to modernise Liberal thinking within the framework of its traditional concerns for individual freedom.

The culmination of Churchill's attempts to entice the Liberals followed the 1951 election, when he offered Davies the post of Education Minister in the Cabinet. Davies turned down the offer after consultations showed that apart from Bonham Carter the party would not accept it.[40] This was one of Davies' major achievements: had he joined Churchill's Cabinet, it is possible that the party would have entirely disintegrated.

Violet Bonham Carter (1887–1969)

Asquith's daughter by his first wife, Violet Bonham Carter was a passionate Liberal and the embodiment of the Asquithian tradition in the party after his death. She was president of the Women's Liberal Federation in 1923–25 and 1939–45 and party president in 1945. After being unsuccessful in standing for Parliament for Wells in 1945 and Colne Valley in 1950, where she had Conservative support, she was made a life peer in 1964.

She was an active member of the League of Nations Union, and was vice-chairman of the United European Movement from 1947. A fine orator – she spearheaded her father's successful election campaigns in Paisley in the early 1920s – she later became a frequent and popular broadcaster. In 1958 her son Mark won the Torrington by-election, the first Liberal by-election gain since 1929.

Despite the party's woolly and centrist image with the electorate, there were many in the party who saw Liberalism as fundamentally distinct not only from the socialism of the Labour Party, but also from the Tories' acceptance of the welfare state and the mixed economy. Traditionalists and economic liberals objected to the Conservatives on free-trade grounds and, more broadly, saw the two main parties as the defenders of monopolistic and protectionist big business and trade union vested interests, while the Liberals alone defended competition, enterprise, small business and the consumer. This current strongly influenced the party's outlook in the early 1950s, making it something of a counterforce to the prevailing Keynesian consensus, which also of course had its advocates in the party.

In the 1950s the party was to the right of the Labour and Conservative parties on economic matters, so much so that there was an exodus of the more left-wing Liberals to the Labour Party, and the Radical Reform Group was formed in 1953 to resist the laissez-faire trend. *The Economist* argued that the Liberals should move to the right of the Conservatives and harness middle-class discontent. Many of the party's old guard had stuck with the Liberals out of loyalty to free trade, but many of the younger figures who kept the party going in the 1940s and 1950s were also libertarian in their outlook. After 1951 all the members of the tiny parliamentary party leaned towards the economic right. Party intellectuals such as Elliott Dodds and the Unservile State Group were concerned with updating rather than replacing the party's traditional libertarian concerns. Mavericks such as Edward Martell, Air Vice Marshal Don Bennett, and Lord Moynihan were later to drift into anti-trade union and right-wing causes.

A vocal ideological libertarian faction led by Sir Alfred Suenson-Taylor (Lord Grantchester), Oliver Smedley, S. W. Alexander and others, attempted to rally the party behind free trade and market economics. Suenson-Taylor was a key sponsor of F. A. Hayek's activities, including the Mont Pelerin Society, established in 1947 as an international network to promote economic liberalism on the back of Hayek's *The Road to Serfdom* (1944). Smedley has been described as 'fervent and obsessive in his belief in the beneficence of the free market'. In 1955, together with a Conservative, Anthony Fisher, he set up the Institute of Economic Affairs (IEA), which was to become the intellectual powerhouse of the neo-liberal counter-revolution in the 1970s. In the early days the IEA was strongly associated with the Liberal Party; Arthur Seldon, who, with Ralph Harris, was to be its driving force, was another active Liberal during this period.[41]

Post-war party assemblies saw fierce debates over trade and subsidies. The economic liberal zealots led by Smedley agitated tirelessly for uncompromising free trade, the abolition of subsidies and assured markets, and a general rolling back of the welfare state. The Smedleyites carried resolutions in favour of unilateral free trade and the abandonment of agricultural subsidies at the 1953 assembly over the loud protests of rural candidates, led by Jeremy Thorpe, who argued that this was a sure vote-loser in agricultural constituencies. This was the high-water mark of the economic liberals, but the debate continued to arouse strong passions throughout the 1950s.

Gwilym Lloyd-George (1894–1967) and Megan Lloyd George (1902–66)

Two of Lloyd George's children made political careers as Liberals although, as their father predicted, Gwilym gravitated to the Conservatives and Megan to the Labour Party. While Gwilym followed a successful ministerial career, Megan, who inherited a good deal of the Welsh Wizard's charm and charisma, never held office and remained politically unfulfilled.

Gwilym was mild, humorous and popular. He was elected as MP for Pembrokeshire in 1922, holding the seat with a short break until 1950. Briefly holding junior office in the National Government in 1931, like Megan he followed his father into the oppositionist Liberal 'family group' after the 1931 election. He worked his way up the ministerial ladder in the wartime coalition to manage the coal industry as Minister of Fuel and Power. By 1945 he was de facto a Conservative, although he continued to stand for election as a 'Liberal and Conservative', from 1951 to 1957 sitting for Newcastle North. He served as Minister of Food (1952–54) and Home Secretary and Welsh Minister (1954–57).

Megan, Lloyd George's youngest child, was brought up in Downing Street and accompanied him on the international political circuit. They enjoyed a close, if at times turbulent, relationship, complicated by Megan's feud with Frances Stevenson, her former governess and Lloyd George's long-time secretary, mistress and eventually, wife. Elected to Parliament for Anglesey in 1929, a seat she held until 1951, Megan was a formidable speaker firmly on the radical left of the party, a pioneer of women's rights and Welsh home rule. She was the only well-known Liberal elected in 1945, but was not chosen as leader. The two *grandes dames*, Megan and Lady Violet Bonham Carter, represented the enduring tension in the party between the Lloyd George and Asquith traditions. Megan increasingly veered towards Labour, finally joining that party in 1955. She captured Carmarthen from the Liberals at a by-election in 1957 and held the seat until her death. She had a secret affair with the Labour MP Philip Noel-Baker for nearly twenty years.[42]

There is considerable debate about when the Liberals reached rock bottom and when the party's fortunes began to recover. The party was very depressed in the period after the 1951 election. Membership was falling, for example in the Western Counties region from over 10,000 in 1949 to 2,660 in 1952. Funding of the party headquarters was also in decline, totalling just £30,000 in 1950–51 and falling steadily to £17,000 in 1956. The local election low-point was during the 1952–54 period. The Liberals' Gallup poll rating actually improved after the 1951 election, reaching 10 per cent in early 1953 but in 1954 was back to 6–7 per cent, and did not begin to recover until mid-1957. Defections continued, most notably those of Dingle Foot, who resigned as a candidate in 1953 and joined Labour in 1955, and Megan Lloyd George, who resigned as deputy leader in 1952 and supported Labour at the 1955 election.

In 1952 Byers launched another initiative to stimulate the revival of the party's grassroots ('Operation Basic') and in 1953, for the first time, a director-general, Herbert Harris, was brought in to rebuild the organisation. The Liberals' local election performance began to improve from 1954, with spectacular gains in Blackpool. In December 1954 in Inverness, a popular Liberal candidate, John Bannerman, came close to achieving the party's first by-election gain since the late 1920s. The 1955 general election was judged a moderate success because the party held all of its six seats and performed creditably in Devon and Cornwall. Membership was increasing and university Liberal associations were thriving.

1955 general election (26 May)			
	Votes	%	MPs
Liberal	722,402	2.7	6
Conservative	**13,310,891**	**49.7**	**345**
Labour	12,405,254	46.3	277
Others	321,182	1.2	2
Total	26,759,729		630
Average vote per Liberal candidate (%)			15.1
Strong Liberal performances (20% or above in three-cornered contests, 33.3% or above in straight fights)			19

The Liberals' recovery in 1953–57 was patchy and hesitant; in truth it was more of an end to a long period of decline than a significant step forward. There were a number of reasons for this change. 'Operation Basic' and the recruitment campaigns of the 1940s were successful in bringing new blood into the party; there were stirrings of what would become known as 'community politics' in a small number of English towns and cities; in areas where Labour was weak, the Liberals were able to take advantage of dissatisfaction with an old-fashioned, largely aristocratic Conservative government; and there were still pockets of Liberal strength, like Inverness, which generated occasional moments of optimism. It remained to be seen whether this period was the start of a more significant revival or another step on the path to oblivion.

Conclusion: how and why did the Liberal Party survive against the odds?
Many Liberals had contemplated, and even expected, the demise of the party at various times during the period covered by this chapter, and yet by 1955 there were modest grounds for believing that the party might have a future after all. How had it managed to survive?

The Liberal Party had never ceased to own a presence in the House of Commons, thanks to its few redoubts in rural Wales, the Pennine textile belt, and the West Country, as well as the indulgence of the Conservative Party in not running candidates against many of its surviving MPs. The Conservatives feared that in opposing some of the remaining Liberal MPs they would hand the seats to Labour, but in the long view this was surely one of the biggest strategic blunders they committed. It was also helped by the absence of competing fourth parties; if the rise of the Welsh and Scottish Nationalists from the 1960s had happened significantly earlier this could have spelled disaster for the Liberals.

Many Liberals still felt that there were profound ideological differences separating them from the other two parties. In particular, free trade served as a symbolic issue that was critical in preventing the party from following the Simonite route of incorporation into the Conservative Party in the 1930s and 1940s, and these ideas were still a potent factor into the 1950s. It was such deep-seated resistance to the Conservative outlook that explained the rejection of Churchill's offer to Davies of a Cabinet seat in 1951.[43] Similarly, the left of the party found it difficult to reconcile itself to the socialist rhetoric and trade-union domination of the Labour Party. The Liberals were able throughout the period to retain the loyalty of enough opinion-leaders, wealthy donors, and local activists to keep going and to bring in new blood. As one veteran has put it, the party was 'kept alive by a rump of mostly elderly "awkward Nonconformists" dedicated to their vision of Liberalism'.[44]

Finally, the Liberals continued to hold on to a residual electoral base throughout the period that gave them the potential for growth as political circumstances improved in the mid-1950s. The 1945 and 1950 general elections, although regarded as disastrous at the time, probably played a vital part in rallying the Liberal vote and local organisation, which might otherwise have collapsed completely, as it almost did in 1951. Yet even in 1951 the party held the loyalty of around 7 per cent of the electorate[45] and at this time Gallup found that about one third of voters said that they might vote Liberal if the Liberals had a chance of gaining a majority.[46] The Liberals never quite descended to minor party status.[47] They had declined massively since 1929, but they did not lose their foothold as the third party in the political system – or, as it turned out, their capacity to recover.

Further reading

For the period from 1929–35 there is much of interest in Trevor Wilson's *The Downfall of the Liberal Party* (Collins, 1966), although its overall analysis and tone are now rather dated. The second Labour government, subsequent National Government and the 1931 election are covered in detail in Philip Williamson's *National Crisis and National Government* (CUP, 1992).

The contribution of Herbert Samuel is highlighted in the definitive, though rather turgid, biography by Bernard Wasserstein, *Herbert Samuel: A political life* (Clarendon Press, 1992). David Dutton's biography of Sir John Simon, *Simon* (Aurum Press, 1992), is balanced, insightful and engagingly written. The best book covering the development of Liberal policy on international affairs and the party's stance on appeasement is Richard Grayson's well-researched and convincing *Liberals, International Relations and Appeasement: A Study of the Liberal Party, 1919–1939* (Routledge, 2001).

The contribution of Sir Archibald Sinclair is covered by Gerard De Groot in *Liberal Crusader: The life of Sir Archibald Sinclair* (C. Hurst and Co., 1993). Sinclair's contribution to the direction of the air war during the 1940–45 period is laid out in Ian Hunter's edited collection of the correspondence between Churchill and Sinclair, *Winston and Archie* (Politico's, 2005).

The declining years of Lloyd George's political contribution is covered brilliantly by Anthony Lentin's *Lloyd George and the Lost Peace* (Palgrave, 2001). The best sketch of Lloyd George during this period is presented by his personal private secretary, in Colin Cross's edited collection of A. J. Sylvester's diaries: *Life with Lloyd George* (Barnes and Noble, 1975). David Dutton's *Liberals in Schism: A History of the National Liberal Party* (I. B. Tauris, 2008) is a thorough and readable account of the history of the Simonites.

Graham Stewart's *Burying Caesar – Churchill, Chamberlain and the Battle for the Conservative Party* (Phoenix, 1999) provides a very clear and readable account of the general politics of the 1930s. There are two general histories which contain useful sections covering this period. Peter Joyce's *Realignment of the Left* (Macmillan, 1999) examines the relationship between the Liberal and Labour parties during the twentieth century and has a useful two chapters covering the periods from 1929 until the late 1950s. David Dutton's *A History of the Liberal Party* (Palgrave Macmillan, 2004) is one of the best single-volume histories of the party.

For an eyewitness account of these dramatic years in the party's fortunes, the two final volumes of Lady Violet Bonham Carter's diaries and letters, *Champion Redoubtable* and *Daring to Hope* (Weidenfeld and Nicolson, 1998 and 2000*)* are unbeatable.

Notes

1 Just before the election Lloyd George expected to win between 80 and 100 seats. See Philip Williamson, *National Crisis and National Government – British Politics, the Economy and the Empire 1926–1932* (CUP, 1992), p. 24.

2 The constraints of the party's limited inter-war base persisted into the 1990s. See Andrew Russell and Edward Fieldhouse, *Neither Left Nor Right? The Liberal Democrats and the Electorate* (Manchester University Press, 2004).

3 For a comprehensive analysis of this process, see Frank Trentmann, *Free Trade Nation – Commerce, Consumption and Civil Society in Modern Britain* (OUP, 2008).

4 Peter Clarke, *Hope and Glory* (Penguin, 1996), pp. 155–56.

5 Imperial policy and especially India played a key role alongside the economy in the political realignments of 1930–31. See Williamson, *National Crisis*, especially chapter 5.

6 Ibid., pp. 251–52.

7 MacDonald's opposition to an election ended after the Conservatives pledged to support him as Prime Minister in a post-election National Government (24 September), but he still worked hard to keep the Samuelites on board.

8 Simon finally abandoned free trade in a speech on 15 September. Leslie Hore-Belisha, encouraged by the Tories and MacDonald, organised a petition of Simonite Liberals which gathered twenty-five signatures.

9 Williamson, *National Crisis*, pp. 394–95. More generally on Runciman, see David Wrench, '"Very Peculiar Circumstances": Walter Runciman and the National Government, 1931–33', *Twentieth Century British History* (2000), vol. 11, no. 1, pp. 61–82.

10 For a detailed analysis of the 1931 election see Andrew Thorpe, *The British General Election of 1931* (Clarendon Press, 1991).

11 Thorpe, *General Election of 1931*, pp. 61–62. Garry Tregidga's study of the Liberal Party in south-west England shows the strong attachment to free trade among many local activists in the 1930s: Garry Tregidga, *The Liberal Party in South-West Britain since 1918* (University of Exeter Press, 2000), pp. 76–77, 130.

12 *Ownership for All: The Liberal Enquiry into the Distribution of Property* (1938); Arthur Seldon, *Capitalism* (Blackwell, 1990), p. 35; and see John Meadowcroft and Jaime Reynolds 'Liberals and the New Right – Arthur Seldon and the Liberal Antecedents of the Institute of Economic Affairs', *Journal of Liberal History* 47, summer 2005.

13 Keynes ceased most of his Liberal Party activities in the 1930s. However he sat on the Liberal benches in the House of Lords from 1942.

14 Tregidga, *Liberal Party in South-West Britain*, p. 83.

15 See Roy Harrod, *The Prof – A Personal Memoir of Lord Cherwell* (Macmillan, 1959), pp. 243–48.

16 Liberals and Liberal Nationals won 24 urban seats in 1931; no less than 14 were ports and 6 others had significant export or shipping industries. All but one had been lost by 1945.

17 See H. M. Hyde, *Strong for Service – the Life of Lord Nathan of Churt* (W. H. Allen, 1968); Elsie Janner, *Barnett Janner - A Personal Portrait* (Robson Books, 1984); and Geoffrey Alderman, *London Jewry and London Politics 1889–1986* (Routledge, 1989).

18 Gillian Peele and Chris Cook, *The Politics of Reappraisal 1918–1939* (Macmillan, 1975), p. 177 and Chapter 7.

19 Liberals won only five rural English seats, by tiny majorities in straight fights with the Tories in 1935. Liberals were prominent in the wave of anti-tithe payment protests in the 1930s, but it retained an all-party character.

20 Quoted in the *Dictionary of National Biography, 1961–1970*, p. 950.

21 Lord Boothby, *My Yesterday, Your Tomorrow* (Hutchinson, 1962), p. 253.

22 Thus he attended some of the War Cabinet meetings in May 1940, providing support for Churchill in resisting Halifax's suggestion that a compromise peace with Germany should be explored after the fall of France. See Ian Kershaw, *Fateful Choices: Ten Decisions that Changed the World 1940–41* (Penguin, 2007), pp. 39, 49.

23 *Radical Action – Its purpose and its programme* (c. 1942).

24 Ian Hunter, 'The Final Quest for Liberal Reunion 1943–46', *Journal of Liberal History* 32, autumn 2001.

25 Jose Harris, *William Beveridge – A Biography* (Clarendon Press, 1977). Harris, p. 448, states that Beveridge served as Liberal leader in the Lords, but this seems to be incorrect.

26 Tony Greaves, *Journal of Liberal History* 9, winter 1995–96, p. 4; see also Harris, *William Beveridge*, pp. 446–47.

27 Letter 17 November 1947 – see *Journal of Liberal History* 27, summer 2000, p. 8.

28 There is a letter between Sinclair and Churchill dated 11 May 1940 which indicated that Davies had informally agreed to accept the Liberal whip, but no public announcement of Davies' conversion was made until 1942.

29 Emlyn Hooson, 'Clement Davies', *Journal of Liberal History* 24, autumn 1999.

30 The Liberal candidates in 1945 were younger and included a higher proportion of ex-service people than the other two parties; see R. B. MacCallum and Alison Readman, *The British General Election of 1945* (1947), p. 86.

31 See Robert Ingham, 'Clement Davies: a brief reply', *Journal of Liberal History* 26, spring 2000. Davies's reply to the Queen's Speech in 1945 welcomed the end of 'Tory reaction' and challenged the Labour government to take a radical and determined road.

32 *The Times*, 22 October 1946.

33 Mark Pottle (ed.), *Daring to Hope – The Diaries and Letters of Violet Bonham Carter 1946–69* (Weidenfeld and Nicolson, 2000), pp. 28–29 and 77–79.

34 Michael Steed, 'The Liberal Party' in H. M. Drucker, (ed.), *Multi-Party Britain* (Macmillan, 1979), pp. 81–82.

35 The Liberals were also unlucky with the location of by-elections in this period. Between 1945 and 1955 only two by-elections took place in constituencies where the Liberals were traditionally strong: Paisley (1948) and Inverness (1954). In the period 1955–65 an average of two by-elections a year took place in traditional strongholds, or otherwise promising constituencies.

36 Frank Bealey, J. Blondel and W. P. McCann, *Constituency Politics: a study of Newcastle-under-Lyme* (Faber and Faber, 1965), p. 103.

37 *Journal of Liberal History* 41, winter 2003–04, p. 25.

38 If the Liberal vote had been 1 per cent higher, the Labour majority would have been seventeen. See Jaime Reynolds, 'Impacts of Reunification', *Journal of Liberal History* 32, autumn 2001.

39 *Journal of Liberal History* 27, p. 10 (quoting letter to G. Murray, 11 May 1950) and 24, autumn 1999, p. 81.

40 J. Graham Jones, 'Churchill, Clement Davies and the Ministry of Education', *Journal of Liberal History* 27, summer 2000.

41 See Jonathan Parry, 'What if the Liberal Party had broken through from the Right?' in Duncan Brack and Iain Dale (eds.) *Prime Minister Portillo – and other things that never happened* (Politico's, 2003); and Meadowcroft and Reynolds, 'Liberals and the New Right'.

42 J. Graham Jones, 'A Breach in the Family', *Journal of Liberal History* 25, winter 1999–2000, and Mervyn Jones, *A Radical Life – the Biography of Megan Lloyd George* (Hutchinson, 1991).

43 Davies had written in 1949: 'Do not run away with the idea that Liberalism provides the middle way between the other two, still less that is a compromise between them. Liberalism is a distinct creed – a distinct philosophy, distinct from Socialism, from Communism, and from Conservatism.' *Journal of Liberal History* 27, p. 8.

44 William Wallace, 'Why Didn't the Liberal Party Die?', *Journal of Liberal History* 16, September 1997, p. 5.

45 Steed, 'The Liberal Party', p. 82.

46 Ibid, p. 84.

47 Although they were neglected as such in R. T. Mackenzie's classic *British Political Parties* (Heinemann, 1955), even at their nadir the Liberals remained in a different league electorally from the Communist, Independent Labour and other minor parties.

Chapter 8

Liberal Revival (1956–1974)

Robert Ingham

The period from 1956 to 1974 witnessed a modest underlying advance in the Liberal Party's fortunes, in stark contrast to the relentless decline of earlier decades, overlaid by a dramatic pattern of spectacular revivals and dizzying declines. High points, such as the Orpington by-election win in 1962 and the February 1974 election result, in which over six million people voted Liberal, were followed by disappointments; and the party's performance in the 1970 election was redolent of the disasters of the early 1950s.

Undoubtedly, however, the party was stronger at the end of 1974 than it had been eighteen years before. There were more Liberal MPs, and none of them were dependent on Conservative support for their seats; the party's local government base had been transformed; and there had been a definite break with the Victorian free trade and Nonconformist legacy in favour of clearer support for more up-to-date concepts, such as British membership of the European Economic Community (EEC). The Liberal Party was still a long way from the centre of the political stage, but at least it was back on the platform and clearly there to stay. The main question the party faced in 1974 was not whether it would survive, but whether its support was based on anything more than transient dissent aimed at the governing party.

Grimond's inheritance

Reynolds and Hunter have shown in the previous chapter that the first signs of a Liberal revival can be detected in 1953–54, with a modest increase in the number of Liberal councillors, a strong performance in the Inverness by-election of 1954 and an increase in the average vote per candidate in the 1955 general election. It only became evident with hindsight, however, that the Liberal Party's long winter was coming to an end. Poor election results still outweighed good, most seats went uncontested, even at by-elections, and the party leadership paid little attention to local government and did not systematically monitor local election results.

What these indications show, however, is that Jo Grimond did not initiate the Liberal revival and nor was his tenure as Liberal leader a period of unblemished success. Indeed, the party's parliamentary nadir came in 1957 with the loss of Carmarthen at a by-election, as a result of which the Liberals were reduced to just five MPs. Grimond ensured, however, that the modest recovery of the mid-1950s was translated into a much more significant advance. His achievement was to supply a positive answer to the question of whether the Liberal Party would survive, and pose new questions about what the revived party now aimed to achieve.

Jo Grimond's accession as Liberal leader in 1956 was untroubled. Although many Liberals appreciated the dedication with which Clement Davies had led the party during a difficult decade, and disliked the way in which he was manoeuvred from office by colleagues tired of waiting for him to resign, there was no resistance to his departure. Davies was over seventy years old, plagued by alcoholism and ill-health, overworked by years as the Liberal standard-bearer in Parliament, and regarded by many younger party members as out of touch and old-fashioned. Grimond, with his youth, good looks, and family links with the Asquiths, seemed the ideal replacement. In fact, he was the only plausible candidate from a tiny field. The four other Liberal MPs, excluding Davies, either owed their seats to arrangements with the Conservative Party, and were thus highly vulnerable to defeat, or were heavily committed to non-parliamentary work, or both.

Jo Grimond (1913–93)

Joseph Grimond was born on 29 July 1913 in St Andrews, the son of a Dundee jute manufacturer. Educated at Eton and Balliol College, Oxford, where he graduated with a first in philosophy, politics and economics, he married Laura Bonham Carter, daughter of Violet, in 1938. Grimond was called to the bar in 1937 and served in Northern Ireland and Europe during the Second World War, rising to the rank of major.

Grimond stood unsuccessfully as Liberal candidate for Orkney and Shetland in 1945 before being elected five years later. He served as Liberal Chief Whip from his election until he became party leader in 1956. Charismatic, telegenic, and able to convey a 'modern' image despite his background, Grimond reinvigorated the Liberal Party with fresh ideas and attracted a new generation of activists to the party. He took advantage of the first stirrings of a Liberal revival and dissatisfaction with the two main parties to reverse the long-term decline in Liberal support. Advocating the 'realignment of the left' in British politics, whereby the Liberals would form a new political grouping with moderate elements in the Labour Party and left-wing Tories, he hoped that a hung parliament could lead to a Liberal breakthrough. The prospect seemed tantalisingly close in 1964, when Labour was elected with a wafer-thin majority, but Grimond's ambitions were dashed when Labour comfortably won the 1966 election and the Liberals made only modest gains, remaining largely a party of the 'Celtic fringe'.

After retiring from the leadership in 1967 Grimond took on the role of elder statesman, although not without causing controversy, for example in mooting an electoral pact with the Scottish Nationalists and attacking the post-war consensus on social welfare. He served briefly as interim party leader after Jeremy Thorpe's resignation in 1976.

Grimond retired from the House of Commons in 1983 and was elevated to the Lords. He died on 24 October 1993.

Weak in Parliament, riven by internal policy disputes and damaged by a succession of high-profile defections, the Liberal Party which Grimond inherited was in a sorry state, notwithstanding its often exaggerated optimism for the future. Nor was it the case that problems at the top obscured strength at a local level. Fewer than 200 active constituency associations were in existence in the mid-1950s.[1] The party's income which came primarily from donations, especially at the annual assembly, bottomed out at less than £17,000 in 1956, and the party headquarters announced its impending closure in February 1957, before constituency associations rallied round to provide further funds. These bodies were traditionally reluctant to provide financial support to the central party. Even by 1961 associations contributed, on average, less than £28 per annum to headquarters, despite a requirement on them each to pay £100, something only fifty-six managed in that year.

Paradoxically, it was the weakness of the party's national structures which helped local outposts to weather the storms of decline. Cut adrift from any prospect of centrally provided grants, some Liberal associations withered away but others built up their membership and income and developed their own ideas about how to fight and win election campaigns. This independence was to provide Grimond and his successors with numerous headaches in future, however, as local activists often resisted being led.

Now that the Liberal decline appeared to have been halted, Grimond's aim was to improve significantly the party's performance at the next general election. From a stronger position, it was hoped, the party would attract further support from people who were minded to vote Liberal only if the party had a better chance of winning. With the reversal of the pernicious 'wasted vote' argument, the Liberals could aspire to a speedy return to government. Grimond began to rally his disparate resources and commence the march back to political relevance.

Suez

The Suez crisis presented an immediate opportunity for Grimond to make his mark as party leader, both with Liberals and with the wider public. On 26 July 1956 Egypt's President Nasser summarily nationalised the Suez Canal Company, prompting a secret plot (the Sèvres Protocol) between the UK, France and Israel for military intervention to take control of the Canal and, it was hoped, topple Nasser. The reaction of the Liberal leadership to Nasser's action, and the Conservative government's response, was initially mixed.[2] Lady Violet Bonham Carter recorded in her diary that Grimond's view, with which she disagreed, was for 'going it alone' to take the Canal.[3] By August, however, Grimond was advocating talks with Nasser to achieve a compromise solution and by November he was the Liberal leader. In Parliament, the Liberals had at first given their backing to the Eden government's response to Nasser, but Grimond deftly led them into

243

outright opposition to military action, despite the reservations of Arthur Holt, in particular, who owed his Bolton seat to a pact with the Conservatives.

Grimond's parliamentary performances at this time began to draw the attention of the public, as well as the respect of fellow MPs. He was adept at delivering the polite, yet devastating turn of phrase. When the government claimed that its decision to send troops into Suez had been vindicated by the establishment of a United Nations task force, Grimond observed that this was 'rather like a burglar's claiming that his skill and violence have compelled the police to improve their methods'.[4]

The Suez episode demonstrated that Grimond could provide his party with a decisive lead, a welcome break from the recent past. It also emphasised what was to become a prominent theme in the party's appeal in the years ahead – a commitment to internationalism and the United Nations. For years derided as a dying relic of the Victorian era, the Liberals could now portray themselves as more modern and forward-thinking in their outlook than the Conservative Party, which was seemingly rooted in the imperialist era of gunboat diplomacy.

The immediate impact of Suez on the Liberal Party was slight – the party's poll rating drifted down from 10 to 7 per cent from September 1956 to spring 1957 – but in the long term two key changes were apparent. The view of some senior Liberals (including Violet Bonham Carter) that the Conservative Party was increasingly being 'liberalised' and was the natural ally of the Liberal Party against Labour was shattered by Prime Minister Eden's decision to side-step the United Nations and resort to military action in Egypt. Although the Huddersfield and Bolton arrangements were to continue at the 1959 election, and there was talk of further deals, the Liberal and Conservative parties began moving apart, the Liberals with renewed hope of what they could achieve without Tory backing and the Conservatives in realisation that their aim of extinguishing the Liberal Party could no longer be achieved. Secondly, a small but significant number of people were energised into becoming Liberal activists as a result of Suez and the Liberals' reaction. They brought new ideas into the party and freshened up Liberal associations which, in many cases, had struggled along during the 1950s with the same small set of active members. Throughout his leadership Grimond inspired people to join, and become active in, the Liberal Party; in later decades, many of the party's leading figures, David Steel being the most prominent, recalled that Grimond's leadership had influenced their decision to join the party.[5]

Pacts and deals

From 1918 onwards Liberals and Conservatives pooled their resources in many parts of the country to take on Labour. From the Conservative perspective, such arrangements were crucial during periods when the two major parties were evenly matched in general elections – for example, in the early 1950s. Many Liberals saw electoral arrangements as essential to the survival of the party, despite the party's independence being compromised as a result.

In Bolton, a formal pact was signed by representatives of the two parties to ensure that Arthur Holt was given a free run in Bolton West in 1951 and the two subsequent general elections and that no Liberal intervened in Bolton East. The deal in Huddersfield, from which Donald Wade benefited, was less formal but equally effective. Welsh Liberals denied that deals were done to ensure that Conservatives did not oppose Liberal MPs in the Principality in the mid-1950s, but the Conservatives undoubtedly preferred to keep right-wing Liberals in Parliament rather than run the risk of letting Labour in.

There were talks between senior Conservatives and Liberals prior to both the 1955 and 1959 elections about seats from which the Conservatives would refrain from standing candidates in return for Liberals standing down elsewhere. No agreement was reached on either occasion because the Conservatives did not believe that the Liberal Party headquarters could enforce such deals in the event of opposition from the rank and file.

Deals, formal or otherwise, with Labour were less common, but pacts did operate at local government level in Southport and Stockport and the Liberals benefited from the absence of Labour candidates in the 1945 general election, including in constituencies such as Buckrose, Cornwall North, Cumberland North and Dorset North.

Rethinking Liberal policy

As a politician, Jo Grimond was principally interested in ideas rather than the minutiae of party organisation or elections. Between 1957 and 1964 he overhauled Liberal Party policy in its entirety. The Liberal Party had never been short of policies, but, ever since Lloyd George had undertaken a similar exercise in the 1920s, they had lacked coherence and thrust. This reflected an unwillingness or inability on the part of Grimond's predecessors to manage the party's complex institutional structure, which encouraged a messy form of policy-making by committee.

In theory, the assembly was principally responsible for deciding party policy, although its relationship with the parliamentary party was not clear and it also shared some policy-making functions with the Party Council. This body was, in effect, an assembly of grandees, meeting every three months and was never popular with Liberal parliamentarians. The council appointed an Executive Committee which was largely administrative, but also claimed policy-making responsibilities. The Executive was too large to be effective and the rules determining who could attend and vote at the assembly were not enforced.[6] In consequence, different Liberal institutions made a variety of often conflicting policy statements each year, and even the most committed Liberals would struggle to state with confidence what Liberal policy was on even major economic and social issues at any particular time.

Uninterested in finding ways of reforming the party's constitution, and rightly sceptical about how long it would take to pilot new policies through the existing machinery, Grimond used his authority as leader to bypass the Council, Executive and assembly. This was first evident when he developed a new policy of opposition to an independent UK nuclear deterrent over the Christmas holiday at the end of 1956, simply announcing it to the media in February 1957. The Party Council's endorsement was conspicuous by its absence and not until the 1958 assembly was Grimond's policy formally adopted by his party.[7] As with opposition to Suez, this new Liberal initiative was eye-catching, attracted some much needed publicity to the party, and appealed to sections of the electorate.

Grimond also got to grips with Liberal policy on European cooperation, at a time when the two main parties were at best ambiguous about the creation of the EEC by the Treaty of Rome in 1957. Despite the Liberals' enthusiasm for internationalism, the party's support for UK membership of the EEC was not a foregone conclusion. Some of the free-trade wing of the party were adamantly opposed to supporting an organisation which would impose tariffs on the imports of non-members, and there was also some idealistic support for a 'world government' which would transcend regional initiatives. Grimond seemed at first sceptical about the EEC, and the 1959 election manifesto placed more emphasis on the UK joining the European Free Trade Area. When the issue arose in Parliament, however, Grimond came down in favour of membership of the EEC and the party followed him. Grimond correctly judged that the bulk of his party would support an initiative which was aimed at tying German and French fortunes together, harking back to the Cobdenite approach to free trade as an antidote to conflict. In Parliament, he could use Liberal enthusiasm for the EEC to expose fault lines in the main parties. Clear leadership tended to marginalise the economic liberals in his party, many of whom drifted into insignificance, or in some cases gravitated towards the right of the Conservative Party.

Another tactic deployed by Grimond was to use a small team of trusted allies, including his brother-in-law, Mark Bonham Carter, and former Liberal MP Frank Byers, to act as an unofficial executive committee, acting on behalf of the leader. Again this way of working proved unpopular with the stalwarts on the constitutional Executive Committee, but it was often necessary to ensure that timely decisions were taken on financial and organisational matters.Grimond also emulated Lloyd George in establishing a number of commissions to review party policy in areas such as housing, local government, social security and education. These involved prominent academics, which added to the credibility of their conclusions. Some, such as Professor Michael Fogarty, went on to become party spokesmen, although remaining outside Parliament.

Under Grimond, devolution also became a central theme of the Liberal message. The party had long argued for Welsh and Scottish devolution, as well as the establishment of a Highland Development Agency, and these ideas were given fresh impetus. The Liberals advocated the establishment of regional development organisations in other parts of the country. These policies were particularly resonant in the more remote parts of the UK, such as south-west England and the far north of Scotland.

Unservile State and New Orbits

Innovative thinking was not the sole preserve of Grimond and the policy commissions he appointed. There had been a long tradition in the Liberal Party of think-tanks being established independently of the party leadership, often with the involvement of Liberal academics or prominent activists whose parliamentary ambitions had been frustrated. Grimond himself had been president of the Radical Reform Group, which had combated the party's economic right wing in the early 1950s.

Even at its lowest ebb, the Liberal Party continued to attract intellectual input. The Oxford Liberal Group, formed in 1953, was particularly important. Its books, *Unservile State* in 1957 and *Radical Alternative* in 1962, comprised high-quality essays from leading Liberal academics. A series of Unservile State pamphlets in the early 1960s complemented the work of Grimond's policy commissions.

Also significant was the New Orbits group, which emerged from the party's youth and students' organisations in 1957. The group inspired the policy on industrial planning adopted at the 1961 assembly, strongly backed Grimond's line on nuclear weapons, was in favour of UK membership of the EEC, and promoted what were then radical policies on divorce and censorship. The group also began considering the relationship between the Liberal Party and its larger competitors, calling, as early as 1958, for a realignment of the left and proposing a strategy to achieve this.

Perhaps the group's most important contribution was to revolutionise the way in which the party presented itself to the public. The New Orbits team was responsible for improvements to the organisation of the party assembly, after the shambolic experience of the 1958 gathering at Torquay, as well as a modernisation of the design of party publications. Liberal publications in the early 1950s lacked visual appeal; New Orbits material grabbed the eye with bright colours, unusual images and attractive page layouts. The group's approach was adopted by the party as a whole and Liberal campaign material in the 1960s was bright, memorable and often witty.

One notable aspect of the Grimond era was the heterogeneity of the party's ideology. A Liberal slant was given to the fashionable nostrums of economic planning but at the same time the economic liberalism of the 1950s, some of which Grimond himself favoured, was not forgotten. The intellectuals now orbiting the Liberal Party, however distantly, were given free rein to propose innovative solutions to the country's increasing economic woes. During the 1960s there were some surprising debates within the party on issues such as health and education vouchers, and the sale of council houses, which anticipated an age to come.

Liberalism in Manchester

The Liberal Party declined more slowly in Manchester than in other northern cities. The city's last Liberal MPs were defeated in 1931 and there were Conservative-backed Liberal aldermen on the city council into the 1960s. The party's revival in Manchester began in the late 1950s. Cheetham ward was won in the 1960 local elections, presaging further victories in the early 1960s, mostly in the south of the city.

Manchester Young Liberals were particularly active at this time and included a number of talented parliamentary candidates, including Dennis Wrigley and Terry Maher. They later helped revive the Liberal associations in a number of north-west constituencies and set up Northern Radical Publications. Like the New Orbits group they were strong supporters of the realignment concept.

One factor in the survival and renewal of the Liberal Party in Manchester was the friendly stance of the *Manchester Guardian*, historically seen by many as the conscience of the Liberal Party.

The army of liberation

From 1955 the Liberal Party had begun to appreciate the strategic value of fighting by-election campaigns in promising areas. Ordinary Liberal members started to flock to help in campaigns, particularly once *Liberal News* had scented the possibility of a good result. Not all went well – Carmarthen was embarrassingly lost in 1957 to former Liberal MP Lady Megan Lloyd George, now standing for Labour – but the Liberal leadership lived in hope of a vacancy in a seat where a combination of a strong Liberal tradition, a good candidate, and an influx of help would secure victory. The breakthrough nearly came at Rochdale in February 1958, where Ludovic Kennedy pushed Labour close and the Conservative vote collapsed. The momentum thus created helped the Liberals in the even more promising Torrington by-election, on 21 March 1958.

The succession of George Lambert, MP for Torrington in Devon, to the peerage had provided the opportunity long sought by the Liberal leadership. Lambert, scion of a distinguished Liberal family, had sat as a Conservative and National Liberal, but there was a history of friction between Conservative and National Liberal activists in the constituency.[8] The by-election campaign reinvigorated the local Liberal association and in Mark Bonham Carter the party found an exceptional candidate.

Bonham Carter squeaked home by 219 votes. By later standards it was hardly a surprise, but as the first Liberal by-election gain since 1929 it was a watershed for Liberal activists. Violet Bonham Carter spoke of the Liberals liberating their territory from enemy occupation and, at a celebratory luncheon at the National Liberal Club, reprised her 'hold on – hold out – we are coming' speech which she had made after her father's election for Paisley in 1920.[9]

Victory in Torrington was the highlight of what could later be seen as the first, brief, Liberal revival of the post-war era. The Liberals' opinion poll rating touched a record 19 per cent in May 1958 but drifted downwards thereafter. The Conservatives had no doubt that the Liberals were benefiting from dissatisfaction among their supporters with the relatively high level of inflation and the government's difficulties in dealing with the trade unions. Liberal propaganda at that time focused strongly on these issues.

After Torrington, the Liberal leadership was desperate for another winnable seat to fall vacant, to help build momentum before the general election due by 1960. Opportunities, however, were scarce. In June the Liberals came a distant second in Argyll and polled respectably at Weston-super-Mare; there was another promising result at Aberdeenshire East in November; and two more distant second placings in Southend West and Galloway in 1959. In none of these seats did the Liberals have a sniff of victory. As the imminence of a general election focused debate on the proposals of the main parties the Liberals declined to just 5 per cent in the polls, lower than at any time during Grimond's leadership.

The Liberal Party entered the 1959 general election campaign with some grounds for optimism, but the results offered hope for the future rather than immediate satisfaction. The party's parliamentary strength remained at six. Jeremy Thorpe narrowly gained North Devon but Torrington was lost. There were a number of near-misses, mostly in traditional areas such as Merionethshire and North Cornwall, as well as promising results in less traditional seats, such as Finchley, Southport and Cheadle. In truth, the 1959 election caught the Liberals in a state of transition. The rethinking of party policy had only just begun and the party's manifesto was as uninspiring as its immediate predecessors. Although the party was becoming stronger, it was still in a weaker state than in the late 1940s and could compete with the main parties, in organisational terms, in only a handful of constituencies. Its manifesto appeal for the return of a significant number of Liberal MPs to moderate the influence of the main parties was hardly a rallying cry. A long hard road lay ahead before the Liberals could seriously contend for power.

1959 general election (8 October)			
	Votes	%	MPs
Liberal	1,640,760	5.9	6
Conservative	**13,750,875**	**49.4**	**365**
Labour	12,216,172	43.8	258
Others	254,845	0.9	1
Total	27,862,652		630
Average vote per Liberal candidate (%)			16.9
Strong Liberal performances (20% or above)			46

Hopes ascending

The results of the 1959 election demonstrated the enormous distance between the Liberals and political power. With six seats, two still dependent on Conservative support, the party was only marginally better off than in 1951. Grimond felt keenly the absence of Mark Bonham Carter from Parliament and, as he never returned to the Commons, the party lost a potential future leader. The party's rapid decline in Wales was worrying and, although he had been comfortably re-elected, there were fears that Clement Davies' health would not hold for the duration of the Parliament and that Montgomery might be lost in a by-election.

In terms of national politics, the 1959 Parliament offered the Liberals advantageous conditions in which to make progress. The Tories had dismissed the gloom of imperial and economic decline by replacing the ailing Anthony Eden with Harold Macmillan. 'Supermac' swept all before him in the 1959 election, not least with the unmatchable 'never had it so good' slogan. Married to a duke's daughter, but respected on the left for his successful spell as housing minister in the early 1950s and for his earlier interest in social policy, he seemed the perfect Conservative leader. After 1960, however, he began to lose his touch. Economic growth stalled and a pay pause was introduced. Splits in the government emerged and were handled badly. Macmillan began to appear old, ill and out of touch.

Meanwhile, the Labour Party was distracted by a prolonged bout of internal faction fighting. A third successive election defeat brought the squabbling between left and right in the party to a head. Bitter policy battles were waged over nuclear disarmament and the EEC, and leader Hugh Gaitskell tried and failed to reform the party's constitution by removing the infamous Clause IV, the commitment to the nationalisation of key industries. All of this tended to blunt the Labour Party's impact as an effective opposition, although it should not be overlooked that the party made four net gains in by-elections during the Parliament, compared to one by the Liberals, and also made substantial gains in local elections.

Still, by-elections were the Liberal Party's best hope for the next few years and again attention turned to any which offered the prospect of victory. The Liberals had contested less than 40 per cent of parliamentary by-elections during the 1955 Parliament but were now determined to fight on a broader front: 80 per cent of by-elections featured a Liberal candidate during the 1959 Parliament. Although this helped raise the party's profile, it entailed fighting in seats which had little or no Liberal organisation and therefore risked some poor results.

The first significant by-election came at Bolton East in November 1960. The Liberals' decision to fight the seat, with Frank Byers as a high-profile candidate, signalled the end of the electoral pacts in Bolton and Huddersfield. Byers came third, although with a creditable 24.8 per cent of the vote. Good results followed, in particular strong second places at Tiverton in 1960, Paisley in 1961 and Blackpool North on 13 March 1962, the latter a constituency in which the Liberals had made spectacular gains in local government. The day after the voters of Blackpool North went to the poll, their counterparts in Orpington were to deliver the Liberal Party's biggest fillip for decades.

With sharper policies, Grimond's increasing media impact, and opportunities to snipe at both government and official opposition, the Liberals were ready to strike. But where? The by-election at Orpington, called for 14 March 1962, did not seem at first to offer much hope of anything but a decent second place. Agent Pratap Chitnis was confident of victory, however, especially given that it would be a lengthy campaign and, as time went on, it became increasingly apparent that this would not be a normal by-election. The Liberal candidate, Eric Lubbock (a local man, in contrast to Peter Goldman, the Conservative), made an enormous impact and the Liberal campaign, managed by Chitnis, was slick and well-staffed. The result was a sensation. The Liberals, third in 1959, benefited from a 29.8 per cent swing to take the seat with a majority of 7,855. 'My God ... an incredible result', was Grimond's immediate reaction on television.

Eric Lubbock (1928–)

Lubbock was born on 29 September 1928. Both of his grandfathers had been Liberal MPs, but Lubbock was not involved in politics until he won a seat on Orpington District Council in 1961. One year later he became, at short notice, the Liberal candidate for the parliamentary constituency, which he won in a sensational by-election upset.

Lubbock served as the party's Chief Whip but lost his seat in 1970. He became the fourth Baron Avebury on the death of a cousin in 1971 and has since been an active member of the House of Lords, focusing on civil liberties and human rights issues.

The Liberal leadership immediately asked Tim Joyce, a professional public relations consultant, Liberal candidate, and New Orbits stalwart, to find out why Orpington had voted Liberal. His conclusion was simple. The Liberals had gradually, over several years, built up a strong presence in local government, outpolling the Conservatives in the 1961 local elections; this had been the main factor in the rise in the Liberal vote from 12.5 per cent in 1955 to 21.2 per cent in 1959, which had provided the springboard to success at the by-election.

This was not what Grimond and his colleagues wanted to hear. Although the party had finally set up a Local Government Department in 1960, funded out of the pocket of Richard Wainwright, the candidate for Colne Valley, the leadership remained almost entirely uninterested in local elections. The contrary is sometimes claimed, because Grimond once said that: 'every time a local Liberal councillor gets a bus stop moved to a better place he strikes a blow for the Liberal Party';[10] but the party Executive Committee barely discussed local elections during the 1959 Parliament.

Grimond was instead convinced that Orpington demonstrated the rise of a new social group, uncommitted to either main party. These individuals, comprising young, suburban, middle-class couples, their income derived from city office jobs, had thrown off the class-based nostrums of their parents and were forward-looking and seeking new ideas. 'Orpington man' was looking for a modern political party and he was tempted by Grimond's Liberals. If the party could win the support of Orpington man at the next general election, swathes of Conservative seats in the Home Counties and even around the UK's other big cities could swing to the Liberals. It was an enticing prospect, apparently backed by a detailed analysis of the 1959 election results, but the reality was to prove disappointing.

Was Orpington man anything more than a myth? Certainly the Liberals did not make gains in suburbia in 1964, but the party's share of the vote did increase significantly in many constituencies in the Home Counties and in the suburbs of Manchester, and major gains were made in local government elections in these areas too. The party had been recruiting well in such areas since the 1940s and some of the biggest and best-resourced Liberal associations were to be found within commuting distance of London. Grimond's political intuition had detected that the Liberal Party was beginning to marshal the support of opponents to the Conservatives in areas where Labour was weak, which helps explain how the Liberals failed to make much impact at that time in parts of the Home Counties where Labour was strong, such as Croydon and Watford.

Hopes descending

Already in good heart before the Orpington result, the Liberal Party reached a febrile state of excitement by mid-1962 which was sustained into 1963. The Liberals' Gallup poll rating was above 20 per cent for most of 1962, peaking at 25 per cent after Orpington. A recruitment campaign was organised to capitalise on Lubbock's victory. It aimed to strengthen constituency associations, publicise Liberal policy more widely, and make inroads into Labour support. The campaign was successful in the short run. It was claimed that Liberal membership peaked at over 350,000 in 1963, a far cry from the 76,000 ten years earlier, although it should be remembered that the party did not keep central membership records at this time.[11] In 1964 the national party's income topped £70,000, four times more than in the late 1950s but still far less than the funds at the disposal of the two main parties.[12] However, Liberals genuinely thought that a breakthrough was imminent when Grimond told them at the 1963 assembly that he was marching the party 'towards the sound of gunfire'.

The party's local election performance, which had been strong in 1960 and 1961, was so remarkable in 1962 that it even began to register with the party leadership. The total number of Liberal councillors nearly tripled between 1960 and 1963. The number of Liberal councillors in the traditional local government heartlands of Lancashire, Cheshire and the West Riding of Yorkshire increased by over 50 per cent but, more significantly, there was an explosion in Liberal representation in south-east England. The counties of Essex, Kent, Surrey, Sussex, Hampshire, the Isle of Wight and Berkshire could between them muster only eight Liberal borough and urban district councillors in 1956; by 1963 there were 470. Liberals controlled nine councils in 1963 and were the largest party on a further twenty-six; the Liberals were the dominant influence on councils in Orpington, Potters Bar, Maidenhead, Aldershot and East Grinstead, a remarkable change in the party's electoral base.

To some extent this represented protest voting against the government, but the Liberals' success also demonstrated a new willingness on the part of activists to get involved with local politics. Council wards were easier, and cheaper, for small groups of Liberals to canvass and leaflet, and annual elections made it easier for a party campaign to gather momentum, and for defeat to be easier to take. This change in tactics had gone unnoticed at headquarters until Pratap Chitnis and, later, Michael Meadowcroft began visiting local councillors on the establishment of the Local Government Department. They identified some of the campaigning tactics which were proving successful in some areas – such as regular ward leaflets focusing on local issues and 'grumble sheets' on which the local populace were asked to raise issues they wanted resolved – and, through local government conferences and newsletters, encouraged their take-up throughout the country.[13] As will be seen later, their work ultimately led to the formation of the Association of Liberal Councillors and the party assembly's endorsement of 'community politics' in 1970.

A by-election victory had catapulted the Liberal Party into the centre of the political limelight, and further victories were required to maintain the party's momentum into the next general election. Only one such success was forthcoming, however, when Emlyn Hooson held Montgomery following the death of Clement Davies in 1962. It was a good result, achieved with a 9.3 per cent swing to the Liberals, but it failed to grab the headlines. The Orpington sensation was not followed up. Aside from Montgomery, there was only one more by-election during the 1959 Parliament in a seat at which the Liberals had polled more than 20 per cent at the previous general election. This fell at Colne Valley in March 1963 and, although Richard Wainwright stormed from third place to within sight of victory, Labour held on by 2,000 votes. The disappointment expressed at the failure to win Chippenham, where the Liberals had claimed only 16.9 per cent of the vote in 1959, and Derbyshire West and Leicester North East, which the Liberals had not even fought then, showed the level to which expectations had been raised.

The national political landscape began to change radically during 1963, to the detriment of the Liberal Party. Harold Wilson was elected leader of the Labour Party following the death of Hugh Gaitskell in January and, through some deft leadership, succeeded in sidelining ideological disputes to launch an assault on power. Wilson was more telegenic than his predecessor and, like his Liberal counterpart, was a good communicator with the public, a master of the barbed retort, and had that essential characteristic for a 1960s leader, a modern image. In contrast stood Sir Alec Douglas-Home, who replaced Macmillan as Prime Minister and Conservative leader in October 1963. Douglas-Home was an aristocrat, hurriedly smuggled back into the Commons from the Lords on becoming Prime Minister, but his basic decency and lack of pretension proved endearing and helped rally the Conservative Party. For most voters the choice in 1964 concerned which of these two men should lead the country. Many of the voters who dallied with the Liberals in local elections or by-elections had no intention of voting Liberal in a general election, no matter the appeal of Grimond, except perhaps in the forty-six constituencies where the Liberals had taken over 20 per cent of the poll in 1959.

By 1964 it was undeniable that the Liberals were going backwards. The party failed to gain even 20 per cent of the vote in any of the eight by-elections it fought in the autumn of 1963 and during 1964, the most worrying results being at Sudbury and Woodbridge, where the Liberal vote was lower than in the previous general election, and at Devizes, regarded as fertile territory for the party, where Michael Fogarty lost his deposit. The elections to the new Greater London Council (GLC), and the councils of the newly created London boroughs, in April 1964 proved particularly disappointing.

Liberal strongholds, including Finchley and Orpington, were subsumed in much larger boroughs, and the Liberals' representation in the capital was reduced from 168 borough councillors to sixteen. No Liberals were elected to the GLC. It was a stark demonstration of how much more difficult it was for the Liberals, with their limited resources, to make an impact over large areas and when the national political contest was becoming more intense.

Compared with 1959, the result of the 1964 election was nevertheless worthy of celebration. The Liberals fielded 365 candidates, the most since 1950, and the average poll per candidate, 18.5 per cent, was the best for nineteen years. Nine MPs were returned, all in three-cornered contests. Although Huddersfield West and Bolton West were lost, after the abandonment of the local arrangements with the Conservatives, Bodmin, Inverness, Ross and Cromarty and Caithness and Sutherland were all gained. The Liberals came within 5,000 votes of victory in thirteen seats, including a very narrow defeat at Colne Valley.

1964 general election (15 October)			
	Votes	%	MPs
Liberal	3,099,283	11.2	9
Conservative	12,002,642	43.4	304
Labour	**12,205,808**	**44.1**	**317**
Others	349,415	1.2	0
Total	27,657,148		630
Average vote per Liberal candidate (%)			18.5
Strong Liberal performances (20% or above)			128

Unsurprisingly, however, given the expectations raised by the Orpington triumph, Liberals were disappointed rather than jubilant. There had been no big breakthrough, merely an incremental improvement which promised, at best, more of the same at the next election. The myth of 'Orpington man' had been cruelly exposed. The Liberals' main gains had been in areas of traditional support, particularly in Grimond's backyard in the Scottish Highlands where the new policy on regional development had been strongly advocated.

There was another lesson hidden in the results of the 1964 elections. For the first time, the national party had targeted resources into a handful of constituencies, with the proviso that money should be spent sensibly and yield tangible benefits, such as increased party membership. Targeting (known as 'special aid') was a factor in Russell Johnston's victory at Inverness and also helped develop Colne Valley, Cornwall North and Aberdeenshire West which were to be Liberal gains in 1966. Special aid was ineffective elsewhere, however; the Liberal vote in Rochdale fell in 1964, despite targeted resources from headquarters.

Targeting was controversial in the Liberal Party, as it tended to reduce the autonomy of constituency associations. Serious debate about whether, and how, it should be done was evaded; Jeremy Thorpe raised most of the money from the Rowntree Trust and other donors and distributed it himself, with the assistance of Ted Wheeler, an experienced agent, and one or two others. The ruthless manner with which Thorpe approached the task – insisting, occasionally, that parliamentary candidates he did not rate should be replaced, and denying money to others – would have caused a storm if the operation had not been carried out with considerable discretion. The party's Executive Committee was only made aware of Thorpe's scheme in October 1963, some eighteen months after it had been established, and there was strong criticism of its unconstitutional nature. Grimond, habitually bored by organisational matters, was no doubt happy for an energetic colleague to get on with helping the election effort. Over the years, targeting became an ever more significant element of the Liberal Party's electoral strategy.

Hopes dashed

Labour was returned to power in 1964 with a majority of only four; the Conservatives had made a tremendous recovery from their low point in 1962, although not sufficient for Douglas-Home to return to Downing Street. The parliamentary arithmetic permitted Labour to govern without resort to a coalition or agreement with another party, but only for a time; by-election losses could be expected to take their toll, and Leyton was lost to the Conservatives as early as January 1965. It was anticipated that another general election would soon be called.

Grimond had repositioned his party, long seen as a more natural ally of the Conservatives, on the left of British politics. From 1958 he had advocated the 'realignment of the left' in British politics, a rather nebulous concept which came into its own during the 1964 Parliament because of Labour's narrow majority. Grimond's vision was of a coming together of Liberals and Labour moderates, with moderate Conservatives thrown in for good measure, to form a progressive grouping which would appeal to a clear majority of the British people and alienate extremists of the left and right. In June 1965 Grimond called for cooperation between the Liberal and Labour parties and held private talks with Harold Wilson, but nothing was likely to happen before the next general election clarified matters.[14]

Many Liberal activists embraced the concept of realignment, as it offered the party a route back to power reminiscent of the great 'progressive' combination of 1906, when the Liberal and Labour parties had combined to smite the Tories. It also reflected a change in the nature of Liberal support: the party now drew its voters evenly from the other two parties, rather than being primarily a party of the right, as it had been under Clement Davies.[15] Not all Liberals were enthusiastic about realignment, however. Emlyn Hooson was a noted opponent of Grimond's views, and Nancy Seear was cheered at the 1965 assembly when she warned Grimond against 'a-whoring after foreign women'. Some in the Labour Party were tempted by a new combination which would secure them victory in the struggle against the Bevanite left and their successors. Grimond underestimated tribal loyalties, however, especially in the Labour Party. Any enthusiasm for cooperation with the Liberals was unlikely to entail mass defection at that stage, and wilted after Wilson became leader. Grimond was also, typically, unwilling to consider the practicalities of realignment; the vision remained just that.

Looking back, it can now be seen that Grimond was ahead of his time, anticipating the formation of the Social Democratic Party and its alliance with the Liberals in 1981. Sixteen years earlier, Grimond hoped Labour would remain the largest party at the next general election but lose its majority and that, buoyed by further gains, the Liberals would have a role in government which would help bring realignment about. There was little reason to expect such an outcome. Wilson, one of the most adept electioneers of the century, was dedicated to returning Labour to power with an increased majority, so that they could 'get on with the job'. The Conservatives had changed leader again, with Edward Heath replacing Douglas-Home, and were not well prepared for another election. The Conservatives led in the polls in only four months between the 1964 and 1966 elections. In by-elections, Labour held all three seats the party defended after the Leyton defeat, including a crucial marginal, Hull North, in January 1966. The Liberals claimed one victory, when David Steel ousted the Conservatives at Roxburgh, Selkirk & Peebles in March 1965. His victory was based on a strong performance in the preceding general election, and the constituency had been Liberal as recently as 1951. In only one other by-election during the Parliament did the Liberal poll top 20 per cent, and in eight of the eleven by-elections during the period where the comparison is possible the Liberal vote fell when compared to the 1964 election.

The result of the 1966 election was the end of the road for Grimond's leadership of the Liberal Party. Although the Liberals again increased their representation, to twelve, gaining Colne Valley, at last, Cornwall North, Aberdeenshire West, and Cheadle, and holding Roxburgh, Selkirk & Peebles (though losing Cardiganshire and Caithness & Sutherland), Labour secured a parliamentary majority of ninety-seven. There had again been no big Liberal breakthrough and Grimond's realignment strategy lay in tatters.

1966 general election (31 March)			
	Votes	%	MPs
Liberal	2,327,457	8.5	12
Conservative	11,418,455	41.9	253
Labour	**13,096,629**	**48.0**	**364**
Others	422,206	1.5	1
Total	27,264,747		630
Average vote per Liberal candidate (%)			16.1
Strong Liberal performances (20% or above)			66

Grimond may not have launched the first post-war Liberal revival, and was perhaps naive in his assessment of what was required to challenge the two main parties at parliamentary elections in the 1960s, but his impact on the Liberal Party was immense. He breathed new life into its leadership, established popular, credible and durable policies on a wide range of issues, inspired activists, and, more than any Liberal leader since Lloyd George, made an impact on the electorate in terms of the things he said, and the way he said them. Without him the Liberals would probably have survived and might eventually have prospered, but the party's development, and the course of British political history, would have been considerably different.

Thorpe in charge?

Grimond had talked wistfully about resigning after the 1964 election, because of the burden of shouldering the vast bulk of the party's parliamentary and media work, as well as the inevitable tours of the country to bolster morale in Liberal associations. The party's failure to make more progress in 1966 cemented Grimond's intention to resign immediately. He was persuaded to stay on until January 1967, when the party faced a novel situation – a contested election for the leadership.[16]

That the electorate for the leadership contest would consist of the twelve Liberal MPs was not questioned, but senior figures in the party outside Parliament protested at the decision to hold the ballot straight away, thus preventing them from influencing the outcome. Three candidates were nominated: Jeremy Thorpe, Emlyn Hooson and Eric Lubbock.

Thorpe was the clear favourite. He had been in Parliament the longest and had been prominent in the party before then. He was the most charismatic of the three and was respected for his energy and determination, best illustrated by his long campaign to capture North Devon from the Conservatives and turn it into an apparently safe Liberal seat. Despite these attributes, Thorpe was not universally well regarded. Lord Beaumont, then vice-chairman of the party, recorded that several senior figures at party headquarters worked to keep Thorpe out of the leadership and tried to persuade Richard Wainwright to stand. Distrust of Thorpe was inspired by his secretive fund-raising for the special aid scheme; a suspicion that, although committed to the Liberal Party, his interest in Liberalism and the development of Liberal ideas was shallow; doubts about whether his Edwardian image, which was hopelessly unrepresentative of the modern Liberal Party, would win votes; and the concerns of some that his private life hid dark secrets, the exposure of which would damage the party.

In the election, which took place on 18 January 1967, Thorpe won six votes and his rivals three apiece. All of Hooson's voters gave Lubbock as their second preference; all of Lubbock's plumped second for Hooson. Stalemate was avoided when Hooson and Lubbock agreed to retire in favour of Thorpe. The result helped to ensure that the next leadership election would be conducted very differently – by a ballot of party members – and that Thorpe would have to work hard to unite his parliamentary party, knowing that half of them had not been prepared to give him any support. He must also have been aware that if Mark Bonham Carter or Frank Byers had returned to the Commons, either of them, rather than him, would now be Liberal leader.

Thorpe's in-tray contained a number of difficult challenges. The first was to prepare the party for the next general election. Unfortunately, the party failed to take advantage of the growing unpopularity of the Wilson government; it became apparent that the Liberals found it easier to prosper when the Conservatives were in power. The party's poll rating remained stuck at between 10 and 15 per cent throughout the Parliament, and unlike during the Macmillan years, by-elections provided little help. Whereas the Conservatives made a series of gains in places as unlikely as Walthamstow and Oldham, the Liberals managed more than 20 per cent of the poll in only one by-election during the Parliament. This came in Birmingham Ladywood in 1969, where community campaigner Wallace Lawler achieved a 32 per cent swing to capture the seat from Labour and win the Liberals their first seat in the country's second city since 1886. This victory was another sign of the potency of local government work and was seized on by the growing number of proponents of community politics within the party, but it was hardly a typical seat. Slum clearance work had significantly reduced the size of the electorate and the seat was due to be abolished with the next review of constituency boundaries.

In local government, the gains made during the early 1960s were generally not maintained, although the party did not return to the nadir of the 1950s. Individual Liberals, using community politics techniques, could still make an impact, one notable example being Michael Meadowcroft, who was elected to Leeds City Council for an inner-city ward in 1968. Institutionally, the party was not in good shape to improve on the 1966 election result. The party's finances were in a dire condition for the remainder of the decade and the party even had to move its headquarters away from Westminster, to the Strand, to help make ends meet. Despite this, Pratap Chitnis resigned as the party's director in 1969 in protest at Thorpe's unwillingness to make the further cuts necessary to reduce an overdraft which never fell below £50,000 during the 1966 Parliament. Much of the party's election fund in 1970 came from the deep pockets of Sir Jack Hayward, a supporter of Thorpe rather than the Liberal cause, after Thorpe had helped Hayward buy Lundy Island in 1968.[17] Thorpe's personal control of the money from Hayward, and further donations over the years, brought him repeatedly into conflict with the party organisation.

Thorpe also faced an immediate challenge to his leadership from the activities of the Young Liberals, who were among the most vocal critics of what they saw as his lack of ideological direction. Under Grimond, and particularly in the early 1960s, the Liberals had almost become fashionable. Grimond's fresh thinking and irreverent attitude chimed with the times and appealed to politically aware young people and students, especially those radicalised by opposition to the Vietnam War and the conflict between the superpowers. During the long years of decline the Liberal Party had been enthusiastic in its encouragement of young recruits to the party, often amazed that anyone in the modern era should wish to join. The party's youth and students' organisations were entitled to representation on the Party Council and their policy pronouncements were treated with a respect which must have inspired envy in their counterparts in the two main parties.

With Tony Greaves, George Kiloh and Terry Lacey at the forefront, the Young Liberals began rethinking the ideological basis for liberalism, with some surprising results as far as the party leadership was concerned. The Liberal Party wanted employees to own shares in the firms for which they worked; the Young Liberals, nicknamed the 'Red Guards' in 1966 (in ironic reference to the zealots of Mao's cultural revolution), advocated workers' control of nationalised industries. The Liberal Party opposed an independent UK nuclear deterrent; the Young Liberals advocated withdrawal from NATO, non-alignment in the Cold War, and cuts in defence spending.[18] The Young Liberals also enthusiastically embraced the 1960s counter-culture, which provided another reason for them to attract considerable media coverage and embarrass the party leadership.

It was repeatedly emphasised that the Young Liberals' policy ideas did not represent official policy. Some senior Liberals went as far as to brand the Young Liberals as socialists or Maoists. This helped ensure that relations between the party and its youth wing remained frosty for the remainder of the decade, the nadir being reached during Louis Eaks' chairmanship of the Young Liberals in 1969–70. One of the issues the Young Liberals had explored was the legitimacy of direct action; Eaks went a step further by claiming responsibility for the sabotage of cricket grounds during the all-white South African team's tour of England. Some inflammatory statements about Israel caused further consternation among the party leadership and Eaks was asked to resign. Further turmoil was saved by Eaks' defeat by Tony Greaves in the election for the chairmanship of the Young Liberals in 1970.

Conflict between Thorpe and the Young Liberals came to a head in 1968 when Thorpe spoke out against what he regarded as their support for 'Marxism in a new dress'. Behind the scenes, plots were hatched to oust Thorpe, but a meeting of the party's Executive Committee strongly backed his leadership and confirmed him in his position.[19] The leadership counter-attacked with an attempt to change the party's constitution to reduce the power of the assembly and give more influence over policy-making to parliamentary candidates and others in whom the leadership could have more trust. This move succeeded only in further alienating a significant tranche of the party from Thorpe and his allies.

Thorpe was keen to disassociate himself from the wider excesses of the Young Liberals, but he had few policy ideas of his own to promote. In Parliament, Liberals were vigorous in opposition to Labour's Immigration Bill, and Thorpe's most original policy contributions related to Commonwealth affairs (to which a sizeable chunk of his volume of reminiscences is dedicated). At the 1966 assembly he suggested that sanctions against Ian Smith's white regime in Rhodesia should be backed by force to disable supply lines from South Africa. The 'Bomber Thorpe' speech was ridiculed by the government but won support within the Liberal Party.[20] He also campaigned to allow Ugandan Asians to settle in the UK, describing Idi Amin as a 'black Hitler' at the 1972 assembly. Thorpe also maintained the party's support for UK membership of the EEC, saving the government from defeat in the House of Commons on the second reading of the legislation to implement UK entry in 1972.

Finally, although Thorpe had more able lieutenants in the House of Commons than Grimond had ever been able to rely on – including Russell Johnston, David Steel, John Pardoe and Richard Wainwright – he was also handicapped by some liabilities. Alasdair Mackenzie, the taciturn member for Ross & Cromarty, could hardly be regarded as a mainstream Liberal, and nor were Wallace Lawler's Liberal credentials entirely trusted by his colleagues. Worst of all was Peter Bessell, MP for Bodmin and a close friend of Thorpe. Bessell, a charming but irresponsible businessman, was in dire financial straits throughout the Parliament and was forced to stand down when on the verge of bankruptcy. He had caused anger within the party, and hilarity without, by claiming in 1965 that Jo Grimond was about to become Speaker and that he would not be averse to taking Grimond's place at the summit of the Liberal Party.

Liberal peers

During the middle of the twentieth century, the Liberal Party's tiny band of hereditary peers was increased only in coronation honours – for example, Sir Archibald Sinclair was made Viscount Thurso in 1953. When life peerages were introduced in 1958, Harold Macmillan decided not to offer them to Liberals. This decision was reversed by Harold Wilson, no doubt mindful of his narrow Commons majority, in 1964.

The first three Liberal life peers were Frank Byers, John Foot and Lady Violet Bonham Carter, the last being a nomination of the Prime Minister rather than the Liberal leader. Byers soon replaced Lord Rea as Liberal leader in the Lords. Violet Bonham Carter's elevation to the peerage was particularly poignant given her decades of commitment to the Liberal Party and her narrow defeat when standing for election at Colne Valley in 1951. A second tranche of Liberal peers was created in 1967, including Nancy Seear, another stalwart Liberal candidate and popular figure within the party.

With hindsight, therefore, it was hardly surprising that the Liberal Party should suffer an awful result, teetering on the brink of disastrous, at the 1970 election. At the time, however, coming after a series of improved general election results dating back to the early 1950s, the set-back was a severe blow. While Edward Heath celebrated victory for the Conservatives, the Liberals mourned a reduction in strength from thirteen to six MPs, with Wainwright and Lubbock among the defeated. Of the six victors, three commanded majorities of less than 1,000, including Steel and Thorpe himself, who clung on in North Devon by only 369 votes. It was a lesson he was not to forget, and he devoted himself to his constituency in subsequent general elections. The average Liberal poll per candidate fell from 16.1 per cent to 13.5 per cent, and 184 of the 332 candidates lost their deposits. Near misses, other than the seats lost, were few: only in Cardiganshire did a

Liberal come within 2,500 votes of victory. The Nuffield election study for 1970 concluded that the party's poor result was due 'in part at least to a lack of weight among its leaders, who never found words to harness the disillusion or apathy of the moderate mass of the British electorate'.[21]

1970 general election (18 June)			
	Votes	%	MPs
Liberal	2,117,035	7.5	6
Conservative	**13,145,123**	**46.4**	**330**
Labour	12,208,758	43.1	288
Others	834,618	2.9	6
Total	28,305,534		630
Average vote per Liberal candidate (%)			13.5
Strong Liberal performances (20% or above)			41

Community politics

In 1970 the party assembly passed a resolution committing the party to adopt 'community politics', a new form of political strategy. As well as extreme left-wing slogans, the intellectual ferment of the Young Liberals had developed the concept of community politics, based on neighbourhood campaigns in the US and, more recently, the UK.[22] Community politics involved local people organising campaigns relating to local issues – the construction of the motorway network proving a frequent inspiration in the UK – and thereby taking power at a local level themselves. Liberals, in favour of devolving decision-making to the lowest possible level, could help such campaigns without taking them over.

That was the theory; in practice, Liberals in many areas had been using local issues as a way to build up support in individual wards since the mid-1950s. In Liverpool, for example, Cyril Carr had used local newsletters, christened *Focus*, since 1965 to secure his own election in Church Ward. Carr persuaded Trevor Jones, then involved with a campaign against the extension of the M62 into the Liverpool suburbs, to join the Liberals. Their activism helped the Liberals take control of Liverpool council, albeit briefly, for the first time in 1973. Similar results were evident elsewhere. In Kearsley, Lancashire, the Liberals controlled the council from 1965, the key party leaders having first been persuaded to join the Liberal Party after campaigning against the proposed route of the M6.

Community politics resolution, 1970

The following resolution on strategy was passed by the Liberal Party assembly in 1970:

This assembly, recognising that, in a world in which Liberal values are increasingly under attack, the need for a political party dedicated to the promotion of Liberal principles and Liberal policies is of ever-growing importance; expresses its determination to maintain the independence of the Liberal Party in opposition to both Conservatism and Socialism, and to develop its power and influence through democratic and constitutional methods at international, national and local levels.

It therefore calls on Liberals to continue to effect their political aims within the organisations of the Party and, in suitable cases, to work with other bodies to achieve reforms, subject to the requirements of the Party Constitution.

In determining the organisational strategy to achieve Liberal aims, this assembly endorses the following objectives as of prime importance:

(1) A dual approach to politics, acting both inside and outside the institutions of the political establishment.

(2) A primary strategic emphasis on Community Politics; our role as political activists is to help organise people in communities to take and use power, to use our political skills to redress grievances, and to represent people at all levels of the political structure.

(3) A national strategy based on:

    (a) The recognition of the need for a comprehensive and coherent organisational strategy covering all aspects of our Party's work;

    (b) A national commitment to build a Liberal power base in the major cities of this country;

    (c) The provision of an aggressive political lead on issues of moral concern, injustice and oppression and the use of these campaigns to publicise Liberal attitudes and policies. We aim to identify with the under-privileged of this country and the world;

    (d) The building of a national image to capture people's imagination as a credible political movement, with local roots and local successes;

(4) A strategy for political development aimed at involving Liberals and the public in a continuing debate about policies and principles and at developing a comprehensive framework for Liberal policies;

(5) The development by Regional Parties of appropriate strategies in the regions and their integration into a national whole;

(6) The creation of a party structure and organisation which is tailored to this strategy;

(7) The creation of a Liberal organisation in every constituency, an organisation with the two-fold aim of:

    (a) Producing in every constituency an organisation capable of strongly contesting local government and parliamentary elections;

    (b) Increasing, through enlarged membership, the financial support given by constituencies to the Party;

(8) The development of area organisations to deploy material resources and personnel to contest all parliamentary by-elections in which Liberal effort can be advantageously made;

(9) The implementation by the national organisation of a plan to contest the next
    general election on the broadest possible front.

To this end, the assembly calls on the National Executive Committee, in collaboration with the Standing Committee, to institute a feasibility study of the
organisational strategy of the Party in relation to material resources and political
priorities, to act upon its findings and report progress to the 1971 Assembly.

Community politics was thus backed by a combination of Young Liberal theoreticians and
hardened local government campaigners. Both were distant from the party leadership,
which generally remained sceptical about the link between local and national politics. The
leadership was not expected to support the community politics resolution; Peter Hain,
then a leading Young Liberal, famously declared that 'the party leadership does not understand what community politics is all about, and if they did they wouldn't like it'.

Thorpe and his colleagues no doubt were not masters of the theory, but they recognised the elements of traditional liberalism in what was being proposed. Percy Harris
had used some of the tactics, such as leaflets on local issues and surgeries for dealing with
casework, in Bethnal Green before the Second World War. They also appreciated that
support for the concept came not just from the Young Liberals but from many well-
respected councillors and provincial leaders. Perhaps most importantly, the party was
bereft of a strategy, and community politics deserved a whirl.

Although community politics was not invented in 1970, that year's assembly marked
a turning point in the history of the Liberal Party. Until then its sole goal had been to
claim power at Westminster, however unlikely that seemed. It had no declared strategy
for achieving that aim: the 'broad front' and 'narrow front' had both been tried at general
elections and found wanting; the targeting of resources had worked to a limited extent
in 1964 and 1966 but had failed in 1970. Now the party had a second aim: to help local
people take power in their own communities. In reality, this was usually interpreted
as helping Liberals win local council seats; many Liberals regarded this as community
politics, to the annoyance of the theoreticians. This strategic change set the tone for the
party's second revival and its subsequent development during the rest of the century.

Community politics: expression of Liberalism or convenient tactic?

The Liberal Party's decision to embrace community politics triggered a rash of writing in the 1970s about what the strategy entailed, including a volume of essays edited
by Peter Hain, who was shortly to depart the Liberal Party for Labour. What became
evident was that there was little consensus within the party about how Liberals were
supposed to help people take power for themselves. If taken to its logical conclusion,
didn't this concept spell the end of party politics and the Liberal Party itself? And what if
a community sought to pursue illiberal aims, such as overt discrimination towards ethnic
minorities – should Liberals help? Could people be led away from populism and yet still
be empowered to act for themselves in the political arena?

One practical approach was to advocate the devolution of decision-making within localities, something Liberal councils could implement. Not all did, however; neighbourhood councils might simply empower the same people who were already involved in local politics, rather than the population as a whole, and could be costly and bureaucratic.

Although claimed by the Liberal Party, community politics is not exclusively liberal. Community politics techniques were also employed by the Communist Party and its offshoots, such as Lawrence Daly of the Fife Socialist League, in the 1940s and 1950s. However, community politics has remained at the heart of Liberal, and Liberal Democrat, strategy ever since 1970.

A second revival

Thorpe was not heavily engaged in political life in the year after the 1970 election, following the death of his first wife, and there was little sign of a Liberal revival in 1971, or through much of 1972. The party's poll ratings were worse than at any time since the mid-1950s, beginning to recover only at the very end of 1972. By-elections were mostly avoided, and the handful contested produced results even worse than had been achieved in 1970.

Britain into Europe

On 17 February 1972, five Liberal votes were crucial in ensuring that the European Communities Bill was given a second reading in the House of Commons.

Labour voted against the bill, which provided the legal authority for the UK to join the EEC. Although in October 1971 sixty-nine Labour MPs, led by Roy Jenkins, had rebelled against a three-line whip to vote in favour of a motion approving the government's decision in principle to join the EEC, in February 1972 it seemed possible that in the light of a continued Conservative back-bench revolt the government could be defeated, possibly causing it to resign. Accordingly, on the latter occasion, only five Labour MPs, including Christopher Mayhew, who was later to join the Liberal Party, abstained on the second reading of the bill.

After the vote, Thorpe wrote 'the Liberal Party pioneered the movement towards European unity in this country, and it is a sign of the cynicism to which politics has now sunk that we should have been expected to throttle it tonight'. He drew attention to the pro-Europeans in the Labour Party, such as Roy Jenkins, who had voted against their convictions. Many of these would later join the SDP.

National political factors were again beginning to favour the Liberal Party, however. Heath's pledge to break the post-war consensus on full employment in the face of accelerating inflation was soon abandoned, industrial relations worsened, and unemployment continued to rise. Disaffected Conservative voters again showed their willingness to kick their own government by supporting the Liberals; and this time, unlike in the early 1960s, the Labour vote often proved weak too. Harold Wilson's image as an energetic, imaginative leader of modern Britain had been severely tarnished during his six years in government, which had caused disillusionment among some Labour supporters and increased interest in pressure groups as a means to challenge the status quo on specific issues.

The first stirring of the second revival came at Rochdale, where a by-election was held in October 1972. The conditions for a Liberal victory were clearly in place. Ludovic Kennedy had nearly won the seat for the Liberals in 1958; the party had claimed second place in the preceding general election; there was a strong Liberal tradition in local government, which had survived the decades of decline; and the Liberal candidate was the irrepressible Cyril Smith, a former Labour councillor with a formidable personal following. His victory, by over 5,000 votes from Labour, was followed by something far more unexpected. Employing pavement politics techniques, helped by Trevor 'The Vote' Jones, in a quintessentially Conservative constituency, in December the young Graham Tope captured the south London suburban seat of Sutton & Cheam by over 7,000 votes. The Liberal bandwagon was rolling and Thorpe was able to capitalise, using his prowess in media appearances to good effect.

The glorious vision of a Liberal breakthrough again materialised. Rebel Labour MP Dick Taverne, having resigned his seat and left the party, successfully defended Lincoln in March 1973 as a 'Democratic Labour' candidate, with surreptitious Liberal backing. Taverne was later to become a prominent member of the Social Democratic Party. The Liberals came from nowhere to take nearly 40 per cent of the vote in Chester-le-Street on the same day as the Lincoln by-election before doing the same at Manchester Exchange in June 1973. Neither could be considered promising Liberal territory. One month later, Clement Freud won the Isle of Ely seat and David Austick claimed Ripon. Hove was the scene of another strong Liberal performance in November 1973 and on the same day Alan Beith took Berwick, the last of five Liberal by-election gains in just over a year. Finally, although the Liberal share of the vote in the 1973 local elections was nothing special, the overall figures hid a number of areas of strength, the most significant of which was Liverpool, where the Liberals won forty-eight seats and became the largest party on the city council.

The Liberal Party entered the February 1974 election on a high. No less than 517 Liberal candidates came forward, the most since 1906. Thorpe presided over press conferences from his constituency, where he was determined to increase his slim majority. His energetic campaigning style again proved popular and his assertion that the Liberals would work with anyone of moderate opinion to get the country back on the rails contrasted well with the background of extremism and class conflict which marked the 'Who Governs Britain?' election, played out against a backdrop of industrial strife and recent experiences of power cuts. The Liberal manifesto was sober and detailed. It celebrated community politics – which it described as 'an attempt to involve people in the decisions that affect their daily lives at the time when the individual viewpoint can really be expressed effectively' – and called for 'the largest possible representation of the "general interest"'.

The Liberal manifesto, February 1974

In a personal introduction to the February 1974 manifesto, Thorpe wrote:

People are now bewildered, frightened and often angry. The first business of any Government should be to draw the nation together and to chart the course towards a new society based on fairness and tolerance.

The role of the Liberal Party at this election is to act as a catalyst in bringing this about by securing the largest possible representation of the 'general interest'. And you, the elector, can help us in this task by rejecting the sterile class conflict of two discredited parties and voting in a new era of reconciliation. It will take courage, but the five Liberal by-election victories in the last fifteen months, during which period we have secured more votes than any other party, shows that it can be done.

Every Liberal vote cast at this election will be a nail in the coffin of the old two-party system of confrontation and a step towards national unity and reconstruction.

The party achieved its best result since 1929, with over six million people voting Liberal, an average of 23.6 per cent of the poll per candidate. Austick and Tope lost their seats but five more were gained, bringing the total number of Liberal MPs to fourteen. There were a host of near misses, which encouraged optimism that, next time, the long-awaited breakthrough would finally happen.

February 1974 general election (28 February)			
	Votes	%	MPs
Liberal	6,059,519	19.3	14
Conservative	11,872,180	37.9	297
Labour	**11,645,616**	**37.2**	**301**
SNP	633,180	2.0	7
Plaid Cymru	171,374	0.5	2
Others	940,113	3.0	14
Total	31,321,982		635
Average vote per Liberal candidate (%)			23.6
Strong Liberal performances (20% or above)			333

For the first time since the 1920s, the election failed to produce a party with an overall majority in the Commons. The Conservatives polled more votes than Labour but won four fewer seats, and Heath, as the incumbent Prime Minister, invited Thorpe to Downing Street to discuss the terms on which the Conservatives and Liberals could cooperate. Heath offered the Liberals a full coalition including a seat in the Cabinet. Thorpe insisted on electoral reform; Heath conceded a Speaker's Conference on the subject, but did not pledge government support for whatever it recommended. Thorpe was not convinced that he should support Heath, not least because the Conservatives were the clear losers from the election. The Liberal Party reacted with horror to the thought of a coalition with the Conservatives and the notion was rejected at a meeting of Liberal MPs on 4 March. Irrespective of what was offered, Thorpe could not have carried his party into coalition.[23]

There was no alternative but for Wilson to return to power, with a minority government. Rather as in 1964, another election would soon be required, and the country returned to the polls in October. This proved a financial strain on the Liberal Party, living hand to mouth as ever, but Thorpe was determined to capitalise on the February result, perhaps mindful of how Grimond's leadership had foundered on the rocks of the 1966 result. For the first time, the party sought to field a candidate in every constituency in England, Wales and Scotland, in the end contesting all but four seats. In his personal message to the British electorate, Thorpe explained how a Liberal government was possible – the first time the party had been able to aim for outright victory since 1950. Under the graphic, if prosaic, slogan 'one more heave', the Liberals went once more into battle.

Again, however, the party found itself squeezed by the realities of the two-party system. Faced with a choice between a Conservative and Labour government, the public plumped – just – for Labour. It was all too easy to portray a Liberal vote as a waste of effort which would not influence the outcome of the great debate. The result for the Liberals was disappointing, but far from catastrophic. Bodmin and Hazel Grove were lost; and Christopher Mayhew, the former Navy Minister who had defected from Labour, failed to gain Bath, having abandoned his Woolwich East constituency. On the plus side, David Penhaligon gained Truro, and the Liberal vote per candidate was a respectable 18.9 per cent. The party had not yet found the knack of turning near-misses at one election into gains at the next, however. Leominster, Skipton, Newbury and Hereford were among the seats again waiting for one more Liberal heave.

October 1974 general election (10 October)			
	Votes	%	MPs
Liberal	5,346,704	18.3	13
Conservative	10,462,565	35.8	277
Labour	**11,457,079**	**39.2**	**319**
SNP	839,617	2.9	11
Plaid Cymru	166,321	0.6	3
Others	916,818	3.1	12
Total	29,189,104		635
Average vote per Liberal candidate (%)			18.9
Strong Liberal performances (20% or above)			189

1956–74: what changed?

In 1955, 96 per cent of voters backed Conservative or Labour candidates and 98.6 per cent of the seats in the House of Commons were won by those parties. Nineteen years later the UK's political duopoly, if not under threat, was discernibly weakening. The 'minority parties' claimed 25 per cent of the vote in the February 1974 election and there were thirty-seven MPs from parties other than the big two.

The Liberals were not the sole beneficiaries of this change in the political landscape and nor were they the only party to suffer from the new-found fickleness of the electorate. The Scottish National Party (SNP), which had attracted just 21,000 votes in the 1964 election, won seven seats in February 1974 and eleven in the general election eight months later, before being reduced to just two seats in 1979. The SNP was able to replace the Liberals in a handful of Scottish constituencies, such as the Western Isles. In Wales, Plaid Cymru was more successful in supplanting the Liberals in most of their Welsh-speaking strongholds in the west and north.

With their background as a party of government, conviction that all reasonable people could be persuaded to vote Liberal (and that most people were reasonable), and natural optimism, Liberals sometimes struggled to make sense of what the electorate was telling them. Twice during this period senior Liberals talked of forcing their way back towards government, and yet from 1967 to 1972 the party seemed no better off than in the darkest days in the 1950s.

By 1974 the Liberal Party had become adept at attracting protest votes, especially at mid-term by-elections during spells of Conservative government, and, as a consequence, its support was highly volatile. Only 52 per cent of the people voting Liberal in 1964 stayed with the party in the general election of 1966, and less than 1 per cent of the electorate in 1970 had voted Liberal both in that year's general election and in 1959. Grimond had once dismissed the criticism that his party was merely a receptacle for protest votes by quipping that 'there's a lot to protest about', but there was no long-term future for a party which relied on taking advantage of Conservatives voting against their government during mid-term, when it mattered least. It was certainly not going to help during the period of Labour government which stretched from 1974; recent experience suggested that the Liberals would not retain the support of previously disaffected Conservatives and would struggle to attract disillusioned Labour supporters when Labour was in power.

The charge of Poujadism stung the Liberals;[24] the 1950s French movement had briefly exploited disaffection with the Fourth Republic before disintegrating. Liberals knew they shared little with those populist small farmers and shopkeepers – after all, they had principles and policies aplenty – but how could they build up a significant, more broadly based, core vote and consistently challenge the main parties, not just in a handful of seats or sporadically at by-elections? This was to be the challenge of the next period in the party's history.

Further reading

There are few books dedicated to this period in the Liberal Party's history. Mark Egan, *Coming into Focus: The Transformation of the Liberal Party 1945–64* (VDM Verlag, 2009), is a detailed assessment of how the Liberal Party changed to focus its resources on local government during the 1950s and 1960s. J. S. Rasmussen, *The Liberal Party: a study of retrenchment and revival* (University of Wisconsin, 1965), focuses on the national party's institutional structure at the time of the 1959 election, and Alan Watkins, *The Liberal Dilemma* (MacGibbon and Kee, 1966), gives a journalist's perspective of the later period of Grimond's leadership. *Liberal Party Politics in Britain* by US academic Arthur Cyr (J. Calder, 1977) is flawed but interesting and has a good introduction by Michael Steed. The political situation after the 1964 election is covered in David Dutton, 'Anticipating 'the Project': Lib-Lab Relations in the Era of Jo Grimond', *Contemporary British History*, Vol. 20, No. 1, March 2006, pp. 101–17.

Grimond produced a volume of *Memoirs* (Heinemann, 1979) and has been the subject of two biographies, *Jo Grimond: Towards the Sound of Gunfire*, by Michael McManus (Birlinn, 2001), and *Liberal Lion: Jo Grimond – A Political Life*, by Peter Barberis (I. B. Tauris, 2005). Thorpe has written a patchy volume of reminiscences, *In My Own Time* (Politico's, 1999), and has been the subject of two books which, although focusing on his later criminal trial and acquittal, are useful sources on his leadership – *Jeremy Thorpe: a Secret Life*, by Lewis Chester, Magnus Linklater and David May (Deutsch, 1979), and *Rinkagate: The Rise and Fall of Jeremy Thorpe*, by Simon Freeman and Barrie Penrose (Bloomsbury, 1996). *Daring to Hope*, the last volume of Lady Violet Bonham Carter's diaries and letters, edited by Mark Pottle (Widenfeld and Nicolson, 2000), contains some typically snappy impressions and judgements.

Notes

1   J. S. Rasmussen, *The Liberal Party: a study of retrenchment and revival* (Universoty of Wisconsin, 1965), p. 20.

2   For a detailed analysis see Michael McManus, 'Liberals and the Suez Crisis', *Journal of Liberal History* 42, spring 2004.

3   Mark Pottle (ed.), *Daring to Hope: the Diaries and Letters of Violet Bonham Carter* (Weidenfeld and Nicolson, 2000), p. 170.

4   HC Deb, 8 November 1956, c293.

5   For more examples see Duncan Brack (ed.) *Why I am a Liberal Democrat* (Liberal Democrat Publications, 1996), pp. 6 (Jack Ainslie), 21 (Lord Beaumont), 34 (Sir Menzies Campbell), 41 (Chris Davies), 42 (Jenny Dawe), 55 (Jonathan Fryer), 90 (Gordon Lishman), 95 (Terry Maher), 96 (Christopher Mason), 100 (Catherine Millar), 109 (Monroe Palmer), 121 (Adrian Slade), 122–23 (Michael Steed), 130 (Paul Tyler), 133 (Mike Wallace) and 135 (Lord Wallace).

6   See Rasmussen, *The Liberal Party*, pp.62–80 for a fuller discussion of the national party's institutional structure; and Appendix 1 of this book.

7   Rasmussen, *The Liberal Party*, pp. 123–28.

8   Garry Tregidga, *The Liberal Party in South-West Britain* (University of Exeter Press, 2000), pp. 65, 75.

9   Pottle, *Daring to Hope*, p. 202.

10 Cited in Alan Watkins, *The Liberal Dilemma* (MacGibbon and Kee, 1966), p. 108.

11 Robert Ingham, 'Liberal Party Membership', *Journal of Liberal History* 32, autumn 2001.

12 Robert McKenzie, *British Political Parties*, 2nd edn. (Heinemann, 1963), pp. 653–59.

13 Letter by Michael Meadowcroft, *Journal of Liberal History* 48, autumn 2005, pp. 44–45.

14 See David Dutton, *A History of the Liberal Party* (Palgrave Macmillan, 2004), pp. 203–06, for a fuller discussion.

15 Robert Ingham, 'Battle of Ideas or Absence of Leadership?', *Journal of Liberal History* 47, summer 2005.

16 The events surrounding the 1967 leadership election are recounted in Tim Beaumont, 'The election of Jeremy Thorpe to the Liberal Leadership', *Journal of Liberal History* 15, June 1997, pp. 5–6.

17 David Butler and Michael Pinto-Duschinsky, *The British General Election of 1970* (Macmillan, 1971), p. 115. Hayward gave the island to the National Trust.

18 Also see Ruth Fox, 'Young Liberal influence and its effects, 1970–74', *Journal of Liberal History* 14, spring 1997, and Peter Hellyer, 'Young Liberals: the "Red Guard" era', *Journal of Liberal History* 17, winter 1997–98.

19 Lewis Chester, Magnus Linklater, and David May, *Jeremy Thorpe: a Secret Life* (Deutsch, 1979), pp. 88–91.

20 Jeremy Thorpe, *In My Own Time* (Politico's, 1999), pp. 171–75.

21 Butler and Pinto-Duschinsky, *The British General Election of 1970*, p. 117.

22 For more see John Meadowcroft, 'The Origins of Community Politics', *Journal of Liberal History* 28, autumn 2000, and letters in response from Michael Meadowcroft and Robert Ingham in issue 30, spring 2001, pp. 25–26.

23 Thorpe, *In My Own Time*, pp. 113–17.

24 See comment by Judith Hart MP in *The Guardian*, 31 May 1962, quoted in William Wallace, 'The Liberal Revival 1955–66', unpublished PhD thesis, Cornell University, p. 49. Also see obituary of Sir Cyril Smith in *The Guardian*, 3 September 2010.

Chapter 9

Breaking the Mould (1974–1988)

Matt Cole

The most divisive issues for Liberals in the twentieth century have been matters of strategy rather than policy; most difficult of all has been the question of how the Liberals, relegated to third-party status, should stand in relation to the larger parties. Should they present themselves as equidistant between the Conservatives and Labour, or as natural allies of one or the other? And how closely should the Liberals work with other parties, whether in Parliament or in election campaigns?

The fear of eradication and the prospect of office have induced some Liberals to go further in these matters than others, and also to open up divisions, not merely about what the party stands for on a particular issue, but what, fundamentally, it is for. This challenge arose in most of the decades of the twentieth century, but was the predominant feature of Liberal politics in the second half of the 1970s and the 1980s, the period characterised by historian Chris Cook as one of 'pacts and alliances'. Starting with cross-party co-operation in the campaign for European Economic Community membership in the 1975 referendum, this period also included the Lib–Lab Pact of 1977–78 and the SDP–Liberal Alliance of 1981–87, which boldly promised to 'break the mould' of British politics, and finished with the merger of the two Alliance parties in 1988.

The Liberal Party's condition in 1988 was in some respects similar to that of 1974: it had on both occasions been bitterly disappointed by the results of a general election at which great expectations had been generated; it was divided, impoverished and at a low ebb in the polls; and on both occasions these conditions prompted questions about the party's structure and leadership. The difference is that whereas in 1974 the party reassessed its finances and organisation and then renewed its leadership, in 1988 it dissolved itself altogether in a merger which was the culmination of the intervening decade's controversial attempts at collaboration with outsiders. Some regarded this as the natural completion of a process started by Jo Grimond and dating back through the Radical Reform Group of the 1950s to the old Liberal–Labour progressive alliance of the Edwardian era. This feeling of destiny was expressed by David Steel, who was gratified that with the merger 'the great majority of us had found the means to realise our common future'.[1] Others, such as Michael Meadowcroft, argued at the time of the merger that the Lib–Lab Pact marked the point of departure from the true faith because 'the Liberal leadership thereafter never again promoted Liberalism as a distinctive and essential philosophy',[2] and that the merger meant that a new Liberal movement would therefore have to be formed. Did this period, then, witness the fulfilment, or the abandonment, of modern Liberalism?

1974–76: From Thorpe to Steel

As the dust settled after the 1974 general elections, an anti-climactic pall hung over the Liberal Party, at least at the national level. The elections had shown that nearly one voter in five supported the party (although polling evidence revealed that the Liberals still struggled to retain support from one election to the next), and the rewards in terms of parliamentary representation had been cruelly similar to earlier elections at which fewer than one voter in ten had been Liberal. Though surviving on an implausible over-all majority of just four seats in the Commons, Labour Prime Minister Harold Wilson neither asked for nor expected co-operation from the Liberals, and seemed intent upon serving a full term in office. Widespread talk earlier in the year of a 'national government' involving the Liberals, and Thorpe's assertion that 'one more heave' would secure the seats needed to achieve this, had come to nothing.

The most immediate problem for the party was the state of its finances. Membership had peaked, and the bills from two election campaigns had to be paid. In January 1975 the party Executive commissioned Colne Valley MP and former accountant Richard Wainwright to write a report recommending reforms. Wainwright confirmed that 'the LPO [Liberal Party Organisation] is heading for a financial breakdown', made worse by high inflation and 'the virtual disappearance of the wealthy supporters who guaranteed the overdraft in 1969'.[3] His report argued that whilst he had been asked to budget for up to £100,000 a year, LPO revenues only allowed for £70,000 expenditure, and he recommended the decentralisation of many LPO functions to regional offices and, most controversially, the suspension of six senior posts, including that of the Head of the LPO. Most of Wainwright's findings were accepted by the Executive, but this last was rejected on the casting vote of the chairman, Ken Vaus. The Head of the LPO, Ted Wheeler, nonetheless resigned, much to Wainwright's satisfaction, as he later confided to the incoming party General Secretary Sir Hugh Jones that the proposed abolition 'had been conceived as a device to get rid of the incumbent'. On taking over, Jones found that 'the whole affair had left the reputation of Party Headquarters in tatters'.[4]

An opportunity to improve the profile of the Liberal Party was provided by the referendum on the UK's membership of the EEC in June 1975. The campaign brought together politicians of all parties, but the Liberals were keen to demonstrate their distinctively united position in favour of membership. The tension between the appeals of inter-party co-operation and competition reflected the arguments which were to characterise the party's development up to and including the merger.

During the campaign, Liberal Party headquarters sought to maximise Liberal exposure and to press the claim made in a book published for the referendum by Jo Grimond that 'the Liberal Party is the only Party which from the outset maintained that Britain should have signed the Treaty of Rome and joined the Coal and Steel Communities and the Common Market'.[5] The Liberals were the only party to issue a full manifesto for the referendum, and, unlike those in the Labour and Conservative parties, the tiny number of anti-membership Liberals 'refrained from embarrassing the Party', according to the main academic study of the campaign. This also noted that, to the annoyance of others in the 'Yes' camp, 'throughout the campaign [the Liberals] stressed their specific party role', and that 'at one stage Liberal pro-Marketeers were actually encouraged from the centre to use the referendum very much for Liberal Party ends'.[6]

The referendum campaign also had a longer term effect: leading Liberals and social democrats in the Labour Party enjoyed the experience of working together in the campaign, and saw the potential appeal of collaboration in the future. As vice-president of the 'Britain in Europe' campaign, Grimond worked with its president, Roy Jenkins, and his fellow vice-president, Shirley Williams, both Labour Cabinet ministers who later formed the SDP. Other MPs active in the campaign who later became Social Democrats included Bill Rodgers, John Roper and Dickson Mabon. Jeremy Thorpe remembered that 'in particular we rather enjoyed inter-party rallies',[7] and Jenkins reflected ten years after the campaign that 'it did have a certain effect in making some of us, certainly including me, believe there was something a bit beyond the high banks of these narrow canals of traditional party politics'.[8] The referendum had thrown the potential benefits of inter-party co-operation in terms of publicity and leadership recruitment into sharp relief for some Liberals; but for others it had highlighted dangers to the clarity of the Liberal message and the independence of the party.

However, the most significant development in the party's history at this time was the resignation of Jeremy Thorpe as party leader and the election in his place of David Steel. This was an episode which damaged the short-term prospects of the party, but which ultimately gave rise to a leadership clearly committed to the inter-party co-operation which shaped the party's future.

Thorpe announced the end of his nine-year tenure as leader on 10 May 1976, but the pressure upon him to resign, for both political and personal reasons, had been building for years. Throughout his leadership Thorpe had been accused of showmanship without substance, and of a refusal to consult widely within the party which led to frivolous and volatile policy-making. Michael Meadowcroft, who had worked for the party when Thorpe was Treasurer, regarded him as 'autocratic', and Grimond's speechwriter William Wallace found himself frozen out of Thorpe's inner circle and became 'increasingly suspicious of what was going on as the years went by'.[9] The collapse of Liberal parliamentary representation in 1970 and the disappointments of 1974, combined with doubts about Thorpe's judgement following the collapse of the London and County Securities Bank, of which he was a director, in 1973, led to further questions about whether Thorpe was fit to take the party forward.

It was allegations about Thorpe's private life, however, which forced him to stand down. A male model, Norman Scott, claimed that Thorpe had had an affair with him, and had paid him to keep it secret. These claims were denied by Thorpe and had been dismissed by a confidential party inquiry in 1971; but when they resurfaced after Scott appeared in court on an unrelated matter, and correspondence was published in the press giving further details of the closeness of the two men's relationship, Thorpe was obliged to resign.[10] The resignation split the party at all levels; many MPs, candidates and activists regarded Thorpe's departure as a coup in which disloyal colleagues had fallen for a homophobic conspiracy promoted by the Tory press; others believed that Thorpe himself had betrayed the party and that his resignation was vital to its survival. These bitter divisions were not eased by the accusation that party money had been used to pay Scott, or by Thorpe's later trial and acquittal for conspiracy to murder Scott. The business session of the 1978 Liberal assembly became 'an intense and at times bitter debate on the Parliamentary Party's alleged failure to stand behind Jeremy Thorpe', in the words of the party's General Secretary.

The process of replacing Thorpe set the pattern, subsequently followed by the two main parties, of opening up the election of the leader to ordinary party members rather than just MPs. This procedure, devised by Cyril Smith, reflected differences of culture in the party; while few wanted to retain the system used in 1967, some, like David Steel and Lord Byers, were still anxious about the influence which might be exercised by radical activists.[11] On the other hand, many of the activists were concerned that in a simple postal ballot of all members, recent recruits and armchair members could be as influential as seasoned and informed campaigners.

David Steel (1938–)

The longest serving Liberal leader after Asquith, Steel was born in Kircaldy, the son of a Church of Scotland minister. Educated in Scotland and Kenya, he joined the Liberal Party at Edinburgh University. Shortly after leaving university, he was selected for Roxburgh, Selkirk & Peebles. He failed to win the seat in the 1964 election, but triumphed in the by-election in March 1965; 'It's Boy David', was the *Daily Express* headline.

Steel quickly earned a reputation for skilful parliamentary negotiation with the passage of his private member's bill, the 1967 Abortion Act. In 1970 he became Liberal Chief Whip and in 1974 foreign affairs spokesman. In 1966–69 he served as president of the British Anti-Apartheid Movement; in 1970 his campaigning against the South African rugby tour jeopardised his majority in his rugby-loving constituency.

After winning the party leadership in 1976 Steel set about making the Liberals a party of power through co-operation with other parties: in the Lib-Lab Pact, the SDP-Liberal Alliance and the merger of the Liberals and Social Democrats. Steel faced criticism within his own party from those concerned about Liberal independence, but ironically was feared by David Owen, and others in the SDP, as aiming to take their party over. He nonetheless succeeded in his aim of demonstrating that the Liberal Party could work with others in the pursuit of common aims, and was not merely a fringe political movement.

Steel acted briefly as interim joint leader of the merged party, the Social and Liberal Democrats, and then served as the party's foreign affairs spokesman until 1994.

He retired from the Commons in 1997, becoming Lord Steel of Aikwood. He was a member of the new Scottish Parliament during its first term, in 1999–2003, serving as its Presiding Officer (speaker).

The solution was a system in which a large minority of MPs had to nominate a candidate, and the votes cast in constituency associations were weighted in proportion to the strength of Liberal support in each constituency at the preceding general election. A special assembly on 12 June 1976 approved a system in which ten votes were allocated to each Liberal association, with a further ten votes if the association had existed for more than a year, and an additional vote for each 500 votes won by the Liberal candidate for the constituency at the last general election.

The two candidates – former Chief Whip and foreign affairs spokesman David Steel and treasury spokesman John Pardoe – were divided by style much more than by substance. Their election literature revealed few differences on policy but included ambitious targets for the party's development; whereas Steel promised eight million Liberal votes at the next election, Pardoe urged the adoption of candidates in all seats, with 'commando' teams setting up associations in barren areas, and a programme of 2,000 public meetings to raise party income from £112,000 to £200,000. Steel, Stuart Mole later wrote, appealed to the Liberal head, with his focus on parliamentary elections, while Pardoe's focus on activism appealed to the heart. Most commentators share Roy Douglas's assumption that the party activists tended to support Pardoe while the rank and file backed Steel. As is common where policy positions are shared by candidates, the contest was not always personally cordial.[12] Perhaps because of a desire among more cautious members for an apparently predictable, restrained successor to Thorpe, Steel won the contest convincingly, securing 12,541 votes to Pardoe's 7,032 when the result was announced on 7 July.

John Pardoe (1934–)

After graduating from Cambridge University, where he performed in the Footlights revue alongside Jonathan Miller, Pardoe was originally a Labour activist, but joined the Liberal Party in 1959, and in 1964 fought Margaret Thatcher in Finchley. In 1966 he captured North Cornwall, and was one of only six survivors of the 1970 general election rout.

In 1976 Pardoe lost to David Steel in the leadership election, but as Treasury spokesman he had a major role in the Lib-Lab Pact, during which he had a fiery relationship with Chancellor Denis Healy. During the trial of Jeremy Thorpe Pardoe spoke out in support of the former leader whose constituency bordered his. Like Thorpe, Pardoe lost his seat in 1979 and never sought a return to the Commons, working instead in television and business.

He criticised David Steel for his failure to persuade Roy Jenkins to join the Liberal Party rather than form the SDP, but undertook roles in both the 1983 and 1987 election campaigns. In 1987 he became highly critical of the dual Alliance leadership after being the national campaign manager.

Steel had always flirted with the idea of engaging in pacts with other parties, and at one stage suggested an electoral deal with the Scottish Nationalists. A week after Thorpe's resignation he put his strategy clearly before the Commons, to many of whose non-Liberal members he would appeal over the coming decade: 'there are occasionally small "l" liberals to be found on particular issues outside the Liberal Party, and we should never fear to co-operate with them effectively to promote some part of our cause'.[13] This was fair warning to his critics. Eighteen months later, at the height of the controversy over the Lib-Lab Pact, he quoted these remarks to Liberal candidates and added: 'no one can say they did not know where I stood'.[14]

1976–79: The Lib-Lab Pact

Steel reiterated his ambitions in his first speech as leader to the Liberal assembly in September 1976. 'We must not give the impression of being afraid to soil our hands with the responsibilities of sharing power', he declared as some delegates waved 'No Coalition' banners. 'We must be bold enough to deploy the coalition case positively.'[15] However, the LPO's annual report to the assembly cautioned the leader that 'the Liberal Party can and will flourish, always provided that it does not sacrifice its Liberal principles to those who would merely seek power through expediency'. Steel's opportunity to change the priorities and image of the party arose promptly; before the end of the year the Labour government, led by James Callaghan, lost its overall majority in the Commons as a result of by-election defeats, and it was only a matter of time before a challenge from the new leader of the Opposition, Margaret Thatcher, drove Callaghan to seek support from beyond his own ranks.

The thirteen Liberal MPs were an obvious source. An arrangement arrived at in the first instance for a single parliamentary division was quickly extended to the end of the session and eventually the Liberals found themselves drawn into supporting the Labour government for nearly eighteen months. Though Steel defended the Lib-Lab Pact both during and after its operation, its benefits were doubted by many Liberals from the outset, and by most of the party not much more than halfway through its lifetime. Why it continued, and what were its effects, are therefore significant questions.

The particular occasion of the first arrangement in which Liberal MPs supported Callaghan's government was a vote of no confidence tabled by Thatcher on 23 March 1977, but Steel had looked forward to the opportunity for years, and his reaction to it set the tone of Liberal politics for years to come. The reasons for going into a pact were both national and partisan, tactical and strategic. Even the Liberals most suspicious of co-operation with other parties could see the attractions of sustaining Callaghan in office: a general election would expose the Liberals' financial and political vulnerability, whereas an arrangement with Callaghan would provide stability for the nation at a time of economic crisis on terms at least partly determined by Liberals; they would also demonstrate the practicality of the sort of co-operation entailed by the electoral reform promoted by the party. The questions were how long the co-operation should continue and at what price, and it was immediately clear that Steel would accept a lower price for a longer agreement than many of his colleagues. Although the tension between these views was present throughout the pact, there were three phases in the development of the arrangement. The first was one of relative harmony within and between the partners; the second one of crisis, which broke the trust underpinning the pact; and the last period was one in which the spirit of the pact had gone, though it lived on in practice. In all three phases Liberals secured achievements, but they were of diminishing significance and came at increasing cost.

Having won the confidence vote on 23 March, Callaghan and Steel drew up an agreement for the remainder of the parliamentary session which was accepted by all Liberal MPs, even though some were surprised at its limited benefits for their party. There would be a Joint Consultative Committee between Labour ministers and their counterparts in the 'Shadow Administration', as the Liberal MPs and peers involved came to call themselves; Liberal proposals on worker participation, homelessness and small businesses were to be given a serious hearing, and – most tantalising of all – the issue of proportional representation for elections to the proposed devolved bodies in Scotland and Wales and for direct elections to the European Parliament was to be put before the Commons. Steel was in bullish mood about the opportunity, writing to Liberal candidates:

> Admire the photos of the Liberal MPs in the *Daily Mail*! When did photographs of all the MPs last appear on the front page of a popular daily? You will have a difficult time. You will have resignations in your constituency. (You would have had from others if we had sided with the Tories.) Don't be defensive. Be aggressive. Go all out to detail the bridling of socialism. Forget the textual analysis of the Agreement. It's what we make of it that matters.[16]

However, little was guaranteed, and the votes on PR were to be free votes so that Labour MPs would be at liberty to oppose the measure. From the outset there were Liberals who took John Pardoe's view that: 'David was determined to do a deal at all costs'. Labour ministers agreed, as one source reported, that: 'the "terms" were heard with some incredulity by the Cabinet' and 'the [Labour] Party had simply undertaken to do what it had anyway intended to do and desist from what it could not do'.[17]

Cyril Smith declared his opposition to the pact early on, and from the outset former leader Jo Grimond and David Penhaligon, the MP for Truro, were extremely sceptical and supported the project only out of loyalty to colleagues. Most of the anxiety at this stage, however, was about the details of policy or the length of the agreement. Steel was able to persuade his colleagues at a weekend meeting of MPs in late June that 'the results to date have been worthwhile and beneficial to the nation but that any future agreement still depends on the government pursuing policies which will bring down the rate of inflation and provide the necessary economic stability for the country'.[18] In July Steel convinced his fellow MPs to continue the pact into another parliamentary session based upon a ten-point agreement which promised a free Commons vote on PR for European elections and consideration of profit-sharing in industry.

For four months Steel unquestionably had the support of most of the party; party headquarters noted confidently that 'initial reactions we have received are, with relatively few exceptions, favourable' and that 'the Party will stand solidly with the Parliamentary Party and the Leader'.[19] Shadow Administration and Joint Consultative Committee meetings went ahead and senior Liberals in the Lords wrote to Steel calling for a more stable and longer-term agreement. There was even a remarkable historical continuum provided by a letter from Sir George Schuster, a former Liberal National MP, who said: 'in listening to what you said last night I felt for the first time that public expression was given to a true Liberal message'.[20] Yet there remained among Liberals a body of sceptical opinion which feared for Liberal independence, and by the summer, Steel recalled, 'the Party was extremely restless' following very poor local election results in May, when three-quarters of the Liberals' county council seats were lost.[21] In September the Association of Liberal Councillors told the Liberal assembly that the party was 'bleeding to death'.

During autumn 1977 the pact was tested to destruction, though this would not be publicly evident until later. The delicate balance of opinion within the Liberal Party was reflected in the annual report to the assembly, which argued that 'the sudden re-emergence of the Liberal Party on to the national stage as a result of the Agreement with the Government has enabled the Party to wield a degree of real and immediate influence more in line with its electoral support at the last election' but also acknowledged that 'it has strained our meagre resources to the limit'. Cyril Smith's attempt to have the agreement renegotiated was voted down by 716 to 385 at the assembly in September, but Steel was obliged by an assembly resolution to promise that in the coming vote on PR in European elections, 'we will be watching the division lists most carefully. We have a right to expect the substantial majority of Labour members – and especially Ministers whose continuance in office depends on us – to support the Government's recommendation'.

The same month Liberal MPs were infuriated to see a study into the grievances of small businesses – for which they had pressed the government since the first days of the pact – set up with no recognition of their role in its establishment; Steel was obliged to release a retrospective press statement claiming the credit for his colleagues. Former Labour minister Christopher Mayhew, who had defected to the Liberals three years earlier, convinced the Liberal assembly at Brighton to pass a resolution demanding that a 'substantial majority' of Labour MPs must support PR for the European elections in order for the pact to continue.

October saw a reshuffle of the Shadow Administration in which doubters made way for more solid supporters of the pact: Smith, who had resigned as employment spokesman, was replaced by Baroness Seear, and Grimond stepped down from his responsibility for energy policy, which was handed to Lord Avebury. In November, a Party Council meeting at Derby insisted that if Labour MPs did not endorse PR for Europe, then a special assembly would have to be called to review the pact. Everything now depended upon the Commons vote on the introduction of PR on 13 December.

The vote for PR in European elections was lost by 319 to 222. Conservative whipping against the bill did damage, but more significant to the Liberals was Labour's lukewarm response. Although a majority of Labour MPs voting – 147 to 122 – supported the bill, fewer than half of the Parliamentary Labour Party voted for it, and eleven ministers, four of them Cabinet members, voted against it. This was hardly the 'best endeavours' of the government which Liberal MPs had been promised in July.

An immediate meeting of Liberal MPs decided to continue with the pact by only six votes to four. To achieve this, Steel was obliged to pretend that Callaghan was going to see the Queen to call an election, a prank which made some of his colleagues feel physically sick. The pact was now doomed.

A special assembly was called to meet in Blackpool in January 1978 to discuss the situation. Conscious of the hostile reaction he was likely to face, Steel secured a long run-in of over a month to the assembly, carefully crafted a resolution for debate which gave him discretion over how and when to end the pact, and wrote a stern letter to Liberal candidates on his view of the best way forward: 'I am not going to change course now. I think the Party would be crazy to change course but you are entitled to do so if you wish at the special assembly.' In the New Year a note of anxiety replaced the bravado of the previous month as he urged candidates to: 'please ensure if you or your constituency delegates are speaking that nothing is said thoughtlessly which can be picked up and used against ourselves in the future by our enemies'. Regretting that the discussion has taken him away from other activities, he warned that 'there must soon come an end to this discussion of our strategy in favour of more effective promotion of it'. On the other side of the debate, the activists' magazine *Liberator* argued that 'somehow or other the Liberal Party must find a way of deciding when to get out of the pact', and complained that 'the problem in all of this, of course, is to ensure that David Steel listens to the party, rather than blindly pursuing his obsession with coalition'.[22]

The Blackpool assembly approved the continuation of the pact by 1,727 votes to 520, but it exposed publicly the divisions within the party. Steel continued to insist that: 'I have to place on record that the Prime Minister delivered exactly what he undertook to deliver on PR', to delegates' cries of 'rubbish!'; but even Richard Wainwright, who opened the debate with a speech supposed to bridge the two factions, referred to the 'perverse sectarian Labour vote in favour of gerrymandering', and the tone of the debate was more important than the substance of the resolution which was agreed. Although Steel was granted the freedom to continue with the pact for the remainder of the session, most delegates regarded this as allowing the pact a dignified demise in preference to administering a lethal injection; it was not an encouragement to attempt to revive it. *The Times* observed that 'neither the wording of the motion nor the mood in the conference hall suggested that the delegates were voting to continue it indefinitely'.[23]

There were occasional minor triumphs over budget measures, or opportunities to advertise Liberal novelties such as a land bank, but few of these ideas came to fruition. One or two MPs, such as Sir Russell Johnston, urged Steel to press on with the pact, hoping that Labour would repent on PR for Europe and the proposed devolved bodies in Scotland and Wales, but these measures were again defeated by Labour peers in April. The balance of party opinion tipped in favour of the sceptics, and only courtesy and electoral necessity restrained the Liberals from ending the pact straight away. The lesson for Steel was clear: much of the Liberal Party would support his strategy of inter-party co-operation, but the circumstances had to be right, and the rewards had to be delivered. In particular, the promise of electoral reform – always central to the Liberals' idea of politics – was sacrosanct.

Publicly, the pact ended with a whimper: in May Steel acknowledged that it would not continue beyond the parliamentary session; in June he told Scottish Liberals wearily that 'it has been an appallingly difficult time for Liberals. We face an electorate brainwashed into seeing politics as a contest between a pair of mighty adversaries', and called for an autumn election. At the end of July Liberal opposition lost the government a vote on the dock labour scheme; but it was not until August that Alan Beith, as Chief Whip, gave notice that all joint meetings were at an end.

For sceptics this experiment in co-operation had been costly and largely fruitless. In electoral terms, as well as losing hard-won council representation, the Liberals lost ground at every parliamentary by-election during the pact, losing over 10 per cent of the vote in half of the contests between April 1977 and May 1978. The party's Gallup poll rating fell into single figures for the first time in five years in August 1977, not to rise again until the 1979 general election campaign.[24] In reality the tangible rewards in terms of policy were at best thin, although a number of Liberal demands had received serious discussion and had been the subject of clear legislative proposals, a situation upon which the party could build in the future.

Such was the opposition to the Lib-Lab Pact in the party that Steel later acknowledged that: 'it's fair to describe it as a Steel/Callaghan Pact' because 'the Liberals, as usual, were difficult and had to be cajoled along'.[25] For Steel, however, a precedent had been set: he opened 1979 with a party political broadcast quoting Bill Rodgers and Edward Heath on the virtues of inter-party co-operation and the need for a statutory incomes policy, and went on to argue at the general election in May that the Liberals had 'knocked sense into Labour' and to appeal for a 'Liberal wedge' to split the two main parties' control of the Commons. The argument over co-operation would surely return.

1979–81: the formation of the Alliance

In view of the difficulties caused by the Lib-Lab Pact, the Liberals' reasonable performance in the 1979 election constituted the rescue of survival from the jaws of oblivion. Going into the election, morale in the parliamentary party was low; as Steel has written: 'When we left the Liberal dining table for the last time we suspected few of the fourteen would be back'.[26] In the event, all but three returned.

There were a number of reasons for the partial recovery. Firstly, the party had time to distance itself from Labour and prepare its organisation because of Prime Minister

Callaghan's misjudgement in deferring the election from autumn 1978, when most had expected it. Between then and May 1979, Liberal support in Gallup polls rose from 6 to almost 14 per cent, and in March the party's campaigning resilience was confirmed by David Alton's by-election victory at Liverpool Edge Hill. Coming on the day after the government's defeat in the Commons, this was a priceless morale-booster, particularly for Liberals fighting Labour, who had suffered most during the pact.

The second reason for the recovery was an effective national campaign which, despite brutal attacks from the Conservative popular press, projected an image which consolidated Liberal support. The Liberal manifesto, which set out the distinctive Liberal position on the constitution and Europe, and stressed the party's concern to take action on the environment, received what was described in the main study of the campaign as 'a cautious welcome from the press';[27] *The Guardian* gave it forty-two points for new ideas, compared to eleven for Labour and nine for the Conservatives, and *The Economist* declared it the best of the three.

Steel took particular pride in his television performances as the basis of the party's appeal, and his final broadcast was described by the chief study of the election as 'one of the most powerful heard in an election'. Two of the three Liberal losses could in large part be attributed to the trial of Jeremy Thorpe – Thorpe's own defeat and that of his constituency neighbour John Pardoe (the third was Montgomeryshire). The number of remaining Liberal MPs, however, was not directly linked to the party's national share of the vote (though 14 per cent was a creditable outcome), nor even to the movement in that share. It was determined by the individual ability of incumbent MPs to hold their seats. The continuing Liberal MPs' limpet-like persistence in retaining local support was reflected in the fact that only two of the eleven lost any vote share, though the party nationally lost 4.5 per cent. Had the swing in the three parties' vote shares in their seats replicated that of the change in the rest of the country since October 1974, only five of the Liberal MPs would have survived.[28]

1979 general election (3 May)			
	Votes	*%*	*MPs*
Liberal	4,313,804	13.8	11
Conservative	**13,697,923**	**43.9**	**339**
Labour	11,532,218	36.9	269
SNP	504,259	1.6	2
Plaid Cymru	132,544	0.4	2
Others	1,040,614	3.3	12
Total	*31,221,362*		*635*

Taking heart from this showing, Steel continued with his efforts at realignment. Even during the 1979 election campaign he had swapped experiences with Roy Jenkins and Lord Carrington at the memorial service for Reginald Maudling in Westminster Abbey. Within weeks of the election, Jenkins was to make a more formal approach to Steel.

He invited Steel to dinner at his home in Brussels (where he had been President of the European Commission since 1977) to mull over the new political scene and to explore 'future political arrangements' between the left and centre of British politics on which Jenkins was to give the BBC Dimbleby Lecture later that year. 'Roy and I agreed', said Steel, 'that some new organisation founded mainly on a mass exodus from the Labour Party but linking up in alliance with us would stand the best chance of "breaking the mould" of British politics'. Steel denied the accusation that he discouraged Jenkins from joining the Liberals,[29] but he did express a view which would have infuriated some of his more sceptical colleagues: 'we as a party were still not cracking the Labour strongholds. Something "extra" was needed to achieve that. Roy and his colleagues, I thought, could provide it.'[30]

Roy Jenkins (1920–2003)

Jenkins was first elected to Parliament for Southwark in 1948, but took over as MP for the Birmingham seat of Stetchford in 1950. He became a minister in 1964 and went on to be a liberalising Home Secretary and an effective Chancellor of the Exchequer in Labour governments in the 1960s and 1970s.

In the 1950s Jenkins became an early advocate of British entry to the EEC, and in July 1971 led a major Labour rebellion against a three-line whip to support the legislation taking the UK into Europe. This stance cost him the Labour leadership contest of 1976, and he subsequently resigned from the Commons to take up the role of President of the European Commission in 1977–81.

During this period he discussed with David Steel the formation of a new party which could attract defectors from other parties and those alienated from politics, but would work closely with the Liberals to reform the sclerotic political system. He also stayed in touch with allies in the Labour Party, increasingly concerned over the growing dominance of left-wing activists after the 1979 election, and the adoption of leftist defence and economic policies, and opposition to EEC membership. Jenkins, together with former Cabinet ministers David Owen, Bill Rodgers and Shirley Williams, came to be nicknamed the 'Gang of Four', after the group of rebels led by Mao's widow in China after his death in 1976.

After the creation of the SDP in 1981, Jenkins returned to Parliament in the Glasgow Hillhead by-election of 1982 and was elected the first leader of the new party. Jenkins suffered criticism for his leadership of the SDP and the Alliance in 1983, however, and resigned after the general election. After losing Hillhead in 1987, Jenkins supported the merger of the Liberals and Social Democrats and subsequently became Liberal Democrat leader in the Lords until 1997, and Chancellor of Oxford University. He chaired the independent inquiry on electoral reform established by the Blair government in 1997–98.

Throughout his career he enjoyed writing as much as politics, and was the author of several political biographies, his subjects including, among others, Asquith, Churchill and Gladstone.

This resort to dalliances with former foes in preference to backing the successes of Liberal community politicians in northern Labour fiefdoms was bold. At the same time, Steel had been contacted by David Marquand, former aide to Jenkins and until 1977 a Labour MP, but now Professor of Contemporary History and Politics at Salford University. Marquand came to see Steel in the Commons for 'a long talk about the prospects of a social democratic breakaway from the Labour Party and its possible relationship with the Liberals', and after meeting Steel (who on this occasion did advise Marquand not to join the Liberals until the possibility of a new party had been explored), urged Jenkins to 'toughen up the draft of what was to become the Dimbleby Lecture, to make it more a call to action and less an academic disquisition on the history of the party system'.[31]

The Dimbleby Lecture was delivered on 22 November (Jenkins had sent Steel a draft in advance) under the title 'Home Thoughts from Abroad', and it made public the renewed debate over the possibility of party realignment on the British centre-left. In the wake of its 1979 defeat, the Labour Party had embarked upon a bitter and extended internal struggle over its identity and structure, in the course of which Michael Foot beat moderate candidate Denis Healey to the leadership, the trade unions won the largest share of control over any future leadership choice, and policy shifted decisively in favour of increased public ownership, withdrawal from the EEC and unilateral nuclear disarmament.[32] Jenkins expressed concern, in the lecture, at the decline of the 'radical centre', and proposed proportional representation as a key element of the solution to Britain's problems.

Although there was considerable interest in the broadsheet press, the lecture was easily dismissed as the musings of an erudite but elder statesman on the political sidelines, and reaction in the political parties was muted. Jo Grimond expressed wariness of 'renegade Labour life peers and other social democrats who had been discredited', and challenged Jenkins to 'come down into battle. Let him shove with the rest of us. All too many social democrats have gone off into banking, consultancy, TV, academic life etc.'[33] Shirley Williams dismissed the idea of a new third party; only Bill Rodgers, a former transport minister, went as far as to tell Labour colleagues that their party had a year in which to make itself electable again, a deadline of which he reminded them six months later.

Steel and Jenkins continued throughout 1980 to meet and plan, to cultivate media interest in their project, and to coax their more cautious colleagues towards some form of realignment. Steel told a meeting in the new year at his own university, Edinburgh, that he looked forward to the Liberals forming the core of a new party, and in April appealed to social democrats in a Liberal Party pamphlet *Labour at Eighty – Time to Retire*. He took pleasure in the fact that a hypothetical alliance between his party and a new centre party was winning 29 per cent in some opinion polls. But Jenkins had only established formal contact with a small number of social democrats in the Labour Party – mostly outside Parliament – and had still to persuade the so-called 'Gang of Three' leading Labour social democrats – Bill Rodgers, Shirley Williams and David Owen – to abandon their party.

The Gang of Three

David Owen (1938–) was elected Labour MP for Plymouth Sutton in 1966, and in 1974 became MP for Plymouth Devonport. He was a junior minister in 1968 and shadow defence minister after 1970, but resigned in 1972 over Harold Wilson's opposition to British membership of the EEC. When Labour returned to power in 1974 Owen joined the government, becoming Foreign Secretary in 1977–79.

Owen joined Shirley Williams and Bill Rodgers as the 'Gang of Three' opposing Labour's unilateralist and anti-European drift in 1980–81. With Roy Jenkins they founded the SDP in March 1981, and Owen became its leader after the 1983 election. His relationship with David Steel was tense partly because Owen was stridently opposed to any merger between the Alliance parties.

When, in January 1988, the SDP voted to form the Liberal Democrats, Owen launched his 'continuing' SDP, which competed with the Liberal Democrats at elections until its demise in 1990. Owen retired from the Commons in 1992, took a seat in the Lords as a crossbencher and between 1992 and 1995 was the EU's co-chairman of the Conference for the Former Yugoslavia.

Bill Rodgers (1928–) was, during 1960–62, the full-time organiser for the Campaign for Democratic Socialism, established to help Hugh Gaitskell oppose moves to commit the Labour Party to unilateral nuclear disarmament. He first became a Labour MP in 1962, served as a junior minister under Harold Wilson and as Secretary of State for Transport in the Callaghan government of 1976–79. He was one of the foremost critics of the Labour left in the years after the party's 1979 defeat.

After the formation of the Alliance, he negotiated the allocation of seats between the SDP and Liberals, but after the loss of his Stockton-on-Tees seat in 1983 his influence waned. He supported merger between the Liberals and SDP, and after 1987 took up senior positions with the Royal Institute of British Architects and the Advertising Standards Authority. As Lord Rodgers of Quarry Bank, he led the Liberal Democrats in the Lords between 1997 and 2001.

Shirley Williams (1930–) was the daughter of author and peace campaigner Vera Brittain, and was first elected as the Labour MP for Stevenage in 1964. She was a very popular Cabinet minister, holding the offices of Secretary of State for Prices and Consumer Affairs, and for Education, in the 1974–79 government, at the end of which she lost her seat.

Although she initially dismissed the idea of a new centre party, Williams was one of the key figures in the creation of the SDP, and became the party's first elected MP when she won the Crosby by-election in 1981. Williams again lost her seat in 1983, but was SDP president during the next Parliament, and fought Cambridge in 1987. She entered the House of Lords in 1993.

Williams supported merger, and led the Liberal Democrat peers from 2001 to 2004. She also broadened her activity beyond British politics, taking up a Professorship at

Harvard from 1988 to 2001. She became an adviser on security matters to Gordon Brown's Labour government from 2007 to 2010.

The recruitment of the Gang of Three was to rely upon the actions of their Labour colleagues rather than those of Steel, from whom they maintained a studied distance. Following a special conference in May 1980 which proposed that the Labour Party should oppose EEC membership, they issued a public threat to leave if the policy were officially adopted. They did not respond to a speech made by Jenkins to the press gallery the next day calling for a new centre party, though on the same day Williams asserted that such a party would have 'no roots, no principles, no philosophy and no values'.[34] It was when Labour's autumn conference agenda emerged over the summer – indicating that the National Executive Committee was committed to increasing the power of constituency activists over councillors, MPs and the leadership – that they acted. An open letter was sent by Rodgers, Owen and Williams to *The Guardian* rejecting the idea of a centre party, but envisaging the possibility of 'a new democratic socialist party' which they might support. Steel wrote an open reply in the same paper calling on the Gang to 'end your dialogue with the deaf and start talking to us'. None of the three replied.

Steel had growing difficulties to tackle in his own party. Though he had assured Jenkins that he had 'overwhelming support in the Liberal Party' for his view, he must have known this was optimistic. After a Party Council meeting at Worcester in May which Steel described as 'troublesome', anxiety had been building among sceptics as to the possible effects upon the Liberal Party of any breakaway from Labour and Steel's likely reaction to it. Michael Meadowcroft was commissioned to write a booklet for the September assembly in Blackpool which delivered a warning that 'there has been relatively little rigorous thinking about Liberal philosophy and its broad application during the last decade.' He went on:

> Confusion within the party over the underlying principles of cooperation with other parties, and over the priorities to be stressed in considering cooperation, both in 1974 and during the Lib-Lab Pact of 1977–78, reflected this lack of attention to basics. The uncertain response to the dilemma of the social democrats within the Labour Party has also displayed confusion about those principles we hold in common and about the most significant differences of perspective.[35]

At a fringe meeting at the assembly, Meadowcroft debated realignment with Marquand, and stressed that the key objectives of social democracy and liberalism were largely mutually exclusive – the one centralist and statist, the other localised and libertarian. Marquand made the case for 'a broad-based progressive coalition' and insisted 'we share the same fundamental values'. Marquand's view was to win in the assembly hall and in the future, but as David Steel's speechwriter remarked as the Alliance approached its first general election, 'the Meadowcroft analysis cannot in any sense be discounted'.[36]

Michael Meadowcroft (1942–)

Meadowcroft joined the Young Liberals in 1958 and was by 1962 working in the Local Government Office at Liberal headquarters. In 1968 he became the Liberal Regional Officer in Yorkshire and a Leeds city councillor, later also becoming a West Yorkshire county councillor. In 1983 he was elected MP for Leeds West.

Meadowcroft was regarded by fellow Yorkshire Liberal MP Richard Wainwright as 'the consummate politician', and by David Steel's speechwriter Jeremy Josephs as 'a sort of political guru', partly for his extensive pamphleteering on Liberal identity. He was a leading enthusiast of community politics and northern Liberalism, and a critic of the Liberal leadership when he saw it drifting from its radical principles in the Lib-Lab Pact, the Alliance and the merger with the SDP.

Although he lost his parliamentary seat in 1987, he was president-elect of the Liberal Party at the time of the merger debate, and became the most high-profile figure to oppose merger and to support the breakaway Liberal Party afterwards. Meadowcroft was president of the 'continuing' Liberal Party from 1989 to 2005, but joined the Liberal Democrats in October 2007.

It was the deterioration in relations within the Labour Party which generated further developments, with the Labour conference in September 1980 confirming the constitutional changes of the previous year's gathering, as well as anti-nuclear defence, anti-EEC and pro-nationalisation positions. In November left-winger Michael Foot took over as Labour leader, and the future direction of the party rested on the decision of one more conference: a special meeting at Wembley in January 1981 to determine the system of election of future Labour leaders. Its conclusion gave the largest influence (40 per cent) in the process to the block votes of the trade unions; Labour MPs were left with only 30 per cent of the electoral college which was set up, and constituency parties the remaining 30 per cent. Many moderate members of the Labour Party – some at the highest levels – did not resist these moves, or refused to support the alternative of 'one member, one vote' elections. They acted in effect as midwives at the birth of the SDP and therefore of the Alliance.

The day after the conference, on 25 January 1981, Jenkins and the Gang of Three, now inevitably the 'Gang of Four', issued a statement – the 'Limehouse Declaration' – calling upon social democrats in the Labour Party to join a Council for Social Democracy (CSD). The statement ended – at Jenkins's insistence – with the phrase: 'we believe that the need for a realignment of British politics must now be faced'. Within weeks the CSD had 25,000 supporters, including fourteen MPs (thirteen Labour and one Conservative), a putative alliance between it and the Liberals led both the main parties in most polls, and the launch of a fully fledged political party now seemed inevitable. Amid a blaze of newspaper and TV coverage estimated to be worth £20 million, on 26 March 1981 the Social Democratic Party (SDP) was launched by the Gang of Four.

The reactions of the two main parties were predictably dismissive or embittered; among Liberals, those who shared Steel's enthusiasm for alliances were emboldened, and in the atmosphere of euphoria, novelty and uncertainty about what the SDP would constitute, sceptics mostly reserved judgement. Even so, Cyril Smith had already declared on television that any party into which the CSD formed itself should be 'strangled at birth'.[37]

Ignoring critics such as Smith, Steel took the opportunity to forge ahead with negotiations, and between April and June produced a joint statement of principles with the SDP leadership confirming that 'our two parties wish to avoid fighting each other in elections'.[38] In July there came the first electoral test of the SDP's strength, when Jenkins fought a by-election in the unpromising safe Labour seat of Warrington, winning 42 per cent of the vote and reducing a Labour majority of over 10,000 to under 2,000. The Liberal Party supported Jenkins, and Liberal MPs brought coachloads of activists from Merseyside, Yorkshire and further afield to work for him. Jenkins's narrow defeat was a potent martyrdom – his speech at the count called it 'my first defeat in thirty years in politics' but 'the greatest victory in which I have ever participated' – which resonated with the experience of Liberals used to fighting from a losing position. It created the best possible atmosphere for the formal approval of the alliance at the Liberal assembly in Llandudno in September.

At the assembly the momentum towards endorsement of the Alliance, driven forward by excitable press interest and a packed fringe meeting addressed by Jenkins and Jo Grimond the night before the vote, was unstoppable. Concerns about the independence of the Liberal Party were downplayed, and a mere 112 delegates out of over 2,000 voted against forming an alliance with the SDP, with only isolated figures speaking against it. Famously, Steel allowed his elation to get the better of him and in his closing speech to the assembly called upon Liberals to 'go back to your constituencies and prepare for government'.

The political impact was immediate. The Alliance topped the opinion polls for months, reaching 51 per cent in December 1981, and won two parliamentary by-elections, in Croydon North West in October and in Crosby in November 1981; the latter contest saw Gang of Four member Shirley Williams return to Parliament after having lost her seat in 1979. As with the Liberal revival a decade earlier, the electorate seemed to respond well to a moderate consensual approach in the face of the ideological polarisation of Tories and Labour.

1981–87: Alliance tensions

The formation of the Alliance, however, did not resolve the central problem which divided both the parties within it: the purpose of the arrangement. Although Steel and Jenkins had conceived of the Alliance as a stepping stone to the formation of a single party, sceptics in both the Liberal Party and the SDP saw it as a limited electoral arrangement between two distinct and permanently separate parties. Cyril Smith accepted the Alliance on the grounds that having failed to strangle the SDP the next best option was to marry it; David Owen expressed a similar view from the Social Democrats' side, urging that 'we should guard against our two-party Alliance becoming before the next election, de facto, a single Alliance Party':

> Before establishing the SDP some thought was given to whether Britain would be better governed by having four parties – Labour, Social Democrat, Liberal and Conservative. There were important arguments of principle about the identity of our new party, as well as a political argument about the long-term appeal of the new party and of the Liberals, which tended towards four parties. We believed, and expressed this belief in the Limehouse Declaration, that there was a definable philosophy of social democracy that was unrepresented by any party in British politics, and that it would provide the electoral basis for a totally new party.[39]

Owen pointed to the fact that most members of the new party had never been involved in politics before as evidence that the SDP had 'identified and mobilised a new political constituency in the country'. He made this case the basis of his bid for the leadership of the SDP in a contest with Jenkins after the latter had re-entered the Commons as winner of the Glasgow Hillhead by-election in March 1982. Though Owen lost, he showed that 44 per cent of the SDP's members were prepared to back his more robust view of the party's long-term independence. This strategic dispute within both Alliance parties was reflected in three problems which became running sores between 1981 and the 1983 general election – candidate selection, policy and leadership, all of which exemplified differences of culture and approach between the two parties.

The question of candidate selection had been a source of controversy since the prospect of an electoral pact had been raised. Established Liberal candidates were unsurprisingly reluctant to abandon their campaigns for office in favour of unknown newcomers or, worse still, sitting MPs whom they had been seeking to remove. Conversely, those Liberals who recognised little difference between themselves and the SDP and whose priority it was to cement their relationship as closely as possible were prepared for the party to make more sacrifices than some of their colleagues. The tension this produced was immediately demonstrated in the Croydon North West by-election in October 1981, at which sitting Liberal candidate Bill Pitt successfully rallied his local activists and elements of the press to resist sustained pressure from Steel and the SDP urging him to stand down in favour of Shirley Williams. Pitt won the by-election to become the first new MP of the Alliance era, giving strength to the demands of Liberals suspicious of such pressure and keen to resist the 'political celebrity' culture of the SDP leadership.

When negotiations about which of the two parties should fight each parliamentary seat got under way in earnest this resistance was replicated in every region. At issue was the number of seats to be fought – the SDP sought parity, whereas sceptical Liberals such as Tony Greaves talked in terms of the new party fighting as few as 100 – and in particular the claims of each party to the most winnable seats. Bill Rodgers, who led the SDP negotiating team, became frustrated that 'everything was slow going because the Liberals were unorganised', and eventually suspended discussions at the end of 1981. It was not until autumn the following year – less than a year before the next election – that seat allocation was finally concluded, and in the end the SDP fought 311 seats and the Liberals 322. In four seats Liberals declined to stand down in favour of SDP candidates, and some Liberal MPs refused to support SDP candidates in certain seats.

In the following Parliament, from 1983 to 1987, seat distribution was described in one academic account as 'the main preoccupation' of the Alliance,[40] and was, Rodgers remembered, 'in some ways more stressful' than before 1983.[41] The controversy was made more complex by the use of 'joint selection' in some seats, so that Liberals and Social Democrats in the constituency would all vote as to who their candidate would be. Owen regarded this process as a stalking horse for merger, and was pleased to see his Chief Whip John Cartwright warn that 'any political party which gives up its right to choose its candidates in accordance with its own constitution inevitably surrenders its right to a continued independent existence'.[42] Nonetheless, some eighty seats chose their Alliance candidates in this way for the 1987 general election and still more used 'joint closed selection' in which members of both parties chose from a shortlist drawn from only one party. The outcome was slightly to restore Liberal superiority, with 327 Liberal candidates coming forward to the SDP's 306.

Like arguments about candidate selection, the policy differences between the SDP and Liberals were not so great as was often supposed by outside observers, but where they existed, their significance was amplified because they reflected the debate about the wider relationship between the parties.

In fact much of the initial criticism of the SDP had been, perhaps inevitably for a new organisation started at national level, its absence of detailed policy. Its initial statement, 'Twelve Tasks for Social Democrats', committed the party in general terms to constitutional reform, a mixed economy, 'multilateral, not unilateral' disarmament and membership of the EEC. However, satirical propaganda joked that the SDP would 'take the politics out of politics', and Denis Healey dismissed the Twelve Tasks as including everything except being kind to dogs. Some early research suggested that 'on any one issue, between 34 and 68 per cent of SDP supporters are ignorant about where the party stands' and even that most Social Democrats disagreed with EEC membership.[43] In practice, on many issues the SDP appeared simply to defend the post-war Butskellite mixed-economy consensus rather than anything more radical; Lord Dahrendorf, one of its sympathisers, accused the party of 'wanting a better yesterday'.[44] On other topics, however, particularly over constitutional reform, the SDP came to share the analysis of its Liberal colleagues.

Having agreed to fight elections together, the two Alliance parties needed to draw up a joint manifesto. As the SDP's policy profile sharpened, Liberals such as Meadowcroft and Social Democrats like Owen emphasised the distinctive qualities of their own party's position, and the need to protect it from being diluted or blurred by the other half of the Alliance. The Social Democrats were keener on economic growth than on the environmental protection many Liberals feared it would jeopardise; Liberals were opposed to nuclear power whereas the SDP favoured it; Social Democrats were planners where Liberals were decentralisers. In Meadowcroft's words: 'the vast expanse of soulless council estates, the confusion of mobility with roads, and above all the wanton destruction of urban neighbourliness, are the products of the social democratic consensus of the post-war years'.[45]

The most high-profile split between the parties' official positions, however, was in the field of defence. The stated position of the SDP had from the outset been in favour of retaining the UK's independent nuclear deterrent – one of the central issues on which the Gang of Four had left the Labour Party – while the Liberals had long been more sceptical about nuclear defence and there was a significant unilateralist strand within the party. Although in 1984 the party had reversed its opposition to the British nuclear deterrent, in 1981 and 1984 the Liberal assembly voted against the siting of US cruise missiles in Britain.

At the 1983 election the issue was managed deftly enough. Although in 1982 there had been some tension during the Falklands War, with the Liberals being somewhat more sceptical than their SDP colleagues, the manifesto for the following year's election paid tribute to the courage of the troops who had fought in that conflict, and accepted membership of NATO and 'the need for a nuclear component in the NATO deterrent'. It stressed that 'our defence polices reject both Labour's one-sided disarmament and the Conservatives' escalation of the nuclear arms race' and called for a 150-km-wide nuclear-weapons-free zone to be established in Europe.

Over the next four years, however, circumstances made such a compromise impossible. Firstly, the leadership of the SDP passed from Roy Jenkins to David Owen, the former defence minister and Foreign Secretary whose commitment to a British nuclear defence capability had been a more decisive factor in his decision to leave the Labour Party than had been the case for Jenkins. Owen had once reacted angrily when accused by the Conservatives of being 'soft' on nuclear defence, saying that he would prefer to be accused of marital infidelity. Shortly after becoming SDP leader he wrote that 'the objective, political and strategic considerations continue to reinforce the view that Britain should remain as long as financially feasible a nuclear-weapons state' and that greater European co-operation in defence was the best way of counter-balancing the Cold War superpowers.[46]

Secondly, the issue arose during the 1983 Parliament of how and whether Britain's Polaris nuclear missiles should be replaced in the coming decade. Labour's position was that there should be no replacement, while the Conservatives were committed to the new Trident missile system; the Alliance had to find a distinctive and united response. In 1984, the two leaders set up a Joint Commission on Defence and Disarmament, but by early 1986 Owen was becoming worried by reports that its SDP members were looking for a compromise solution on a replacement for Polaris; he concluded that the Commission was 'up to no good'.[47] Following (inaccurate) press reports in May that the

Commission would come out against any replacement of Polaris, Owen spoke out. At a meeting of the Council for Social Democracy at Southport he loaded his rejection of the Commission's view with the added implication that the SDP's independent appeal was at stake:

> There are voices that tell me that our policy ... should be determined not on the basis of facts, not on the merits, but on whether we can find a form of words which will keep various strands of the party happy, and even more importantly, keep our Liberal partners with us as well. I must tell you bluntly, that if that becomes the guiding principle, then we too will become vulnerable to the Thatcher challenge.

'No leader of any political party', he went on, 'can stand before the British electorate and refuse to answer the question' of what to do about replacing Polaris. The 'fudging and mudging' of the Commission's position 'would get and would deserve a belly laugh from the British electorate'. The Owenite party newspaper, *The Social Democrat*, pointed up 'the clear differences of opinion' within the Commission.

Owen's passionate stance on nuclear defence was clear, but the underlying issue for him was whether the SDP had any long-term role in British politics. As David Watt, a friend of Owen's, wrote in *The Times*, 'an agreement at all costs suits the Liberal mergerites and those who want to cut Dr Owen down to size'.[48] Owen himself believed that 'the question was whether we had yet become a Liberal Party Mark II'.[49] Liberal critics of the Alliance, and others who simply disagreed with Owen over nuclear defence, took exactly the same view as him about the significance of the debate: upon it rested not merely the policies of the parties, but also their relationship to each other.

Owen's public criticisms of the Commission before it had even produced its report infuriated its SDP members, however, who had not been consulted about his remarks; they reacted against what they saw as his growing tendency to run the party as a one-man band. In June Shirley Williams, president of the SDP, made it clear on BBC Radio 4 that: 'it does not follow that what the leader says is the same and identical with the policy of the party'. In the light of the very public row, the Alliance dropped sharply in the opinion polls. Owen and Steel decided that they needed to demonstrate Alliance unity, and lit on the idea of Anglo-French cooperation over nuclear weapons, building on the Commission's support for greater European collaboration on defence.

The SDP's support for an independent British nuclear deterrent, and for investigation of the practicality of a 'European minimum deterrent', was backed by the party's National Committee and its September conference in Harrogate. The mood at the Liberal assembly at Eastbourne, however, was very different. Delegates were sceptical of the new proposal (there was no evidence that anyone, including the French, actually wanted it) and concerned at what they saw as Owen's attempt to scupper the Commission's findings and railroad Steel into a different policy, and also at the priority Steel appeared to be affording to demonstrating Alliance coherence rather than defending his own party's policy. In a tense debate, the assembly split evenly over the issue, with MPs Michael Meadowcroft, Archy Kirkwood and Simon Hughes promoting a resolution calling for a non-nuclear approach to any European co-operation over defence. Meadowcroft insisted that it was important to assert the assembly's right to make policy as the starting point for negotiations with the SDP; Hughes demolished the credibility of the 'Euro-bomb' proposal; and Tony Greaves declared that 'this is a debate about values and principles and the soul of the Liberal Party. If we abandon those what is our contribution? We may as well join the SDP.'[30] The assembly voted by 652 to 625 to welcome European cooperation over defence policy 'provided that such a defence capability is non-nuclear'; this was widely (though inaccurately) reported in the media as a vote for unilateralism. Steel described the decision in his leader's speech at the end of the assembly as 'a breathtaking misjudgement'.[31]

Simon Hughes (1951–)

Born in Cheshire, Hughes was educated in Cardiff, Brecon, Selwyn College, Cambridge, and the College of Europe in Bruges; he subsequently practised as a barrister. He joined the Liberal Party at university and fought GLC and council seats in Bermondsey in the early 1980s.

He was selected to fight the Bermondsey by-election in February 1983. In a bitter campaign, fought against the background of an acrimonious split in the Labour Party (with a 'Real Bermondsey Labour' candidate opposing the official, left-wing, Labour candidate Peter Tatchell), Hughes won the seat with the highest swing between two parties in British political history – 50.9 per cent from Labour to Liberal. An energetic community campaigner, he has held the seat ever since, and helped to build up the party's strength on Southwark council, which it ran in 2002–10.

Within the Liberal Party and Liberal Democrats, Hughes rapidly gained a reputation as the darling of the radical activists, opposing the leadership on a number of occasions, most notably over the proposal for European cooperation over nuclear weapons in the Alliance defence commission report of 1986. It was his speech more than any other which swung the Eastbourne assembly against the platform. He was also instrumental, as environment spokesman for the Liberal Party in 1983–87 and the Liberal Democrats in 1990–94, in establishing the party as the greenest of the main parties.

He stood for the Liberal Democrat leadership in 1999, coming second, and in 2006, coming third. He served as the president of the party in 2004–08, and in 2010 he was elected as the parliamentary party's deputy leader.

The row over nuclear weapons damaged the credibility of the Alliance less than a year before the next general election, undermining the credibility and public appeal it had built up after by-election victories at Portsmouth South in 1984, Brecon & Radnor in 1985 and Ryedale in 1986, together with good local election results. Those sceptical about the possibility of the parties working more closely together, especially the Owenites in the SDP, pointed to the natural cleavage between Liberal and Social

Democrat ideologies which had been exposed; others blamed the failure of leadership by both Owen, artificially generating conflict and unwilling to make any compromise, and Steel, too willing to make concessions to achieve an Alliance policy at the expense of Liberal independence.[52]

There were differences between the SDP and the Liberals about other policy issues, including nuclear energy and industrial relations, in particular the miners' strike of 1984–85. Although at the formation of the SDP it had been generally assumed that the new party would occupy a position to the left of the Liberals, in fact Owen took his party steadily to the right, coming to believe that much of what Mrs Thatcher was doing in terms of breaking the power of the unions, introducing competition into public services and privatising nationalised industries, was correct in principle, even if not always in detail. This caused some problems within the SDP, as Jenkins and his followers generally opposed this rightward shift in approach.

The two Alliance parties came increasingly to differ over future strategy in the event of the election of a House of Commons with no overall majority; Owen and his allies in the SDP gave the impression of being ready to work with the Conservatives under Thatcher much more easily than with Neil Kinnock's Labour Party, whereas the reverse was true for Steel and most Liberals. These were issues on which Liberals and Social Democrats had sincere and sometimes contrasting convictions, but the impact of these debates was far greater because they heralded future arguments over the relationship between the parties. Each time Liberal and Social Democrat opinion differed, anti-mergerites in both parties took a stand on it as a matter of party identity; mergerites compromised so as to prove the common ground and goodwill they shared.

1983–87: The two Davids

Inevitably, the media's interest in the tensions within the Alliance focused on the question of which of the two party leaders led the Alliance and how they got along with each other. The relationship between David Steel and Roy Jenkins was not without its difficulties, but these were eased by their personal amity, their difference in age and their common purpose in bringing their parties closer together. As early as March 1982 the two leaders agreed that although Steel would take a leading campaigning role in the coming election, Jenkins, being so much more experienced, would be the Alliance's 'Prime Minister designate'.

This ran counter to strong opinion poll evidence that Steel was more popular among members of both parties and among voters, however, and during the 1983 election, Steel became worried by Jenkins's poor media impact and the 'ornate gothic constructions' of his speech. Even the SDP's MPs and staff expressed misgivings about his effectiveness as the campaign approached. Steel convened a meeting at his Ettrick Bridge home during the campaign where he tried to persuade Jenkins to abandon the title of Prime Minister Designate; the attempt was unsuccessful, though at a press conference it was acknowledged that the Liberal leader would have a higher profile in the remainder of the campaign.

Alliance opinion poll ratings improved to the point where the Liberals and Social Democrats were jointly challenging Labour for second place in the popular vote; Margaret Thatcher became worried enough to intervene on her old enemy's behalf, insisting that the Labour Party would never die, and praising the courage of those who had stayed in Labour to fight the left. Although he was understandably anxious at Jenkins's electoral weaknesses, Steel could reassure himself with the thought that in the long run Jenkins shared his view of the two parties' destiny; and secondly that – given Jenkins was nearly twenty years his senior – Steel could reasonably expect to inherit the leadership of any merged party that would eventually be created.

The Alliance manifesto – boldly sub-titled 'Programme for Government' – offered core Liberal commitments such as reform of the Lords and the electoral system, and familiar social democrat strategies such as increased government borrowing and a statutory incomes policy to tackle inflation. The campaign, however, often struck a negative note, highlighting the big parties' weaknesses rather than the distinctive appeal of the Alliance; Thatcher and Foot were parodied in billboard posters as the Tin Man and the Straw Man from the Wizard of Oz, with the captions 'I wish I had a heart' and 'I wish I had a brain'.

The final result of the 1983 election was a bitter disappointment, with Liberal and SDP candidates gaining 25.4 per cent of the vote – the highest poll of any third party since 1923, and within almost 2 per cent of Labour – and yet winning only twenty-three parliamentary seats, six SDP and seventeen Liberal. For all its fanfare, the SDP had added little to the parliamentary outcome, securing a smaller share of votes per seat than the Liberals, and losing all but four of the seats of defecting Labour and Conservative MPs, and gaining only one new one; all of its by-election gains were lost apart from Roy Jenkins's seat. Apart from the MPs, only one other SDP candidate was in the list of the top fifty seats, by share of the vote, achieved by Alliance candidates, and at the following election in 1987 only sixteen Social Democrats figured in the fifty most attainable seats for the Alliance. Even a 5 per cent uniform swing from the Conservatives to the Alliance (an optimistic prospect on top of the groundbreaking 1983 poll) would deliver only ten new SDP seats.

1983 general election (9 June)			
	Votes	%	MPs
Liberal-SDP Alliance	7,780,949	25.4	23
Liberal			17
SDP			6
Conservative	**13,012,316**	**42.4**	**397**
Labour	8,456,934	27.6	209
SNP	331,975	1.1	2
Plaid Cymru	125,309	0.4	2
Others	953,826	3.1	17
Total	30,661,309		650

In the wake of the 1983 election Liberals sceptical about the Alliance – reinforced in Parliament by the election of Michael Meadowcroft as MP for Leeds West – sought to retrieve control of the party and subjected Steel to 'a barrage of criticism'[53] about the dual leadership. Over the summer, David Alton and Cyril Smith circulated a strategy paper calling for the election of a deputy leader. Steel had taken a sabbatical to recover from the election and was so taken aback by the criticism on his return that he wrote a letter of resignation, only to withdraw it the following day.

The main leadership problem after 1983, however, was Steel's relationship with the new leader of the SDP, David Owen, who took over from Roy Jenkins without a contest. Steel had worked well with Owen during the Lib-Lab Pact, describing him as being 'absolutely straight' about the introduction of proportional representation and 'effusive' about Steel's performance at the Blackpool assembly but in the context of the Alliance their relationship deteriorated because Owen was so strongly opposed to merger. Steel acknowledged his irritation at being presented on the satirical TV show *Spitting Image* as a squeaky-voiced, smaller junior partner tucked into the top pocket of Owen's dinner jacket.

As the 1983–87 Parliament progressed, Steel's frustration at Owen's resistance to joint candidate selection or policy convergence grew; privately he told Robert Mugabe, Prime Minister of Zimbabwe, that Owen was harder to deal with than Mugabe's rival former guerrilla leader, Joshua Nkomo. Publicly he said that Owen was 'not the easiest person in the world to work with. He never has been in any post he has held',[54] and compared their relationship to the marriage of Sybil Thorndike to Lewis Casson; when asked if she had ever considered leaving her husband, Thorndike answered: 'divorce, never; murder, often'.

Owen was widely regarded as a talented but conceited man who gave little credit to others' opinions; the main academic study of the SDP places his personality somewhere between those of Napoleon and of Baron Munchausen. Owen took pleasure in repeating the comment of his former Cabinet colleague Denis Healey that 'the good fairies gave the young doctor almost everything: thick dark locks, matinee idol features, a lightning intelligence – unfortunately the bad fairy made him a shit'.[55] Roy Jenkins declared in the middle of the row over defence that Owen was 'not fit to hold public office',[56] and also likened him to the Javanese upas tree, poisoning all life around it. Owen himself said that his initial relations with Steel as leader were 'edgy but civil' but acknowledged publicly that they were 'not bosom pals' and recalled that when a child's letter asking Owen what he would do if the world were ending went accidentally to Steel's office, the latter passed it on with a note saying that the end of the world was 'more your department'.[57]

Rivalry and distrust between political leaders is as unremarkable as it is – usually – manageable. What made the relationship between Steel and Owen especially hard to resolve were their divergent agendas for the future of their parties. On policy matters they shared a good deal of common ground, even where elements of their parties were at odds; but on merger they were irreconcilable, and suspected one another of manipulation in pursuit of their respective agendas. Owen believed Steel was conspiring with pro-merger Social Democrats to undermine the SDP's distinct identity, for example by leaking the conclusions of the Joint Commission on Defence and Disarmament in 1986. Liberals resented Owen's dismissal of the report, and Steel distrusted Owen's promises to consider merger in the future. Though he vetoed any discussion of merger at the SDP's Salford conference in 1983, Owen gave assurances two years later that 'after the next election the issue of merger or of a closer relationship will come back on the agenda and rightly so'.[58] The fact that Steel and Owen were almost exact contemporaries in age and parliamentary experience also meant that Steel could not even look to time to offer a route out of the confrontation.

The uneasy relationship between the leaders and their parties, and between the pro- and anti-mergerites in both parties, was maintained until the 1987 general election. The year began with a high-profile Alliance rally at the Barbican Centre in London, at which the Alliance team and programme for government were launched. By-election victories for the SDP in Greenwich in February and for the Liberals in Truro in March (following the death of Liberal MP David Penhaligon in a car accident) were encouraging, particularly the Greenwich result, where the SDP took a seat from Labour for the first time. Local election results in May were also positive, with the Alliance polling the equivalent of a national vote of 27 per cent (to Labour's 31 per cent and the Conservatives' 40 per cent). This was the highest base from which any third party had launched a general election campaign since the 1920s.

On the back of the local election results, Mrs Thatcher called the general election for 11 June 1987. During the campaign, the two Alliance leaders held daily joint press conferences in the morning and public 'Ask the Alliance' meetings in the evenings to reinforce the impression of unity. However, at the end of the second week of campaigning Steel asserted that it was 'unimaginable' that the Alliance would support a Thatcher minority government, while the next day Owen said the Labour Party failed on 'the one fundamental issue' of 'the security of our country.'[59]

The faltering campaign, the opening broadcast of which featured extended soft-focus film of Greenwich by-election winner Rosie Barnes petting a rabbit in a field, struggled to stimulate any improvement in the Alliance's poll rating, and the dual leadership, described politely in academic commentary as producing a 'blurred image', came in for particular criticism. An exasperated Des Wilson, chair of the Alliance Planning Group, later wrote that: 'I cannot believe there is anybody who was centrally involved in the Alliance campaign who would wish to repeat the experience of having two leaders in two buses in two different parts of the country with two different views on strategy, effectively conducting two different campaigns'; John Pardoe, who chaired the campaign committee, went as far as to say that: 'I did not much want to be governed by either and the thought of being governed by both was too appalling for words.'[60]

The election campaign saw a decline from the 25 per cent share of support which the Alliance had enjoyed in 1983 to 22 per cent. When the results came in – with only five Social Democrats and seventeen Liberals in the Commons – the two leaders drew their own conclusions; Steel declared on election night that 'we must undergo our internal debate about the future of the Alliance',[61] while Owen told the press the next morning that 'the endless examining of our own navels on whether or not we should exist is probably one of our greatest weaknesses. I have never doubted that we should exist.'[62] 'We' meant, as it always did for Owen, the SDP. The end of the Alliance had begun.

1987 general election (11 June)			
	Votes	%	MPs
Liberal-SDP Alliance	7,341,651	22.6	22
Liberal			17
SDP			5
Conservative	13,760,935	42.2	376
Labour	10,029,270	30.8	229
SNP	416,473	1.3	3
Plaid Cymru	123,599	0.4	3
Others	858,276	2.6	17
Total	32,530,204		650

1987–88: Merger

The process by which the Liberals and Social Democrats became the Liberal Democrats lasted only nine months, but involved three identifiable phases: a 'warm-up' phase; an intense negotiating phase, during which the process came close to collapse; and the completion of the merger. It was a debate the parties would inevitably engage in at some point, but its conduct, the overall outcome, and its impact upon the fortunes of the party which eventually emerged need not have been so damaging as turned out to be the case.

Following the 1987 general election, battle lines were drawn in both parties (but especially in the SDP) between the pro- and anti-merger camps. Before the SDP conference and Liberal assembly of the autumn, a phoney war was conducted, partly in private but also in the media, over how the parties' relationship should develop and how the question should be decided. David Owen's press conference on the morrow of the general election poll indicating that he would resist merger was supported by the *Social Democrat*, which condemned early moves by Steel to consider merger as splitting the Alliance, and claimed that all SDP MPs were resisting merger. Within two days, however, Shirley Williams and Roy Jenkins called publicly for merger, and leading paid officials of the party departed to start the 'Yes to Unity' campaign.

Among Liberals the debate was more layered and nuanced, focusing upon the form of merger and the compromises which it would entail rather than outright opposition; Tony Greaves told his local press that he hoped merger would take the form of Owen and his supporters disappearing into the wilderness because there was no need for the SDP: 'I do not think they have brought anything extra which would not have been achieved by the more Liberal-minded members of the SDP joining the Liberal Party'. He also called for Steel to resign, a demand which became associated with doubts about merger for some Liberals.[63] On the same day, five days after the 1987 election, Steel formally opened the protracted and rancorous public debate with an open memorandum to colleagues calling for the 'democratic fusion' of the parties, and was encouraged by the large body of approving correspondence he received from Liberal activists.[64]

At the end of June the SDP National Committee ordered a ballot of party members, offering the alternatives of opening merger talks or Owen's option of 'a closer constitutional framework for the Alliance, short of merger'. At this time Charles Kennedy broke away from the other SDP MPs to support the merger cause. In August the result of the ballot showed that 57 per cent favoured negotiations aimed at merger; in an early sign of the toll merger would take on membership, a quarter of SDP members did not vote. Owen promptly resigned, to be replaced by Robert Maclennan; although Maclennan had campaigned against merger, he accepted the verdict of the membership.

Robert Maclenann (1936–)

Maclennan was born in 1936 in Glasgow. Educated at Glasgow Academy, Oxford, Cambridge and Columbia, he became a barrister. At the 1966 election he defeated the Liberal MP George Mackie to take Caithness & Sutherland for Labour. He was a junior minister in the Department of Prices and Consumer Protection in 1974–79.

He was one of the first MPs to join the new Council for Social Democracy in 1981, and helped to draft the SDP's constitution; unlike most of his SDP colleagues, he held his seat in 1983 and 1987. Although he campaigned against merger in the original ballot in 1987, unlike Owen and his followers he was not opposed to it in principle; he just thought it was premature. Distressed at the acrimonious split within the SDP, he tried hard to dissuade Owen from resigning as leader, and hoped that the merger process could be made to create a party of which Owen could still be a member. He was persuaded by Shirley Williams to stand for the leadership after Owen's resignation, and was elected unopposed. He led the SDP negotiating team in the merger talks.

Together with David Steel, he served as the Social and Liberal Democrats' joint interim leader until a leadership election could be held, and was the Liberal Democrats' president in 1994–98. In 1996–97 he negotiated the eponymous agreement with Robin Cook, for Labour, on an agreed package of constitutional reforms the new government would implement after the 1997 election. He stood down from the Commons in 2001 and is now a Liberal Democrat peer.

The following month both the SDP's conference at Portsmouth and the Liberal assembly at Harrogate voted to open negotiations for merger. Some misgivings were expressed at Harrogate about the pace and direction of the process, but very few delegates opposed it outright. In the SDP however, Owen made it clear that he would continue a separate party with the support of those – including two of his five MPs – who did not want merger, whatever the result of the negotiations. It was a strategy which was to undermine the work of the joint negotiating team of representatives from both parties, which began at the end of September.

It was in this second, negotiating, phase that tensions among Liberals came to a head. The joint negotiating team included both enthusiasts and sceptics for the merger, but the Social Democrats wholly opposed to merger – Owen and his closest allies – were absent. This led to a preoccupation on the part of some of the SDP members of the team with the likely reaction of Owen and his supporters to the outcome, a preoccupation which was resented by some Liberals.

The central areas of argument were twofold: the party's constitution and its initial policy platform. The SDP's insistence that the principle of 'one member, one vote' for leadership elections – on which their founders had broken with Labour in 1981 – should be enshrined in the constitution of the new party was accepted without much difficulty by the Liberals, but disputes about the power of activists within the new party caused more problems. Social Democrat negotiators were keen to avoid replicating the Liberal Party Council, which they regarded as dominated by activists unrepresentative of the wider membership; the eventual compromise was reached of having two conferences each year, but compared to the SDP, conferences had greater power over the policy-making process. For their part, the Liberal attachment to a decentralised structure for the party was expressed in agreement on a federal structure, with 'state' parties in England, Scotland and Wales.

Another key constitutional question – the new party's name – was chiefly symbolic, but nonetheless fiercely contested. It was this which was raised with David Steel more often than any other in the correspondence he received from activists over the summer. New SDP leader Robert Maclennan objected to the name 'Liberal Democrats', which most Liberals favoured because, it was said, he envisaged Owen on the day of the party's launch like an usher at a wedding, saying: 'Liberal Democrats this side; Social Democrats this side'. In Maclennan's view, the name would have to stress the SDP's incorporation into the party. Steel, on the other hand, received written demands from his MPs that the term 'Liberal' should remain in the party's title, and Tony Greaves wrote in his *Liberal News* column that he did not mind what the name of the merged party was, so long as it could be shortened to 'Liberal'. The title 'Social and Liberal Democrats' which was ultimately adopted proved cumbersome and unnerved some Liberals, especially when later shortened to 'Democrats'. By September 1990, when the now-familiar 'Liberal Democrat' name had been agreed, pollsters Gallup found that three-quarters of respondents either did not know the party's name or got it wrong.

The argument over policy concerned how far the party needed to commit itself to specific positions at its launch and what those positions might be. Again Maclennan pressed for clear commitments which would reassure potential defectors to Owen's 'continuing' SDP. His negotiating team insisted that a commitment to membership of NATO should appear in the preamble to the new party's constitution, in the face of considerable Liberal disquiet, but it was the policy statement *Voices and Choices for All* which he published with Steel (without consultation with their negotiating teams, who focused only on structures) in January 1988 which caused uproar. It proposed, among other policies, the replacement of the Polaris missile system with Trident, the ending of universal child benefit and mortgage tax relief and the extension of VAT to children's clothes. Protest erupted from Liberals and Social Democrats alike; the Liberal Party president and chairman met Steel to threaten that the National Executive would disown the statement, at least one MP publicly described it as 'loopy' and one senior party official told *The Times*: 'it's incorrect that there is controversy within the Liberal Party about the document. We're all against it.'[65] A press conference to launch *Voices and Choices for All* was postponed at the last moment, after the document had already been released; *The Guardian*'s leading article despaired that 'fiasco is too mild a word'.[66]

In *The Independent* Peter Jenkins had already written that 'the fights within the Alliance are fights about nothing. The protagonists are engaged in tearing apart the stuff of a dead dream.'[67] Ten days before the Liberal assembly met to finally accept or reject the outcome of the merger negotiations, the divisions within and between the parties had been thrown into sharp relief. Disagreements over the structure and the name of the new party had led four Liberal members of the joint negotiating team, and one Social Democrat, to walk out, but the negotiations at least concluded with agreement on a draft constitution.[68]

By the time the assembly met in Blackpool on 23 January, an identifiable core of anti-merger opinion had developed around former MP and party president-elect Michael Meadowcroft, Tony Greaves and fellow radicals, particularly Young Liberals or members of the Association of Liberal Councillors from the north. They mounted a rearguard action against the 'Merger Now' campaign based upon what they regarded as the centralised nature of the new constitution and their experience of the negotiating process. Meadowcroft warned that 'in a single merged party the option of being loyal to a separate Liberal identity is not available';[69] Greaves reflected after the *Voices and Choices for All* episode that 'this week's events have been first distressing and then astonishing. And full of lessons.'[70] Their campaign had started too late, however; at the assembly, only 385 of over 2,500 delegates voted against the merger package, and a week later the Council for Social Democracy at Sheffield followed suit.

Meadowcroft told the delegates at Blackpool that the Liberal Party had been 'on hire purchase' for seven years. It was to be the last of many times over the years since 1974 that he would appeal to Liberals to assert their independence. Ballots of both parties' members followed. Meadowcroft and Greaves continued to argue 'the case for Liberal renewal' but Blackpool had effectively resolved the issue. 88 per cent of those voting in the Liberal ballot approved the merger but, echoing the SDP's experience eight months earlier, nearly half of Liberal members failed to return their ballot papers. The SDP ballot confirmed the decision, and the Social and Liberal Democrats was launched on 3 March 1988. In the following months, Owen's 'continuing' SDP and Meadowcroft's independent Liberal Party both came into existence, to challenge the merged party for the centre ground.

The controversy over merger was the culmination of a debate which had continued since before 1974 – the question of whether, and if so how, Liberals should co-operate with other parties, and especially with social democrats. In one sense the merger represented the fulfilment of the co-operators' project; Steel called it his proudest moment as a member of the Liberal Party when, 'after 120 years of history, it decided in a mature, deeply serious but completely good-humoured way to take this new step forward'.[71] For the negotiators Tony Greaves and Rachael Pitchford, 'the roots and traditions of Liberalism have been denied', and 'the party appears to have no underlying message or idea of what it stands for and the electorate don't either'.[72]

The course of the merger set back membership and morale and damaged the public's perception of the party. However, the previous fourteen years had shown that the Liberals could gain between a fifth and a quarter of the vote, win thousands of council seats, and play a part in government. The merger also removed the tensions between the Owenites and those in both parties favouring merger, ending a debate which was an inevitable consequence of the formation of a new centre party. However, given its predictability, it is something of an understatement to say that the merger process could have been better managed.

The end of the Alliance was variously described as a Greek tragedy and a civil war, but even these metaphors do not wholly capture what were in fact concurrent, and sometimes bitter, battles within the two parties about their future direction. A better comparison would be the one alluded to by Maclennan: a row between and within two families at a wedding. The merger had opened a Pandora's box of personal animosities, structural tensions and ideological schisms which the Alliance's opponents had always warned about. Many members of both parties left, some into the two breakaway factions but most leaving politics altogether, and the Social and Liberal Democrats started life in a parlous condition in virtually every respect. But, like Pandora's box, the fragile spirit of hope remained.

Further reading

General studies covering this period of the party's history include Chris Cook's *A Short History of the Liberal Party: the Road Back to Power* (Palgrave Macmillan, 2010); David Dutton, *A History of the Liberal Party* (Palgrave Macmillan, 2004); and Roy Douglas, *Liberals: the History of the Liberal and Liberal Democrat Parties* (Hambledon and London, 2005). There is also a useful brief summary by Stephen Ingle, 'Liberals and Social Democrats: End of a Chapter or End of the Book?' in *Talking Politics* vol. 1, no. 2 (winter 1988/89). *Liberal Party Politics* (OUP, 1983), edited by Vernon Bogdanor, contains a series of authoritative chapters on the state of the party in the early stages of the Alliance. The main study of the SDP is by Ivor Crewe and Anthony King, *SDP: the Birth, Life and Death of the Social Democratic Party* (OUP, 1995) – which takes a very downbeat view of the party's impact; more optimistic contemporary commentaries from journalists include Ian Bradley's *Breaking the Mould?* (Martin Robertson, 1981) and Hugh Stephenson's *Claret and Chips: the Rise of the SDP* (Michael Joseph, 1982). Bradley also published *The Strange Rebirth of Liberal Britain* (Chatto and Windus, 1985) which puts the party's fortunes in recent historical context. The first commentary on the Lib-Lab Pact is *The Pact: The Inside Story of the Lib-Lab Government, 1977–78* (Quartet, 1978) by two more journalists, Simon Hoggart and Alistair Michie.

Publications by activists of the period worth reading include *Liberalism Today and Tomorrow* by Michael Meadowcroft (Coventry Liberal Association, 1989) and the detailed account *Merger: the Inside Story* by Rachael Pitchford and Tony Greaves (Liberal Renewal, 1989), both critical of David Steel's leadership of the Liberals. A more favourable account can be found in *Inside the Alliance* (John Martin, 1983) by Jeremy Josephs, Steel's former speech-writer. *The SDP Story* (Hartswood 1987) by Dennis Outwin, a former member of the Council for Social Democracy, is brief but thoughtful, and conveys contemporary atmosphere.

There is a wealth of material written by and about the leading figures in the Liberal Party and SDP during this period. Biographies of Jeremy Thorpe focusing on the Scott affair include *Jeremy Thorpe: A Secret Life* (Fontana, 1979) by Lewis Chester, Magnus Linklater and David May, and *Rinkagate: The Rise and Fall of Jeremy Thorpe* (Bloomsbury, 1996) by Simon Freeman and Barrie Penrose. Thorpe's own account of his work, *In My Own Time: Reminiscences of a Liberal Leader* (Politico's, 1999), focuses on his political career, but offers little substantial new insight. Steel's experiences of the Lib-Lab Pact are set out in his *A House Divided* (Weidenfeld and Nicolson, 1980) and his full autobiography is *Against Goliath: David Steel's Story* (Weidenfeld and Nicolson, 1989). Leading Social Democrat memoirs include *A Life at the Centre* (Macmillan, 1991) by Roy Jenkins, *Fourth Among Equals* (Politico's, 2000) by Bill Rodgers, and David Owen's *Time to Declare* (Penguin, 1990), which give contrasting accounts of the relationships at the top of the Alliance. In addition, Shirley Williams devotes some of *Climbing the Bookshelves* (Virago, 2009) to her experience with the SDP. David Marquand, *The Progressive Dilemma* (Heinemann, 1991) includes a chapter on Owen which recognises both his strengths and weaknesses in the context of the progressive tradition.

Among the memoirs of backbench Liberal MPs, Sir Cyril Smith's *Big Cyril* (W. H. Allen, 1977) goes into some depth about Liberal fortunes in the 1970s; Annette Penhaligon wrote *Penhaligon* (Bloomsbury, 1989), the biography of her husband David, Liberal MP for Truro; and Sir Alan Beith's *A View From the North* (Northumbria University Press, 2008) is particularly valuable as the testimony of the longest-serving Liberal and Liberal Democrat MP. Richard Wainwright's contribution to the Liberal Party is set out in *Richard Wainwright, the Liberals and Liberal Democrats: Unfinished Business* (Manchester University Press, 2011) by Matt Cole – Chapters 10–14 focus on his parliamentary career during the period covered by this chapter.

The perspective of Liberals outside Parliament is reflected in *Campaigning Face to Face* (Book Guild, 2007) by Sir Hugh Jones, the Liberal Party Secretary-General and then Treasurer 1977–87, and *Battle for Power* (Sphere, 1987) by Des Wilson, party president in 1986–87 and chair of the Liberals' general election campaign committee in 1987.

Notes

1 David Steel, *Against Goliath: David Steel's Story* (Weidenfeld and Nicolson, 1989), p. 294.

2 Michael Meadowcroft, *Liberalism Today and Tomorrow* (Coventry Liberal Association, 1989), p. 4.

3 Richard Wainwright, Report to LPO Executive, 20 March 1975.

4 Hugh Jones, *Campaigning Face to Face* (Book Guild, 2007), p. 59.

5 Jo Grimond and Brian Neve, *The Referendum* (Rex Collings, 1975), p. 1.

6 David Butler and Uwe Kitzinger, *The 1975 Referendum* (Macmillan, 1996), pp. 81, 175 and 130. On the last of these pages is a memorandum from Liberal HQ to constituency associations dated March 1975 which states that 'there must be no joint campaigns' and tells activists 'to maintain a distinct and different image for the Liberal Party throughout the campaign and beyond'. Richard Wainwright's report on party finance suggested that advertising space in *Liberal News* could be sold to both the 'Yes' and the 'No' campaigns.

7 Jeremy Thorpe, *In My Own Time* (Politico's, 1999), p. 193.

8 Cited in Philip Whitehead, *The Writing on the Wall: Britain in the Seventies* (Michael Joseph, 1985), p. 139.

9 Interview with Wallace, 19 January 2009.

10 The fullest accounts of the Thorpe resignation are: Lewis Chester, Magnus Linklater and David May, *Jeremy Thorpe: A Secret Life* (Fontana, 1979) and Simon Freeman and Barrie Penrose, *Rinkagate: The Rise and Fall of Jeremy Thorpe* (Bloomsbury, 1996). Thorpe's own account of his life, *In My Own Time,* discusses his leadership of the party only briefly, mentioning 'the so-called Norman Scott Affair' just once (pp. 134–37).

11 Interview with Sir Cyril Smith, 8 January 2000. Smith reported that Byers was 'totally opposed to the membership of the party selecting the leader' because he feared the consequences of MPs and party members expressing divergent views. See also Smith's *Big Cyril* (W. H. Allen, 1977), pp. 219–21, on this and the leadership contest.

12 See Wainwright papers, file 8/19, London School of Economics and Steel, *Against Goliath*, pp. 114–15, in which Steel confirms that Pardoe nicknamed him 'traffic cop' and Cyril Smith said Steel 'couldn't make a bang with a firework in both hands'; Steel satisfied himself with likening Pardoe to A. A. Milne's Tigger and – to Pardoe's fury – suggesting to the press that he wore a hairpiece.

13 David Steel, *A House Divided* (Weidenfeld and Nicolson, 1980), p. 22.

14 David Steel, letter to Liberal candidates, 16 December 1977.

15 Alistair Michie and Simon Hoggart, *The Pact: the Inside Story of the Lib–Lab Government, 1977–78* (Quartet, 1978), p. 149. The assembly was held on 14–18 September.

16 David Steel to Liberal candidates, 24 March 1977.

17 Whitehead, *The Writing on the Wall*, p. 259.

18 Liberal Party press release, 27 June 1977.

19 Undated note in Liberal Party Papers, File 19/3, London School of Economics.

20 Sir George Schuster to David Steel, 16 June 1977. Schuster (1881–1982) had been a Liberal candidate before World War One, Liberal National MP for Walsall in 1938–45, and a close friend of Asquith and Violet Bonham Carter.

21 Steel, *Against Goliath*, p. 134.

22 *Liberator*, December–January 1977–78, p. 1.

23 'The Liberals set their course', *The Times*, 23 January 1978.

24 Philippa Norris, *British By-elections: the Volatile Electorate* (Clarendon, 1990), Appendix. In fairness it should be pointed out that in no by-election of the October 1974 Parliament did any Liberal candidate match the party's performance at the preceding general election, but the decline became much more marked after April 1977. Only in one of the previous contests had the drop in the vote exceeded 10 per cent. See also Anthony King (ed.), *British Political Opinion 1937–2000* (Politico's, 2001), pp. 11–13, on Gallup's monthly poll ratings.

25 Quoted in Mark Oaten, *Coalitions* (Harriman House, 2007) p. 193.

26 Steel, *Against Goliath*, p. 148.

27 David Butler and Dennis Kavanagh, *The British General Election of 1979* (Macmillan, 1979), p. 159.

28 The two MPs who lost vote share were Richard Wainwright and Geraint Howells, although Wainwright increased the size of his majority, and Howells's vote was almost unaffected. The five 'survivors' had the national vote swing come into effect in Liberal seats would have been Wainwright, Howells, Jo Grimond, David Steel and Cyril Smith.

29 'Jenkins "never asked to join the Liberals"', *The Guardian*, 16 September 1981.

30 Steel, *Against Goliath*, pp. 216–17.

31 David Marquand to David Steel, 11 December 1987, in which he reminds Steel of their earlier meeting.

32 The moderate Labour perspective on these events is set out in Austin Mitchell's *Four Years in the Death of the Labour Party* (Methuen, 1983). A less partisan account is to be found in David Kogan and Maurice Kogan, *The Battle for the Labour Party* (Fontana, 1982).

33 Grimond was reviewing the Dimbleby Lecture for *The Listener*; cited in Steel, *Against Goliath*, p. 217.

34 Williams made this remark in a broadcast, but it was reported in *The Times*, 9 June 1980.

35 Michael Meadowcroft, *Liberal Values for a New Decade* (Liberal Publications Department, 1980), p. 1.

36 Josephs, *Inside the Alliance*, p. 88.

37 Cited in Ian Bradley, *Breaking the Mould?* (Martin Robertson, 1981), p. 90.

38 'A Fresh Start for Britain: statement of principles commended by a joint working party of Liberals and Social Democrats', 16 June 1981

39 David Owen, 'The Enabling Society' in Wayland Kennet (ed.), *The Rebirth of Britain* (Weidenfeld and Nicolson, 1982), pp. 241–42.

40 Byron Criddle, 'Candidates', in Butler and Kavanagh, *The British General Election of 1987*, p. 196.

41 Bill Rodgers, *Fourth Among Equals* (Politico's, 2000), p. 227. Pages 222–28 of this memoir explore the issues of candidate selection in more detail.

42 David Owen, *Time to Declare* (Penguin, 1992), pp. 601–02.

43 Bradley, *Breaking the Mould?*, p. 148.

44 Quoted in Jeremy Josephs, *Inside the Alliance* (John Martin, 1983), pp. 85–86.

45 *Alliance* magazine, September 1982.

46 David Owen, *A Future that will Work* (Penguin, 1984), p. 154 and Chapter 9, 'European Security Responsibilities' passim.

47 Owen, *Time to Declare*, p. 642.

48 David Watt, 'When it's best to disagree', *The Times*, 6 June 1986.

49 Owen, *Time to Declare*, p. 654.

50 Des Wilson, *Battle for Power: the inside story of the Alliance and the 1987 General Election* (Sphere, 1987), p. 49.

51 Steel, *Against Goliath*, p. 273

52 A particularly detailed account of this view of the episode, identifying nine leadership mistakes in managing the decision over defence, is given by Duncan Brack in Chapter 15 of Duncan Brack (ed.), *President Gore and Other Things that Never Happened* (Politico's, 2006).

53 Steel, *Against Goliath*, p. 249.

54 Ibid., pp. 185 and 266.

55 Owen, *Time to Declare*, p. 624.

56 Steel, *Against Goliath*, p. 266.

57 Owen, *Time to Declare*, p. 611.

58 Steel, *Against Goliath*, p. 282.

59 Butler and Kavanagh, *The British General Election of 1987*, p. 115.

60 Ivor Crewe and Martin Harrop (eds.), *Political Communications: The General Election of 1987* (CUP, 1989), p. 58.

61 Butler and Kavanagh, *The British General Election of 1987*, p. 122.

62 Owen, *Time to Declare*, p. 707.

63 *Lancashire Evening Telegraph*, 16 June 1987.

64 Dozens of examples of this correspondence can be seen in the Steel papers at the LSE archives, file A/5/3, including letters from a wide variety of activists as well as leading academics supporting the Alliance such as Professors David Marquand and Richard Layard.

65 Quoted in Rachael Pitchford and Tony Greaves, *Merger: the Inside Story* (Liberal Renewal, 1989), p. 131.

66 *The Guardian*, 14 January 1988.

67 *The Independent*, 22 December 1987.

68 The SDP negotiator John Grant, always a sceptic over merger, left on 9 December 1987 because of repeated policy disputes and what he saw as 'a Liberal takeover'; the following month four of the eight negotiators elected by the Liberal assembly resigned. For Michael Meadowcroft the breaking point was the proposed commitment of the new party from the outset to NATO; for Rachael Pitchford, Tony Greaves and Peter Knowlson it was the proposed name of the party.

69 Michael Meadowcroft, 'A case of political suicide', *The Times*, 14 January 1988.

70 Tony Greaves, 'Liberals must remain true – and not become blue', *The Guardian*, 15 January 1988.

71 Steel, *Against Goliath*, p. 293.
72 Pitchford and Greaves, *Merger: the Inside Story*, p. 143.

Chapter 10

From Protest to Power: The Liberal Democrats (1988–2010)

Duncan Brack

If the story of the Liberal Party throughout the twentieth century was dramatic in its ups and downs, the history of the merged party, the Liberal Democrats, has proved just as remarkable, and over a much shorter period – from near-extinction, through a failed realignment of the left, a period of rapidly changing leaders, and finally into government, all in the space of just twenty-two years.

The history of the Liberal Democrats up until the 2010 election can be considered in five phases: survival, 1988–92; an attempt to realign the left, 1992–99; a return to a more traditional approach of protest politics, 1999–2005; a period of instability, including two leadership elections, 2005–07; and the search for a definition in the wake of the disintegration of New Labour, 2007–10. These are all familiar themes from earlier periods of post-war Liberal history; what made a major difference in this period, at least from 1997 onwards, is that the party finally succeeded in targeting its vote, overcoming, at least to a certain extent, the drawbacks of the first-past-the-post system. In turn this led to the Liberal Democrats gaining enough MPs to hold the balance of power after the 2010 election. A constant underlying theme, therefore, is of the steadily increasing campaigning effectiveness of the party.

Survival: the edge of the precipice, 1988–89

The Social and Liberal Democrats formally came into existence on 3 March 1988. The new party faced a troubled beginning; in David Dutton's words, it was 'founded more on the ruins of its predecessors than as the beneficiaries of their respective political traditions'.[1] The merger process had been long-drawn-out, often acrimonious and at time farcical; it had sapped the morale and loyalty of party members, and damaged the party's public image, to a greater extent than was realised at the time. The local elections two months later saw the party's vote fall to 18 per cent, 5 per cent down on the previous year's general election and a full 9 per cent fall on the 1987 local elections.

The two Alliance parties' leaders, David Steel and Robert Maclennan, acted as interim leaders of the SLD until a postal ballot could be held for the new leader, which took place after the local elections. Two Liberal MPs, Alan Beith and Paddy Ashdown, stood for election, and on 28 July Ashdown was elected by a wide margin, 41,401 (72 per cent) to 16,202 (28 per cent). Neither were particularly well known outside the party, but Ashdown had been the favourite from the outset, with his appeal to south-western members (one of the biggest party regions), activists, Social Democrats (he appeared to be less of a traditional Liberal) and radical Liberals (who remembered his pre-vious opposition to nuclear weapons) clearly outstripping Beith's support from his more traditional Liberal and northern base. Ashdown had based his leadership campaign on the need to rethink the party's approach. His underlying theme was that choice and indi-vidual freedoms were the entitlement of every citizen, but that with that came rights and responsibilities. Specific areas of new thinking included looking at the social security system, putting green politics at the top of the agenda, and using the market wherever possible to promote prosperity. In a sign of things to come, Ashdown argued for the Grimondite approach of a realignment of the left, in which the new party would over-take the Labour Party as the main radical alternative to the Conservatives.[2]

Paddy Ashdown (1941–)

Paddy Ashdown, leader of the Liberal Democrats from 1988 to 1999, created, out of the wreckage of the Liberal-SDP Alliance, a professional, modernised and effective Liberal Party. He took the party through the wrangles over its name and collapsing support in the opinion polls to a new respectability, impressive local election and by-election victories and – finally overcoming the barriers of the first-past-the-post electoral sys-tem – a greater number of Commons seats than at any time since 1929. And yet his grand strategy of working with the Labour Party, based on a common progressive agenda, to change the face of British politics forever – 'the project' – ultimately ended in failure.

Ashdown came into the party as an outsider, with no long record of political activ-ism; he abandoned a career in the services (including the Special Boat Squadron) and the Foreign Office to return to Britain, join the Liberal Party and fight the seemingly hopeless seat of Yeovil, which he won, at the second attempt, in 1983. He built a reputa-tion on the activist wing of the party, opposing the siting of US cruise missiles in Britain, and proved an effective parliamentary spokesman on trade and industry and education. He once observed that he never felt happy in the chamber of the House of Commons unless both of the other two parties were attacking him.

His career as leader can be divided into three phases, following the plan he himself had mapped out on becoming leader: 'The first was survival from a point of near extinc-tion; the second was to build a political force with the strength, policy and positions to matter again in British politics; and the third was to get on to the field and play in what I believed would become a very fluid period of politics.'[3] Strategic planning of this sort was typical of Ashdown, one of the characteristics almost everyone who worked with him remembered – he always had a plan, and a position paper, and when he achieved one objective he was often already looking ahead to the next. He was fascinated by ideas, and published a series of books and pamphlets; his conference speeches often challenged party orthodoxies, particularly in the early years.

Ashdown succeeded in finding positions for his party which were liberal, principled and distinctive. Many of these were on international issues, on which he established a strong personal reputation. He stood down from the Commons in 2001, becoming a peer. From 2002 to 2006 he served as High Representative and EU Special Representative for Bosnia and Herzegovina. He played a full part in the Liberal Democrats' 2010 election campaign and, with some reluctance, supported the party's participation in the coalition government.

The party's first task was simple: survival. As Ashdown put it later, 'we were heavily in debt, the headquarters staff demoralised and leaving in droves, the party in the country was in the midst of an identity crisis, and we were all punch-drunk from the succession of blows we had inflicted on ourselves over the last eighteen months'.[4] More than once in its first two years of life, the SLD came very close to disappearing completely. It was not until late 1989 that the party leadership could be sure they would still have a party to lead into the next election, and not until the Eastbourne by-election in October 1990 that the outside world started to believe it too.

In its early years, the party faced three major threats. The first was its internal weakness in organisation, finance and membership, which had all suffered severely from the divisions and accompanying infighting of the merger process. The pre-merger Liberal Party and SDP claimed about 150,000 members between them (though, as the Liberal Party did not possess a centralised membership system, the Liberal membership figure of 100,000 was always somewhat suspect), but only 80,000 ballot papers had been issued for the new party's leadership election.

The party's membership income was accordingly much lower than had been anticipated, and it had lost most of the donors, both individual and corporate, that the Alliance had enjoyed. Finances were precarious; for most of its first eighteen months the party teetered on the edge of bankruptcy. In July 1988, just half an hour before the leadership election result was due to be announced, the Inland Revenue had sent two officers round to threaten to close down party HQ because of unpaid national insurance contributions. Plans had been made to recruit a headquarters staff of fifty, but first recruitment was frozen and then staff were sacked. After the electoral crisis of summer 1989, HQ staff numbers were cut by more than half, to just fifteen. Federal Executive members had to pledge their own assets as security for a bank loan. Both were drastic steps, but they finally started to stabilise the party's financial situation.

The second major challenge faced by the Social and Liberal Democrats was to establish itself as the UK's undisputed third party. The merger outcome had not proved acceptable to a significant group of Social Democrats led by David Owen; he, together with two other of his MPs, Rosie Barnes and John Cartwright, and perhaps 10,000 or so SDP members, refused to join the new party and instead formed the 'continuing SDP'.

As Ivor Crewe and Tony King observed, this was probably what Owen had wanted all along: a completely independent party, unencumbered by messy compromises with Alliance partners, able to fight and win elections against all comers – and a party, furthermore, in which Owen could propound his political strategy without restraint from the other members of the Gang of Four, or, indeed, from anyone else. 'This strategy appealed to the Owenites', argued Crewe and King, 'and they adopted it. It can only be described, however, as being completely potty.'[5]

Given the British electoral system, it was difficult enough for a third party to prosper, as the SLD was finding – but Owen was trying to establish a fourth, and one, furthermore, without a significant membership, campaigning strength or clear policy prospectus. The idea that the 'continuing SDP' could ever mount a serious challenge was fantasy – but what it could do was damage the SLD. In the first two by-elections the Owenite party fought – in Kensington in July 1988 and in Epping Forest in December 1988 – it was beaten into fourth place by the SLD, but in the third by-election, in Richmond, North Yorkshire, in February 1989, the Owenites were lucky: the contest fell in an area where they had retained a reasonable number of local members and where their candidate, a local farmer, was popular and effective. As a result, they clearly outpolled the SLD, handing victory to the Conservative candidate, the future party leader William Hague. If the SLD and Owenites had combined behind one candidate, they could have won the seat easily.

Ashdown immediately proposed that the two parties put aside their differences and come together to beat the Tories; a few days later he suggested a process of joint open selection for parliamentary candidates, a proposal that caused some unhappiness at the party's spring conference a week later. But it was an astute move; Owen refused point-blank to contemplate any kind of cooperation – as Ashdown had believed he would – with the result that the media, and the electorate, came to see him, not the SLD, as the problem. In the end, Richmond was a false dawn for the 'continuing SDP' – they lacked the strength to fight elections seriously in most areas, and were trounced in local and European elections and successive by-elections. After being beaten into seventh place in the Bootle by-election in May 1990, with less than half the vote of the Monster Raving Loony Cavern Rock Party, Owen and his colleagues announced that the 'continuing SDP' was being wound up. As Crewe and King put it, 'it was perhaps appropriate that what one journalist had dubbed "the Monster Raving Ego Party" should in the end have been destroyed by the Monster Raving Loony Party'.[6]

Owen did not stand at the 1992 election, arguing instead for a vote for the Conservatives. Cartwright and Barnes fought the 1992 election as independent Social Democrats, and lost. Other 'continuing SDP' members drifted back into the Liberal Democrats, or over to the other main parties; many left politics entirely.

The Liberal anti-mergerites never caused the SLD anything like the same problems, though they continue to exist today. They were even smaller in number than the Owenites, and lacked any MPs; their best-known figure was Michael Meadowcroft,

Liberal MP for Leeds West 1983–87. They retained councillors in a few areas, most notably Liverpool and Exeter, and fought a handful of parliamentary seats, generally losing their deposits. Again, over time, some of their activists, including Meadowcroft, joined the Liberal Democrats.

No sooner did the Owenite menace seem to be fading, however, than a new threat emerged to take its place. Desperately short of money, in 1989 the SLD threw most of its campaigning resources into the county council elections in May, with reasonable results: a vote share of 19 per cent, slightly up on the previous year. But in turn this meant that the party mounted almost no central campaign at all for the European elections that took place a month later. And here they were faced with a new opponent: the Green Party.

Environmental issues had been slowly rising up the political agenda, both in the UK and world-wide, since the early 1960s. in the 1970s the Liberal Party had been the first of the major parties to respond; Ashdown had emphasised green themes in his leadership election, and SLD policy-making had begun to develop a strong environmental approach. None of this, however, was visible to the electorate in mid-1989. Their attention was captured instead by the imaginative and well-funded campaign of the Green Party. Founded in 1972, the Greens had not hitherto had much of an impact, but in 1989 a combination of Margaret Thatcher's declining popularity, ineffective SLD and Labour campaigns, rising concerns over environmental issues and an election for a European Parliament which most voters probably saw as irrelevant to their day-to-day lives led to a dramatic result: the Greens achieved 15 per cent of the vote. The SLD came fourth, with a mere 6.4 per cent. In only one seat, Cornwall & Plymouth, did the party manage a good second place; everywhere else its candidates were beaten into fourth place, or, in fifteen constituencies, fifth, by nationalists, Owenites or independents.

It was the new party's bleakest hour. On election day itself, Ashdown recorded in his diary that 'I am plagued by the nightmare that the party that started with Gladstone will end with Ashdown'; and after the results were announced three days later, 'to bed about 3.00. I couldn't sleep a wink. We are in a very black position indeed.'[7] For most of the rest of the year the party sank beneath the Greens in the opinion polls; throughout the summer it was polling at about 4 per cent – fairly close, as was pointed out, to being within the margin of error of zero.[8] In the end, however, as with the Owenite SDP, the Greens lacked the resources and campaigning strength on the ground to mobilise support in local or general elections, and by early 1990 their challenge had clearly faded.

The financial and electoral crises of summer 1989 were bad enough, but they helped to bring to a head the third challenge faced by the party: confusion over its identity. Was the new party to be Liberal, Social Democratic or something else entirely? In practice, the argument was conducted over what the party was to be called.

The formal name agreed in the merger negotiations, Social and Liberal Democrats, was clumsy and forgettable (in summer 1988, Ashdown was recognised in France by an English visitor as the 'leader of that party no one knows the name of!'[9]). In keeping with his desire for a new approach, Ashdown was happy to support a short title of 'Democrats', and this was endorsed by the party's first conference, in September 1988. The decision to drop the historic name 'Liberal', however, caused deep unhappiness among many Liberals, particularly (though not only) those who had supported Alan Beith in the leadership election; many of them refused to use 'Democrats', preferring to retain the term 'Social and Liberal Democrats'. The electoral disaster of the 1989 Euro-elections brought the issue to a head; several MPs (mostly Beith supporters) threatened to adopt the name 'Liberal Democrat' unilaterally, promising to resign the whip – or even, in the case of Geraint Howells, resign from the Commons – if their wishes were not implemented. Ashdown gradually became convinced that they were right over the name. 'Being a relative outsider compared to the older MPs,' as he put it later:

> I had, in my rush to create the new party, failed to understand that a political party is about more than plans and priorities and policies and a chromium-played organisation. It also has a heart and a history and a soul – especially a very old party like the Liberals. Alan Beith and the other 'Name' rebels understood this better than me. They were right, and I had nearly wrecked the party by becoming too attached to my own vision and ignoring the fact that political parties are, at root, human organisations and not machines.[10]

Ashdown stood firm, however, against the parliamentary party deciding the name of the party by themselves. The party's democratic structures had decided on 'Democrats' in 1988; they should decide on whatever should replace it. Although opposed by most former SDP members, Ashdown persuaded the Federal Executive to conduct an all-member ballot on the name in the autumn, and 'Liberal Democrats' was chosen by a clear majority. Some members threatened to resign over the issue, but in the end few did.

Survival: rebuilding credibility, 1989–92

By the autumn of 1989, the worst seemed to be over. In July the massacre at Tiananmen Square had given Ashdown the opportunity to develop a distinctive policy stance for the Liberal Democrats, in calling for UK passports to be given to all Hong Kong citizens. The policy was not particularly popular with the public, but it was principled and different, the constant quest of third-party leaders: as Ashdown said later, 'I would sell my grandmother for some distinctiveness for the party'.[11] The September conference was surprisingly upbeat, and Ashdown's closing speech was particularly well received. Just before the conference he had published *Citizen's Britain*, an attempt to map out 'a coherent new agenda for the liberal left in Britain based on shifting power from the state producer to the citizen consumer'.[12] The book foreshadowed many of the approaches which came to be adopted by the Liberal Democrats, including an emphasis on investment in education.

One major benefit of the merger was that it provided a democratic means of resolving the policy differences inherited from the Alliance days, for example over nuclear power and nuclear weapons, and these began to be settled from September 1989 onwards.

Under the new party's constitution, the conference was (and still is) sovereign in terms of policy-making, but the Federal Policy Committee had a key role in producing policy papers for conference debate, thus effectively controlling the terms of the debate and the details of the policy; it also produced election manifestos. Ashdown chose to chair the FPC himself, and led a thorough overhaul of the party's programme; unlike David Steel, but in common with Jo Grimond, he was always fascinated by ideas, and his views largely helped to determine the direction and main themes of the party throughout the 1990s. Although this led to a few clashes with the FPC and conference (who both tended to be less market-oriented than Ashdown in economic and social policy), he was able to stamp his ideas firmly on the party largely because of the respect and admiration he earned from members, thanks to his personal charisma and successful efforts to rebuild the party. 'Ordinary party members will take things from him for which they would have lynched David Owen,' commented *The Economist* in 1991.[13] In addition, although there was often fierce debate over specific policy details, there was general agreement on its broad thrust, and Ashdown never faced any coherent and consistent challenge to his policy agenda.

Although in organisational terms the merged party borrowed heavily from the SDP, in ideological and policy terms, the Liberal Democrats were effectively a modernised Liberal Party, with a policy platform built around Liberalism. In practice, the social democracy of the SDP (excluding the later versions of Owen's social market) had not differed markedly from the social liberalism of the early 1980s Liberal Party. The main difference lay over attitudes to the state, where Liberals were more sceptical of the dangers of state power than the SDP tended to be, and more attracted to means to constrain it, such as decentralisation.[14]

Five main themes, three of them familiar from earlier periods, came to characterise the Liberal Democrat policy platform in the run-up to the 1992 election. British participation in the European Community had been one of the key issues underlying the SDP's split from the Labour Party, and one in which their Liberal allies were wholly in agreement; the Liberal Democrats fully supported European integration and, in particular, British entry to the single European currency. Also familiar from earlier manifestos was a comprehensive package of constitutional reform, aiming to give more power to the individual and reducing the degree of centralisation in government. Environmental policies, including opposition to nuclear power and a shift in taxation from income and employment to pollution and resource use, also featured strongly; throughout the 1990s the Liberal Democrats became widely regarded as the greenest of the three major parties.

Economic policy became more market-oriented than the Alliance position; the party called for independence for the Bank of England in setting interest rates, thereby helping to promote long-term stability, and for greater competition, particularly in the privatised utilities. These were not, however, signs of a non-interventionist approach to economics in general; the 1992 manifesto contained an ambitious reflationary plan designed to bring down unemployment. The second new theme was the need to invest in public services, particularly in education, and the commitment to raise taxes to pay for it, including increasing the standard rate of income tax by one penny for education. Initially viewed by commentators as a risky move, in fact it proved to be a popular selling point. The party was also critical of much of the Conservative government's introduction of market mechanisms into public services. Overall, the platform was clearly left of centre, opposed to much of what the Conservative government stood for.

Under Ashdown's leadership the party slowly recovered its credibility in the public eye. As the threats from the Owenites and the Greens faded, and as Thatcher's Conservatives grew ever more unpopular, particularly after the introduction of the poll tax in April 1990 (the much-resented replacement for the rates as a system of local taxation; instead of paying a tax linked to property values, every resident paid the same), electoral success returned. In October 1990 a parliamentary by-election took place in Eastbourne as a result of the IRA's assassination of the Conservative MP Ian Gow, a close associate of Mrs Thatcher. Ashdown's initial instinct was to declare that the Liberal Democrats would not contest the by-election, in order not to give the IRA the satisfaction of disrupting parliamentary politics, but he was firmly told he was wrong by the party's Campaigns Director, Chris Rennard. In reality, Eastbourne was a gift: a seat with a solid local government base (the Alliance had run the council in 1986–88), a respectable, though distant, second place in the 1987 election, and with Labour well behind in third place. The party was able to mobilise the anti-Thatcher and anti-poll-tax vote, and on 18 October David Bellotti won the seat with a 20 per cent swing from the Conservatives.

Chris Rennard (1960–)

Former party leader Charles Kennedy has described Chris Rennard as 'a quite extraordinary figure in British politics'. Conservative commentator and publisher Iain Dale claimed in June 2011 that Rennard 'is probably the most formidable and feared political campaigner of the last twenty years'. For two decades he was the mastermind behind the Liberal Democrats' increasingly effective parliamentary campaigning, in by-elections and general elections.

Born and educated in Liverpool, Rennard was drawn into local Liberal campaigning as a schoolboy; he was the agent for the successful Edge Hill by-election in 1979 and helped the local Liberals take control of the council in 1980–83. After university he became one of the Liberal Party's national area agents. From 1989 to 2003 he was the Liberal Democrats' Campaigns Director and from 2003 to 2009 the party's Chief Executive.

He developed the campaigning techniques he had started to learn in Liverpool into a ruthlessly effective election machine. He is credited with a string of by-election victories and near-misses, and in the general elections of 1992 and 1997 he oversaw the party's target seat campaign, which resulted, in 1997, in the Liberal Democrats more than doubling its number of MPs. He also directed the party's general election campaigns in 2001 and 2005, which further increased the number of seats. In the 2001 election, there was a near-perfect match between those seats which followed his campaigning template, and won, and those which did not, and lost. This significantly reinforced his standing within the party, and gave him the authority to largely determine the party's messaging and strategy in the 2001–05 Parliament, under Kennedy's hands-off leadership.

He entered the House of Lords in 1999. Although no longer employed by the party, he still contributes to party strategy and has become a frequent media commentator on elections and politics.

The Eastbourne result provided a much-needed morale boost for the party, and, even more importantly, helped to underline the Liberal Democrats' recovery in the public eye; it showed not only that the party had survived the assaults of the merger (self-inflicted), the Owenites and the Greens, but that it was capable of reaching parts of the electorate that the official opposition, Labour, could not. It also contributed to Mrs Thatcher's downfall, as Conservative MPs increasingly feared that her continued leadership would cost them their seats; five weeks later she resigned as Conservative leader.

Her replacement by John Major led to a Conservative recovery in the polls, but mostly at Labour's expense. On 7 March 1991 the Ribble Valley by-election gave the Liberal Democrats another chance. Although the seat was the thirteenth safest Conservative constituency in the country, after a campaign dominated by the single issue of the poll tax, the Liberal Democrats easily captured it. As Mike Carr, the winner, said in his victory speech, 'here lies the poll tax, killed in Ribble Valley'; two weeks later the government announced it would be scrapped and replaced by Council Tax.

The local elections two months later provided emphatic evidence of the party's recovery with a vote share of 22 per cent, and in November the party won a third by-election, Kincardine & Deeside, from the Conservatives. The party thus entered 1992 in good heart, though this was briefly interrupted by the threatened revelation by the *News of the World* of an affair Ashdown had had with his secretary five years earlier. After an initial attempt to suppress the story through injunctions, Ashdown decided to announce the facts to the press himself. This was the right strategy; although the issue clearly caused him and his family considerable pain (and the *Sun*'s nickname of 'Paddy Pantsdown' stuck to him for years afterwards), his dignified handling of the story actually led to his personal ratings rising. As the 1992 election campaign finally kicked off in early March, Ashdown was the party's strongest asset.

The party's manifesto, *Changing Britain for Good*, based its proposals on the five themes outlined above. It was well received: 'The Liberal Democrat essay far outdistances its competitors with a fizz of ideas and an absence of fudge,' stated *The Guardian*;[15] and *The Independent* believed that 'across a spectrum of issues, the Liberal Democrats are more in sympathy with the spirit of the times than either of the two big parties.'[16] Under election director Des Wilson, the party fought an effective campaign, targeting its resources on the seats in which it hoped to do well. Starting at about 16 per cent in the opinion polls, the party steadily moved upwards, hitting 21 per cent by the beginning of April. From being treated as an also-ran by the media at the start of the campaign, the party had firmly established itself as an important, albeit third-placed, contender by the middle.

However, this was a mixed blessing, as the near neck-and-neck polling of Labour and the Conservatives (though, as it turned out, the polls consistently over-estimated Labour's support) led journalists to focus on the Liberal Democrats purely in terms of which other party they would support in the event of a hung parliament. Ashdown declined to answer, focusing instead on policy demands, mainly the introduction of proportional representation. In retrospect, he recognised this as a mistake, making him 'look as though I was more interested in what was good for the Lib Dems than in what was good for the country'.[17] It also allowed the Conservatives to run scare stories about the supposed instability of hung parliaments; and although the electorate possessed no enthusiasm for the Conservatives, they proved even less keen on seeing the Labour leader Neil Kinnock in Downing Street. Support began to ebb away from both Labour and the Liberal Democrats, though most opinion polls failed to pick this up, mostly continuing to predict a hung parliament.

After the raised expectations of the campaign, the result of the 1992 election came as something of a disappointment to Liberal Democrats – and Labour – as the Conservatives pulled clearly ahead, winning a majority of twenty-one over all other parties combined. Just under six million voters supported the Liberal Democrats. The party ended with twenty seats, losing all three of its by-election gains and three further seats (two of them in Wales, reducing the Welsh party to just one MP), and gaining four, all in the West and South West. Compared to the previous general election, in 1987, this represented a net loss of 4.8 per cent of the vote and two seats. Compared to the dark days of 1988–89, however, it was a triumph. The party had survived.

1992 general election (8 April)			
	Votes	*%*	*MPs*
Liberal Democrat	5,999,606	17.8	20
Conservative	**14,093,007**	**41.9**	**336**
Labour	11,560,484	34.4	271
SNP	629,564	1.9	3
Plaid Cymru	156,796	0.5	4
Others	1,174,617	3.5	17
Total	*33,614,074*		*651*

The 'project': realigning the left? 1992–94

Having survived and securely established themselves as the third force in British politics, what were the Liberal Democrats to do next? Ashdown's aim was the realignment of the left, a common theme of previous Liberal leaders, including Grimond's call for a realignment of the left in the 1960s, the formation of the Lib-Lab Pact in the 1970s, and the alliance with the SDP in the 1980s. The idea was based on the notion that there was usually a clear anti-Conservative majority in the country, and it was only the division between the progressive parties, Labour and the Liberal Democrats, that allowed the Tories to gain power; this seemed particularly true in 1992, after thirteen years of Conservative administration. Ashdown was always careful not to talk about realignment in terms of electoral pacts or alliances, however, which would have been too controversial (particularly after the acrimonious end of the Liberal-SDP Alliance); instead, in 1987, he had maintained that: 'The realignment of the Left in Britain has always been seen in terms of realignment of political forces. This is a pity, since what we need is a fresh assembly of new ideas.'[18]

Although there had been some contacts with Labour politicians and sympathisers before 1992, it was Labour's fourth successive defeat that provided the main opportunity for action. Exactly a month after the election, on 9 May, Ashdown delivered what became known as the 'Chard speech', given to an audience of only forty or fifty in a small town in his constituency; he said later that he believed it was the most important speech of his leadership. Arguing that the Liberal Democrats needed to 'work with others to assemble the ideas around which a non-socialist alternative to the Conservatives can be constructed', he called for a national electoral reform commission and for Labour to be more open to constitutional reform and a market economy, more pluralist and less a creature of the trade unions.[19]

The speech was deeply unpopular with Liberal Democrat MPs (one took to referring to it as a 'burnt offering'), partly because at the time Labour seemed finished and about to descend, in the wake of Neil Kinnock's resignation as leader, into another bout of infighting. The Liberal Democrat peers, however, were more supportive, and a strategy debate at the autumn conference went Ashdown's way. However, there was very little response from Labour; although some of its leadership, including Robin Cook and Peter Mandelson, were open to approaches from the Liberal Democrats, the new leader elected in July, John Smith, was determined to maintain his independence and believed that Labour was still capable of winning on its own.

Events during the autumn and winter of 1992 seemed to suggest he was right. First, 'Black Wednesday', which saw the pound forced out of the European Exchange Rate Mechanism after a concerted speculative attack, destroyed the Conservatives' reputation for economic competence. The government then started to tear itself apart over Europe; the passage of the legislation allowing British accession to the Maastricht Treaty of European Union in 1992–93 saw the Tories lose their majority in the Commons after a Eurosceptic rebellion. On a number of occasions the bill only survived thanks to Liberal Democrat votes, a stance which caused some unhappiness within the party (and vitriolic attacks from Labour) but was entirely consistent with the party's long-standing position on Europe (twenty years before, Jeremy Thorpe's small band of Liberal MPs had similarly kept the legislation implementing British entry to the European Community alive), and its support for the Maastricht Treaty itself. Neither development led to any improvement in relations with the Labour Party, however, as Labour opened up a commanding lead in the opinion polls over the Conservatives.

The collapse in Conservative support also paid dividends for the Liberal Democrats, and the party started to make significant electoral gains, particularly in southern England. There were significant swings away from the Conservatives in local government elections in 1993 and 1994; the party's vote share increased to 25 per cent and 27 per cent, and in many urban areas, Liberal Democrats became the main opposition to Labour. Parliamentary by-elections were even more encouraging: in 1993 the party won Newbury and Christchurch, on huge swings from the Tories, and in June 1994 Eastleigh. On the same day the party won its first-ever seats in the European Parliament: Somerset & North Devon and Cornwall & Plymouth.

Ashdown's stock as leader also rose, partly as a result of his growing reputation as a foreign affairs commentator; in 1992 he began a series of visits to the war zones in Bosnia, where conflict had broken out in April, and eventually played a major part in building public support for the NATO-led action that ended, in 1995, the Serbian attempt to destroy the Bosnian state.

Liberal Democrat election campaigning

The first-past-the-post electoral system discriminates fiercely against 'third parties', and particularly against those whose support is spread fairly evenly throughout the country. Thus in 1983, although attracting over a quarter of the national vote, the Liberal-SDP Alliance gained only a handful of seats. The problem faced by the Liberal Democrats was how the party could raise its vote in any particular constituency above the national average vote of 15–20 per cent to the 35–40 per cent level generally needed to win.

The solution Chris Rennard and his colleagues developed was to apply systematically the successful community politics-type campaigning the party had employed, at least in some areas, from the 1960s. Parliamentary election campaigns came to be built on the back of a long background period of intensive local campaigning, with the candidate presented as the local advocate, ready to take up citizens' grievances. Winning local council seats was a key part of this strategy; and also, as more Liberal Democrat MPs were elected through the 1990s, there also seemed to be a 'contagion effect', with neighbouring constituencies benefiting in turn. The more people could see Liberal Democrats being elected, on their council or in nearby seats, the more likely they were to think of them as potential victors in their own area.

None of this was new, of course – Paddy Ashdown, for example, had built up the Yeovil Liberals in much the same way from 1976 to his election in 1983. What Rennard did was to apply the techniques systematically across the party. Training sessions in campaigning skills for party activists and candidates were delivered with growing frequency, and resources were increasingly targeted on winnable seats, not just during the election campaign but – much more importantly – in the years leading up to it. In the 1992 election, for example, roughly £120,000 out of the party's campaign expenditure of £3 million was spent on target seats; by 2005, this had grown to £2 million out of a total of £4.5 million.[20]

This approach to fighting elections was a rational – and effective – way of overcoming the challenges of the first-past-the-post system. Some Liberal Democrats worried, however, that the intensive focus on local issues and the candidate as local champion came at the cost of blurring the party's national image; national policies were often downplayed or ignored, and the campaign was built round the candidate rather than the party. This possibly partly helps to explain why the party lost seats in 2010 (see Chapter 11). Thanks to the TV debates, specific Liberal Democrat policies, particularly on immigration and Trident, were subjected to much greater scrutiny than before. Lacking any firm ideological attachment to the party and its platform, a proportion of its local voters possibly began to detach themselves when they found out what these actually were. This could help to explain why the party's vote rose in scores of seats where it had no realistic chance of winning – on the back of a stronger national message – but fell in many of the seats it was defending. An additional explanation may be simply that the other parties were starting to copy the Liberal Democrats' successful local campaigning techniques themselves.

The Liberal Democrats now face the challenge of adapting this campaigning style to being in government. With a level in national opinion polls well below its support at the 2010 election, the party seems likely to have every need of Chris Rennard's campaigning techniques.

The 'project': surviving New Labour, 1994–97

The political situation shifted again with the sudden death of John Smith in May 1994, and his replacement as Labour leader by Tony Blair in July. This presented both an opportunity and a challenge to the Liberal Democrats. On the one hand, Blair, influenced partly by Peter Mandelson, was far more open to some form of cooperation with the Liberal Democrats than Smith had been; indeed, Ashdown had discussed the issue with him as early as July 1993. On the other hand, he seemed likely to move the Labour Party decisively to the centre, colonising the Liberal Democrats' growing base of support. Initially the latter seemed to be more likely; in the second half of 1994 the party's support in the opinion polls fell from 23 to 13 per cent. This was, as Ashdown later remembered, 'the deepest and most desperate point of depression in my whole leadership of the party'.[21] As he complained to his ally Lord Holme in August, 'I have been building the party to fill a certain gap in politics, which I know is there and which would give us real electoral appeal. But then along comes Blair with all the power of Labour behind him, and fills exactly the space I have been aiming at for the last seven years!'[22]

He was soon encouraged, however, by an approach from Blair, who, following Roy Jenkins (whom he regarded as a mentor), recognised the strength of the argument that the historic split in the British left had handed power to the Conservatives: 'the twentieth century had been a Tory century precisely because good and talented people who should have been together were instead in separate parties fighting each other'.[23] In September 1994 Ashdown and Blair began what was to become a five-year series of meetings and discussions about how to get rid of the Tories and how best to work together both before and after a potential election victory.

Despite the fall in its opinion poll ratings, the party on the ground succeeded in withstanding the New Labour challenge – partly because it took some time for the electorate to lose their distrust of Labour and partly because in many areas the Liberal Democrats were clearly better placed than Labour to dislodge the Conservatives, and thus benefited from the electorate's rapidly accelerating desertion of the Tories. Local elections continued to show the party polling much higher than its national ratings; the Conservatives sustained such huge losses that after the 1995 elections the Liberal Democrats became the second party of local government in terms of numbers of councillors, a position they retained until 1999. In July 1995 the party fought off a strong challenge from Labour to win the Littleborough & Saddleworth by-election from the Conservatives. In 1995 and 1996 the defections of two Conservative MPs, Emma Nicholson and Peter Thurnham, both helped to thrust the party back into the limelight and suggested that some at least of the departing Tory vote might prefer the Liberal Democrats to Labour; they were joined in due course by several Conservative MEPs and former MPs. Nicholson's defection in particular came at a fortunate time, December 1995, when the party was doing particularly badly in the polls (13 per cent to Labour's 55 per cent); Ashdown later reckoned it ranked with the 1990 Eastbourne by-election as one of the key moments that gave 'the party a desperately needed profile and a role. The Lib Dems were the Heineken Party: we could reach parts of the Tory Party which New Labour, even with Blair, couldn't reach.'[24]

In the background Ashdown and Blair continued to explore the possibilities of cooperation. In due course they agreed that while it made no sense for their parties to stop fighting each other in areas of the country where they were the two main contenders, in general they should focus their attacks on the Conservatives rather than each other. In public each party would show respect for the other, and coordinate attacks in Parliament. This public display of cooperation included a formal abandonment of 'equidistance' by the Liberal Democrat conference in 1995, a decision reached after extensive consultation within the party by Ashdown. Although several of the party's MPs were strongly opposed, in general the activists were less so; many of them were councillors, comfortable with operating in coalition with other parties in local authorities. Liberal Democrat policy positions were, with a few exceptions, much closer to Labour's than to the Tories, and the government was so unpopular by 1995 that it was ludicrous to pretend that the Liberal Democrats were indifferent, or 'equidistant', between them and the official opposition.

In fact, cooperation between Labour and the Liberal Democrats extended further than most realised at the time. In the run-up to the 1997 election the two parties agreed a (secret) list of Tory key seats in which one party had little chance of winning and would therefore not invest resources, so as to give the other a clear run. Also as a result of joint discussions, during the election the *Daily Mirror* published a list of twenty-two seats where, if Labour voters backed the Liberal Democrats, the Conservatives would be defeated; in the event the party won twenty of them.[25]

Blair and Ashdown also agreed to collaborate on policy areas where they hoped to work together. The key outcome was a series of talks on constitutional reform led by Robin Cook, for Labour, and Robert Maclennan, for the Liberal Democrats; this was given the go-ahead in March 1996, though the talks were not publicly announced until October. In March 1997 the group reached agreement on a package of proposals including incorporation of the European Convention on Human Rights into UK law, freedom of information legislation, devolution to Scotland and Wales (and elections by proportional representation to their parliaments), an elected authority for London, removal of the hereditary peers from the House of Lords, proportional representation for the European elections, and a referendum on voting reform for Westminster elections, comprising a choice between the existing first-past-the-post system and a proportional alternative, to be agreed by a commission on voting systems. Most of this had been Liberal Democrat policy for years (or was a watered-down version of it), but much was new for Labour. Blair saw it as part of his programme of modernising the Labour Party, and the position of the constitutional modernisers within Labour, such as Robin Cook, was thus strengthened.

The Cook–Maclennan process was public, and in general was cautiously welcomed by Liberal Democrats. What was discussed in secret, however – and which would have alarmed many party members – was something much more dramatic, what Ashdown called 'the big thing', an agreement to fight the election on a common platform on at least two or three major issues. 'If, as it appears', Ashdown confided to his diary in April 1996, 'I have more in common with Blair than he has with his left wing, surely the logical thing is for us to create a new, more powerful alternative force which would be unified around a broadly liberal agenda'.[26] Ashdown went so far as to draft successive versions of a 'Partnership for Britain's Future', covering constitutional reform along the Cook–Maclennan lines, cleaning up politics (after several examples of corruption and dishonest conduct among MPs which came to characterise the last years of the Tory government), the reform of welfare systems and economic policy reform, including investing in education, awarding independence to the Bank of England, and adherence to the criteria for entry into the single European currency. From July 1996 Blair and Ashdown started to talk about Liberal Democrat participation in a Labour government; Peter Mandelson later claimed that this would have involved including two Liberal Democrat MPs, Alan Beith and Menzies Campbell, in Blair's first Cabinet.[27] Blair even sprang on a surprised Ashdown the idea of merger between the parties; Ashdown responded by saying 'that may be a long-term destination … that may happen, say, ten years from now, probably under someone else's leadership'.[28]

In the end, the 'big thing' was too big a step. What worried Ashdown and his colleagues was Blair's refusal to commit firmly to the introduction of proportional representation for Westminster elections – the absolute bottom line for the Liberal Democrats, who could not be expected to tie themselves to a much bigger partner without being able to survive its eventual fall. Ashdown's diaries record in painstaking detail a long series of meetings in which Blair was first educated about what PR meant and the different systems through which it could be introduced, and then prevaricated, hinting at his own possible conversion to it (or maybe to something weaker, such as the alternative vote), but stressing the opposition he would face in the Parliamentary Labour Party. By January 1997, the very small number of Liberal Democrat colleagues who were kept in the loop by Ashdown were unanimously urging him to drop the project, but he persevered, despite Richard Holme's warning that: 'You must not get carried away with the film script you have written in your head – two strong people standing up and shaping history.'[29]

In the end, policy cooperation extended only as far as the Cook–Maclennan agreement. The Liberal Democrat manifesto for the 1997 election built on its predecessor of 1992, stressing as before the party's commitment to constitutional reform, Europe (including entry to the single currency) and the environment. The commitment to invest in public services was developed further, with increases in income tax (both the basic and top rates) to pay for them; the issue was given a much higher profile than in 1992, and hammered home repeatedly in a highly focused campaign. As in 1992, this platform received praise; *The Independent* called the party's manifesto the most challenging of the three, saying that politics without the Liberal Democrats would be 'intolerable', while Peter Riddell in *The Times* enjoyed its 'refreshing candour' and admired Ashdown's willingness to leap where Tony Blair feared to tread.[30]

The general election was finally called for 1 May 1997, John Major leaving it almost as late as he could, in search of a Conservative revival in the polls. The revival never came, and the Conservatives went down to their worst result in a century and a half, losing a quarter of their vote and half of their seats. Their losses were exaggerated by tactical voting in many areas, assisted by the covert cooperation between Liberal Democrats and Labour mentioned above – though this helped Labour more than the Liberal Democrats; in many seats where Labour could not win, their vote still increased, sometimes denying the seats to the Liberal Democrats. After a strong campaign by Ashdown, which saw the party's vote rise from 10–11 per cent at the beginning of the campaign to as high as 19 per cent in some polls, the final share of the vote was 16.8 per cent, actually a slight fall from 1992. A combination of tactical voting and much more ruthless targeting of resources on winnable constituencies, however, saw the party jump from twenty-four seats to forty-six, the highest for any third party since 1929. Had the Liberal Democrat vote risen evenly across the country, the party would have won only twenty-eight seats.[31] Two of the four by-election gains were retained; Christchurch was the only loss to the Conservatives, while Littleborough & Saddleworth, along with Rochdale, were lost to Labour. These were more than compensated, however, by twenty-five gains from the Conservatives, all but seven in southern England; in Devon and Cornwall the party's vote rose to 35 per cent, higher than both the other two parties.

1997 general election (1 May)			
	Votes	%	MPs
Liberal Democrat	5,242,947	16.8	46
Conservative	9,600,943	30.7	165
Labour	**13,518,167**	**43.2**	**419**
SNP	621,550	2.0	6
Plaid Cymru	161,030	0.5	4
Others	2,141,647	6.8	19
Total	31,286,284		659

As late as election day, Blair and Ashdown were still talking about whether they could entertain any form of cooperation; Blair declared that he was 'absolutely determined to mend the schism that occurred in the progressive forces in British politics at the start of this century'.[32] He hinted at a coalition, though Ashdown pointed out that it would be unacceptable for Liberal Democrat ministers simply to implement a Labour programme; by then it was obvious that Labour was going to win with a large majority. By the next day, however, Blair had changed his tone, talking merely of a 'framework for co-operation'. Robin Cook later confirmed that Gordon Brown (Labour's Shadow Chancellor) and John Prescott (its deputy leader) had both made clear to Blair overnight their virulent opposition to any role for Ashdown or his colleagues in government. In any case, the size of Labour's majority destroyed any argument for it.

The 'project': last chance, 1997–99

The 'project', however, was by no means dead, and Ashdown was determined to adopt a stance of 'constructive opposition' – opposing the new government where the Liberal Democrats disagreed with them, but working with Labour where they agreed, especially over constitutional reform. Blair seemed to share this approach; on the day after polling day, he declared that 'I am absolutely determined to change politics with you and heal the schism. If we allow ourselves to get into a position where we play conventional politics, the schism will just reopen.'[33]

Ashdown assessed his key priorities as implementing the Cook–Maclennan Agreement, placing Liberal Democrats on Cabinet committees and acquiring rights of access and input to the preparation of key government papers. In the end the two leaders opted for a single Joint Cabinet Committee between the two parties. Announced on 22 July, the Committee, which comprised five members from each party, was initially to discuss constitutional reform, but its remit could move on to other areas, such as Northern Ireland or Europe. The announcement of the JCC came as a shock to the party, most of whom were not aware of the close relationship Blair and Ashdown had built up over the preceding three years. Ashdown later admitted that he deliberately bounced them into it – 'I am absolutely convinced that we would never have got the party into the Joint Cabinet Committee … if I had gone through a consensual process'[34] – using some of the political capital he had accumulated with party members over the preceding nine years to try and achieve something with the platform he had built. Many of the party's MPs were strongly opposed.

A key stumbling block to further co-operation, however, was Blair's continued refusal to commit to proportional representation for Westminster elections. Over the summer he again raised the issue of merger, seeing it as a way of tying the Liberal Democrats into the Labour project; the alternative, as he confessed to Ashdown in June, was introducing PR, sacrificing Labour's majority, seeing the Liberal Democrats more than treble their number of seats and enabling them to form an alternative coalition if they wanted. Ashdown was understandably exasperated; he thought Blair had committed himself more firmly to PR and should welcome it for its own sake, if he genuinely believed his own rhetoric about a new, more pluralist, style of politics. Ashdown instead suggested a deal by which Liberal Democrats would agree to a coalition with Labour on the basis of an agreed policy programme, including PR. By July he thought he had convinced Blair; he started making plans for a special party conference in November to approve the entry of Liberal Democrat ministers into government.

In September, Ashdown hinted at the possibility of coalition in an interview with the *New Statesman*, with the intent of gauging the level of opposition the idea would rouse. By then the party was beginning to turn more decisively against Labour, with the growing evidence of the government's centralising approach to politics, its determination to stick to the Major government's spending plans, thus putting public services under pressure, and the lack of any announcements on PR or British entry into the European single currency; this was not what the Liberal Democrats had fought the election for. Ashdown's approach came in for growing criticism at the party conference in September and thereafter.

As Ashdown had anticipated, the greater the delay in forming a coalition, the less possible it became, as the government steadily became less palatable to Liberal Democrat sensibilities. But for Blair the moment never seemed ripe. In the autumn he delayed making a decision until the spring, partly because he was under pressure from within his own party over the Labour manifesto commitment to a referendum on an alternative electoral system, a pledge which few Labour MPs really supported. In December, however, the government finally announced the establishment of an independent commission on voting reform, to be chaired by Roy Jenkins. In turn this weakened Ashdown's chances of getting a coalition through his own party; if the government was doing what Liberal Democrats wanted on constitutional reform anyway, why tie the party in to the rest of its agenda, with an increasing proportion of which it disagreed?

In March 1998 Blair decided that he needed to delay a decision on coalition yet again, this time until after the publication of the Jenkins commission's report; as before, the reason he gave was opposition from Brown and Prescott. At the same time antagonism was mounting within the Liberal Democrats; the party's spring conference the same month agreed what later became known as the 'triple lock' procedure for agreeing to 'any substantial proposal which could affect the party's independence of political action'. The support of the parliamentary party and Federal Executive would be needed for any such proposal; failing a three-quarters majority in each body, a special conference would be held; and failing a two-thirds majority there, an all-member ballot would need to be organised. Ashdown was fully aware that the mechanism was explicitly designed to tie his hands, and he initially determined to oppose it; he was talked out of it by his advisers, aware that this was much better than the alternative resolution that had been submitted to the conference (but had not been chosen for debate), which was to rule out any coalitions for the lifetime of the parliament.

Throughout the summer Ashdown attempted to nail Blair down to a commitment to a PR referendum, and other aspects of the Cook–Maclennan Agreement. But despite a long series of meetings Blair seemed ever less likely to reach a final decision. Richard Holme described the process as like 'being condemned to attend endless repeats of *Hamlet*'; Ashdown noted in his diary that 'waiting for Blair is like waiting for Godot'.[35] In September Blair agreed with Ashdown to hold a referendum on PR before the next election (having previously declared that it would have to wait until after the election), but six weeks later, on the eve of publication of the Jenkins report, Blair changed his mind yet again, feeling that he could not overcome opposition in the Cabinet and did not want to risk splitting the government. When, on 29 October, the Jenkins report was published, advocating an additional member system of PR, Blair's response was entirely neutral, with no commitment to a referendum; later that day Jack Straw, the Home Secretary, rubbished it publicly, and did so again in a Commons debate on the report the following week.

Effectively this was the end of the project. As Ashdown complained to Blair:

> I am ... at the end of my tether. It's always us who put the propositions to you. Then you and I agree how to go forward. Then, at the last moment, it's discovered you can't. Then we – never you – go off and find a different way to keep the project on track and the whole depressing cycle starts over again. Frankly I don't know how long we can keep doing this and, anyway, I'm not sure it's worth doing at all if it falls flat on its face again.[36]

Ashdown tried once more to extract a promise from Blair to state publicly that he would hold a referendum on the Jenkins proposals, but failed. Despite this, Ashdown could not quite accept that the project was dead. In November he and Blair announced the extension of the remit of the JCC, following a review of its work and effectiveness; the remit was eventually extended to cover a number of specific European policy issues. The move roused predictable opposition within the party, but Ashdown won support for it from the parliamentary party and, narrowly, from the party's committees.

Despite delays, the government was making progress on several constitutional reform issues that had been included in the Cook–Maclennan Agreement, including devolution for Scotland and Wales, PR for the European elections and first-stage reform of the House of Lords. Nevertheless, Ashdown was aware that he had failed in his main objective, achieving PR for Westminster elections, and after the government's hostile response to the Jenkins report he determined to resign the leadership; he had agreed with his wife before the 1997 election that he would step down as leader at some point before the following election. He delayed the announcement until the extension of the JCC's remit had been agreed, finally revealing his intentions on 20 January 1999.

Who are the Liberal Democrats?

'We see that the image of the Liberal Democrats that was often conveyed by the media in times past as predominantly sandal-wearing, bearded male eccentrics concerned about marginal issues is far from the truth. While we did not ask our respondents about their footwear or shaving habits, we did ask them enough about their background and attitudes to know that such an image is a caricature. Liberal Democrat members are relatively mature, highly educated professionals whose attitudes reflect the core beliefs of modern Liberal Democracy.'[37]

During the 1990s the membership of Britain's three main political parties were studied in some detail. The data showed that Liberal Democrat members were predominantly male (like the Conservatives but unlike Labour) with an average age of fifty-nine (older than Labour, younger than the Conservatives). Liberal Democrats were the most highly educated of the three: 42 per cent had a degree, compared to 30 per cent of Labour members and 19 per cent of Conservatives. 46 per cent of the party membership worked, or had worked, in the public and 10 per cent in the voluntary sector, no less than 74 per cent in professional occupations.

Party members strongly supported constitutional reform, industrial democracy and European integration: two-thirds believed that the UK should join the euro. An overwhelming majority favoured increased taxation and government spending and the redistribution of income and wealth, but they were not collectivists, also favouring free markets and individual responsibility. Very strong support was evident for environmental policy, including higher taxes for car users. Members were socially liberal on issues such as abortion and sexuality, but less so on issues of crime, such as sentencing policy. 80 per cent of members thought that the party should stand by its principles, even it meant losing an election.

In common with other parties, levels of political activism fell throughout the 1990s, though even in 1999, 30 per cent of Liber Democrat members saw themselves as very or fairly active within the party (compared to 17 per cent of Conservatives and 25 per cent of Labour). Party members' willingness to campaign both during and between elections was an important factor in the party's growing ability to target its resources and win seats, which paid such dividends in the 1997 election.

Ashdown's resignation was to take effect in August, with the leadership election due to kick off after the European elections in June. He therefore had the satisfaction of seeing the party do well in the first elections to the new Scottish Parliament and Welsh Assembly in May. In Scotland the party won 17 seats (out of 129) and formed a coalition government with Labour, with the Scottish Liberal Democrat leader Jim Wallace becoming Deputy First Minister and his colleague Ross Finnie joining him in the Scottish Cabinet (of eleven) as Minister for Rural Affairs. Ironically, this was a considerable boost to the principle of co-operation with Labour, but came too late to have any effect south of the border. In Wales the party won six seats; Labour at first formed a minority administration but in 2000 also entered a coalition with the Liberal Democrats. In the local elections held on the same day the party won 25 per cent of the vote, losing seats to the Conservatives but making significant gains from Labour.

A month later the introduction of PR helped the party increase its representation in the European Parliament from two to ten MEPs, the largest national contingent in the European Liberal group. The Liberal Democrats won only 12.1 per cent of the vote, however, and there were substantial votes for 'fourth parties', including the UK Independence Party and the Greens, who both won seats. This was perhaps the first sign that the party would face difficulties in contesting PR elections, where its normal campaigning style, focusing on targeting resources, promoting local candidates and squeezing the third-placed party, would not work – though European elections were particularly challenging, taking place over huge regional constituencies, for a legislature that the electorate was largely ignorant of and with the party fighting on a pro-European platform that was not especially attractive to many of its local supporters, particularly in south-west England.

Ashdown's resignation as leader took most MPs by surprise. He decided not to support any successor, and the group of MPs around Ashdown fragmented; Menzies Campbell, Don Foster and Nick Harvey all at times contemplated standing, but all in the end decided against. The clear favourite from the beginning was Charles Kennedy, who, as a former party president and a frequent performer on television, had a high profile among the party membership. His main challenger turned out to be Simon Hughes, from the party's activist left; although Hughes fought a more professional campaign than many had expected, and seemed to be catching Kennedy towards the end of the election, he started too late and could not overcome Kennedy's strong support among the armchair membership. Most of the party's MPs supported Kennedy, partly from an aversion to Hughes, who could be seen as erratic and populist, and partly because they could see who was likely to win. In common with most other leadership elections, ideological factors did not distinguish the candidates, and none of them was enthusiastic about pursuing closer links with Labour. In the final round of the election, after the votes of David Rendel, Jackie Ballard and Malcolm Bruce were eliminated, Kennedy beat Hughes by 28,425 to 21,833.

Ashdown's leadership was over. That night he recorded in his diary: 'I left the celebrations quietly and walked back to the House feeling just a tinge of sadness that I am no longer a leader of one of the great British political parties. But this was more than offset by the feeling of having cast off a very heavy burden ... I felt very contented.'[38]

Ashdown and the 'project': assessment

In the short history of the Liberal Democrats, Paddy Ashdown plays a highly significant role. It is not unreasonable to suggest that the party would not have survived its early years at all without him, or at least would have taken much longer to recover. In the second phase of his leadership, 1992–97, he successfully rode the rising tide of support for centre-left sentiment and the rejection of the Conservative government that not only swept Labour into power in 1997 but delivered the highest number of seats for a third party for seventy years. Under a less skilled leader, the Liberal Democrats could easily have been squeezed out by Blair's New Labour. The abandonment of equidistance can thus be seen as an – ultimately successful – attempt to become part of the movement for change rather a casualty of it.

In contrast, the third phase of the Ashdown leadership, 1997–99, was a failure, as Ashdown freely admits: although several aspects of the Cook–Maclennan constitutional reform agenda were implemented – though sometimes in partial and, to Liberal Democrats, unsatisfactory ways (such as reforming the Lords only to the extent of removing (most of the) hereditary peers' right to vote) – the big prize, PR for Westminster, was never even close. Ashdown later blamed a series of factors: Blair's overriding objective in his first term, which was to get elected for a second, rather than achieve anything as fundamental as reforming the political system; Blair's overestimation of his ability to charm away opposition in his own party; and his underestimation of the strength of that opposition to any deal with the Liberal Democrats.[39] Ashdown felt that that was due in part to the fact that Blair was an outsider in Labour politics, not someone who had grown up in the tribal traditions of the party – a characteristic that Ashdown also shared in relation to the Liberal Democrats, and which arguably led him to the same error, to underestimate the strength of his own party's opposition to a deal with Labour, which became steadily more apparent throughout 1997 and 1998.

Was Blair ever serious about his half-promises and hints to Ashdown? Ashdown thought he was, arguing that he would hardly have spent so much time on all those discussions and meetings, even after he had become Prime Minister, if he had not been genuinely committed to it. Furthermore, Prescott and Brown clearly believed it too, as revealed in the depth of their opposition; Prescott was reported to have warned that 'the day that man [Ashdown] walks through the door is the day that I walk out of it'.[40] Richard Holme told Ashdown that he believed Blair meant it – 'but then, the best seducers always do!'[41] However, even if Blair had whole-heartedly supported Ashdown's aims, he enjoyed very little support in his Cabinet, and would have risked a split in his own party if he had pushed the issue. At the very least, as Ashdown believed, 'although I think he spoke the truth when he said that partnership with the Lib Dems was the big thing he wanted to do to reshape British politics, it never was the *next* thing he wanted to do. Hence the delays, which in the end killed us.'[42]

The result of the last phase of Ashdown's leadership, as Tony Greaves has observed, 'was that Liberal Democrats loved their leader but, insofar as they sensed his strategy, most wanted none of it. The "what if" question must be how much more could have been achieved if all that time at the top and personal energy had been spent on something other than "The Project".[43] But was there a realistic alternative? Like Grimond and Steel before him, Ashdown was driven inexorably by the logic of the realignment/ co-operation strategy. However well the Liberal Democrats performed in elections – and Ashdown hardly neglected that aspect of party strategy – it never seemed remotely feasible that the party would leap straight to majority government from third position, or even replace one of the two bigger parties as the main opposition. Sooner or later the party would hold the balance of power, and in the political circumstances of the 1990s, it was inconceivable that the Liberal Democrats could have reached an arrangement with anyone other than the Labour Party. Indeed, Ashdown was not particularly aiming for a hung parliament, in which, he thought, any attempt to bring in PR would be seen as weakness on the part of the bigger coalition partner; he wanted to introduce it from a position of strength, with both parties of the left genuinely behind it. His problem was that most of the Labour Party was never committed to PR at all, and saw no point in making any concessions to Ashdown's party once they commanded a 179-seat majority in the House of Commons. But Ashdown was always going to try; he possessed neither the temperament nor the patience to sit quietly on the sidelines, snatching what chances he could to advance incrementally.

No comprehensive and objective assessment of the 'project' with Labour has yet been carried out. It is not clear what, if anything, the JCC ever achieved, but it can certainly be argued that the Cook–Maclennan Agreement had a direct impact in the shape of the constitutional reforms Blair implemented after 1997. Probably Labour would have devolved power to Scotland without any prompting from the Liberal Democrats, but Labour's attachment to Welsh devolution and to proportional representation for the European elections was much weaker and these policies may not have been implemented in the absence of the agreement. Thus Ashdown and the Liberal Democrats contributed to permanent and profound changes in the way in which Britain is governed. And in the final analysis, if Ashdown had delivered on proportional representation, the third phase of his leadership would have been seen as a triumphant success. It was a calculated strategy, but in that respect it failed.

1999–2001: Edging away from Labour

If the party had deliberately set out to choose a leader who was as different as possible from Paddy Ashdown as his successor, they could hardly have done better than Charles Kennedy, the victor of the leadership election of July–August 1999. Where Ashdown was driven, energetic and hyperactive, Kennedy was relaxed and laid-back – a considerable part of his attraction after the last years of the Ashdown leadership. Kennedy opted for the default position for leaders of third parties: opposing both the government and the main opposition, and looking out for opportunities to distinguish the party from both. He was to find them increasingly in opposition to New Labour's authoritarian and centralising approach to politics, and, above all else, over the war in Iraq.

Charles Kennedy (1959–)

Kennedy was born in Inverness, the son and grandson of Highland crofters. His entry into Parliament was sudden; at Easter 1983, when he was in the middle of a postgraduate degree in the US, he unexpectedly gained the SDP nomination for Ross, Cromarty & Skye, and in June won the seat from the Liberals' fourth place in 1979, defeating the sitting Conservative minister and becoming the country's youngest MP at the age of twenty-three.

He soon acquired a reputation as a gifted communicator, both on the conference platform and on TV, reaching not just the usual political audiences, but also a wider public with appearances on programmes such as *Wogan* and *Have I Got News for You*. At an early stage, he was tipped as a future leader. After the 1987 general election, alone among the SDP's MPs, he stood up to his leader, David Owen, to back merger with the Liberal Party. He was president of the Liberal Democrats in 1990–94, and was the obvious contender for the leadership when Ashdown decided to go.

Kennedy's style as leader was very different from that of Ashdown. He was far more collegiate; and he disliked, and actively avoided, confrontation. This meant he suffered none of the leadership defeats at conference that Ashdown had experienced on a number of occasions; since Kennedy never actually adopted a position on a key conference vote, he could not be defeated. Initially a refreshing change from Ashdown's, this approach eventually, however, came to be seen as one of directionless inertia. It was the party's drift and lack of direction as much as his alcoholism that brought an end to his leadership in 2006.

After stepping down as leader, Kennedy declined to take a party spokesmanship. He was one of the few MPs not to support the coalition in 2010, abstaining in the final vote.

Kennedy's first two years as leader were a success. He gave the party the quiet life it had been seeking after the Ashdown years; he edged gradually away from the relationship with Labour, allowing the Joint Cabinet Committee to complete its work on drawing up a common negotiating position for the next stage of EU integration, but then finally abandoning it after the 2001 general election. Any of the other four leadership contenders would also have ended the association, but by simply letting the JCC wither on the vine rather than pulling out at once, Kennedy was able simultaneously to reassure his own party, avoid creating bad blood with Blair, and ensure that the Liberal Democrats were still associated with Labour during the 2001 election, when there was still plenty of anti-Tory tactical voting.

Similarly, he adopted a very different approach to the possibility of a Labour–Liberal Democrat coalition in Wales than Ashdown would have done. After the Assembly elections in 1999 Labour had formed a minority government, but in February 2000 they faced defeat on a vote of no confidence in the First Secretary, Alun Michael. Kennedy came in for heavy lobbying in favour of a deal from both Blair and Ashdown, but refused to intervene, leaving the decision to the Liberal Democrat group in the Assembly; as he said to Blair: 'You don't understand. It's not my decision; it's their decision. It's devolved.'[44] He was thus able to demonstrate both his understanding of the politics of devolution and his independence from Labour, along with a very different leadership style to that of his predecessor. And in the end, in October 2000, the new Labour leader, Rhodri Morgan, negotiated a coalition with the Liberal Democrats, agreeing in the process to no fewer than 114 Liberal Democrat manifesto commitments, including smaller school class sizes, free school milk, a bigger student hardship fund, a larger health budget and a freeze in NHS prescription charges.

Kennedy again displayed good judgment over his decision to take on the Conservatives over their policy on immigration and asylum during the Romsey by-election in May 2000. Although the Tory leader William Hague was at the time taking his party decisively to the right, it seemed unlikely that the Liberal Democrats could win what was one of the opposition Conservatives' fifty safest seats. But win it they did, after a campaign focusing on the damage Conservative governments' underfunding of public services had caused and specifically attacking Hague's 'saloon-bar language' and 'gutter politics' on immigration and asylum.[45] The party won Romsey on an 18 per cent swing from the Conservatives, squeezing the Labour vote down to under 4 per cent. It was an excellent and largely unexpected result, overshadowing sizeable Conservative gains in the local elections held the same day, and undermining Hague's position as Tory leader. Kennedy had turned the contest into a personal trial between the two leaders, and come off better. He reprised the theme in a poster in the 2001 general election, with the slogan: 'I jump on injustice. Not bandwagons.'

Kennedy came over well in the 2001 election, his image as an ordinary and likeable individual contrasting positively with the professional politicians Blair and Hague. The party made the most of his style of politics, presenting him as open, down to earth and straightforward, the antithesis of spin. The policy platform presented in the manifesto was a straightforward development of the Ashdown themes, adjusted for the first four years of the New Labour government. Thus policy on taxation began to change away from simply raising revenue for expenditure on public services, and concentrated on being more fair, in line with Labour's perceived failure to reduce levels of inequality; this included replacing Council Tax with a local income tax (a long-held Liberal policy) and raising the top rate of income tax. Environmental policy continued as a strong theme (Kennedy had devoted almost the whole of his spring 2000 conference speech to the environment), and the commitment to Europe also remained clear, although as Eurosceptic feelings spread throughout the UK, policy proposals tended to focus on the need to democratise the EU's institutions.

What was new was a stress on 'freedom', reflected in the title of the manifesto (*Freedom, Justice, Honesty*). The party promised to reduce the number of centrally set targets for public services, reduce restrictions on local government, and end unnecessary regulation of business – all in response to the perceived 'nanny-state' governmental style of New Labour. This was a natural stance for the Liberal Democrats to adopt, given their decentralist ethos, but it did not imply any hostility to the concept of state provision of services; in autumn 1998 the party conference had heavily defeated a proposal from the leadership for 'neighbourhood schools trusts', a similar idea in some ways to the academies later introduced by the Labour government.

No one expected the Liberal Democrats to do well in the election – the standard orthodoxy being that Liberals lost votes under periods of Labour government – and perhaps as a result neither Kennedy nor his policies were subjected to particularly close scrutiny. However, with the Conservatives still deeply unpopular, anti-Tory tactical voting still in evidence (aided by continued covert cooperation between Labour and the Liberal Democrats), and the shine coming off New Labour, the party clearly had an opportunity. The campaign added about five points to the Liberal Democrats' starting position, resulting in a vote share of 18.3 per cent, the first increase in the third-party vote since 1983. Two seats were lost to the Conservatives, and seven (including Romsey) gained, with one more gained from Labour; the party thus ended up with fifty-two seats in total. In regional terms, the party's share of the vote evened out slightly, seeing its largest increases in Scotland (an impressive achievement given that it was in government in Edinburgh), northern England, the East Midlands, and London. With gains in North Norfolk and Chesterfield, for the first time since 1929 the party had at least one MP in every region. The result was very creditable, and a success in particular for Kennedy; opinion polls showed that he was the only one of the three main party leaders to have improved his personal rating during the campaign.

2001 general election (7 June)			
	Votes	%	MPs
Liberal Democrat	4,814,321	18.3	52
Conservative	8,357,615	31.7	166
Labour	**10,724,953**	**40.7**	**413**
SNP	464,314	1.8	5
Plaid Cymru	195,893	0.7	4
Others	1,811,108	6.8	19
Total	26,368,204		659

2001–05: Protest politics

The 2001–05 Parliament was defined by the events of 11 September 2001 and the response to it, in particular Tony Blair's decision to join the US invasion of Iraq in 2003. The Liberal Democrats were presented with their best chance for a generation, holding a policy position – opposition to the war – which was both unique among the three main parties and popular in the country. The fact that they failed to make the most of this opportunity was due largely to a failure of leadership.

From the beginning the Liberal Democrats struck a different note from the other two parties. Although they supported the invasion of Afghanistan in October–November 2001, they carefully differentiated their response from the Conservatives, whose new leader Iain Duncan Smith had offered unqualified support to the government and US President Bush; they stressed the necessity of acting in accordance with international law and drew attention to the need to understand and deal with the root causes of terrorism. They consistently opposed the steady infringements of civil liberties introduced by the government in the name of the war on terror, including in particular detention without trial.

During 2002 the US invasion of Iraq grew steadily nearer. Kennedy was critical of the US approach from the beginning, particularly its emphasis on regime change; as with Afghanistan, this was in sharp contrast to the Conservatives, who, with a few exceptions, were enthusiastic backers of Blair and Bush. The September 2002 Liberal Democrat conference called on the government to participate in military action only as a last resort and under a clear UN mandate, and only after a debate and vote in Parliament. At the end of the conference, Kennedy committed himself to a strategy of replacing the Conservatives – then trailing the Labour Party badly in the opinion polls – as the main opposition party: 'The prize is very great. There is no law that says when the Conservative Party is down it must come up again. And there is no law which says the Liberal Democrats need forever remain third among Britain's political parties.'[46]

Kennedy was careful not to portray his party as opposed to war in all circumstances, and by instinct he was cautious and concerned to maintain party unity. The approach of the major anti-war march on 15 February 2003, however, forced him to come off the fence; it was clear it was going to be very widely supported, even if its organisers, the Stop the War Coalition, were an alliance of far left and radical Muslim groups. The party's Federal Executive unanimously called for Liberal Democrat participation, but the foreign affairs spokesman, Menzies Campbell, and several other MPs were opposed, fearing association with anti-American and far left groups. In the end Kennedy took the decision to participate without consulting Campbell or anyone else, following a *Guardian* lunch at which journalists criticised his prevarication. About 3,000 party members joined the march, and Kennedy was the most senior politician to address the rally, though he stressed the need for a UN resolution authorising action rather than straightforward opposition to the war.

Kennedy's stance drew heavy criticism from the Conservative Party and the right-wing press, many of whom likened his position to Neville Chamberlain's appeasement of Hitler; yet opinion polls suggested significant public support. He also succeeded in keeping his party together; although there were a few Liberal Democrat supporters of the eventual British participation in the invasion, none were of any significance, with the exception of Paddy Ashdown (who was then safely out of the way in Bosnia, and refused to make any public comment, though he sent a private letter of support to Blair). The emphasis on the need for a UN resolution was key to party unity; the Liberal Democrats had always been strong supporters of the international rule of law, and even those who could see the value of removing Saddam Hussein from power were opposed to doing it without a UN mandate. In the end there was no UN resolution and the Liberal Democrats were the only major party not to split on the issue in the House of Commons vote on 18 March 2003 ('the Liberal Democrats – unified, as ever, in opportunism and error', as Tony Blair put it).[47]

In the end the military action against Iraq was short in duration, but the aftermath, including the failure of the US-led coalition effectively to reconstruct the country, mounting terrorist atrocities, and the lack of any evidence of Iraqi weapons of mass destruction, steadily alienated British public opinion and seriously undermined trust in Tony Blair. In 2004 Kennedy declined to participate in the Butler inquiry into the failures of intelligence, on the grounds that it was to exclude the political decisions taken on the basis of the available intelligence. This was an astute move, as the Butler inquiry was widely regarded as unlikely to be particularly critical of the Prime Minister (though in the end it was).

As the only party to have opposed the war, the Liberal Democrats reaped electoral rewards in local elections in 2002–04, beating Labour into third place in 2004 on a notional country-wide vote of 29 per cent. Although the Conservatives also gained council seats in each of the three elections, Liberal Democrats gradually replaced them as the opposition to Labour in the main cities; in 2003, for example, there were no Tory councillors elected in Manchester, Newcastle or Liverpool and only one in Sheffield. The Liberal Democrats steadily gained control of several northern cities, in 2004 gaining Newcastle and Leeds (jointly with the Conservatives), adding these to Liverpool, which had been won in 1998.

The Scottish and Welsh elections in 2003 were not so positive; in a pattern that was to become more evident in the 2005 and 2010 general elections, Labour support held up more strongly in the two nations than in England. The Liberal Democrat outcome was unchanged in each case, with seventeen seats in the Scottish Parliament and six in the Welsh Assembly; in Scotland another Liberal Democrat–Labour coalition was agreed, but in Wales the Labour Party won just enough seats to govern independently. Much more striking was the result of the by-election in Brent East in September; hitherto a safe Labour seat, the Liberal Democrats capitalised on the deep levels of anger and distrust of Blair that were evident; party leaflets regularly featured pictures of Blair and Bush together. Starting from a poor third place, but helped by a weak Conservative campaign and a low turn-out, the party won the seat on a 29 per cent swing; it was the first seat Labour had lost in a by-election for fifteen years. The relegation of the Tories to a distant third place was a major contributory factor to their MPs' overthrow of Iain Duncan Smith a month later, and his replacement by Michael Howard.

Liberal Democrats in power: Scotland and Wales

The establishment of the Scottish Parliament and Welsh Assembly in 1999, and the fact that their elections were conducted by proportional representation, gave the Liberal Democrats opportunities to share power and implement policies in both nations.

In Scotland, the party formed a coalition government with Labour from 1999 to 2007. The Scottish Liberal Democrat leaders Jim Wallace (until 2005) and Nicol Stephen (from 2005) served as Deputy First Ministers; the post was combined with Minister for Justice, 1999–2003, and Minister for Enterprise and Lifelong Learning, 2003–07. Ross Finnie joined them in the Cabinet throughout the period, as Minister for Rural Affairs 1999–2003 and for Environment and Rural Development 2003–07. From 2003 the party had a third Cabinet post as Minister for Transport, held by Nicol Stephen 2003–05, and Tavish Scott 2005–07. There were also two Liberal Democrat junior ministers throughout the period.

The coalition is generally recognised as having succeeded in producing political stability in the new Parliament and also in implementing many Liberal Democrat policies, including free personal care for the elderly, a different system of university student finance to England (no up-front tuition fees, but a contribution, after graduation, to a fund for assisting poorer students), free prescriptions and eye tests, more liberal freedom of information provisions and proportional representation for local elections. None of these seem likely to have been implemented by a solely Labour administration. The Liberal Democrats were widely regarded as having played their hand well, at least until 2007; indeed, Henry McLeish, Labour First Minister 2000–01, reckoned that 'the Liberal Democrats have probably gained more from devolution than any other party'.[48]

In Wales, Labour also failed to gain a majority in 1999, and after a period of minority government the party chose coalition with the Liberal Democrats in October 2000. The Welsh Liberal Democrat leader Mike German served as Deputy First Minister and Minister first for Economic Development and later for Rural Affairs. His colleague Jenny Randerson joined him in the Cabinet as Minister for Culture, and the party also had one junior minister. As in Scotland, the Liberal Democrats were able to implement a significant number of policies; indeed, they claimed that 80 per cent of the policies in their manifesto would be introduced. Specific achievements included smaller school class sizes, free school milk, a bigger student hardship fund, a larger health budget and a freeze in NHS prescription charges.

In the European elections in 2004 the party increased its vote to 14.9 per cent and gained two more MEPs, but was beaten into fourth place by an unexpectedly strong performance by the UK Independence Party. The Greater London Assembly elections were better, with a strong third place, and a gain of one seat, to five. As in 2003, by-elections proved even more fruitful; in July the party won the safe Labour seat of Leicester South (the victor, Parmjit Singh Gill, becoming the first Liberal Democrat MP from an ethnic minority) and just failed to gain the even safer Labour constituency of Birmingham Hodge Hill. In September Labour just held on again in Hartlepool. Labour had learned from its defeat in Brent East; their campaigns were much shorter (in Brent Labour had delayed the poll for several months, allowing the Liberal Democrats to build up their organisation), much more targeted on Liberal Democrat policies (including in particular the party's policy on crime and policing, which Labour regularly attacked as 'soft on crime'), and more personal. Nevertheless, the results were another boost to Liberal Democrat credibility, particularly in comparison to the Conservatives, who were forced into poor third places in Leicester South and Hodge Hill and fourth, behind UKIP, in Hartlepool. The Liberal Democrats increasingly began to seem like the main opposition to Labour; in July *The Sun* paid the party the compliment of describing it as 'the most dangerous party in Britain',[49] while in September *The Guardian* declared that if it had had a vote in Hartlepool it would have been cast for the Liberal Democrats: 'We still support most of the aims of this Government. The Liberal Democrats, though, are the one party to have consistently opposed the war and to have consistently tried to hold the executive to account. This election is about the effectiveness of Parliament.'[50]

As is normal for third parties, most of the press attention the Liberal Democrats attracted focused on the leader. Kennedy's collegiate style of leadership, however, was allowing other figures to rise to prominence, including in particular the foreign affairs spokesman (and deputy leader from February 2003), Menzies Campbell, who played a prominent role in the party's response to the Iraq War, and Vince Cable, Treasury spokesman from autumn 2003.

In the background, however, there was increasing concern over the leader himself. While Kennedy's fondness for drink had been an open secret since his university days, very few party members knew how seriously it had begun to affect him. He missed key events and debates in Parliament; on other occasions he appeared, but obviously the worse for wear. In July 2003, he even went so far as to organise a press conference to announce that he was standing down as leader temporarily to seek medical treatment for alcoholism – but he cancelled it at the last moment and the episode stayed a secret until the publication of his biography in 2007. In March 2004 he missed the budget speech, ostensibly because of illness, and appeared ill and pale at the party's spring conference a few days later; rumours began to circulate about him standing down as leader, either temporarily or permanently. In a private meeting with party managers a few days afterwards he admitted that he was an alcoholic, though it was steadfastly denied in public. His office became used to keeping him out of sight when he was drunk, which increased his isolation from other Liberal Democrat MPs, undermining his support among his colleagues. Critics within the parliamentary party were always deterred from acting, however, both because he either claimed that he had his drinking under control or was about to seek help (and in fact his alcoholism was not a consistent problem), and because the party was doing well in the polls and no one wanted a leadership election in embarrassing circumstances in the run-up to the general election.

Nevertheless, Kennedy's leadership style was increasingly unsuited to the higher profile role the party was playing. Kennedy never seemed to have a clear agenda for his leadership; although, like Paddy Ashdown, he chaired the party's Federal Policy Committee, unlike his predecessor he gave it no clear lead. The book he published in 2000, *The Future of Politics*, although designed to answer the question 'What makes this

Kennedy fellow tick? … Why is he a Liberal Democrat?'[51] revealed only, as his biographer put it, 'a startling lack of original thinking on policy or a strand of political thought that was identifiably his own'.[52] Against this background the publication, in August 2004, of *The Orange Book: Reclaiming Liberalism*, by David Laws MP and Paul Marshall,[53] can be seen as an attempt to give the party direction. The book was heavily trailed before its appearance, *The Guardian*, for example, leading an article with the claim that the 'Liberal Democrats are set to be shaken by a controversial call from the party's young Turks to adopt new "tough liberal" policies which are pro-market and more Eurosceptic and place new responsibilities on persistent offenders'.[54]

Despite *The Orange Book*'s pre-release spin and the tone of some its chapters, in fact its contents were almost entirely in line with existing party policy. Almost the only new proposal was Laws's call for a social insurance basis for health care, an idea which had been rejected by the party in 2002. Issuing a call for such a major revision of policy, accompanied by the broad criticism of the party's approach as 'nanny-state Liberalism', could well have been acceptable two or three years before an election, or immediately after one – but to do so just before a campaign struck many in the party as unnecessarily divisive and likely only to give ammunition to the party's opponents (as it did, with Labour canvassers in the Hartlepool by-election claiming that the Liberal Democrats wished to privatise the NHS). Laws was subject to bitter criticism within the parliamentary party and the book's conference launch meeting was cancelled.

Social versus economic liberals?

There have always been divisions within British Liberalism over the appropriate balance between the market and the state. 'Classical' or 'economic' liberals, often harking back to the party's approach throughout the nineteenth century, have tended to rank individual freedom above material equality and to argue that the state's sphere has to be strictly limited. 'Social liberals', looking back in their turn to the New Liberal interventionist social policies of the early twentieth century, have argued that poverty, unemployment, ill-health, disability and a lack of education are serious enough constraints on freedom that state action, including redistributive taxation, is justified to redress them. Both groups have been aware of the dangers of the growth in the size of the state; economic liberals have generally concluded that this should lead to an attempt to reduce it, whereas social liberals have tended to argue that it should be constrained (for example through a written constitution) and decentralised, to make it more accountable and participative.

Since Jo Grimond's leadership, at least, the Liberal Party and then the Liberal Democrats adopted a predominantly social-liberal approach; in the 1980s the Liberal Party's Alliance with the SDP, and the championing of the free market by Margaret Thatcher, helped to minimise the attractiveness of a more economic-liberal approach. The development of New Labour's centralised and bureaucratic model of the state, however, helped to revive interest in an alternative version of Liberalism, leading to the publication of *The Orange Book: Reclaiming Liberalism* in 2004. Its main message was clearly pro-market; its main editor, David Laws MP, complained that 'in the decades up to the 1980s, the Liberal belief in economic Liberalism was progressively eroded by forms of soggy socialism and corporatism, which have too often been falsely perceived as a necessary corollary of social liberalism'.[55] Laws called for the party to draw on its economic-liberal heritage to address public service delivery, introducing more choice, competition and consumer power.

The publication of *The Orange Book* led, three years later, to the appearance of an explicitly social-liberal alternative: *Reinventing the State: Social Liberalism for the 21st Century.*[56] The book made the case for state action in a series of areas where market solutions were inadequate, including in particular the need to reduce income and wealth inequality and to tackle climate change. A major theme of the book was localism, and a series of chapters explored how decision-making and public service provision could be decentralised. 'It is about reinventing the British state so that it delivers social justice and environmental sustainability through a decentralised and participatory democracy.'[57]

Although the two books were certainly different in tone and message, the extent of policy disagreement between them was limited, and several MPs contributed chapters to both. In reality there is a spectrum of opinion within the party, and many party members would decline to be identified by either label. After the 2005 election the supposed divisions became a short-hand, in the eyes of the media, for all sorts of other disagreements within the party, including the normal tensions that always exist between the parliamentary leadership and the grassroots activists. 'Economic liberals', or *'Orange Bookers'*, became equated with parliamentary 'modernisers', eager to short-circuit the party's internal democratic structures and put more power into the hands of the MPs, while 'social liberals' were portrayed as the grassroots activists unwilling to compromise the purity of their beliefs in the pursuit of power, happier to stay in opposition as a party of protest.

The Orange Book had little influence on the manifesto prepared for the 2005 election, which was in any case well advanced by the time of its publication. There were few significant differences from the 2001 platform: in the face of Labour's substantial injection of resources into public services, the party's commitment to increase the basic rate of income tax was dropped, but otherwise taxation policy stayed broadly the same, concentrating on creating a fairer system. The extra revenue that would be generated from a higher top rate would help to pay for free personal care for elderly and disabled people and the abolition of university tuition and top-up fees – an important commitment, given that Labour had broken its 2001 promise not to introduce them. The party also promised to abolish the Department of Trade and Industry, cut subsidies to industry, and scrap plans to introduce compulsory identity cards. As before, environmental policy was a consistent theme throughout. The manifesto particularly criticised Tony Blair's style of government: centralising and interfering, micro-managing public services, and concentrating too much power in the hands of the Prime Minister.

The party was able to display its proposals much more extensively than before thanks to a last-minute donation of over £2 million from a businessman, Michael Brown. This was by far and away the largest donation the party had ever received, though it arrived too late for it to be used to maximum effect; the money could have been much more valuable if it could have been deployed in target seats in the years running up to the election. (After the election, it transpired that Brown had acquired the money dishonestly; fortunately for the Liberal Democrats, a court ruled that they had carried out sufficient checks on the donation to have satisfied the Electoral Commission's procedures.)

In contrast with the 2001 election, the 2005 contest saw a much greater focus on the Liberal Democrats, largely because the government went into the campaign with a smaller lead over the Conservatives, and the Liberal Democrats were starting from a stronger base in the polls, 21 per cent. Initially the party suffered from this attention. The low point was the launch of the manifesto at the start of the campaign, where Kennedy proved incapable of explaining the details of the party's policy on local income tax. He tried to shrug this off as a result of the birth of his son three days before, but in reality he was hung-over and under-prepared. Although Kennedy's performance improved later in the campaign, voters did not see him as a potential Prime Minister, a question that had not been an issue in 2001. He also lacked a coherent message; thanks to the events of the preceding Parliament, for the first time in years the electorate were able to identify a number of specific policies, including opposition to the war in Iraq, tuition fees and the Council Tax, as being Liberal Democrat positions, but at the same time they entirely failed to grasp any underlying connections between them. Voters knew what the party was *against*, but had no idea what it was *for* – and neither the manifesto nor Kennedy's own campaign gave them much of a clue.

As Labour failed to establish a clear lead in the opinion polls, they were able to play on the electorate's fear of a Conservative victory under Michael Howard to convince wavering Labour voters not to switch to the Liberal Democrats – even in seats where in reality the Lib Dems were much better placed to defeat sitting Tories. In the end the party increased its share of the vote to 22 per cent, the highest figure since 1987, but a much smaller rise over the campaign than in previous elections. The party did particularly well among students and Muslim voters and, as in 2001, the best results were in areas of Labour strength; in the North of England the Liberal Democrat vote rose by 6.2 per cent and in Scotland by 6.3 per cent, beating the SNP and the Tories to take second place. This resulted in sixty-two seats, the highest number of Liberal MPs since 1923. The party gained eleven seats from Labour, almost all in urban areas, and lost one, while one seat was gained from Plaid Cymru. Three were gained from the Conservatives, but five were lost, and the so-called 'decapitation strategy' aimed at high-profile Conservatives in vulnerable seats completely failed. It was a good result; but given what had happened in the previous four years, the unpopularity of Tony Blair and the lack of appeal of the Conservatives under Michael Howard, many had hoped for much better.

2005 general election (5 May)			
	Votes	*%*	*MPs*
Liberal Democrat	5,985,454	22.0	62
Conservative	8,784,915	32.4	198
Labour	**9,552,436**	**35.2**	**356**
SNP	412,267	1.5	6
Plaid Cymru	174,838	0.6	3
Others	2,238,600	8.2	21
Total	*27,148,510*		*646*

Who votes for the Liberal Democrats?

As the Liberal Party revived in the 1960s and 1970s, it was often seen in voting studies as nothing more than a repository for protest votes. Support for the party was regarded as highly volatile, with little consistency in its bases of electoral support. This was always, however, something of an exaggeration, and became even more so throughout the 1980s and 1990s. Even in its darkest days, the party always did better in rural constituencies. It also retained its historic link with Nonconformism (although by 2005 this factor seemed to have disappeared). The party found it easier to attract middle-class voters than working-class ones, and the higher the level of education of a voter, whatever their class, the more likely they were to vote Liberal; the party did particularly well among those educated to degree level.

This social base placed the party closer to the Conservatives than to Labour, explaining why it tended to do worse under periods of Labour government. From 1997 onwards, however, this changed; the Liberal Democrats gained votes in all the three elections under the Blair and Brown governments, and gained seats in 2001 and 2005, including several from Labour.

Analyses of the social bases of Liberal Democrat support showed no great change, however; the party continued to poll strongest among professional and managerial voters and weakest among routine and semi-routine workers, and small employers. In 2005 45 per cent of those in full-time education, and 33 per cent of those with a university degree (compared with 15 per cent of those with no educational qualification), voted Liberal Democrat. One marked change in 2005 was the party's strong performance among Muslim voters, in the wake of the war in Iraq; this was much less of a factor in 2010.

Iraq was probably the major factor moving voters away from Labour in the 2005 election; over a quarter of 2001 Labour supporters who strongly disapproved of Britain's involvement switched to the Liberal Democrats. Disappointment with the performance of the public services also helped, but in contrast with Iraq, Labour voters disaffected with their former party over this issue were almost as likely to switch to the Conservatives.

The key point underlying these changes in voting patterns was that by 1997 the Liberal Democrats were seen as ideologically closer to Labour than to the Conservatives. This was a marked change from earlier periods; in 1974 more than three times as many people saw the Liberal Party as closer to the Conservatives than to Labour, and even in 1979, after the Liberals had kept the Labour government in power for eighteen months through the Lib-Lab Pact, voters saw the party as slightly closer to the Tories. In the 1980s and early 1990s, again the party was seen as closer to the Conservatives, but by 1997 this had changed decisively; three times as many people saw the Liberal Democrats as closer to Labour. This was even more marked in 2001 and about the same in 2005. Thus the party was well placed to benefit from the collapse in Labour support from 2007 onwards.

However, as the psephologist John Curtice observed, this situation obviously posed dangers in the event of a hung parliament: 'protesting Labour voters might want to bring Labour to heel, but they may be less happy to see Liberal Democrat MPs help remove Labour from office'.[58]

2005–06: Changing leaders I – from Kennedy to Campbell

The twenty months following the 2005 election were to see the most unstable period the party had known, with three leaders and two leadership elections. It was triggered by the outcome of the election itself, and a widespread feeling in the party and outside that the Liberal Democrats had failed to realise a historic opportunity.

A long drawn-out reshuffle of the Shadow Cabinet first unsettled the parliamentary party, and then angered several veterans, as they were dropped in favour of MPs who had only just been elected. A number of MPs started what looked like manoeuvring for the leadership, and at the end of June Kennedy threatened to sack any front-bench spokesman who plotted against him or spread rumours about his alcoholism. In September the party conference revealed a level of unhappiness with the leadership among the wider party, and frustration that the election results had not been better; the perception of drift and lack of direction became widespread. The leadership suffered two defeats in conference debates (which, while not unknown, were not common) and divisions seemed to be opening up between the so-called 'economic liberals' and 'social liberals'. In reality the differences were not that wide, and the defeats were over relatively minor policy issues, but there was no clear leadership on offer to damp them down and take the party in any particular direction.

A series of cancelled appearances by Kennedy in November brought matters to a head. Faced with an increasingly intrusive press, and accumulating discontent with Kennedy's lacklustre leadership, several MPs began to talk about resigning from the Shadow Cabinet unless the matter was resolved. News of the plan leaked out, however, and Kennedy was able to face down his critics, though many of them told him to his face that his position was untenable. Over the Christmas recess MPs' discontent again began to grow, and half the members of the Shadow Cabinet signed a letter asking Kennedy to reconsider his position. On 5 January 2006 ITN informed Kennedy that it would be running a story about his drinking. Pre-empting it, Kennedy revealed at a hastily organised press conference that he had successfully sought professional help for alcoholism, and announced that since he felt it only fair that party members should have a say in the matter, he was calling a leadership election in which he would be a candidate. Most of the parliamentary party, however, were not prepared to tolerate this, and in the face of a majority of MPs preparing to state that they would not serve under him, Kennedy finally resigned the leadership on 7 January.

Why did it all go wrong? There are two views. The first, expressed in the title of Greg Hurst's biography, *Charles Kennedy: A Tragic Flaw*, is that Kennedy would have been a fine leader if he had not been brought down by drink. It was his alcoholism that muffled his undoubted talents as a communicator, robbed him of the dynamism any third-party leader needs to be effective and forced those around him systematically to cover up, isolating him from his potential supporters in the party. This was the most commonly offered explanation at the time of his resignation.

The alternative view, held by some of those at the centre of the party, but less generally admitted, was that Kennedy's drinking was a symptom of his problem, not a cause: that he was not an effective leader, drunk or sober, and he knew it; he drank partly out of recognition of his own under-performance.[59] His basic problem was that he had no agenda for his leadership, no obvious reason to be leader and no idea of the direction he wanted the party to go in. Although he could often display good judgment when forced to make a decision – for example, over the Romsey by-election, withdrawal from the JCC or the refusal to participate in the Butler Inquiry – in between these points, or away from the pressure of election campaigns, he too often simply lapsed into inertia. In 2003 he was lucky over Iraq; without the boost that opposition to the war gave to the Liberal Democrats, it is likely that the hollowness at the centre of his leadership would have been exposed earlier. In the end, Iraq carried him through the 2005 election, but the lack of coherence of the party message was obvious.

Kennedy's resignation proved deeply traumatic for the party, leaving scars that took time to heal. Most of the grassroots party membership had no idea either of Kennedy's drink problem or of his broader failures of leadership, and were affronted by what they saw as an MPs' plot to get rid of a popular and ostensibly effective leader. Indeed, in the summer of 2006 there was media speculation about a Kennedy come-back should his successor Menzies Campbell prove a disappointment, but in time this faded.

The leadership contest triggered by Kennedy's departure saw four possible contenders: the deputy leader, Menzies Campbell, the party president, Simon Hughes, the former MEP Chris Huhne, who had only been elected to Parliament the previous year, and the home affairs spokesman, Mark Oaten. Oaten failed to attract enough MPs to nominate him, however, and withdrew. A few days later his political career effectively came to an end after the *News of the World* published details of his visits to a male prostitute; the paper was presumably frustrated at not being able to use the information against a leadership candidate, or even leader. Hughes' campaign was destabilised in turn by intercepted phone messages forcing him to admit in a newspaper interview that he was bisexual. Remarkably, despite all this, in February the party managed to win the Dunfermline & West Fife by-election from Labour, suggesting, perhaps, that the electorate cared less about Westminster goings-on than journalists and politicians tend to believe.

Campbell led the field from the start, attracting the support of a majority of the MPs; a respected deputy leader and foreign affairs spokesman, he seemed to promise the stability the party needed. He was also sixty-four years old, and would clearly not be leader for long, an added attraction for some potential younger future leadership hopefuls. Huhne fought a energetic and effective campaign, and gained 32 per cent of the first-preference votes to Campbell's 45 per cent and Hughes' 23 per cent. After redistributing Hughes' votes, Campbell was the winner by 29,697 (58 per cent) to 21,628 (42 per cent).

On 2 March 2006, Menzies Campbell thus became the third leader of the Liberal Democrats, and the party looked forward to a period of stability and calm. It was not to get it.

Sir Menzies Campbell (1941–)

Walter Menzies Campbell – usually known as 'Ming' – was born in Greenock. He was a champion athlete, representing Britain at the Tokyo Olympics in 1966; he pursued a legal career. He became interested in Liberal politics after Jo Grimond's attack on the Suez debacle in 1956, and the party's support for Scottish home rule, and in 1987 he won North East Fife, at the third attempt; the seat was more or less the same as that represented by Asquith from 1886 to 1918. He rose to prominence in the Liberal Democrats in particular as foreign affairs spokesman (1997–2006), where he gained a reputation as a knowledgeable and articulate performer.

Campbell was close to Ashdown, and supported his efforts to build closer relationships with the Labour Party; he enjoyed close personal relationships with many Scottish Labour figures, partly from his time at university. In 1999 he contemplated standing for the leadership against Charles Kennedy, but decided that he did not have sufficient backing. In February 2003 he was elected deputy leader by the party's MPs. He was elected leader in March 2006.

Although he helped to stabilise the party and improve its organisation, he failed to communicate its message effectively in Parliament and to the public; his age and his innate caution told against him. Like Roy Jenkins, he found it difficult to adjust to the more exposed position of the leader, in Parliament and the press, after the more rarefied world of foreign policy. Gordon Brown's failure to call an election in 2007 spelled the end of Campbell's leadership, and he announced his resignation in October. Since standing down, he has played no formal role in the parliamentary party.

2006–07: Changing leaders II – from Campbell to Clegg

Campbell's immediate tasks were to stabilise the party, after the disruption of the previous six months, to professionalise its organisation and to give it direction. It was obvious that Blair would hand over the Labour leadership in the next year or so, and the party could then be faced with a snap general election called by the incoming Prime Minister. In terms both of policy and organisation, it had to be ready.

To a considerable extent Campbell achieved all three aims. He took the party organisation seriously, chairing meetings effectively and imposing a sense of purpose. In terms of policy, he largely adopted the agenda begun under Kennedy's notional leadership after the 2005 election. After a passionate but good-natured debate at the 2006 autumn conference, the commitment to a higher top rate of tax was dropped, on the basis that it looked like an attack on aspiration, and the basic rate of tax was to be cut substantially, paid for by ending exemptions for higher-rate taxpayers and introducing new environmental taxes; the new package was in fact more redistributive than the old one. In the spring 2007 conference, Campbell intervened in a debate over the UK's nuclear deterrent, successfully defending his position, of a reduction in the number of warheads, against a proposal for the immediate scrapping of the Trident missile force. After Gordon Brown's arrival as Prime Minister in June raised the prospect of a general election in the autumn, a draft manifesto was approved by the Federal Policy Committee and parliamentary party immediately after the September conference. The party organisation was in good shape to fight an election in October.

In terms of party management, then, Campbell's record was in many ways a good one. Unfortunately for him, this counted for little in the outside world, where he failed to build an image as an effective and charismatic leader. His age proved to be a problem; although he was only sixty-four when he was elected leader, he looked older than his years (treatment for cancer in 2002–03 may have been partly to blame) and he acted old, with an old-fashioned turn of phrase. He was mercilessly lampooned in the media, in a way that would have been regarded as unacceptable if it had been directed against a politician on the basis of their gender or race; as Vince Cable put it, 'to see cartoonists in otherwise liberal newspapers depict a sixty-five year-old as a geriatric has-been with a Zimmer frame went way beyond political wit'.[60]

A well-respected foreign affairs spokesman, Campbell found it difficult to adjust to the rough and tumble of Prime Minister's questions, and the more hostile line of questioning of media interviews; he had too much respect for intellectual argument for simple soundbites to come easily. In fact he worked hard at his communications style and was getting much better by the end of his leadership, but it came too late; in today's media-intensive world, initial images are set very quickly and are difficult to dislodge once formed. In addition, he was innately cautious, too much so for the leader of the third party. On a number of occasions, he took his time reaching decisions, only to find that the ground had shifted under his feet before he could announce them. His preference for consultation before he reached conclusions sometimes stopped him making the snap decision that might have served better.

Campbell's own ratings never reached the levels that Kennedy had attained. As one commentator put in in September 2006:

Sir Menzies, elected on the basis that a steady pair of hands was the best replacement for a shaky pair of hands, has struggled to make an impact with the public ... In the top job, he has seemed ill at ease and unsure of himself except when he is on the territory of foreign affairs ... he has been wounded by polls suggesting that voters still preferred Kennedy drunk to Campbell sober ... He likes to think of himself as a statesman. He needs to remember that a leader also has to be a salesman.[61]

The final one of Campbell's problems became evident during 2007; he lacked solid support in the parliamentary party. His closest adviser, Archy Kirkwood, had stepped down from the Commons in 2005 and was a relatively new peer. Although the vast majority of the party's MPs had supported him in the leadership election, there was no real inner circle committed to the Campbell leadership; as an obvious caretaker leader never likely to do more than one election, most of them were looking ahead to his successor. This increasingly became a problem, particularly after poor election results in May 2007. The English local elections brought an end to six years of steady gains, with losses of almost 250 councillors. Although a notional UK-wide vote of 26 per cent was quite respectable, the party now had far more councillors to lose, and the result looked bad. In the Scottish elections the party lost one MSP; coupled with losses by Labour and a major advance by the SNP, this was enough to bring the Labour–Liberal Democrat coalition to an end. In Wales the party won the same six seats it had at the previous two elections; Labour defeats opened up the possibility of a coalition, but the Welsh Liberal Democrats could not agree on the right course of action and by the time they had reached a conclusion Labour had negotiated a deal with Plaid Cymru.

The party's rating in the opinion polls started to slide, down from 20 per cent in April to 15 per cent in August, lower than at any point since 2002, and to 11 per cent in October. A number of MPs and peers started to try to destabilise Campbell, briefing the press against him and hoping to trigger a new leadership election. The Liberal Democrat peers were a particular problem, as Campbell had alienated many of them by supporting the idea of a referendum on British membership of the EU. This seemed like a neat solution to the problem caused by the campaign, by the Conservatives, UKIP and others, for a referendum on the European constitution. Most, though not all, Liberal Democrats opposed the latter referendum, partly because it would probably be lost; by calling for an 'in/out' vote (which was more likely to be won), Campbell could give a nod to the growing public Euroscepticism while at the same time defending the European cause. Many Liberal Democrat peers, however, who had experienced the European question as a defining issue of their time in politics in the 1960s, 1970s and 1980s, tended to be a good deal more pro-EU than their counterparts in the Commons and were not impressed.

(The issue continued to cause problems for Campbell's successor when, in March 2008, Parliament voted on the ratification of the Lisbon Treaty, the final outcome of the long drawn-out process of agreeing an EU constitution. When the Liberal Democrat amendment to the Commons motion calling for an in/out referendum was not selected, the new leader, Nick Clegg, imposed a three-line whip for abstention on the Conservative amendment for a referendum on the treaty. Thirteen MPs, mostly with small majorities and/or largely Eurosceptic electorates, defied the whip to vote for the amendment; this included three front-bench spokesmen, who resigned. The Liberal Democrat peers, however, opposed both versions of the referendum. The party's public stance on Europe ended up looking, to say the least, confused.)

In the end it was Gordon Brown's decision not to call an election in 2007 that finished Campbell's leadership. Although by mid-2007 many of the party's MPs had doubts about their leader, it made no sense to try to remove him on the eve of an election. When that was postponed for at least a further two years, entirely new possibilities opened up. The hostile background briefing increased, and Campbell reached the end of his tether; as he put it later, 'what frustrated me most was how the media's obsession with my age obscured the party's radical policy agenda and the progress it had made under my leadership'.[62] Faced with a queue of party grandees asking him whether he could tolerate the situation for a further two years, on 15 October he resigned the party leadership. In the end, even his own office did not try to dissuade him from going.

The party's deputy leader Vince Cable took over as acting leader until Campbell's successor could be elected, and became a surprise hit with the media, scoring points against Gordon Brown in the Commons (including deploying the memorable phrase, 'The House has noticed the Prime Minister's remarkable transformation in the last few weeks from Stalin to Mr Bean'). His earlier repeated, but generally ignored, warnings about the extent of the debt problems, both public and private, facing the economy seemed to be coming true, as in the autumn Northern Rock became the first British bank for 150 years to suffer a bank run – the first signs in Britain of the world-wide credit crunch.

Just two candidates fought the second Liberal Democrat leadership election in less than two years: Nick Clegg, the Shadow Home Secretary, and Chris Huhne, the Shadow Environment Secretary. Both were former MEPs; both had only been elected to the Commons in 2005. Huhne was older and had greater political experience, having fought parliamentary seats for the SDP, but from the outset Clegg was seen as the more likely winner and attracted the support of most of the MPs. After a hard-fought election, however, he won only by a very narrow margin, by 20,988 to 20,477 on a 64 per cent turnout. On 18 December 2007 Nick Clegg thus became the fourth leader of the Liberal Democrats.

Nick Clegg (1967–)

The speed of Nick Clegg's rise to prominence within the Liberal Democrats has been without precedent: from virtually unknown to MEP to MP to party leader within the space of ten years.

Clegg has a thoroughly international family background; his ancestors on his father's side include the Russian writer Baroness Moura Budberg (the so-called 'Mata Hari of

Russia', and the mistress of, among others, H. G. Wells and Maxim Gorky), while his Dutch mother was as a girl interned with her family by the Japanese in Indonesia during the war. In 1994 he joined the European Commission, working first on aid for Central Asia and then in Trade Commissioner Leon Brittan's private office.

In 1999 he was elected to the European Parliament for the East Midlands, the first Liberal parliamentarian to be elected in the region since 1931. He served as trade and industry spokesman for the European Liberal group. He decided not to seek a second term, seeing Westminster as the crucial battleground for the cause of European politics in Britain, and in 2004 was selected to succeed Richard Allan, the Liberal Democrat MP for Sheffield Hallam.

After winning the seat in 2005, Clegg was appointed as the Liberal Democrat spokesperson on Europe, and then Shadow Home Secretary. He succeeded Menzies Campbell as leader in December 2007, declaring himself, in his acceptance speech, to be 'a liberal by temperament, by instinct and by upbringing'. He announced his priorities as defending civil liberties, devolving the running of public services to parents, pupils and patients, and protecting the environment.

2007–10: Searching for a definition

Nick Clegg's assumption of the leadership stopped the slide in the opinion polls and stabilised party morale – which came as a distinct relief after two leadership resignations and elections in as many years – and the Liberal Democrats performed strongly in the local elections in 2008 and 2009, beating Labour into third place on both occasions. The party did particularly well in urban areas, picking up much of the collapsing Labour vote under Brown's increasingly unpopular leadership; by the beginning of 2010, the Liberal Democrats were responsible, either by themselves or in coalition, for running seven of the ten biggest British cities outside London, including Sheffield, the city of Clegg's constituency. The big winners in the rest of country, however, were the Conservatives, who opened up a substantial gap in the polls with the government and appeared headed for an overall majority at the election which had to come by June 2010. The London elections in 2008 were more of a disappointment, with the Liberal Democrats losing two of their five seats on the London Assembly, and in the European elections in 2009 the party again finished in fourth place, with 13.7 per cent of the vote and eleven MEPs. Parliamentary by-elections, which had so often helped to give the party a boost in times of need, were not kind. In only one during 2008–09 – Henley, in June 2008 – did the party start in second place, and given how well the Conservatives were doing by then (having won Crewe & Nantwich from the government the month before) victory never seemed very likely; the Conservatives held the seat comfortably.

The world-wide credit crunch and the bail-out of a series of British banks by the government in 2008–09 resulted in a major deterioration in public finances. Gordon Brown was widely held to have performed well in the crisis, at least initially, and Labour support recovered slightly in the second half of 2008. The Liberal Democrats did well, too, largely thanks to the reputation of the party's deputy leader and Shadow Chancellor, Vince Cable, 'the sage of the credit crunch', as the *Daily Telegraph* described him[63] (though Tory MPs joked that his reputation was exaggerated, having predicted the last nine out of one recessions[64]). However, Liberal Democrat policy, which had largely relied on promising higher public expenditure in key areas, clearly had to change. In any case, Labour's pouring of public money into public services, often with disappointing outcomes, coupled with the government's increasing degree of control from the centre and the stifling of local initiatives, had undermined support for central state activity.

This process led to tensions within the party, particularly between the so-called 'economic liberals' and 'social liberals'. Typically, the leadership election of 2007 had not been fought on particularly ideological grounds, and gave no real clue to the direction of party policy under either contestant. After the election Clegg argued that he was both a social and an economic liberal. As he said in his first major speech as party leader, in January 2008: 'Marrying our proud traditions of economic and social liberalism, refusing to accept that one comes at the cost of the other. On that point, if not all others, the controversial *Orange Book* in 2004 was surely right.'[65] In the superficial sense that economic growth and social justice were not mutually exclusive, this was of course correct, but there were real differences of opinion within the party over levels of taxation and public expenditure and degrees of state intervention. It was another part of the same speech that gave more of a hint to where Clegg would try to take the party, with a call for the establishment of free schools, not run by local authorities, and a requirement for the NHS to pay for private treatment for patients where maximum waiting times were exceeded. This appeared to mark a decision to try to roll back the frontiers of the state, a distinctly economic-liberal approach.

It is not clear whether Clegg came into office with a clear plan and determination to move the party in this direction, or whether it simply seemed a sensible response at the time to the disintegration of New Labour and the attempt by the Conservative leader David Cameron to portray himself as a liberal Conservative in an attempt to attract Liberal Democrat supporters. After the 2010 election, and the party's decision to enter a coalition with the Conservatives, most commentators found it easier to present it as the former, conspiracy stories about takeovers of the party by a small *Orange Book* clique making a better story. It is also plausible, however, that Clegg was simply reacting to circumstances, in a way that his predecessors had always done. He did not consistently follow an economic-liberal approach, for example releasing, in December 2008, proposals for a 'green road out of the recession' which involved significant extra investment in home insulation, housing and transport.

Having said that, it is also the case that Clegg was the first Liberal Democrat leader not to have been active in politics under Thatcher's and Major's Conservative governments; his instincts always appeared to be more hostile to Labour and economic-liberal than were Ashdown's, Kennedy's or Campbell's. This was reinforced by the economic-liberal tendencies of the majority of the Liberal Democrat Shadow Cabinet, in contrast to the wider parliamentary party, and the party membership as a whole. Nevertheless, Clegg won support for his approach at the autumn 2008 conference, with the adoption of a (slightly vague) proposal to cut public expenditure and levels of taxation. In turn this led to a sharp rise in the number of self-identified social liberals standing, successfully, for election to the Federal Policy Committee and to the launch, in spring 2009, of the Social Liberal Forum. The new organisation attracted the support of several MPs and leading activists, though it went out of its way not to be seen as an anti-leadership body.

A more bitter argument developed over the party's policy on university tuition fees, which had been an important feature of the 2005 manifesto. Neither Clegg nor Cable had ever been convinced of the policy, seeing it as an unjustified subsidy for the middle classes when there were higher priorities in education spending, and they used the squeeze on public expenditure to try to move the party away from it. They were opposed, however, by a clear majority of the FPC, who argued for its retention partly on the grounds of principle (access to education should be free) and partly of pragmatism (the policy was widely seen as contributing to the party's gaining a string of university seats in 2005). Clegg was heavily defeated at an FPC vote on a draft policy paper in January 2009; had his proposal been put to the spring conference two months later, it would have been defeated even more overwhelmingly.

Another attempt to downgrade the policy in summer 2009 led to a semi-public row between Clegg and the FPC, contributing to a generally unhappy autumn conference, unusually for the last main conference before an election. The feeling was also stoked by Vince Cable's unveiling of his proposals for a 'mansion tax', a 1 per cent tax on homes worth £1 million or more. Although most party activists were probably happy to see a radical and redistributionist policy, the threshold was set too low for several of the MPs' constituencies, and furthermore, it was launched without all its details being settled and with virtually no consultation with Cable's colleagues. After the conference the proposal was revised, with the threshold being raised to £2 million, after full consultation with the parliamentary party and FPC. Supporters of the party's democratic policy-making processes, which were often criticised by the leadership for being long-winded, enjoyed pointing out that had the policy been put to the FPC in the first place, it could have been road-tested, its problems ironed out and put to the conference in a markedly less slapdash manner.

By this stage, however, Clegg was commanding increasing respect from his party. Like Ashdown, after initial difficulties (such as the split over the European referendum) Clegg steadily improved his performance and began to demonstrate that he was able to grab the limelight for the party in the way that Campbell had never managed. During the scandal over MPs' expenses he was at the forefront of the demand for reform, and in May 2009 he defied convention to call for the resignation of the Speaker of the House of Commons, Michael Martin, following the Speaker's dogged defence of the existing system. In April 2009, on the back of a high-profile media campaign led by the actress

Joanna Lumley, he scored a notable victory over the government when Conservative and rebel Labour MPs voted for a Liberal Democrat motion on settlement rights for retired Gurkha soldiers. He also started to question the role of British troops in Afghanistan. This all helped to push the Liberal Democrats' poll ratings higher, to 20 per cent by December 2009.

Clegg's ally Danny Alexander was put in charge of the preparations for the 2010 manifesto. Unlike its 2005 predecessor, it attempted to present a coherent underpinning to its proposals, using the theme of 'fairness', aiming to distribute power – economic, social, political and financial – more fairly. Using the slogan 'Change that works for you', it highlighted four key commitments: fair taxes (including raising the income tax threshold, paid for by ending tax allowances and environmental taxes); a fair future (breaking up the banks, 'honesty about the tough choices needed to cut the deficit', and boosting employment by investment in low-carbon infrastructure); a fair chance for every child (including the 'pupil premium', extra resources for schools taking on children from disadvantaged backgrounds); and 'a fair deal' (political reform: giving electors the right to sack corrupt MPs, restoring civil liberties, and constitutional reform).

As before, the manifesto was carefully costed, and included a cautious approach to cutting the public sector deficit, with no reductions before 2011–12, and the establishment of a cross-party Council on Financial Stability to agree the scale and speed of more radical spending cuts. Tuition fees were to be abolished, but only over a six-year period, the FPC's concession to Clegg and the state of the public finances. Again as with previous manifestos, the 2010 version had a strong green element, with ambitious targets for curbing climate change, including a commitment to a zero-carbon Britain by 2050. On immigration, one of the key issues that emerged during the campaign, the party proposed a regional points-based system to direct immigrants to where they were needed, and an earned amnesty for illegal immigrants who had been in Britain for ten years, but spoke English and had no criminal record. On Trident, another campaign issue, the party ruled out a like-for-like replacement in favor of unspecified alternatives.

Having trailed the Conservatives by at times up to thirty points in the opinion polls since early 2008, by the beginning of the campaign Labour had closed the gap to a mere five points, with the Liberal Democrats polling about 20 per cent. Although there was widespread dislike of Gordon Brown, particularly in southern England, there was no great conviction that David Cameron's Conservatives would be all that much better. A hung parliament thus looked a possibility from the start.

In the event the election campaign was unlike anything Britain had seen before, thanks to the country's first-ever television debates between the three main party leaders, which brought to life what had started as a rather lacklustre campaign. Clegg performed strongly, particularly in the first debate; his message that real change was needed clearly resonated with the electorate, and the argument that only the Liberal Democrats, with no record of failure in government, could deliver it seemed to strike a chord. 'I agree with Nick' became a widespread slogan (after Brown used it several times in the debate), and 'Cleggmania' became a phenomenon; the party shot up in the opinion polls, reaching as high as 34 per cent on a couple of occasions, ahead of both the other two parties. The Liberal Democrat 'surge' became the highlight of the election, and was itself covered at length in the media, helping to perpetuate the phenomenon. As a result, the Liberal Democrats came under sustained attack from the right-wing press, particularly over the party's stance on immigration. Many of the stories the tabloids used were fed to the press by Conservative HQ; 'we did a pretty comprehensive job on them', admitted one of Cameron's team later, 'however dirty it was'.[66]

Towards the end of the campaign, and after stronger performances by both the other leaders, the Liberal Democrat surge receded somewhat, but the most pessimistic of the eve-of-poll predictions still saw the party gaining 26 per cent of the vote. The results of the election therefore came as a considerable shock: 23 per cent of the vote and only fifty-seven seats, a net loss of six. Fourteen seats were lost, all but two to the Conservatives, and eight gained, five from Labour and three from the Conservatives. In some respects the party was unlucky, failing to gain or hold no less than twelve seats by less than 1,000 votes in each case (though another five were gained or held by less than 1,000).

2010 general election (5 May)			
	Votes	*%*	*MPs*
Liberal Democrat	**6,836,824**	**23.0**	**57**
Conservative	**10,703,754**	**36.1**	**306**
Labour	8,609,527	29.0	258
SNP	491,386	1.7	6
Plaid Cymru	165,394	0.6	3
Others	2,884,895	9.7	20
Total	*29,691,780*		*650*

Several reasons have been put forward for the dashed Liberal Democrat hopes, though it is still not clear whether the opinion polls had over-estimated the party's vote through-out the contest. What became clear later was the ephemeral nature of much of the Liberal Democrat support during the campaign. Closer analysis revealed that those who said they were planning to vote for the party were also those least likely to be sure about their choice, least likely that they would vote at all, and most likely not to have voted at the previous election (the strongest determinant of turn-out at the next one).

As in the 1992 election, the fact that the polls pointed steadily to a hung parliament as the most likely outcome may have scared some voters back to their traditional loyalties – a move reinforced by many of the main newspapers, particularly the wide-circulation *Daily Mail*, arguing strongly against a vote for the Liberal Democrats and warning of the likely chaos of a hung parliament. Possibly, also, the rapid increase in the party's stand-ing in the polls helped to undermine its own targeting strategy, convincing candidates and voters in what were in reality unwinnable seats that they had a chance and deterring them moving to help in more winnable prospects.

Despite the disappointments, the Liberal Democrats had performed creditably. The party polled particularly well with women and young people, winning, for example, 34 per cent of women aged 18–24 – ahead of both other parties, and 8 per cent up on 2005. In only one region did the party's vote fall: Scotland, by 3.7 per cent, although this led to no net loss of seats. Its final UK-wide vote of 23.0 per cent was 1 per cent up on 2005, only the second time that the Liberal vote had increased under a Labour government, the second-best Liberal result since 1929 (after 1983), and the third election in a row in which the Liberal Democrat vote had risen. By comparison, the Labour vote of 29.0 per cent was their second-worst result since 1918 (when they fought only half the seats), and the Conservative vote of 36.1 per cent was their fifth lowest since 1918. For the first time since Labour supplanted the Liberals as the main non-Conservative Party in the 1920s, the combined Conservative and Labour vote fell to below two-thirds of the total.

And of course, the most arresting feature of the 2010 election was that after all the speculation, it had indeed resulted in a hung parliament, the first since February 1974. A new era in the party's history was about to begin.

Conclusion

The story of the Liberal Democrats from 1988 to 2010, from near-oblivion to entry into government, has been a dramatic one. A number of key factors can be identified as having contributed to the party's survival and success.[67]

First, although the Liberal Democrats have never managed to win as much as 10 per cent of Parliamentary constituencies, they have been much more successful at local level. The Liberal Party had built up its local strength to almost 1,500 councillors by the time the SDP was formed in 1983; the Alliance took this to over 3,500 by 1987. For most of the lifetime of the Liberal Democrats, the party has had over 4,000 councillors, briefly topping 5,000 in 1996–97, 22 per cent of the UK total. Importantly, this has been supplemented since 1999 by Liberal Democrat MSPs and AMs in Scotland, Wales and London, all giving the party a presence throughout the country, gaining it credibility and profile. Local Liberal Democrats have had a focus for their efforts and, in most areas, a taste of electoral success and a demonstration of the way in which effective campaigning and organisation can lead to results. There was a strong correlation between local government success and many of the Westminster seats gained in the 1997 and subsequent general elections.

A good local government record does not, however, generally produce national headlines. Parliamentary by-elections have always been helpful, and sometimes vital, to the party's national image. Eastbourne in 1990 demonstrated that the party had survived (and contributed to Mrs Thatcher's downfall). Newbury and Christchurch in 1993 showed that the Liberal Democrats could challenge the Conservatives even in their strongholds, while Brent East in 2003 and Leicester South in 2004 achieved the same with respect to Labour. In 2006, Dunfermline & West Fife rescued the party from the aftermath of the resignation of Charles Kennedy. Every one of the party's eleven by-election victories between 1990 and 2006 helped build profile, poll ratings, credibility, morale and funds.

As the Liberal Party and the Alliance learned, however, by-election victories are no guarantee of general election success. From 1997 onwards the Liberal Democrats have managed to win significantly greater numbers of seats than their predecessors, often on smaller proportions of the national vote. This has been the outcome of a combination of intensive local campaigning – both contributing to and reinforced by local government success – and an increasing targeting of resources on winnable seats, together with a steadily more professional party organisation.

The role of the party leader has often been crucial. In smaller political parties the media has, perhaps inevitably, always tended to focus on the leader to the exclusion of his or her colleagues. Compared to other parties, therefore, the Liberal Democrat leader occupies a larger part of the kaleidoscope of impressions that together form the overall image of the party in the mind of the electorate – along with the party's national policies, its local record and its local representatives. Overall, the party has been well served by its leaders, particularly during general election campaigns, which is when most electors see and hear them; Ashdown, Kennedy and Clegg all performed creditably in the general elections in which they led the party, except for the opening of the 2005 campaign. This in turn, of course, places a greater premium on their effectiveness, which is why Kennedy's and Campbell's perceived shortcomings caused such concern.

The party also succeeded in sharpening its definition, developing policies that the electorate came to recognise as distinctly Liberal Democrat – including, in particular, support for investment in education, opposition to university tuition fees, opposition to the war in Iraq and support for green policies (from 1995 onwards, the party always came first or second in opinion polls measuring which party the electorate thought was best on the environment – this was true of no other policy area). It also strengthened its social bases of support, appealing most strongly to the educated middle classes, particularly those working in the professions and the public sector. It came clearly to be seen as a party of the centre-left – which was not the case in the 1970s or 1980s – well placing it to pick up the support of discontented Labour voters after 1997.

All of these factors ensured that the Liberal Democrats were the main beneficiaries from the accelerating decline in support for the other two major parties. In the 1951 election, almost 97 per cent of the votes cast were for the Conservative and Labour parties. By February 1974 this had fallen to 75 per cent, by 1983 to 70 per cent, and by 2010 to 65 per cent. The reasons for this dealignment of the electorate are multiple, and often contested, but what is clear is that the Liberal Party, the Alliance and now the Liberal Democrats have been the main beneficiaries, capturing the lion's share of the remaining vote, and even more of the remaining seats in Parliament. The party has successfully positioned itself as the major alternative to the Tory–Labour duopoly.

Furthermore, it has managed to do this despite having a series of overall strategies that have varied quite significantly – from replacing Labour as the main opposition party (1988) to working with them to unseat the Conservatives (1994–97) to 'construc-tive opposition' (1997–2001) to replacing the Conservatives as the main opposition party (2002) to holding the balance of power (2010). Whether these were ever really credible strategies is more open to question; in reality they were all, of course, responses to exter-nal developments over which the party had little or no control.

As the journalist David Walter put it, 'the party's position has been that of a surfer, waiting patiently for the right wave to rise and then using all its skills to stay upright and to travel as far and as fast as possible'.[68] In the lifetime of the party it has proved increasingly able to keep its balance and to ride the political waves. In 2010, they took the Liberal Democrats into government.

Further reading

General studies covering the period from 1988 to 2010 include David Dutton, *A History of the Liberal Party* (Palgrave Macmillan, 2004) and Chris Cook, *A Short History of the Liberal Party: the Road Back to Power* (Palgrave Macmillan, 2010), the latter taking the story up to July 2010.

The only comprehensive study of all aspects of the party, including policy, organisa-tion and strategy is the now dated *The Liberal Democrats*, by Don MacIver (Prentice Hall Harvester Wheatsheaf, 1996), though a special issue of *Political Quarterly* in 2007 (78:1, January–March 2007), edited by Richard S. Grayson, has valuable content on many aspects. Andrew Russell and Edward Fieldhouse, *Neither Left nor Right? The Liberal Democrats and the Electorate* (Manchester University Press, 2005) contains a detailed examination of the Liberal Democrats' electoral support in 1997 and 2001, and contains several interesting case studies of constituency campaigns. Paul Whiteley, Patrick Seyd and Antony Billinghurst, *Third Force Politics: Liberal Democrats at the Grassroots* (OUP, 2006) contains a detailed analysis of the party membership and its attitudes in the 1990s.

On ideology, Kevin Hickson (ed.), *The Political Thought of the Liberals and Liberal Democrats since 1945* (Manchester University Press, 2009), contains contributions from a wide range of academics and Liberal Democrat activists. Tudor Jones, *The Revival of British Liberalism: From Grimond to Clegg* (Palgrave Macmillan, 2011) examines Liberal ideas as they have been embodied in the writings of Liberal politicians and thinkers and in party policy and strategy. The economic-liberal book that sparked off the ideological debate within the party in 2004 – *The Orange Book: Reclaiming Liberalism*, by Paul Marshall and David Laws (eds.) (Profile Books, 2004), and its social-liberal riposte, *Reinventing the State: Social Liberalism for the 21st Century*, by Duncan Brack, Richard Grayson and David Howarth (eds.) (Politico's, 2007) – are both worth reading.

All the Liberal Democrat leaders now have biographies or autobiographies: Paddy Ashdown, *A Fortunate Life* (Aurum Press, 2009); Greg Hurst, *Charles Kennedy: A Tragic Flaw* (Politico's, 2006); Menzies Campbell, *My Autobiography* (Hodder and Stoughton, 2008); and Chris Bowers, *Nick Clegg: The Biography* (Biteback, 2011). Paddy Ashdown's *The Ashdown*

Diaries (Penguin, 2000 (vol. 1, 1988–97) and 2001 (vol. 2, 1997–99)) are invaluable source material for the Liberal Democrat side of 'The Project'. Sir Alan Beith's *A View From the North* (Northumbria University Press, 2008) gives the party's longest-serving MP's perspective.

Notes

1   David Dutton, *A History of the Liberal Party* (Palgrave Macmillan, 2004), p. 269.

2   See Harriet Smith, 'The 1988 Leadership Campaign', *Journal of Liberal History* 24 (autumn 1999).

3   Paddy Ashdown, *The Ashdown Diaries: Volume Two, 1997–1999* (Penguin, 2001), p. 494.

4   Paddy Ashdown, *A Fortunate Life* (Aurum Press, 2009), p. 237.

5   Ivor Crewe and Anthony King, *SDP: The Birth, Life and Death of the Social Democratic Party* (OUP, 1995), p. 450.

6   Ibid., p. 440.

7   Paddy Ashdown, *The Ashdown Diaries: Volume One, 1988–1997* (Penguin, 2000), pp. 50–51.

8   All opinion poll ratings in this chapter are taken from the Ipsos-MORI series, available at: http://www.ipsos-mori.com/researchspecialisms/socialresearch/specareas/politics/trends.aspx

9   Ashdown, *A Fortunate Life*, p. 237.

10   Ibid., p. 246.

11   Ashdown, *The Ashdown Diaries Volume Two*, p. 495.

12   Ashdown, *A Fortunate Life*, p. 250.

13   'Paddy's people', *Economist* 14 September 1991.

14   This argument is further developed in Richard S. Grayson, 'Social democracy or social liberalism? Ideological sources of Liberal Democrat policy', *Political Quarterly* vol. 78:1, January – March 2007.

15   Leader, *Guardian* 19 March 1992.

16   Leader ('The case for the Lib Dems'), *The Independent*, 8 April 1992.

17   Ashdown, *A Fortunate Life*, p. 260.

18   Smith, 'The 1988 Leadership Campaign', p. 20.

19   Paddy Ashdown, 'A broader movement dedicated to winning the battle of ideas', 9 May 1992, in Duncan Brack and Tony Little (eds.), *Great Liberal Speeches* (Politico's, 2001), p. 427.

20   Chris Rennard, pers. comm. The periods over which this expenditure was incurred were not the same, so the figures are not strictly comparable; but they are illustrative of the general trend.

21   Interview with Paddy Ashdown, *Journal of Liberal History* 30 (spring 2001), p. 7.

22   Ashdown, *The Ashdown Diaries Volume One*, p. 273.

23   Tony Blair, *A Journey* (Hutchinson, 2010), p. 119.

24   Ashdown, *The Ashdown Diaries Volume Two*, p. 497. The reference to Heineken relates to a popular advertisement for a brand of beer.

25 Ashdown, *A Fortunate Life*, pp. 277–78.

26 Ashdown, *The Ashdown Diaries Volume One*, p. 419.

27 Peter Mandelson, *The Third Man* (Harper Press, 2011), p. 256.

28 Ashdown, *The Ashdown Diaries Volume One*, p. 452.

29 Ibid., p. 449.

30 David Butler and Denis Kavanagh, *The British General Election of 1997* (Macmillan, 1997), p. 178.

31 Dutton, *A History of the Liberal Party*, p. 285.

32 Ashdown, *The Ashdown Diaries Volume One*, p. 555.

33 Ibid., p. 559.

34 Interview with Paddy Ashdown, *Journal of Liberal History* 30 (spring 2001), p. 13.

35 Ashdown, *The Ashdown Diaries Volume Two*, pp. 254–55.

36 Ibid., p. 319.

37 Paul Whiteley, Patrick Seyd and Antony Billinghurst, *Third Force Politics: Liberal Democrats at the Grassroots* (OUP, 2006), p. 47.

38 Ashdown, *The Ashdown Diaries Volume Two*, pp. 489–90.

39 Ashdown, *A Fortunate Life*, pp. 323–25.

40 Andrew Rawnsley, *Servants of the People: The Inside Story of New Labour* (Penguin, 2000), p. 199.

41 Ashdown, *A Fortunate Life*, p. 322.

42 Ibid., p. 323.

43 *Journal of Liberal History* 30 (spring 2001), p. 28.

44 Greg Hurst, *Charles Kennedy: A Tragic Flaw* (Politico's, 2006), p. 112.

45 Ibid., p. 116.

46 Ibid., p. 156.

47 Ibid., p. 164.

48 Henry McLeish, *Scotland First: Truth and Consequences* (Mainstream, 2004), p. 219, cited in Martin Laffin, 'The Scottish Liberal Democrats', *Political Quarterly* vol. 78:1, January – March 2007.

49 *The Sun*, 17 July 2004.

50 *The Guardian*, 30 September 2004.

51 Charles Kennedy, *The Future of Politics* (HarperCollins, 2000), p. xii.

52 Hurst, *Charles Kennedy*, p. 119.

53 Paul Marshall and David Laws (eds.), *The Orange Book: Reclaiming Liberalism* (Profile Books, 2004).

54 Patrick Wintour, 'Lib Dem radicals call for pro-market switch', *The Guardian*, 4 August 2004.

55 Marshall and Laws, *The Orange Book*, p. 29.

56 Duncan Brack, Richard S. Grayson and David Howarth MP (eds.), *Reinventing the State: Social Liberalism for the 21ˢᵗ Century* (Politico's, 2007).

57 Ibid., p. ix.

58 John Curtice, 'New Labour, New Protest? How the Liberal Democrats profited from Blair's mistakes,' *Political Quarterly* vol. 78:1, January – March 2007.

59 This is explored in more detail in Duncan Brack, 'Liberal Democrat Leadership: The Cases of Ashdown and Kennedy', *Political Quarterly* 78:1, January–March 2007. A summary of both views is put in Dennis Kavanagh and Philip Cowley, *The British General Election of 2010* (Palgrave Macmillan, 2010), pp. 98–99.

60 Vince Cable, *Free Radical* (Atlantic Books, 2009), p. 287.

61 Andrew Rawnsley, 'Burst out of the pinstripes and show us some passion', *Observer*, 17 September 2006.

62 Menzies Campbell, *My Autobiography* (Hodder and Stoughton, 2008), p. 299.

63 Chris Cook, *A Short History of the Liberal Party: the Road Back to Power* (Palgrave Macmillan, 2010), p. 298.

64 Kavanagh and Cowley, *The British General Election of 2010*, p. 105.

65 'Clegg calls for radical grassroots innovation in public services', speech to the 'Setting the Agenda' conference, 12 January 2008.

66 Kavanagh and Cowley, *The British General Election of 2010*, p. 167.

67 Much of this argument is taken from Chris Rennard, 'From Protest to Power – The Progress of the Liberal Democrats', in Dominic Wring, Roger Mortimore and Simon Atkinson (eds.), *Political Communications in Britain: The Leader Debates, the Campaign and the Media in the 2010 General Election* (Palgrave Macmillan, 2011).

68 David Walter, *The Strange Rebirth of Liberal England* (Politico's, 2003), p. 3.

Chapter 11

Into Government: Coalition (2010–2011)

Philip Cowley and Martin Ryder

Every Liberal Democrat leader had dreamed of an election leading to a hung parliament. Given that the party was unlikely ever to be able to make the leap straight from third place to majority status, an interim stage, where it performed well enough to deny any other party the chance to govern by itself, and was then able to use this leverage to implement at least some Liberal Democrat policies, in particular reform of the electoral system, was always the best that could be hoped for. The outcome of the 2010 general election, however, was far from ideal; indeed, as Paddy Ashdown described it, the electorate had contrived to come up with 'an instrument of excruciating torture for the Liberal Democrats, where our hearts and emotions went one way but the mathematics the other'.[1] In terms of values and policies, almost everyone – including most Liberal Democrats – assumed that the party was closer to Labour than to the Conservatives, yet the election outcome made any arrangement with the Labour Party very difficult. The Conservatives were twenty seats short of a majority, Labour sixty-eight. With fifty-seven seats, the Liberal Democrats held the balance of power, but not evenly – they could put the Conservatives in, either as a minority government or through a coalition, but they would have to rely on support from other parties to do the same for Labour.

Negotiating the coalition

The Liberal Democrat leader Nick Clegg had come under pressure throughout the campaign to reveal his intentions in the event of a hung parliament. His initial line was to say that any party that came ahead in both seats and votes should have the first chance at forming a government, though he later added the rider that should Labour come third in votes but top in seats (a possibility given the vagaries of the first-past-the-post system, and the apparent surge in Lib Dem support during the campaign), he would not support Gordon Brown remaining in Downing Street. Accordingly, speaking outside party headquarters on the morning of Friday 7 May, Clegg announced that he would talk first to the Conservatives.

The Liberal Democrats had been preparing for this, in secret, for the previous six months. In December 2009, Clegg had appointed a group of four MPs to act as the party's negotiating team should one be needed: Danny Alexander and David Laws, both close ideological allies of Clegg, Chris Huhne, his leadership opponent, and Andrew Stunell, the party's former Chief Whip and a reassuring figure to the grassroots. The group had met on several occasions before the election to talk through scenarios and desirable outcomes.

The Conservatives began to think seriously about their options in the case of a hung parliament in the middle of the election, after the first television debate and the Liberal Democrat surge in the polls. Although their initial assumption was that a minority government would be the best outcome, possibly with a 'confidence and supply' arrangement with the Liberal Democrats (through which the party would support the government on confidence votes and key decisions such as the budget, but remain outside government), David Cameron became increasingly attracted to the idea of a coalition, given the economic situation and the desirability of a full-term parliament. Accordingly, on the Friday afternoon, Cameron made a 'big, open and comprehensive offer' to the Liberal Democrats; although he did not use the word 'coalition', he explicitly stated that he was willing to go further than simply a confidence and supply agreement. The first of a series of meetings between the two parties' negotiating teams took place that evening.

The Labour Party had made very few preparations for a hung parliament, but when Gordon Brown saw the chance of staying in power he jumped at it. In this he was encouraged by Transport Secretary Andrew Adonis, himself a former Liberal Democrat, and Peter Mandelson, a veteran of the Ashdown–Blair 'project'; other Labour Cabinet members were less enthusiastic. Brown rang Clegg on the Friday afternoon, and an exploratory meeting between the Liberal Democrat negotiating team and Labour representatives took place on the Saturday morning – though, unlike the talks with the Conservatives, this was not made public at the time.

These were the opening moves in what was to prove to be four days of negotiations, meetings and phone calls between the three parties' negotiating teams, leaders, ex-leaders and other politicians. The Liberal Democrat leadership was careful to keep the party informed, and the parliamentary party and Federal Executive met almost daily – in sharp contrast to the other two parties, where the negotiations were essentially run only by the leaderships.

The negotiations have been detailed in several books, one by Liberal Democrat negotiator David Laws.[2] The Conservative and Liberal Democrat teams got on well, and made good progress. By the Monday, however, the talks seemed to be breaking down over the issue of electoral reform, where the most the Conservatives would offer was a free vote in the Commons on a referendum on replacing first-past-the-post with the alternative vote (AV) – not a proportional system but one which was expected, in most cases, to result in a slightly less disproportional outcome.

At the same time, discussions with Labour were proceeding behind the scenes. The Liberal Democrats were distinctly unenthusiastic about any deal which would see Gordon Brown – an unpopular prime minister who had just been rejected by the electorate – remain in power. On the Monday morning Brown promised Clegg that he would resign as leader of the Labour Party, with the new leader to be elected by September. One of the blockages to a Labour–Liberal Democrat deal having been removed, formal negotiations between the two parties began that evening, shortly after Brown's public announcement of his intention to resign.

This in turn increased the pressure on the Conservatives. A phone conversation between Clegg and Cameron on the Monday afternoon gave rise to the impression that Brown was offering the Liberal Democrats immediate legislation for AV and a referendum on a proper system of proportional representation. In fact Brown had not offered this – he had talked rather vaguely about a multiple-option referendum – and Clegg never explicitly claimed he did, but Cameron was certainly left with that impression, and he used the threat of AV being imposed by a Labour–Liberal Democrat coalition to persuade first his Shadow Cabinet and then his parliamentary party to back a Conservative offer of a referendum on AV as part of a coalition deal. Whether Clegg deliberately misled Cameron over the Labour 'offer', whether Cameron deliberately misled his party to force them into the deal, or whether it was simple confusion has not been established.

The new Conservative offer, together with the lack of any progress in the negotiations with Labour, proved to be enough for Clegg and his team; on Monday evening, they effectively opted for coalition with the Conservatives. They kept the negotiations going throughout Tuesday, however, hoping that the possibility of a deal with Labour would help to extract further concessions from the Conservatives. This strategy ended when Brown finally lost hope and resigned as Prime Minister, shortly after 7pm. An hour later David Cameron accepted the Queen's invitation to form a government.

A joint meeting of the Liberal Democrat MPs, peers and Federal Executive took place that evening to debate the four-page draft coalition agreement hammered out by the Conservative and Liberal Democrat negotiating teams. Under the terms of the 'triple lock' procedure agreed in 1998 (see Chapter 10), both the MPs and the Federal Executive had to support the proposal for a coalition, and if either failed to do so by a three-quarters majority, the support would be needed of a special conference (which, in turn, if it failed to vote for coalition by a two-thirds majority, would need to put the proposition to a ballot of party members). The emotionally charged meeting saw displays of support, concern and hyperbole, but almost no substantive opposition. Charles Kennedy said that he could not support the agreement, but offered no alternative, and only former MP and Executive member David Rendel opposed it outright, on the grounds that it failed to contain any guarantee of proportional representation. Shortly after midnight, the MPs voted for the proposal by 50 to 0 (with 7 abstaining or absent), and the Executive by 27 to 1.

The first of the three locks had been cleared so decisively that there was no need for the second or third, but the Executive had already agreed to organise a special conference regardless of the first-stage votes, on the basis that entry into coalition was so momentous a decision that the party's grassroots should have a chance to have their say. The conference took place the following Sunday, 16 May. Out of the thirty-eight speakers in the three-and-a-half-hour-long debate, just six opposed the coalition, and only about twenty representatives, out of well over 1,500, voted against.

The conference, together with the efforts made to consult the parliamentary party and Federal Executive, was an astute piece of party management. Although unhappiness with the coalition was to become more widespread within the party later in the year, no one could complain that they had been bounced into the decision; the party as a whole had signed up to the deal.

Why did the coalition form?

The commentary on the formation of the coalition displayed a curious characteristic: although almost no one had predicted it, after it had happened almost everyone agreed that it had been inevitable.[3] There are several reasons why the Liberal Democrats in the end opted for coalition, and coalition with the Conservatives.

Even before the election, in the light of the dire economic situation, the Liberal Democrat negotiating team had concluded that coalition would be preferable to a looser arrangement, such as a confidence and supply agreement. If the party were merely to support a minority government, the chances of the Liberal Democrats being blamed for the public spending cuts that would probably follow (or the possible economic chaos that might result from a failure to tackle the public sector deficit) while failing to reap any of the rewards of actually being in government, able to implement party policies, seemed too high; furthermore, they would be vulnerable at any time to the prime minister calling a snap election. As they talked through the options during the negotiations, by the Monday the parliamentary party had come to agree that confidence and supply was not attractive: Liberal Democrats would 'take all the responsibility and get no power ... all the downside and none of the upside at all'.[4]

Refusal to make any kind of deal with any party risked a rapid second election and the charge that the Liberal Democrats preferred to remain a party of protest, outside government. That left only coalition, with Labour or the Conservatives. There are four main reasons why the party went with the Tories.

First, simple electoral arithmetic. A Conservative–Liberal Democrat coalition would enjoy a clear majority in the House of Commons; a Labour–Liberal Democrat one would be just short. Although it might be possible to add in the votes of the other putative 'progressive' parties (the Scottish and Welsh nationalists, the SDLP, Green and Alliance Party of Northern Ireland MPs), any such arrangement would be highly vulnerable to defection or parliamentary rebellion.

Second, a significant portion of the Labour Party did not want coalition with the Liberal Democrats. Although some members of the Labour negotiating team, notably Adonis and Mandelson, as well as Brown, were genuine in their desire for a deal, it was clear that others were not. And the negotiations were conducted against a background of Labour MPs and ex-ministers coming out in public to call for their party to have nothing to do with any such arrangement – partly out of dislike of the Liberal Democrats, partly out of opposition to electoral reform, and partly out of a feeling that after such a clear rejection by the electorate, Labour had no moral case for staying in government. The Liberal Democrats themselves were wary of the public response to a government being formed by the two parties which had both lost seats in the election. Trying to win parliamentary votes with a coalition commanding a minority of seats and with plenty of disaffected MPs in the larger partner did not look enticing.

Third, because the Liberal Democrats felt the Conservatives offered them a better deal. The Conservatives conceded to them on many of the key Liberal Democrat manifesto pledges, including their four key priorities of raising the income tax threshold, banking reform, the 'pupil premium' for schools, and various constitutional reforms, including the referendum on AV. Similarly, the Conservatives had given up several of their policies disliked by Liberal Democrats, including inheritance tax cuts, renegotiating elements of the Lisbon Treaty and scrapping the Human Rights Act. Indeed, the Liberal Democrat negotiators felt that their counterparts were quite happy to abandon some of their more right-wing populist policies and marginalise their own right wing, and were more keen to get into government than to defend their own platform, with a few 'red line' exceptions.

The key issue for the Conservatives was the speed of reducing the public-sector deficit. Although the Liberal Democrats had fought the election on a platform of resisting immediate cuts, and aiming only to halve the deficit by 2013–14, their negotiators accepted the Conservative alternative of a package of immediate cuts and an elimination of the deficit by the end of the Parliament. This came as a surprise to the Conservative team; George Osborne, the Shadow Chancellor, is reported to have said: 'This should be the happiest day of our lives, because it's all our policy that's being agreed'.[5] Yet the Liberal Democrat view was not as clear as the party's manifesto had made out. Vince Cable had argued for a tougher stance on the deficit during the drafting of the manifesto, in late 2009, and during the election campaign Clegg had come to agree with him, in the light of the growing turmoil in the financial markets, though he kept this quiet at the time. The Liberal Democrat team were aware that whatever deal they reached would have to be credible to the markets, particularly in the light of the growing sovereign debt crisis in Greece and other European countries, or it could cause serious economic instability in the short term, and undermine the case for hung parliaments, and coalition governments, for years to come.

Other Conservative red lines included immigration, where the Liberal Democrats accepted a limit on the number of non-EU economic migrants (not Liberal Democrat policy, but an issue on which they had come under attack during the election); and Europe, where agreements not to join the euro or to transfer any further powers to the EU (neither of which Liberal Democrats had committed to), and to referendums before any future transfer of powers, were balanced by a commitment to play a positive role in Europe. A number of Liberal Democrat policies were also dropped, including the mansion tax.

Liberal Democrat policies in the coalition programme

Key Liberal Democrat manifesto pledges incorporated in the coalition programme included: raising the income tax threshold to £10,000 over the course of the Parliament; introducing the pupil premium to give extra resources to schools taking on children from disadvantaged backgrounds; restoration of the earnings links for the state pension; a banking levy and reform of the banking system; investment in renewable energy; an immediate cancellation of plans for a third runway at Heathrow airport; an end to the detention of children for immigration purposes; the dropping of plans for identity cards; agreement to reach the UN target of 0.7 per cent of GNP for overseas aid by 2013; reform of the House of Lords; and the introduction of a fixed-term parliament of five years.

A number of issues where agreement could not be reached were referred to reviews, and in three areas Liberal Democrat MPs were to be allowed to abstain in parliamentary votes: higher education funding, nuclear power, and tax breaks for married couples. On Trident, Liberal Democrats accepted the case for the replacement of Trident, but were allowed to 'continue to make the case for alternatives' to a like-for-like replacement.

All this was considerably better than the Labour alternative. Indeed, the Liberal Democrat negotiating team felt that their Labour counterparts in reality offered them very little; a document prepared by Gordon Brown's office on Sunday evening was, in the words of one Liberal Democrat aide, 'basically the Labour manifesto. They said we'll carry on everything that we're doing and we'll have a few reviews.'[6] They were unwilling to fully fund the pupil premium, increase the income tax allowance, introduce a banking levy or restore the pension–earnings link. On key economic issues, the Labour negotiators appeared not to have the authority to reach any agreement, suggesting instead separate discussions with the Chancellor, Alistair Darling – to the exasperation of the Liberal Democrat team, which had the power to negotiate on behalf of their party as a whole and could not see why their Labour counterparts did not. (In fact, at Brown's suggestion, Vince Cable did hold an unauthorised meeting with Darling on the Tuesday morning, but without result; both men agreed they could do little to influence the outcome.)

Furthermore, the Labour negotiators themselves seemed divided; although the document they tabled for discussion on the Monday did make a concession towards the Liberal Democrats' new desire to move faster on deficit reduction, this was opposed by one of their number, Ed Balls, in the talks that evening. Similarly, Balls cast doubt on the Labour Party's ability to deliver its own MPs in voting for a referendum on AV – an intervention viewed at the time by the Liberal Democrats as a deliberate wrecking move.[7]

The final factor underlying the attractiveness of the deal with the Conservatives was the positive personal chemistry between David Cameron and Nick Clegg, and the almost total lack of it between Clegg and Gordon Brown. The importance of this can exaggerated, but it certainly helped.

Some of the Labour negotiators have since argued that the Liberal Democrat team was never serious about a deal with Labour, and only engaged in talks because it helped to increase the pressure on the Conservatives. That seems unlikely; there was a clear desire among the Liberal Democrat parliamentary party for genuine negotiations with Labour, and probably a majority of them would have preferred such a deal had it been feasible. The Liberal Democrat negotiating team themselves, before the election, had expected the Labour option to be more likely. It was a combination of the factors outlined above that made even the most staunch supporter of a 'progressive' coalition come to accept that, under the circumstances, the deal with the Conservatives was better. Even Paddy Ashdown, who had spent so much of his time as leader pursuing the 'project' with Tony Blair, spoke up in favour of the Tory deal at the party's meeting on the Tuesday night. 'Fuck it!' he said, after reading the coalition agreement. 'If this is what you're going to fight for – even with the bloody Tories – you'd better count me in.'[8]

Yet the Liberal Democrat leadership of 2010 was also much better disposed towards the Conservatives than Ashdown – or Kennedy or Campbell – would have been. Unlike his predecessors, Clegg had only been politically active under a Labour government; he had none of their shared experience of opposing Conservative governments with Labour, and had come to distrust New Labour's centralising approach and contempt for civil liberties. A combination of a slight rightward shift in the Liberal Democrat position under his leadership, and a major move towards the centre by the Conservatives under Cameron, had brought the two parties (indeed, in practice, all three parties) closer together in policy terms than at any election for decades.[9] Commentators' surprise at the formation of the coalition reflected their disregard of this growing policy consensus.

The coalition's first year

The coalition government came into being in the early hours of Wednesday 12 May 2010. For the first time in sixty-five years Liberals took their places in British government.

Five out of twenty-two Cabinet posts went to the Liberal Democrats: Nick Clegg (Deputy Prime Minister, with particular responsibility for constitutional reform), Vince Cable (Business, Innovation and Skills), Chris Huhne (Energy and Climate Change), Danny Alexander (Scotland) and David Laws (Chief Secretary to the Treasury). The party gained control of two of the key areas it was interested in, constitutional reform and environment policy (Huhne's department being the stronger of the two government environment departments); Scotland made sense given that there was only one Scottish Conservative MP to eleven Liberal Democrats; and Business was an obvious place to put Vince Cable if it was felt that the Chancellor had to be from the same party as the Prime Minister. Clegg apparently had Transport in mind for Laws, but Laws argued for the Chief Secretary post, pointing out that the Liberal Democrats needed to have as much input as possible into key spending decisions, to ensure that party priorities were protected.

Seventeen days after the formation of the coalition, however, on 29 May, Laws resigned after accusations of misuse of parliamentary expenses. He was replaced by Danny Alexander, with Michael Moore being made Secretary of State for Scotland. Laws' resignation was a blow to the party, removing one competent minister and putting another one, Alexander, into a position where he would have less time to spend following up Liberal Democrat input government-wide.

Ten Liberal Democrats were given junior ministerial posts, and a further seven gained other government offices (Deputy Leader of the Commons, law officers or whips). The total allocation of posts was rather higher than the proportion of government MPs contributed by the party (16 per cent). The decision was taken to have Liberal Democrat ministers in almost every department (the exceptions were Environment, International Development, and Culture, Media and Sport, and the Northern Irish and Welsh Offices) rather than have the party 'own' particular ministries (as tends to be the case in some European coalition governments), with the aim of the party being able to influence every area of government policy.

In forming the coalition, the party was aware that it faced a dilemma: it needed simultaneously to demonstrate that coalition government could deliver effective government, and in particular deal with the deficit, while at the same time preserving the Liberal Democrats' identity, distinct from their coalition partners. The leadership decided that the former was the more urgent task, particularly given Britain's lack of familiarity with coalitions, while the latter objective could wait for later, nearer the next election. Thus Liberal Democrat ministers went to some lengths to demonstrate unity with their Conservative colleagues, starting with the joint press conference given by the two leaders on the Wednesday after polling day, where their mutual rapport was obvious. Later in May David Laws defended the government's emergency budget, including a £6 billion package of immediate cuts, with enthusiasm. On occasion the party leadership gave the impression that coalition policies were better than their own party's; as the introduction to the full coalition programme (an expansion of the original shorter document, published on 20 May), claimed: 'We have found that a combination of our parties' best ideas and attitudes has produced a programme for government that is more radical and comprehensive than our individual manifestos'.[10] At the Liberal Democrat conference in September, Clegg claimed that the coalition was 'more than the sum of our parts'.[11]

The problem with this strategy was that the more Liberal Democrats attempted to demonstrate unity with their coalition partners, the less they looked any different from the Conservatives, and the more they had to defend policies they had campaigned against only weeks before. This contributed to a growing unhappiness among Liberal Democrat backbenchers, with the first significant rebellion taking place in June over the emergency budget's increase in VAT, a policy which had been explicitly opposed by the party during the election, and had not been included in the coalition programme, though it was defended as necessary to the deficit reduction plans. Although opinion polls immediately after the formation of the government showed general public support for the coalition, this seemed to benefit the Conservatives more than the Liberal Democrats; by the end of July, Liberal Democrat support had fallen from 24 per cent at the election to 14 per cent, while Conservative support had risen from 37 to 40 per cent.[12] Conservative voters appeared to like the way in which the Liberal Democrats were moderating their own party's right wing, whereas many of those who had voted Liberal Democrat in May were unhappy with their party forming part of a Tory-led government. Clegg's net approval rating fell from +53 during the election to +30 after the formation of the coalition to +13 in July.[13]

By and large the coalition worked well for its first six months. Although there were several parliamentary Liberal Democrat rebellions, they were small and almost never threatened the government's majority. Conservative MPs, particularly those on the right, also rebelled, but on different issues. Even the announcement of the government's comprehensive spending review in October, which set out the aim of cutting almost 20 per cent from public expenditure over four years – substantially more than Mrs Thatcher's government had achieved thirty years earlier – failed to cause much of a problem; after all, tackling the deficit was one of the main reasons the coalition had come together, and opinion polls suggested that people mostly understood and agreed with the government's aims.

The Liberal Democrats faced a much worse problem over university tuition fees. Although reversing the Labour government's introduction of top-up and tuition fees had been a key commitment of the party's manifestos in 2005 and 2010, the party's leadership had never been convinced that it should be a priority; Clegg had lost an argument over this with the Federal Policy Committee in the drafting of the manifesto (see Chapter 10). The Liberal Democrat negotiating team made no attempt to fight for the party's position during the talks; indeed, they had concluded before the election that 'on tuition fees we should seek agreement on part-time students and leave the rest. We will have clear yellow water with the other [parties] on raising the tuition fee cap, so let us not cause ourselves more headaches.'[14] The coalition programme had parked the issue by simply allowing Liberal Democrat MPs to abstain if the government's response to the Browne Report on higher education funding, expected in the autumn, was not acceptable.

Yet the minister responsible for deciding the government's response to the Browne Report was himself a Liberal Democrat, Vince Cable – who, if anything, was even more sceptical of his party's policy than Clegg. Accordingly, when the report was published in October, he endorsed its main thrust, that tuition fees would have to be raised. His own proposals, published a few weeks later, did not accept Browne's solution of lifting the cap on fees entirely, but raised the ceiling to a maximum of £9,000 from the previous level of £3,290, though any university charging more than £6,000 would have to undertake a series of measures to encourage applications from students from poorer backgrounds. There were many attractive features of Cable's proposals, including the fact that no student would have to face any up-front costs, a raising of the post-university minimum income below which repayment was not required, and the extension of the system to part-time students (who, previously, had had to pay up-front fees); but all this was overwhelmed, in the public reaction, by the near-trebling of the cap.

Clegg and Cable were convinced that the system they were introducing was better than the one it was replacing, and initially intended to vote for it, but in the teeth of strong opposition from their back-benchers announced that they were prepared to abstain to preserve party unity – as the coalition agreement permitted – as long as the rest of the parliamentary party followed suit. The rebels would not be dissuaded, however, and, fearing defeat in the Commons, the Liberal Democrat ministers decided to vote for the rise in the cap. In the end, on 9 December, the party split three ways: twenty-eight Liberal Democrat MPs, mostly ministers, voted for; twenty-one, including party president Tim Farron and former leaders Charles Kennedy and Menzies Campbell, voted against; and eight, including deputy leader Simon Hughes, abstained or were absent. The government carried the vote by a reduced majority.

This would have been bad enough if the damage had been confined within the party. But during the election campaign every Liberal Democrat MP had signed a pledge, promoted by the National Union of Students, to vote against any increase in the tuition fees cap. Thus the issue became not just about higher education policy, but a matter of trust. Student demonstrations before the vote, which were well-supported and occasionally violent, were targeted particularly at Clegg and the Liberal Democrats. The party's opinion poll rating fell further, to 11 per cent in December, and Clegg's approval rating sank even more, from a net +5 in October to −12 in December and −23 in January. Liberal Democrats worried that this was the equivalent of their party's Iraq War, a decision which would damage their image and reputation long after the details of the policy had been forgotten.

Their fears seemed to be justified in May 2011, after the English local, Scottish and Welsh elections and the referendum on the reform of the voting system. The election results were much worse than the party had expected. In England, the Liberal Democrats lost over 40 per cent of the council seats they were defending and lost control of nine councils out of nineteen; in terms of local authority strength, this took the party back to its 1993 level. The overall projected national vote was just 15 per cent, worse than the Liberal Democrat performance in any local election; indeed, worse than any result since the last local elections the Liberal Party had contested before the formation of the SDP (13 per cent in 1980). The losses were particularly heavy in the northern cities which the party had taken from Labour over the preceding ten years; Hull, Leeds, Liverpool, Newcastle and Sheffield were all lost to Labour, generally by wide margins. In northern England, more dependent on the public sector than the south, the coalition's cuts programme was deeply unpopular, and in any case there were few Conservative councillors left to bear the brunt of the Labour assault.

In Scotland, in the face of a exceptional performance by the SNP, and even greater antipathy towards the Tories, the Liberal Democrat performance was catastrophic, falling from seventeen to five MSPs; every mainland constituency was lost and the party's vote more than halved, to 7.9 per cent. Scottish leader Tavish Scott resigned the day after the elections. The Welsh result was not as bad; the party lost one AM out of six and its vote fell from 14.8 to 10.6 per cent. Although there had been some talk of a coalition with the Labour Party in Cardiff, Labour won thirty out of the sixty seats and decided to govern alone.

Liberal Democrat misery was compounded when the AV referendum was lost, by 32.1 per cent to 67.9 per cent, on a 41 per cent turn-out. After a promising start, the Yes campaign had been outperformed and outspent by the No campaign, which had been supported solidly by the Conservatives and roughly half Labour's MPs.

There were a few crumbs of comfort for the party. In England, the local results were better everywhere the party had MPs; almost all of them would have held their seats even on the same vote. In absolute numbers, the party's vote actually went up – but the Conservative and Labour votes increased even more. In retrospect the decision to hold the AV referendum on the same day as the local elections was a mistake (though no one argued against it at the time). Instead of the normal low turn-out boosting the chances of the Yes campaign along with those of the Liberal Democrats, the reverse seemed to have happened; Conservative voters who would not normally have bothered to cast local votes turned out to defeat AV and voted for their party at the same time. Unexpectedly, the Conservatives actually gained councillors. A sizeable proportion of Labour and former Liberal Democrat voters had also clearly used their vote to both punish the Liberal Democrats in the elections and vote against AV.

However bad the results, however, the Liberal Democrats were still clearly committed to the coalition; although in the aftermath of the election, a few former councillors called on Nick Clegg to resign as leader, no major party figure joined them or called for withdrawal from the government. The steps taken, during the coalition negotiations, to ensure that the party was fully committed to the deal had paid dividends.

What party members now wanted was for their leadership to ensure that the party became much more distinctive from its Conservative colleagues. This was beginning to happen in any event; the tactics used by Conservative ministers, including David Cameron, during the AV referendum campaign caused offence to many Liberal Democrats and brought an end to any post-negotiation honeymoon. Clegg signalled a change of approach in a speech the week after the election:

> The current government is a coalition of necessity ... It is not a 'national' government, but it is a government formed in the national interest ... In the next phase of the coalition, both partners will be able to be clearer in their identities ... You will see a strong liberal identity in a strong coalition government. You might even call it muscular liberalism.[15]

A particular flashpoint developed over the coalition's proposals for reform of the National Health Service, outlined in a white paper published in July 2010. Growing numbers of health professionals came out against the potentially far-reaching reforms, which seemed to threaten gradual privatisation of health service management and much greater local variability in treatment. Although the white paper had been approved by the party leadership, as well as the Liberal Democrat health minister, Paul Burstow, some of the party's MPs had opposed it from the beginning, particularly as the coalition programme had promised the opposite, an end to any top-down reorganisations of the NHS. At the Liberal Democrat spring conference in March 2011, in the face of a major revolt, the leadership decided to accept a resolution largely hostile to the reforms, and in the following months argued for major revisions to the white paper. In June, Cameron and Clegg announced a series of substantial changes to the proposals; although Cameron was probably happy to ditch what were in any case becoming deeply unpopular reforms, clever footwork by Clegg ensured that the Liberal Democrats gained much of the credit. The party's leadership appeared to be learning how to distinguish the party from its coalition partners.

Conclusion: the impact of the coalition

In terms of policy, the coalition programme appeared to be a reasonably clear win for the party. One analysis suggested that 75 per cent of Liberal Democrat manifesto commitments had been included, against only 60 per cent of the Conservatives'.[16] Another study concluded that 'the overall left–right placement of the coalition agreement was closer to the Liberal Democrat manifesto than to the Conservative one ... Liberal Democrat achievements in the negotiations were impressive'.[17] In the coalition's first year, the party was able to point to a number of specifically Liberal Democrat measures which had been implemented, including an increase in the income tax threshold, the restoration of the state pension–earnings link and the introduction of the pupil premium.

Yet the programme itself is not necessarily the same as government policy; it cannot cover every eventuality, and in a number of areas the coalition has tried to implement policies which were not included in the programme, such as the NHS reforms. This problem will get worse over time, as the original commitments are either implemented or abandoned as unworkable, and new issues arise to which responses are required.

The distribution of ministries was not such a clear win for the Liberal Democrats, leaving them without control of any of the major spending departments such as health or education. Constitutional reform and climate change are important issues for the party, and areas where they can already point to some achievements, but are less salient to the general public. One of the party's Cabinet ministers mainly appears in public to defend spending cuts and another is largely invisible outside Scotland. The evidence suggests that Liberal Democrat junior ministers, usually isolated in Conservative-led departments, have found it difficult to demonstrate clear achievements; on many occasions they may have stopped the Conservatives implementing unattractive policies, but this is not usually visible to the public.

On the other hand, the party has clearly demonstrated that coalition government can work, and can work well. A study of the operation of the government over its first year suggested that it had been successful in managing relations between coalition partners, directing the business of government and reviving Cabinet decision-making, with much less micro-management from the centre than under its New Labour predecessor.[18] One weakness the party faced in elections – that there is no point in voting for the Liberal Democrats because they will never get into government – has been well and truly eradicated.

The problem, of course, is that a sizeable proportion of people who voted Liberal Democrat in May 2010 did *not* wish the party to get into government – or, at least, not into one with the Conservatives. To a large extent this was an inevitable outcome of having to choose, and the party could well have lost just as much support from joining a coalition with Labour, or, indeed, if it had stayed outside government entirely. It was a particularly unwelcome decision, however, to the sizeable number of voters who had switched away from Labour to the Liberal Democrats from 2003 onwards. What is not yet clear is whether the Liberal Democrats can win back some of their previous support, or attract new supporters to replace their old ones.

The key to the Liberal Democrat performance at the 2015 election will be the extent to which the party manages to demonstrate that the coalition is not simply another Tory government, that Liberal Democrat priorities have featured in the government's programme and would not have done so without the party's involvement, that their distinctiveness can be demonstrated without at the same time triggering a Conservative backlash and breaking up the coalition – and that the government's economic record is better than that of Labour. This is a tall order – but at the very least, after decades in which the party's chances depended primarily on the actions of others, the Liberal Democrats now have their future rather more in their own hands.

Further reading

The two key insiders' accounts of the coalition negotiations are David Laws, *22 Days in May: The Birth of the Lib Dem–Conservative Coalition*, which covers his two and half weeks in government as well as the negotiations, and Rob Wilson, *5 Days to Power: The Journey to Coalition Britain*, written after extensive interviews with key players from all three parties (both Biteback, 2010). Chapter 10, 'Five Days in May', in Dennis Kavanagh and Philip Cowley, *The British General Election of 2010* (Palgrave Macmillan, 2010), gives a concise account.

Academic analyses of the coalition and its impact on government are likely to appear with ever-increasing frequency, but so far are mainly confined to academic journals. One exception is Vernon Bogdanor, *The Coalition and the Constitution* (Hart, 2011) which examines the effect of previous hung parliaments and coalitions and speculates on the outcome of the Liberal Democrat–Conservative government.

Notes

1   Rob Wilson, *5 Days to Power: The Journey to Coalition Britain* (Biteback, 2010), p. 100.

2   David Laws, *22 Days in May: The Birth of the Lib Dem–Conservative Coalition* (Biteback, 2010);
     see also Wilson, *5 Days to Power* and Chapter 10, 'Five Days in May', in Dennis Kavanagh and
     Philip Cowley, *The British General Election of 2010* (Palgrave Macmillan, 2010).

3   See, in particular, Tim Bale, 'I *don't* agree with Nick: Retrodicting the Conservative–Liberal
     Democrat Coalition', *Political Quarterly* 82:2, April–June 2011.

4   Wilson, *5 Days to Power*, p. 203.

5   Ibid., p. 171.

6   Ibid., p. 226.

7   Laws, *22 Days in May*, p. 153.

8   Kavanagh and Cowley, *The British General Election of 2010*, p. 220.

9   For a comparative analysis of election manifestos, see Marc Debus, 'Portfolio Allocation and
     Policy Compromises: How and Why the Conservatives and the Liberal Democrats Formed a
     Coalition Government', *Political Quarterly* 82:2, April–June 2011, p. 298.

10   HM Government, *The Coalition: Our Programme for Government* (May 2010), p. 8.

11   Full speech available at www.libdemvoice.org/full-text-nick-cleggs-speech-to-liberal-
     democrat-autumn-conference-21236.html

12   All opinion poll ratings in this chapter are taken from the Ipsos-MORI series, available at:
     http://www.ipsos-mori.com/researchspecialisms/socialresearch/specareas/politics/trends.
     aspx

13   Net approval = those approving minus those disapproving. All figures: Ipsos-MORI,
     available at www.ipsos-mori.com/researchpublications/researcharchive/poll.
     aspx?oItemID=88&view=wide

14   Wilson, *5 Days to Power*, p. 45.

15   Nick Clegg speech, 11 May 2011, 'One Year In: Coalition and Liberal Politics'.

16   'Inside Story: How Coalition Government Works' (Constitution Unit, June 2011).

17   Thomas Quinn, Judith Bara and John Bartle, 'The UK Coalition Agreement of 2010: Who
     Won?', *Journal of Elections, Public Opinions and Parties* 21:2, May 2011, p. 309.

18   'Inside Story: How Coalition Government Works'.

Party Organisation from 1859

Sarah Whitehead and Duncan Brack

Formation of the Liberal Party

The meeting between Whigs, radicals and Peelites at Willis's Rooms in June 1859 may indeed have marked the official birth of the Liberal Party in Parliament (see David Brown's assessment in Chapter 2), but the evolution of a homogeneous and effective Liberal organisation throughout the country was much slower.

Local Liberal associations where they did exist were often financially independent of the central party and relied upon candidates to fund their own campaigns, thus leaving many associations relatively free to exercise their own judgement in relation to the selection of candidates and the fighting of elections.[1] Indeed, in the absence of any meaningful chain of command, local associations frequently resisted central interference, while other constituencies remained inactive, failing to respond to the challenge posed by the extension of the franchise and relying on the traditional influence of political patronage to ensure electoral success.

1860: Liberal Central Association

In response to a general lethargy in some seats, in 1860 the party leadership formed the Liberal Registration Association, in order to maintain the upkeep of the electoral register in areas where the registration of Liberal supporters had been neglected. The Association, initially based at Victoria Street in London, also helped interview potential candidates.[2] Later renamed the Liberal Central Association, illustrating the increasing desire to establish greater communication between the central party and local associations, the organisation later moved to Parliament Street, Westminster, in offices which served as a base to receive visitors from the constituencies.

Originally, the chairman of the LCA was the leader of the Liberal MPs in the House of Commons, but this role was later assumed by the Chief Whip. In effect, the LCA headquarters served as a whips' office, taking care of the needs of the Parliamentary Liberal Party as well as attempting to provide some assistance to local Liberals. In addition to parliamentary duties, the Chief Whip was also responsible for administering limited grants to poorer constituencies and recommending candidates to those areas without a suitable contender. He was assisted in this task by the appointment of a principal parliamentary agent, but the LCA had few resources and thus it was difficult for the organisation to exert its influence in seats where local Liberals resisted any interference from above.

1877: National Liberal Federation

The dramatic Liberal defeat of 1874 impressed upon radicals within the party the need to establish a more effective organisation to ensure electoral success, particularly following the extension of the franchise in 1867 (see Chapters 3 and 4).

The model for the subsequent reorganisation of the party outside Parliament was provided by the Birmingham Liberal Association: a 'caucus' of radical politicians led by Joseph Chamberlain, who argued that all Liberal associations should join a federated union with the aim of presenting a united front on the key political issues of the day. The National Liberal Federation, formed in May 1877, also provided a representative body to impart the views of the wider party to the Liberal leadership, thus facilitating the 'participation of all members of the party in the formation and direction of its policy'.[3] Chamberlain and his followers wanted the new alliance of local Liberal associations to remain entirely separate from the Whig-dominated parliamentary party, while Whigs, such as the then Liberal leader Lord Hartington, saw the formation of the NLF as a direct attempt by radicals to challenge the power of the Whig elite and exert more influence over the party leadership. From the outset this ensured a tense relationship between the Liberal leadership and the party's rank and file and established a tradition whereby activists would often seek to assert their independence from the central party.

Within the first month of its foundation, forty-six local associations had joined the NLF, which was initially based in Birmingham. The city's Liberals took key positions in the new organisation and Joseph Chamberlain was appointed as the first NLF president. A series of vice-presidents were appointed from the largest Liberal associations across the country, but it was the Birmingham association which provided the NLF with its first treasurer and secretary.

Appointed as the NLF's secretary in July 1877, Francis Schnadhorst also served as the secretary of the Birmingham Liberal Association and played a major role in the future organisation of the party. Working over the next sixteen years to create new Liberal associations and introduce them into the Federation, Schnadhorst was also able to help establish a more effective working relationship between the NLF, representing party activists, and the LCA, representing the parliamentary party.

When the NLF moved its headquarters from Birmingham to London in 1886, after Chamberlain split from the party over home rule, the two organisations found themselves working more closely with one another, a development facilitated by the NLF taking offices at 41–42 Parliament Street, next door to the LCA.[4] In addition to his secretarial role within the NLF, Schnadhorst was also appointed as the LCA's secretary, thus cementing the increased co-operation between the two wings of the party. Despite this, there remained a certain amount of overlap in the activities undertaken by the two bodies, with the Chief Whip remaining in charge of party funds and the LCA continuing to help some local associations find suitable candidates, despite NLF efforts in this respect.

In its early years, the NLF focused on helping to build up Liberal organisations in dormant constituencies and the dissemination of party propaganda, as well as arranging ad hoc meetings in support of various Liberal campaigns. By 1891 the NLF had become sufficiently influential for Gladstone to endorse the policies agreed by Federation conferences as the basis for his election programme, particularly in the 1891 'Newcastle Programme'.

The official activities of the NLF were divided between a Council, a General Committee and an Executive. The Council, a forerunner to the modern party conference, was the party's main policy-making body. It met at least once a year and was attended by MPs, members of the NLF Executive and delegates from local Liberal associations. Before the First World War, local groups were permitted to send one delegate for every 1,000 voters in their constituency but following the extension of the franchise in 1918 this was reduced to one representative for every 2,000.

The General Committee comprised all NLF officers, plus representatives from various federated associations, who added an additional twenty-five members to the group.[5] The Committee's overall role was to appoint the NLF's Executive, to promote the aims of the Federation, to summon an annual meeting of the Council, organise further meetings as necessary and put key political questions to local Liberal associations when a united response was required. Despite its remit to canvass the views of local associations on critical national issues, however, the General Committee did not have the authority to decide the subsequent response on behalf of the party. The administrative work of the General Committee was executed by three sub-committees. One dealt with organisational matters and another with finance, while the Liberal Publications Department evolved from a third committee which co-ordinated the production of political pamphlets.

In addition to the dissemination of party propaganda, the NLF also worked to strengthen its base of local Liberal associations and by the time the Liberal Council first met at Leeds in January 1879, 101 associations had been federated.

The creation of the NLF also led to the emergence of the Women's Liberal Federation and the Scottish Liberal Association in 1877. A series of regional Liberal associations also naturally evolved, with organisations in areas like the Home Counties, the Midlands and the West Country in existence by the 1890s.

Party organisation and the Asquith/Lloyd George split

The structure of the NLF remained largely unchanged until 1936, although the parliamentary party went through dramatic changes in the years following the wartime split between Lloyd George and Asquith in 1916. Despite the decision of Lloyd George's followers to fight the 1918 general election as Coalition Liberals against Asquith's official

Liberal group, the NLF was keen to avoid a permanent division within the party and thus sent election material to every local Liberal association, regardless of their affiliation.[6]

But such gestures did not prevent Lloyd George establishing his own political headquarters in 1922, following the fall of his coalition government. His decision to take offices at 18 Abingdon Street in Westminster, paid for from his private political fund, was particularly galling as the headquarters of the official Liberal Party, still under Asquith's command, was then sited at 21 Abingdon Street.[7]

The Liberals continued to face immense financial difficulties in the early 1920s, as the party divided at both a parliamentary and constituency level and continued to see its vote steadily decline. After 1923, when Lloyd George was uneasily reunited with his former party in defence of free trade, Liberal organisers hoped that his personal fund would provide a much-needed source of financial support, but were disappointed at his reluctance to make his resources available to them. Despite providing limited finance for the 1923 and 1924 election campaigns, Lloyd George insisted that the efficiency of the party organisation be improved before more money changed hands. Desperate to avert the disappearance of the Liberals altogether, Asquith bowed to his demand, but despite the establishment of a special committee under Sir Alfred Mond to review the structure of the party, Lloyd George refused to accept its findings, complaining that the Liberal headquarters continued to be dominated by supporters of Asquith.

In a further attempt to try and solve the party's financial problems Asquith established the Million Fund in 1925, with the aim of attracting smaller donations from a greater number of sources, rather than relying on larger amounts given by a limited group of wealthy benefactors. Unfortunately potential donors were reluctant to part with their money, given rumours that the party had access to Lloyd George's private fund, which supposedly amounted to millions of pounds.

The appointment of Lloyd George as Liberal leader in 1926, following Asquith's retirement, caused a further rupture in the organisation, with many Asquithians abandoning the party's headquarters in disgust and forming the Liberal Council under the direction of Viscount Grey. The Council continued to provide an alternative source of funds to certain candidates for some time.

1936: Liberal Party Organisation

The Liberals' dismal showing in the 1935 election was partly (though optimistically) blamed upon the decay of local constituency associations. Not only had worsening election results affected the vitality of Liberal associations but there had been defections of activists to both main parties and to the Simonite Liberals. In several areas, Liberal associations were supporting Liberal National MPs and were effectively lost to the Liberal Party.

To revive the ailing party's fortunes, Sinclair appointed a reorganisation committee under the chairmanship of Lord Meston to review the role of uncoordinated bodies such as the LCA and NLF, with the aim of creating a single policy-making body within the party.

The proposals, adopted by a Liberal Party convention in June 1936, saw the NLF replaced with a new body, the Liberal Party Organisation (LPO). This incorporated all existing bodies within the party, except the LCA, which continued to provide a secretariat and an office for the Liberal leader and the Chief Whip. The whips' office also retained some responsibility for selecting and placing candidates.

Responsibility for policy-making fell to the newly created Liberal assembly, which replaced the annual Liberal Council meetings. Delegates attending the assembly included MPs, candidates and representatives from the constituencies, who were elected in proportion to the size of their local associations, rather than on the number of voters in each area, as previously. Each Liberal association was initially permitted to send four delegates to the assembly, plus an additional representative for every 100 subscribing members, up to a maximum of twenty in all.[8]

The work of the assembly involved considering resolutions on public policy proposed by affiliated constituency associations, the newly-created Liberal Council or any recognised unit within the party such as the League of Young Liberals. The assembly also elected party officers, reviewed the activities and progress of the party and ratified its annual accounts.

Responsibility for making short-term policy statements fell within the remit of the new Liberal Council, which met quarterly. It comprised the officers of the party, plus five MPs, including the Chief Whip, and five members of the House of Lords. Representatives of affiliated constituency associations were elected to the Council through their area federations, for a maximum of thirty per area. A further thirty members from the party as a whole were elected by the assembly. The Women's Liberal Federation, the League of Young Liberals, the Society of Certificated and Associated Liberal Agents, and the National Union of Liberal Clubs were also represented, along with party donors.

The first duty of the Council, as listed in the party's 1936 constitution, was to do 'everything in its power' to stimulate Liberalism in each part of the country,[9] a task that was aided by maintaining a staff of organisers to work with the area federations and help local associations. The Council also had to express the views of Liberals on current political questions, raise money, maintain a party headquarters and staff, organise publicity, propaganda and publications and, finally, ensure that Liberal candidates were adopted in as many constituencies as possible, although the whip's office continued to play a role in this.

The day-to-day activities of the Council were carried out by a series of standing committees, including an Executive Committee, an Organisation and Affiliation Committee (which maintained contact with the area federations and received periodic reports from them) and a Committee on Publications, which was responsible for directing a publications department and information bureau, at the service of the parliamentary party. As such, this committee maintained contact with the whips' office.

At a local level, each constituency association was responsible for maintaining an agent or an organiser if possible and for ensuring that Liberal supporters turned out to vote. Local associations were also responsible for carrying out propaganda work through the organisation of meetings and lectures and by focusing campaigning activities around a parliamentary candidate. Only party members over the age of eighteen were permitted to select both candidates and officers of the party.[10]

The reorganisation of the Liberal Party in 1936 has been criticised by some historians who argue that the replacement of the NLF by the LPO was cosmetic rather than a structural overhaul, with authority remaining divided between various parts of the party.[11]

1946: *Coats off for the Future!*

In the wake of the electoral battering of the 1945 general election, the new leader, Clement Davies, appointed a committee to look at the reconstruction of the party and address those areas overlooked by Meston. Its report, entitled *Coats off for the Future!*, was presented to the assembly in 1946, amid fears that the world was 'faced with the possible eclipse of British Liberalism'.[12] It was critical of the lack of co-ordination between different elements of the party such as the party headquarters and the area federations. The division of responsibility between the LCA and the LPO over the selection of candidates and financing of campaigns was highlighted as a particular failing which aggravated the overall 'uncertainty of control'.[13]

The report also found the party's policy-making machinery to be inadequate and identified an overall lack of finance as a key problem; the party lacked professional staff, including agents. Even the home of the party's headquarters at Gayfere Street came in for criticism, the report concluding that the division of the organisation across three separate houses made 'effective supervision impossible' and created 'an unfavourable impression upon visitors'.[14] The reconstruction committee recommended that an executive officer be appointed to run the headquarters, although the party did not appoint its first general director, Herbert Harris, until 1953.

The report also recommended the recruitment of more professional staff and an end to the division of command between the whips' office and the LPO on matters concerning the selection and placing of candidates. The establishment of an appeals department to look at modern fundraising techniques was suggested and, echoing the concept of Asquith's Million Fund, it was also decided that the raising of funds should be placed on a more democratic and popular basis, with contributions to be attracted from a multitude of individuals, rather than a handful of large donors. Under Davies' leadership, attempts were made to raise additional resources, with the establishment of a Foundation Fund in May 1946, aimed at accumulating £125,000 through the sale of Liberal bonds over a five-year period.[15] A small weekly paper, *Liberal News*, was also published for supporters to buy and keep as a receipt of their weekly contribution to party funds. The scheme had the benefit of providing the party with a regular income without the trouble and expense of keeping detailed records.[16]

On policy, *Coats off for the Future!* recommended that the Liberal assembly should continue to hold ultimate sovereignty, but it was suggested that a permanent committee be established to operate like a Shadow Cabinet and issue policy statements on matters of urgency. The membership of the committee would be largely determined by the leader. The proposal was accepted, although the Council rejected a recommendation to name the new body the 'Grand Committee', and insisted on having a greater say in who the party leader could select to serve on it.[17]

In addition to reviewing the party's structure, Clement Davies and his Chief Whip, Frank Byers, worked to boost activity within the dormant constituencies so that by the time of the party's 1947 assembly there were 500 local Liberal associations, compared to just 200 only eight months earlier.[18] But despite Davies' best efforts, the party continued to struggle to recruit candidates and win support.

1959: Grimond's Organisation Committee

Recognising that the party needed an increasingly streamlined structure in the aftermath of the disappointing 1959 election result, Jo Grimond proposed that a special committee, established to prepare for the contest, should continue on a permanent basis and take responsibility for improving party organisation and 'increasing the impact of Liberalism upon the electorate'.[19] Although not included in the party's constitution, the new committee was accepted by the Executive and given the general task of overseeing day-to-day operations at Liberal headquarters and co-ordinating local election campaigns. But within days of its permanent adoption, the small group, chaired by Frank Byers, caused controversy by proposing a major restructuring of the party, including calling for the dismissal of the party's general director, Herbert Harris. He was subsequently dismissed by the Executive, but many within the rank and file were unhappy about the status of Grimond's powerful new committee and one of the party's treasurers resigned in protest at its functions.

During the course of 1960, the committee, initially comprising two MPs, two former MPs and the head of the party's local government department, continued to attract suspicion by accumulating more powers for itself, including within the field of policy. Party activists became increasingly concerned about the concentration of power within the hands of a small group whose members were closely acquainted with the party's leadership, and eventually pressure led to the functions of the committee being placed on a constitutional basis. Subsequently christened the Organisation Committee, the body officially became a sub-committee of the party's Executive, which was then charged with the task of selecting its members.[20]

A Standing Committee, later renamed the Policy Committee, was later established to coordinate party policy-making, including approving the texts of election manifestos, drawing on the resolutions adopted by the assembly. The party leader, however, retained a veto over the content of the manifesto; radicals in the party made sporadic attempts to remove the veto, but to no avail. The Policy Committee also established a series of policy panels of experts from within the party to consider specific areas of policy, advise party spokesmen and, occasionally, publish policy booklets.

The president of the party – the voice of party members in the country – was elected by assembly delegates. The president was originally responsible for chairing the assembly, but after the shambles of the 1958 assembly in Torquay, during which the 76-year-old president, Arthur Comyns Carr, insisted on placing his notes between his mouth and the microphone, thus rendering him largely inaudible, a series of reforms were instituted. An Assembly Committee, elected by the Council, was created to select the agendas for the assemblies and to provide chairs for the sessions.

1967 and 1976: electing a leader

Before the First World War, the Liberal Party was often in government and its leadership was regularly determined by whoever was asked by the monarch to form an administration and succeeded in doing so. Later, Liberal MPs sporadically elected a chairman of the parliamentary party to lead them in the Commons, with the successful candidate then also speaking on behalf of all Liberals in the country. But as the party fell further into decline following the Great War, the prospect of another Liberal government became increasingly unlikely and thus some began to question whether it remained legitimate for a small number of MPs to determine who had the best qualities to lead the party. Major rifts within the parliamentary party also prompted some within the rank and file to question the judgement of MPs in selecting their leader. Lloyd George's assumption of the leadership in 1926 was not welcome by those still loyal to Asquith, even after his death, and prompted calls for Liberal activists to have a say in the selection of their party's chief.[21] Ramsay Muir, appointed chairman of the NLF in 1931, was particularly critical of the parliamentary party's role in appointing the leader, arguing that Liberal MPs no longer represented the views of the rank and file.

Jo Grimond's popular appointment in 1956, following an evident rank and file desire for Clement Davies to retire, dampened the demands for change, but the question remained of whether a small group of MPs could legitimately select a leader on behalf of the party as a whole. The furore surrounding the hasty election of Jeremy Thorpe in 1967, who was supported by just six out of twelve Liberal MPs, only days after Grimond's retirement, ensured that the old system could not continue.[22] Thus in July 1976, David Steel became the first leader of the Liberal Party to be elected by a vote of its entire membership – a ground-breaking move for any major political party in the UK.

Reflecting the concerns of the activists that the votes of the armchair members would swamp their own – supposedly more politically aware – voice, the system was not a simple one-member, one-vote arrangement. An electoral college was effectively created, in which ten votes were allocated to each Liberal association, with a further ten votes if the association had existed for more than a year, and an additional vote for each 500 votes won by the Liberal candidate for the constituency at the last general election. Thus campaigning activity and hard work were rewarded with a greater say over the leadership. It was left up to local associations to decide how to ballot their membership;

some did so by a postal vote of the entire membership, others by allocating votes to any members who turned up to an association meeting held to conduct the vote.

1981: The Social Democratic Party

The founders of the SDP in 1981 were determined to create a structure which would avoid the kind of left-wing militant take-over which had helped to drive many of them out of the Labour Party. Its set-up was accordingly significantly more centralised and managerialist than that of the Liberal Party.

Individual members joined the party nationally, a proportion of their subscription being remitted to their area party (typically covering three or four parliamentary constituencies) – the reverse of the Liberal system, in which individuals joined their local associations, which then affiliated to the national party. Area parties elected representatives to the Council for Social Democracy, the party's policy-making body, which met three times a year; its total voting membership was intentionally small (about 400) to instil a sense of cohesion and to discourage the development of factions. Area parties were responsible for selecting parliamentary candidates, by a postal ballot of all their members – selection of candidates by a small clique of activists was thereby avoided.

The most powerful bodies in the party were the National Committee and the Policy Committee (which was elected by the National Committee); both were designed to be dominated by the parliamentary party, though councillors, peers and ordinary party members were also represented. The Policy Committee tightly controlled the party's policy-making process; it was responsible not only for submitting policy papers to the Council but also for approving any policy resolutions that the Council independently adopted, and it also drew up election manifestos. In fact throughout the SDP's existence there was very little internal dissent over policy positions – which was partly why the vicious infighting over the merger process in 1987–88 came as such a shock to the outside world, and to many of the party's members.

The principle of one member, one vote was enshrined throughout the SDP; party members had the right to vote for the party leader, president, members of the National Committee and their area's representatives to the Council. Another principle was positive discrimination for women in elections for Council representatives and National Committee members. The new party also introduced modern techniques for administering its membership (including a centralised membership database) and fund-raising.

Crewe and King, the authors of the main study of the SDP, concluded that:

> In modern times a party constitution needs to combine three principles which are not readily compatible. The first is internal party democracy: sovereignty must be vested in the party membership. The second is organisational effectiveness: only leaders and a small executive can take initiatives, respond quickly to events, represent the party to the public and run it from day to day. The third is a measure of independence for

the party's MPs, who owe their position both to the party that nominated them and to the ordinary voters who elected them ... [The SDP] probably brought these principles into better balance than the old parties had done.[23]

1988: the formation of the Liberal Democrats

The Liberal Party organisation of the 1980s was still based on the constitution agreed in 1936, encompassing the same tensions between activists and the central party evident in the nineteenth century, including decentralised decision-making and funding, which made it difficult to ensure that there were adequate resources for the national party as well as central influence over candidate selection; and a preponderance of councils and committees, some of whose members were essentially self-appointed. Merging this structure with the more modern and centralised Social Democratic Party was not an easy task, as Chapter 9 shows. Nevertheless, the new party's constitution was approved by all-member ballots of both parties as part of the decision to merge, and the Social and Liberal Democrats came into existence on 3 March 1988.

The new constitution contained a provision that it would be subject to a thorough review after the first general election faced by the new party, and this was accordingly conducted in 1992–93, though individual changes had been made earlier (including the deletion of the reference to NATO in the preamble to the constitution, passed in 1989 after the party had agreed its first defence policy paper, and the change in the party's name to 'Liberal Democrats', also in 1989). The review's changes included a simplification of the rather cumbersome policy-making process and a decentralisation of power down to the regional parties in England, together with a host of more minor modifications. The description that follows is based on the revised constitution.

In essence, while the philosophy of the merged party is essentially Liberal (as Duncan Brack argues in Chapter 10), in its organisation it borrowed much from the SDP, though it has always been less centralised and more membership-driven than the Social Democrats.

The party structure is federal, with state parties existing in England, Scotland and Wales. The federal party, which operated until August 2010 from the SDP's former headquarters at 4 Cowley Street in Westminster, is responsible for the preparation of UK policy, the conduct of parliamentary elections and fundraising.

The state parties are responsible for the selection procedures for parliamentary candidates and arrangements for the collection and renewal of party membership. Every person who joins the party automatically becomes a member of their local party, relevant state party and the federal party. Individuals living in Northern Ireland or outside the UK can join the federal party directly. (The Liberal Democrats do not fight elections in Northern Ireland, deferring instead to their sister party, the Alliance Party of Northern Ireland.) The Scottish and Welsh parties, which possess their own headquarters and staff, are responsible for election campaigns in their own nations, while the English party essentially contracts with the federal party for most of its functions, retaining only a small office in federal HQ. In addition, the English party contains eleven regional parties, most of which possess a small staff and headquarters. Local parties are responsible for selecting parliamentary and local election candidates and for fighting campaigns, though a feature of the party's evolution has been the growing extent to which 'target' seats are given additional financial help from the centre.

A biannual federal party conference retains sovereignty over the Liberal Democrats' policy-making, though the Federal Policy Committee oversees the process, and is responsible for the preparation of policy papers (which are submitted to conference for debate) and the preparation of UK and European election manifestos. State parties are responsible for the preparation of policy on matters which would be the responsibility of a state parliament in a federal United Kingdom; in practice this is generally taken to mean the responsibilities of the Scottish Parliament and Welsh Assembly. Any state party can 'pass up' responsibility for policy-making to the federal party, and the English state party has done so.

Conference representatives are elected by local parties in rough proportion to the local party's membership, though the allocation is generous enough that very few local parties have contested elections. The Liberal Democrat conference has a reputation in the media for an anarchic readiness to vote against its leadership, and it has certainly done so more often than Labour or Conservative conferences, which are little more than leadership rallies. This reputation is often exaggerated – the number of leadership defeats in the party's history is tiny – but it is true to say that conference representatives tend to pride themselves on their independence, and will vote against the leadership if they think it is wrong. As one election agent put it, 'If ever we lose our ability to embarrass the leadership as a party, even when we are in government, then we won't be the Liberal Party I joined'.[24] The conference therefore acts, to an extent, as a constraint on the leadership.

Conference representatives elect the majority of members of the three key committees which run the federal party: the Federal Conference Committee (which selects conference agendas), Federal Policy Committee and Federal Executive (which oversees overall management, finance and campaigning). MPs, peers, MEPs, councillors and the state parties are all also represented, in different combinations. The president of the party chairs the Federal Executive, and an MP chairs the Federal Policy Committee; up until 2010, this was always the leader, though it does not have to be. State parties largely mirror this kind of committee and conference structure within their own organisations.

At various times Liberal Democrat leaders have attempted to centralise control over the network of party committees, much in the way that Jo Grimond tried to do in the Liberal Party. Paddy Ashdown established separate structures, under his control, for running general election campaigns, and a 'Chief Officers Group' was established as a loose coordinating group of committee chairs and leading parliamentarians under Charles Kennedy, and in a more formal way under Nick Clegg. In general, though, the party possesses considerable reserves of loyalty to its leadership, and has never been factionalised to any significant degree; although leaders may have occasional difficulties over specific issues, if they are diligent enough at party management they have usually managed to get their own way.

As Stephen Ingle has argued, the 'philosophy of participation' is clearly reflected within the structure of the Liberal Democrats, which uses a one-member, one-vote system to elect both the leader and the president. Proportional representation, in the form of the single transferable vote, is used in internal elections, and the decentralised nature of the party emphasises its commitment to subsidiarity and participation.[25] John Stevenson has argued that the more regular and systematic organisation of the SDP was one of the most important features the merged party inherited, with the computerisation of membership records one example of how efficiency was improved.[26] Other features taken from the SDP include the more deliberative policy-making process, based on policy papers produced by working groups of experts from within the party, and positive discrimination for women, in elections to federal committees and the selection of parliamentary candidates. The number of women Liberal Democrat MPs has remained disappointingly low, however, leading in 2001 to the creation of the Campaign for Gender Balance (later, the Gender Balance Task Force) aiming to provide additional support to women hoping to become MPs.

Party structure has not changed substantially since the constitutional review in 1992–93, but it has been significantly influenced by the growth in the size of the party, and in particular the increased resources that brought in the form of 'Short money' (at least until the party entered government in 2010). Financial assistance allocated to opposition parties in Parliament in rough proportion to their vote share and number of seats, this enabled the number of central party staff, mainly based in Parliament, to expand substantially. The outcome was an increasing professionalism in the party's policy-making, campaigning and press operations.

This took place alongside a substantial increase in the proportion of resources devoted to building up the party's campaigning capacity in the seats it hoped to win at the next election, a strategy particularly associated with Chris (now Lord) Rennard, the party's Campaigns Director and then Chief Executive from 1989 to 2009. Inevitably this involved a closer degree of control over campaigning techniques and strategies from the centre, reinforcing the overall tendency for an increase in central control by the party leadership. Delivering the electoral success it did, however, there were few complaints about this from the party membership, though concern has been expressed that the ruthless concentration on local issues has muffled the party's national message (see Chapter 10).

Conclusion

The organisation of the Liberal Democrats is influenced by a range of different factors, many of which also affected the Liberal Party in years past.

In the mid-nineteenth century, the extension of the franchise forced Liberals to campaign more aggressively and to build up a wider party organisation outside Parliament in order to achieve electoral success. The mutual suspicion which initially character-ised the relationship between the NLF and the Whig-dominated parliamentary party developed into one in which the Liberal rank and file continued fiercely to protect their independence and refused to be deferential to the party's leaders, resisting the imposition of professional workers and organisational structures they thought would give parlia-mentarians undue influence over the party's affairs. In his book on the Liberal Party, Rasmussen argued that the suspicion with which the rank and file viewed its leaders, combined with their interest in policy, 'made the party's history one of clashes between the parliamentary party and mass party'.[27]

The independence of the NLF from the central party also saw a plethora of differ-ent, overlapping organisations develop within the party, with various Liberal leaders seeking to reorganise the party along more efficient lines at different times. The need to reinvigorate the party became all the more imperative after Liberalism fell into decline in the aftermath of the Great War, but splits within the parliamentary party in 1916 and 1931 undermined the Liberal leadership and led the rank and file to question whether the dwindling number of Liberal MPs should be responsible for electing the party's leader.

Unlike the other two parties, the Liberals relied on neither business nor the unions as central sources of funding and, as support for the party dwindled, so too did the party's finances. This emphasised the increased need for the party to seek smaller contributions from a greater number of members, rather than from a handful of wealthy donors, and threw local party associations back on to their own resources, helping to reinforce the spirit of local independence.

Many of these issues, particularly organisational structure and finance, were never satisfactorily resolved by the Liberal Party. But in combination with the strong organi-sational roots of the SDP, the Liberal Democrats were set up so as to enable the rank and file to retain its independence and have an input into policy, but in a more structured and well-defined manner than hitherto.

Entry into government poses new challenges, which the party is beginning to tackle. The extent to which this organisational structure can satisfactorily contain the tensions between the leadership and activists which are bound to develop is now being put to the test.

Notes

1   H. J. Hanham, *Elections and Party Management: Politics in the Time of Disraeli and Gladstone* (Longman, 1959), p. 347.

2   John Vincent, *The Formation of the Liberal Party 1857–1868* (Constable, 1966), p. 82.

3   Third annual report of the National Liberal Federation, Birmingham 1881, cited in F. H. Herrick, 'The Origins of the National Liberal Federation', *Journal of Modern History,* Vol. 17, No. 2, June 1945, p. 128.

4   B. M. McGill, 'Francis Schnadhorst and the Liberal Party Organisation', *Journal of Modern History*, Vol. 34, No. 1, March 1962.

5   Herrick, 'The Origins of the National Liberal Federation', p. 127.

6   Roy Douglas, *The History of the Liberal Party, 1895–1970* (Fairleigh Dickinson University Press, 1971), p. 127.

7   Trevor Wilson, *The Downfall of the Liberal Party 1914–1935* (Collins, 1966), p. 112.

8   *Constitution of the Liberal Party* (1936), p. 4.

9   Ibid, p. 7.

10 Ibid, p. 10.

11 Chris Cook, *A Short History of the Liberal Party: The Road Back to Power* (Palgrave Macmillan, 2010), p. 122.

12 Liberal Reconstruction Committee, *Coats off for the Future!* (1946), p. 3.

13 Ibid., p.7.

14 Ibid., p. 8.

15 J. S. Rasmussen, *The Liberal Party: A Study of Retrenchment and Revival* (University of Wisconsin, 1965), p. 14.

16 Ibid.

17 Ibid., p. 80.

18 Ibid., p. 14.

19 *Liberal News*, 17 December 1959, cited in Rasmussen, *The Liberal Party*, p. 77.

20 Rasmussen, *The Liberal Party*, p. 79.

21 Ibid., p. 36.

22 See Robert Ingham, 'Liberal Leaderships', *Journal of Liberal History* 23, summer 1999.

23 Ivor Crewe and Anthony King, *SDP: The Birth, Life and Death of the Social Democratic Party* (OUP, 1995), pp. 236–37.

24 Andrew Russell and Edward Fieldhouse, *Neither Left nor Right? The Liberal Democrats and the Electorate* (Manchester University Press, 2005), p. 74.

25 Stephen Ingle, 'Party Organisation' in Don MacIver (ed.), *The Liberal Democrats* (Prentice Hall Harvester Wheatsheaf, 1996), p. 114.

26 John Stevenson, *Third-Party Politics since 1945: Liberals, Alliance and Liberal Democrats* (Blackwell, 1993), pp. 114–15.

27 Rasmussen, *The Liberal Party*, p. 267.

Appendix 2

The Liberal Vote 1832–2010

Election	Total MPs	Liberal candidates	Liberal MPs elected (unopposed)	% of total UK seats	Forfeited deposits	Total Liberal vote	% of total UK vote
1832	658	636	441 (109)	67.0	–	554,719	67.0
1835	658	538	385 (154)	58.5	–	349,868	55.2
1837	658	510	344 (115)	52.3	–	418,331	51.7
1841	658	388	271 (113)	41.2	–	273,902	46.9
1847	656	393	292 (136)	44.5	–	259,311	53.8
1852	654	488	324 (95)	49.5	–	430,882	57.9
1857	654	507	377 (176)	57.6	–	464,127	64.8
1859	654	465	356 (183)	54.4	–	372,117	65.8
1865	658	516	369 (161)	56.1	–	508,821	59.5
1868	658	600	387 (212)	58.8	–	1,428,776	61.2
1874	652	489	242 (52)	37.1	–	1,281,159	52.0
1880	652	499	352 (41)	54.0	–	1,836,423	55.7
1885	670	572	319 (14)	47.6	–	2,199,998	47.4
1886	670	449	192 (40)	28.7	–	1,244,683	45.5
1892	670	532	272 (13)	40.6	–	2,088,019	45.4
1895	670	447	177 (11)	26.4	–	1,765,266	45.7
1900	670	402	183 (22)	27.3	–	1,572,323	44.6
1906	670	536	399 (27)	59.6	–	2,751,057	48.9
1910 (J)	670	511	274 (1)	40.9	–	2,866,157	43.0
1910 (D)	670	467	272 (35)	40.1	–	2,293,869	43.8
1918	707	421	161 (27)	22.8	44	2,754,448	26.8
Coalition		145[1]	133 (23)	18.8		1,455,640	14.2
Asquithian		276	28 (4)[2]	4.0		1,298,808	12.6
1922	615	485	115 (10)	18.7	32	4,139,460	28.7
National		151	53 (4)	8.6		1,471,317	10.2
Asquithian		334	62 (6)	10.1		2,668,143	18.5
1923	615	457	158 (11)	25.7	8	4,301,481	29.6
1924	615	339	40 (6)	6.5	30	2,928,737	17.6
1929	615	513	59 (0)	9.6	25	5,308,738	23.4
1931 (exc. Lib Nat)	615	117	36 (5)	6.0	6	1,476,123	6.8
Liberals (Samuelite)		111	32 (5)	5.4		1,372,595	6.3
Ind Lib[3]		6	4 (0)	0.7		103,528	0.5
Lib Nat (Simonite)		41	35 (7)	5.7		809,302	3.7
1935	615	161	21 (0)	3.4	40	1,443,093	6.6
1945	640	306	12 (0)	1.9	76	2,252,430	9.0

Election	Total MPs	Liberal candidates	Liberal MPs elected (unopposed)	% of total UK seats	Forfeited deposits	Total Liberal vote	% of total UK vote
1950	625	475	9	1.4	319	2,621,487	9.1
1951	625	109	6	1.0	66	730,546	2.6
1955	630	110	6	1.0	60	722,402	2.7
1959	630	216	6	1.0	55	1,640,760	5.9
1964	630	365	9	1.4	52	3,099,283	11.2
1966	630	311	12	1.9	104	2,327,457	8.5
1970	630	332	6	1.0	184	2,117,035	7.5
1974 (Feb)	635	517	14	2.2	23	6,059,519	19.3
1974 (Oct)	635	619	13	2.0	125	5,346,704	18.3
1979	635	577	11	1.7	303	4,313,804	13.8
1983	650	633	23	3.5	11	7,780,949	25.4
Liberal		322	17	2.6		4,210,115	13.7
SDP		311	6	0.9		3,570,834	11.6
1987	650	633	22	4.2	1	7,341,633	22.6
Liberal		327	17	2.6		4,173,450	12.8
SDP		306	5	0.8		3,168,183	9.7
1992	651	632	20	3.1	11	5,999,606	17.8
1997	659	639	46	7.0	13	5,242,947	16.8
2001	659	639	52	7.9	1	4,814,321	18.3
2005	646	626	62	9.6	1	5,985,454	22.0
2010	650	631	57	8.8	0	6,836,248	23.0

Notes

1   Excludes fourteen candidates who received the 'coupon' but repudiated it.

2   Slight over-estimation of non-Coalition Liberals, as nine candidates who had not received the 'coupon' accepted the coalition whip upon election.

3   The Lloyd George family group.

Sources

F. W. S. Craig, *British Electoral Facts 1832–1987* (Ashgate, 1989)

Colin Rallings and Michael Thrasher, *British Electoral Facts 1832–2006* (Ashgate, 2007)

House of Commons Library Research Paper 01/54, *General Election Results 7 June 2001* (2001)

House of Commons Library Research Paper 05/33, *General Election 2005* (2005)

House of Commons Library Research Paper 10/36, *General Election 2010* (2011)

Appendix 3

Liberal Leaders

Party leaders as they exist today are largely a twentieth-century innovation. In the eighteenth century, all Prime Ministers represent aspects of the Whig tradition (see Chapter 1), but by their close association with George III, Lord Bute, Lord North and William Pitt the Younger are generally seen as more representative of what became the Conservative tradition. Selection of a premier by the monarch made that man the leader of his party, if he was able to form a government. Until the advent of Fox, it would be hard to identify a continuing formal opposition and leader of the opposition; hence there are some gaps in the table below.

Even in the nineteenth century, there was no formal process of election of a party leader, and the party in each House of Parliament had its own leader, with claims to parity between the two Houses. Towards the end of the century, the leader in the Commons came gradually to be regarded as the leader of the party as a whole.

Consequently, the table below must be treated as an approximation only.

Whigs			
1721–42	Sir Robert Walpole		
1742–43	Earl of Wilmington		
1743–54	Henry Pelham		
1754–56	Duke of Newcastle		
1756–57	Duke of Devonshire		
1763–65	George Grenville		
1765–66	Marquess of Rockingham		
1766–68	Earl of Chatham		
1768–70	Duke of Grafton		
1782	Marquess of Rockingham		
1782–83	Earl of Shelburne		
1783	Duke of Portland		
1783–1806	Charles James Fox[1]		
	House of Commons		*House of Lords*
1806–07	Charles Grey, Viscount Howick	1806–07	Lord Grenville
1807–17	George Ponsonby	1807–09	Duke of Portland
1817–21	George Tierney		
1830–34	John Spencer, Viscount Althorp	1830–34	Earl Grey (Charles Grey)
1834–55	Lord John Russell	1834–42	Lord Melbourne
		1842–55	Marquess of Lansdowne
1855–58	Henry John Temple, Viscount Palmerston	1855–59	Earl Granville

Liberals	
1859–65	Henry John Temple, Viscount Palmerston
1865–66	Earl Russell
1867–75	William Ewart Gladstone
1875–80	Earl Granville and Spencer Compton Cavendish, Marquess of Hartington (joint leadership)
1880–94	William Ewart Gladstone
1894–96	Archibald Philip Primrose, Earl of Rosebery
1896–99	Sir William Vernon Harcourt
1899–1908	Sir Henry Campbell-Bannerman
1908–26	Herbert Henry Asquith[2]
1926–31	David Lloyd George
1931–35	Sir Herbert Samuel
1935–45	Sir Archibald Sinclair
1945–56	Clement Davies
1956–67	Jo Grimond
1967–76	Jeremy Thorpe
1976	Jo Grimond[3]
1976–88	David Steel
Social Democratic Party	
1981–83	Roy Jenkins
1983–87	David Owen
1987–88	Robert Maclennan
Liberal Democrats	
1988	Robert Maclennan and David Steel (joint interim leaders)
1988–99	Paddy Ashdown
1999–2006	Charles Kennedy
2006–07	Sir Menzies Campbell
2007–	Nick Clegg

Notes

1 Fox was Foreign Secretary in the Whig administrations of 1783 and 1806, and was generally regarded as leader of the opposition to Pitt during parts of the intervening period.

2 David Lloyd George replaced Asquith as Prime Minister in 1916, although the latter continued as leader of the official Liberal Party. Asquith lost his seat at the 1918 election and Donald Maclean, who was elected as chairman of the Liberal parliamentary party, acted as the party's leader in the Commons until Asquith was returned to Parliament at the Paisley by-election in 1920.

3 Grimond briefly served as caretaker leader during the summer of 1976 after Thorpe resigned over the Scott affair.

Appendix 4

Liberal Timeline

1642–46, 1648 The English Civil Wars establish the supremacy of Parliament over the monarchy. Intensive debates begin on the proper form of government and the appropriate limitations on its authority, from which Liberalism ultimately derives. The terms Whig and Tory are first used.

1649–60 The execution of Charles I is followed by a republican government, which proves unable to devise acceptable forms of accountability and settle the degree of religious toleration which is compatible with national unity.

1660 Restoration of the monarchy.

1678–81 The Exclusion Crisis, from which the first Whig and Tory parties emerge. Whigs favour the exclusion of James, Duke of York, from the succession to the crown because he is a Roman Catholic.

1685 James II succeeds Charles II.

1688 The Glorious Revolution: William of Orange and Mary overthrow James at the invitation of the predominantly Whig nobility.

1689 The Bill of Rights and Toleration Act passed.

1690 Publication of Locke's *Two Treatises of Government*, a foundation document of Whig/Liberal philosophy.

1715 Jacobite rebellion fails, ensuring continued Whig hegemony.

1721 The Whig Robert Walpole becomes the first Prime Minister.

1742 Fall of Walpole.

1745 Final Jacobite rebellion fails, allowing for the gradual recovery of Tory respectability.

1760 Accession of George III. He plays an active role in British politics, with profound consequences for the development of parties.

1763 John Wilkes challenges the authority of general warrants.

1770 Edmund Burke publishes *Thoughts on the Cause of the Present Discontent.*

1776 American Declaration of Independence. Whigs tend to side with the colonial rebels.

1783 William Pitt the Younger becomes Prime Minister. The duel between Pitt and Charles James Fox comes to define the conflict between the Tories and Whigs.

1789 The French Revolution, welcomed by Fox, begins.

1791 Thomas Paine publishes *Rights of Man.*

1792 Mary Wollstonecraft publishes *A Vindication of the Rights of Woman.*

1793 Outbreak of war with France.

1806 Death of Fox. Death of Pitt.

1815 The end of the Napoleonic Wars. Corn laws introduced.

1819 The Peterloo Massacre.

1829 Catholic emancipation.

1830 After a long period of Tory dominance, the Whigs return to power under Earl Grey.

1832 Passage of Great Reform Act. Liberals of various hues win the resulting general election. Earl Grey continues as Prime Minister.

1834 William IV dismisses Grey and appoints Peel as Prime Minister of a brief minority Conservative administration.

1835 Liberals win general election. Lord Melbourne becomes Prime Minister, following meeting of liberals at Lichfield House.

1838 Anti-Corn Law League established. People's Charter drafted.

1841 Conservatives under Peel win general election and return to power.

1846 Repeal of the Corn Laws splits Conservatives. Peel resigns and is replaced by the Whig Lord John Russell.

1847 Liberals (more accurately, a combination of Whigs, radicals and Peelites) win general election. Russell continues as Prime Minister of a Whig administration.

1852 Russell's government collapses and is replaced by a minority Conservative administration under Derby. The liberals are again victorious in a general election and Lord Aberdeen is appointed Prime Minister of a coalition of Whigs, radicals and Peelites.

1855 Aberdeen resigns over the conduct of the Crimean War. Lord Palmerston becomes Prime Minister.

1857 Liberals win general election. Palmerston continues as Prime Minister, but resigns in 1858 following Orsini plot.

1859 The Liberal Party formed on 6 June, when Whigs, Peelites and radicals meet at Willis's Rooms in St James Street, London, to unite in opposition to the Conservatives. Palmerston becomes first Liberal Prime Minister.

1865 On Palmerston's death shortly after a general election victory, Earl Russell succeeds as leader.

1866 Russell's government falls as a result of internal disputes over electoral reform.

1867 Disraeli's government passes Second Reform Act.

1868 Liberals win general election and William Gladstone becomes Prime Minister.

1869 Irish Church Act leads to disestablishment of Church of Ireland.

1870 Forster's Elementary Education Act establishes school boards to oversee primary schools.

1872 Secret ballot introduced.

1874 Conservatives, led by Disraeli, win general election.

1877 National Liberal Federation formed.

1879 Gladstone's first Midlothian campaign.

1880 Liberals, under Gladstone, win election and return to power. Compulsory primary education introduced.

1884 Liberals enact Third Reform Act.

1885 General election results in a hung parliament. Gladstone forms his third administration with support from the Irish nationalists.

1886 Liberal Party splits over home rule for Ireland. Conservatives, together with their Liberal Unionist allies, dominate government for the next twenty years. Women's Liberal Federation formed.

1891 National Liberal Federation meets in Newcastle; its resolutions form the basis of the 1892 election manifesto.

1892 General election results in another hung parliament. Gladstone forms his fourth and last government, with Irish nationalist support.

1894 Gladstone resigns. Lord Rosebery becomes Prime Minister.

1895 Unionists win general election.

1896 Sir William Harcourt replaces Rosebery as Liberal leader.

1899 Sir Henry Campbell-Bannerman replaces Harcourt as Liberal leader.

1900 Unionists win general election.

1903 Joseph Chamberlain begins his tariff reform campaign, which divides the Unionists. Herbert Gladstone negotiates secret electoral pact with the newly formed Labour Party.

1904 Winston Churchill, among other Unionist free traders, crosses the floor to join the Liberal Party.

1905 Balfour resigns as Prime Minister; Campbell-Bannerman appointed.

1906 Liberals win a landslide election victory. Free school meals introduced.

1908 Campbell-Bannerman resigns due to ill health and is succeeded as Prime Minister by H. H. Asquith. Labour exchanges introduced.

1909 David Lloyd George's 'People's Budget' rejected by the House of Lords, prompting a constitutional crisis. Old age pensions paid for the first time. Trade Boards Act introduces first minimum wage in certain occupations.

1910 Two general elections fought, on the basis of 'peers versus people', to resolve the crisis over the budget and the power of the Lords. The Liberals remain in power with the support of Labour and the Irish nationalists.

1911 National Insurance and Parliament Acts passed; the supremacy of the House of Commons is established.

1913 Lloyd George launches his land campaign.

1914 First World War declared.

1915 Asquith forms coalition with the Conservatives.

1916 Mounting unhappiness with Asquith's conduct of the war leads to his replacement by Lloyd George as Prime Minister of the coalition government, largely at the behest of the Conservatives.

1917 Maurice debate deepens divisions between Asquith and Lloyd George Liberals.

1918 'Coupon' election sees landslide victory for Lloyd George's coalition; Asquithians are crushed, Asquith himself losing his seat.

1920 Asquith returns to Commons in Paisley by-election.

1921 First Liberal Summer School held at Grasmere.

1922 Conservative backbenchers rebel and bring the coalition to an end. The two Liberal factions are outpolled by the Labour Party in the election that follows.

1923 Liberal factions reunite to fight election in support of free trade, following Prime Minister Stanley Baldwin's decision to introduce tariffs. Liberals win 158 seats but are now clearly the third party, behind Labour as well as the Conservatives.

1924 Liberal support for the first Labour (minority) government splits the party; Liberals reduced to forty seats in the general election after the fall of the government.

1926 General Strike. Asquith retires and Lloyd George takes over as leader.

1928 Lloyd George leads revival in party thinking. *Britain's Industrial Future* (the 'Yellow Book') puts forward ideas for stimulating the economy and reducing unemployment.

1929 Liberals win over five million votes but only fifty-nine seats. Second Labour government again leads to growing divisions within the Liberal Party.

1931 Financial crisis leads to formation of National Government. Liberals split three ways: mainstream party, under Sir Herbert Samuel, supports the coalition if it remains true to free trade; followers of Sir John Simon pledge unconditional support to National Government; Lloyd George's small independent group opposes continuation of coalition when it calls an election. Landslide election victory for National Government.

1932 Samuelites leave the government when tariffs are introduced. The Simonites are reconstituted as a new political party, the Liberal Nationals.

1935 Liberals reduced to twenty-one MPs at general election. Sir Archibald Sinclair replaces the defeated Samuel as leader.

1936–39 Sinclair increasingly critical of policy of appeasement and government's failure to rearm.

1939 Sinclair declines offer to join National Government at outbreak of war.

1940 When Chamberlain's government falls, the Liberal Party joins the new coalition under Churchill, with Sinclair serving as Secretary of State for Air.

1944 Sir William Beveridge, author of the influential report on the need for a comprehensive social security system, elected as a Liberal MP at a by-election.

1945 Coalition dissolved as election called after the end of the war in Europe. Liberals win just twelve seats in general election. Clement Davies elected to replace the defeated Sinclair, but proves incapable of preventing the further decline of the party, as MPs and activists defect to right and left.

1950 Liberals reduced to nine seats in general election.

1951 Liberals win just six seats in general election. Davies rejects Churchill's offer of a Cabinet seat.

1956 Davies retires and Jo Grimond becomes Liberal leader; attacks Conservative government over Suez crisis.

1957 Liberals reach parliamentary nadir when former Liberal MP Megan Lloyd George wins Carmarthen for Labour, leaving the Liberals with just five MPs.

1958 By-election victory at Torrington – the party's first by-election gain for twenty-nine years – signals Liberal revival is under way.

1962 Eric Lubbock wins spectacular by-election victory at Orpington.

1964 Liberals win nine seats in general election. Narrow Labour majority encourages Grimond to pursue his strategy of realignment of the left.

1966 Liberals win twelve seats in general election, but large Labour majority renders Grimond's strategy irrelevant.

1967 Grimond retires. Jeremy Thorpe takes over the party leadership.

1970 Election sees the Liberals slip back to six seats again. Liberal assembly adopts the new strategy of community politics.

1971 Labour Party splits over Europe; Roy Jenkins leads rebellion against three-line whip to support Conservative Prime Minister Ted Heath in British entry to EEC.

1972 Liberal votes instrumental in ensuring survival of legislation implementing UK entry to EEC.

1972–73 Mounting unpopularity of Heath's governments leads to second Liberal post-war revival, with five by-election gains.

1974 Miners' strike triggers the indecisive 'who governs Britain' election (February), in which the Liberals poll six million votes but win only fourteen seats. Heath invites Thorpe to discuss the possibility of a coalition, but fails to offer guarantees of proportional representation. Minority Labour government survives until second election in October gives it narrow majority; Liberals slip back to thirteen seats.

1975 Referendum on Britain's continued membership of the EEC, in which Liberals campaign alongside senior politicians from other parties, including several Labour ministers who go on to found the Social Democratic Party.

1976 Allegations about Jeremy Thorpe's private life reach the public domain and lead to his resignation. David Steel elected in his place in first all-member election for the leadership of a major British party.

1977 March – Steel and Labour Prime Minister Callaghan negotiate Lib-Lab Pact after government loses its majority after by-election defeats.

1978 August – Lib-Lab Pact brought to an end.

1979 Liberals win eleven seats at general election.

1981 Moderate Labour leaders Roy Jenkins, David Owen, Shirley Williams and Bill Rodgers (the 'Gang of Four') break away from Labour to form the Social Democratic Party (SDP) on 26 March. Liberal Party and SDP form an alliance, agreeing to fight elections on a common platform with joint candidates. Alliance's first by-election victories in Croydon North West in October and Crosby in November. Poll in December shows 51 per cent support for Alliance.

1983 Alliances wins 25.4 per cent vote in general election, but only twenty-three seats. Jenkins resigns as leader of the SDP, to be replaced by David Owen.

1986 Rows between the two parties on defence issues damage the Alliance in the run-up to the 1987 election.

1987 The Alliance's vote share drops to 22.6 per cent in the general election, and Steel proposes a merger of the two parties. Owen opposes merger, but loses the SDP ballot on opening negotiations, and is replaced as party leader by Robert Maclennan.

1988 Merger approved by special conferences and postal votes of both parties and the new party, the Social and Liberal Democrats, comes into being on 3 March. Paddy Ashdown elected leader in July.

1989 SLD beaten into fourth place by the Green Party in the European elections. 'Liberal Democrats' adopted as party name.

1990 Eastbourne by-election victory demonstrates Liberal Democrats' survival and undermines Margaret Thatcher's leadership of the Conservatives; she resigns five weeks later.

1991 Liberal Democrat victory in Ribble Valley by-election spells end of poll tax.

1992 General election sees Liberal Democrats wins 17.8 per cent of the vote and twenty seats. After the election, in a speech at Chard, Ashdown signals the end of his party's 'equidistance' between the two main parties, and indicates that he would be prepared to work with Labour to defeat the Conservatives.

1992–93 Liberal Democrat votes ensure survival of legislation implementing Maastricht Treaty of European Union in Commons after Conservative Eurosceptic rebellion.

1994 Liberal Democrats win first-ever seats in the European Parliament.

1995 Collapse in Conservative support leaves Liberal Democrats as second party of local government (until 1998), with over 5,000 councillors.

1996–97 Talks over possible cooperation with Labour lead to Cook–Maclennan Agreement, setting out constitutional reforms the two parties aim to implement.

1997 Despite winning smaller share of the vote than in 1992 (16.8 per cent), Liberal Democrats win forty-six seats in general election. Size of Labour majority destroys case for coalition, but Joint Cabinet Committee formed between Labour and Liberal Democrats, initially to discuss constitutional reform.

1998 Commission on reform of voting system under Roy Jenkins reports; government's failure to support it effectively ends attempts at further cooperation between Liberals Democrats and Labour.

1999 In January, Ashdown announces intention to resign, and is replaced by Charles Kennedy in August. In May elections for new Scottish Parliament see Liberal Democrats win seventeen seats and form coalition government with Labour; the party wins six seats in the Welsh Assembly. In June, Liberal Democrats win ten seats in European elections (now conducted under PR).

2000 Liberal Democrats win Romsey by-election from Conservatives. New Labour leader in Wales negotiates coalition government with Liberal Democrats.

2001 Election sees Liberal Democrats increase vote share to 18.3 per cent, winning fifty-two seats.

2003 Liberal Democrats alone among major parties in opposing UK participation in US-led invasion of Iraq. Elections in Scotland and Wales see no change in Liberal Democrat numbers; coalition with Labour continues in Scotland, but in Wales Labour wins enough seats to govern alone.

2004 Local elections see Liberal Democrats outpoll Labour. Twelve Liberal Democrats elected in European elections but party falls to fourth place behind UK Independence Party.

2005 General election sees party's vote rise to 22 per cent; it wins sixty-two seats, the highest number of Liberal MPs since 1923.

2005–06 Growing evidence of Kennedy's alcoholism leads to two attempts by MPs to encourage him to resign; the second, in January 2006, is successful.

2006 In February, Liberal Democrats win Dunfermline & West Fife by-election in middle of leadership campaign. In March, Sir Menzies Campbell elected leader.

2007 Scottish and English local elections see losses, and end of Liberal Democrat – Labour coalition in Scotland; in Wales, party retains same six seats. Party's fall in the opinion polls, and unhappiness with Campbell's performance, leads him to resign as leader in October. Nick Clegg elected as leader in December.

2009 European elections see eleven Liberal Democrats elected (a notional increase on a smaller number of seats), but the party again in fourth place.

2010 General election campaign transformed by Britain's first-ever television debates. Clegg performs exceptionally, leading to polls temporarily showing Liberal Democrats in the lead. Final result sees party increase vote to 23 per cent but lose seats to fifty-seven. Hung parliament leads to coalition with Conservatives; five Liberal Democrats enter Cabinet. In December, party splits three ways over government proposals to increase tuition fees despite party's election pledge not to; opinion poll ratings fall sharply.

2011 English local elections see Liberal Democrats win 15 per cent of vote, losing 40 per cent of defended seats. In Scottish elections, party falls to five MSPs; in Wales, party loses one AM to end with five. Referendum on replacing first-past-the-post with the alternative vote lost by margin of two to one.

Index

Acland, Richard: 223; founding member of
Common Wealth, 225; movement to Labour
Party, 226

Addington, Henry: administration of, 28

Addison, Christopher: 156; defection to Labour
Party (1929), 185

Adonis, Andrew: activity during Coalition
negotiations (2010), 362; British Transport
Secretary, 360

Afghanistan: 90, 350; invasion, 333; Panjdeh
Incident (1885), 106; Second Anglo-Afghan
War (1878–80), 98, 106

Alexander, Danny: 360; Chief Secretary to the
Treasury, 366; role in creation of Liberal
Democrats' election manifesto (2010), 350;
Secretary of State for Scotland, 365

Alexander, S. W.: 234

Alton, David: 295

Amin, Idi: opposition to, 259–60

Anne I: reign of, 14

Anti-Corn Law League (ACLL): 56; formed
(1838–9), 44, 55; ideology of, 82; supporters
of, 44, 55

Arch, Joseph: background of, 105; organiser of
National Agricultural Labourers' Union, 105;
vice-president of NLF, 131

Ashdown, Paddy: 312, 317, 320, 322, 324–5,
328–9, 353, 383; background of, 318; *Citizen's
Britain* (1989), 312; EU Special Representative
for Bosnia and Herzegovina, 309, 333; leader
of Liberal Democrats, 308, 314, 329, 348, 359;
resignation of (1997), 326–7; service in Special
Boat Service, 308; support for formation of
Coalition Government (2010), 365

Asquith, Herbert Henry: 118, 120, 122, 152,
157, 163, 178, 186, 191–2, 201, 211, 375;
administration of, xii, 153, 157, 160, 164, 173;
background of, 153; British Home Secretary,
117; Chancellor of the Exchequer, 153, 157;
death of (1928), 154; electoral campaign of
(1997), 322–3; family of, 153, 181, 190, 229,
233; leadership campaign of, 4; 'Partnership

for Britain's Future', 321; resignation as
Liberal Party leader (1918), 153–4; retirement
(1926), 185; role in establishing Million Fund
(1925), 376; speeches of, 162–3; supporters of,
179–80, 189–90, 192, 209, 212, 216, 218, 221

Attlee, Clement: administration of, 227

Attwood, Thomas: founder of Birmingham
Political Union, 34

Austick, David: electoral performance (1973),
265; loss of parliamentary seat, 266

Austria: 70; Vienna, 61

Bagehot, Walter: 62; *The English Constitution*
(1867), 51, 79

Baldwin, Stanley: administration of, 186, 221;
resignation of (1929), 209

Balfour, Arthur: administration of, 156; creation
of Committee of Imperial Defence, 166;
Education Act (1902), 152

Ballard, Jackie: 327

Balls, Ed: 364

Bannerman, John: electoral performance (1955),
236

Bank of England: 313

Barnes, Rosie: 309

Beaverbrook, Lord: Minister for Aircraft
Production, 225

Beith, Alan: 321; Liberal Democrat leadership
candidacy (1988), 308, 312

Bellotti, David: electoral performance (1990), 314

Bentham, Jeremy: 42; advocate of utilitarianism,
3, 54; theories of, 54

Benn, Sir Ernest: *Manifesto on British Liberty*, 225

Bevan, Aneurin: supporters of, 255

Beveridge, Sir William: background of, 226;
Beveridge Report (1942), xii, 2, 218, 225, 227;
Director of London School of Economic, 226;
recruitment to Liberal Party (1944), 226

Birkett, Norman: loss of parliamentary seat, 217

Birmingham Political Union: members of, 34

Bismarck, Otto von: 155; role in formation of
German Empire, 83–4, 138